The Man Who Changed China

The Man Who
Changed China

The Life and Legacy of Jiang Zemin

ROBERT LAWRENCE KUHN

Crown Publishers / New York

Published by Crown Publishers, New York, New York.
Member of the Crown Publishing Group, a division of Random House, Inc.
www.crownpublishing.com

CROWN is a trademark and the Crown colophon is a registered trademark
of Random House, Inc.

Printed in the United States of America

Design by Leonard Henderson

Library of Congress Cataloging-in-Publication Data
Kuhn, Robert Lawrence
The man who changed China : the life and legacy of Jiang Zemin / Robert Lawrence Kuhn.
Includes bibliographical references.
1. Jiang Zemin, 1926– 2. Heads of state—China—Biography. 3. China—Politics and government—1976– I. Title: Life and legacy of Jiang Zemin. II. Title.
DS779.29.J53K85   2004
951.05'9'092—dc22   2004013162

ISBN 1-4000-5474-5

10   9   8   7   6   5   4   3   2   1

First Edition

Contents

The Man Who Changed China

Introduction

The Life of Jiang Zemin

IT IS SAID THAT JIANG ZEMIN WAS not a visionary founder of the nation like Mao Zedong or a daring reformer of society like Deng Xiaoping; Mao and Deng changed China, but Jiang did not. His impact, critics claim, was as modest as it was accidental; he simply maintained social stability and enjoyed the good fortune of a growing economy.

That is the assumption.

Here are the facts.

ON SEPTEMBER 11, 2001, at midnight in Beijing and noon in New York, just hours after the horrific attacks on America, President Jiang Zemin sent an urgent message to President George W. Bush. He was one of the first world leaders to do so.

"On behalf of the Chinese government and people," he wrote, "I would like to express sincere sympathy to you, and through you, to the U.S. Government and people, and condolences to the family members of the victims. The Chinese government consistently condemns and opposes all manner of terrorist violence."

The next evening President Jiang spoke with President Bush and again strongly condemned "the appalling terrorist attacks," pledging, "We are ready to provide all necessary support and assistance to the U.S. side." That same day, at the United Nations in New York, China voted for the U.S.-sponsored Security Council resolution against terrorism. Under instructions from Beijing, China's UN representative said, "Yesterday's attacks, which stunned the world, took place in the United States, but represented an open challenge to the international community as a whole." China's diplomatic support was clear and firm, aiding the United States in forming a worldwide coalition against terrorism.

Almost immediately after the attack, China dispatched thirty-two counterterrorism specialists to the United States to provide unprecedented access to China's detailed intelligence about the Taliban and Osama bin Laden's al-Qaeda network, a stunning turnabout in U.S.-China relations. Over the next months, as America planned its counterattack, Chinese teams met regularly with their U.S. counterparts. Jiang Zemin's China closed its borders with Afghanistan and its longtime friend Pakistan to prevent al-Qaeda and Taliban leaders from using China as an escape route. China also worked quietly to encourage Pakistan and Central Asian nations to cooperate with America. These proactive behaviors were all the more remarkable considering China's bright-line policy of not violating national sovereignty and noninterference with other countries' internal affairs.

In October, at a joint news conference with President Bush in Shanghai, President Jiang stated that China and the United States "share common responsibility and interest . . . with the international community to combat terrorism." In November, in an unambiguous signal of support, China allowed a U.S. aircraft carrier to stop in Hong Kong en route to the war in Afghanistan.

Jiang's support seemed surprising, considering his behavior after May 7, 1999, when five satellite-guided bombs, dropped from a U.S. Air Force B-2 Stealth bomber flying nonstop from Missouri, destroyed the Chinese embassy in Yugoslavia and killed three Chinese journalists. All across China outrage erupted on the streets and in the media; a firestorm of anti-American anger was fueled by an entrenched conviction that America sought to contain China and frustrate its historic resurgence. As thousands of Chinese students encircled the U.S. embassy in Beijing, hurling rocks along with their epithets, Jiang castigated the United States for its "deliberate provocations."

He told Russian president Boris Yeltsin that the NATO air strikes on Yugoslavia were an example of America's "absolute gun-boat policy" that should "arouse the vigilance of statesmen all over the world." He then ratcheted up the rhetoric, pronouncing that "the U.S.-led NATO must bear full responsibility for the atrocity, or the Chinese people will not leave the matter at that." The next day, when meeting with Russian special envoy Viktor Chernomyrdin, Jiang stated that "the Chinese people have expressed their indignation through demonstrations, rallies, statements and forums, showing their passion, will and great patriotic power." Defiantly he proclaimed, "The great People's Republic of China will never be bullied, the great Chinese nation will never be humiliated, and the great Chinese people will never be conquered."

Jiang's response to September 11 also seemed surprising when compared to his reaction just five months earlier, when a U.S. Navy EP-3E Aries II surveillance plane, monitoring electronic signals off China's coast, collided with a Chinese F-8 fighter jet that crashed into the South China Sea, disintegrated, and killed its pilot. The damaged U.S. aircraft was forced to make an unauthorized emergency landing on the Chinese island of Hainan, and as news of the incident spread, waves of Chinese nationalism and student rage flooded the Internet, inundated radio, television, and the press, and poured onto the streets. Once again Jiang personified China's outrage. "The United States should apologize to the Chinese for this incident," he said, "and bear all responsibilities for the consequences."

Although President Jiang's September 11 feelings of "sympathy and condolences" seemed to be an about-face from his indignant ire over the embassy bombing and airplane collision, they were not. Without understanding his real beliefs, one might assume that Jiang's castigations of America were calculating and opportunistic, that he took advantage of these unfortunate accidents to rouse anti-American sentiments. Such an assumption would be false, a simplistic judgment based on misunderstanding China.

Appreciating how Jiang thinks requires understanding Chinese history and culture, an awareness of the milieu in which he was born, grew up, worked, and lived. The themes that emerge show why, in context, Jiang Zemin's statements about the embassy bombing, the airplane collision, and the September 11 attacks were all drawn from the same philosophical well, each consistent with his overarching vision of China and his long-standing feelings about America.

Although he opposes what he calls American "unilateralism," Jiang appreciates American culture and ideals. While many Americans criticize Jiang for being anti-American, some Chinese derogate him for being pro-American. Jiang is not pro-American, but he does understand America. He is, above all, a Chinese patriot who believes that America can help China grow strong and that good relations between America and China are vital for peace and prosperity in the twenty-first century.

IN 1989 CHINA WAS ENGULFED in its largest crisis since the founding of the People's Republic forty years earlier. As the world watched, huge masses of student protesters gathered in Tiananmen Square in the heart of Beijing, China's capital. In open defiance of their government, they rallied around a homemade replica of the Statue of Liberty and urged Western journalists to share their story with the world. The government reacted, first by imposing martial law, and then by employing force, and the tragedy that ensued drew international censure. In the havoc of the season, the position of general secretary of the Central Committee of the Communist Party of China (Party or CPC), the top job in the country, was given to a former engineer known for his loyalty, tact, cultural values, and intellectual interests. A portly man with a receding hairline and large spectacles, Jiang Zemin was regarded by nearly everyone as a mere transitional figure, someone to hold the place until a new strongman emerged.

A decade later Jiang Zemin was still in place, stronger than ever with the additional titles of chairman of the Central Military Commission and president of China. Though it had taken years of policy renovation, consensus building, deft maneuvering, and political infighting, he had surprised the world, transforming his country into an economic superpower. Under Jiang's leadership, the country had changed in ways that few had thought possible but that, in May 1999, were put to a severe test, literally by fire.

In the spring NATO armed forces, led by the United States, commenced air strikes to force Yugoslav president Slobodan Milosevic to stop Serbian attacks on ethnic Albanians in Kosovo. On May 7 a U.S. B-2 bomber, loaded with forty thousand pounds of ordnance, made one such run. Among its targets was a Serbian military supply building whose detailed coordinates were fed into the bomber's state-of-the-art guidance systems and coordinated with the U.S. military's meter-accurate global positioning satellites.

Of the nine thousand bombs and missiles dropped by NATO forces on Yugoslavia between March 24 and May 6, 1999, only seven had hit the wrong targets. That day five more landed on the Chinese embassy in Belgrade. The bombs destroyed the building and killed those three Chinese journalists. Twenty more people were injured. NATO announced that the bombs had not actually been off target; the problem was that the target itself was wrong. In explaining how one could mistake the large, prominent embassy for a military supply center, spokesmen blamed "faulty information," saying that CIA officials had given military planners incorrect data—or as American intelligence put it, "old maps."

Within an hour of the blast President Jiang convened an emergency meeting of his country's top officials. Present were all seven members of the Politburo Standing Committee, the Party's most senior decision-making body that runs the country, as well as the heads of all relevant ministries and agencies, including the Central Military Commission, the Foreign Ministry, and the Information Office. A rapid response was needed, but providing one would require delicate balance.

Wang Guangya, then vice minister of foreign affairs and more recently China's ambassador to the United Nations, recalled the sensitivities. "We recognized," he said, "that this incident would send shock waves through the populace, especially the young people. The students would surely react."

To the Chinese people, the bombing was a national insult, and virtually everyone assumed that it had been deliberate. Angry crowds began forming in Beijing, focusing their fury on a compound in an eastern, tree-lined section of the city—the U.S. embassy—where the U.S. ambassador to China, James Sasser, was holed up as a virtual hostage. As the crowds grew larger and more belligerent, China watchers realized that the demonstrations were spontaneous.

Back at Zhongnanhai (meaning, literally, "Center [and] South Sea"), the walled-off area of unassuming buildings, Chinese structures, tranquil lakes, and elegant grounds where China's senior leaders live and work, the irony of the situation was noted. For years the U.S. government had criticized China for not being responsive to its people's wishes. Now, listening to public opinion would mean taking an even stronger anti-American stance.

"Tell the U.S. government the Chinese people are not easy to humiliate," a middle-aged man outside the U.S. embassy shouted at a Western reporter. "China is not Kosovo, and it is not Iraq."

After listening to reports from the scene and asking questions, Jiang solicited opinions, individually, from almost everyone in the room. "After all the input was given and all the discussions taken," Wang Guangya remembered, "it was left to President Jiang to weigh the long-term interests of the country against the short-term emotions of the people. This was not easy, although it was clear that China would have to respond sharply. Our sovereignty had been violated and the norms of international law flouted—and we knew that the Chinese public would be watching us.

"But," added Wang, a graduate of the School of Advanced International Studies at Johns Hopkins University, "we also knew that the students could overreact and set themselves on a counterproductive course of action. We all recognized right away that the major challenge we faced was not how to deal with the Americans—that was the easy part—but how to deal with our own citizens, particularly our students, how to prevent inappropriate behavior, how to persuade them not to overreact."

Jiang expected that public anger would peak early and decline quickly, and he did not want to condemn America excessively and exacerbate relations. Together the leaders planned a course of action. The first step would be to cut off negotiations on China's entry into the World Trade Organization (WTO), suspend military and arms control talks with Washington, and demand that America compensate China for losses sustained in the attack. The second would have the country's vice president, Hu Jintao, make a televised address with a dual purpose: to express the seriousness with which the Chinese government viewed the incident and to urge citizens to exercise restraint in their reactions. "Jiang believed," Wang recounted, "that although China had suffered a great wrong, we shouldn't jeopardize our future by an out-of-proportion response."

But Jiang underestimated the power of the people's fury. With senior leadership cloistered away for three days of virtually nonstop meetings, some sardonic Beijingers rang up the emergency line at the police department to report three missing persons: Jiang Zemin, Zhu Rongji, and Li Peng.

"Here at the Foreign Ministry," Wang said, "we received an avalanche of biting, hostile criticism from our own people. Mountains of letters piled up, our switchboards were jammed, and our ministry's website was almost incapacitated with e-mails. It's ironic that Americans say that there is no freedom of expression in China.

"A few would have had us declare war on NATO or America, or retaliate with a missile attack against NATO's headquarters," Wang continued. "Early on Russian president Boris Yeltsin made extreme remarks, and some took his unfiltered comments to advocate a military alliance between China and Russia to confront the United States."

Against this backdrop of heated debate, Jiang stressed the need for economic progress and social stability. He urged the continuation of current foreign policy in the interests of China itself as well as world peace.

Moderation was not popular. The Chinese people, long wary of foreign aggression, viewed the deaths of three Chinese citizens on a symbolic piece of Chinese territory by NATO forces as an egregious affront. Jiang now realized that the Party had to take the lead in expressing such nationalism or risk losing control of the volatile situation.

His challenge was not limited to preserving the stability of the social order but also involved sustaining his personal power within it. It was no secret that President Jiang and Premier Zhu Rongji believed that good relations with the United States were necessary to transform China's economy and improve its people's lives, a position with which some of their colleagues, especially Li Peng, disagreed.

The public was not on their side either: ordinary Chinese had become steadily more anti-American in their attitudes, and this change of heart narrowed Jiang's maneuvering room. A 1995 poll of Chinese young people had 87 percent naming the United States as the country "least friendly" to China and 57 percent stating the country about which they felt most negative was the United States.

Jiang did not escape censure. To many Chinese, their president seemed inordinately quiet, even reticent, in the face of the American outrage. Public expressions of disgust at Jiang's apparent passivity spread. Not all the protest banners condemned America; some now ridiculed their own leader. One read "Slave of the American Master." Another said, "Jiang Zemin—the Turtle That Pulls in Its Head." A college student on his third day of besieging the U.S. embassy put it this way: "Even if the government forbids protests, we'll still demonstrate until the Americans give us a good answer."

Though personal preservation did not drive his decision-making, Jiang had to wonder whether his conservative colleagues, perhaps in concert with elements in the military, could turn the rapidly growing anti-American demonstrations against him, weakening his control. Some spoke with nostalgia for Mao Zedong, praising his actions during the Korean War in thwarting the United States. "Now everyone is saying Mao was great after all," asserted one army colonel. "Let the world's proletariat unite and smash U.S. imperialism. The embassy attack woke up the Chinese people; it should also wake up Jiang and Zhu."

Faced with the unnerving prospect of tens of thousands of Chinese marching through the streets, Jiang decided to assuage, rather than oppose, the mounting public anger. He moved to channel the outrage, seeking alignment between the protesters and the government. He wanted to make sure that his country remained stable and that his administration remained secure. General Fu Quanyou, chief of the General Staff, pledged fidelity to the Party and to Jiang and vowed to "defend state sovereignty and territorial integrity and ensure that they are not infringed upon."

State media praised the students for backing the government. Party-supported student unions rented buses to transport students to the embassy district in an effort to avoid masses of young people marching across Beijing and drawing workers to join their cause, as had happened in 1989. The government certainly did not want protesting students stopping off around Zhongnanhai, or heading there in the first place, to vilify their "weak" leaders for not "standing up to America."

On May 9 Vice President Hu Jintao, who would become Jiang's successor, appeared on national television. Hu condemned the bombing as a "criminal act" that violated international law and said that the Chinese government "firmly supports and protects . . . all legal protest activities." But he also added that it would "prevent overreaction." This was the first time most people had heard Hu speak. The next generation's leader projected a strong, resolute personality.

While other Chinese leaders kept a low profile, Hu sought to encourage students, yet at the same time calm them, as they vented their rage against America. He had built his political base as a former head of the Communist Youth League and was the youngest senior leader. Channeling student rage was essential for containing the crisis, and the Youth League, with which Hu maintained ties, helped provide students with demonstration banners and transportation to the American diplomatic compound.

President Jiang refused to take a hotline call from President Bill Clinton, who telephoned to offer his apologies. "I was dumbfounded and deeply upset by the mistake and immediately called Jiang Zemin to apologize," remembered Clinton, who called the tragic bombing "the worst political setback of the conflict." But the Chinese leadership had decided that any apology by the United States must be made officially as a nation and should not be exchanged privately between leaders. Waiving diplomatic ceremony, Clinton "publicly and repeatedly apologized."

That same day Clinton sent a formal letter to Jiang expressing "regret and condolences on behalf of the American people" for the bombing. He emphasized that the attack "was in no way willful, was not intentional and was clearly a mistake."

"I don't blame people for being upset about it; I'm upset about it," Clinton said. "We need some sense of proportion here."

Across China, the irate crowds grew more raucous. Students and workers continued to hurl rocks and garbage at the U.S. embassy, smashing the few remaining windows. Protest marches were staged at U.S. missions in other cities. The U.S. State Department warned American citizens not to travel to China and advised those already there to avoid crowds.

After three days of siege Ambassador James Sasser gave an on-the-spot report. "We're inside the embassy here and we're surrounded by a cordon of police," he said. "The embassy building itself is a structure that's been damaged by missiles thrown in, breaking windows, and Molotov cocktails have set at least two fires in the embassy yesterday." Sasser added that although President Clinton had issued a formal apology and Secretary of State Madeleine Albright had gone to the Chinese embassy in Washington to express the profound condolences of the American government, neither gesture had been reported by the Chinese media.

Hours after the bombing Ding Guangen, head of the Party's Publicity (Propaganda) Department, had called a meeting of newspaper editors to discuss their coverage. From that moment every newspaper—from the trendy *Beijing Youth Daily* to *People's Daily,* the Party mouthpiece—devoted multiple pages to the bombings, all expressing identical views, often using the same turns of phrase to do so. With headlines screaming "Shock-Outrage-Protest" or "The Bomb Attack Was Premeditated," the Chinese press retreated from its forays into diversity and spoke with a single stentorian voice.

Virtually every newspaper published similar columns by similar experts, all of whom offered "proof" that the bombing had been intentional. Television programs that normally attacked corruption now vilified America.

To the West, it looked like a propaganda campaign to sway the people's opinions. The opposite was true: Although the media could never challenge or contradict the Party or the government, most Chinese dismissed the notion that it could manipulate their thoughts or opinions anymore. Instead, the public was dictating what the media broadcasted and published. The headlines, outrage, and expert opinions all gave the masses precisely what they wanted to read and hear, just as the market-driven press did in the West. An intentional bombing only confirmed what most Chinese already believed: that America sought to contain and control China and would stop at nothing to do so.

By contrast, many Americans blamed the Chinese government for stirring up anti-U.S. hostility. They naïvely interpreted the Chinese media coverage as Beijing taking advantage of the situation, and concluded that the bombing provided a handy excuse for Chinese leaders to do what many Westerners feared they wanted to do all along—commence expansionist, nationalistic aggression.

Polls showed that as many as 90 percent of Chinese did not believe NATO's explanation that the bombing had been an accident, a statistic borne out by conversations with sophisticated Chinese. It seemed implausible, they said, that a country as technologically advanced as America could make such a stupid mistake.

Boris Yeltsin telephoned Jiang to pronounce his "strongest condemnation," adding that "the stance of Russia is totally the same as that of China." Jiang called the attack "an utmost barbarous act" and said that the two countries would strengthen cooperation in international issues, including Kosovo. Both agreed that military interference in sovereign countries was wrong and dangerous. Going to *Guangming Daily* to mourn and praise two of the dead journalists, Jiang said the attack "seriously infringed on Chinese sovereignty and constitute[d] an open provocation of the 1.2 billion Chinese people" and was "a gross violation of international norms and the working rights of journalists."

Although Clinton had apologized personally to Jiang, the feeling remained that NATO and America had yet to apologize officially to China. Relations deteriorated further when China canceled normal military contact with the United States and broke off consultations on weapons proliferation, arms control, human rights, and international security.

At an emotion-laden ceremony where he welcomed home embassy staff members from Yugoslavia and conferred the title of "revolutionary martyr" on the three dead journalists, Jiang praised the Chinese people's indignation, which he said evinced the "great patriotism and cohesive force" of the Chinese nation, and stressed that China "can never be bullied!" For the first time in three years, Jiang called America "hegemonist," a derogatory term that China reserves for its enemies. He accused the United States of using its economic and technological superiority to pursue "power politics and to wantonly interfere in the internal affairs of other countries." He said that the United States must "make formal apologies, thoroughly investigate the bombing and punish those responsible," warning, "Otherwise the Chinese people will never let the matter go."

At the same time Jiang asked the Chinese people to channel their rightful ire into building the country's economic, defense, and national strength. He asserted that social stability must be maintained, noting that China had to be "vigilant to the attempts of hostile forces from both home and abroad to create chaos and undermine the socialist modernization drive." Jiang's reference to "hostile forces" at "home" was not missed.

On May 14, after a week of tense silence, Jiang accepted a telephone call from Clinton. During the thirty-minute conversation Clinton again expressed his sincere regrets for the tragedy and offered his condolences to the injured embassy staff and family members of the deceased.

Clinton later described this first post-bombing conversation with Jiang. "I apologized again and told him that I was sure he didn't believe I would knowingly attack his embassy. Jiang replied that he knew I wouldn't do that but said he did believe that there were people in the Pentagon or the CIA who didn't favor my outreach to China and could have rigged the maps intentionally to cause a rift between us. Jiang had a hard time believing that a nation as technologically advanced as we were could make such a mistake." Clinton then mused, "I had a hard time believing it too, but that's what happened."

Clinton promised Jiang that there would be an investigation of the bombing and that he would let the Chinese people know the truth as soon as possible. Jiang "took note" of the regrets and the promises, using a diplomatic expression that suggested Beijing was finally willing to acknowledge Clinton's repeated apologies. Stating that the protests were spontaneous, Jiang told Clinton that it was up to America to repair the damaged ties between the two countries.

The fever of the crisis broke the following day when China's state media reported Clinton's apology. It was featured prominently on the front pages of all the national newspapers, alongside Jiang's appeal to the Chinese people to channel their anger into making China strong enough to resist such affronts in the future.

In the West, the delay in widely reporting the apologies was seen as proof that the Chinese government encouraged the violent protests, but in truth the outrage had come first from the Chinese people, not from their leaders. Violence would have erupted regardless of what the government did or said. The four-day lapse between the first American apology and the Chinese media's broad coverage of it had given the country's citizens a chance to express and dissipate their nationalistic anger. By the time the apology was finally reported, passions had run their course and the population was ready for resolution.

Western pundits assumed that the bombing would set back U.S.-China relations for years and bolster conservative factions in the Party. They were wrong; what happened was the reverse. Jiang used the crisis to strengthen his leadership and his reform-minded agenda. In its aftermath, the Chinese media unabashedly praised his handling of the crisis.

In mid-June the American side of the story was presented to the Chinese people in a complete and relatively balanced manner. China Central Television's (CCTV) *National News*, the most widely watched program in China, devoted a significant portion of its broadcast to the issue. The government was now working to defuse the confrontation, as Jiang had advocated from the beginning. "Most Chinese people believe [the bombing] was deliberately planned," said one government foreign policy adviser. "We needed time to release that kind of emotion."

The Chinese people's response to the tragedy reflected a complex attitude toward America. During the protests at the U.S. embassy, one undergraduate could be heard vociferously berating a reporter about America's condescending belief that its political system should be imposed on every country in the world. When the reporter asked how long his ranting would continue, the young man matter-of-factly replied that he couldn't stay around much longer. He had to go home, he explained, to study for his upcoming GRE, the entrance exam for American graduate schools.

Like many people in the world, Chinese aspire to live as Americans do, even as they resent the power that they believe America holds over them. Chinese feelings are reflected in the following joke: "Since World War II, why has every country in the world had a revolution except the United States? Because the U.S. is the only country without an American embassy."

American insensitivity and egocentric naïveté do not help. James Sasser relates an incident from a 1997 congressional visit to Beijing. After a senior official briefed the delegation on China's domestic and international issues, he invited questions. "I just want to know," one member of Congress inquired, "if you've accepted Jesus Christ as your personal savior." The Chinese official, Sasser recalls, looked stunned.

In 1989 Chinese students had appealed to America for help against their own government. Ten years later they were freely lambasting their leaders for not standing up to America. Back then political freedom had been at stake. This time it was national pride. The demonstrators in Tiananmen had been more outward-looking than their leaders; now it was precisely the opposite: Jiang Zemin and his government were more outward-looking than were their nationalistic critics and citizenry. In one short decade, neatly spanning the tenure of one man's power, the country had undergone an astonishing transformation.

IT IS ALMOST IMPOSSIBLE to comprehend the changes that have occurred in China during Jiang Zemin's term of leadership. The dramatic improvement in the standard of living of most Chinese, and in the strength and vitality of the country, is evidenced in almost every city and town. The Chinese economy, based on purchasing power, is now the second largest in the world; in thirty years it may well be the largest. Chinese corporations are selling electronics around the world and Chinese entrepreneurs are building private businesses on the Internet.

Problems of unemployment, corruption, income disparity, and a primitive legal system are real, continuing, and troubling, but there is a newfound dynamism and self-assurance among the people. Material well-being is only part of the reason. Another is that they no longer fear to speak their minds. Hundreds of millions use cell phones, even for transmitting political jokes. More than a billion Chinese watch television, choosing from dozens of channels. The diversity in dress and entertainment, the art forms from film to fashion, the flexibility in personal behaviors—job choice, unrestricted travel, sex education—all confirm the magnitude of the changes. China won the bid to host the 2008 Olympics, launched its first astronaut, instituted measured legal and political reform, revitalized its armed forces, and is involved in every major foreign affairs issue. Domestically confident and internationally respected, China has become a leader among the great nations of the world.

Jiang Zemin's life and leadership sweep through almost eighty tumultuous years of Chinese history and personify it. His story is an epic of war, deprivation, revolution, political turmoil, social convulsion, economic reform, national transformation, and international resurgence. By examining his life and legacy, we experience the clash between China's traditional culture and chaotic history, and the enormity of the Chinese people's struggles, traumas, aspirations, challenges, and triumphs.

In a sense, Jiang's early skeptics got it right: He was a transitional figure—but not in the way they had meant it. With unshakable if paternalistic vision, backroom political skills that no one anticipated, and a persistence that can only be called indefatigable, Jiang Zemin became an unexpected agent of change, effecting the transition from a traumatized society to a stable, confident, prosperous country rapidly ascending in the New World Order. The skeptics misunderstood and underestimated the man, the man who changed China.

Part One

Grounding

1926–1989

Chapter 1

1926 – 1943

"My Background Is My Family"

NINETEEN TWENTY-SIX, THE YEAR OF THE TIGER, was a time of great uncertainty for China. Fifteen years had passed since the overthrow of the Qing dynasty and the founding of the republic, but warlords and other political factions still dueled with the Nationalist (Kuomintang) government for primacy, while to the east, the Japanese were making unsettling noises of war. In the ancient city of Yangzhou on the banks of the Grand Canal, 150 miles northwest of Shanghai in Jiangsu province, a young couple named Jiang Shijun and Wu Yueqing had a third child. The date was August 17.

Appropriately for a society that values family so highly, it is the custom in China for the surname to come first rather than last as it does in the West. Since the Chinese have no common pool of first names from which to choose, babies are given names that are individual reflections of who they are. A name can refer to any number of things, from ancestral heritage to a proud parent's hope for the future, and it generally consists of one or two characters, each representing a separate idea. It is not unusual for the given names of siblings, and even cousins of the same generation, to start with the same first character, thus strengthening the family identity. This was the case in the Jiang family, and the new baby, a boy, was given a name like his siblings before him that started with the character *ze*, which translates into "benefit" or "help." It is the same character as the *ze* in Mao Zedong, but where Mao's given name literally means "benefit the East" (which some might call perfect foresight and others perfect irony), Jiang Zemin's given name, taken from the writings of Confucius, means "benefit the people."

"The making of a leader takes more than the person himself," Jiang Zehui, the president's sister, later reflected. "It involves the historical and cultural background of a family. One cannot understand President Jiang without understanding three things about him: his family heritage, his cultural roots, and his revolutionary background. It's not by accident that Third Brother [San Ge], as I've always called Jiang Zemin, has become a state leader."

The same could be said about almost any Chinese leader of a certain age, but perhaps in no other case are the three elements so intimately entwined. Jiang's last name means "river" and was derived from a poor village in a lush, mountainous area of eastern China. But exactly which poor village is the Jiang family's ancestral home is a matter of controversy. At one point President Jiang, a bit embarrassed by the dispute between two dueling villages, asked both sides to "stop guessing." If one were to ask, he would say that his hometown is Yangzhou, the city of his birth.

With a history stretching back some 2,500 years, Yangzhou was a center of culture and commerce. The Han canal, which runs through it and links the Yangtze River with the Huai River, is the oldest in China; it was constructed in the year 486 B.C. In his *Travels* Marco Polo wrote that when he arrived in Yangzhou, he felt as if he had ventured into a wonderland, and there were those who believed that the city produced the most beautiful women in the country. Emperors would seek their brides there, an honor to which other Chinese cities also lay claim.

Even discounting the legends, Yangzhou has a rich and storied past. In the Ming and Qing dynasties, it was a favorite destination of wealthy businessmen and high officials, many of whom had homes there. Its Slim West Lake area contained numerous establishments to fulfill every desire, from restaurants and teahouses to bookstores and brothels. During the evenings the city was alight with festivities as tourist boats cruised the rivers accompanied by the music of flutes. "Those rich with tens of thousands of dollars," goes one ancient saying, "must ride cranes to Yangzhou."

During the Qing dynasty a creative and intellectual movement known as the Yangzhou School flourished in the city. Local officials sponsored poetry contests, and every afternoon audiences would assemble to listen to storytellers present dramatic narrations of Chinese classics. It was also the era of the Eight Eccentrics, a group of innovative Yangzhou artists whose actual number was closer to fifteen. Using various forms of expression, from drawings and paintings to poems and essays, they established subtle links between art and politics and railed against social evils and imperial control. Rather than adhering to the old brushstroke conventions, they created a new naturalistic style. In this way they changed the course of Chinese art, becoming forerunners of modern Chinese culture.

Shi Kefa, a celebrated figure in Yangzhou history, is one of Jiang Zemin's heroes and role models. Born in 1602, Shi Kefa witnessed the decline of the increasingly weak and corrupt Ming dynasty. He rose to the rank of general, and when Manchu invaders conquered Beijing and established the Qing dynasty in 1645, he refused to acknowledge their authority. Instead, he went to Yangzhou to prepare its defense. The day after he arrived the Qing army laid siege to the city. Though he faced overwhelming odds, Shi Kefa refused to surrender. "I have already determined to die if the city is breached," he informed his Qing counterpart. "No matter how you may kill me, I do not worry about my life."

A week later Yangzhou was invaded. Shi Kefa was arrested and put to death, becoming the first high official of the South Ming dynasty to perish at his post. Over time his legend grew, until his death was deemed so solemn "that all of earth, heaven, gods and ghosts were moved."

To Jiang Zemin, Shi Kefa represented the highest Chinese ideals: patriotism, diligence, commitment, honesty, morality, and self-sacrifice. In a 1991 interview with Russian media, Jiang reaffirmed his allegiance to the city of his birth and to its most famous citizen. "I am a native of Yangzhou," he said. "At the foot of Meiling Mountain, there is the Hat and Clothes Tomb of Shi Kefa. At the tomb, there is also an antithetical couplet that reads: 'Plum flowers shed tears of a fallen nation. Half of the moon radiates my hometown sentiments.' "

"When I was a student in Yangzhou," Jiang recalled in 1995, "I was shocked to see and hear about the evil acts of the Japanese aggressors. Every time I saw the tombstone of Shi Kefa with my classmates [they often visited on Sundays], I felt strong anti-Japanese and patriotic emotions and became determined to engage in revolutionary struggle." It is said that Jiang Zemin meditates on the "eight virtues" of Shi Kefa.

Yangzhou has long been eclipsed by other cities, a fate that helped preserve its quaint charm. A description of the place, written in 1934, encapsulated both pros and cons of Jiang's hometown. "The city lacks the sort of splendid roads one finds in a major city. The honking cars, the blazing lights, the Western-style buildings soaring into the clouds. It also bears no traces of occupation by the blue-eyed, and no missionaries. It could be said to be an utterly Chinese place and certainly is spared the insults and oppression of imperialism to which those big cities are subject."

Jiang has always been proud of his origins and continues to speak with a noticeable Yangzhou accent. One of his favorite writers, Zhu Ziqing, also comes from Yangzhou, and his work expresses the complex relationship that locals have with their city. A classmate of Jiang's father, Zhu wrote a well-known essay, "I Am a Yangzhou Man." In it, he refers movingly to the city.

"My family's relationship with Yangzhou by and large fits what the ancients say," he wrote. " 'Born here, died here, sang and wept here.' "

Until Jiang was seven, his family lived in a spacious home on Tianjia Lane, a street bordering the Grand Canal in the city's exclusive Dongquan district. The street name is said to have arisen during the late Ming dynasty, when a beautiful, talented girl from a family known as Tian—*jia* is the Chinese word for "family"—became a favorite of the emperor and was promoted to the rank of imperial concubine. (She was skilled, it is said, at the fascinating territorial game Go.)

Built in the classical Chinese design around an inner courtyard, the gray-brick Jiang house featured doorframes with intricate stone carvings and was lined with books and works of art. It was a home befitting Jiang Zemin's grandfather, Jiang Shixi, a scholar and businessman. Jiang Shixi was also a doctor of traditional Chinese medicine, a poet, a musician, a political activist, and an ardent nationalist. Though he died when Jiang Zemin was only seven, his values and beliefs had a lasting impact on the household. "Our family has been a family of letters," Jiang Zehui observed, "with a deep commitment to learning and a love of literature and art. From one generation to another, our family has had tradition in our education and discipline in our upbringing."

Grandfather Jiang's residence housed a rich but not expensive collection of paintings, ancient books, and calligraphies (the artistic writing of Chinese characters). He played various musical instruments, including the lute, and he liked to sing; he enjoyed Chinese chess and took pleasure in painting. Most of all, he loved writing poetry. "Our grandfather was a wonderful poet," said Jiang Zehui, who bears a striking similarity to her famous brother. "I have a book of Grandfather Jiang's poems, which reflects the society in which he lived. Sadly, the original calligraphies were destroyed during the political madness of the Cultural Revolution."

At times Grandfather Jiang's life was difficult. Two of his sons died in childhood during a famine in the last years of the Qing dynasty. His medical practice, while highly respected, did not make enough money to support the family. In 1919, at the age of forty-nine, he left medicine and, with little experience, entered the world of commerce; the Chinese now refer to such a change as "jumping into the sea." He joined the Grand Canal Shipping Company and later became the company's representative in Yangzhou. It was during this period that he moved the family to the comfortable house where Jiang Zemin was born.

"My grandfather was not a landlord, nor was he a capitalist," explained President Jiang, more than eighty years later. "But he was educated, cultured, and very talented. In the old days, when ships were sailing on the Yangtze River, their propellers often became entangled with weeds, the grasses that grew wildly in the water. He invented a machine that could cut these weeds, which he sold—for less than it was worth—to a well-known businessman."

In his early years Jiang was just another boy in a home brimming with children. In his nuclear family alone there were three sons and two daughters. Each was expected, as had been expected of their father before them, to be a "dragon," or distinguished person. The house was full of books, music, art, and political discussion—all of which would imprint Jiang Zemin.

When Grandfather Jiang died at the age of sixty-three, financial constraints forced the family to move to humbler surroundings, but the spiritual loss was greater than the material one. Grandfather Jiang had been a powerful, vigorous figure. Though much occupied with business, he never forsook his love of art and literature—he had many artistic and scholarly friends—and took pride in honing his calligraphic skills. Like many intellectuals of his day, he had been politically active, writing articles that took strong nationalistic positions. Early in the century he had decried the weakness of the Qing dynasty. Later he lamented Japanese incursions into China and committed dissident acts against a scheming imperial general. He even set his nationalistic writings to music so that his fervent, defiant messages would reach more people by way of these satirical songs.

At the funeral Jiang Zemin's uncle, Jiang Shangqing, recited a poem he had written, titled "Mourning Father." "You have given the world your best," he said. "But you never wanted to stand out above others."

His words described the family's philosophy. Like his siblings and cousins, Jiang Zemin was taught to excel while remaining humble. By the time of his grandfather's death, he had started school at the prestigious Xionghua Guan Primary School, about a twenty-minute walk from his home. The school's curriculum combined modern and traditional elements. The traditional program was constructed around four arts—literature, music, calligraphy, and Chinese chess—subjects Jiang would enjoy throughout his life.

It was here that he acquired his ongoing passion for music, learning to play a variety of instruments including the bamboo flute, the piano, and the *erhu*, a two-stringed Chinese violin that dates back over a thousand years. Many decades later President Jiang would be sitting in the audience when a noted *erhu* player had a mental breakdown and could not continue. Jiang walked up

江绍岳　　赵氏
（石泽）
（1870－1933）（1873－1956）

Family tree of the Jiang family, drawn by Jiang Zehui, August 2004.

JIANG FAMILY TREE

Jiang Shaoyue (aka Shixi)
(1870–1933)

Mrs. Jiang (aka Ms. Fan)
(1873–1956)

First Son: Jiang Shijun (Guanqian, 1894–1973)
Wife: Wu Yueqing (1897–1977)

- Jiang Zejun (Zhejun) — son
- Jiang Zefen — daughter
- Jiang Zemin — son (adopted by Shangqing)
- Jiang Zekuan (Wu Dexin) — son
- Jiang Zenan (Zelan) — daughter

Second Son: Jiang Shijie (died young)

Third Son: Jiang Shihao (died young)

Daughter: Jiang Shiying (1906–1948)
Husband: Liang Muyuan

Fifth Son: Jiang Shixiong (Mutao, 1909–1966)
Wife: Yang Guifen (1911–1944)

- Jiang Zequn — daughter
- Jiang Qiaosheng — son (died young)
- Jiang Qingsheng — son

Sixth Son: Jiang Shihou (Shangqing, 1911–1939)
Wife: Wang Zhelan (1911–1985)

- Jiang Zeling — daughter
- Jiang Zehui — daughter
- Jiang Zemin — adopted son

Seventh Son: Jiang Shibo (Shufeng, 1914–1993)
Wife: Hu Qide (1916–1983)

- Jiang Zezhong (Zhezhong) — son
- Jiang Pan — daughter

onstage, requested the *erhu*, sat down in a chair, and played a well-known piece.

The Chinese classics formed the core of Jiang's early education. Every day—even before he was old enough to begin school—his father would require him to recite lines from the great masters of the Tang and Song dynasties, poems that were seeded with wise sayings and practical advice.

In keeping with his classical training, Jiang also had extensive lessons in calligraphy, learning to draw traditional Chinese characters in a way that integrated verbal and visual ideas. Though the Chinese mainland adopted a simplified system for writing characters after 1949, President Jiang still used the traditional style (as do Taiwan and Hong Kong) and to this day will present his personal inscriptions to organizations, events, or projects he wants to support.

Every day when class was over, Jiang would sing a song that, decades later, still affected him: "Now after school I am going home. Mom is waiting for me. So please don't dally and loiter around. Have you remembered clearly what the teacher said today? Administering the country and the world in the future all depends on us. So let us work hard. See you tomorrow, classmates!" School songs would hold lifelong meaning for Jiang. One time (when he was China's president), he became so frustrated when he couldn't remember certain verses that he called an old classmate in America to refresh his memory.

But school could provide only a temporary shelter from the realities of the outside world. The Japanese were coming. Weeks after Jiang started his first year of education in 1931, Japan began its brutal incursions into Manchuria. In 1932, seeking a base to invade inland China, Japan launched the Battle of Shanghai, where Japanese aircraft carriers saw action for the first time.

Closer to home, the city of Yangzhou was embroiled in a literary uproar. In 1934, when Jiang was eight, a book titled *Idle Talk on Yangzhou*, written by a government official named Yi Junzuo, was published in Shanghai. Denouncing what he saw as prevailing trends of decadence and apathy, Yi portrayed Yangzhou as a stagnant place, a breeding ground for passive, indolent people. "Yangzhou," he wrote, "is like a great family in decline." Yi raised the highly charged issue of collaboration with the Japanese and, for good measure, made reference to an eighth-century poet who once claimed that "prostitutes throughout the country have all been trained in Yangzhou."

The people of the city were enraged, and the Committee for the Investigation of Yi Junzuo was formed. Led by a remarkable woman, a mother of ten who had founded an anti–foot binding association and a girls' school, the group succeeded in forcing Yi to apologize publicly and pay a fine of $800. The offending book was banned, and the publisher agreed to destroy its printing plates along with all remaining copies.

But silencing the critics was not the same as solving the problem. Yi's book was not merely a diatribe against Yangzhou but also a critique of the country. Even as Japanese troops advanced from the north, Communist and Nationalist forces continued to battle each other. In August 1935, during its year-long, 6,000-mile strategic retreat called the Long March, the Communists proposed to stop the civil war and form a united front to fight their common Japanese enemy, but the bitter adversaries were unable to put aside their differences.

"Chinese should not fight Chinese," chanted student protesters. The internal conflict came to a head in December 1936. Unhappy with Nationalist leader Chiang Kai-shek's focus on destroying the Communists rather than defeating the Japanese, Nationalist soldiers, led by General Zhang Xueliang, staged a minor coup. They kidnapped Chiang as he was visiting the ancient city of Xi'an and kept him prisoner until he agreed to form a coalition with the Communists to confront the foreign invaders.

Jiang Zemin was ten years old at the time, and as part of his secondary school entrance exams, he wrote an essay approving Zhang's bold action. The Jiang household was a political one, and the boy already knew on which side his allegiance lay. In the spring of 1937 he graduated from primary school with exam scores that placed him in the top ten percent. That summer he started Yangzhou Middle School, which in his year accepted only fifty of eighteen hundred applicants from all Jiangsu province.

Based on a Western model, the school offered six years of demanding education. It had already produced politicians, scientists, and intellectuals, including Zhu Ziqing, the literary giant who later refused to eat American-supplied relief grain. Mao himself would praise the symbolic patriotic act, saying that Zhu "embodied the heroic spirit of the Chinese people."

In school Jiang memorized numerous classical Chinese poems, many of which he could recite by heart into old age. One favorite was "My Cottage Unroofed by an Autumn Gale" by the Tang dynasty poet Du Fu, who lived in the eighth century. Jiang would quote the last stanza, which is among the most admired in Chinese poetry.

> *Could I get mansions covering ten thousand miles,*
> *I'd house all scholars poor and make them beam with smiles.*

In wind and rain these mansions would stand like mountains high.
Alas! Should these houses appear before my eye,
Frozen in my unroofed cot, content I'd die.

JIANG HAS ALWAYS LOVED PATRIOTIC poems. On public occasions and in private meetings he would refer to the Ming dynasty poet Gu Yanwu, who said, "Every man has a share of responsibility for the fate of his country." He often recounted the story of the Song dynasty prime minister Wen Tianxiang, who refused to surrender to his country's enemy and wrote the famous lines: "Since olden days there is no man but suffers death; let me but leave a loyal heart shining in the pages of history."

Jiang would recall the Song dynasty general Yuefei, whose deeds of courage were memorialized in his stirring nationalistic poem, *Manjianghong:* "You can spend thirty years pursuing worthless fame, or traveling eight thousand miles night and day fighting for your country. Decide wisely, lest you regret having wasted your youth. . . ." Later, as leader of China, Jiang could look back and say, "When we were students, these works were rooted in our hearts and made us love our country."

Jiang also grew to love Russian and Western literature. He read many works that had been translated into Chinese, including *War and Peace, Anna Karenina,* and *Les Misérables.* Later, as president, he would pay homage to his literary heroes during trips abroad. In Russia he visited Tolstoy's home, and in France he went to the place in Marseilles where Alexandre Dumas wrote *The Count of Monte Cristo.* Yangzhou Middle School also introduced Jiang to American culture. He learned the speeches of Thomas Jefferson and Abraham Lincoln, and to this day he can recite the Gettysburg Address, which he did to great effect as mayor of Shanghai.

"I had three kinds of education," Jiang reflected. "The first was Chinese philosophy, particularly Confucius and Mencius; from elementary school on I began to recite the three-character scriptures. My second kind was bourgeois education, especially Western science. My third was Marxist education."

"OUR JIANG FAMILY WAS A LARGE ONE," recalled Jiang Zehui, the president's sister. "All of us—grandparents, their four sons and a daughter, with all their spouses and grandchildren—lived together. None had separate households."

Arrangements like this gave rise to the Chinese term *Big Family (da jia).* The ties in such Big Families run deep and can be complicated. Jiang Zemin may have been born to the family's oldest son, Jiang Shijun, but in a sense, he belonged to the entire clan.

"Sure it was crowded, but there were benefits in living so tightly together," said Jiang Zehui. "Grandpa passed on his cultural passions, even to the generation of Third Brother and me, as if the love of literature and art could be encoded in our genes. Look at Grandpa's children: my father, my Oldest Uncle, and my Seventh Uncle all excelled at classical literature and poetry. My father was Sixth Son, and my Oldest Uncle, First Son, was Jiang Zemin's father."

What? If the fathers of Jiang Zehui and Jiang Zemin were *brothers,* wouldn't that make Jiang Zehui the president's *cousin,* not his sister?

"Jiang Zemin," she said slowly, savoring the paradox, "is truly my Third *Brother*—this is no figure of speech or Chinese custom. To explain why, I must start the story with my birth.

"It was 1938, also the Year of the Tiger," she began. "Jiang Zemin was twelve at the time, and so Third Brother and I, being twelve years apart [a complete zodiac cycle], are both 'Tigers.' The Japanese had invaded, and China was in collective agony when I was born in my grandmother's home in the countryside, on a small islet in the Yangtze River."

With the men gone, Grandmother Fan, who was from a family of farmers, had taken charge, moving the entire Jiang household to avoid the Japanese air raids. She gathered up her daughters-in-law and her grandchildren from their comfortable home in Yangzhou and hurried them off to her native village, an unassuming rural area not far away but not likely to be attacked.

Jiang Zehui's father, Jiang Shangqing, who was Jiang Zemin's uncle, was not often home. He was a revolutionary, and that was how he became so significant to Jiang Zemin.

In 1928, at the age of seventeen, Jiang Shangqing had secretly joined the Communist Youth. He studied literature at Shanghai Arts University and took up his pen as if it were a gun, writing numerous poems and essays and establishing periodicals and newsletters to criticize the corrupt government and spread revolutionary fire. The Nationalists were already determined to eradicate Communism, and the young man was denounced by a disloyal colleague. Jiang Shangqing was arrested and imprisoned for his beliefs, and refusing to betray others, he spent the next few years in and out of jail. Though he was nearly executed on several occasions, his determination never wavered. In prison or out, he continued to work relentlessly for the cause.

In 1932 the Communists helped secure his release. (By this time he was a full-fledged member of the Party.) He returned home to recuperate from his imprisonment and plunged right back into the revolution. He started a radical journal and, undaunted when local authorities shut it down, started another one. The police persecuted him, driving him from one teaching job to the next, but he continued to maintain his Communist ties, sometimes under the nose of Nationalist officials.

Notwithstanding his progressive ideas and underground activities, Jiang Zemin's uncle maintained close ties with his family. In 1935, at the age of twenty-four, he allowed his mother to arrange his marriage to her niece, Wang Zhelan, at a time when many young revolutionaries were casting aside such cultural traditions. For Jiang Shangqing, the old ways could harmonize with and even strengthen the new ones. It was a philosophy that Jiang Zemin would later share.

IN 1937 THE CONFLICT WITH JAPAN escalated into full-scale war, and the course of Jiang Shangqing's life changed forever. "My heart is heavy, my eyes are sullen," he wrote in a poem. "I dream of my wandering. My night poem is filled with tears and drowned with sorrows. Raindrops on the palm leaves are like my solitary heart of indignation. Old books won't give me power. Horses tread outside like violent drumming."

Like many young patriots, Jiang Shangqing joined the Communist army. At first his duties centered on journalism and education—areas of his expertise. He organized anti-Japanese propaganda teams and work troops, encouraging the people to unite and fight the invaders. Then in 1938 a Kuomintang official named Sheng Zijin, who recognized the importance of Communists to the war effort, asked that some Party members be sent to work with him. The Party sent seven men to Sheng, who was stationed in Anhui province, with secret instructions to organize a Party branch in the occupied area and ensure that Communists controlled the anti-Japanese bases there. This covert unit was led by Jiang Shangqing. His official role was secretary general to Sheng and chief commander of the public security headquarters—effectively the number two Nationalist in the region—but he was operating undercover as the special Party secretary in northeast Anhui. (In the Communist system of governance, Party secretaries are always the most senior official for the area or function.)

It was a tricky role to play. At any moment the Nationalist government could discover that he was a spy. At the same time, to many Communists, he appeared to have gone over to the other side. In his official capacity he worked with Sheng, who appointed him political director of the Fifth Guerrilla district. All the while Jiang Shangqing was converting the local population to Communism. He also managed to persuade Sheng to incorporate two Communist-led guerrilla groups into the Kuomintang army.

As Jiang Shangqing's fortunes rose, those of his country declined. In the fall of 1937 the Japanese army escalated its attacks on China's coastal regions. In December Shanghai fell. In another month the Japanese took the Yangtze River valley all the way to Nanjing. Jiang Zemin's school in Yangzhou was requisitioned by Japanese troops, who converted the gymnasium into a horse stable. Books were torched; teachers and students were dismissed.

Still, the city could consider itself lucky. The takeover had been relatively bloodless. Only fifty miles away the citizens of Nanjing faced devastation. The Japanese slaughtered an estimated 40,000 to 60,000 people in a city of one million. Bodies lined the streets, as burning, looting, and torture became the order of the day. The appalling events would later come to be called the Rape of Nanking in the West (Nanjing Massacre in China), in large part because of the atrocities that were committed there against women.

As many as twenty thousand Chinese females of all ages—from seven-year-old girls to seventy-year-old grandmothers—were raped, many gang-raped by groups of soldiers. The crimes were committed in broad daylight, often in front of husbands and children. The usual practice, condoned by the Japanese army, was to murder the women afterward. Sometimes the procedure involved cutting off their breasts or disemboweling them with bayonets. Every rank, from foot soldiers to senior officers, participated. The story is told of one group of Japanese soldiers who raped and killed a pregnant woman, then ripped out the fetus and stuck it on a bayonet. When they presented the trophy to their commanding officer, he laughed.

Coming almost two years before Germany invaded Poland, triggering World War II in Europe, and four years before Japanese bombers attacked Pearl Harbor, commencing the War in the Pacific, the enormity of the Nanjing Massacre went largely unnoticed in the West. When other Chinese cities fell, the treatment by the Japanese and the response from overseas were similar. Rape, pillage, and murder marked the fall of Beijing, Shanghai, Hankow (Wuhan), and Canton (Guangzhou). Before the bloodletting was over, more than 2.5 million people would lie dead. Japanese atrocities were gruesome and legion. Women were forced into sexual slavery, and biological weapons were tested on civilians. To the Chinese, the lesson was clear: If their country was to survive, they would have to take charge of their own destiny.

As the war progressed, Jiang Shangqing became vice principal of Anhui Anti-Japanese Military Academy. He started a daily newspaper, which soon became the mouthpiece for anti-Japanese activities. Battlefield news was reported, and articles and speeches of Communist leaders were published, including Mao's essay "Persistent War."

He was also instrumental in helping to plant the seeds for an eventual Communist takeover. In January 1939 Zhang Aiping, a division commander of the New Fourth Army who would later become China's minister of defense, sandwiched the Nationalist area under Sheng Zijin between two of his army units. Jiang Shangqing advised Sheng to form a united anti-Japanese front with the Communists.

When Zhang Aiping and Jiang Shangqing met for the first time, there was instant affinity. Zhang recognized Jiang, who was wearing dark glasses, but before he could say "Shangqing," Jiang had already greeted him as "Aiping." Others present assumed that they were old friends. Zhang was only one year older than Jiang and they had similar interests and experiences. They had different accents but shared the same ambition. They discussed strategies for winning over Sheng Zijin, whether to play good-guy/bad-guy or two good guys. In the end, virtually surrounded, Sheng could not resist their "offer."

In June of the same year Jiang Shangqing was ambushed and captured by a group of Nationalist soldiers. The leader of the group, a former bandit named Zhu Shilin, held a grudge against Sheng Zijin, who had earlier initiated a campaign against banditry, during which Zhu's brother was killed. When Zhu discovered that Jiang Shangqing was Sheng's secretary, he told his soldiers to execute him. His commander intervened, however, and ordered that the prisoner be set free, shaking Jiang's hand and wishing him well.

Sheng Zijin was so relieved that his protégé had escaped that he held a banquet in his honor. In his speech Jiang Shangqing promised to fight to the end, proclaiming that he would shed his last drop of blood for the great patriotic cause of defeating the Japanese. On July 29, while riding back from a meeting, Sheng Zijin's party was ambushed again—this time by local civilian forces. It was just after sunset when Jiang Shangqing, who was leading the way and completely unprepared, was hit by a shower of shells and blown off the white horse he was riding. He fell to the ground dead, a martyr at the age of twenty-eight.

At the large memorial service, Sheng Zijin eulogized the young man as a "wonder of versatile talents" who had "unparalleled boldness." Zhang Aiping mourned the "loss of a great friend and comrade-in-arms" who "sacrificed his life for our country." "Our revolutionary mansion lost a major pillar," he said. An anti-Japanese choral group sang "A Big Falling Star," a song composed in his honor. It was the first of many accolades. Buried locally, Jiang Shangqing's body was moved to the Martyrs' Graveyard in the early 1950s after the Communists took over.

The greatest honor, however, came from his older brother, Jiang Shijun, Jiang Zemin's father. Jiang Shangqing had left two young daughters but no son. Traditional Chinese culture is very filial—it centers on perpetuating the family line and venerating one's ancestors. Because daughters join the families of their husbands, these obligations are fulfilled by sons. For Jiang Shangqing, the chain was broken.

So important was the need for a son in old Chinese culture that a custom was developed to solve the problem. If a man had more than one son and his brother died without a male heir, the living brother would give one of his own sons to the surviving members of the deceased's family. Jiang Shijun did not hesitate. He and his wife, Wu Yueqing, offered their son, Jiang Zemin, to Jiang Shangqing's widow, Wang Zhelan. "I wish his son to follow his father," Jiang Shijun said at the time, "and take revenge upon the evil enemy." The boy was thirteen.

"To understand President Jiang Zemin," Jiang Zehui stated, "one must appreciate his adoptive father, my real father, Jiang Shangqing. His life and death symbolized the tumultuous time in which Third Brother grew up."

In a practical sense, the adoption hardly changed Jiang Zemin's life. Though the family had fled to the countryside and now lived in poverty, they still maintained one household and the culture of the Big Family. Jiang Zemin had grown up regarding Wang Zhelan as a very close aunt, and his cousins, Jiang Zelin and Jiang Zehui, as sisters. His biological mother continued to love him as if he still belonged to her. After he was adopted, the balance changed only slightly.

"For the rest of his life, President Jiang would call his biological mother 'Mama' and his adoptive mother 'Niang,'" explained Jiang Zehui. "In our culture, both mean 'mother.' However, there is a subtle difference in terms of intimacy and closeness. 'Niang' is a little more intimate, a closer term of endearment." (The difference between the two terms is akin to the one in English between Mother and Mom.)

In another sense, Jiang Zemin's life changed completely. With the formal ceremony that marked his adoption, he became the legal son of a Communist hero and martyr. Though he could not know it then, the death of his adoptive father would one day become an immortal story of the Communist revolution. Later on this would give Jiang Zemin a "revolutionary family background" that strengthened his Party credentials and energized his political career, helping set in motion a chain of events that would one day lead him to China's presidency.

"Jiang Zemin," Jiang Zehui repeated, "is truly my Third Brother."

She was correct three times over. Chinese families number their children according to their birth order, regardless of gender. As the third grandchild born into the Big Family, Jiang Zemin was already Third Brother in the extended household. He was also the third child born into his biological family. When he was adopted by Jiang Shangqing's family, in a sense, he became the third child again—in time if not age. "Even today, we still call him San Ge," said Jiang Zehui. "He may be the Party general secretary and state president, but to his family he will always be San Ge, Third Brother."

"For the first eleven years of my life all I remember is unending want and deprivation," recalled Jiang Zehui. "Our family had little to eat, sometimes no food at all. However, we were a proud intellectual family, and no matter how poor we were, the family always prized learning and culture. Education, in school and at home, was the heart of our family values. We all grew up well because of this."

As the war raged, life in the Big Family became increasingly difficult. Jiang Zemin's education was disrupted, the Jiang men were away at war, and the family suffered material hardship. Everyone was forced to find work; even the women had to get jobs. Jiang Zemin's adoptive mother had come from a relatively well-off family and had never worked before, but like the rest of the family, she dedicated herself to helping make ends meet.

The women learned to adapt to their new roles. As the oldest, Jiang Zemin's natural mother became responsible for managing the affairs of the family. Wu Yueqing had been born into a peasant family but had received a good education and was conversant with classical literature, poetry, modern fiction, and history. In addition, she was firm and able in dealing with the outside world, a skill considered "man's work."

In the late fall of 1939 Wang Zhelan, Jiang Zemin's adoptive mother, became so distraught over her husband's death that she felt compelled to make the arduous journey to northeastern Anhui province to visit the place where he had been killed. She had never traveled far from home by herself, and there was no man at home to accompany her. Seeing how sad her sister-in-law was, Wu Yueqing offered to go along.

Japanese soldiers or prowling bandits were everywhere, and young, pretty Wang Zhelan was sure to attract unwanted male attention. The trek across the lawless territories would take many days; to get to their destination they would have to pass through many blockades and several different lines of control from Kuomintang-run regions to Japanese-occupied areas to places of ungoverned anarchy.

Though "Elder Aunt," Jiang Zemin's biological mother, was over forty and not in top physical condition, she was determined to protect her twenty-eight-year-old sister-in-law. Cleverly, she decided that Wang Zhelan should disguise herself as a man.

"No matter what happens," Elder Aunt instructed her, "you must not say a word. You cannot let on that you are a woman. Whatever the situation, I will handle it."

Wang Zhelan dutifully put on men's clothing and a man's hat, and the two women headed north. Nowadays it does not take long to travel from Yangzhou to northeastern Anhui, probably four to five hours by car, but in the rickshaw that Elder Aunt rented, the trip was grueling—150 miles traversing country dirt roads under terrifying conditions.

It was quite a feat, for in the vacuum of war China had descended into chaos. In theory the Kuomintang ran the country, but in truth it had been carved into various competing sectors. In addition to the Kuomintang and the Communists, there were regional warlords, local militias, pillaging bandits, random gangs, and above all the Japanese. The two women were often stopped and interrogated by all variety of battle-hardened men. Each time Elder Aunt handled the situation with aplomb. The two women made their pilgrimage and returned home without major incident. "We will always respect our Elder Aunt," Jiang Zehui said, "Jiang Zemin's mother."

Young Jiang Zemin came to view China as "a nation ridden with disasters." For all the days of his youth, all that he knew was that his once-proud country had fallen into bondage and disgrace. "I spent my adolescent period in Yangzhou," he would later recall, "when the nation was in dire straits and disasters encompassed us. It was just what our national anthem says: 'The peoples of China are in the most critical time, [and] everyone must speak out in defiance.' It was the strong patriotic influence of the anti-Japanese spirit that motivated me, even in middle school, to participate in student movements." It was an emotional imprint that would last a lifetime.

Like so many others, he began to feel that the only hope for his country was a Communist revolution. To many Chinese, Communism has been less about economic systems than about liberty, unity, equality, and stability. For Jiang Zemin, Communism had even greater appeal. "My family were all revolutionaries," Jiang Zehui noted. "My father, uncles, and even Jiang Zejun, who was Jiang Zemin's older brother, all went out to join the revolution, fighting both the Japanese invaders and the Chinese Nationalists."

BY THE TIME SCHOOL RESUMED at the end of 1939, the war had left its mark on Jiang Zemin's psyche. According to rules laid down by the Japanese colonial authorities, the Japanese language became a required part of the curriculum. Although Jiang sat in Japanese class every day, he barely learned enough to get by, an unusual lapse for a boy with a good ear for languages. Years later he would regret his adult inability, but never his youthful defiance—"I would speak better Japanese today," President Jiang would say, "if I had not been forced to learn it under the occupation." At the time he found solace in studying English instead.

Jiang Zemin was a promising student, and the family spared no effort to support his education. Under financial pressure, his adoptive mother begged friends and acquaintances to help her find a job. Finally she found work at Xionghua Guan Primary School, from which Jiang Zemin and his sister had graduated. Sometimes a teacher, sometimes an administrator, she took on various duties including cleaning the classrooms.

Jiang's diligent study paid off; he was one of the leading students in his middle school, getting excellent scores in almost every subject, his favorite being science. Influenced by family tradition and under his uncles' coaching, he also continued chess, calligraphy, painting, and singing. He had a natural talent for playing musical instruments, and he progressed on the piano, guitar, flute, and *erhu*.

In the spring of 1943, two months shy of his seventeenth birthday, Jiang Zemin graduated from Yangzhou Middle School and prepared to leave his family. A place was waiting for him at Nanjing Central University, the most prestigious institute of higher learning in Jiangsu province. There Jiang would develop two of his lifelong passions: scientific knowledge and political activism. The end of the war was coming, and a new era was about to begin.

Chapter 2

1 9 4 3 – 1 9 4 7

"I Am a Patriot"

JIANG ZEMIN WAS ONE OF EIGHT STUDENTS admitted into Nanjing Central University's machinery and electronics department. He shared a room with three other first-year students in his program, all of them older. "My first impression was that Jiang was just a youth, really very young, barely beyond a child," remembered one of his roommates, Tong Zonghai, who at nineteen was the oldest of the group. "But we soon found out he would not be our 'Little Brother.'"

"Our first conversation was about our hometowns and families," said Tong. "He made me feel comfortable. I felt I could trust him."

University life provided a partial refuge from the mayhem of war. At times chaos could seem worlds away; in truth it was right on campus. Six years earlier the Japanese army had invaded and sequestered large sections of the university grounds, converting them into a military camp. "There were so many humiliations," Tong said wistfully.

The parklike campus had originally belonged to an American Christian school and was luxurious by the standards of the day. Jiang's dormitory had a grand exterior in the traditional style of the Forbidden City, while the interior had Western lighting and ventilation. Although the rooms themselves were cramped—four single beds and one desk for all the roommates to share—they were not unpleasant. Jiang's and Tong's beds faced each other across a narrow walkway.

Jiang took to university life with enthusiasm. The math, science, and engineering courses in the first and second years made for a rigorous course load. Jiang studied hard, often deciphering by himself what had been taught in class, then helping his classmates understand the material. They formed deep bonds during long hours of classes and homework, especially when solving problem sets that were assigned on a weekly and sometimes daily basis. Jiang hated to leave any problem unsolved and tried again and again to figure out the intractable ones.

Jiang had an active social life. Students thought him interesting and humorous, and he made friends easily. Money was tight, and if students needed something, they had to plan and save before they could buy it. Jiang did not have many clothes, but he appeared neat and clean. He picked his close friends carefully, and in spite of his young age, many sought his advice.

"Jiang led a simple life," said Tong Zonghai. "And he became our leader."

One of Jiang's roommates was the son of a wealthy man from Yangzhou. When the boy's father came to see his son at school, the pair invited Jiang to dinner at an expensive restaurant, but when he learned that the other roommates had not been asked, he politely declined. The father and son insisted that he join them, but Jiang continued to say no. Giving in, the father said, "If you come with us, I'll invite your two other roommates as well." Only then did Jiang agree to go.

"I was quite glad to go along as a result of Jiang's stubbornness," added Tong, who six decades later bore a bespectacled resemblance to the Chinese president.

Like typical students, Jiang and his roommates talked and played music late into the night. Jiang also liked doing physical exercise, particularly chin-ups.

"You want to know the happiest moment of Jiang Zemin's college days?" asked Tong Zonghai with a grin. "It was a chin-up competition, which Jiang won. We used the doorframe beam in our room as a makeshift horizontal bar. The competition was Jiang's idea."

The chin-up contests became frequent events, and every time they occurred—always at Jiang's suggestion—he would win. At his peak he could do two dozen.

"He didn't try to get away with partials," Tong added. "In every repetition he'd pull high enough so that he got his chin above the beam."

As pleasant as academic life was, the real world still intruded. Because Nanjing was then the capital of China's puppet government, led by Wang Jingwei and propped up by the Japanese occupation army, Nanjing Central students were in the constant presence of the protracted conflict. Japanese soldiers were everywhere, walking with the swagger of conquerors. Political issues were never far from student minds, and students found strength in numbers and a growing desire to try to fix their country's problems.

In mid-December of Jiang's first year opium abuse became the focus of student frustration. Under the Kuomintang drugs had been strictly forbidden. Anyone caught smoking opium was thrown in jail; some were beaten to death on the spot. Under the Japanese the situation was reversed. The occupiers actively trafficked in the drug, stimulating its use among the locals as a way to weaken and incapacitate them—as well as to make money. "After the Japanese conquered Nanjing," Tong recalled, "opium houses sprang up like bamboo shoots after a spring rain. They were everywhere. Obviously, the Japanese encouraged them. We despised their vicious, poisonous policy."

To the students, smoking opium became a hated symbol of the prolonged stupor into which their nation had fallen. One day after class Jiang Zemin came bounding into his dorm room. Student leaders, he reported, were planning to take action. "Last night a few of our classmates went out to close down the opium houses," an agitated Jiang told his roommates, "but the depraved owners called in the Japanese military police to beat them up. Several students were injured." With the backing of the Japanese occupiers, the opium house owners had no fear of reprisals.

"Tonight," whispered Jiang, "we're going out en masse—the more the better. All of us should go."

It was not a simple decision. In 1943 Nanjing was under the tight control of the Japanese, who employed the infamous Three All policy—Burn All, Kill All, Take All—to control the Chinese. If a Japanese soldier did not like the way a person looked, he could fabricate charges to arrest, imprison, torture, and kill him. "We were slaves," Tong Zonghai said.

It took bravery to demonstrate against policies that were supported by the Japanese, but that night thousands took to the streets in protest. Most of the students had been born in the 1920s and had lived their whole lives in the shadow of Japanese oppression. "We were very young when we witnessed the brutalities of the invaders," said Tong. "All our lives we'd heard the humiliating news of our trampled sovereignty and the haunting wails of our brothers and sisters."

Even before the war against Japan, Chinese students had turned time and again to protest as a way of effecting change, often with powerful results. From the founding of the republic to the May Fourth Movement of 1919, the first nationalistic mass movement in modern China, China's young intellectuals had not hesitated to voice their opinion about their country's future. During these demonstrations the students often sang a tune called "The Song of Graduation."

Fellow students, rise up, rise up.
Let's shoulder the fate of our country.
Listen, listen.
Hear the mourning and groaning of our fellow countrymen.
Look, look.
See our country being taken inch by inch.
Fellow students, rise up, rise up . . .

The final lines go, "Should we choose to fight and struggle? We want to be masters of our country. We are willing to fight on the battlefield until death."

Years of subjugation and disappointment had left their mark on Jiang's generation, who came of age determined to fight for their country. For some, the antidrug campaign became a platform for expressing their long-suppressed rage and hatred of the Japanese. Almost sixty years later those two former roommates, Tong Zonghai and Jiang Zemin, could still remember all the verses of "The Song of Graduation." Over the years Jiang would sing the tune on many occasions, including on CBS's *60 Minutes*.

As eager as his roommates were to suppress the opium, they did not immediately join Jiang's call to action. Many of the opium house owners were members of criminal gangs and, in addition to the Japanese, had powerful Chinese collaborators as behind-the-scene backers. The students feared revenge, even physical violence.

"Of course, we were worried," said Tong. "The owners were gangsters. We were only a bunch of kids. How could we fight them? Sure, we supported the 'idea' of smashing those evil places. However, when it came to really doing it, we were afraid. And what if we'd actually succeed in trashing some opium houses? What then? We'd be identified, blacklisted, picked off one by one."

But Jiang persisted. "A small group won't work," he pleaded with his friends. "Come with us. No matter what, we've got to go tonight." He made passionate references to Chinese history, culture, and character, until two of his roommates agreed to join him. The third said that he would stay behind. "In case something happens to you guys," he told them, "at least I can send messages to your families."

That evening, when the drug-selling business was at its peak, hundreds convened on the university's sports field where students from other Nanjing universities and middle and high schools were also gathering. Soon a throng of a thousand students began walking toward town along Taiping Road, a name that means "peace." They headed for the Confucius Temple, around which many of the opium houses were concentrated.

"It was a bitterly cold night," recalled Tong. "We raised our right arms boldly and clenched our fists defiantly while singing protest songs and shouting slogans. We wanted to attract bystanders to our cause, and although it was now dark, many people gathered along the streets to watch. As we marched, our ranks swelled—students were constantly joining us, as if by magnetism, so that our total number grew to about four thousand."

"We felt powerful," exulted Tong in remembrance. "So many were with us."

At first the still-seventeen-year-old Jiang Zemin walked with his roommates, but he then began moving up and down through the mass of marchers, helping to maintain communication between different sections of the procession.

"There was sweat all over his face," Tong said.

At every opium house, the students lectured the intoxicated customers about the harm of doing drugs and admonished them to quit. They also criticized the owners for the immorality of their trade, saying that it would hurt the Chinese people for generations to come. Selling opium, the students asserted, was a crime. They demanded that the owners hand over their opium and assorted drug paraphernalia. Some gave in without protest, but others tried to resist.

"If the owners gave us the drugs and smoking utensils, we would leave," Tong recalled. "If they didn't, we'd start breaking the utensils, literally smashing them on the ground, and we'd seize the drugs. We rented some rickshaws to carry away our 'spoils.' On our way back to the university, when we reached an open square near the original National Congress Hall on Guofu Road, we unloaded all the confiscated stuff from the carts and burned it in a gigantic barn fire."

Throughout the night the students were trailed by Chinese collaborators and Japanese military police shouldering loaded rifles, but they marched on, chanting slogans and singing songs, crowding together against the frigid winter winds. And when the opium and its supporting equipment were torched and burned, they shouted and applauded raucously, not stopping until they grew hoarse and tired.

A student leader, Li Enyu, spoke out. "Our actions today are courageous and victorious," he said to the assembly. "We taught a lesson to those selling and smoking drugs. Opium is China's disgrace; it has brought nothing but shame to our country."

Li then referred to the Opium War of 1840 against the British, which had led to the nineteenth-century carving up of China by foreign imperialists and ultimately to the country's occupation by Japan. It was a long litany of slights and humiliations, symbolized above all by opium, which the students had so triumphantly destroyed.

"We should never forget this historical lesson," Li Enyu orated as Jiang Zemin stood transfixed. Patriotic fervor, Jiang realized, could prevail.

Li Enyu's words of fury seemed aimed at the British, but his real target was the Japanese. "What breaks my heart is that even today there are still so many people smoking opium in our city," he concluded. "We should stand up as proud Chinese. As our ancestors said, 'Every person has a share of responsibility for the fate of his country.' "

Still surrounded by Japanese troops, two thousand students defiantly sang "Song of Graduation." Sensing power for the first time, they realized that if they joined forces, they could overcome seemingly insurmountable odds. For Jiang Zemin, the moment held several valuable lessons. It taught him that the force of a crowd was both to be admired and to be feared. It also taught him the necessity of taking risks. Finally, he learned the difference between symbolic change and real change. The lessons would last a lifetime.

"He also recognized," Tong reflected, "that the essence of our movement went beyond drugs. Even at his young age Jiang took responsibility as a Chinese citizen and fought on the front line at the risk of his life." Decades later President Jiang would focus on educating young people about patriotism. If one doesn't know Chinese history, he would say, one cannot understand today's China. He would also have another task: how to reconcile his personal participation in student movements, and the ardor, idealism, and change-making patriotism of his youthful protests, with his government's suppression or squelching of what for all the world seemed to be similar student movements, energized by the same kind of ardor, idealism, and change-making patriotism.

For a generation of Nanjing students, the Communists, who unbeknownst to Jiang and Tong had instigated the antidrug march, provided a means to express their idealistic rage and growing political awareness. That night Jiang Zemin had participated in his first overt political act. It was also the first time that he had personally witnessed how Chinese could fight back and win. And he relished taking an active, coordinating part. In a society that traditionally awarded seniority by age, it was unusual for a seventeen-year-old to play such a role. Although Jiang would only later learn of the Communist involvement behind the protests, his fate was already being linked to the Party and to the cause that his martyred adoptive father had left unfinished.

ON SEPTEMBER 2, 1945, JAPAN surrendered, and the long, debilitating war was finally over. Chinese students were in high spirits. They anticipated a bright future, but when the Nationalist government turned its overdue attention to higher education, the outcome was devastating. On September 26 the Kuomintang issued a regulation titled "Reexamination Procedures of College Students in Fallen Areas." Everything that had existed under Japanese rule was labeled "collaborationist" and "illegitimate," including all educational institutions that had been located in enemy-occupied areas.

The Ministry of Education decreed that any credits earned at such schools during the war years were invalid. All college students had to be reexamined, attend "political training" sessions, and write a twenty-thousand-word essay based on their study of Chiang Kai-shek's article "The Fate of China." If they did not attend, they could not graduate. Worse, they would have to take a qualification exam so that the authorities could judge if they were even competent enough to continue their education. If they passed, they would still have to take separate exams in each of the courses they had taken previously to determine if they should be given credit.

"Can you imagine how we felt?" asked Tong, his ferocity unabated after more than half a century. "What a travesty! For years we had endured occupation. Now we were being punished by our own government. We were miserable."

Tong learned that there was an alternative. Through a friend with high connections in the Kuomintang (KMT), he discovered that the academic credits of KMT members were being retroactively reinstated. "My friend told me that joining the KMT seemed a simple solution for the mess," he recalled. "He was going to try to arrange for me to join, too. Frankly, I was thrilled."

Tong returned to his dorm to share the good news and to get Jiang and his two other roommates to join the KMT, assuming that they would be as happy as he was. To Tong's surprise, Jiang would have none of it and became furious. "The KMT is so corrupt that even common people know it," he said. "Everyone can see through them. How could you join? You are such a fool!"

Jiang attacked another fallacy in Tong's idea. "Our 'illegitimate student' status applies to many, not just us," he continued. "We've got to find a solution for everybody.

"As for our education," Jiang reasoned, "it doesn't make sense that the knowledge we've learned is considered 'illegitimate.' What's the distinction between 'legitimate' and 'illegitimate' knowledge? Knowledge can't be divided into legitimate or illegitimate categories. It's either correct or incorrect. Science is science, period! We've done nothing wrong." Still in his teens, Jiang was not cowed by pressure. He could think abstractly, in terms of theory and practice, a talent that would serve him well by the end of the long century.

When Tong flushed and said nothing, Jiang changed his tone; perhaps he had been too hard on his friend. "We will eventually find an appropriate solution," he said gently. "Don't be discouraged. Cheer up!" Tong did not join the KMT.

Meanwhile the Communist Party was trying to gain political advantage in the political void that had been left by the end of the war. It encouraged students from six Shanghai universities to organize their own unions to demonstrate against the KMT's education policies. On October 6, 1945, angry protesters marched through Shanghai's main thoroughfares, holding aloft signs, banners, and flags rejecting the government's position on student accreditation. They hung posters in conspicuous places and distributed leaflets in Chinese and English. In addition, the Communists organized demonstrations, circulated petitions, and conducted press conferences with reporters from domestic and foreign newspapers.

Later that month the Kuomintang Ministry of Education issued a mandate that Nanjing Central University would be closed and combined with Shanghai Jiaotong University and Chongqing Jiaotong University. Though Jiang and Tong eventually ended up at the newly created institution, which took the name Shanghai Jiaotong University and was said to have the best engineering school in China, they first found themselves living in temporary quarters in Shanghai.

"They didn't know what to do with us," said Tong with a smile of satisfaction. "Because students from Nanjing Central University had gained valuable experience in negotiating with the government during the student movements, we caused headaches for the Ministry of Education in Nanjing. Maybe that's why they transferred us to Shanghai."

Life in postwar Shanghai was more stringent than it had been in Nanjing. Inflation skyrocketed, caused by mismanagement of the currency, graft, competing factions within the government, and the resurgence of civil war. Corrupt officials, under the guise of repatriating property from the Japanese, expropriated property for themselves. They used traitors from the deposed puppet government to further their personal interests. After the victory over

Japan, the Chinese people hoped that the Kuomintang could reconstruct the government into a disciplined one, but instead many KMT officials became noted for their avarice. A saying at the time listed the Five Items of corruption—houses, cars, money, women, and gold.

In a struggle to survive, Jiang used his little spare time to teach algebra and trigonometry at a night school run by the Shanghai Youth Society. He also tutored the children of rich families. University students were eligible to apply for supplies donated by a relief agency of the United Nations, and Jiang supplemented his earnings with these contributions of powdered milk, bread, and used clothes.

Throughout the war student resentment against the Nationalist government had been growing. Wang Huijiong, a lifelong friend of Jiang Zemin from their university days together, remembered the ill will. "Jiang and I grew up with the same background. Old China was a semifeudal, semicolonial, oppressed country. The Kuomintang government made Chinese Communists their primary enemy, and our real enemy, the Japanese, they made secondary. This aggravated many patriotic people."

During a visit to Shanghai, Chiang Kai-shek found himself confronted with students protesting the annulment of academic credits. Many of the demonstrators, including Jiang, were from Shanghai Jiaotong University. Although their own credits had been reinstated, they were demonstrating on behalf of other, less fortunate students. In March 1946 the petitioners prevailed. Realizing that student demonstrations would not abate, the Nationalist government ordered the Ministry of Education to change its reexamination policy.

The fight was Jiang Zemin's first experience in a protest under the overt leadership of the Communist Party. From then on he became part of the backbone of the student movement. In January 1946 he helped organize a demonstration when a music teacher and three students were killed in Kunming by KMT agents carrying out reprisals against those opposing the civil war. While many participants were workers, the most spirited were students, who shouted slogans until their throats cracked. During a memorial service one after another came up to the podium, often in tears, to denounce the KMT for starting the civil war and for its brutal crackdown on the student movements. The KMT secret police kept close watch on the demonstration, and when they began moving to arrest participants, the students scattered.

"Since Jiang had invited me to join," Tong Zonghai recalled, "he felt responsible for my safety. When the police started coming against us, he pulled me aside and said, 'Leave by yourself or in a very small group. Don't follow the crowd. Just go back to school directly. We don't need to meet again.' Because we departed in different directions, it was impossible for the secret police to follow us all. Jiang was not only a good organizer, he was also thoughtful in protecting his classmates and clever in his street-wise strategy."

A month later Jiang was a student leader of a demonstration that illustrated the complexity of the situation. Called the Anti-Soviet Movement, the rallies seemed, on the surface, to express Chinese patriotism. In reality, they formed part of the ongoing power struggle between the Kuomintang and the Communists. In order to garner public support, the KMT sought to stir up anti-Soviet emotions in the hope of undermining the Communist Party in China. The KMT appeal was to patriotism. The Soviet Union, it said, was yet another foreign power plotting to control China, usurp Chinese land, and steal Chinese property.

The flashpoint of the movement was the death of Zhang Xinfu, a government official who had been killed during a conflict with Soviet engineers over the rights to a Manchurian manufacturing plant. The Japanese had built the factory and supplied it with advanced equipment, which they abandoned in their defeat. In the waning days of the war, the Soviet army had invaded Manchuria and was now squabbling with the Chinese over the spoils of victory. Zhang Xinfu had been killed trying to stop the Soviets from seizing the plant's equipment.

The Kuomintang portrayed the Soviets as foreign invaders with links to Chinese Communists—it seemed the perfect pretext for suppressing the Communist Party. To Party members and their sympathizers, it was an obvious ploy, but it took an ominous turn when they learned that KMT organizers were planning to incite the anti-Soviet marchers to destroy the building that housed the Russian-owned *Contemporary Daily* newspaper and to ransack the nearby Soviet Union's consulate general office. "Because most people didn't realize the KMT's hidden agenda," said Tong, "they participated out of patriotism."

A group of pro-Communist students, including Jiang Zemin, shrewdly decided that rather than try to stop the anti-Soviet protest—which they couldn't do since the Chinese masses had been galvanized by the "Zhang Xinfu incident"—the thing to do was to join it, then to redirect it. In doing so, they would appear loyal to the KMT government, while preventing damage to the Soviet Union, the Communists' chief ally.

An estimated thirty thousand students and others attended the memorial service to honor Zhang Xinfu. Afterward a giant procession marched through the streets of downtown Shanghai, intent on showing its anti-Soviet fervor. But before the protesters reached the offices of *Contemporary Daily* and the Soviet consulate, two large groups of seemingly oblivious students appeared at both ends of the street where the two buildings were located, impeding all access. The swarm of demonstrators were physically unable to approach the newspaper office or the consulate.

KMT leaders were confused. They could not push their way through, and the students blocking them, whose real plan was to protect the Soviet institutions, appeared to be supporting the demonstration. Protesters in the back of the increasingly tense crowd had no idea what was going on in the front and kept yelling, "Move! Move! What's the matter?" But after shouting a few anti-Soviet slogans, most of the demonstrators lost their patience and flowed on to the side streets. The Soviet structures remained untouched.

"On the surface," Tong observed when remembering the incident, "we students responded to the government's call and supported the march. Beneath the surface, we furthered our own objectives—protecting the Soviet properties and containing the people's emotions. Everything had two meanings, surface and subsurface."

It was the sort of strategy that Jiang would rely on throughout his career. The plan worked like a classic kung fu move, deflecting the power of the mighty rather than confronting it head on. More than fifty years into the future, Jiang Zemin would have another opportunity to redirect Chinese fury at foreigners—but then the foreigners would be American and Jiang would be president.

IN THE SPRING OF 1946, as church bells chimed across campus, Jiang was walking with Zhang Gongwei, whom he had met three years earlier when they marched together in the Nanjing antidrug campaign. Among Jiang's schoolmates, Zhang Gongwei was one of his closest friends. They were both from Yangzhou, where Zhang had known of Jiang's literate family and of the martyrdom of Jiang Shangqing, Jiang's adoptive father. Zhang was vice chairman of the student association—with the support of the underground Communist Party—and had the air of a professional revolutionary.

Though laughing and appearing carefree, they couldn't shake their residual bitterness over what they sarcastically termed the "fake student movement," of which Zhang had been the "general commander"—which included three thousand students and professors breaking into the railway station and commandeering a train to Nanjing to deliver their petitions to the KMT government. They remembered how they had shouted the slogans "Science Is No Fake!" and "Learning Is No Fake," and how earlier, during their antidrug demonstration in Nanjing, they had stopped solemnly at the bronze statue of Sun Yat-sen and mourned the father of the Chinese Republic.

In April 1946, four months shy of his twentieth birthday, Jiang Zemin joined the Communist Party. He was sponsored by Wang Jiaqiu, a classmate from both Nanjing and Shanghai. The Shanghai Committee of the Communist Party had been established less than a year before, but already the organization was growing in strength and numbers, recruiting many students who would later figure prominently in Chinese politics and in the senior collective leadership of which Jiang Zemin would become the core.

On June 23 of that year, some fifty thousand students, teachers, office workers, and laborers from more than three hundred organizations assembled at the Northern Railway Station in Shanghai to march for peace and in opposition to the civil war. The rally, coordinated by the Party, was the culmination of an increasingly volatile and competitive series of political activities that had been building since April. While the ostensible goal was "peace," the real purpose was to gain ground in the ongoing battle between Communists and Nationalists for the people's support. By late June the antiwar protests had begun tilting against the KMT and, by extension, against America, which had allied itself with the Kuomintang throughout World War II and in its aftermath.

To Jiang's young sisters, however, the young revolutionary remained a play pal. One of Jiang Zehui's first memories of her brother dates from this period. For the summer vacation, Jiang returned home to Yangzhou, and the two little girls, clamoring for his attention, asked him to demonstrate his strength.

"He stretched out his two arms at about a forty-five-degree angle to the floor," Jiang Zehui remembered, "and asked my sister and me to each grab on to one of his arms. My brother then proceeded to lift both of us up until his arms were parallel with the floor."

The two delighted children hung from his arms like monkeys from a tree, while Jiang Zemin held the position "like a gymnast," Jiang Zehui recalled, "for what seemed like hours. He was really proud of his strength."

Jiang was also building political muscle. He became so deeply immersed in politics that he even began involving his family in the illegal activities. Wang Jiaqiu, on behalf of the Nanjing Communist Party, asked Jiang if he would help their old friend Li Enyu, who had led the anti-opium demonstration. Li was wanted by the Kuomintang for being a Communist organizer, and he needed to go underground and find a safe place to stay. Without hesitating, Jiang offered to hide him in his aunt's home.

Li Enyu moved in under the pretext that he would tutor Jiang's cousin. Jiang and Li had not seen each other for three years, but the friendship, forged in common cause, had not diminished. Li introduced Jiang to progressive and revolutionary works, and the two often discussed them. One favorite was Ai Siqi's *Philosophy for the Masses,* published in 1934, which Mao had used in preparing his two famous essays, "On Practice" and "On Contradiction." Li Enyu, whom Jiang regarded as a "big brother," had extensive knowledge of Communist ideology and helped to expand Jiang's understanding of political theory.

Jiang helped Li Enyu survive. This was not easy, given the economic woes facing the country and Li's need to remain hidden. Sometimes the two would eat with Jiang's aunt; at other times Jiang would share provisions he received from the United Nations or buy simple food with money earned from his tutoring. Li stayed under Jiang's care and protection until November 1948, when the Communists had gained near control of the country.

In later years Li Enyu became principal of Nanjing Middle School; he suffered terribly during the Cultural Revolution—he was not released until 1975—and he died of cancer in 1978, sadly before he could witness the youngster whom he taught Communist theory become general secretary of the world's largest Communist Party. In July 1998, on the twentieth anniversary of his death, President Jiang wrote an article "In Memory of Comrade Li Enyu."

"Jiang invited me to come to his aunt's home to meet with Li," said Tong Zonghai, "because he wanted to help me improve myself. Jiang was always encouraging his friends to upgrade their knowledge. It was very secretive; Jiang never would have made the offer if I were not very trustworthy. Through Jiang's introduction, I too became a friend of Li Enyu; the three of us had many discussions about life, belief, and values, and occasionally Communist theories. In this sense, I consider Jiang Zemin my ideological mentor."

When President Jiang would later stress that the Chinese people should uphold their "collectivist spirit," and not focus solely on their individual futures, it was a direct expression of his student-protest experiences. "It sounds so familiar to me," said Tong. "Jiang's collectivist spirit is deep-rooted. He saw the power of working together."

Reflecting back, Tong said that even though Jiang played an increasingly active and central role in the protests, petitions, rallies, and marches, he obviously did not do it alone. "One person couldn't make such a difference," Tong asserted. "Jiang wasn't even one of the main leaders. Credit must go to the underground Communist Party."

Jiang would take calculated risks, Tong noted, but he was not impulsive or hotheaded. He approached critical matters cautiously and was careful about how he expressed himself. "Sometimes during the Japanese occupation," Tong recalled, "I would find myself humming anti-Japanese songs. If I sang a little too loudly, Jiang would remind me to lower my voice. 'Be careful!' he would say. 'If spies or collaborators hear you, you'll be in big trouble.' "

Similarly, when Tong once heard Jiang singing a particularly stirring piece and asked about it, Jiang claimed not to know its title. A few years later Tong learned that it was the Communist Internationale. Even by the time the two graduated, Tong still would not know that Jiang had joined the underground Communist Party. "I only knew he was progressive in his political ideas," remarked Tong. "Jiang didn't even try to pressure his roommate!"

In the fall of 1946 Jiang, Tong, and their classmates were allowed to enter Shanghai Jiaotong University officially, matriculating as fourth-year engineering students.

It was a time of uncertainty. Even the university had been considering a draconian cutback, which could have closed down all but its engineering curriculm. Jiang continued participating in public protests, especially in support of education. The demonstrations advocated financial aid for needy students and destitute professors (and cutbacks in military spending); the previous summer, students had organized the "Respect Teachers" movement to raise money for the cause.

In spite of heavy outside activities, Jiang continued to excel in his studies. The Engineering College consisted of three departments: machinery, electric power, and civil. Jiang took courses in the first two, which were ranked among the top in the university, and he specialized in power generation and transportation.

It was a rigorous academic program. Not only did students have to take almost forty hours of coursework each week, they also had to complete numerous assignments and experiments every day. Each month there was an assessment test. In some courses, every chapter of the textbook was tested. Grades were determined strictly: All the assessment tests plus the final, weighted heavily, were added up and averaged.

With all the demands on his time—which included reading literature, participating in student movements, and working for the Communist Party—Jiang developed a reputation for not attending classes as often as did the other students. Yet because of these absences, he was all the more diligent, making up for what he missed in class by pushing himself extra hard at night.

Jiang never exaggerated his academic prowess. "Wang Huijiong was the one whom our department chairman liked to ask questions," Jiang freely told friends, including Wang, decades later. "He had all the answers, perfect answers. He loved studying and was very diligent. He was our class leader.

"We were in the same lab group," Jiang remembered, referring to Wang. "To this very day, I still have my lab notebooks. I've also kept our textbook on radio engineering. When I look at them—for example, one experiment on alternating current—memories flood back.

"Everything was in English," Jiang continued, "textbooks, lab reports, lectures, exams—this greatly benefited our language skills. Professor Wang is especially fluent; his English is wonderful—better than mine."

"How long has it been?" Jiang asked Wang wistfully in late 2003. "Fifty-seven years?" As his old lab partner nodded, Jiang Zemin gazed at Wang Huijiong—respectfully, admiringly, almost deferentially. It was as if their Zhongnanhai dinner dematerialized and more than half a century collapsed, so that the two buddies were back at Shanghai Jiaotong University and Wang was once again the class leader.

Jiang has also admitted that other students were better engineers. Comparing himself with a classmate who would become a leader in what was then a thorny technology, Jiang noted that although "I threw myself into the study of furnaces along with Zhu Linwu . . . I am ashamed to say I never reached his level."

In college Jiang maintained his love for music and literature. Even when he was engaged in revolutionary activities, he found ways to practice his skills. He often played the *erhu* as an accompanist when students put on mini-plays in support of Communist ideas, and whenever there was a class meeting, he led the singing. Classmates called him "the director."

When Jiang was low in spirit, he did not confide in his roommates. Rather, he would sit cross-legged on his bed and read sad poems from the Tang and Song dynasties. As he read aloud, he would sigh and make audible exclamations.

"No matter how troubled he might have been," Tong Zonghai remembered, "Jiang would never vent or lose his temper. When Jiang recited classical poetry, he usually had a specific poem that reflected his mood. When he was happy, he would choose cheerful poems. Generally speaking, he's an optimist."

One of Jiang's professors at Shanghai Jiaotong University was Zhu Wuhua, an electronics expert who also came from Yangzhou. Once while he was enrolled in Professor Zhu's class, Jiang decided to visit his teacher at home. For a Chinese student, bound by the hierarchies of the day, this was a bold move. During his visit the two men talked about many things, including their mutual hometown.

Jiang would remember that even though Professor Zhu was a well-established scholar, he still seized every possible moment to study. Whenever he found himself with free time, he would use it to read or write. That Zhu Wuhua had an unending love of learning and diligently sought new knowledge made him one of Jiang Zemin's role models.

There was another reason as well. Just before leaving the house, Jiang happened to speak with the professor's wife, a woman with little education. He was struck by the loving relationship between the two, and the fact that in spite of their differences, they had the utmost respect for each other. The visit left a lasting impression.

Another of Jiang's favorite professors was Gu Yuxiu, a remarkable scientist and scholar who had graduated from MIT with a Ph.D. in electromechanical engineering and was one of China's most distinguished academicians. "Jiang must have been good in mathematics to have done well in Professor Gu's class," reminisced Wang Huijiong, who would become an international scholar. "It was one of the toughest in the school." Gu Yuxiu was also a celebrated playwright and master poet, who wrote thirteen modern dramas and more than eight thousand poems.

Throughout his life Jiang took the time to remember old friends and teachers. In October 1997, when on a state visit to the United States, President Jiang sent word that he would like to see Professor Gu, who had emigrated to America and was living in Philadelphia. By then Gu Yuxiu was ninety-five years old, but he began making travel plans to meet his old student in Washington or New York, as he had done on a similar trip two years earlier. But this time Jiang insisted on going to Philadelphia to honor his mentor.

When Jiang entered the professor's modest apartment, he apologized for not coming sooner. "Today," said Jiang, who must have been nursing two years' worth of guilt, "I come here to visit you."

Another of his professors died in 1993, just two days before he had planned to visit him. "I got up very early this morning so that I could pay my respect to my teachers," President Jiang said sadly at Jiaotong University. "Unfortunately, Professor Shen Shangxian just passed away. . . . We Chinese have a great tradition: No matter what your position or status, you should always respect your teachers. If all of us nationwide can maintain this wonderful tradition and appreciate knowledge and talent, our country will have a bright future."

JIANG ZEMIN, JUST TWENTY YEARS old in his last year of college, spent an increasing amount of time on political activities. On Christmas Eve 1946 two drunken U.S. Marines raped a teenage girl, a student at Beijing University. Editorials filled the Chinese press, equating the rape with the "violation" of Chinese sovereignty—a common metaphor that had now materialized into a literal event. The incident inflamed students across China and spawned the Movement Protesting American Brutality. Even while American and Chinese authorities tried to downplay the rape, five thousand demonstrators marched in Beijing shouting anti-American slogans. This protest was followed, in more than twenty cities, by marches, rallies, and classroom strikes. Schools in Beijing, Shanghai, Nanjing, and Tianjin had begun to coordinate their political actions. In Shanghai, Jiang joined the demonstrations.

Throughout the spring Jiang attended protest after protest. April through June saw many rallies against the grinding civil war. In May demonstrations against famine swept parts of the country. Called the Anti-Hunger Movement, the month-long series of political activities began on the twenty-eighth anniversary of the May Fourth Movement, linking Jiang's generation of student protesters to their celebrated forerunners.

"It's difficult for non-Chinese to understand the emotions of the people at this turbulent time," said Wang Huijiong, the senior class leader. "All intellectuals, even if they weren't Communists, were against Chiang Kai-shek and his KMT party. The primary reason was corruption. The KMT further antagonized the students by arresting their leaders—again, even those who weren't Communists. I wasn't a Communist; I didn't join the Party until after the Cultural Revolution."

On May 30, 1947, Mao Zedong published an article praising the students' demands for food, peace, and freedom, and their battles against hunger, civil war, and prosecution. Society's sympathy is for the students, Mao wrote, the high tides of student movements will surely push all people forward.

A short time later, in the summer of 1947, Jiang Zemin graduated. Though only twenty-one years old, he had such a broad range of knowledge that his classmates called him "Dr. Jiang." On his graduation program, his friends wrote words of remembrance.

"Brother Jiang Zemin, the renowned classroom 'doctor.' "

"His grades are often among the top, and he is especially good at math; he enjoys debates and often turns out to be the winner—because of all this, we grant him the 'doctor' title."

"He loves sports and is especially fond of the horizontal bars and sprinting."

"Lately he enjoys writing poems and playing music, just like 'Grandpa Jiang.' "

Jiang Zemin had received two very different but, to him, equally important kinds of education. One was in Western science and engineering; the other was in Marxism and revolutionary theory. By the time he finished his formal education, he had succeeded in becoming both "professional" and "Red," a particularly useful combination for beginning his long, steady climb upward in the Communist hierarchy.

Chapter 3

1947 – 1955

"I Am an Engineer"

IN SPITE OF HIS DEGREE in electrical engineering from one of the most prestigious programs in the country, Jiang had difficulty finding a job. He heard about openings at power plants in northeast China but couldn't travel there because of the civil war and lack of transportation. With little else to do, he and his friend, Tong Zonghai, took on a variety of odd jobs and, in their free time, hung around the school, hoping an opportunity might materialize on the departmental bulletin board.

"Jiang and I had an agreement," Tong remembered. "If he found any posting that fit my qualifications, he'd tell me, and if I found any that fit his, I'd tell him."

But soon, with Jiang occupied elsewhere, checking the bulletin board became Tong's responsibility. In August he came across a notice, posted by a former professor, from the Shanghai Haining Corporation, a Chinese-American joint venture in the food business. "When I found Jiang," recalled Tong, "we headed straight to the professor's office." The next day, armed with letters of recommendation, the two friends went to the company, where a corporate executive greeted them cordially.

"Obviously," Tong observed, looking back, "we had already been introduced." He then added with a smile, "Who could have known that by finding Jiang Zemin his first job, I set him on a course that would ultimately lead to his becoming Party general secretary and China's president?"

Shanghai Haining was a well-known company that produced ice cream and fruit-flavored ices, which were sold in supermarkets and grocery stores. Its most famous label, Mei Nu, or Beautiful Girl, was a household name with a large market share in ice-based products. With its vast refrigeration equipment—it had the largest cold-storage facilities among all foreign firms in the city—the factory needed two generators to maintain power supplies. Jiang Zemin and Tong Zonghai began their apprenticeships in the engineering division of that department.

The factory was located in the city's Hongkou district, a once-prosperous business section. After Japanese invaders devastated the area in 1937, it deteriorated into a poor neighborhood for migrant workers from Jiangsu, some of whom worked on the factory's assembly line. Because he came from the same province and could speak the dialect, Jiang got along well with these laborers in spite of the differences in their educational backgrounds.

One day a worker asked Jiang to repair a broken motor. "I was shocked," he remembered fifty years later, the realization still vivid. "I had no idea how to do such a thing. After all, I was a university graduate, and not one of all my calculus, physics, and engineering classes dealt with fixing things." From now on Jiang Zemin would have to get very good at "fixing things."

The winter of 1947–48 was particularly harsh. Severe food shortages caused by the war broke out around the country; in Shanghai some five hundred people succumbed to starvation. As the civil war slogged on, the Kuomintang lost more and more ground to the Communists, and Shanghai became the linchpin in a last-ditch KMT effort to retain control over a portion of China. Chiang Kai-shek's strategy was to retreat south of the Yangtze River so that he could form a defensive line. To supplement its food supply, the government bought out the Shanghai Haining food factory, compensating its American owners $300,000. Jiang worked on the transaction, participating in negotiations with shareholders and evaluation of the company, and facilitated the equity transfer to the Chinese.

Jiang Zemin, Communist activist, now found himself working for the Nationalists. The company—renamed Number One Army Provisions Plant—was ordered to increase its production of cereal-based foodstuffs to supply the Kuomintang army, which was by then in full retreat.

Four months after beginning work Tong Zonghai decided to take a position at a power plant in Huangshi, hundreds of miles up the Yangtze River in Hubei province. At five A.M. on the morning of Tong's departure, Jiang Zemin and Li Enyu, who was still staying with Jiang's aunt, went to the Shanghai wharf to bid their friend farewell.

The political situation in China was still volatile, and Jiang was, technically speaking, working for the Nationalist government. In frequent letters he encouraged Tong to befriend local Communists, but he also urged him not to reveal his true beliefs. Jiang's caution was both wise and typical. "About five months after I moved to Huangshi," said Tong, "I finally got in touch with underground Communists. I participated in underground work in 1948, and joined the Party in early 1949." But the local Communist branch also exercised caution, advising Tong to stop writing to Jiang for fear of compromising their mutual safety. The KMT secret police were monitoring the mail, and such contact could jeopardize not only their lives but also those of others. For years their friendship was over.

They were right to be concerned. In May 1948 the Kuomintang Shanghai Garrison issued an arrest warrant for another university friend, Zhang Gongwei, a student organizer. Two tense months of playing hide-and-seek with the authorities followed. Many times the young man narrowly escaped capture and death until finally the Communist Party arranged for his escape by sea along with that of eight other fugitives. Zhang was told to meet his contact at a prominent department store—a place deemed too busy to draw attention from government agents. From there they would go to the docks.

At the appointed time and place Zhang Gongwei was waiting, but when no one came, he grew anxious. Suddenly an American-style jeep zoomed up, and his heart began pounding. Could the operation have been compromised? he wondered.

Zhang was about to make a run for it, when a young man stepped out of the vehicle. It was Jiang Zemin. He grabbed Zhang and whispered, "Come with me." Jiang hit the gas and sped off to the designated wharf, but just before reaching it, he pulled off the road and parked in the shadows. "Gongwei," he said, "I have to leave you here. Go to the boat. The others are waiting."

Though they did not know it at the time, the need for such secrecy was nearing an end. In 1946 Mao Zedong had predicted that it would take five years to overcome the Nationalists, but by mid-1947 the civil war had already begun to tilt in his favor. By 1948 KMT forces were losing battle after battle across the country. In the Dabie mountain area near the Anhui-Jiangsu border, not far from where Jiang Shangqing had been ambushed a decade earlier, a forty-three-year-old officer named Deng Xiaoping led 200,000 troops to a major victory. In the fall of 1948 in Manchuria, the Nationalists lost nearly half a million soldiers.

In January 1949 Beijing was taken. The Communist Party Central Committee instructed its Shanghai operatives to protect factories, offices, and schools from destruction by the Nationalists. The underground Party was also expected to coordinate with the People's Liberation Army (PLA) to maintain order and restore production as soon as the city was won. On April 20 peace talks between the Communists and the Kuomintang broke down. The next day Mao Zedong issued the order "Marching Toward the Whole Country!" which aimed at "steadfastly and completely killing off all reactionary Nationalist forces that were resisting." More than a million PLA soldiers crossed the Yangtze River and marched inland and south.

Throughout the spring the PLA fought from one victory to another. The tide of refugees flowed to Taiwan as Communist forces overwhelmed the Nationalist capital of Nanjing. In Shanghai the KMT took revenge by attacking various Communist groups and executing two Jiaotong University students in a police station. The situation became more volatile in early May. As the PLA reached the outskirts of the city, Jiang Zemin worried that Nationalist forces would try to take his factory's heavy equipment in their evacuation to Taiwan. "We won't allow them to take what's ours," Jiang told his workers. "We'd have nothing to eat but the bitter northwest wind."

Jiang put his good relationship with the factory workers to the test. "I am here today to seek your advice," he told them. "All of you are more senior than I. We workers depend on these machines for our livelihood. No matter who wins, no matter who owns the factory, we all need to earn a living. If our machines are taken away, we won't be able to feed our families." The laborers asked Jiang to suggest a plan. With four years' experience of student protests under his belt, he organized the workers into three shifts to guard the factory continuously. They also moved the trucks off premises and hid the small tools.

In the end, his careful planning proved unnecessary. The Nationalist forces were so disorganized that, aside from the Central Bank's reserves of gold and silver, they managed to take little else with them. There was no time for wide-scale looting, and at the food factory Jiang and his workers faced no confrontation. The battle for Shanghai lasted only two weeks. On May 25 the PLA entered the city and within two days had taken all of it. But the war continued. When the Nationalists later bombed the Shanghai power plant, Jiang personally started his factory's backup power generators to prevent the ice cream from melting and spoiling—a contribution to Liberation of which he would always remain proud.

THE DAYS OF RISK WERE OVER; the underground surfaced. Jiang no longer had to hide his Communist affiliation but would now benefit from it. Because of his efforts in securing the factory, he was appointed the plant's Communist representative and put in charge of production. At the same time he served as the associate engineer, director of work assignments, and director of the power supply section.

After the takeover, the plant became part of the Yimin Corporation and was renamed Factory Number One of Shanghai Yimin Food Company. Everything was under the Department of East China Industry. One day in September 1949 a department minister and up-and-coming Party leader named Wang Daohan arrived at the factory for a formal inspection. The visit revealed a creaky but clean dairy plant, filled with the smell of fresh ice cream and something even better: a young man with potential.

"Jiang was full of vigor," Wang said, recalling their first encounter. "He was a Party member and seemed trustworthy. My impression was that he had promise.

"The Communists had just captured Shanghai from the Kuomintang," Wang continued. "It was one month before the founding of the People's Re-public, and I was responsible for heavy industry under the Shanghai Military Control Commission. One of the corporations we controlled was Yimin, where Jiang was working in one of its food factories. When I met Jiang, he was only twenty-three.

"Jiang was waiting for me in the office of Yimin's general manager," Wang continued. "After some brief generalities about the factory, Jiang was the one who presented their new business strategy, including a detailed report about sourcing raw materials and ideas for product distribution. A large dairy farm was Yimin's sourcing partner, and so with a stable milk supply and ample production capacity, the key to the factory's success would be marketing—finding customers for Yimin's ice cream, ice pops, and biscuits. Jiang organized marketing teams to focus on supermarkets and groceries."

After presenting the report, Jiang and several managers accompanied Wang to the plant floor, where they observed Yimin's production lines, then the best in Shanghai. "Jiang was enthusiastic and energetic," recalled Wang, "a hardworking professional."

Wang, just thirty-four, and Jiang took an instant liking to each other as they discussed new ways to distribute frozen treats to Shanghai's war-exhausted citizens. Although Jiang was already on the fast track at Yimin—he was direc-tor of technology and support and deputy general manager—the association with Wang would speed his promotion to general manager. Furthering the connection was the fact that Wang was married to the president of the Yimin Corporation, who was Jiang's boss's boss.

"I ran all the industries in Shanghai," noted Wang. "My wife managed a large holding company under me, and Jiang worked for one of her subsidiaries."

Jiang Zemin and Wang Daohan soon discovered that they shared many things in common. Both were graduates of Shanghai Jiaotong University; both had been underground Communists; Jiang worked for Wang's wife; Jiang and Wang had similar skills and energy levels; and they shared a kinship to Jiang Shangqing, Jiang Zemin's foster father. Wang had been in charge of military logistics and had served under Zhang Aiping in the guerrilla wars, as had Jiang Shangqing.

"Because Jiang was a senior executive in the factory that reported to my wife," Wang recalled, "they grew close and Jiang became a frequent visitor to my home. My wife was nine years older than Jiang, and we began treating him like our younger brother. In addition to business, we spoke about other things, such as our families. Jiang's heritage was not insignificant: he was the adopted son of Jiang Shangqing, the Communist martyr. Comrade Shangqing and I didn't know each other personally, but I had heard of his exploits and sacrifice."

Jiang came to confide in Wang's wife through the bright challenges and dark trials, professional and personal, of his early career; and the deepening friendship between Wang Daohan and Jiang Zemin developed into a lifelong bond that would change the lives of both men. As Wang advanced in the Party and the government, he took Jiang along with him. Wang Daohan would go on to become mayor of Shanghai; his protégé, following in his footsteps, would one day surpass him. The distribution of ice cream in Shanghai would change the course of history in China.

On October 1, 1949, from a podium high above Tiananmen Square in central Beijing, Mao Zedong proclaimed the founding of the People's Republic of China. He promised the masses a "New China" without foreign occupation or civil war. But peace would not come easily, and prosperity would take a long time to achieve. The exhilaration of Shanghai's Communists was soon tempered by the suspicious attitudes of their liberators. To the soldiers of the PLA, hardened by years of rural living and personal deprivation, the sophisticated Westernized comrades from Shanghai, though Party members, were too bourgeois for their taste.

Adding to the tension was the fact that the city was in a state of chaos. Prices inflated rapidly, and unemployment was high. There were shortages of rice, coal, cotton, and other necessities. Doing even the simplest errand required standing in an excruciatingly long line. "Food for three people," Mao declared, trying to help, "must be shared by five people." But as dissatisfaction grew, demonstrators took to the streets.

Before long the Communists were resorting to some of the same coercive tactics used previously by the Kuomintang. A round of witchhunts targeted "enemy agents, counterrevolutionaries and political bandits." Shanghai authorities decreed that all formerly underground Party members were required to experience a period of "training and rectification" in order to purge any vestiges of old ways of thinking. The sessions consisted of intense interrogations designed to ferret out Nationalist agents and expose bourgeois thinkers.

Having supported the Communist cause at great personal risk for the last six years, Jiang Zemin was insulted by the "training and rectification" and resented the fact that his work at the factory would be interrupted. Food production would slow at a time when people were starving. Nonetheless Jiang was taken to Songjiang, a city south of Shanghai, where in spite of his irritation, he submitted to the sessions and was deemed a success. After only a month he was back at his old post at the Yimin plant and given two new titles: first deputy factory director and, more important, Party branch secretary, his first position of formal leadership in the Communist Party.

Following the Communist revolution, Chinese enterprises developed a dual governance structure—a Party side and an administrative or business side. From the early 1950s until the late 1990s, the Party side had the most power. As Party chief of Yimin, Jiang effectively controlled the enterprise and would soon come to lead the business side as well. Though in his mid-twenties, his leadership of the Yimin Food Factory would make him a member of Shanghai's industrial elite, a platform that would serve him well for his rise in the Party. In February 1951 he attended the First People's Congress of Hongkou district, Shanghai, as an official representative.

For Jiang Zemin and other "Third Generation" leaders who would rise to prominence in the 1980s, factory work became the key to their elevation. Many were technocrats who had come up through the system by managing state-owned enterprises such as factories or research institutes. This was in sharp contrast to earlier generations of leaders. In Deng Xiaoping's "Second Generation," personal advancement had come through military hardships and victories, while Mao's "First Generation" had wrestled with founding ideology, a struggle that had resulted in a Chinese version of Marxist-Leninism.

As head of the Yimin Food Factory, Jiang implemented new policies and programs. The Mei Nu (Beautiful Girl) brand name was scrapped in favor of Guangming (Bright), reflecting the political shift from bourgeoisie to proletariat. Guangming is still one of the most famous brands in the food industry.

A fervent Communist, Jiang insisted that his workers sing revolutionary songs on their breaks. In 1950, when the government was trying to nationalize the power supply, Jiang took advantage of the many outages to lead renditions of "We Workers Have the Power." Later, as a senior leader, he was known to burst into this song when visiting factories. At the same time he understood the importance of the marketplace and sought to expand Yimin's share of it through creative advertising.

As a manager, Jiang tried to ease the lives of his employees. He upgraded the food service in the dining facilities, and night-shift workers were given free meals. Employees were also permitted to take food home for their families, a common practice. (Enterprises would purchase food, such as eggs, in bulk and distribute it as a way of supplementing meager incomes.) Jiang organized cultural events, such as mini-plays and musicals that were performed at the factory, and provided areas for recreational activities. He had begun to develop his trademark style of management: attending to the interests of his superiors while caring for the needs of his subordinates.

Within months of Jiang's promotion to factory director, Yimin's output target was exceeded. The factory became a model of production, and soon another food plant, which produced the Meilin brand of canned food, was merged and brought under his supervision.

OUTSIDE OF WORK, JIANG's thoughts turned to family. In December 1949, at the age of twenty-three, he married his high school sweetheart, Wang Yeping, whom he had known almost all his life. There was said to be "an innocent affection between them from childhood." Wang was a niece of Jiang's adoptive mother, a biological second cousin through marriage (not blood), bringing the extended family even closer.

Jiang Zehui recalled their courtship: "When Third Brother moved from Nanjing to Shanghai to attend Jiaotong University, he would often visit my grandma, my mother's mother, and my uncle, Wang Yeping's father. Both of them liked Third Brother very much. In 1949, when my mother moved to Shanghai, she was happy to see Third Brother and her niece dating happily."

It seems to have been a case of opposites attracting. While Jiang was gregarious and self-confident, his new bride was quiet, accommodating, and unassuming. Wang Yeping was also talented and educated and had attended Shanghai's Foreign Languages College.

In the Party's efforts to reform Chinese society and uproot its feudal traditions, marriage laws were liberalized. Before the takeover, husbands had dominated wives, but under the new system, wives were considered equal to their husbands, and divorce was permissible. One unintended consequence of this reform was that while married women were expected to join the poorly paid workforce, their domestic chores, by tradition, remained undiminished.

Jiang's bride had a background similar to his own. Her paternal grandfather was a successful businessman in Shanghai in the 1920s and 1930s and a collector of antiques and classical paintings. Her father traveled to America and spoke fluent English. He owned a modestly successful arts and crafts factory, but after his early death, the family fortune disappeared.

At the time and for years after, a false rumor circulated that Jiang's new wife was the relative of a senior Communist leader whose surname also happened to be Wang. In China more than seven percent of the population are named Wang.

About a hundred guests attended the three-hour marriage ceremony and dinner, which took place at an elaborate Shanghai restaurant in the heart of the city near the Bund, the grand riverfront avenue that has been called a museum of world architecture because of its many styles of buildings.

"According to custom," remembered Wang Huijiong, "guests brought small packages of money, some wrapped in red envelopes. It didn't balance the cost of the wedding, of course. Jiang and I each attended the other's weddings; I was one of the two witnesses at his ceremony.

"Jiang and I became even closer after graduation," recalled Wang, "but it was difficult to maintain regular contact because of the pressures of our new jobs, the stress of the times, and prior to the revolution, the dangers of exposing our Communist or anti-Kuomintang views. Once we met on the street and were embarrassed we hadn't talked in a while. After I left Shanghai in 1956, we lost contact for over twenty years."

In 1951 the young couple had their first son, whom they named Mianheng, which means "gentle and persevering." Their second son arrived in 1954; they called him Miankang, or "gentle and healthy." In spite of his responsibilities at the factory and at home, Jiang continued to take care of his younger sisters, even pampering them when he could. Decades later Jiang Zehui still smiled at the memory of one special gift she received from her beloved Third Brother.

"For physical education, we were required to wear sports shoes," she recounted. "And since many of our Yangzhou classmates were from well-to-do families, they wore fashionable sneakers and loved showing them off. My sister and I were so envious. We didn't have sneakers because we couldn't afford them. This was a big deal to us, so my sister and I decided to write to Third Brother in Shanghai and tell him of our 'plight.' Almost immediately two pairs of sneakers arrived in the mail! I can never forget how happy I was. Now I bragged that my sneakers were even better than those of my schoolmates. 'My sneakers are from Shanghai,' I said proudly. 'Yours are only from Yangzhou.'"

The two girls began spending their summer and winter vacations with Jiang and his new wife in the Yimin dormitory. He treated them to a variety of activities, from showing them how the famous Bright ice pops were made to teaching them how to ballroom dance.

"Third Brother would always be arranging activities for us," Jiang Zehui recalled with almost girlish glee. "Sometimes he'd take us to Jiang Wan stadium to watch sports, or to the parks where we'd just enjoy the scenery. Even though he was busy at the factory, whenever he had free time, mostly on Sundays, he'd find something fun for us to do."

Jiang and his wife lived in a small apartment on the second floor of the factory dorm. It had one bedroom and a small loft, but in spite of their cramped quarters, they always welcomed family. When Jiang Zehui's mother moved to Shanghai to work at a bank, she lived with the couple for five years.

Jiang suggested that Jiang Zehui and her sister move to Shanghai to be with their mother, but Seventh Uncle argued that Yangzhou Middle School would provide the best traditional education, and he feared that Shanghai would offer too many temptations. "Even though I was a little resentful that I didn't spend much time with my mother," Jiang Zehui reflected, "I had a great time in Yangzhou and received an excellent education. Seventh Uncle was like a father to me. He and my real father were only three years apart; they had fought together in the war and had had the same friends. After the war ended, Seventh Uncle became a professor of foreign literature, later specializing in Russian literature and classical Chinese poetry."

MEANWHILE THE NEW CHINESE government was being put to the test. Three days after the founding of the People's Republic, the U.S. government declared its continued support for the Kuomintang regime. On June 25, 1950, the North Korean army, led by Kim Il-Sung, the autocratic "Great Leader" of the Democratic People's Republic of Korea, invaded the southern part of that peninsula, known as the Republic of Korea. America came to the aid of its South Korean allies, ordered the U.S. Seventh Fleet to patrol the Taiwan Straits, and marched troops to the Yalu River, which forms the border between Korea and China. The Chinese government, already anxious over American incursions, joined forces with the North. In the West the conflict was called the "Korean War." In China it was known as the "War to Resist U.S. Aggression and Aid Korea."

For many Chinese citizens, regardless of their degree of participation, the war seemed a turning point. After interminable years of subjugation and humiliation, China was finally under the control of a unified and truly independent government. Mao Zedong ordered his troops to drive American forces back from China's borders. After three years of hurling wave after wave of human sacrifices at their American enemy, China managed to end the war in a stalemate. Though it came at a cost of 700,000 to one million Chinese lives, including that of Mao's own son, the Chinese still view the war with pride. The signing of the Korean Armistice Agreement marked an end to the long period during which China had always come out worse at the negotiating table. Many Chinese credited the Communists, particularly Mao, with the country's reemergence as a world power. Sino-American relations had hit an all-time low.

IN 1951 WANG DAOHAN TRANSFERRED Jiang Zemin to the China (later Shanghai) Soap Factory. When he arrived, the plant was operating at half capacity and losing money. Jiang, only twenty-five, was made the company's deputy director. One of his first tasks was to prepare for its nationalization.

With a ruined economy and large cities on the brink of collapse, government control was the swiftest way to institute reform. Extreme measures to control resources, enterprises, and land were put in place, establishing a command economy that was born as much out of necessity as to conform to Marxist-Leninist ideology. Based on the Soviet model, the state would own all the means of production and determine in advance how much each factory would produce. At the same time the Communists initiated politically motivated mass movements that were intended to purify the Party and unify the country.

China had entered its "Soviet Period," as Mao tried to make Marxist-

Leninism work for his country. Central planners in Beijing, copying their counterparts in Moscow, pushed the collectivization of agriculture, the development of heavy industry, and the setting of production targets for each factory. (A planned economy is when the government requires, say, fishermen to produce an inviolate quota of two hundred pounds per day, but comes not to care whether the catch of the day is composed of fish, shells, mud, or rocks, just so long as those two hundred pounds are delivered, weighed, documented, and reported to superiors.)

More than 400,000 Soviet specialists streamed into China to supervise the installation and operation of factories, and tens of thousands of Chinese were sent to Russia to study their methods. In retrospect, it may seem odd that a newly liberated China would allow itself to become so heavily dependent on the Soviet Union, which was, after all, a foreign power, but Mao and his top ministers were ideologues who believed ardently in the unifying elixir of socialism.

In early 1953 Wang Daohan was promoted to vice minister of the recently established First Ministry of Machine-Building Industry in Beijing. In adapting the Soviet structure, the Ministry was required to set higher production levels, establish new enterprises, and organize research and development. Wang's mandate was to centralize the best technologies for manufacturing heavy machinery and electrical equipment. Seeking to assemble the best talents for this national effort, he transferred Jiang Zemin to the ministry's Number Two Design Institute in Shanghai as head of a new electrical power equipment department. It was a lateral move for Jiang, who was then twenty-six, but it enabled him to develop his skills in a technically demanding environment.

About a year later the State Council instructed the Machine-Building Ministry to draft its first five-year plan. Because of its significance, Wang recommended that Jiang be transferred to Beijing to participate in its drafting. Again the move did not entail a promotion, but it gave Jiang a firsthand perspective on making government policy.

At the time efficiency was assumed to be proportional to size: the larger the factory, it was believed, the higher its productivity. In 1955, on the fifth anniversary of the signing of the Treaty of Sino–Soviet Union Friendship, Mao Zedong sent a telegram to Soviet leaders expressing "sincere thanks to the Soviet Government, which has aided China in building 156 large industry enterprises." One of the most significant was the First Automotive Works in

Changchun, about five hundred miles northeast of Beijing in Jilin province, which would later develop into the country's leading manufacturer of cars and trucks. For more than seven years the massive factory would be home to Jiang Zemin. It was there that he would further develop his managerial skills and come to understand something of centralized planning and totalitarian rule.

Chapter 4

1955 – 1962

"I Love Talent"

CONSTRUCTION OF THE SPRAWLING Changchun auto plant began on July 15, 1953. Designed by Soviet experts and located on former sorghum fields on the outskirts of the city, it was to be modeled after what was then the Stalin Automobile Works near Moscow. In November 1954, when Jiang Zemin was assigned to Changchun, the factory had not yet been completed, but the government was already preparing for opening day.

"We made a major commitment to build China's first automotive factory," explained Wang Daohan, Jiang's lifelong adviser. "And we needed our best people with the best training."

The Machine-Building Ministry made plans to send more than seven hundred technicians to study in the Soviet Union. To prepare, Jiang was enrolled in a Russian language immersion course held in a Changchun suburb. In April 1955 he and a dozen others took the Trans-Siberian Railroad west on the long journey to Moscow. There Jiang practiced Russian whenever he could—at formal meetings with mentors and in casual encounters with strangers. A lover of languages, he never felt a wisp of self-consciousness, and he encouraged his more reticent colleagues to follow his example.

"To succeed here, we must listen more closely and speak more frequently," he admonished them. "And never be embarrassed." In addition to learning the advanced technology that he would need on the job, Jiang reveled in Russia's cultural richness. He had enjoyed Russian literature in translation; now he read his favorite masterpieces in their original language. He learned numerous Russian songs, and he loved the hearty food, especially a type of black bread called *khleh*.

In spite of his delight in his new surroundings, Jiang was often homesick.

He could not bring his wife and children with him, and he knew they were struggling to cope with his absence back in Shanghai. When he felt sad, he played the *erhu* and sang Chinese songs, a form of self-therapy that enabled him to express his melancholy.

The Stalin Automobile Works was, in typical Soviet fashion, a gigantic facility. Jiang's assignment was to learn about energy resources, power conservation, and the management of power stations and networks. He spent most days in the central control room, sitting on a stool before a vast array of dials, gauges, panels, and instruments that monitored the plant's massive power supplies.

WHILE JIANG WAS IN MOSCOW, not far from where he was apprenticing, an event took place that would shake the Communist world. On February 26, 1956, Soviet leader Nikita Khrushchev dared to attack former Soviet dictator Joseph Stalin, dead barely three years, in a radical speech. Delivered to shocked delegates at a closed session of the Twentieth Party Congress, it was a denunciation of Stalin's "grave abuse of power." Stalin had "caused untold harm," said Khrushchev, by choosing "the path of repression and physical annihilation, not only against actual enemies, but also against individuals who had not committed any crimes." The brutality and repression had been possible, Khrushchev added, "because Stalin himself, using all conceivable methods, promoted the glorification of his own person."

"Comrades," Khrushchev concluded, "we must abolish the cult of the individual."

Future historians would consider the speech one of the most important of the twentieth century, but at the time its full significance was not understood. While the Soviet Union was renouncing the "cult of personality," China was embracing it and would come to worship Mao even more than Russia had Stalin, to even more grievous effect.

A FEW WEEKS BEFORE he was called home for the opening of the factory, Jiang was invited to a reception held in honor of Marshal Zhu De, the former commander-in-chief of the Communist armed forces. Zhu had come to Moscow on an official visit and wanted to meet with Chinese students and professionals studying and training in the Soviet capital. When Jiang arrived at the reception, he was astonished to see his old friend Zhang Gongwei, whom he had not laid eyes on since he helped him escape arrest eight years before.

"I never thought I'd ever see you again," Jiang said.

"I didn't want to ask about you," said Zhang, "because I feared what I might find."

The two longtime friends embraced and, oblivious to the festivities around them, reminisced about the old days.

Zhang had succeeded in evading the Kuomintang in part by changing his name, a common practice for underground Communists. In the years to come, as the two progressed in their different careers, Jiang would persist in calling his old friend "Gongwei," even though the rest of the world knew him as Professor Yu Li, a distinguished expert in mining technology.

WHEN JIANG RETURNED FROM the Soviet Union in the spring of 1956, he went to Yangzhou to visit his family. His grandmother was ill, and he had come to pay his respects. She would die two months later, but for the moment the Big Family was happily reunited. Jiang Zehui was particularly pleased to see her Third Brother. "I had graduated from middle school and was preparing to take my college entrance exams," she recalled. "Third Brother was very interested in the schools I was applying to. In China, attending the right school is extremely important."

Months later Jiang Zehui was disappointed to find that she had been rejected by her top three choices: Beijing, Nanjing, and Shanghai Jiaotong Universities, three of the most selective schools in the country. She had not applied to a backup, and at the time the policy for students without a placement was that they would be assigned a college and a major by the government. Jiang Zehui had wanted to study psychology and philosophy. Instead, she was assigned to Anhui Agriculture University as a forestry science major, a field about which she knew and cared nothing.

"I felt dejected, miserable, and I refused to go," she remembered. "But Seventh Uncle and Third Brother both encouraged me. Third Brother sent me a letter in which he wrote, 'We have a saying in Chinese that every one of the thirty-six professions produces its own leading authority. You should definitely go and become the leading authority in forestry science.' "

The message was clear: The Jiang family made the best of circumstances, whatever they might be, and strove to be the best, however they could. Jiang Zehui followed her brother's advice and grew to love her accidental career. She would become one of the world's foremost experts on bamboo and rattan, and president of the Chinese Academy of Forestry.

"When I was in college, Third Brother was working in Changchun," Jiang Zehui remembered, "and each month he sent me more than ten yuan for support. He also sent ten yuan to my sister. That was a lot of money back then—his salary was very low. He also had to support his parents, his wife and two sons, and his mother-in-law who had moved in with them. But he never missed a month."

When Jiang Zemin walked into the gleaming new plant, he had already been named section chief of the power supplies department with two laboratories and a hundred employees reporting to him. Around July 15, 1956, when the plant's first vehicle, a Liberation brand truck, rolled off the assembly line, Jiang was named deputy division chief, a normal promotion. Since one of his supervisors was Russian and the other was not a Party member, Jiang was also named Party secretary of the power supplies department.

Before they met him, his subordinates were apprehensive. Many had never left their native Manchuria, and this Shanghai-educated boss seemed daunting—wunderkind, intellectual, expert, and Party cadre (Party official or functionary). But on his first day an ebullient Jiang Zemin showed up in a blue work gown and started talking to people, asking about everything from their backgrounds and specialties to their hobbies and families. Before long he earned an endearing nickname: "the Magic Chatterer."

A former technician recalled his first encounter with the new boss. "I told Jiang that I liked listening to music, especially Peking Opera. He became excited: 'Very good. I like Peking Opera, too.' He asked, 'Do you know how to sing Li Duokui's "Catching the Golden Turtle"?' "

When the man said yes, Jiang threw his arm around his shoulder and said, "Let's sing it together!"

Another colleague, Chen Yunheng, had more sensitive concerns. As chief power engineer, he was Jiang's boss, but he was not a Party member and that could have made things awkward. "I was worried," he recalled, "whether I could get along well with my vice director who was a Party member." Politics was always sensitive in the revolutionized country. "But Jiang Zemin was easy to work with," Chen added. "He didn't carry that superior air and was kind to us non-Party members."

Jiang liked to say, "I love talent." At the time experts who did not belong to the Party were regarded with suspicion. While other managers were afraid to give them responsibilities, Jiang took the chance. About one innovative engineer who had been unable to advance because his father had owned a small store and was thus considered a capitalist, he said: "What his father was has nothing to do with what he is!" With Jiang's support, the man later made important contributions and won several prizes.

Fang Mingsong, a chief engineer interested in mathematics and automation, remembered that Jiang was not the most talented developer, but he understood and appreciated other people's skills. "Regarding technology," Fang said, "Jiang Zemin himself did not make many improvements. But as director of power supplies, he brought out everyone's potential. That was no easy task. Jiang respected intellectuals. I never felt the kind of pressure normally associated with a Party leader. He put me at ease."

Jiang made several close friends in Changchun, one in particular. Shen Yongyan was also a power engineer, responsible for installing equipment. They were both *Jiangzheren*—or people from Jiangsu and Zhejiang provinces. The two areas are often lumped together because their food, accent, and culture are similar.

"Jiang and I considered ourselves country fellows," Shen recalled. "We were young when we met: he was thirty, I was twenty-nine. I often visited him at home. Since there wasn't much to do in the evening, we spent time talking. He had financial burdens. We were very open with each other."

At lunchtime the two would avoid the cafeteria line by bringing food from home. They ate quickly and often played table tennis. Years later a hint of their good-spirited rivalry surfaced. "Jiang liked to play table tennis," Shen said, "even though his technique, which was more slicing than driving, was just so-so."

Jiang's wife, Wang Yeping, and the couple's two young sons relocated to Changchun, where she found a job in the Party office at the same factory. The Jiang family was assigned a fourth-floor apartment that had three rooms and an entrance foyer, but the space housed seven people, including Jiang's mother and his wife's parents. Still, compared to many Chinese dwellings of the time, it was considered comfortable, having central heating, a gas stove, a private toilet, and double-glazed windows to keep out the frigid winter weather of the Manchurian plains.

Virtually all of the thirty thousand workers at the plant lived in similar red brick dormitories. The plant provided the classic cradle-to-grave services that, in future decades, would put unbearable burdens on state-owned enterprises. These included a kindergarten for children, shops with discounted prices, and medical services. Some state-owned enterprises literally maintained company graveyards.

Inside the factory the future seemed bright, particularly for Jiang. He got on well with his Russian supervisor; the two often sang Russian folk songs. One of Jiang's duties was escorting visiting delegations around the plant; when three of his former professors showed up, it was a special honor to give them a tour and treat them to dinner. Jiang's work was going well, and First Automotive Works fulfilled its initial quota of vehicles.

THE IDYLL WAS NOT to last. Under Chairman Mao the political situation in China was becoming more volatile. In 1956 Mao launched the Hundred Flowers Campaign, a call for intellectuals to voice their true feelings. "Let a hundred flowers bloom," he proclaimed, quoting a Chinese poem; "let a hundred schools of thought contend." By reaching out to intellectuals, Mao hoped to promote new forms of art and cultural institutions, a lifelong passion. Premier Zhou Enlai sought constructive criticism of the central government. "The government needs criticism from its people," Zhou said in a 1956 speech. "Without this criticism the government will not be able to function as the people's democratic dictatorship." What happened was tragedy: the momentary flash of freedom turned into a means for flushing out, and then eliminating, all opposition.

At first, suspicious intellectuals figured that Mao's appeal was a ruse and virtually no one spoke out, but when Mao began reprimanding those who did *not* offer "heathy criticism," many succumbed to their pent-up yearnings and presented what they thought were honest, helpful ideas for improving governance. But when the proffered advice began including democracy, human rights, and suggestions that the Party should "open up," and when the number of critical missives reached avalanche proportions (during a six-week period in mid-1957 millions of letters streamed into central authorities), Mao took it personally and badly. Not without reason, the Great Helmsman characterized the criticism as a blatant attack on his own leadership and became resentful and enraged. Egged on by those who sought to accrue power, Mao labeled the opposition "Rightists" and decided to accelerate his nascent Anti-Rightist Campaign.

Sweeping accusations were initiated against these so-called Rightists. Blaming intellectuals for all manner of ills, Mao ordered the letter writers, who were now branded counterrevolutionaries (the worst of all sins), arrested and punished. At its onset, only a few thousand people were purged, but the Anti-Rightist Campaign fed on its own vitriol and soon the condemned swelled to more than half a million. The best a Rightist could hope for was demotion and "reeducation through labor." Some were beaten and imprisoned, others maimed and even killed.

Beijing took the opportunity to test Party loyalty. As Party chief of his department, Jiang was given a "quota of Rightists" to strike from his staff. He had many intellectuals whose opinions and critiques he respected and found useful. While neighboring work units rushed to purge and punish, Jiang was conflicted.

"There must be something wrong," he confided to Shen Yongyan, who had just joined the Party. "How come there are so many Rightists among us? Where did they all come from? How come all these intellectuals, trained and educated by the Party, have suddenly become Rightists? This is impossible. We should try to save as many as we can."

Because of Jiang's reluctance, none of his subordinates were removed initially. In contrast, the infrastructure construction department, which was only slightly larger than Jiang's department, denounced eleven staff members for being Rightists. As time went on, Jiang's lack of enthusiasm for the official campaign became obvious and dangerous. Several zealots, already jealous of Jiang's success, began asking a question opposite of the one he had asked Shen. "How come," the whispers went, "there are so many 'intellectuals' in the power supplies department and no Rightists?"

In the end, Jiang succumbed to the pressure and purged two people— probably the minimum he could give up and still protect his own position. One man had quasi-religious ideas, but Jiang was at a loss to name another. At the time the power supplies laboratories had two different kinds of lathes. One was Soviet made and had arrived recently; the other had been imported from America prior to 1949. It was a difference between the two pieces of equipment that would lead Jiang to his second Rightist, Ge Dongqing, a mid-level manager. His offense consisted of observing that the Soviet lathe "made more noise" than the American one.

"How could *anyone* doubt the accuracy of Ge Dongqing's comment?" asked Shen Yongyan with a sarcastic chuckle years later. "The two lathes, Soviet and American, were sitting right next to each other, so it was obvious which one made more noise! Only a deaf man could doubt it."

But in those tense times praising anything American was enough to ruin a man's career. Had the "made more noise" comment circulated before Jiang reported it, his own career might have been ruined. If he wanted proof, he had only to look to his own family. His older sister, Jiang Zefen, an elementary school teacher in Jiangsu province, spoke up on behalf of a man whom she believed had been wrongly accused. She was labeled a Rightist for her trouble. Even though another teacher came to her defense, she was downgraded to "temporary teacher" and reassigned to a peasants' school. Later she was sent back home and forced to live on eight yuan a month.

Denounced by Jiang, the lathe-labeling Ge Dongqing was stripped of his managerial position and forced to toil as a physical laborer. He was also subjected to frequent self-criticisms and "struggle sessions."

Jiang remained haunted with guilt for the role he played in Ge's downfall. "After decades, even to the present day, Jiang deeply regretted his actions against Ge Dongqing," Shen Yongyan recounted. "And Jiang has apologized to him several times. When the Rightists were rehabilitated in 1962, Jiang saw to it that Ge was the first to be reinstated."

Having met his quota, Jiang tried to protect the other workers in his care. One young technician was indiscreet when offering critical ideas. When Jiang found out, he chastised him severely, but then followed up with a heart-to-heart talk.

"I was prepared to die," the technician, who later emigrated to America, recalled. "I was so scared that I even considered suicide when my friend told me that I had been labeled a Rightist and that Jiang needed to talk to me. When waiting to meet him, I was so nervous that I literally began shaking with fear."

But after reprimanding the young man, Jiang simply asked him to admit his errors and work hard. In any other division, he would have been purged.

"His advice not only got me through the Anti-Rightist Campaign," the man observed, "it helped me through the even more devastating Cultural Revolution. Jiang's advice probably saved my life."

Not satiated by the Anti-Rightist Campaign of 1957, Mao followed up with the Anti-Rightist Deviation Movement in 1959. A once-great leader who was revered for founding New China, Mao had allowed ideological fanaticism and personal megalomania to shatter millions of lives. For the young Jiang Zemin, it was a firsthand lesson in the dangers of abusing authority. It was also an education in being politically astute.

"He never got a sufficient number of Rightists," Shen Yongyan observed. "He was not aggressive in criticism meetings—the so-called 'struggle sessions'—against Rightists. The tone of his speeches was always too studied, too calm. His lack of zeal was so obvious that I worried about what might happen to him. Yet Jiang survived; his political instincts must have been good."

When meeting old colleagues from First Automotive Works decades later in 2000, President Jiang remembered one man by his willingness to protect others. "Comrade Lei Wen is an old Party member and a man of integrity," Jiang said. "During the political campaigns [Anti-Rightist and Cultural Revolution], he had the courage to distinguish clearly between right and wrong, and he shielded many good comrades."

The next assault came quickly in the form of the Great Leap Forward, Mao's disastrous campaign to accelerate the country's agricultural and industrial production in a ludicrously short period of time—he imagined China could catch Britain within fifteen years. Begun in 1958, Mao's plan, which he rooted in Communist theory, had a lofty goal, bizarre economics, and horrendous results. He proclaimed that labor-intensive methods of production, which stressed manpower over machines, could be as effective as expensive technology. He aggregated vast masses of peasants into large-scale rural communes for collective farming. Numerous small backyard steel furnaces dotted every village; according to the delusion of the Great Leap Forward, they would eliminate the need to build large factories.

Mao campaigned to promote his preposterous vision. In February 1958 his traveling propaganda show arrived at the Changchun auto plant. In a reckless attempt to please the chairman, managers set wildly unrealistic goals, promising forty thousand trucks a year, a fourfold increase in production, while chopping costs in half. In five years, they boasted, eight times the number of vehicles would be rolling off assembly lines. Anyone who doubted these figures, however fantastical, was labeled a Rightist. Jiang, who was sure the promises could never be fulfilled, tried to express his disapproval in subtle ways; he knew that any overt criticism would be punished swiftly.

First Automotive Works rolled and cut its own steel, a process that consumed huge amounts of power. By mid-1958 the factory was equipped with a new power plant to achieve its overly ambitious goals, and Jiang was placed in charge of it. As the factory's outlandish production targets were forced higher, its demand for power grew proportionally. Jiang pushed the generating equipment to its limits and beyond. Even then the amount of steel fell short of what was needed, and its quality was often poor for making cars and trucks.

Inferior materials were sometimes pressed into service in a desperate effort to meet the targets. Air pumps and parts of cars were constructed of wood and, when that ran out, bamboo. Truck frames were welded together out of many small pieces of metal when larger ones were not available. Everyone, including Jiang and Shen, was mobilized to produce Red Flag cars, manually hammering inferior steel into even more inferior car bodies. Even as they pushed themselves to their limit, they were dismayed by the quality of their work.

In another aberration, the Great Leap Forward promoted homegrown ideas that produced harebrained products, such as the Ultrasonic Wave, a supposedly breakthrough technology that used a vibrating metal powered by compressed air. "To power engineers, it was ridiculous," recalled Shen Yongyan. "Yet everyone was lauding this Communist-created technique and adding 'ultrasonic devices' to all sorts of machines, from cutting tools to food cookers. The only real results were that air pressure throughout the factory dropped and productivity along with it."

Daring to dissent, Jiang spoke out against the Ultrasonic Wave, using a book written in 1930 by an Englishman to make his point. Not only did the work show that foreigners had already invented this so-called revolutionary technology years before, it also proved that the technique itself was nothing but the conversion of electrical power into pure noise. "Jiang was determined to expose this nonsense device," said Shen. "But the Party secretary did not support us. At that time Party secretaries were the real decision-makers, even on technical matters."

To a trained engineer like Jiang, this approach was reprehensible. Thirty years later he would mention the Ultrasonic Wave movement in a talk, still upset by the faulty thought process to which he had been subjected. "I was not against experimentation," he said of the time. "The issue was that we must have a scientific attitude."

In 1958 the president of First Automotive Works promised the Party Central Committee that the factory would produce 250 cars in each eight-hour shift. The design capacity at the time was 50. In 1964 a vice minister laughed out loud when Shen Yongyan told him where he worked. "You people are such braggarts," the minister said. "How could you think you'd produce five times your capacity?"

With all the energy going into steel manufacturing, China's farm program began to languish. In an effort to shore up the buckling agricultural sector, 500 million farm workers from 740,000 cooperatives were compressed into 26,000 communes and ordered to increase food production by 50 percent. Like the auto workers, the farm workers had insufficient resources and limited expertise. By early 1959 famine was widespread, and over the next three years malnutrition, starvation, and associated diseases became pandemic. It is not known how many Chinese died in the world-record famine. The number is said to be at least 20 million people and possibly as high as 50 million.

Workers from the Changchun factory were conscripted to help the farmers in the countryside. They devoted their summers to fighting droughts or containing floodwaters. In the winter they repaired dikes and irrigation systems and lived in cargo trains to do so. Although he was the boss, Jiang preferred to sit with his crew on the deck of an open truck during the long rides rather than up front in the cab. To buoy spirits, he would lead workers in rousing songs as they rumbled for hours on bumpy roads. "If you want to do a good job," he often said, "you must be with people. Without people you can accomplish nothing!"

In late 1958 and early 1959, prompted by deteriorating relations with the Soviet Union, First Automotive Works was restructured. Seven departments were merged to form the new power subfactory, which had about a thousand employees and serviced all the power needs for all the plants in the enterprise. Jiang Zemin was named the general manager.

Upon taking over, Jiang established two top priorities: uninterrupted service and worker safety. "Power is the heart of the factory," he told his workers. "If anything goes wrong here, all machines will halt and production will stop. We must ensure that the heart works normally." Regarding safety, he was relentless, stressing it at virtually every meeting and supporting others who did the same. One crotchety safety engineer, Zhao Hongqing, was so strict with his inspections and stubborn on his reports that he had alienated his fellow workers and was not admitted into the Communist Party. "Lao [Old] Zhao," Jiang said to the man, using the Chinese honorific "old" before his colleague's name signifying friendship and respect, "I'm fully in favor of your joining the Party. As long as you are the one who inspects for safety, I am at ease."

Every day Jiang walked the floor in his blue work gown, chatting with workers and inquiring about their machines. He developed a reputation for asking about anything he did not understand and for never pretending to know something that he did not. He also looked out for his crew, on the job and off. In 1960 a young engineer with whom he worked wanted to get married but could not because there was no home available for newlyweds. Jiang, who was still living in the small three-room apartment with six other family members, offered one of the rooms to his colleague, and the young couple lived with the crowded Jiang family for the next two years.

This was a selfless act to be sure, and perfectly praiseworthy as an epitome of egalitarian Communist ideology. But what was the effect on the Jiang family, and on others like his who were so committed to the Communist ideal that they felt compelled to make such sacrifices? When political passion, like religious fervor, becomes so overwhelming as to suppress natural concerns for one's own family, such severe belief systems have a way of turning dangerous and destructive, as Mao's mass movements unhappily confirmed. Though the minor inconveniences of a still more crowded apartment may seem trivial compared to other kinds of more serious sacrifices, it suggests an inculcated mental framework that subjugates the individual to the collective. Jiang's generosity must be admired, but the belief system that inspired it must be watched.

IN 1960, REACTING TO Chinese criticism of Soviet "revisionism" and a spate of increasingly hostile border disputes, Nikita Khrushchev ordered all Russian experts and advisers to leave China. Their departure could not have happened at a worse time. The Great Leap Forward had destroyed the country's economy. In Changchun the auto factory was in deep trouble. There was never enough steel, never enough power, never enough fuel, and never enough food. Workers on the factory floor were collapsing from hunger. Coal was in short supply, and central planners in Beijing, in an act of desperation, decided to convert the power plants in some of its major factories to heavy crude oil. Changchun, located near the Daqing oil fields in Heilongjiang province, was chosen to be an innovator in the conversion process. The Soviet experts had the technology, but now they were gone.

Zhou Jiannan, vice minister of the Machine-Building Ministry, arrived at First Automotive Works and gave management a frightening timetable to convert the power generating system: three months. There was no margin for error to pass the winter safely. Jiang was given total responsibility (as chief commander) for the seemingly impossible task, and his friend Shen Yongyan was sent to Daqing to secure the crude oil and ship it back to Changchun.

The deadline seemed absurd, even dangerous, but Jiang knew the consequences of questioning such a directive. He sprang into action, assembling the best group of technicians. When they heard their assignment, they were staggered. Some worried about accidents working with crude oil; others didn't understand the technology; all agreed that three months was absurd. Jiang reassured them that even the most unfamiliar technologies could be mastered with enough diligence, and he encouraged them not to worry about making mistakes. "We shouldn't carry too much burden on ourselves," he said. "We must work hard to learn new things. Even if we run into problems, everyone will understand."

Jiang devised a plan. The first step was to build reserve tanks. Four huge vessels, each capable of holding a thousand tons of petroleum, were hurriedly assembled. The technicians scoured Russian manuals that had been left behind. Three shifts worked around the clock; the number of laborers jumped from two hundred to one thousand; many dropped from exhaustion, hunger, and illness. Although Jiang himself was sick, he stayed at the site, resting only a few hours a day. He was obsessed with details, forcing subordinates to check and recheck data. Remarkably, after three and a half months, the conversion was completed, almost on schedule.

Nonstop work, minimal sleep, irregular eating, and unremitting pressure caused Jiang's health to suffer. He had continuous stomach pain and often pressed down on his right side to alleviate it. He may also have contracted hepatitis. Later he would admonish workers in other factories not to neglect their food as he had done. Unintended consequences aside, the conversion was a triumph and a milestone. Jiang Zemin would consider it one of his life's great achievements.

"When you're young and endure such a difficult experience, whenever you recall it in later life, you feel proud," Jiang said about the experience. "When we finished, we began to burn petroleum to provide power, and a hundred thousand people had heat for the harsh Changchun winter. It's a pity I'm not a novelist. Otherwise I'd have written a book about the project."

It was not just a personal success but a political one as well. The project was so important to Beijing that Vice Minister Zhou Jiannan remained in Changchun for the entirety of the conversion. During that time Zhou became so impressed with Jiang's ability and leadership that he later helped transfer and promote him. Leaving the Changchun factory would be a major move in Jiang's career. Without the high-profile conversion project, it might never have happened.

When the Russians left, Jiang lost his conversation partner, but he soon befriended the Chinese-Russian translator, Liu Renwei, who was the night-shift foreman in the boiler room. Jiang would get to work early, just as the foreman finished his work, so he could speak Russian and learn production at the same time. Almost three decades later, at the end of 1989, Jiang Zemin as the new Party general secretary hosted a reunion with his Russian mentor from Moscow and Liu Renwei. For six hours the trio spoke Russian and sang Russian songs.

Jiang would never forget the Soviet experts with whom he worked. When Chinese automotive delegations visited Russia in the 1990s, he asked Shen Yongyan to have delegation members ask about those Soviet experts who were still alive. As the Chinese leader, Jiang not only sent his personal regards, he also inquired if they needed help. Jiang would tell Shen, "They contributed tremendously to Chinese socialist construction. We shouldn't forget them."

FOR THE TIME BEING, however, Jiang had more mundane problems to handle. The three-year famine had caused such food shortages that to survive, factory workers were compelled to grow crops around the dormitories. Workers in one of Jiang's shops managed to grow enough beans to supply each person with about forty pounds. They gave their director, who had done none of the gardening, a smaller share, but he was not pleased with his allocation.

When Jiang heard of the squabbling, he was furious. "The workers grew the beans and gave you some for free," he told the man. "This is already good enough. How could you argue about getting too little?"

Jiang then ordered him to make a self-criticism in front of the staff.

"This is not a shame," he reassured the director. "You represent the Party among the workers, and the only way the Party grows stronger is with the support of ordinary people. Showing off and putting yourself above others is never allowed."

True to his principles, Jiang lived simply. Although he enjoyed some special privileges of a thirteenth-rank official, his salary was still only 150 yuan a month. Combined with his wife's earnings, the family lived on 200 yuan. Considering the times and the very low cost of living, it was a reasonable sum, but Jiang had many people to support, including relatives in his extended family. Once when the factory managed to get some melons for staff and workers, the Party secretary gave Jiang an early opportunity to buy some for his children. "No thanks," Jiang replied. "I can't afford it."

"You earn so much each month," the secretary said. "What are you saving up for?"

"You don't know?" Jiang asked. "You see this sweater I have on? I got it when I was in college. I can't afford a new one. My older brother's son is at college; I have to send him five yuan every month. I also help my sisters. I have to conserve where I can."

Jiang often went hungry. "If only I could have one egg a day," he said at the time, "I would be very satisfied."

He paid attention when workers began complaining about the canteen. He asked local Party leaders to institute a prohibition against Party officials ordering special meals and cutting in line ahead of others. Although Jiang usually brought his lunch from home, on days when he did eat in the cafeteria, he instructed the staff to keep a detailed record of what he consumed. Accounts came due at the end of the month, and Jiang always paid his in full.

By 1961 some of China's senior leaders, including Deng Xiaoping and Chen Yun, tried to reverse some of the damaging policies of Mao's Great Leap Forward. A limited, rural-based, free-market system, which included private vegetable gardens and a merit-based pay system, was permitted. At the same time many factory managers were chastised or even fired for submitting false production reports, which they had generated in response to Beijing's unreasonable production quotas.

Jiang had personal projects, too. In 1956 his Russian mentor at the Stalin Automotive Works had asked him to translate his book, *The Optimal Use of Electrical Power in Machine-Building Factories,* into Chinese. When the Soviet Union began recalling its advisers from China in 1959, the project became practical as well: Chinese engineers now needed all the technical help they could get.

Jiang began translating the technical treatise, but before he could finish it, he would be transferred to another assignment. It was not until 1965 that he would finally finish, sending the handwritten translation to Shen Yongyan for proofreading and editing.

"When the Cultural Revolution started [1966], I certainly couldn't work on a foreign book," Shen explained. "It was far too risky, literally life threatening. Most books were burned, especially foreign ones."

IN SPITE OF THE HARDSHIPS he endured there, Jiang Zemin would always have fond memories of Changchun. In the early 1980s a visitor knocked, unannounced, on the door of his apartment in Beijing. Jiang was late for a meeting so his sister answered the door and told the stranger that her brother was not in. "My name is Lei Wen," the man said, "from First Automotive Works." No sooner had he spoken than Jiang appeared with a big smile.

Because of Jiang's prior engagement, the two could only chat briefly, but Jiang told the man something he had wanted to say for a long time. "Lao [Old] Lei," he said, "I've felt very sorry that I left so much work for you when I left. You must forgive me."

During his years at the factory, Jiang Zemin became a true leader, guiding by example without condescension and correcting subordinates' mistakes without rancor. He would never hesitate to ask questions, or lose an opportunity to break into song. In doing so, he won not only the respect of his workers but their friendship as well. He played bridge with the staff during lunch, rotating from room to room, and when he lost at table tennis, he would get in line with everyone else to wait for the next turn. He played hide-and-seek games and participated in rowing races in a nearby lake. He was also there in times of trouble, visiting colleagues in the hospital and helping with the funerals of their parents. He was infrequently confrontational, rarely devious, and decidedly not pompous.

Jiang accomplished difficult goals under arduous conditions. He won positive notice from Beijing when many of his peers cracked under the production strain or political pressure. Such a talented man could not be expected to remain in Changchun, and in 1962, having matured as an industrial manager, it was time to move on.

In 1990, Party General Secretary Jiang Zemin made an exception to his early policy of not writing personal inscriptions—he feared they could cause a "negative impression"—by writing one in his own calligraphy for the published annals of First Automotive Works. As Jiang explained to Shen Yongyan, "After all, I worked at the factory for over six years. If I don't write the inscription at your request, my old colleagues may misunderstand."

Chapter 5

1962 – 1976

"A Period of Unprecedented Destruction"

JIANG ZEMIN MANAGED TO SURVIVE the Anti-Rightist Campaign and Great Leap Forward relatively unscathed, and in 1962 all thoughts were on the future. Again the catalyst was Wang Daohan. The two had remained close over the years; whenever Jiang went to Beijing on business, he would visit Wang and his wife. Wang was then vice minister of the Machine-Building Ministry, and with the economy beginning to rally, he wanted his protégé closer to the center of action. Wang transferred the thirty-six-year-old Jiang from Changchun to Shanghai and made him first deputy director of the Shanghai Electrical Equipment Research Institute, a job engaging his managerial and technical skills.

"There were more than seven hundred people working there," recalled Zeng Peiyan, who joined the Institute in the same year and who, decades later, would become one of President Jiang's leading ministers. "Young people and technicians all liked to communicate with Jiang. He was an organizer as well as an expert. He often came to our laboratories to find out how our research was going."

Wang also arranged for Jiang's wife, Wang Yeping, to be hired as a general affairs secretary at the same institute. Over the next twenty years she would gradually rise in rank to become director of research. At work she was warm and low key, and after work she would rush home to care for her family. Since money was tight, she shopped the markets, bargaining with street vendors to save pennies.

Shanghai was an island of relative prosperity in a country devastated by the Great Leap Forward. Still, life was hard. Although he had been promoted, Jiang's salary remained low. He and his wife packed their own lunches and, sending their boys to school, took a bus to work. Several times a week they sought the shortest lines to buy necessities. One benefit of Jiang's new job, however, was a modern two-bedroom apartment in a new staff dormitory. To have their own apartment in Shanghai had been their family dream, and here they would live for more than twenty years.

Optimism was in the air; it seemed the political movements were finally receding. Pragmatic Party officials, led by Liu Shaoqi, who had succeeded Mao as head of state in 1959, and Deng Xiaoping, became increasingly bold in confronting the radical Leftists. (In China, the political labels "Left" and "Right" mean the reverse of what they do in America with respect to "conservative" or "liberal" views. Leftists are conservatives; they seek to retain the pure socialist system and political controls promulgated by Mao Zedong. Rightists are liberals, who seek to change the system to be more in line with the free-market economies and open democratic governments of the West. Throughout his career, Deng Xiaoping fought both extreme Leftism and extreme Rightism. Jiang Zemin, following in Deng's footsteps, would do likewise.)

In February 1962 Liu Shaoqi told a meeting of seven thousand Party officials that only 30 percent of the country's abysmal condition could be blamed on natural disasters. The other 70 percent, he said, had been caused by human error. Many senior leaders, including Mao and Liu, made self-criticism. Deng blamed lack of experience and said all should share responsibility. Mao, who continued to be revered as the founder of New China, was uncharacteristically docile at the meeting, but the critique may have rankled him. It would take him four years to launch his counterattack on Liu and Deng and exact his revenge, but when he did, he would almost succeed in taking down the entire country with them.

For the moment people attempted to adopt practical approaches for solving problems. One of the more innovative areas was the First Ministry of Machine-Building Industry, run by a protégé of Liu Shaoqi, Bo Yibo, who developed a merit-based environment, the kind of place where a man like Jiang Zemin could thrive.

"One of Jiang's main tasks at the Research Institute was to develop international collaboration," recalled Shen Yongyan, who visited Jiang soon after his appointment. "He told me that the director of the institute was not interested in this area." With his love of languages, especially English, and his open-minded curiosity, Jiang was a natural. He visited several countries, and his international perspective began to develop.

In 1965 Jiang was a member of a delegation that the ministry sent to attend a technical convention in Japan. Since there were no diplomatic relations be-tween China and Japan and hence no direct flights, the delegation stopped off in Hong Kong, where Jiang was impressed by the island's prosperity and rapid development. All of its industries—textiles, electronics, shipping, real estate, tourism—were booming. Hong Kong's exports exceeded those of all China by six times! The contrast with Shanghai, supposedly China's commercial center, was startling. The island's elegant department stories and modern skyscrapers showed Jiang what a Chinese city could achieve.

His demeanor on the trip and subsequent report impressed his superiors, and in mid-1965 the ministry intended to transfer him to Beijing to help manage production of the nation's electrical machinery, but a more important assignment opened up. The Wuhan Thermal Power Machinery Research In-stitute, a key project that included an atomic energy research center, had just been completed, and Wang Daohan suggested that Jiang, not yet thirty-nine years old but with a strong track record in power engineering, be made both director of the new institute and deputy Party secretary. Holding both posi-tions would give Jiang a great deal of authority, and the appointment would elevate him to the category of high-ranking official.

Jiang had mixed feelings about the assignment. He would be the boss of the new institute with more than three hundred employees, but he had rel-ished the prospect of working in Beijing. A downside was that his family could not accompany him; they stayed in Shanghai—the start of a twenty-year separation. Though Jiang was permitted a one-month leave per year to spend with them, his absence would take an emotional toll, particularly on his wife. Another negative was that Wuhan, the capital of Hubei province, was out of the political mainstream, but events would soon prove that to be a blessing. For the next several years the political mainstream would be the last place that anyone would want to be.

The first hint of impending doom came on November 10, 1965, when a Shanghai newspaper published a caustic review of a play titled *Hai Rui Dis-missed from Office*, written by a vice mayor of Beijing. The reviewer, a man named Yao Wenyuan, claimed that the work was a veiled attack on Chairman Mao and suggested darkly that certain senior Party officials were behind it. As it turned out, Yao himself was a puppet of others, particularly Mao's wife, Jiang Qing, and a Shanghai propagandist named Zhang Chunqiao. The three, along with a factory security guard named Wang Hongwen, would come to be known, infamously, as the Gang of Four.

By March 1966 the Gang of Four's attempts to manipulate Mao in his dotage were succeeding. "Your orders are being ignored," they warned him gravely, "and your authority is being usurped." Mao thought he could hasten China's development by purifying its ideology, but what became known as the Cultural Revolution was the product of his sad and vainglorious belief, in the twilight of his turbulent career, that he had to rerevolutionize China—and this meant reaffirming his potency and asserting his preeminence, particularly over Liu Shaoqi and Deng Xiaoping. Begun as an effort to prevent China from going the "revisionist" way of Khrushchev's Soviet Union, the Cultural Revolution dissolved into a decade of colossal chaos and decimated the country. Those whom Mao hoped to help—workers, farmers, peasants—became all the more destitute.

As he had done in the past, Mao turned to the people, urging them to denounce their leaders and the Party's Central Committee, which he termed "the palace of hell." Later that year Liu Shaoqi, president of China, and Deng Xiaoping, general secretary of the Party, were labeled, respectively, "the biggest capitalist" and "the second biggest capitalist." Both were purged. Liu and his wife endured protracted physical and mental torment. When jailers refused to give him medication for his diabetes, Liu Shaoqi died. Deng Xiaoping found a better fate, though not without bearing long hardships.

Similar punishment was meted out to intellectuals and professionals throughout the country. At first they refused to believe that such madness could last, but the Cultural Revolution quickly spiraled out of control, having been taken over by radicals and opportunists and energized by fundamentalist fervor. The worship of Mao, a true charismatic figure whose persona was wildly distorted, terrorized the nation. Young Red Guards, most with scant education, waved their little red books of Mao's quotations as if they were divinely inspired and stood in judgment over anyone they deemed counterrevolutionary. Virulently, they screamed their divisive slogans: "Destroy the four olds!' (i.e., expunge old ideas, old culture, old customs, and old habits), "Better poor under Communism than rich under capitalism," and "Always loyal to Chairman Mao."

Universities were shut down, and professors were exiled to farms to clean pigpens and work in rice paddies. Progress ground to a halt as "revolutionary committees" took over the few institutions that remained open. People began turning on one another—worker against worker, friend against friend, child against parent. An entire generation was lost as millions were purged and civilization was trashed. "The absurd activities that downgraded and even destroyed fine culture and art," Jiang would exclaim three decades later, "are all erroneous."

At first Jiang's main concern was for his family in Shanghai. By November 1966 he realized that the anarchy was spreading—not passing, as most had expected—and in December he asked for a short leave to see his wife and children. He may have decided to go by way of Beijing, a significant detour, to get a firsthand sense of what was happening.

When Jiang arrived in the capital, he learned that the entire senior leadership of his ministry had been or was about to be purged and shipped to the countryside. Wang Daohan, along with many of Jiang's friends, was banished. Most were gone for a decade or longer.

The scene in Shanghai was equally disturbing. Surging masses of Red Guards swarmed in front of Party headquarters and chanted slogans demanding that Chen Pixian, the Shanghai Party secretary, and Cao Diqiu, the city's mayor, be removed. Both men had stellar revolutionary records but were attacked, it was said, because Chen refused to denounce Liu Shaoqi and Deng Xiaoping. On December 30 rioters broke through the army-guarded barricades and ransacked the Shanghai Party offices in what became known as the Kanping Incident. Soon afterward, Chen was made to endure three struggle sessions and show trials that were broadcast live on national television. Then he, like so many others, was purged. Jiang later called the mayhem, some of which he witnessed, "a period of unprecedented destruction." (There are unconfirmed reports that Jiang met with Chen Pixian at this time, after being escorted through the sea of red flags and angry mobs of Red Guards, and that the relationship would come to provide key support at crucial moments in Jiang's later career.)

In January 1967 Jiang returned to Wuhan to find that the frigid blasts of the Cultural Revolution had, as if with the winter, swept in. He kept a low profile, wearing cast-off army clothes to blend in, but as director of the Institute, he made an easy target. "Big character" slogans denouncing him were plastered on the walls. "Jiang is expert but not Red," read one of them. He was accused of being a professional, a revisionist, and a capitalist roader. His own words—"We must love what we are doing"—were used to evidence his guilt, and he was criticized for repeating General Chen Yi's statement "Professionalism is Red; they are two sides of the same coin."

In Jiang Zemin the Red Guards found plenty to attack: intellectual background, cultural upbringing, elite education, apprenticeship in the Soviet Union. The fact that he spoke different languages "proved" that he "worshipped foreign ways." They also accused him of leading a "bourgeois lifestyle."

Jiang was indeed mindful of his appearance. On occasion he would comb his hair and tidy his clothes in public. His friends sometimes made good-natured fun of this habit: "A small comb for a big head," they would say. Jiang would smile and joke back: "It's human nature to look beautiful."

Jiang stoically absorbed the criticisms. Compared with classmates and colleagues, he knew he was fortunate. He had not been purged, exiled, or jailed. He had two saving graces: he had been born into a "Red" family, and he was focusing on scientific research. In the lingo of the Cultural Revolution, he was being "set aside" but not "pulled down." Nonetheless he was incensed: he had worked so hard to build the country and the Party. "The wall posters were unbearable," Jiang would later tell family and friends. "There was no way to argue with them. It was an ordeal and a test for me."

Perhaps the height of mortification arrived in the form of a college student, Liu Zhenhua, who had been selected by the Red Guards to investigate and examine Jiang. During the interrogation Jiang was frank. "You young people must keep a clear head," he told the nervous student. "In our socialist country there are all types of people. You must learn how to use your own mind to analyze problems and find the truth." When Liu leveled the charge of "bourgeois living" at him, Jiang was indignant.

"Ridiculous!" he fired back. "I live in a dorm. My blanket is worm-eaten. My briefcase is falling apart. Check all my possessions!"

Secretly, Liu told a friend that he was very thankful for Jiang's advice.

Nonetheless, Jiang was denounced, removed from his position as director, and made to stand trial. He was forced to confess his wrongdoings and write self-criticizing reports. Though he might have been alternatively fuming and laughing inside, Jiang tried to act in a straightforward and upright manner, not giving the hooligans any excuse to attack him further. Even so he refused to implicate others in order to lighten the load on himself, and after a while his attackers seemed to run out of things of which to accuse him.

What accounts for Jiang's relatively light treatment? First, he was sufficiently distant from Beijing and Shanghai, which were seen as the incubators of those "capitalist roaders" who allegedly opposed Mao and undermined Communism. Also, Jiang's personal behavior was beyond reproach; he had few possessions and never paraded an ostentatious style of life. To confuse his tormentors, Jiang highlighted his Communist martyr father while downplaying his cultural upbringing and elite education. Though

Jiang did not know it at the time, his old school, Yangzhou Middle School, was an early target of the Red Guards, who defaced the "feudal" building with bright red graffiti.

Jiang did his best to help the institute staff. His office director, Yang, a Party loyalist who had worked as a guard in Zhongnanhai for ten years, took it upon himself to write letters to the CPC Central Committee criticizing the Gang of Four, for which he was thanked by being branded a reactionary. "Comrade Yang," Jiang said, "you are indeed a good comrade. You must believe that as long as our senior leaders are alive, as long as the People's Liberation Army remains, the sky won't fall down. Eventually, you will be cleared and appreciated."

During his suspension Jiang organized lectures and courses for his technical staff, a minor miracle considering the anti-intellectual political climate. Included were lessons in English and Russian, which attracted more than a hundred students. He also enhanced his own understanding of both nuclear engineering and Marxism-Leninism. For once with enough time, he read avidly, particularly English-language texts, including, ironically and cleverly, the translated works of Mao Zedong. After all, how could he be criticized for reading Mao? In another effort at self-improvement, Jiang learned to swim, a skill that would become his primary exercise in years to come.

In September Jiang visited some new institute employees and noticed that four of them were jammed into a tiny room. Addressing a recent graduate named Hua Mingchun, who was barely in his twenties, he said, "Little Hua, why don't you live with me?" On hearing this, the recent arrival did not know how to respond and just smiled nervously. "It's not a big deal," said Jiang. "The director should just be like everyone else. A leader should never seek special treatment." When Hua arrived at Jiang's room, he was surprised to find that Jiang had already rearranged the two single beds and put his small desk between them so that it could be shared.

In 1967 the violence of the Cultural Revolution peaked. "One day," recalled Hua Mingchun, "I asked Director Jiang if he wanted to go out and watch the different Red Guard factions fighting. He patted my shoulder and said, 'Little Hua, you're still young; you should spend your time studying. If we don't have knowledge, we won't be able to build our country.'"

Prior to Hua moving in, Jiang had spent all his time after work studying in his room. His bed was always piled high with books. Now that he had a roommate, he stayed in his office to read and did not return to his room until very late, almost always after Hua had gone to sleep. "He always opened the door gently," said Hua. "He never turned on the light. He got ready for bed in the dark."

Hua shared a room with Jiang for three years, and he never saw Jiang smoke or drink alcohol. He did, however, remember Jiang's wide-framed glasses and, oddly enough, some problems with his hair. "Some people in our Institute accused Jiang of wearing his hair too long," said Hua. "They said his style was from the [pre-revolutionary] 1930s."

Jiang had no choice but to get his hair cropped, but when he returned, he heard the same complaint—his hair was still not short enough. So back to the barber he went and asked for a politically correct buzz cut. Scratching his virtually bald head, he asked his roommate, "Little Hua, how is my hair now?"

Hua could not avoid laughing, "Well, Director Jiang," he said, "short hair will prevent others from *jiu bianzi* [literally, pulling a braid or pigtail; metaphorically, seizing upon someone's mistakes or shortcomings]. Trust me, this time no one can criticize your hair."

During his years in Wuhan Jiang had few possessions—his old leather briefcase; a synthetic tote bag; a small flower-patterned cotton blanket; an old mosquito net; a small radio; a kerosene stove. The Institute did not have a canteen, so to eat the singles went next door to the Wuhan boiler factory. Sometimes when he was too busy with work or study, Jiang would leave a note for Hua and ask him to bring back a bowl of rice. Other times he would use his kerosene stove to cook noodle soup. "We had kerosene in our institute," Hua noted. "But Jiang always went to the store to buy the little kerosene he needed."

"Personal things are personal things," Jiang said, "and Institute's are Institute's. We must keep them separate.' "

"This seemed to me a little excessive," said Hua.

In 1968 more people joined the Institute, and with no housing available, two moved in with Jiang and Hua. "We should share both comfort and hardship," Jiang told Hua. No matter how noisy the room—his roommates talked and played cards—if Jiang was there and not sleeping, he was always reading. Once when a roommate's family came to visit, Jiang suggested that everyone else find another place to sleep for a couple of nights so that the family could have some private time together.

Years later (1991) Hua Mingchun was surprised to learn that Jiang Zemin was Jiang Shangqing's son. "We lived in one tiny room for over three years," said Hua at the time, "but he never mentioned to me that he was the son of a martyr."

ON OCTOBER 9, 1967, Premier Zhou Enlai, one of the lone voices of reason during the calamitous period, visited Wuhan. The institute staff was asked to line the streets to welcome the great man, and Jiang, like the rest of his colleagues, considered it an honor. Just before Zhou arrived, however, Jiang and six senior managers, all of whom had been suspended, were forcibly confined to an empty room. For Jiang, it was a bitter disappointment. "Today," he said, "my biggest regret is that I was not able to see Premier Zhou." Jiang's friends had never seen him so depressed.

After almost two years of official inactivity, Jiang was required to submit to a strict investigation by the Party, which concluded that it could not find any serious problems with his personal background or political behavior. As a result, Jiang was transferred to a May Seventh Cadre School, named after the day when Mao first issued his call for intellectuals to experience the manual labor of peasants. Located on a farm, the "school" used physical hardships, considered to be the refining fire of political purity, in the rehabilitation process. Eating dinner meant slurping noodles from coarsely made bowls while squatting, peasant style, on the floor. Decades later Jiang would remember the farm's "dusty, muddy, bumpy, country road."

Jiang lived on the farm for well over a year. True to his nature, he made the best of it and struck up several friendships. Along with the required pig raising and wheat growing, he passed the time playing musical instruments, practicing calligraphy, and painting. Once again his cultural interests maintained his spirits. Change was coming, and cadre school was the first step in Jiang's return.

FOR MANY OTHERS, INCLUDING members of Jiang's own family, the era was more devastating. His father's brother, Fifth Uncle, who had once risked his life working for an underground press during the war, was crushed to death during a mass gathering typical of the period. His sister, Jiang Zehui, was packed off to work on a farm. "I was a counselor who supervised students at the University," she recalled without rancor. "When the rebellion started, the students didn't know what they were doing, so the first people they attacked were the people they knew."

Because her husband had studied in the Soviet Union, he was considered a spy and also purged. "Everyone was suspected of everything," said Jiang Zehui. "You were whatever they labeled you."

In early 1971 Jiang Zehui and her husband were still living in rural exile when they were given leave to visit her in-laws in Nanjing for the Chinese New Year. Jiang Zemin happened also to be in Nanjing at the time (staying at the home of his older brother, Jiang Zejun) and, not knowing where his brother-in-law's parents lived, searched frantically to locate them.

"When he finally found us," Jiang Zehui remembered, "he anxiously bunched up his questions. He wanted to know everything at once. 'Were you cleared of all charges?' 'Have you been reinstated?' 'How is your life now?' " Jiang told his sister that Party inquisitors had completed their investigations and that he had been cleared. "He seemed frustrated by the futility of it all," she said, "though he wasn't bitter."

Jiang Zemin's two sons, Jiang Mianheng and Jiang Miankang, were also victimized by the times. Their studies, like his own three decades earlier, were disrupted by political upheavals. For Jiang, it had been the invading Japanese; for his sons, it was the self-immolating Cultural Revolution. Though on occasion they were able to visit their father while he was "set aside" in Wuhan, the Cultural Revolution changed their lives. When Mianheng, at fourteen, graduated from middle school, he was consigned to the countryside where he, along with innumerable others of the educated class, underwent a regimen of "rustification." Mianheng worked as a laborer in a grain storage area, spending his days shouldering large sacks of flour. His younger brother, Miankang, left lower middle school in 1968 and joined the army. The boys would not have the chance to complete their education until 1979.

Jiang Zemin adopted a philosophical attitude toward the trauma that his family and the country had undergone. "We who experienced the Cultural Revolution harbored harsh feelings toward those who had tortured us physically and tormented us emotionally," Jiang Zehui explained. "Third Brother encouraged me to try to understand the historical perspective and be kind to others—even to those who had moved against us. He said, 'If you could win their hearts, they would be at peace with you.' "

"President Jiang and I rarely speak of the Cultural Revolution," explained Wang Huijiong. "We don't need to. We can't forget the suffering. We can't forget the mangled lives and lost generation. We can't forget the terrible harm to China. We can't forget the radical Leftists. We were both intellectuals, professionals—there is no need to say more."

IN APRIL 1969 THE Ninth Party Congress redistributed power among competing factions, reestablishing a modicum of stability and anointing Lin Biao, a military leader, as Mao's successor. The Cultural Revolution was on the wane, and although Mao and the Gang of Four were still in charge, the rehabilitation of purged officials quietly began.

Jiang left the Cadre School in 1970 and returned to Beijing. After a transitional period in the Office of Struggle, Criticism, and Reform, he became vice director of the Bureau of Foreign Affairs of the First Ministry of Machine-Building Industry, his first formal governmental position. The move marked a fundamental shift in his career, from industry to politics. What he has called his "twenty-three years of frontline workplace experiences" and his "grass roots period" had concluded, and a new era had commenced.

During the Cultural Revolution Zhou Enlai had been placed in charge of the country's foreign affairs. In 1970, following the premier's advice, Mao began to explore new strategies in foreign policy, particularly in resisting the Soviet Union, with whom relations were frigid. A series of armed skirmishes had again broken out along their long, contested border, and China wanted to gain leverage against her powerful, nuclear-armed neighbor.

Considered a pariah state at the time, China had little diplomatic strength. One of the few countries that supported China was Romania, and to consolidate ties, China agreed to a request by the Romanian government, which was trying to reduce its own dependence on the Soviet Union, to help build fifteen machinery factories. This quasi-alliance between Romania and China, based on the ancient principle that "the enemy of my enemy is my friend," provided the only counterweight to Soviet dominance of the Communist world.

The project was accorded the highest priority. Zhou Enlai gave the assignment to the Machine-Building Ministry, which selected the forty-four-year-old Jiang Zemin to lead its delegation to Romania. The purpose of the trip was to conduct a feasibility study for constructing those fifteen factories, and after an intensive course in Romanian, Jiang departed for Eastern Europe. The last time he had gone abroad, he was the student; now he was the teacher.

Jiang's language skills were an essential aspect of his leadership. He seized every chance to practice Romanian, and when his newest language failed him, he could still speak Russian with East Europeans and English with West

Europeans. He found the Romanian people to be spirited and open-minded, and he liked being with them. It was Jiang's first official responsibility in foreign relations, and his superiors back in China, hungry for international success of any kind, judged it to be a diplomatic coup. Jiang later recalled that the experience "opened my eyes to see the world." It marked the beginning of what would become a major legacy of his career: the fostering of goodwill between China and the rest of the world.

In September 1971, while Jiang and his team were in Romania, Lin Biao tried to launch a military coup that included an attempt to assassinate Mao. The coup failed, and Lin fled the country with his family, only to die in an airplane crash in Mongolia. The confusion enabled Zhou Enlai to expand his own powers, and he quietly began to rehabilitate some who had been purged.

The Lin Biao incident also exposed the Party's propaganda machine as a house of cards. During the early stages of the Cultural Revolution, Chinese media had praised Lin as "Mao's closest comrade-in-arms and best student." Suddenly he was a traitor. Perhaps other things the media had been asserting were wrong, too. The fearsome fog of the Cultural Revolution was beginning to lift.

Deng Xiaoping, still in exile at a tractor plant, wrote letters to Mao, admitting his errors and pleading to be reinstated. With Zhou Enlai in bad health, Mao needed help, and in March 1973 Deng resumed his position as vice premier. He immediately began implementing long-overdue reforms, including reductions in China's ponderous and costly armed forces. Zhou and Deng enjoyed a good working relationship, and under their leadership the government began to return to normal.

After having achieved China's objectives in Romania, Jiang reassumed his position as vice director of his ministry's Bureau of Foreign Affairs. Shortly after his return from Bucharest, he went on holiday to Changchun to visit his old friends at the automotive factory. For nearly five years he had been unable to communicate with Shen Yongyan, who joyfully arranged a suite for him in the factory guesthouse.

"Lao [Old] Shen," Jiang said on seeing the spacious quarters. "What do you mean by this? I can't stay in a suite. Please get me a standard room."

It was not humility; it was anxiety. Having been criticized and denounced during the Cultural Revolution, Jiang refused to accept the suite. "He was a little more reserved," Shen recalled. "Not as ebullient as I'd known him; he was being extra cautious after those terrible years."

One facet of China's new strategy was its historic decision to begin normalizing relations with the United States. Through Romanian (and Pakistani) backchannels, facilitated in part by Jiang's work in Bucharest, secret negotiations between China and America progressed with surprising speed. On February 21, 1972, President Richard Nixon began his path-breaking trip to China. Nixon met with Chairman Mao and had daily talks with Premier Zhou. Like so many of its officials sent to the countryside, China itself was being rehabilitated.

In March 1973 China finalized agreements with Romania to build the fifteen factories. Jiang was responsible for organizing and implementing the project, which would include an exhibition on socialism in Bucharest. Though the Cultural Revolution was technically over, foreign affairs remained a challenge. The trick was to do a competent job, while avoiding the still-potent accusations of "Rightist," "revisionist," or "worshipper of foreign things." Now as in the future, Jiang's experience and pitch-perfect sense of Party vagaries would be invaluable.

Even as his career was taking off, Jiang's personal life remained lonely. He continued to live in a drab Beijing dormitory, while his wife and family resided in Shanghai. Most of the time he took his meals in the office cafeteria with other midlevel bureaucrats. He made steady progress in his job and was eventually promoted to director.

Jiang avoided the extreme politics of both Left and Right, and he was beginning to express himself more freely. From time to time officials were asked to move temporarily from their run-down dwellings to more decent quarters in order to impress (or not to appall) important visitors. Jiang decried the cover-up. "Intellectuals cannot alter reality to suit the situation," he said later, remembering the practice. "We are burdened to face facts as they really are."

IN 1975 DENG XIAOPING was executive vice premier but since the ultra-Leftist Gang of Four still controlled propaganda—they had disbanded the ministry but operated the machine—he created a competing force at the State Council, the Political Research Office. Using this new resource, Deng prepared an important article—"On the Overall Work Plan for the Country and the Party"—in which he sought to shift the Party's emphasis from class struggle to economic productivity. Deng was assisted by Hu Qiaomu, Mao's former secretary, and Deng Liqun, who would later become his sharpest conservative critic. They were in turn assisted by a young Party theorist, Teng Wensheng, who fifteen years later would become Jiang Zemin's speechwriter and head of research.

Though Deng tried to integrate Mao's ideas into the article, Mao came to conclude that Deng was playing games with his words in order to move the country in a direction opposite to that which Mao had dictated. Even before the article was published, it became "evidence" of Deng Xiaoping's "major crimes." Deng was purged again—he was last seen giving a eulogy at Zhou Enlai's funeral in January 1976—but this time, mercifully for China, his exile would not last very long.

Chapter 6

1976 – 1985

"It Was My Habit to Learn on the Job"

A S SOME CHINESE SAW IT, 1976 was a year when the heavens sparkled and the earth groaned. In March a huge meteor exploded over Jilin province, enveloping five hundred square miles with streams of lights and showers of rocks. In July the deadliest earthquake of the twentieth century obliterated Tangshan, killing 240,000 people.

Cataclysmic developments were also occurring on the political scene. On January 8 Zhou Enlai died after a protracted battle with cancer, and 1.5 million people stood in line to view his coffin. Eight months later, on September 9, at ten minutes past midnight, Mao Zedong, the Great Helmsman, died at the age of eighty-three. His death meant the end of an era. Across the country people wore black ribbons and white flowers; they wept tears of genuine sorrow but also waited anxiously for what would follow.

Within hours of Mao's demise, China's senior leaders were meeting in various combinations, seeking alliances and plotting strategies. Although Mao had named Hua Guofeng his successor, the Gang of Four, led by Mao's widow, Jiang Qing, attempted to maintain their power by discrediting him. In response, Hua Guofeng joined with moderate Party and army leaders, and on October 6 he authorized the arrest of each of the Four in a coordinated raid that also secured the national radio station and *People's Daily* newspaper. The tyranny of ultra-Leftism was over.

Certain Leftists, however, refused to recognize the new leadership in Beijing. Many of them were concentrated in Shanghai, which had been the Gang of Four's base of power. The renegades had an armed militia of more than 30,000 troops and 80,000 weapons, and they commandeered local media to prevent the transmission of any news from Beijing. Forces loyal to the central government surrounded the city, while leaders invited representatives of the

Shanghai Revolutionary Committee to Beijing for discussions. Those who were willing to abandon their support for the Gang of Four were offered amnesty, and many agreed to the terms.

The Party Central Committee assigned a fourteen-person Working Group to restore order in Shanghai. Among its members was Jiang Zemin, now fifty years old, and though he was a natural candidate considering his knowledge of the city's industry and enterprises, he was caught by surprise. Jiang had mixed feelings, but no choice, about accepting the job. He was pleased to live with his wife and sons, but the work was fraught with competing interests and hidden snares. It seemed more like a career interruption than a promotion. Jiang quietly sought the advice of Wang Daohan, but since Wang had not yet been reinstated, he was careful not to say too much.

Jiang's assignment was to revive the city's industry and transport, which had been controlled by the Gang of Four and their cronies. In the city where he had once protested against the Kuomintang, Jiang now held authority to decide the fate of thousands. It was a daunting task: Many had fallen prey to purges; others had jobs they did not deserve. Close examination of each case would be required.

Jiang set to work in an organized, rational manner tempered by political savvy. His first initiative was to restore key people to their positions, and to remove those who had been illegitimately appointed. He targeted those enterprises that seemed the most recalcitrant and suggested loyal groups to take them over. Gang of Four acolytes were arrested or investigated. Concerned that sudden change could be disrupting, Jiang slowly helped reinstate rules of efficient management that the Cultural Revolution had eliminated. He also recommended limited incentive systems for workers and brought back commonsense traditions like wearing canvas overalls instead of revolutionary garb for heavy industrial work.

As a member of the Working Group, Jiang was entitled to a car and driver, but the privilege made him uneasy. The family continued to live in the same apartment, which was set among the modest dwellings of ordinary workers. He was sensitive to criticism and did not want children staring at his car or neighbors talking behind his back, so he asked his driver to drop him off a few blocks from home, and he would walk the rest of the way like everybody else.

The Working Group was a great success. Jiang spent a year in Shanghai, and on his return to Beijing, he resumed his post as director of the Foreign Affairs Bureau of the Machine-Building Ministry. The next few years were to be frustrating ones. Politics was in transition, and although the Gang of Four were incarcerated, the country seemed stagnant. Hua Guofeng, who had been appointed Party chairman in August 1977, resisted any changes. He was known for his Two Whatevers—"Whatever Chairman Mao decided we uphold; whatever Chairman Mao instructed we do."

Jiang Zemin was ill suited to this reactionary environment. Over the next year he was passed over for two vice-minister positions. So many officials were being rehabilitated that there was now a glut of candidates for choice jobs. At fifty-two, Jiang was in career crisis. He considered leaving government to teach in a university, a move he would consider again more than a decade later.

Fortunately, change was coming. Deng Xiaoping, reemerging from his second purge following Mao's death, became one of three vice chairmen under Hua Guofeng, and as Deng's fortunes rose so would Jiang's. Though they could not know it at the time, Deng and Jiang would become inextricably linked in leadership.

In response to Hua's Two Whatevers, Deng countered with "Seek truth from facts" and "Practice is the only standard to test truth." The former was a more rational understanding of Mao's original idea, which had lain dormant during two decades of raging ideological fever. The latter sparked a national debate. Deng's powerful aphorisms challenged Mao's insistence that Communist ideology was the supreme arbiter for all decision-making in China, and everyone understood that new thinking was afoot.

"I was honored to have been a drafter of one of the most important articles in modern times," recalled Teng Wensheng. Titled "Liberate Your Thoughts, Seek Truth from Facts, Get United, and Move the Country Forward," the paper was produced by Deng Xiaoping for a working session of the CPC Central Committee in November and December of 1978. Deng himself prepared the outline; Hu Qiaomu helped with revisions. The article made two powerful points: Stay away from old doctrines, and let part of the people get rich first—breaking the sacred dogma of total equality for all classes. "This is very courageous," Teng Wensheng remembered thinking at the time. Deng's article set the tone for the crucial Party plenary, coming in late December, which would become a turning point in Chinese history and change the country for good.

IN A STROKE OF good timing, Jiang's longtime mentor, Wang Daohan, returned to politics in late 1978. After years in purgatory toiling as a low-level bureaucrat,

Wang was reinstated into the Party and restored to his former position as vice minister for foreign economic relations in the First Ministry of Machine-Building Industry.

It had been a protracted, traumatic period for Wang—thirteen years, more like an era—during which Jiang did all he could to help his friend. Wang's wife, who had suffered from kidney failure for years, died in 1965. Prior to her death Jiang and his wife often visited the Wang home; Jiang never forgot how the terminally ill woman, his former boss, had counseled and comforted him in the early 1950s.

Throughout the turbulent years, the families maintained contact. With Jiang in Wuhan, Jiang's wife gave Wang's daughter shelter in Shanghai after her father had been purged and exiled. This was not without risk, since any contact with the excommunicated Wang could have given a handy excuse to those who sought to bring Jiang down.

By the middle 1970s Wang Daohan was back in Beijing, living quietly, and Jiang met with him frequently. This was still dangerous, since Wang had not yet been rehabilitated.

"We were strictly old friends," recalled Wang. "Sure, we'd talk politics— we both knew that the Gang of Four had to be removed and that China needed new leaders—but we'd also talk about world economics, modern technology, literature. Jiang told me about Shakespeare's great plays (I had time on my hands and read a great deal). I appreciated how much Jiang knew, and even during the hardest of times how eager he was to learn."

Following the devastating earthquake in Tangshan, and while the Gang of Four was still in power, Jiang had moved into Wang's home. "Beijing was feeling the aftershocks, and people living in tall buildings were nervous," Wang explained. "Many sought low-story houses as temporary shelters. Jiang and his mother stayed at my house for a few days. At that time she was living with Jiang in a third-floor apartment in a high-rise building, and I used to visit them often. Jiang's mother cooked wonderful Yangzhou cuisine and treated me like a son. Every time I visited, she would prepare her best dishes, such as shredded roasted tofu and the tennis-ball-size "Lion's Head" meatballs that are deep-fried and braised with vegetables. She was a well-educated woman who loved to read, especially classical Chinese novels—she enjoyed discussing the characters."

On December 18, 1978, the Third Plenary Session of the Eleventh Party Congress jolted the country out of its malaise. Hua Guofeng's Two Whatevers were repudiated, and Hua himself, in the fashion of the time, offered self-criticism. The transitional period was over, and Deng Xiaoping assumed power. It was a majestic moment: Deng would now institute and energize the greatest growth spurt in the country's history.

While Mao was an idealist, Deng was a realist. "Black cat, white cat," he said famously, "whichever catches mice is a good cat." (Or, "It doesn't matter if the cat is black or white, what's important is that it can catch mice.") In China subtle phrasing can convey enormous meaning, and no one missed the pragmatic message about this or that political system—socialism or capitalism—in Deng's memorable remark about black and white cats.

Deng's speech "Emancipate the Mind, Seek Truth from Facts, Unite and Look Forward" became the Party's new manifesto as its mission changed almost overnight from class struggle to economic development. Among other reforms, the government adopted an "Opening Up" or open-door policy, welcoming the participation of foreign interests (trade and investment) in the modernization process. It also began the gradual loosening of Chinese society and the slow flowering of personal freedoms. The Four Modernizations—agriculture, industry, national defense, science and technology—became the cornerstone of Deng's program. From here on the achievement of economic goals would be the measure of success or the mark of failure. Policies and careers would rise or fall on the quantifiable test of growth and development. "If we do not start reform," Deng said, "then our goal to modernize socialism will be buried."

Deng restored the family farm, introduced market economics, and praised consumer goods. He promoted trade with Taiwan, South Korea, Hong Kong, Singapore, and Japan. He also challenged ideological dogma. Beijing issued study documents on the nature of truth, and debate was encouraged throughout society. Never again would one person's thoughts—not Mao's, not Marx's, not even Deng's—be accepted blindly and unconditionally.

Later, Deng would decree that the Party should stop debating whether a given policy was "part" of a socialist or capitalist system, which for decades had been the touchstone of acceptability. He challenged Communist dogma by declaring that a market economy need not mean capitalism. "No longer mention struggles in the ideological sphere," Deng said, meaning that nineteenth-century Marxism could not be transplanted whole hog into twentieth-century China. Deng, who had lost most of his hearing in one ear but none of his humor, spoofed his own deviation from rigid Marxism: "Marx sits up in heaven, and he is very powerful. He sees what we are doing, and he doesn't like it. So he has punished me by making me deaf."

In October 1978, two months before the historic Third Plenary Session of the Eleventh Party Congress, deep in the countryside in the village of Xiaogang, Anhui province, eighteen impoverished farmers held a secret meeting. With their families near starvation, they agreed that they could not survive under the collectivist system of common ownership, and they decided to split the commune's crop land into individual plots and allocate them among its member households, thus adopting a "household contract responsibility system." By working independently, they would now keep the fruits of their own labor, and their rapid success would come to the attention of Deng Xiaoping and help change the course of Chinese history.

On the twentieth anniversary of the "household contract responsibility system," in the fall of 1998, President Jiang came to Xiaogang—now featuring cement roads, brick farmhouses, modern school buildings, and television satellite dishes—and saw a photocopy of the original contract, which the farmers had signed, with their thumb prints, literally in blood. Jiang read their desperate, pioneering words aloud: ". . . If we are successful in the future, we will not ask the state for any money or grain. If we are not [successful], we cadres are willing to risk imprisonment or the death penalty, and [we request] those who remain alive to raise the children [of the punished] until they are eighteen years old." Jiang praised the "vivid and concise" language and took a photograph with the original farmers, who jockeyed with one another for proximity to China's leader.

In January 1979 China and the United States reestablished diplomatic relations. A few weeks later President Jimmy Carter hosted Deng Xiaoping and his wife on a state visit, the first official trip to America of a Chinese leader since the founding of the People's Republic in 1949. Perceptions of China began to change. It was said that the diminutive Deng, who donned a cowboy hat, was someone with whom Americans could "do business."

In April 1979 Deng suggested the establishment of Special Economic Zones, known as SEZs, where foreign investors would be encouraged to build factories to manufacture and export consumer goods. The first such zones, located in Shenzhen, Zhuhai, and Shantou in Guangdong province, and Xiamen in Fujian province, would become prototypes and symbols of reform. China's State Council established two ministerial-level commissions to implement Deng's reforms (import-export and foreign investment). Both were chaired by a revolutionary leader and vice premier named Gu Mu.

In a speech to the Politburo Deng said, "Our chief task now is to discover and promote young and middle-aged officials early in their careers and without limitations." He called for "Four Transformations" to produce the new generation of Communist leaders, seeking those who were "more revolutionary, younger, more knowledgeable, and more specialized."

After hearing of Deng's directives, Wang Daohan, now fully back in power, approached Gu Mu and recommended that Jiang Zemin be given a senior role in the newly formed commissions. (Wang himself had just been offered one of China's most important positions: mayor of Shanghai.) Gu Mu, who had been vice Party secretary in Shanghai in the 1950s, remembered Jiang from the old days, and appointed him vice chairman and Party secretary of the general office of both commissions as well as a member of the Party's "Leading Group" of each commission.

After four years of stagnation, the fifty-four-year-old Jiang was finally a vice minister. Within weeks he was participating as a nonvoting member in a meeting of the Standing Committee of the National People's Congress (NPC), which is technically the highest organ of state power of the People's Republic of China, where he gave a briefing on establishing the Special Economic Zones. He was also elected for the first time as a member of the Chinese People's Political Consultative Conference (CPPCC), which represented China's diverse sectors, groups, minorities, and non-Communist parties in a "patriotic United Front" under the leadership of the Communist Party. (In practical fact, the NPC and CPPCC have always been subservient to the Party, which in any event controls them.)

Jiang's task in structuring the SEZs, which he would later call "pioneers," "windows," and "experimental fields" for the rest of the country, was to maintain a balance between economic progress and social stability. He had to stimulate foreign investment, while ensuring that any economic reform would not destabilize socialism or threaten the interests of the Party. It was hoped that the SEZs would become conduits for the influx of foreign money, materials, and knowhow—but not foreign ideology. To that end, the SEZs would be separated from the rest of the country, quite literally, with barbed-wire fences and guard dogs.

In the fall of 1980 the SEZ commissions were asked to organize a UN-sponsored world tour of import-and-export centers and free trade areas in twelve countries. Jiang was appointed head of the delegation, which was comprised of ten Chinese—Party secretaries from SEZ-designated cities and technical and legal specialists from various ministries—and a West German guide.

In Singapore the delegation faced a less-than-friendly reception; for example, they were not permitted into the manufacturing areas of an airplane parts producer. The next morning, in complaining to local officials, who insisted on speaking English, Jiang found that his translator was unable to keep pace, and so Jiang himself did all the translating—which was most unusual for a delegation head. Jiang was not pleased that these Singaporean-Chinese officials would not speak Chinese, and in the afternoon session he insisted that they do. As a result, the discussions became informative.

The forty-day trip, which took the delegation to Southeast Asia, North America, and Europe, concluded in Geneva, where Jiang briefed UN officials. "Jiang was very diplomatic in his report," remembered delegation member Liu Zifen, Party secretary of Xiamen. "The truth was that except for our talks in Singapore, the trip was unproductive. Everywhere else the meetings lacked substance. Jiang did a great job, though, in promoting China's new reform policy. Later Jiang was the one who pushed for the final decision to start the 2.5-square-kilometer SEZ in Xiamen. As with all of the SEZs, there were disagreements among the central, provincial, and municipal governments over control. . . .

"Jiang was a down-to-earth professional," Liu added. "During our trip he pitched in and did all kinds of work, small and big, and he never put on airs of a senior official."

Though Jiang had spent a fair amount of time in other countries, he was startled by the contrast between China and the rest of the world. He pinpointed the Jurong Industrial Estate in Singapore and the free-trade zone in Shannon, Ireland, as possible models for China to follow, and he began to develop a sense for structuring the SEZs.

Following the delegation's return, Jiang and his team prepared a groundbreaking report. Given the still-fresh nightmare of the Cultural Revolution, the recommendations were daring. Included were policies allowing local governments to authorize tax breaks and land leases and to secure their own foreign funds. In addition, the report suggested that foreign-funded ventures should be permitted to hire and fire workers as they saw fit. These were radical ideas for a Communist country, and only the Politburo, the Party's highest ruling body, had the power to approve them.

The SEZs were controversial and the report caused consternation. Everyone, it seemed, found something to dislike. Hardliners worried about negative influences of foreign capital; ideologues saw distortions in the socialist system; and bureaucrats balked at ceding power to local authorities. The Trade Ministry was opposed, while the Finance Ministry remained skeptical. The idea of a competitive marketplace was at best a cause for anxiety, at worst a source of fear. Jiang refuted these concerns with empirical evidence. It was not a matter of ideology, he said, but of outcomes. The delegation was simply recommending structures and policies that were working elsewhere. It was just the sort of argument that would resonate with Deng Xiaoping.

Jiang made his case before the National People's Congress and succeeded in securing conditional consent to go forward. (His well-received presentation was called eloquent, expressive, logical, and humorous.) The approval was not unanimous, however, and he was told that the SEZs would be watched closely. Nonetheless the decision was a historic breakthrough—for Jiang personally as well as for China. No longer a technocrat, he had leaped to the cutting edge of policymaking: he had become an early implementer of Deng's reforms, the first to make concrete decisions in Shenzhen on behalf of the central government. "All projects in the SEZ," he said, "should be started from a long-term perspective and be consistent with international standards." Jiang Zemin was now a champion of what would become known as "Deng Xiaoping Theory." The role would serve him well.

SOMETIME DURING 1982, AT the end of a meeting, Jiang walked over to General Zhang Aiping, then vice premier and minister of defense. They had met several times before, but this time Jiang had something personal on his mind.

"Do you still remember Jiang Shangqing?" Jiang asked.

"Of course, he was my close friend. Sadly, he died young!"

"He was my adoptive father," Jiang said.

"Really?" Zhang was taken aback. "How come you never mentioned this before?"

"Frankly, I didn't know what to say."

"For years, I've been searching for Shangqing's family. I had no idea that you are his son!"

"When he died, I was only thirteen," Jiang added.

Elated, Zhang asked many questions about Shangqing's relatives.

Then Jiang made his request. "The local government wants to establish a monument for my father. I would like to ask you to write an inscription for it."

On that same day, Zhang Aiping wrote a seven-character inscription: "Tomb of Comrade Jiang Shangqing." On the back would be an epitaph written by the fallen man's colleagues. It had been forty-three years since his death.

IN MARCH 1982 THE two commissions of which Jiang was vice chairman, along with other economics-oriented ministries, were combined into one new superministry known as the Ministry of Foreign Trade and Economics Cooperation, or MOFTEC. Chen Muhua, the only female vice premier at the time, was appointed minister, and when she announced her senior team, Jiang Zemin's name was not on the list. He had been squeezed out again, but this time he had two powerful patrons, Gu Mu on the State Council and Wang Daohan, the mayor of Shanghai. Both went to Zhao Ziyang, then premier, to put in a good word for him. Again Jiang benefited from good timing: The State Council had just decided to authorize the creation of a new Ministry of Electronics Industry.

Zhao Ziyang, an ardent reformist, made it his priority to appoint competent, innovative thinkers. He liked to observe candidates for high office in different settings: visiting them at work, hearing them present reports, and chatting with them at dinners. Jiang excelled in all of these venues. In May 1982, after Zhao interviewed him privately, the Party appointed Jiang Zemin to be first vice minister and Party secretary of the Ministry of Electronics Industry. It was a major promotion. Ironically, Zhao had just accelerated the career of the man who would one day replace him.

At the Twelfth Party Congress in September 1982, Deng Xiaoping's keynote speech was titled "Socialism with Chinese Characteristics," a phrase that would thereafter define the country's program of reform. Deng believed that the theories of Marx and Lenin had to be adapted to Chinese culture, a theme that Jiang would develop in the future. To Westerners, Deng's reforms may have seemed like tentative, baby steps, but in China they were viewed as bold and far-reaching.

At the same Congress Jiang Zemin became the 210th member of the CPC Central Committee, the body that sets policy and elects the Politburo. By entering into the inner sanctum of political power, Jiang had overcome the final barrier to becoming a candidate for high office. He met the four standards of the era almost perfectly: revolutionary heritage, three decades as a knowledgeable manager, technically specialized in several areas, and at the age of fifty-six, still relatively young.

When he took his seat for his first meeting of the Central Committee, Jiang could look around and feel at home. He knew many of the members, including several from the Shanghai underground. There were senior elders who had fought alongside his martyred foster father, Jiang Shangqing, many of whom would become his supporters, particularly General Zhang Aiping. His recent boss, Gu Mu, was vice premier and a member of the Secretariat, the organization that manages Party affairs. Relationships formed the core of Chinese politics, and Jiang was a natural at creating and building them.

CONSUMERISM WAS BEGINNING TO emerge, and the electronics industry had to scramble to meet new demands. It was said that in Mao's era, young people getting married in urban areas wished for a bicycle, a watch, an electric fan, and a radio. By Deng's time, it was a color television, a tape recorder, a washing machine, and a refrigerator. To meet the challenge, Jiang took a self-study crash course in electronics, reading books and papers, attending technical briefings, conversing with experts. When asked about his hobbies at a later press conference, he said, "As an intellectual, I like to read. I read materials related to my job: first, machinery; then electronics." When Jiang visited the Massachusetts Institute of Technology (MIT) on his second visit to United States in June 1983, it was as though he had gone to science heaven. He would note, with some wistfulness, that had his life taken a different course he would have loved to earn a doctorate at MIT.

Representing the electronics ministry, Vice Minister Jiang met with various technology companies, including Hewlett-Packard, with which he signed one of China's first joint ventures. His last stop was in San Francisco, where the head of Hewlett-Packard China, Dr. Liu Chining, offered to host a special Chinese dinner. Apparently, one member of Jiang's delegation had not been able to eat Western food throughout the trip and had remained in his room, missing most of the meetings. (Dr. Liu's home-cooked Chinese noodles did the trick, reviving the man just in time for his return to China.)

Liu picked up the delegation at the airport and on the drive to his home told Jiang that in addition to the Chinese meal he had also arranged a celebration.

"Celebration?" Jiang asked. "For what?"

"For what?" Liu responded. "Are you joking? For your promotion to minister of Electronics Industry, of course."

"Where did you hear that?" said Jiang, astonished. He had not expected it now and had received no official notice.

Liu said that he had heard from friends that Jiang, barely a year after he had joined the Ministry, had been appointed its head. Jiang asked if he could stop and call the Chinese Consulate in San Francisco to check the news. He was apprehensive, though not showing it. He certainly didn't want to attend a celebration if the promotion wasn't real. Only after receiving confirmation could he enjoy the party, particularly a large cake inscribed in his honor. Jiang Zemin was now a full minister.

When Jiang met President Ronald Reagan during this period, he complained about American restrictions on the sale of certain technologies to China.

"We worry that you will use them for military purposes," said Reagan.

"Then why do you sell us wheat?" countered Jiang with a smile. "We use it to feed our soldiers." Reagan and Jiang shared a good laugh.

ALTHOUGH TECHNOLOGY HAD CHANGED a great deal since his graduation, Jiang knew enough electronics to identify needs and opportunities. Explaining his background, he said, "My experience involved the engineering, electronics, and power industries, as well as the export-import business." Jiang never learned any subject comprehensively; he gained enough knowledge to know what to do and who should do it. As he pointed out, "It has been my habit to learn on the job."

At the ministry Jiang was in charge of some fourteen hundred enterprises operating nearly four thousand factories, many of which were military. Under his supervision were 75,000 ministry personnel and nearly three million factory workers. His mandate was to bring China current in computer technology and consumer electronics. It was a colossal task. "Technically," Jiang said, "we are fifteen years behind in industrial production and eight to ten years lagging in science and technology." Factories were in disarray; enterprises could not meet the needs of large-scale production; and electronics imports exceeded exports by a factor of five.

In an August 1983 interview, Jiang was candid. "Our level of production, quality and reliability of products, and even the economic results of our electronics industry, are rather low," he said. "Our scientific research is backward, and the development period for new products is too long. Moreover, our factories are scattered, do not carry on specialized, high-volume mass production, and are not coordinated. None of this is suitable for this industry."

There were distasteful aspects to the job. In November 1982 Jiang investigated a massive smuggling case, the largest since the founding of New China, at the Shenzhen branch of China Electronics Import and Export Corporation. The conspiracy involved tens of thousands of televisions and other consumer electronics items, and *People's Daily* published an exposé stating, "We must raise our awareness and carry this struggle to the end." It was a pioneering move to purify the Party, and it would mark an early battle in Jiang's protracted, often exasperating war against corruption.

Though Jiang remained unspoiled by success, he did take pleasure in his new living quarters. Shen Yongyan, who visited him during this period, recalled that "Jiang was really happy with his apartment," adding, "It was the first time I remember him saying that—I think because it had two bathrooms."

Just after Jiang was appointed minister of Electronics Industry, the two friends spoke again. "Jiang was excited about the increasing importance of electronics in commercial and defense applications," said Shen, "and the long challenge of bringing China up to world-class standards. He also told me, with some satisfaction, that his promotion from vice minister to full minister brought along an important perk—a minister can fly first class during international travel. Jiang said he liked being able to recline and rest on the long flights."

Wang Huijiong, Jiang Zemin's old classmate, also noted some changes. "I could see that Jiang had become more mature," Wang remembered. "He still went out shopping, bought his own vegetables, and led a normal life—he actually liked shopping and thought it useful to check prices. But he had become more cautious. Before he had been, frankly, more action oriented, not impulsive, but aggressive. Now, he had become more considered in his words and deeds."

IN SPITE OF HIS heavy responsibilities, Jiang made time for family. He invited his older sister, Jiang Zefen, who was still struggling to overcome the damage done by the Anti-Rightist Campaign, to move into his apartment. "Most often my brother would come home from work very late," Jiang Zefen remembered. "Our family had finished eating hours before, and when I asked him what he'd like to eat, he'd often ask for a bowl of noodles. For him, work was everything; he had a simple lifestyle."

In 1982, when Jiang Zehui was appointed associate dean of the forestry department at Anhui Agricultural University, she rushed to Beijing to tell Jiang Zemin. "I had worked on farms for ten full years during the Cultural Revolution," she said matter-of-factly. "I was proud of my promotion and couldn't wait to surprise Third Brother." In the Chinese system of public servants, her new rank was equivalent to that of a county supervisor or a division chief in a ministry. On hearing the good news, Jiang gave his sister a congratulatory hug and then some big-brotherly advice. "You are a county leader now," he said. "I want to give you a *duilian* as an encouragement gift."

A *duilian* is a kind of poem consisting of a couplet that contains five to seven Chinese characters per row and is meant to inspire or guide its recipient. The *duilian* that Jiang gave to his sister was written about General Zhu

Geliang, who lived in the third century and is considered China's greatest military strategist.

"*Gong Xin,*" it read in part. "Work to win people's hearts."

"*Shen Shi,*" went the next line. "Judge the hour." In other words, size up the situation.

"I thought about what this *duilian* might mean," said Jiang Zehui, "and how it related to my situation. Since I had become a chief cadre, Third Brother was counseling me that I should learn how to manage people. He wanted me to become an effective leader who could bring people together. Propriety and good sense were also important."

In late 1983 Jiang's salvage-and-expansion plan for China's electronics industry—building an industrial base and increasing 1980 output eightfold by the year 2000—was approved by the State Council. Production of radios and black-and-white televisions was cut back, while that of telephones and color televisions increased. Current international standards would replace outmoded Soviet ones.

Implementing the plan, Jiang made computers and integrated circuits a priority, stressing their military applications. The electronics industry produced China's missiles and satellites, a responsibility that Jiang happily accepted. National pride as well as defense was at stake. In April 1984 a Long March III rocket successfully launched a *Dong fanghong II*—"East is Red"—telecommunications satellite, making China the fifth country to reach geostationary orbit. Jiang, who was present at the launch site, was congratulated by the Politburo and the State Council.

"When Jiang became vice minister, the first thing he did was to set goals and tasks," recalled Zeng Peiyan, who was transferred to the ministry in 1984. "At that time many of the enterprises were redundant and located in mountainous regions [where China had built them in the 1960s fearing an attack by the Soviet Union]. Jiang made many inspection trips to the factories, including on his 'holidays.' We had a slogan: 'Combine R&D with production.'

"Jiang had an early vision that software was key for the future," Zeng added, "and he was the first one in China, as far as I know, to talk about 'knowledge production.' He saw the need to improve human talent by educating and retraining employees. Every year he brought two to three hundred electronics industry leaders to Beijing; he enjoyed mixing with scientists and engineers; some even became his friends."

Jiang constantly communicated upward. He wrote reports for the Party Central Committee, the State Council, and the Central Military Commission that advocated speeding up electronics development to support China's Four Modernizations. Jiang argued that "electronics" had become "microelectronics," especially to support computers and telecommunications. Encouraged by his joint venture with Hewlett-Packard in 1983, he held a great number of international meetings throughout 1984.

Although the grand electronic revolution that Jiang promised did not take place on his watch—years later he admitted that China's electronic development "was not accomplished in line with my original hopes"—his achievements included the conversion of struggling military factories into prosperous producers of consumer goods. Jiang also gained international experience; for example, he sat with Premier Zhao Ziyang and Canadian prime minister Pierre Trudeau for talks on disarmament and East-West relations.

PROPELLED BY DENG XIAOPING's reforms, China finally seemed to be emerging from the long shadow of the Cultural Revolution. The year 1984 marked the thirty-fifth anniversary of the People's Republic, and it was a time of so much optimism that the October event became a mass celebration. In Tiananmen Square students put up a banner greeting Deng by his first name, "Hello Xiaoping," expressing the intimacy that ordinary Chinese felt with their Paramount Leader. It would have been an unthinkable familiarity during Mao Zedong's reign, and it signaled a new, freer atmosphere.

The more relaxed environment suited Jiang Zemin's direct, unpretentious style. To update the revered elder Chen Yun, Jiang brought along an armload of props. Using integrated circuit boards, a microprocessor, and a microscope with which to view them, Jiang helped Chen understand the meaning of the electronics revolution, all the while speaking in the old man's Shanghai dialect. Chen, who was arguably second only to Deng in veneration, appreciated that Jiang not only grasped the latest technology but also had the good grace to make him feel comfortable with unfamiliar material.

People's Daily published a major story on the visit, which portrayed Jiang as both technologically astute and traditionally respectful. Part of the point was to show that the advances being made by Western-oriented intellectuals did not somehow contradict the people's revolution of peasants, farmers, and workers.

Exercising his growing political savvy, Jiang wrote an article for *People's Daily* in which he extended Party general secretary Hu Yaobang's campaign to close ranks in response to minor dissent. Jiang was now advancing the Party line, not just supporting it. By making his strong views known so publicly—the article symbolized his personal commitment—Jiang was confirming his orthodoxy. As an intellectual with an affinity for Western ways, he would regularly have to reaffirm his Communist credentials. Some old-guard elders lacked formal education and harbored lingering suspicion of those who did.

In October 1984, with economic growth its new hallmark, the Central Committee passed a resolution about reform that referred to a "commodity economy with planning." The resolution enshrined Deng's idea of "Socialism with Chinese Characteristics," the bellwether phrase he had first articulated in 1982, and it would henceforth drive reform. It was a milestone: Socialism and the market were no longer contradictory. Moreover, the new creed affirmed that the market was a necessary step in the development of social-ism. From now on Chinese socialism would be a market economy that used public ownership as its industrial base. It was the Party's new formulation of Marxism, and it became the theoretical guideline for subsequent reforms.

That same year Deng's vision of "one country, two systems," crafted to re-solve the contradiction posed by Taiwan, was made law. Diplomatic policy began to change as well. Moving away from simplistic opposition to the American and Soviet superpowers, the government adopted a more textured policy of maintaining Chinese independence and pursuing the country's ini-tiatives peacefully.

MEANWHILE, JIANG ZEMIN WAS feeling less satisfied in his job. Though the elec-tronics industry had fulfilled its annual quota three months early, up 40 per-cent over the previous year, he was frustrated by the turf battles between ministries and the stifling bureaucracy within his own. He was ready for a change.

Wang Daohan's term as mayor of Shanghai was due to expire in 1985, and Beijing was casting about for his replacement. For whatever reason, China's most important commercial center had not thrived—some said that Wang's aging leadership lacked vitality, while others blamed the absence of central government support,

"Of course I participated in the discussions about who should succeed me as mayor of Shanghai," recalled Wang Daohan. "Vice Premier Wan Li, who was close to Premier Zhao, came to consult with me. He presented several strong candidates. I recommended Jiang."

In December 1984 Premier Zhao Ziyang led a delegation to Shanghai for the purpose of accelerating its development, and Jiang was the only minis-ter in the group. Zhao was taken by the ideas of futurist Alvin Toffler and his "Third Wave" of industrial development centered around computers, information, and high tech. If Shanghai were to lead China's Third Wave, Jiang Zemin seemed a perfect fit to be its next mayor.

Don't expect laurels, Wang Daohan cautioned Jiang after the decision was made. Being Shanghai's mayor, he said, was like being the "chief clerk" of a general affairs office. Jiang replied, "I'd be thrilled to be the chief clerk for twelve million people."

With his appointment still a secret, Jiang took the opportunity to get reacquainted with the city he loved. Though he maintained his ministerial responsibilities, he began to consider Shanghai. Reportedly he would don pensioner's clothes as a disguise and walk the city—from the campus where he had studied to the streets where he had marched to the factories where he had worked. Everywhere he saw nothing but Shanghai's faded glory. Surrounded by the city's shabby buildings and defective infrastructure, Jiang Zemin was appalled—and determined to build anew.

Chapter 7

1985 – 1986

"Talk Less and Do More"

THE NAME SHANGHAI MEANS "on the sea," and the city lies on the East China Sea just south of the Yangtze River estuary. In the early twentieth century it was the most prosperous metropolis in Asia, a vibrant international community and the center of finance and trade. Shanghai surpassed such upstarts as Tokyo and Hong Kong and was known as the Pearl of the Orient, the Paris of China, and a paradise for risk-takers. By the 1980s, however, Shanghai had fallen on hard times. From the Japanese invasion and civil war to central planning and the Cultural Revolution, events seemed to have conspired to turn the formerly grand city into an isolated, dilapidated relic.

Even after Deng Xiaoping began his reforms, progress was slow (Shanghai was never designated a Special Economic Zone). While other areas, particularly South China's Guangdong province, were developing with remarkable speed, Shanghai was said to be like a "heavily loaded cart pulled by an old cow." Its growth rate in the 1980–83 period was barely half that of the country as a whole.

Many senior leaders, including Deng, became personally involved in the plan to resurrect the city. On a trip in the spring of 1984 the Paramount Leader stopped in Shanghai after inspecting Shenzhen and found the contrast between the two places stunning. Before reform Shenzhen had been a shantytown; now it was a vigorous, burgeoning metropolis. In contrast, the infrastructure of once-proud Shanghai could not even support the needs of its own people. Overcrowded housing, congested traffic, inferior telecommunications, and environmental pollution all impeded the city's growth. Deng went after city officials. "I come to Shanghai every year," he said. "What I see is always the same. Can't you move faster? Next time I come I expect to see major changes!" (Later Deng would blame himself for not including Shanghai in the first round of SEZs in the early 1980s.)

The problem was political as well as physical. So severe was the stagnation in local government that it had been given a derisive name: Shanghai Comprehensive Syndrome. When Wang Daohan attempted to assert progressive views as mayor, the left-leaning Party secretary responded by ordering an investigation of the *World Economic Herald* newspaper, an advocate for reform whose honorary chairman was Wang himself. The investigation amounted to little, but it evidenced the divisions within the municipal political system. With an expectant Beijing and a suspicious Shanghai watching his every move, the city's next mayor would face challenges and feel pressure.

Though Jiang Zemin seemed like an ideal candidate for the job, his nomination reportedly met with minor resistance, including at least one elder who may have remained apprehensive of the younger man's intellectual bent and Western interests. Neither Premier Zhao Ziyang nor Party general secretary Hu Yaobang knew Jiang very well, and neither said very much. According to the same report, Jiang's supporters were led by at least one other highly respected elder who argued that, in addition to having the talent and experience for the job, Jiang had proven his loyalty to the Party throughout his life. After this, all opposition was withdrawn.

Just before Jiang took office, he visited Yangzhou, his hometown, where he gathered his relatives together and spoke to them bluntly. "In the old days," he said, "when a man attains the Tao [i.e., enlightenment and immortality], even his pets ascend to heaven with him [meaning that when a man gets a top job, all his family, relatives, and friends benefit]. Since Yangzhou and Shanghai are so close, people from the two cities interact frequently. When I start working in Shanghai, you should never hold my signboard [meaning, don't use my name to get preferential treatment]."

In the eyes of the people of Shanghai, Jiang was Beijing's man. It was said at the time that while "observers and officials do not underrate his skills, few are taking bets on whether he will succeed." Undeterred by the modest expectations, the fifty-nine-year-old Jiang set about making his own mark. For his first formal act as mayor, he broke from tradition and held a press conference instead of giving a speech. Relaxed and self-assured, he invited journalists to ask questions. The day before, he had told Shanghai media that the city's development would be founded on three pillars: infrastructure development, foreign capital and exports, and technology and training.

"I have spent twelve and a half days listening to reports and making field trips to sites," he said in response to a reporter's query. "Problems have been piling up for years. We can only solve them one by one. We should talk less and do more."

Shanghai was in such a state of desperation that Jiang's first concern had to be food. He wanted grain reserves for at least three months, and he negotiated the purchase of meat from other cities—provisional measures that would be replaced by the Food Basket Project, designed to provide sufficient staples for the population.

This Project industrialized the breeding of livestock and set aside some thirty thousand acres as a sort of vegetable preserve. Professionals were hired to oversee every phase of the supply system, from seed selection to harvesting and distribution. Such steps provided the foundation for a strategic self-sustaining solution, rather than the stopgap emergency measures on which the city had been relying. "Shanghai people," Jiang would later observe, "are very demanding about getting fresh vegetables."

Jiang's next priority was improving the transportation system. "We must change Shanghai's three faces," he said, introducing his plans to build a new railway station, expand the international airport, and construct a passenger ship terminal at the port. Numerous other construction projects were put into the works as well.

The new mayor's most far-ranging project, however, was laying the groundwork for the future Pudong New Area, an experiment in massive regional development that would have national importance. Jiang placed Wang Daohan in charge of researching the project and drawing up preliminary plans.

At home Jiang faced personal pressures. Though he was reunited with his family, his wife's health had started to deteriorate. His aging mother-in-law also needed care. Then within weeks of Jiang's arrival in Shanghai, his beloved adoptive mother, Wang Zhelan, died in Yangzhou.

Long separated from his extended family, Jiang now resolved to return to his hometown every year for Qingming, the spring festival of mourning the dead. The name literally means "clear and bright," and it is a time to pay respect to one's ancestors by cleaning their gravesites, removing weeds, and sweeping away dirt. Jiang had made a pilgrimage to the tomb of Jiang Shangqing a few months earlier. On the thirtieth anniversary of Jiang Shangqing's death, at the height of the Cultural Revolution, Red Guards had desecrated the martyr's original resting place. In 1982 a new grand memorial had been built with a three-meter-high tombstone, the one engraved by Jiang

Shangqing's commander and friend, General Zhang Aiping, and it was this site that Jiang Zemin went to visit. Now the minister of national defense after having been purged in the 1960s, Zhang would remain one of the mainstays of support behind the new mayor.

SHORTLY BEFORE ASSUMING HIS new position, Jiang had been embarrassed by a silly scandal, mockingly called the "cold dinner incident" in the press. At a reception promoting electronic technology, hundreds of guests brought their own plastic bags and other containers in order to raid the buffet line. Within minutes of the reception's start, all the food disappeared. When second helpings came along, they too were snatched up and squirreled away—along with three hundred stainless steel forks and knives. In the pandemonium, people accosted the waiters and overturned tables and chairs.

The incident was a humiliation for a city already struggling with image problems. "Please bring in the traffic police," read the caption of one cartoonist's drawing, "to ensure safety at the cold dinner banquet." The local Party disciplinary committee issued a report that priced the fiasco at 31,370 yuan—or 26 yuan per person, an amount equal to an engineer's weekly salary.

Jiang was distressed. He had been the minister of electronics industry, and many of the people involved were his former subordinates. In July, two days after he was elected mayor, *People's Daily* reported on Jiang's decision to crack down on the corrupt lifestyles of officials. In doing so, he was fighting long-standing tradition and continuing an unending battle. He started small by promoting the idea of having just "four dishes with one soup" at official banquets instead of more numerous and lavish preparations, but Chinese hosts interpreted this policy as "four large plates with one deep bowl." While managing to stick to the letter of the law, they would offer guests a variety of expensive foods on each of the four plates and a number of delicacies in the deep bowl.

Undaunted, Jiang was a whirlwind of activity, breathing new life into set ways. Earlier Chinese leaders tended to remain in cloistered quarters, issuing rulings based on reports and briefings, or to go on well-planned, highly scripted tours. In contrast, on his second day in office Jiang donned a disguise and walked anonymously among the crowds to check out Shanghai's notorious traffic. Not satisfied with an official report, Jiang and Shanghai Party secretary Rui Xingwen went out to inspect a new residential area, where they visited two apartments and heard an earful of complaints. (Since for every geographical area, the Party secretary, or "Party chief," was ranked first, and the chief administrative officer was ranked second, for a city, the Party secretary was the number one official and the mayor was the number two.)

Jiang helped dockworkers clear away piles of trash, milling around afterward to offer towels and water to the workers. As part of another clean-up campaign, he shoveled watermelon rinds while chatting with street vendors. Jiang peppered his talks with Chinese folk wisdom. Discussing the market economy, he quipped: "When Lao Wang sells his melons, he always says they are sweet. He never says they are bitter."

There was a downside to urban reform, and Beijing was ill prepared to handle its complexities. When the Party agreed to permit the market to set prices, inflation skyrocketed as producers raised prices to exploit pent-up demand. In 1985 Shanghai's retail prices shot up 17 percent, and almost every necessity of life—food, clothing, transportation—suddenly cost more. It came as a rude shock to people who had known stable prices for more than three decades.

The central government was divided about what to do. Premier Zhao Ziyang, leader of the pro-market forces, claimed that the difficulties were temporary, but those more conservative, like senior elder Chen Yun, argued that price controls were needed to maintain social stability. A natural reformer and politically savvy, Jiang sided with the pro-market forces. They seemed to be the wave of the future; conservatives sounded like voices of the past.

As happens with societies in transition, students were beginning to rumble. At Tongji University, discontent with cafeteria food and overcrowded dormitories morphed into protests over the influx of Japanese consumer products, the escalating cost of living, and the pervasiveness of official corruption. In an attempt to defuse the situation, Jiang addressed ten thousand largely friendly students and faculty at the university. Acknowledging the unprecedented rise in consumer prices, he defended the reforms, explaining that the market economy would eventually regulate supply and demand at reasonable prices. The student unrest blew over, but it provided a dress rehearsal for things to come.

Less than a year into his term, and three months before his sixtieth birthday, Jiang unveiled Shanghai's Comprehensive Plan, the result of years of design and debate. The plan focused on three geographical areas: the central urban area, which included the vast Pudong region east of the Pu River; seven satellite cities and towns, which formed the shape of a hand; and a number of towns and villages. The central city would be linked with outlying areas by high-speed trains and highways, while ring roads would connect the satellite cities. Industry would gradually expand outward from the core, while counties and towns developed their own businesses, mainly processing plants for vegetables, eggs, and poultry. "In the next five years," Jiang declared, "Shanghai will experience the greatest changes and fastest development in its history."

These improvements were costly and the government was strapped for money, so Jiang turned to overseas investors for funding. The city raised $3.2 billion from international capital markets, of which $1.4 billion was allocated to subways, bridges, water treatment plants, airport expansion, and telephone exchanges. To construct the bridges, he issued bonds that guaranteed a minimal return on investment of 15 percent, then collected tolls to ensure that the promise could be kept. Even so, there were not enough funds to pay for all the new projects that Jiang envisioned.

AS MAYOR, JIANG'S MANAGEMENT style was rooted in the systematic thinking of an engineer. First he would read or hear reports, then he would listen to expert opinion, then he would conduct on-site research, and finally he would suggest next steps or request further information. He would arrive at the office, like everyone else, at about 8:00 A.M. and often stay late for after-work engagements. His office had more than three thousand books, second in number only to Wang Daohan's. Lunch was often noodle soup at the municipal canteen, earning him the sobriquet "Noodle Mayor." He was never offended.

Decisions were made in the mayor's weekly work meeting, attended by the mayor, vice mayors, and senior staff—about a dozen people. Normally held on Monday, it could last half the day, but lunch was rarely served. Procedures were formal. An agenda would be distributed the previous Friday, and whoever chaired the meeting would manage the time. For each issue the vice mayor in charge of that area spoke first. After discussion the mayor would offer his conclusion. If everyone agreed, the matter would be passed. Otherwise, it would be put aside for a future meeting.

"My office was in the same building as Mayor Jiang's, but on a different floor," remembered Ye Gongqi, vice mayor in charge of finance. "If I needed him, I'd just ring his office. If he wasn't in, I'd schedule a time to see him. Jiang did the same. If he wanted to see me, he'd always call first. It'd be rude for him to just drop by. As the one who was in charge of budgeting, it was natural that I might complain from time to time. There was never enough money to do all we had to do.

"I treated him like a big brother," Ye continued. "I shared thoughts and concerns without reservation. As his chief financial officer, I gave him my honest opinion. He'd never force me to adopt his priorities."

Ye Gongqi worked closely with Jiang Zemin for almost four years. "He is a person of high emotion," said Ye. "When something good happened, he would spontaneously show his exuberance. He'd say to us in meetings or meals, 'Let me sing a song to entertain you.' To sing songs for his subordinates? This was hardly the normal practice of a senior leader! It would come from the heart, welling up out of him like a geyser. Jiang is true to life. When he's excited, he'll express it openly. When something bad happened, perhaps an irresponsible act of an official, he could become very indignant. . . .

"Jiang is transparent," continued Ye. "He acts as he thinks. Some senior officials put on airs. Not Jiang; he's always down to earth. As vice mayor of Shanghai, I was in charge of the two factories—Yimin Food and China Soap—where, many years before, Jiang had worked as a young man. The older staff remembered him as capable and intense. Some of them still kept in touch with him!"

Even as mayor, Jiang's personal life remained modest. He rarely went to restaurants, and unless he was attending a municipal function, he ate at home with his family, treasuring the after-dinner time for reading and studying. His wife, Wang Yeping, did not join Shanghai society, preferring to stay at home. When the family moved to Kang Ping Road No. 165, a guarded area where many senior leaders lived, Wang Yeping felt sad that she had to leave her neighbors of two decades.

The new apartment seemed spacious, with three bedrooms on three stories, about five thousand square feet, but there were *ten* people in the household— two sons, two daughters-in-law, two grandchildren, a mother-in-law, and a maid in addition to Jiang and his wife. Since their hometown of Yangzhou was close to Shanghai, five or six times a year they would find relatives or friends, often in groups, descending on them, since it had become common knowledge that Jiang would always insist that visitors stay at their home. This meant making "beds" on the floor; Wang Yeping herself would go over to the municipal guesthouse to borrow bedding pads and quilts.

With ten mouths to feed, most of the household income went for food. To save money, the Jiangs had porridge *(congee)* and steamed buns for breakfast. Dinner was the main meal of the day, usually with four dishes to share—

three vegetables and one meat or poultry. The whole family sat around the table together. On weekends they might buy a roast duck as a special treat.

With inflation, every citizen felt the pinch, and Jiang was no exception. When he and his wife went to the markets to shop for food, he heard people ranting about the skyrocketing food prices. One day he did the same. "As prices keep going up," he told his staff, "citizens curse the government. You know, I sometimes feel like cursing as well. But I can't ventilate like a normal person. I have a big family; I can barely make ends meet. We can only afford vegetables now; no meat or poultry!"

Jiang's wife almost never bought expensive items, but one time during this period she made a huge exception. Since college it had been Jiang's dream to own a piano, but with his financial burdens it had been impossible. Acting on a long-thought-out plan, she withdrew all their savings from the bank and borrowed additional money from relatives and friends to scrape together 2,000 yuan to purchase a Nie Er piano (a Chinese brand named for a noted composer).

Wang Yeping had little interest in fulfilling other people's ideas of how the First Lady of Shanghai should look or act. Once when she went to an official municipal residence to visit a friend from Beijing, she was stopped at the gate by two security guards who did not recognize her. Wearing an old brown knitted sweater, worn-out black pants, and flat cloth shoes, Wang was pushing her grandson in a cradle cart. One guard required that she fill out a visitor's form, a normal procedure, before he would grant her entry, but the other laughed and said, "Don't make it hard for her—she's just a nanny who can't read. Let her in." Just then Wang's friend came running out exclaiming deferentially, "Comrade Yeping!" Since first names are quite individual in China, everyone knew "Comrade Yeping" was the First Lady of Shanghai (and would turn heads much as "Hi, Hillary" would in Washington during the Clinton administration). The Party chief's wife was not angered or irritated—she only smiled as she walked past the two dumbfounded guards, who now had the story of a lifetime to tell their grandchildren.

AFTER SEVERAL TOP AIDES fell ill with maladies attributed to stress, Jiang initiated a program to improve health and morale. He commissioned research to discern which sports could help to make hardworking middle-aged executives physically fit. When he received two answers—tennis and bowling—he required senior officials to pick one. Neither was not an option.

Earlier, Executive Vice Mayor Zhu had a heart attack at his desk and fell into a vegetative coma that lasted for six months before he died. During this period Jiang visited him in the hospital, disregarding the advice of staff who thought the mayor had better things to do with his time. "Jiang knew that his presence would signal the doctors that this patient was very important," observed Ye Gongqi.

When Zhu's wife became emotionally unstable as a result of the strain, Jiang took it upon himself to look out for the welfare of the couple's daughter. He invited the girl's uncle, who lived in Australia, to come to Shanghai to discuss options for her future. Together they decided that Zhu's daughter should move to Australia. Jiang made arrangements for her trip personally, even calling the mayor of Shenzhen at 10 P.M. when the girl was being detained at the Hong Kong border for having incomplete paperwork. Jiang also helped Zhu's widow find a job in Shanghai, and right before moving to Beijing in 1989, he spoke with Ye Gongqi. "Please watch over the Zhu family," Jiang said to his vice mayor. "I am entrusting their care to you."

When Ye Gongqi collapsed and was hospitalized in Hangzhou, some 140 miles from Shanghai, Jiang made a special trip to visit and help arrange his treatment. In 1992 another of his former vice mayors died of a heart attack. By then Jiang was Party general secretary, and according to protocol, it was not appropriate for someone of his high rank to attend the memorial service. But Jiang insisted on honoring his old colleague and traveled to Shanghai as an ordinary citizen. The media did not report the trip, and he scheduled no other appointments on the visit.

When Tong Zonghai, his college roommate, developed detached retinas, Jiang brought in one of Shanghai's best ophthalmologists for treatment that was unavailable in Tong's hometown.

"Of course I knew that Jiang was the mayor of Shanghai," said Tong, "but I didn't want to take advantage of our friendship. I felt ashamed, but when I ran out of options, I sent him a short telegram. The next day I received a telegram back. 'I have made arrangements for you,' Jiang wrote. 'Please come to Shanghai immediately.' "

By the time Tong arrived in Shanghai, he was virtually blind. Jiang's secretary (personal assistant), Jia Ting'an, met him at the boat, made arrangements for his accommodations, and facilitated his transfer to the hospital. A native of Henan province, Jia had come to Shanghai with Jiang from the Ministry of Electronics Industry. His job was to do just about anything. Whether it was a matter of state or a personal request, Jiang Zemin could always count on Jia Ting'an.

"Jiang came to see me in the hospital," said Tong. "He told me not to worry about being an out-of-town patient [a serious problem in China]. 'Relax and rest well,' he said. 'Don't feel like a stranger because you're not from Shanghai.' On his visit, which caused quite a stir, Jiang brought along leaders of Shanghai's Public Health Bureau. The doctors told me that this was the first time the mayor had come to this hospital. My vision was totally restored."

Compassionate as he was with those he liked and trusted, Jiang could be hard on people whose attitudes and actions he thought harmful to China. In addition to corrupt and irresponsible officials, he criticized those who mourned the days prior to the Communist takeover. Ye Gongqi described them as "Those who would 'rather eat the leftovers that fall from the table of foreigners' as long as they get more food than when they have to work for themselves." In Jiang's view, these people cared only about money, which enraged him.

In May 1986 Jiang Zemin and Shanghai Party chief Rui Xingwen convened a seminar to formulate a "cultural development strategy" for the city, a euphemism for resisting Western values while requesting Western investments. All of China's senior leaders, even those who favored accelerated reform, worried that market freedom would create social disruption. They feared that Western "materialism and decadence" could destabilize Chinese institutions and undermine Party authority. To Jiang, the key was to develop cultural and humanistic standards that would sustain a robust, self-sustaining Chinese socialism.

WHEN QUEEN ELIZABETH II arrived in Shanghai in October 1986, Jiang welcomed her with enthusiasm. The queen held special significance for the Chinese, whose imperial history made people respect regal continuity. Two years earlier, when China and England signed an agreement ensuring Hong Kong's repatriation to China, Deng Xiaoping spoke admiringly of the British monarch. "In my lifetime," he said, "I wish I can meet the queen of England." When he finally met her, Deng, an avid smoker, politely refrained, since she did not like people to smoke in her presence.

It seemed that all China was preparing for the queen's visit, which symbolized the country's reemergence as a world center of culture and grandeur. Jiang immersed himself in the details of her visit to Shanghai. Buildings on the historic Bund were cleaned of any remnants of British colonization. The long highway from Hongqiao International Airport to downtown was widened.

Sprinkler systems were installed in meadows to ensure lush greenery. Every street on the queen's itinerary was festooned with colorful lights. The state guesthouse villa where she would stay was redecorated, and when she asked to see the city from her car, the dark-tinted windows on a special Red flag limousine were changed to clear glass.

As the queen stepped down from her aircraft, fifteen hundred children waved flags and held bouquets and toy pandas. Thousands performed British and Chinese traditional dances. Two children presented flowers to the queen and her husband, Prince Philip. Jiang welcomed the couple in their native tongue.

Since the queen desired to visit Yu Garden, a four-hundred-year-old Chinese arboretum with more than thirty pavilions linked by a maze of corridors and pond-spanning bridges, Jiang suggested that she rest at the Teahouse Pavilion in the middle of the main lake, where he planned an elegant show. A local Chinese folk singer and a famous flautist, Lu Chunling, performed for the queen, while sweet delicacies and Dragon Well tea were served. Earlier that morning Jiang had visited Lu to go over his choice of music, encouraging him to be "well prepared." With Zemin of Shanghai sitting beside Elizabeth of England in the ancient elegance of Yu Garden, against a background of rock gardens and towers with upturned eaves, Lu played Chinese and English songs, including "An English Country Garden." After concluding his brief concert, Lu surprised the queen, who drank two small cups of what is perhaps the best tea in China, by presenting her with one of his seven personal flutes.

About ten days later a different kind of visitor arrived in Shanghai—Erich Honecker, the autocratic ruler of Communist East Germany. Visiting the site of the first national congress of the Communist Party of China, Honecker wrote in the visitor's book, "The birth of the CPC provided a great impetus to the Chinese workers' movement and the revolutionary struggle in the whole world." Later the East German dictator placed a basket of flowers at statues of Karl Marx and Friedrich Engels, and Jiang cohosted a banquet in his honor. Neither could know it then, of course, but within three years Honecker would be forced from office as Communism in his country collapsed.

SOMETIMES MUNICIPAL NEEDS TOOK precedence over personal affairs. When Jiang's foster mother, his Niang, died in 1985, he was attending a critical meeting in Beijing, and so he asked his wife, Wang Yeping, and his son, Mianheng, to organize her funeral. In 1987 Jiang led family members from Shanghai to Yangzhou for an official memorial to his foster mother, and he paid his respects at her tomb. Similarly, when his biological mother had died years earlier, he was unable to handle her funeral personally.

"Third Brother loved his mother very much," said Jiang Zehui, "and he did his best to take care of her." After Jiang's father died in 1973, his mother had gone to stay with him in Beijing. When Jiang worked in Changchun, his parents lived with him for a short time; then they came back to Yangzhou. "Although Third Brother did not live with his parents, he took care of their financial needs," said Jiang Zehui, the family historian. "In her late years his mother could enjoy her son and his family."

IN NOVEMBER 1986 THE State Council approved the Shanghai Comprehensive Plan that Jiang had unveiled the previous May. Shanghai, they pronounced, should become a world-class city with a prosperous economy, advanced technology, advanced culture, and a clean environment. The aim was to build Shanghai into the largest center of industry and trade in Asia—a major challenge for a place where the stock exchange still operated across a single counter and many apartments still did not have toilets.

Shen Yongyan, Jiang's observant friend, noted that Jiang's style of city management in Shanghai was similar to his style of plant management in Changchun. "Take safety," Shen offered. "Although he was extremely busy running the city, every time a serious accident took place, he would drop almost anything to figure out how to prevent similar accidents in the future."

Jiang also established himself as a consensus maker with a talent for building rapport with the right people. One holdover from China's imperial history was the formal trips that senior leaders took to inspect activities of their subordinates. The practice was expanded under the Communist system, and Mao, Deng, and other state leaders made these visits regularly. Strict rules of protocol, determined entirely by rank, were followed, and a myriad of details had to conform: types of accommodations, models of cars, seating arrangement at dinners, even the size of newspaper images. The local official was expected to know his superiors' preferences, hobbies, schools of thought, political orientations, personal goals, and all manner of needs and wishes. To further one's career in the Chinese system, it helped to be good at hosting senior leaders.

By the time he became mayor, Jiang Zemin had already hosted hundreds of such visits and receptions. In Shanghai he entertained virtually all of China's senior leaders, from Deng Xiaoping on down. On one occasion he personally delivered a cake at midnight to a retired official celebrating his eightieth birthday. "This was the last cake at the hotel," Jiang reportedly said. "But I didn't want you to think I had forgotten your birthday."

So considerate was Jiang to President Li Xiannian, who enjoyed returning to Shanghai in winters, that a false rumor arose that Jiang was Li's son-in-law. It was a mark of suspicion to be the relative of a political leader, and the persistence of this rumor suggested that not everyone wished the mayor well.

Though it was politically correct behavior for a city leader to attend to visiting elders, Jiang did so with respect and, in many cases, genuine affection. He also showed concern for the wives of senior leaders, engaging them in conversation, a practice that did not impede prospects for advancing his career.

Jiang was fortunate that Deng Xiaoping, China's Paramount Leader, spent every Chinese New Year in Shanghai. If fate is capricious in awarding its gifts, Deng's visits to Shanghai exemplified such serendipity. There could be no better way for Deng to get to know Jiang—an intimate sense of the person that would later prove pivotal.

Chapter 8

1 9 8 6 – 1 9 8 9

"How Could I Not Know?"

A CROSS CHINA, DISCONTENT WAS brewing. Whether reform was happening too quickly or not broadly enough, frustrations were increasing. While some people got rich, others were suffering; corruption increased; wages did not relate to performance. "Surgeons are no richer than barbers," went one popular saying. In September 1985 Beijing University students protested: "Down with corrupt officials!"

The demonstration took China's leadership by surprise. General Secretary Hu Yaobang sought to address the problems, not attack the demonstrators. He championed the need to fight corruption, promote younger leaders, and—most radically—reform the political system. Initially, Deng Xiaoping gave Hu moderate support for exploring political reform, while also cautioning, "The Party must retain ultimate leadership," and "Decision-making must be cautious to avoid disorder."

Resurgent conservatives, uncomfortable with the rapid pace of reform, seized the opportunity to line up against Hu. At the Party plenum in September 1986 they added the words "strongly oppose bourgeois liberalization" to a document that Hu Yaobang had submitted. However vague the phrase, it was certainly disparaging and contentious and it would stoke the political furnace. ("Bourgeois liberalization" seemed to represent a tendency to move toward Western-style multiparty democracy, which would abrogate the ruling monopoly of the Communist Party; Western-style popular culture, which would overwhelm traditional Chinese culture; and Western-style economic systems, which would do away with socialism.)

Deng did what some called an about-face, but which showed both the clarity of his political commitment and the subtlety of his political sense. "Why do I support this opposition to bourgeois liberalization?" he asked. "The representatives of this liberal thinking are leading us to capitalism, which they call 'modernization.'

"Liberalism is capitalism," he added. "And it contradicts our policies and systems. If we don't stop liberalism, this and other rotten thinking that develop in the course of opening-up would form a powerful force to destroy socialism." With a dual agenda of promoting reform but not weakening socialism, Deng accomplished both by taking up the Leftist-conservatives' own complaint. His strategy relieved pressures against reform (by depriving Leftists of a hot-button issue) while bolstering socialism to withstand opposing pressures from the Rightist-liberals.

Jiang Zemin's strategy was simpler. He sensed danger in the new uncertainty, and rather than support Hu Yaobang's reforms, he adhered tightly to Party precepts. At a mid-August meeting for Party discipline officials, Jiang gave a tough-minded speech on fighting corruption and bureaucracy.

Intellectuals joined the fray, overstressing fault lines in Chinese society. The most outspoken was Fang Lizhi, a respected astrophysicist and vice president of the University of Science and Technology in Hefei, Anhui province. In November 1986 Fang gave a series of startlingly frank lectures and interviews. At Beijing University he attacked the government—to the prolonged applause of students. In a speech at Tongji University in Shanghai he attacked the icons of Communism itself. "I am here to tell you," he said, "that the socialist movement from Marx and Lenin to Stalin and Mao Zedong has been a failure." At Shanghai Jiaotong University, Fang went further. "We can see that democracy is coming," he said. "Democracy is achieved by fighting."

Fang returned to Hefei a hero. On December 5 fifteen hundred students at his university staged a campus protest. "We want free elections!" they shouted. "Long live democracy!" Four days later two thousand students marched through the city streets, chanting, "We'd rather die for democracy!" That night they made calls to fellow students across the country, beseeching them to start their own protests in sympathy. It was the first modern echo of Jiang's own student years.

At Shanghai Jiaotong University, Jiang's alma mater, a small notice was posted, reporting what had happened in Hefei. The next day the notice was gone, torn down. Students were enraged, and in no time two new posters appeared: One retold what had happened in Hefei, and the other denounced the censorship. A threshold had been crossed. Similar posters started sprouting at other Shanghai universities, particularly at Tongji and Fudan.

Each day more and more posters appeared, and more and more students came to read them. On the morning of December 15 the small-lettered wall posters were replaced by big-lettered ones that sprouted all over the campus. It was the first high-profile appearance of "big character" posters since 1979, when they had been banned for their role in inciting the Cultural Revolution. In less than a week the walls at Shanghai Jiaotong University were covered.

University authorities held an emergency meeting in an attempt to pacify angry students, who called for a mass demonstration. One of their demands was that they speak with the mayor. The students knew that Jiang had spoken to students at Tongji University the previous year. He should come to Jiaotong now, they asserted—after all, he was an alumnus. While his staff debated the matter, Jiang decided to go.

Jiang requested detailed information about the students and their concerns. Included in his dossier was a private briefing by the Jiaotong Party secretary. There were some issues that Jiang could handle and ameliorate, such as improving living conditions at the university, but for the most part the changes that the students sought far exceeded his authority. Given these demands—political reform, freedom of the press, relaxing police control—there was no way the two sides could agree.

The encounter took place on December 18. So many people surrounded the cars in Jiang's entourage as they arrived on campus that he was delayed. It was forty years, almost to the day, since Jiang himself had been a student protester in Shanghai. Then the issue had been the rape of a Chinese student by two American Marines, and the protest had helped the Communist cause. Now students were protesting the Party's leadership.

More than three thousand people came to hear Jiang speak. The auditorium overflowed with students; surprised by their own power, they were boisterous and giddy. As Jiang approached the lectern, they began clapping raucously.

Putting on his reading glasses, Jiang unfurled a small piece of paper and spoke in a mild tone. His talk, which touched on the merits of the current five-year economic plan, did not suit the agitated audience, and some began whistling and catcalling. A youthful voice broke through the uproar. "You should listen," it said to Jiang, "before you speak!" The mayor hesitated, and in that moment a chorus of new voices burst forth. Many began to shout protest slogans. The students did not want to hear what Jiang wanted to say.

"Treat us as equals!" yelled one. "We should speak first," bellowed another.

Jiang tried to continue, but people began booing. He stopped, looked sternly at the crowd as if daring them to boo again. They did—more loudly this time. Jiang singled out a student. "Since you seem to have so much to say," he told the young man, "why don't you say it to everyone?" At first the student declined the offer, but his friends egged him on, and he rose to take the microphone. Before he was finished, a line of others formed, each with a question to ask or an opinion to voice.

"Why wasn't the press permitted to report on the demonstrations?" "Why had a guard beat up students?" "How did Jiang get to be mayor?" Emboldened, the students became aggressive, while Jiang sat in the audience and listened. When one student challenged him sharply, he responded angrily. "What is your name?" Jiang asked. "What class are you in?" The authoritarian reflex elicited a chorus of boos. Threats were not conciliatory, the audience admonished the mayor, and not acceptable. Reform was indeed changing China, but not always in ways that its leaders intended.

For the next three hours the students passionately outlined their demands: press freedoms, particularly full and fair coverage of their protests; the right to mount wall posters as part of open debates; legal authorization for demonstrations; and assurance that no retribution would be taken against demonstrators.

The mayor took it all in. When the students were finished, Jiang walked onto the stage to respond. Under the Communist system, he told the students, the press is the "mouthpiece of the Party" and must report that which is beneficial to the masses. He said that he would permit demonstrations as long as they did no harm to the public good. In such cases, no action would be taken against demonstrators. But, he warned, if protesters seized the streets and blocked traffic, they would hurt productivity and retard reforms.

Jiang's words were genuine and moderating, though hardly the radical change that the protesters were demanding. The crowd seemed to rouse itself again. One student, face flushed, snatched the microphone and shouted, "He is a mayor that was appointed, not elected by us. He can't represent the people. We Shanghai people won't consider him our mayor."

Jiang smiled at this outburst, surprising the room into momentary silence. "The first thing I saw when I arrived on campus," he said, "were all the big-character wall newspapers calling for a government 'of the people, by the people, for the people.'"

"Do you know who said that?" a student interrupted him.

"Of course, how could I not know?" Jiang shot back. "It was said by Abraham Lincoln, the sixteenth president of the United States of America, in his famous Gettysburg Address, given on November 19, 1863.

"Now let me ask you a question," Jiang challenged his audience. "Can any of you recite the whole text of this address?"

Before anyone could answer, Jiang began reciting Lincoln's speech in English. It was as if the mayor of Shanghai had become an actor in an American Civil War drama, using his well-honed oratorical skills—a sense of pace and pitch—to portray President Lincoln, imparting meaning and passion to each phrase.

"You really must appreciate Abraham Lincoln's deep intent," counseled Jiang when he finished. "You only know Lincoln's speech in words. You don't know its historical context."

He then compared America and China. With superficial knowledge, Jiang said, one could not fathom how dangerous an American-style democracy might be for China. "Our country has a different culture," he said. "With different values, traditions, and problems." Though their hearts were in the right place, he told the students, they needed to be more patient.

Most were not appeased. They wanted action, not rhetoric, and they interpreted Jiang's arguments as condescending. They began to chant: "Of the people, by the people, for the people . . ." Although the afternoon ended in a frustrating stalemate, Jiang Zemin, former student protester and alumnus, had shown that he was willing to face the younger generation.

The next day the situation worsened when the meeting went unreported in the Shanghai dailies. Most students skipped classes, choosing instead to gather around campus bulletin boards to read uncensored reports of what had happened. Incensed by the commentary, much of which was biased, student leaders began calling for strikes at all Shanghai's universities. That afternoon more than three thousand protesters poured into the streets. Holding banners, putting up posters, and handing out leaflets, they congregated in two central locations, including People's Square. The police made no attempt to interfere. Blocking the entrance to municipal and Party buildings, the students sat and waited.

As dusk approached, Vice Mayor Ye Gongqi urged demonstrators to disperse. "Rush hour is coming," he said. "Please do not tie up traffic." Some protesters heeded his advice, but about two thousand remained, continuing to demand a meeting with the man they had come to see: Jiang Zemin.

Jiang was on his way to his office on the Bund when his driver braked the car so suddenly that the mayor banged his forehead against the window. The injury was superficial but bloody, and it seemed an unfortunate omen for an already confrontational situation. Using a handkerchief as a makeshift bandage, Jiang entered the municipal building through a side door. After his head wound was cleaned and covered—a visible symbol of his harrowing ordeal—he agreed to meet student representatives, who were admitted, one by one, through the heavily guarded front door.

The meeting was little more than a repeat performance of the day before. Jiang was irritated by the street demonstrations, which he called disruptive and intolerable. They threatened the city's annual production targets, on which he had staked his personal credibility, and they offended his deep-rooted belief in the importance of order. He had been willing to disrupt the order of a corrupt and foreign-beholden Kuomintang China forty years earlier, but this was New China, as he saw it, standing on its own, and he was determined to help make his country succeed.

He also surmised that opportunists, both Leftists and Rightists, would try to use the turmoil to their own advantage. Accordingly, Jiang refused to grant any concessions. He did not agree with most student demands, particularly the one regarding freedom of the press, which he saw as threatening the Party's monopoly and the country's stability.

Student leaders left the meeting envisioning a massive protest that would cripple the city during the morning commute, leading to just the sort of chaos that Jiang had warned against. Notwithstanding Hu Yaobang's directive for "mediation and discussion," the mayor ordered police to disperse the bleary-eyed students. But he meant no crackdown. On Jiang's orders, the more than two thousand officers carried no weapons; they guided two thousand students peacefully into buses, which then drove them back to their schools, where special meals had been prepared for them. The dispersal provided an oddly upbeat end to an edgy situation, but many students remained undaunted. "The future belongs to us," some shouted as the buses departed.

Avoiding force may have been a miscalculation. Hours later students were out in even greater numbers. As more than ten thousand protesters flooded downtown Shanghai, the mayor sent word that he was willing to meet with their leaders. The policy from Beijing was to use restraint, and Jiang was advised to defuse the tension through dialogue. Senior leaders were watching closely.

The talks were inconclusive, and the next day, a Sunday, confrontation peaked. The largest demonstrations in almost a decade transfixed the city. More than thirty thousand students—some reports put the number as high as seventy thousand—turned out. When two reporters identified themselves as Americans, they received a round of cheers. Students surrounded another journalist from Voice of America, a principal source of news for many Chinese, and chanted, "America, America!"

As word of the demonstrations spread, factory workers and other laborers joined in support. "We're of one heart with them," said several. A group of workers vandalized a minivan that they believed belonged to the police, overturning the vehicle and spilling gasoline. Observers feared that the situation was about to spiral out of control.

Along with Shanghai Party secretary Rui Xingwen and the minister of public security, Jiang began to effect countermeasures. They summoned eight thousand Party branch secretaries to a massive meeting at Shanghai Stadium and requested that all Party members work to stop the student protests, which included urging parents to persuade their children not to use force. Workers were forbidden to join the demonstrations; those who broke this rule would receive no bonuses. "We cannot allow workers and students to unite," Rui stated in what may have been precisely the reverse of what the prerevolution Communists had prescribed. "Otherwise Shanghai would fall into chaos and drag down the rest of the country."

In the end, the emergency preparations turned out to be largely unnecessary. Just as suddenly as they had started, the demonstrations seemed to lose momentum. Students returned to their classes, and within two days the protests were over.

The official Xinhua News Agency compared the disturbances to those of the Cultural Revolution. It must have been galling for those intellectual, democracy-seeking students to be likened to uneducated, democracy-denying Red Guards. But senior leaders, survivors of the Cultural Revolution, feared turmoil. Chinese history is unambiguous, they said; there is no middle ground between stability and chaos.

"Jiang was sympathetic to the students," remembered Ye Gongqi. "Although naïve, most wanted faster reform and more democracy. This was understandable. Jiang and I, and many others, wanted this, too! But there was more going on here. Since both of us had been leaders in the student movement in the old days, we knew there had to be some people with 'beards and mustaches' [i.e., older people] who manipulated the students in order to drive the movement toward confrontation. This was true in 1986, and it would be true again, with more serious consequences, in 1989."

As Jiang reflected on the protests, he concluded that they had arisen in part because of inadequate ideological education. He would later characterize the student protesters as "simple-minded," noting that they "were not at all like we were in 1946"—a position that would be a challenge to defend.

The punishments handed down evinced how seriously the government regarded social instability. Two people who had instigated the minivan incident were imprisoned for "hooliganism." In China some crimes that in other countries may be considered misdemeanors are simply not tolerated.

True to his word, Jiang did not arrest any students, though some demonstrators were threatened with "administrative punishment"—which could have meant time in China's arduous labor camps. The Shanghai Party began to purge members who had protested. Communist leaders throughout China viewed the incident as a setback for the Party. Though the demonstrators were quiet for now, pockets of unrest continued to smolder in the country's major cities. From here on the power struggle in Beijing centered on the student movement.

In this first round, the main victim was Hu Yaobang. On December 30 Deng Xiaoping convened an emergency meeting, which was critical of Hu. Deng supported "dialogue and persuasion" in dealing with students but warned that if they destabilized the social order, action would have to be taken, thus ratifying Jiang's actions in Shanghai.

"It is said in Shanghai," Deng observed, "that the central government has two conflicting opinions on anti–bourgeois liberalization. They are waiting to see what will come out of this." In the meantime Premier Zhao Ziyang, who may have been lobbying to remove Hu Yaobang for two years, now actively sought to replace his rival.

Senior leaders, including Zhao, met at Deng's home and decided to relieve Hu Yaobang of his position, and a week later, at what seemed to be a standard Politburo meeting, the decision was abruptly formalized. Hu was accused of failing to submit to the Party's collective decisions, particularly the struggle against bourgeois liberalism. Zhao Ziyang was appointed general secretary in Hu's place, and Li Peng was chosen to replace Zhao as premier. After his obligatory self-criticism, Hu went into seclusion. Although he remained a member of the Politburo, he was a beaten man.

After hearing of Hu's ouster, the Shanghai Party closed one newspaper for promoting the now-forbidden "bourgeois liberalization." Two days later it reorganized the editorial board of the *World Economic Herald.*

Considering the thorny circumstances, Jiang had acquitted himself well, demonstrating his personal strength and political resilience in dealing with both the student movement and the hardliners. Although neither side was pleased, tensions were reduced. This impressed China's elders. Furthermore, Jiang was beginning to be known as a new kind of Chinese leader, one who could recite Lincoln's Gettysburg Address in the international language of English. (At one time Jiang could also recite Hamlet's soliloquy "To be or not to be" and Shelley's "Ode to the West Wind.")

"We should persist in taking the Chinese-style socialist road," Jiang said in

January 1987, "break away from traditional economic modes without ever returning to the capitalist road, and adopt a clear-cut stand against bourgeois liberalization. However, we may study and assimilate the positive elements in the capitalist economy."

Jiang was adhering to Deng Xiaoping's proposition of "one center and two basic points," the center being economic growth and the two basic points being reform and opening up on the one hand and resisting bourgeois liberalization [i.e., Western-style democracy] on the other. Jiang's post-demonstration statements, combined with his takeover of the *World Economic Herald,* reinforced his image as a dedicated socialist and enforcer of social stability who was at the same time a thoughtful reformer and internationalist.

In March 1987 Jiang was interviewed by the *Los Angeles Times.* He wore a dress shirt and tie with a zippered sweatsuit jacket, an image that combined a businesslike demeanor with confident informality. Jiang seemed eager to assure foreigners that the purpose of controlling demonstrations was to protect China's policy of opening to the outside world. "If the masses are striking on the street," he asked, "how can we attract foreign investors to Shanghai?" That same month the city's total foreign investment jumped to second place after Guangzhou (the capital of Guangdong province), with $2 billion going into some one hundred projects.

EARLIER IN 1986 JIANG began holding regular meetings with editors of the city's newspapers and electronic media. The fact that Jiang himself took charge of this task—normally, propaganda officials were responsible—shows how deeply he understood the power of the media. When television coverage of burst water mains made city officials look inept, Jiang said that he expected people to understand the problems with Shanghai's infrastructure and to recognize that the city was making progress in resolving them. No matter how bad the disaster, no matter what its cause, Jiang wanted the story reported with a positive spin, particularly regarding the roles of city or Party officials. It was vital for society, Jiang believed, that people have confidence in their leaders. The media's job was as a tool for implementing government policy, not as a check on assessing its effectiveness.

In mid-1987, Jiang's concept of media was put to the test by another encounter with water. An article in *Jiefang Daily,* the official newspaper of the Shanghai Communist Party, told how Jiang had ordered the repair of a broken water pipe near the Shanghai Railway Station. Entitled "Mayor Jiang

Zemin Personally Concerned with Water Leak Case," the highly visible, highly complimentary report noted that when local deputies had complained to him that the pipe had been leaking for more than three months and that no one had done anything about it, Jiang, always the industrial engineer, took charge and ordered that the problem be fixed at once.

A few weeks later, a story broke on the front page of *People's Daily,* the Party's national newspaper, implicitly critical of Jiang's micromanaging style. Creating a clever title, "The Other Side of '*Shi Bi Gong Qing,*'" a well-known reporter named Xu Jingen took a certain "Mayor XX" to task for meddling in the work of the bureaucracy, suggesting that such intervention encouraged dependency, indecisiveness, and passivity at lower levels of government. Though Jiang's name was not mentioned, the Shanghai setting left no doubt that the article was targeting him.

Xu criticized Jiang by playing with a Chinese idiom—*Shi Bi Gong Qing*—which means something like "His Excellency must be personally involved in everything" (or more colloquially, "The boss must handle every detail himself") and is derived from a classic story illustrating how a leader's interest in what seems to be minutiae sometimes reflects deeper insights. Xu's article, however, made it clear that in his opinion this case was "the other side" of such a situation, and that a more effective government would result if a leader would encourage (or coerce) subordinates to solve problems, not override subordinates and solve problems himself. (The writer recognized that many local officials were irresponsible and only good at "kicking the ball from one to another.") Xu quoted an irritated city council delegate: "I wouldn't have expected that such a minor matter couldn't be dealt with unless a city leader got directly involved. If everything in the city were handled in this way, how could Shanghai operate?"

Xu argued that leaders "should deal with broader problems of a general nature" and that "they should not look into every specific and trivial matter personally." Continuing his critique, Xu castigated "our media" for "not paying much attention to this issue" and, worse, for "even publishing articles praising Mayor XX for personally solving problems such as a taxi driver overcharging a passenger." Xu concluded his article by wondering, "Then we should ask ourselves about the director general, division chiefs, and officials of the city's price control department and the managers of the taxi companies—where are they and what are they doing?"

"As soon as I had read the *Jiefang Daily* article about Jiang ordering the repair," Xu Jingen recalled years later, "I was bothered. It wasn't necessary for the mayor of such a large city to worry about such trivial problems as a leaky tap."

Mayor Jiang Zemin, who made it a habit to read news stories carefully, was not amused. Xu's article derided the enormous effort he had been making to deal with the city's many issues. After all, since cities are run on a myriad of minor matters, if a leader pays attention to them, he sets a good example for lower officials to do likewise. If small concerns are not below the mayor's dignity or office, they certainly should not be below theirs. In addition, given the political climate, being mildly mocked on the front page of *People's Daily*—which was required reading for every official in the country—was dangerous. In a hierarchic system where signs of weakness can frighten allies and enliven enemies, politicians must be ever vigilant. Jiang did not take the criticism well.

On July 10, at an enlarged meeting of the Shanghai municipal government, which included officials responsible for media, Jiang went out of his way to read several paragraphs from the *People's Daily* article. Referring to the offending writer by name, Jiang rebutted Xu's criticism and rebuked Xu personally. It was improper, Jiang said, for Xu to have issued his public censure without finding out the real situation. The mayor observed that Xu had no clue how to run a city, much less one the size and complexity of Shanghai, and then suggested that the reporter go out into the real world to see how things were done. "Does he really think that being the mayor of a large city is that easy?" Jiang asked rhetorically, adding, "He must be a [naïve] scholar!" Not satisfied until he was sure that the reporter would get the message, Jiang asked *Jiefang Daily*'s editor in chief, who was at the meeting, to convey his reprimand directly to Xu.

It seemed that Xu Jingen had found Jiang Zemin's Achilles' heel. No one could ever accuse this mayor of being incompetent or lazy, but calling him, in essence, a micromanager and a meddler was a charge more difficult to refute. Jiang's instinctive reaction was to make clear that, from here on, it would behoove the Shanghai media to find little in his leadership style worthy of criticism.

When the red-faced editors returned to their newspaper's offices, they advised Xu that he had better act fast if he valued his job.

"When I heard the mayor's criticism, I became very nervous," Xu remembered. "That I still thought my article to be good journalism was hardly relevant. I had offended the mayor—this was no small matter. Would I be able to continue writing in Shanghai? Would I be able to continue to be a reporter?"

Xu stayed up all that night drafting and redrafting a letter of apology, and he delivered his pleadings, which explained his motivation for writing the article, to the mayor's office early the next morning.

"I didn't quite fully appreciate your efforts to understand citizens' life," Xu wrote to Jiang. "My opinions were rather biased. Please forgive me."

Xu's act of repentance took Jiang by surprise. He read Xu's letter on the evening of July 11 and answered him right off on the morning of July 12. Jiang used a Chinese brush pen to compose a three-page letter in his own calligraphy. In his response, which was apologetic in tone, Jiang said that in general he agreed with Xu's concerns and key points and understood the purpose of the original criticism. Although he disagreed with Xu's use of the "other side" of the Chinese idiom, Jiang expressed "hope" that Xu "wouldn't mind."

"I'll welcome more of your criticisms and suggestions for the work of the municipal government," Jiang encouraged Xu, "including about my own involvement." Jiang added that he knew his work style had shortcomings. "My attitude can be a bit stiff," Jiang confessed, "and I am sometimes too harsh and express myself with biting sarcasm."

Several days later, Zhao Qizheng, then a member of the Standing Committee of the Shanghai Party, told Jiang that Xu had felt nervous after the mayor's criticism, fearing that local newspapers would stop publishing his articles. But as soon as Xu received Jiang's letter, Zhao continued, the reporter was greatly relieved.

Jiang replied, "When offering criticism, we should fully consider the consequences for each of our comrades."

A few days later when Jiang read another of Xu's articles, this one condemning officials who commercialize their power, he told a nearby *Jiefang Daily* photographer (who was covering the mayor's activities) that Xu's article was well written. "Please convey my hearty congratulations to him," Jiang said. By passing on praise through a newspaper employee, who would surely tell everyone within earshot what the mayor had said, Jiang was rehabilitating and bolstering Xu's reputation. "I was deeply moved by the mayor's concern," Xu remembered.

AT A PANEL DISCUSSION at the Thirteenth Party Congress in October 1987, Qiao Shi, who would be elected to the Politburo Standing Committee at the close of the Congress, said that Shanghai's economy should gradually shift from central planning to a market economy, and that this shift would require a drastic change in both ideology and practice.

Jiang agreed. "That's the only way for Shanghai," he said. Jiang told the delegates that he had heard about certain high-level dissatisfaction with the not-lively-enough economy of Shanghai. "Let's do away with that bad name," Jiang said, rising to his feet and speaking in the Shanghai dialect. "Shanghai people have too much business acumen but not enough wisdom."

When another delegate, a local bank president, disagreed with the mayor, Jiang countered: "I'm afraid the days are gone when Shanghai's industry can thrive on mandated cheap raw material from other parts of the country." Then Wang Daohan, the former mayor, interrupted and said, "That's why we must change our old concepts and cast away our old practices." Wang was perhaps the only man in Shanghai who could so confidently interrupt Jiang.

Jiang had fun, too—his kind of fun. He initiated a bimonthly seminar with leading Shanghai scholars. For each session he would raise a hot or sensitive topic and enjoy the discussion.

In the late fall Zhao Ziyang, now the Party general secretary, asked Rui Xingwen to head the Secretariat of the Party's Central Committee, which maintained day-to-day control of Party operations. As a result, Jiang Zemin was promoted to Rui's old position as Shanghai Party secretary, making him the undisputed leader of the city. Customarily, the Party leaders of Beijing and Shanghai, which report directly to the central government, are members of the Politburo. At the still relatively young age of sixty-one, Jiang Zemin joined the highest decision-making body in the Communist Party, the seat of ultimate power.

Under Zhao Ziyang, the Thirteenth Party Congress elaborated the Party's guiding theory, known as "The Primary Stage of Socialism." The idea was that even though current reforms such as the establishment of a market economy might closely resemble capitalism, they were in fact part of a long-term plan to construct socialism. In this manner the Party hoped to harmonize the ideological core of Communism with the market necessities of modernization and reform.

Replacing Jiang as mayor was the little-known Zhu Rongji, a descendant of the first emperor of the Ming dynasty and scion of a rich, landowning family in Hunan province. Not surprisingly, he had spent time in political disgrace (Zhu was denounced as a Rightist in 1957), but once Deng came into power, he rose rapidly through sheer talent. Zhu was tough-minded and known for his bluntness. He got things done, but often at the expense of people's feelings. Everyone, from Party prognosticators to foreign pundits, was surprised when Jiang and Zhu got on well together, balancing each other and forming a complementary team that would one day lead all China.

The two tackled Shanghai's problems with force and efficiency. One trouble spot was the city's immense bureaucracy. One joint venture with foreign investors required no fewer than 126 stamps of approval, known as "chops." The process took fifteen months and involved fourteen offices and nineteen bureaus. "I feel mortified that this sort of thing is still going on," Jiang said. "With such low work efficiency, how can we expect foreigners to come and do business with us? Foreign investors just won't stand for so much red tape." A new office was established to handle similar cases. Under Zhu Rongji the commission could approve any joint venture between $5 million and $30 million. The service was known as "One Window, One Stamp." It made for a dramatic increase in efficiency, and Zhu Rongji became known as "One-Chop Zhu."

Zhu's appointment also meant that Jiang was now free from the daily mayoral grind and could occupy himself with larger political matters. The Thirteenth Party Congress had mandated more dialogue with the people. Jiang had already been holding open discussions with city residents; now he increased these interactions. In one such session, he learned that some ten thousand Shanghai dwellers were packed so tightly that each had an average floor space of only two square meters. As a result, 60 percent of those individuals were moved.

Zhao Ziyang moved ahead with new programs for economic reform. He envisioned the Pearl River Delta in Guangdong province and the Yangtze River Delta around Shanghai as the two "dragon heads" that would drive the development of China's southern and eastern coasts. Partially conceived as a way to catch up with a booming Taiwan, Zhao's policy was summarized by the phrase "Two heads facing abroad; big imports, big exports."

Acting on the new policy, Jiang Zemin led a large delegation of Shanghai's leaders on a fact-finding mission to Guangdong in January 1988. His effort to understand the dynamic province to the south could have been perceived as an embarrassing plea for help from the city that had long been China's center of commerce. Instead, it became a public relations bonanza. By being eager to learn from Guangdong, Jiang was portrayed as a forward-thinking, pragmatic leader.

Upon his return, Jiang convened a grand meeting of ten thousand officials. "The first thing we must do is to liberate our thinking," he said. "Guangdong's rapid development is based on reform, opening-up, clear-cut financial appropriations, decentralized responsibility systems, and the offering of incentives to all enterprises, departments, and managements." In a February meeting he became more specific, calling for structural changes in Shanghai's industrial sector. Authority, he said, had to be dispersed to lower levels of management. He also urged the full use of rural and township businesses with their low labor costs and surplus production capacities. More enterprises needed to be converted into shareholding companies, and more strong brand names needed to be built. In the same month new data showed that from 1985 through 1987 foreign investments in Shanghai had tripled.

The figures were good, but Jiang knew they were not good enough. Concerned how local managers were negotiating with foreign investors, Jiang criticized their short-term focus, which he felt came at the expense of long-range development. "Shanghai people are smart but not intelligent," Jiang quoted a foreign investor as saying. "In ten business negotiations, nine fell through." He instructed his staff to analyze thirty failed cases of business negotiations, and he scolded those in charge for not thinking strategically. He advised local managers to reduce their profit expectations, allowing foreign businesses to have a larger share and thus promoting more ventures.

At the same time Jiang always defended his people to outsiders. When he heard foreign businessmen complain about the Shanghainese being "shrewd" in negotiations, Jiang replied, "Shrewdness is a good thing; I'd rather deal with shrewd people. Hurried agreement would lead both sides to difficulty and unhappiness."

Jiang's attitude made an impression on visiting dignitaries, who would often come to Shanghai after visiting Beijing. Jiang also led official delegations to foreign countries. U.S. senator Dianne Feinstein said that Jiang was "one of the most 'Western' leaders I ever met in China," while Maurice Greenberg, head of AIG (insurance), recalled that in meetings Jiang "asks a great many questions, more like a businessman than a politician."

JIANG'S YEARS IN SHANGHAI were brightened by the arrival of his two grandchildren, Zhicheng, Mianheng's son, in 1986, and Zhiyun, Miankang's daughter, in 1988. As with Jiang Zemin's generation, the first character of their given names was the same, "Zhi," meaning "ambition" or "good goals." *Zhicheng* means something like "With ambition, you can achieve"; *Zhiyun* combines ambition with the imagery of clouds (from a Tang dynasty poem). Zhicheng had little hair when he was a baby, so he was nicknamed "Maotou," meaning No-Hair-Baby (literally, "Hair Head," a cute name contrary to fact); Zhiyun was nicknamed "Meimei," meaning "little sister."

Their grandfather beamed whenever he saw them, which was all the time, of course, since the families lived and ate together in the same large apartment. That made it all the more difficult for Jiang and his wife when their sons and their families went abroad to study and work—which in the case of Mianheng was soon after the birth of his son. "Third Brother and his wife missed their children and grandchildren greatly," recalled Jiang Zehui.

On the eve of the Chinese New Year in early February 1988, Deng Xiaoping was greeted with a standing ovation when he walked vigorously into the Friendship Hall auditorium of the Shanghai Exhibition Center. With Jiang very visibly at his side, Deng was confirming his confidence in the enthusiastic Shanghai Party chief. After watching elaborate performances of song, dance, traditional Peking Opera, and acrobatics, Deng, trailed closely by Jiang, climbed up on the stage to greet the artists, and a photograph of the occasion appeared in major newspapers.

Twelve months later, in early February 1989, a year that would begin with political disputations even before erupting in the Tiananmen turmoil, Jiang would also celebrate the New Year with Deng. In his mid-eighties, Deng had labored a lifetime to see China develop; he had few years remaining and he wanted rapid results. In Shanghai it seemed that Jiang Zemin was delivering.

Expressing his abiding interest in Marxist ideology, Jiang introduced progressive ideas at a March 1988 conference on political values. Building on Mao's foundation, Jiang was revisiting the ideas of socialism and capitalism in the context of the late twentieth century. "There should be no taboo in theoretical study, and theorists should be allowed to speak out freely," Jiang told the audience of a thousand. "We should allow errors in theoretical study as we do in reform." For guidance he looked to history, which, he said, "has proved that rejecting a hundred schools of thought in order to follow a single school of thought will suppress the will of the people, suffocate thought, and result in the destruction of theories."

When Jiang said "no taboo," what he left unsaid, but everyone knew anyway, was something like ". . . provided that the theoretical study is still within Marxism" or ". . . as long as the theorist still professes Marxism." As such, Jiang's "no taboo" does not mean what, say, an American First Amendment attorney arguing a freedom of speech case would mean by that phrase. Nonetheless, Jiang's expression reveals, it seems, the internal struggle of an intrinsic intellectual, a true lover of learning who appreciates the conditions and constraints of scholarly freedoms, even though he cannot deliver the former and he will not loosen the latter. Scholarly freedom is important, Jiang believes, but not as important as the monopolistic power of the Communist Party.

A month later, at the Shanghai People's Congress, Vice Mayor Huang Ju gave a report on a spate of local disasters that put the city leadership under great strain. In December 1987 eleven people had been trampled to death and ninety injured in a ferry accident caused by thick fog. The next month an outbreak of hepatitis, traced to contaminated clams, had afflicted almost 300,000 people and caused several deaths.

At the session several vice mayors made self-criticisms for having improperly carried out their duties. Demerits, disciplinary warnings, and demotions for dereliction of duty were meted out. Jiang felt personally responsible, particularly for the hepatitis epidemic, and he also made a self-criticism. He admitted that he had not paid sufficient attention to public health and should have anticipated the problems that might arise with the burgeoning of the private business sector. "As the main leader of the municipal government," Jiang said, "I should shoulder the responsibility."

In a more lighthearted expression of reform, a Shanghai television station, the Shanghai Women's Federation, and several consumer products companies announced that they would reinstitute the Miss Shanghai beauty pageant, an event not held since the founding of the People's Republic. In addition to massive media attention and hundreds of entrants, the pageant triggered heated debate.

Many Party cadres, especially those worried about poverty and health care, were offended by the 450,000-yuan cost of the contest. Writing letters to newspapers and filing formal objections, they expressed disgust that the Miss Shanghai winner would receive 5,000 yuan, far more than most workers' annual salary. Others, recalling past decadence, suspected that the pageant's real purpose was to "select beautiful girls for certain officials."

Jiang did not want to project the image of an old-fashioned hardliner, which would hurt Shanghai's international ambitions, but he could not ignore the chorus of complaints from Party members. After three weeks of deliberation Jiang canceled the Miss Shanghai beauty pageant, carefully wording his explanation. At present, he said, "conditions are not yet ripe," conveying the idea that while he did not oppose beauty contests in principle, the city had bigger issues to address first.

Chief among them was skyrocketing inflation. A government policy, championed by Zhao Ziyang, was supposed to resolve blatant price distortions by relaxing price controls. It did not work, and panic buying broke out. China's leaders were forced to reverse their policies. "Each time we saw General Secretary Zhao on television," commented one Chinese official, "his hair had gone whiter."

In the second half of 1988 Premier Li Peng determined to freeze prices. New building construction—especially of hotels and office buildings—was virtually stopped, and more than ten thousand projects across China ground to a halt. Li Peng's austerity measures were credited with saving China from Zhao's reforms. In Shanghai Jiang Zemin, who had faithfully followed the previous aggressively reformist policies from Beijing, now faithfully followed the nationally mandated retrenchment. In October he convened a meeting of scholars to examine the nuts and bolts of how to implement Li Peng's austerity program.

IT SEEMED TIME FOR JIANG to reconsider his career. He would turn sixty-three in 1989, and considering the political uncertainty in Beijing, his prospects seemed limited. Traditional posts for retired senior leaders—a vice chairmanship of the National People's Congress or the CPPCC—did not appeal. Instead, Jiang considered making a radical change. He would become a professor at his alma mater, Shanghai Jiaotong University.

Though he could have used his position as Shanghai Party chief to guarantee himself a place at the university, Jiang wanted to win an appointment on his scholarly merits. Recalling his Chinese translation of the Russian book on electrical power, he contacted Shen Yongyan to resuscitate the project. An intellectual at heart, Jiang took pride in the thought of being a published author. He also prepared to give a lecture at the university on "Current Trends in Power Conservation and Energy Development," a topic on which he would write a technical article.

"I was surprised when Jiang called," said Shen. "He was anxious about locating his old manuscript. Frankly, I had no recollection of what had happened to it. Over twenty years had passed, ten of which were consumed by the memory-fogging Cultural Revolution. I told him I'd look."

Shen rummaged through his bookshelves and closets and finally found the forgotten manuscript as if it were an archaeological artifact. But he couldn't find the original Russian book; for personal safety, his wife might have sold it or burned it during the Cultural Revolution.

"Jiang was greatly relieved," said Shen, "and told me that he would contact our former Russian adviser to get another copy of the original Russian." Within a month Jiang had the book and sent it to Shen.

"Please help edit and proofread the manuscript," Jiang beseeched Shen. "This book is so important to me."

"I understood what he was saying," Shen noted wistfully. "In addition to his personal plans for retirement in the academic world, publishing the book would fulfill the long-ago promise that Jiang had made to his Russian mentor.

"I did as Jiang requested," he went on. "It was very complicated, very difficult. Everything—graphics and sketches as well as the translation—had to match the original perfectly."

But while Jiang was making plans for a future outside of politics, a political earthquake rocked everyone's future.

"I had only completed half the manuscript," said Shen, "when I heard the astounding news that my dear friend, Jiang Zemin, had become general secretary of the Communist Party. 'Well,' I thought, 'that's the end of our little book project.' "

Part Two

Leadership

1989–1996

Chapter 9

J A N U A R Y – M A Y   1 9 8 9

"Get Prepared for a Protracted Struggle"

M UCH HAS BEEN MADE OF the sharp political differences among China's senior leaders at the beginning of 1989. In fact, no one of importance disagreed fundamentally with the necessity of reform to spur economic development. The fault line between the so-called "liberals" and "conservatives" was the speed and style of the reforms. Still, the division was seismic, and the epicenter would soon be Tiananmen Square.

To Leftist officials, Deng Xiaoping's aggressive reforms—market orientation, decentralization, and opening up to the outside world—threatened their personal power. Many were entrenched in the system of government control, centralized planning, and state-owned enterprises, and they propounded a conservative ideology to protect these career and life interests. Although their withering criticism was directed at Zhao Ziyang for his liberal "disruptions," many in the Communist system sought to curb Deng Xiaoping's capacity to effect change. In addition, old-time idealists yearned for a return to Communism's "golden age" (the early and mid-1950s before Mao's mass movements roiled the country), when a utopian goal, a shared vision, comradely equality, and Party loyalty were at their peak and unified the country.

As for Jiang Zemin, the last thing on his mind was political advancement. He had decided to retire in Shanghai as a professor. For decades he had been moving around. Now that he had come back to Shanghai, his wife, Wang Yeping, wanted him to stay. She loved the city and spoke the local dialect better than she did Mandarin. The mandatory retirement age for a Shanghai Party secretary was sixty-five, which meant that in a little over two years Jiang would have to quit politics anyway, and the couple could live out the rest of their days in comfort in Shanghai.

Shen Yongyan remembered calling Jiang's office one day in April 1989, and

Jia Ting'an answered. "Jia told me," Shen recalled, "that Jiang was giving a lecture at Jiaotong University." He was preparing for his transition from high-profile public figure to low-key academic.

The tectonic shift began with tragedy. On April 8 the regular Friday meeting of the Politburo, held in Zhongnanhai, began at its usual time, 9:00 A.M. The topic was educational reform. As chair, General Secretary Zhao Ziyang sat at the head of the large oval table that could seat twenty. The man he had replaced, Hu Yaobang, sat toward the middle, not quite across from Jiang Zemin.

Since 1987, when he had been removed from his position, Hu Yaobang almost never spoke at Politburo meetings. He had suffered a heart attack in 1988 and was in poor health. One of his greatest regrets, he told a former aide, was that after his forced resignation as Party general secretary, he had engaged in ritualistic self-criticism, disappointing his intellectual supporters. Hu doubted that people would ever miss him.

Forty minutes into the meeting Hu rose to his feet and interrupted the general secretary.

"Comrade Ziyang," Hu said. "I'm not feeling well. May I leave?"

"Of course," responded Zhao. "Please take care of yourself."

But instead of walking out, Hu sat back down. Almost in slow motion he folded his arms on the table and, without a sound, cradled his head between them.

"Who has the medicine?" Zhao asked, referring to the special packet of drugs that senior leaders were supposed to carry at all times to deal with medical emergencies. "We need nitroglycerin!"

Jiang Zemin spoke up: "I have it! But I've never used it before," he said. "Who knows how nitroglycerin should be given?"

"My father had a heart condition," said Zhu Yuli, an education official. "Let me have it." Jiang ran over to Zhu, who took the medicine and placed it under the sick man's tongue.

Doctors were called, and Hu was taken to Beijing Hospital. For the next week he appeared to be doing better, but on April 15 he suffered a massive myocardial infarction. Ten minutes later he was dead.

That evening China Central Television broadcast the sad news, and within hours students began milling around on campuses across Beijing, wondering how to honor the one man who had stood up for their rights. The next day a group of students from Beijing University entered Tiananmen Square. What began as a memorial to the former general secretary soon transformed itself into a demonstration supporting the liberal values he had espoused. Students slapped together posters and banners that called for ending corruption, promoting democracy, and allowing greater freedom of the press. They also demanded that Hu's record be reexamined and that he be posthumously exonerated.

When word spread about the demonstrations in Beijing, students from East China Normal University in Shanghai hit the streets. Remembering 1986, the city government issued warnings to prevent the movement from getting out of hand. But for Jiang Zemin and Zhu Rongji, the problem was not so much the demonstrations as the way they were being covered in one local newspaper, the *World Economic Herald*. The paper's founder and editor in chief was a Party veteran named Qin Benli, a seventy-year-old gritty intellectual who wore Mao jackets and espoused a simple lifestyle.

Although the city government sponsored the paper, the *Herald* enjoyed an unusual degree of editorial independence. Under the implicit protection of Hu Yaobang and then Zhao Ziyang, the *Herald* had become the vanguard of the media, reporting on reform in the Party and entertaining new ideas in politics. With a circulation of 300,000 largely upscale readers, the paper was influential in setting the tone for national debate.

Four days after Hu's death, *Herald* editors held a symposium titled "Comrade Yaobang Lives with Us Forever" at the Ministry of Culture in Beijing. Determined to challenge the official view of Hu's record, they invited a number of prominent intellectuals to speak. Qin Benli's instructions were that the content of the symposium should be "substantive and not ordinary words of condolence." Accordingly, the participants were frank and outspoken, calling for more democracy and open disclosure.

Certain speakers were publicly critical of Hu Yaobang's opponents in the Politburo. "Some people who were in charge of ideology have no right to mourn Hu," said one participant in an apparent reference to senior Party officials Deng Liqun and Hu Qiaomu. "They stabbed him in the back. They should be tried by history." Another labeled Hu's forced resignation "a nonprocedural grab for power." Many demanded that government leaders admit their errors. They denounced the purification and anti–bourgeois liberalization movements as being contrary to the will of the people. They even criticized Deng Xiaoping, saying that he had distanced himself from the masses.

Qin Benli planned to publish a special insert on the symposium in the

April 24 issue of the *Herald*, two days after the Party's formal memorial service for Hu. The front page would feature a large portrait of the former general secretary along with the headline "People's Memorial Embodies Enormous Prime Force for Reform."

When Jiang got wind of the special insert, he instructed the vice Party secretary for propaganda, Zeng Qinghong, and the director of the Propaganda Department, Chen Zhili (dubbed "the iron lady"), to investigate. The pair met with Qin Benli (April 21) and requested an advance copy of the articles, which the editor promised to deliver by the following morning.

The copy did not arrive until 4:30 P.M. the next day, but it did not take Zeng and Chen long to find parts of it unacceptable. In an emergency meeting at 8:30 that evening, Zeng told the *Herald* editor that certain inciting sections of the insert had to be deleted. It was important, he said, to keep the peace in these sensitive times.

"Since Comrade [Shanghai Party chief] Jiang Zemin hasn't seen the proofs yet," Qin cajoled Zeng, "so the Party and the Propaganda Department are free of any responsibility."

"This isn't about protecting ourselves," Zeng retorted. "It's about protecting society!"

Qin refused to budge.

On April 19, the same day as the *Herald* symposium, students began to block the Xinhuamen, or New China Gate, which marks the formal entrance to Zhongnanhai adjacent to Tiananmen Square on Chang'an Avenue, the Avenue of Eternal Peace, the main thoroughfare that bisects Beijing. The protesters demanded that Hu Yaobang be rehabilitated and that Li Peng come out to talk with them. The next day the students were still there, having received no satisfaction; frustrations rose, and a scuffle with police ensued. The government announced that students were being exploited by "a small group of people" and that their actions were "abnormal."

On the morning of April 22 Hu's memorial service was held in the Great Hall of the People. The ceremony was presided over by President Yang Shangkun with most of China's senior leaders in attendance. Jiang remained in Shanghai, dealing with the deteriorating situation, and sent a wreath to express his condolences.

In Tiananmen Square, the hundred-acre expanse filled with students and citizens expressing their support for Hu's ideals and paying final tribute to the beloved leader. They lifted a giant portrait of him near the Monument of

People's Heroes at the center of the square. Coming from dozens of Beijing schools, the crowd swelled to 100,000. After a sit-in failed to receive any official response, students presented a formal petition. When it became clear that the Party was not going to rehabilitate Hu Yaobang, the students were outraged. They called for a nationwide strike to halt work and classes. Growing in agitation, they marched through the streets of the capital and were applauded by thousands of onlookers.

Leaders grew anxious, fearing violence. Some ten thousand military personnel were brought in for crowd control. A worried Deng Xiaoping remarked that the student movement did not seem to be of the ordinary kind.

In Shanghai the special insert of the *Herald* was slated to be published in two days. When Zeng Qinghong told Jiang of Qin Benli's refusal to censor the inflammatory sections, Jiang called his old mentor, Wang Daohan, who was the honorary chairman of the paper.

"Jiang asked for my help," Wang recalled years later. "I too gave the highest priority to maintaining stability. Leaders needed to explain the danger the country was facing and the safety measures that were necessary."

Together the two men confronted the editor, using the classic strategy of good cop, bad cop. Although Jiang and Qin had enjoyed a good relationship, Jiang did not bother to disguise his anger—he was the bad cop. He wanted to save the *Herald,* which he admired, from embarrassing the Party and destroying itself. Jiang accused Qin of being cavalier about Party discipline, and then he departed, leaving Wang Daohan—the good cop—to persuade Qin to make the desired edits. After some discussion, the editor agreed to remove the offending passages and change the page layouts. The revised edition would be finished by the following afternoon, so that it could be printed, as scheduled, on the morning of April 24.

Wang stayed up until 1:00 A.M., poring over the copy and making final edits. Much to his surprise and dismay, a printed copy of the original, unedited version of the newspaper was delivered to his home later that morning (April 23). Apparently 160,000 copies of the uncensored version had just come off the presses, and several hundred were already on the morning flights to Beijing. Whether Qin had been duplicitous all along in agreeing to make the changes, or whether he later changed his mind under pressure from his young editors, remains a mystery. Qin was not available for comment; his office told callers that he was away, on vacation or out sick (the story apparently changing). Meanwhile, the *Herald* staff distributed as many copies of the original version as possible, hoping that its incendiary content would ignite a freedom-of-the-press firestorm.

The Shanghai Party Committee, headed by Jiang, insisted that Qin Benli substitute the revised copy and layout for the uncut version and recall all remaining issues of the original. Foreign newspapers were now reporting that the *Herald* had been seized and closed down, an unfounded story that the Party later blamed on the *Herald's* Beijing office.

Qin agreed to make the changes for the Monday morning (April 24) edition because, as he acknowledged, he had given his word to Jiang Zemin and Wang Daohan. Yet that same evening (Sunday), Qin convened a secret meeting at his home. He described his talk with Party leaders, then asked his editors for their advice. "If we support the students," one said, "we can change the government—but only if we stick to our principles and publish the original, unedited version."

"I don't think we did anything wrong," Qin responded. "The parts they wanted to delete are precisely the parts we wanted to stress." He said that Deng Xiaoping ought to admit his error in removing Hu from office. Getting Deng "to do a self-criticism [for removing Hu Yaobang] is exactly my aim," Qin told his staff. "If Deng does self-criticism, we'll support him." Otherwise, he implied, we won't.

The next day the edited version of the *Herald* did not appear. A furious Jiang managed to confiscate only twenty thousand copies of the original paper. Readers in Shanghai and Beijing were devouring the articles and calling their friends to spread the word.

Pressured by queries from Beijing, Jiang called the *Herald's* offices demanding an explanation. Again he was assured that the edited version would be printed as planned. Again it did not happen. Wang Daohan resigned from his honorary chairmanship, and the game of promise-the-new-copy continued for another day.

Finally dispensing with pretense on the evening of April 25, *Herald* editors laid out their bold position in a brusque "urgent message" to Party headquarters. "For your information . . . ," it began coldly. The claim was that Qin was ill and unable to produce the edited newspaper. In an argument that challenged logic, the editors explained that they had decided to publish the original, uncorrected version in order *not* to "intensify the conflict." It was an explicit act of defiance. In essence, the audacious editors were saying that the Party had no say in what their newspaper did or did not publish.

"It is the Central Committee's responsibility, not the *World Economic Her-*

ald's," Jiang stated on hearing this news, "to come to a final conclusion about Hu Yaobang."

"I was there!" recalled former Vice Mayor Ye Gongqi. "I am witness. We were promised one thing—that the few offending words would be eliminated—and we discovered another thing—the newspaper was printed with the offending words included. It was not a mistake. We were deceived. We were responsible for the security of Shanghai. What else could we do?"

It was during this period that Jiang Zemin called his sister, Jiang Zehui, then chair of the forestry science department at Anhui Agriculture University, to get an independent assessment of the student movement. "He would ask me about the situation in Anhui," said Jiang Zehui, "where students were just as active as elsewhere. Third Brother and I kept in close touch. I really cared for the students, trying to prevent them from getting too emotional. A few students lost control and were not polite. I'd tell Third Brother what was happening on campus, and I'd give him my observations, truthfully and timely. As family, he knew he could always trust me."

EVEN WITH THE SITUATION in Beijing deteriorating, Zhao Ziyang continued with plans to visit North Korea. It was a mistake. He left the country on April 23, and the next day the standing members of the Beijing Communist Party, led by the ambitious Beijing mayor, Chen Xitong, declared that the student movement was "targeting the central Communist leadership and attempting to overthrow the Communist Party." That night Li Peng presided over the Politburo Standing Committee in lieu of the absent Zhao. Based on reports from the Beijing Party (and perhaps from military intelligence as well), the Standing Committee voted to support the Beijing Party's conclusion that the intent of the student demonstrations was "counterrevolutionary." The label was ominous.

April 23 was also the day when rampant nepotism was given wide exposure. Lists of names and positions of relatives of senior leaders were mounted on wall posters at Beijing and Tsinghua Universities. There was at least one mistake: "Politburo member Jiang Zemin, son-in-law of former President Li Xiannian." No matter how many times Jiang or his staff or his relatives denied this rumor, it continued to be repeated, particularly in foreign reports.

On April 24 sixty thousand students from thirty-eight universities and colleges in Beijing began to strike, stating that they would boycott their classes indefinitely to press their demands for more democracy and a freer press, particularly in response to the crisis at the *World Economic Herald.* Student leaders also said that they would be sending delegations to factories to solicit active support from workers.

The next morning Li Peng, Yang Shangkun, and Li Ximing, the Beijing Party secretary, arrived at Deng Xiaoping's home to report on the deteriorating events. After listening to Li Peng's report, Deng made his defining statement about the nature of the student movement, branding it "turmoil." It was the most inflammatory word he could use in a country still traumatized by the Cultural Revolution. "Turmoil" was a trigger word, and it elevated the danger of the demonstrations to the highest order of magnitude. By contrast, the 1986 student protests had been designated as mere "disturbances." "This is a well-planned plot," Deng said, "whose real aim is to reject the Chinese Communist Party and the socialist system at its most fundamental level. . . . We've got to be explicit and clear in opposing this turmoil."

The Beijing Party drafted an editorial based on Deng's assertions, excoriating students for being "out of order" and labeling their actions "illegal." It also attacked any criticism of the government and called for an end to the "plotted riot." The editorial bore the bellwether title "We Must Clearly and Steadfastly Oppose the Turmoil!" On the evening of April 25, Li Peng ordered CCTV to read the script several times on national news programs. The next morning "Turmoil" was the headline in *People's Daily*.

Zhao Ziyang received copies of the editorial in North Korea. Across the country leaders made their own assessments. Jiang Zemin instructed Zeng Qinghong to contact the Beijing Party to find out the source of the editorial. If Deng Xiaoping was behind it, then the parallel to the 1986 demonstrations that had led to the removal of Hu Yaobang was clear and Zhao Ziyang was finished.

JIANG WAS STILL DEALING with the crisis at the *Herald*. The *People's Daily* editorial arrived on the same evening as the rebellious message from the *Herald*'s editorial staff. The two pieces of paper lay together on his desk, almost like opposing declarations of war. Jiang Zemin knew that he must act.

Editor in chief Qin had to be held responsible. At best he could not control those under him; at worst he had been duplicitous and maliciously insubordinate. In an emergency meeting after midnight on April 25, Shanghai Party leaders decided that *Herald* editors and writers would report to a five-person editorial review board whose members would be named by Jiang. The next afternoon, in a sports stadium packed with cadres, Jiang announced the decision to fire Qin Benli and "rectify" the *Herald*. Referring darkly to those who "are trying to enlist international criticism to lessen our resolve," Jiang said that such tactics would be ineffective. "They will never succeed," he declared. "They cannot shake our determination to maintain stability and unity."

Jiang encouraged everyone to read the "important guidelines" of the *People's Daily* editorial. He also reaffirmed that the Party would "persist in the reform and opening policy" and improve the economy. Then he praised the *Herald* for playing a positive role in propagating reform.

On April 27 the "rectifying group," led by Liu Ji, deputy director of Shanghai's Propaganda Department, entered the *Herald's* offices and found that the conflict was not over. According to procedures, the editorial staff had to sign off on any issue before it could go to press, and this they refused to do for the revised, censored version. The review board had to find a deputy publisher to authorize the proofs so that the new edition could finally be printed.

The next day, when *People's Daily* ran an editorial approving Jiang's action against the *Herald*, the reaction was swift. Thirty-three intellectuals in Beijing signed an open letter of protest to the Party Central Committee. Entitled "Safeguard the Freedom of Press," the letter demanded that "the Shanghai Communist Party should reverse their erroneous decision to remove Qin Benli" and should apologize for their "ill-conceived denouncement" of the speakers at the Hu Yaobang memorial symposium.

The crisis in Beijing was also gathering force. Two hundred thousand students massed in huge parades throughout the city and accused *People's Daily* of "slander." The marches continued for more than twelve hours. By the time they ended, the government agreed to speak with the students, but a three-hour talk ended inconclusively, and the strike continued.

The next day Zhao Ziyang returned from North Korea. Distancing himself from Li Peng's hard line, he decided to take his last stand with the students. Briefed on the suppression of the *Herald*, he was furious. He counted the paper as part of his primary base, and its censorship meant losing an important source of support. Zhao had to take the offensive. His real targets, Deng Xiaoping and Li Peng, were too powerful to attack. Instead, he chose Jiang Zemin.

"The Shanghai Party [Jiang] moved too hastily [in firing Qin Benli] and bungled the matter," Zhao said at the Politburo on May 1. "Their simplistic approach to the problem only made it worse, and they wound up trapping themselves in a bad position." He added, "We need to support their decision anyway, of course."

As it turned out, the watchdog committee was not effective in censoring the *Herald*. The paper's headlines protested Qin's firing, and articles stressing the need for reform continued to appear. To reform-minded people, the *Herald* editors had become heroes, while Jiang was cast as villain. Journalists from most Shanghai newspapers joined demonstrations all along the Bund. Signs calling for Qin's reinstatement were held up alongside those demanding Jiang's resignation.

On May 3 the protests grew larger as seven thousand students and thousands of others challenged the legality of Qin's dismissal. The next day—the seventieth anniversary of the May Fourth Movement of 1919, when students had first marched against oppression and for democracy—thousands more poured into the streets, waving banners and chanting slogans. Their demands ranged from an end of official profiteering and higher pay for teachers to democratic reforms, rule by law, and freedom of the press. In Beijing 200,000 students again filled Tiananmen Square. Representatives from almost fifty Beijing schools published a "New May Fourth Declaration," while members of the city's press corps marched, declaring their support for the deposed *Herald* editor.

Speaking at a conference on Asian banking in Beijing, Zhao Ziyang, still the Party general secretary, called the students "patriotic." In doing so, he shut the door to compromise with his colleagues. For the moment, though, Zhao appeared to be gaining ground. The *Herald's* Beijing branch engaged legal experts to draft a statement of charges against Jiang for removing their editor in chief. Almost five hundred reporters sent letters to the *Herald* expressing their support for Qin. On May 7 the editorial review board rejected an article that claimed the firing of Qin Benli had been illegal. A heated argument ensued, and the newspaper failed to be published at all. But the next day an equally provocative article ran under the headline "Without Press Freedom There Is No Genuine Stability." On May 9 a thousand reporters and editors submitted a petition opposing press control by the government.

Zhao continued to blame Jiang for the uproar, claiming that he had mishandled the volatile situation, while others believed he had not been tough enough. At another Politburo meeting on May 10, Zhao criticized Jiang's decision to take over the *Herald*. The strong backlash, he said, was distracting the people and debilitating the Party. The rest of the Politburo sat mute, waiting for Jiang to respond.

"We tried to estimate the probable fallout over the rectification [takeover] of the *World Economic Herald*," Jiang admitted, "but it turned out to be worse than our estimate." Responding to the charge that his actions had triggered the "big demonstration in Shanghai" with Qin Benli "marching in the front row," Jiang used an earthy saying: "It's not totally a bad thing when some of these liberal elements jump out in the public eye. The problem arises when students and some other intellectuals get drawn in. 'Mixing fish eyes and pearls' makes our work harder."

Zhao Ziyang, feeling the heat, shot back: "The Shanghai Party [Jiang] was hasty and careless in dealing with the *Herald*; it painted itself into a corner and turned a simple issue into a mess."

Jiang remained calm. "We followed Party principles scrupulously in the *Herald* matter," he told the Politburo. "We focused on the big picture and drew a clear distinction between Party members and the general public. Qin Benli tried to deceive the Party by feigning compliance. He violated the most fundamental Party regulations and deserved his punishment. The problem was that the press blew everything out of proportion. The Party's position on the student movement has been absolutely clear: We will never allow protests to disrupt Shanghai's production routine or social order, will never permit the rise of illegal organizations, will ban all illegal demonstrations and marches, will forbid all forms of networking, and will dutifully carry out thought work and guidance among teachers and students. In particular, we will strive to win over the masses in the middle, to defuse confrontations, and to get things settled down as quickly as possible."

Jiang was oblivious to the fact—which would be recognized only in retrospect—that by opposing Zhao Ziyang he was positioning himself to advantage. His candid explanations were an attempt to restore order and survive the political storm, not to angle for higher office. In any event, his actions against the *Herald* were considered decisive by Party elders at a time when being decisive was exactly what China's leaders determined they needed.

Outside, the "turmoil" spread. On May 13 five to six hundred students, mostly from Beijing University, began a hunger strike in Tiananmen Square. Members of the Politburo decided to send Yan Mingfu, a senior Party official, to negotiate with the protesters. Deaf to his pleas for their health and his reprimands that they should uphold "the dignity of the nation," the hunger strikers continued to grow in number. By the end of the night, more than three thousand students were fasting.

The internal struggle also escalated. On May 14 a Hong Kong publication, quoting a high-level inside source, claimed that Zhao Ziyang declared in a Politburo meeting that since the *Herald* incident "has been provoked by the Shanghai Municipal Party Committee, it should be ended by the same Municipal Party Committee." It seemed an overt rebuke to Jiang.

Meanwhile *Herald* editors prepared an unprecedented two-page spread also criticizing Jiang. Foreign censure would be included, as would advertisements supporting Qin. Not surprisingly, the review board refused to allow the issue to be published, stating that the publication had not met its deadline. Jiang ratified the postponement without checking with Beijing.

Jiang's suspension of the *Herald* caused an uproar. Foreign reporters criticized the Shanghai Party chief with a fervor that had previously been reserved only for Li Peng. Two hundred and thirty artists and scholars submitted a petition calling for the reinstatement of Qin and the dismissal of the editorial review board.

The public outcry strengthened Jiang's resolve. Only if Qin admitted his error regarding the Hu Yaobang memorial edition, Jiang stated, would he be restored to his post. Qin was intransigent and called Jiang's actions "perverse behavior." In the end, no one gave in. Qin was never reinstated, and the paper lost its punch.

HUNGER STRIKES CONTINUED in Beijing. The students sought a reversal of the April 26 *People's Daily* editorial and live broadcasts of their meetings, demands that were unacceptable to the government. "I desire rice," the fasting protesters shouted. "But I desire democracy more!" By evening on May 15 more than a hundred hunger strikers had fainted, and people from different segments of society, workers as well as intellectuals, began to display sympathy for the students. A gigantic multitude—800,000 people—now filled Tiananmen Square. Still unwilling to take action, the government once again asked students to return to their campuses.

At 5:40 P.M. that afternoon Yan Mingfu walked alone into Tiananmen Square. Though he had a high fever, he followed his superiors' request. Surging crowds of disheveled students enveloped him as he spoke with great emotion. Yan complimented demonstrators for promoting reform and beseeched them to keep healthy. They were China's future, he said. He praised their patriotism and promised that they would not be punished if they returned to their campuses. Yan urged the students to be patient, hinting that they should wait until a more reasoned evaluation of their protest could take place. He even offered to stay as their hostage so that they could withdraw without worry. His speech was much appreciated by the students, but it had come too late.

The Party would later criticize Yan Mingfu for his actions and for his speech, dismissing him from all his posts, a casualty of the chaos. "I expected it would be difficult," he later reflected. "What I did not expect was that it would be on international television."

On the same day President Mikhail Gorbachev of the Soviet Union flew to Beijing for a long-planned visit. The timing could not have been worse. For a government pursuing international prestige, the massive demonstrations were awkward and humiliating. Gorbachev was welcomed at the airport instead of at the Great Hall of the People in Tiananmen Square, and the plan for the Soviet leader to pay his respects at the Monument of People's Heroes was canceled. The purpose of Gorbachev's visit was the resumption of friendly relations between the Soviet Union and China after thirty years of undeclared cold war. It was a historic moment, and hundreds of journalists had descended on Beijing to cover the story. But when they saw the surging crowds of protesters, they knew they had a far bigger story than a Communist summit.

In Shanghai four thousand students showed solidarity with their fellow students in Beijing by encamping in front of Party headquarters. It was a cold, rainy day, and by nightfall only a few hundred remained. Zhao Ziyang's policy required city leaders to establish "dialogue teams" and enter into discussions with demonstrators. The first encounter in Shanghai took place on May 17. Thirty students representing seventeen schools were invited, and five senior city officials participated. Jiang Zemin was not among them.

His absence stirred up more unrest. For three days ten thousand students paraded through Shanghai carrying banners that read, "Put Jiang on Trial." Within the Party certain groups were also pressuring Jiang to deal with what they called "legitimate demands of the students." They wanted him to speak directly with the protesters and to declare the movement patriotic and lawful. But Jiang had no such power and no such wish. Yet he continued to avoid confrontation.

The protests continued unabated. More than 100,000 demonstrators appeared on the winding streets of Shanghai, snarling traffic and threatening Gorbachev's coming visit. On the Bund waterfront, tens of thousands of students and workers rallied into the evening as another three hundred students, on the steps of City Hall, entered the second day of a hunger strike.

Deng first voiced the military option when meeting at his home with seven elders, Party leaders, and senior army officers. "We old comrades . . . have no choice," Deng Xiaoping said. "At bottom they [our opponents] want to overthrow our state and our Party—that's what's really going on here. If you don't see this point, you can't be clear about what's going on. If you do see it, then you'll know why we need martial law in Beijing." Still transfixed by the chaos of the Cultural Revolution, Deng added, "Some people object to the word [turmoil], but it hits the nail on the head." Martial law gave Li Peng a legal basis for moving the army into the capital. The internal struggle was over. Hardliners had won.

In contrast to Gorbachev's embarrassing visit to Beijing, his six-hour trip to Shanghai was a success. Jiang enjoyed meeting the Soviet leader and handled the volatile situation with aplomb. When Gorbachev's motorcade became entangled with demonstrators en route to a statue of Alexander Pushkin, one of Jiang's favorite poets, Jiang ordered a thousand green-jacketed paramilitary police to secure a small intersection so that Gorbachev and his wife, Raisa, could place bouquets of carnations on the monument. At one point Jiang joked that Gorbachev's arrival had caused Shanghai's weather to change for the better. "I am glad to see," the Soviet leader replied, "that Sino-Soviet weather has also changed for the better."

IN A BREACH OF PROTOCOL, leaders of Shanghai's officially sanctioned "democratic parties," which had always backed the Communist Party (this was, in essence, their mission), issued an open letter to Jiang Zemin. Calling the student movement patriotic and the situation grim, it appealed to Jiang to "handle the reasonable demands of the students within the framework of democracy and the legal system as soon as possible," and it advised him to "make a full, fair, and timely report through the news media." That same day eighty-seven Party members from the Organization Department sent a letter expressing "extreme shock and distress" and recommending, among other suggestions, that Jiang "immediately hold a dialogue with the students and declare the student movement to be patriotic and democratic."

The hunger strike on the Bund was in its third day, and the story was being followed closely by the media. The number of fasting students reached about 450, with some of them starting to faint. Images of medical personnel administering first aid were broadcast on television.

Most members of the media, incensed by the *Herald* affair, had become openly critical of the government. Shanghai's three newspapers and two television stations, as well as other major press units, sent representatives to march and sit with the students in front of the municipal offices. Reporters and editors signed petitions in support of the students, who seemed to be getting the upper hand.

Monitoring the evolving situation in the capital, Jiang Zemin broke his own ban on speaking with the students in Shanghai, working throughout the night to persuade them to abandon their protests. In the very early morning, he made his most valiant effort as he waded into the crowds along the Bund, bullhorn in hand.

"Your patriotic feelings are praiseworthy," he told the students through the bullhorn. "And your reasonable aspirations for opposing corruption, deepening reforms, and promoting democracy are also identical with the goals of the Party and the government. We are striving to achieve these goals. A top priority task now is to protect the health of the students on hunger strike. You represent the future and hopes of our country, and you must remain in good health in order to study well and contribute to building socialism."

Jiang assured them that he and other leaders would continue to hold informal discussions with them. "Such dialogue," he cautioned, "can be held only in a calm and reasonable atmosphere in order to exchange views and reach common understanding." Jiang's moderating move came just after martial law had been declared in Beijing.

By 2:45 A.M. the Shanghai students who had been fasting for five days stopped. Later that day Jiang visited hospitalized students and wished them a speedy recovery. Remarkably, he had achieved a nonviolent end to Shanghai's demonstrations. At the same time, he sent a telegram to the Party Central Committee fully supporting its decision to impose martial law. It was a tricky balancing act, but Jiang was pulling it off.

On May 19 Zhao Ziyang entered Tiananmen Square. With tears in his eyes, he begged the students to end their hunger strike, saying, "We have come too late, and we are sorry." Throughout the day, tension mounted as news of the government's intentions reached student leaders. At seven that evening they decided to end the hunger strike but remain where they were. At 10:00 P.M. a stiff-looking Li Peng spoke, reaffirming the government's stand and calling for "serious measures to end the riot." Two hours later, at midnight, a loudspeaker in Tiananmen announced the imposition of martial law.

More than 100,000 troops had been mustered in an overwhelming show of force. Before morning on May 20 they were in position to enter the city and clear the square. That was when Premier Li Peng and Beijing mayor Chen Xitong issued decrees imposing martial law. Included were strict prohibitions of any type of demonstration, a clampdown on the media, and authorization of the armed police and military to "use all necessary means, including force, to deal with prohibited activities."

In response, some students raised the stakes; ominously, they began using obstructionist measures such as blocking transportation, accosting police and soldiers, and sabotaging public facilities. A few now believed that violence and bloodshed would help their cause.

Jiang continued to send different, though not contradictory, messages. In a television appeal, he voiced support for Li Peng's speech, but his tone was less strident. All avenues of negotiation must be explored, he said, before the government moved against demonstrators. This conciliatory message contrasted with the confrontational threats to the north. Though Western pundits had taken to calling him "one of the leading conservatives in the Politburo" behind Li Peng, Jiang's actions evidenced a more judicious position.

Senior Party officials state that at this time, on May 20, the decision was made to "nominate Jiang Zemin to become the new general secretary of the Central Committee of the CPC." It is claimed that the momentous moment occurred at the residence of Deng Xiaoping and that it was "suggested by Deng with Li Xiannian, Chen Yun, Peng Zhen, Yang Shangkun, Weng Zhen, Li Peng, Qiao Shi, Yao Yilin, and Song Ping." (This assertion does not seem consistent with the sequence of events as described in *The Tiananmen Papers* and used below.)

On May 22 troops tried to enter the capital but were forced back when large numbers of residents and students blocked the streets with hastily erected barricades. In Shanghai six hundred students, along with former editor Qin Benli, marched in a heavy downpour, carrying signs that read, "Li Peng Step Down." That evening in Beijing a large meeting of senior leaders gathered to effect the ouster of Zhao Ziyang.

At the same time, the central government brought the Party secretaries of every province and other senior leaders to Beijing, where they were briefed on the coming purge by four leaders—Yang Shangkun, Li Peng, Qiao Shi, and Yao Yilin. After Jiang Zemin's briefing on May 23, President Yang Shangkun asked to speak with him alone. Wan Li, chairman of the National People's Congress (NPC), was cutting short a visit to North America and returning to Beijing via Shanghai, Yang told Jiang. There was concern that Wan, who said he would protect the "patriotic enthusiasm" of the demonstrators, might use the formal power of the NPC to reverse the removal of Zhao Ziyang and dismiss Li Peng instead. Jiang asked who would meet Wan Li in Shanghai. "You'll be our representative," Yang replied. "You've been handpicked by Comrade Deng Xiaoping."

When Wan's plane landed at the Shanghai airport at 3:00 A.M. on May 25, Jiang was waiting for him on the tarmac with a letter from Deng. He informed the NPC chairman that it was too late to prevent a military response. Until Wan agreed to support the decision, Jiang was under orders to keep him in Shanghai.

Jiang escorted Wan to a suburban guesthouse, personally briefed him, and delivered formal documents. It was common knowledge that Wan Li was flying back to Beijing, so that when it was announced that Wan's detainment in Shanghai was "advised on health grounds by his doctors," insiders knew that martial law would not be reversed. On May 27 Wan Li wrote a formal letter to Party Central stating that he supported the decision to impose martial law.

That same day Deng Xiaoping met with China's eight senior elders to determine Zhao Ziyang's successor as general secretary. The historic determination took five hours.

"After long and careful consideration," Deng told his inner group, "the Shanghai Party secretary, Comrade Jiang Zemin, does indeed seem a proper choice. I think he's up to the task. Comrades Chen Yun, Xiannian, and I all lean toward Comrade Jiang Zemin for general secretary. What do the rest of you think?"

After two elders agreed—based more on their trust of Deng than on their familiarity with Jiang—Li Xiannian said, "It's true that Jiang Zemin lacks experience at the center. But this man has a political mind, is in the prime of life, and can be trusted." According to knowledgeable sources, Li Xiannian and Bo Yibo were instrumental in Deng's decision to appoint Jiang.

Yang Shangkun concurred by emphasizing that "the new leadership team [must] maintain the image of reform and opening and win the trust of the people," adding that if it is "stodgy, rigid or mediocre," the people won't trust it, Party members won't respect it, there will be constant disturbances, and "we can forget about economic growth." For China to seal itself off again, he said, would be "frightening."

Elder Bo Yibo also endorsed the new generation. "As long as we stay out of the way and let them go," he said, "I think they'll do well."

Deng then called a formal vote on the appointment of the new Standing Committee of the Politburo with Jiang Zemin as its general secretary. The agreement was unanimous.

Chapter 10

"I Feel the Heavy Burden on My Shoulders"

W HEN JIANG ZEMIN RECEIVED an urgent message from the Secretariat requesting that he come to Beijing immediately, he hurried to the Shanghai airport. There he found a luxury aircraft waiting for him, but strangely, the car sent to pick him up at Nanyuan Airport in Beijing was an ordinary VW-Santana. His puzzlement grew when the military officer serving as his driver gave him a set of work clothes—perhaps a painter's outfit—to change into. Only then was Jiang told that he would be meeting Deng Xiaoping in his villa in Western Hills. The disguise was a precautionary measure to keep Jiang from being recognized by irate demonstrators.

When Deng offered him the post of general secretary, Jiang was dumbfounded. He expressed profound appreciation to Deng, pledged his loyalty to the Party, and affirmed that he would do whatever the Party requested. "I am afraid," Jiang said, "I am not worthy of the great duty entrusted by the Party."

Jiang had mixed feelings about the offer. He was ambitious but not overly so. He was happy in Shanghai and would later tell friends, "I can't bear to leave!" As he explained to Deng, his minimal experience in Beijing would be a liability, especially when dealing with colleagues who had worked there for decades. "We all support you," Deng replied. "We will help you whatever the difficulty; you do not have to worry." That evening a dazed Jiang Zemin took the same jet back to Shanghai.

On quiet reflection, Jiang wondered what on earth had just happened. Deng had surely offered him the job—it wasn't a dream—and he made it clear that the elders supported the decision. But nothing was formal or official; the elders were still meeting and talking; the Central Committee had not voted—few if any of its members even knew of Deng's offer—and Jiang himself certainly had no power. Anything could happen. Everything, truly, was in flux.

Wang Yeping was subdued when her husband broke the news. The four happy years that they had spent together in Shanghai, after more than two decades apart, would end. She had no political or social ambitions, and the idea of becoming China's most visible woman did not appeal to her at all. A humble researcher, Wang preferred to stay in her beloved hometown. In addition, her health had been deteriorating, and she was apprehensive about taking on new responsibilities. She also feared for their family. If her husband failed in his high-profile job, even if it was not his fault, there was no telling what might happen to them. Jiang did not disagree. "Those in high places," he would later say, "don't survive the winter."

Jiang wondered if he could hold his own among the capital's elite. The position would entail sensitive political maneuvering and protracted factional infighting, and he would be almost entirely dependent on Deng Xiaoping for continuing support. As he had so often done in the past, he called upon Wang Daohan for advice.

With their homes next to each other on Kang Ping Road, Jiang walked the few steps to Wang's front door, knocked, and after a brief greeting, revealed the astonishing news. When they had first met, the biggest thing on Jiang's mind had been how to distribute ice cream in war-torn Shanghai. Now he was discussing whether to become general secretary of the Communist Party of all China. Jiang and Wang sat down and made two lists, the pros and the cons of being the nation's leader in a time of calamitous uncertainty, weighing the chance to stabilize society and build China against the dangers of social tensions and political treachery.

"I knew he was the right choice for general secretary," said Wang, "but I could see his mixed emotions. That's why I encouraged him by writing in my own calligraphy an antithetical couplet by Lin Zexu, the Chinese national hero who led the Opium War against the British in 1840. The main idea was not to be afraid of death if it benefits the country: 'Now that I'm ready to lay down my life for the state, how can personal gain or loss keep me from accepting the mission?'

"The reason I felt he was perfect for the post," Wang continued, "was that Jiang had evinced courage, conviction, and compassion in dealing with the student movements in 1986 and 1989, and with the *Herald* press incident. His strength is to reach out to people; he has the fortitude to face people and discuss issues.

"On the other hand," Wang said, "I was concerned because Jiang didn't have any experience working at the highest levels of the central government, which had many complications and contradictions, especially all the subtle conflicts between different interest groups. It would be tough, dispiriting at times. I used Lin Zexu's poem to tell Jiang that he should not give up the opportunity because of personal concerns. He should take up the great challenge regardless of what lies in store."

Wang's confidence reassured Jiang. Despite his wife's anxieties and his own insecurities, Jiang Zemin resolved to accept Deng Xiaoping's call to duty.

THOUGH THE CHOICE of Jiang surprised many, he was a natural. No one on the Politburo's Standing Committee would have been acceptable to the people and to the elders. Li Peng's doctrinaire approach certainly ruled him out as far as the people were concerned. As Deng reportedly said to Li Peng and Yao Yilin: "If the leadership we present seems rigid, conservative, or mediocre, there will be more trouble in the future. . . . We will never have peace. . . . We must establish credibility among the people."

Moderates were excluded for the opposite reason; in this time of crisis, the elders would reject any leader deemed too liberal. They had just managed to depose Zhao Ziyang and had no intention of replacing him with more of the same.

Jiang had not been associated with what had happened in Beijing—or, as Deng would ensure, what would happen. He had shown good instincts in handling demonstrators in Shanghai, finding conciliation and moderation while not relinquishing any of the Party's power. And his resolute handling of the *Herald* affair had shown conservatives that he was willing to be take action when necessary.

In addition, Deng believed that China's new leadership would require several critical qualities. High on the list was moral integrity. Jiang had accumulated an impressive record fighting corruption, and no hint of scandal had ever attached itself to his name. He had an exemplary Party record and always backed Deng's reformist vision for China. Equally important, Jiang had the technical expertise, political experience, and diplomatic savvy to see it all through. Trained in science with broad cultural knowledge and a facility for languages—Deng considered Jiang an adept intellectual—he presented an attractive image to the outside world. Finally and simply, Jiang was likable, a nice quality for helping heal a divided land.

Jiang's main liability—the fact that he had no strong base of support—now became an asset. "I need someone who doesn't deal in factions," Deng said.

Virtually everyone else at the top belonged to a clique, whereas Jiang, as an outsider, was not politically polarized in any direction. Party leaders could support him without working against their own factions or for those of their rivals.

Also working in Jiang's favor were the many friends he had made along the way. Li Xiannian, the chairman of the CPPCC, who knew Jiang well from Shanghai, may have been the first to recommend him for the leadership position. Chen Pixian, whom Jiang may have helped during and after the Cultural Revolution, was also vocal in his support. Many Party elders, including Chen Yun, were impressed by Jiang's role in quashing the rebellious *Herald*.

Jiang made what he, but few others, knew might be his farewell speech in Shanghai. At the Minhang power station he told workers, "Without electric power, Shanghai cannot have stability." It was not just the city's stability Jiang was now worried about, but the nation's.

At 10:30 on the evening of May 29, a thirty-seven-foot-tall statue, called the Goddess of Democracy and resembling the Statue of Liberty, was wheeled into Tiananmen Square on a half-dozen flatbed bicycles. By noon the next day the presence of the sculpture, created by students from the Central Academy of Fine Arts, reenergized the protesters. Amid euphoric demonstrators and international media, a student read out a "Declaration of the Goddess of Democracy."

The next day, during a meeting in Shanghai, Jiang Zemin was interrupted by an emergency call from Beijing. Within hours he was again flying north.

At the same time Deng broke the news about Jiang to senior Politburo members, a few of whom harbored hopes of being appointed general secretary themselves. The Paramount Leader stressed the importance of reform and opening up. "We've heard all sorts of slogans recently, but nobody shouts 'Down with reform!' China can't possibly fit back into its former isolation," he stated. "That isolation also caused disasters like the Cultural Revolution.

"As soon as the new leadership group can establish its authority, I'm going to retire," Deng asserted. "Party Central leadership has decided that Comrade Jiang Zemin will serve as the general secretary of the Party's Central Committee. I hope everyone will be able to unite around him and not carp at one another. I hope everyone will unite around Comrade Jiang Zemin as the core."

The internal struggle was momentarily over, but the external one was about to turn ugly. From the outset Deng kept his anointed successor behind the scenes and out of the media during the peak of battle. He knew that it was essential to maintain Jiang's image as a moderate if he were to succeed in reuniting the polarized nation.

On June 1 the Politburo and elders received a lengthy report from the Beijing Party Committee. Titled "On the True Nature of the Turmoil," it had been ordered by Li Peng and placed the blame on a number of putative plotters backed by "foreign and domestic hostile forces," including those of Taiwan and the United States. Seizing the moment, Premier Li urged that "we move immediately to clear Tiananmen Square and that we resolutely put an end to the turmoil and the ever-expanding trouble." Deng Xiaoping agreed. "Martial law troops," he suggested, should "begin tonight to carry out the clearing plan and finish it within two days."

Student leaders, sensing the worst, announced that they would compromise to open talks with the government. Their more limited conditions no longer included repudiation of the *People's Daily* editorial. But concessions were coming too late. The next day China's elders voted formally to allow military action to proceed.

"We must be merciless with the tiny minority of riot elements," asserted Li Peng. "The PLA martial law troops, the People's Armed Police, and Public Security are authorized to use any means necessary to deal with people who interfere with the mission. Whatever happens will be the responsibility of those who do not heed warnings."

President Yang Shangkun tried to rein in emotions. "The Martial Law Command must make it quite clear to all units that they are to open fire only as a last resort," he said. "And let me repeat: No bloodshed within Tiananmen Square, period."

For several days Chinese armed forces from provinces outside Beijing had been arriving at staging camps on the outskirts of the city. China's leadership was taking no chances that local troops might sympathize with the students. Small groups of soldiers, disguised in plain clothes, had begun slipping into the city, and on the evening of June 3, 1989, the army received word to enter the city en masse. Their explicit order: Clear Tiananmen Square. As they had before, crowds of angry residents blocked the tanks and heavy transports and alternately taunted and pleaded with the troops.

This time the soldiers did not turn back. As the army forced its way into the center of the city, the first casualties were reported. Late that night tanks and armored vehicles, followed by troops, forced their way into the center of

Beijing. They came from several directions to avoid bottlenecks and assure penetration. A military bulletin to the leadership described one of the early clashes: "Infantrymen led the way, firing into the air. Then the soldiers—with the first two rows in a kneeling position and those in back standing—pointed their weapons at the crowd. At about 10:30 P.M., under a barrage of rocks, the troops opened fire." In accord with President Yang's directive, the troops held their fire in Tiananmen Square, but in other parts of the city hundreds were killed and thousands injured as fighting raged for about twelve hours.

Rain began to fall on the afternoon of June 4. Bodies could be seen on some roadsides. Tanks rumbled through the streets. CCTV announced the enforcement of martial law; TV anchors dressed in dark colors and spoke with sad and mournful voices.

On June 5 a young man in a white shirt, armed with nothing but a large shopping bag, as if he had just loaded up at a discount store, stood defiantly before a long line of tanks, stopping seventeen of them in their tracks. When the lead tank tried to maneuver around the unknown hero, he side-stepped right back into its path, and standing defiantly erect, blocked the mechanized advance. Captured by photojournalists and flashed around the world, the picture made the front page of almost every major news publication. It remains one of the most arresting images of the twentieth century, and it helped galvanize Western opinion against the Chinese government.

THAT EVENING, DEEP IN ZHONGNANHAI (Room 202), Premier Li Peng, Shanghai Party Secretary Jiang Zemin, State Council Secretary General Luo Gan (a close associate of Li Peng), Foreign Minister Qian Qichen, and Propaganda Minister Wang Renzhi held a long meeting. The group summoned Teng Wensheng and another speechwriter to draft an open letter to the country.

"Chairing the meeting was Li Peng; Jiang Zemin hardly said a word," recalled Teng of that critical moment. "Knowing the system, I was puzzled why Jiang was there at all. I had no idea, no clue. I addressed him as 'Secretary Jiang' only because he was the *Shanghai* Party secretary."

Li Peng was the only one to speak substantively about the vital letter, giving a basic outline and primary points. "Please go next door [which was Mao's old meeting room] to write it," Li said. "We will wait for you to finish."

"We'll give you two honorable scholars one and a half hours," added Jiang pleasantly. It was his only comment.

Teng and his partner finished in one hour, returned to Room 202, and read their letter aloud. The group seem satisfied. Only Li Peng made changes, just a few and all of them minor. He asked whether anyone had additional comments; no one did. Then Li Peng said to Teng, "OK, your job is done. You can go." As Teng departed, he still wondered why Jiang was there.

PROTESTS AGAINST THE MILITARY action were heard across China and around the world, but Beijing itself was quiet. After months of agitation and euphoria, an eerie silence descended on the city. The mortality count varied wildly. A report from the Beijing Municipality issued on June 19 stated that 218 civilians, 36 of whom were students, had died, along with 23 soldiers, putting the total death count at 241. Students and foreign reports strongly disagreed; some of their estimates numbered the dead into the several thousands. A reliable count has never been established, but it is closer to the official one. Statistics aside, the nation remained traumatized long after the violence was over. In addition to those killed, thousands were injured or arrested. Some student leaders received up to thirteen years in prison. A small number of other people were executed for crimes committed during this period; according to the government, no one was executed for participating in the student movement per se.

Jiang's activities during the Tiananmen tragedy remain a mystery. Some reports suggest that the new general secretary, while not involved in military operations, "played a sizable role in crisis management." Yet in his detailed, first-person recollections of the events of Tiananmen, James Lilley, the United States Ambassador to China at the time (and former CIA operative), mentions Jiang Zemin only once, and that was in the context of his "handling the protesters with more success" in Shanghai.

Over the ensuing years Jiang sought to distance himself from the bloodshed, offering, by way of contrast, how he dealt with the student movement in Shanghai. "The leadership," Jiang would later say in reference to the calamity, "must be careful and judicious in handling national disturbances." Still, he often acted as an apologist for the men who had taken action that day, asking how Western governments would react if even one-tenth the number of protesters camped out for almost two months in front of the White House, No. 10 Downing Street, or the Élysée Palace.

Though he remained removed, Jiang learned "bloody" lessons while watching the disaster develop. He resolved to practice prevention to ensure that such a thing would never happen on his watch. He believed that riot control should come under the jurisdiction of the police, not the military. He saw the sense in providing advanced training in riot control and using nonlethal weapons, such as rubber bullets, as in Western countries. He also felt that foreign press coverage had exacerbated problems, and he recommended tighter controls in the future. On Jiang's list of priorities, national stability always remained paramount.

As word of the catastrophe in Beijing reached Shanghai, students there exploded with anger and outrage. They erected bus barricades that paralyzed traffic, slashed tires, seized radio stations, and stopped trains. Shanghai leaders issued stern warnings to the rioters, telling them to cease and desist or be punished severely. Police arrested dozens of the most radical students as the Party mobilized some forty thousand cadres and citizens to remove the barriers that had been erected at intersections. Mobile patrols prevented students from blocking traffic. As people grew tired of the turmoil, the strategy began to work. By June 7 Shanghai returned, more or less, to normal. Newspapers wondered why similar tactics had not been tried in Beijing.

In a radio broadcast Mayor Zhu Rongji apologized for not being able to fully protect the people of Shanghai from the results of the riots, and he pointed out that never once had he considered calling in the army. Describing the pro-democracy protesters as "patriotic" rather than counterrevolutionary, the mayor left the impression that he too was distressed by events in the capital. "Things that occurred in Beijing are history," Zhu said. "No one can conceal history. The truth will eventually come to light."

JIANG WOULD NOT BE formally elected to his position for another three weeks. During this time Deng Xiaoping prepared a smooth transition. While he continued to defend the military's actions, he also reiterated his commitment to economic liberalization and openness. Determined to make sure that his policies would continue, Deng asserted that his reforms had not led to the pro-democracy turmoil. Rather, he stated, it was the failure of what he called "political education."

On June 16 Deng met with at least eight elders and senior leaders to explain why the Third Generation collective leadership should have a "core" and to affirm that this core should be Jiang Zemin. After recounting early CPC history, including his choosing and changing two prior successors, Deng said: "A collective leadership must have a core; without a core, no leadership can be strong enough. The core of our first generation of collective leadership was Chairman Mao. Because of that core, the Cultural Revolution did not bring the Communist Party down. Actually, I am the core of the second generation. Because of this core, even though we changed two of our leaders, the Party's exercise of leadership was not affected but always remained stable. The third generation of collective leadership must have a core, too; all you comrades present here should be keenly aware of that necessity and act accordingly. You should make an effort to maintain the core—Comrade Jiang Zemin, as you have agreed. From the very first day it starts to work, the new [Politburo] Standing Committee should make a point of establishing and maintaining this collective leadership and its core."

The notion of a "core leader" emerged in the context of the Tiananmen tragedy. "While paling in comparison to such terms as 'great helmsman' and 'paramount leader' that reflected the majesty and clout of Mao and Deng respectively," wrote Professor Frederick Teiwes of the University of Sidney, "the term 'core' was clearly designed to bolster the position of Jiang Zemin, newly installed against all expectations. . . . It was a higher rhetorical and symbolic position than those granted his predecessors as general secretary, Hu Yaobang and Zhao [Ziyang], who labored under the notion of 'collective successors.' . . . Yet the notion of 'core' was firmly tied to that of the collective leadership of different generations in an effort to balance the need for an authoritative leader with the need to prohibit the type of destructive one-man rule that Mao had exercised in his 'later years.' " Boston University professor Joseph Fewsmith characterizes "core" as "that combination of informal and formal authority that makes a leader the final arbiter of Party issues—the ability, as the Chinese put it, to 'strike the table' and end discussions."

Then Deng announced his intention to leave politics. "I will no longer concern myself with your affairs or interfere with them," he told the hushed group, stating that this was what he had told Li Peng and Yao Yilin earlier, possibly at the time he informed them of the surprising decision of the elders to select Jiang Zemin as the new general secretary. Yet, the Paramount Leader could not disengage so easily. If left on his own too soon, Jiang would fall or fail. Over the next three years, he would remain dependent on Deng's constant presence and occasional intervention.

The final consensus-building step was a meeting of the expanded Politburo, which included leading elders, that took place for three days on June 19–21. On June 24 the CPC Central Committee convened its formal conclave, which would be known as the Fourth Plenary Session of the Thirteenth Party Congress. To the surprise of no one, Zhao Ziyang was officially relieved of his post. He was accused of "very serious mistakes" and "splitting the Party" but was not branded a "counterrevolutionary." Li Peng, who led the prosecution, averred that Zhao "accommodated, encouraged, and supported bourgeois liberalization."

Contrary to time-honored tradition, Zhao gave a spirited defense of his actions and refused to offer self-criticism, all to no avail. The deposed Party chief was placed under house arrest, and Jiang Zemin, who never could have imagined such a moment, was elected to take his place as general secretary of the Central Committee of the Communist Party of China.

"I feel the heavy burden on my shoulders," Jiang said, addressing the session. "I thank you, comrades, for your trust in me. I am determined, together with you, to study hard, strengthen research, and devote all my energy to doing the job."

Helping Jiang Zemin draft his inauguration speech was Teng Wensheng. It would be the first of hundreds of such collaborations. "A few days before his election, Jiang called me up," remembered Teng, who by that time had heard the news. "He told me simply, 'The Central Government wants me to be the Party general secretary. Can you help me prepare a speech?' "

Teng went immediately to Jiang's temporary residence in Zhongnanhai. "We were sitting at his desk, across from each other, while he gave me his ideas. It took about thirty minutes." Teng was a heavy smoker at the time, three packs a day—an occupational hazard, it seems, for speechwriters (and accountants). "Lao [old] Teng," Jiang said, "you are such a heavy smoker—how come?"

"I didn't realize how much Jiang was annoyed by smoke," said Teng. "That day, I decided to quit, though it took me a little time."

A few days later, Teng presented the draft speech to Jiang, who did not make many changes. "From then on," Teng noted in early 2004, "I wrote most of his speeches. I was assigned to him, just as other members of the Policy Research Office were assigned to other members of the Politburo Standing Committee. We spent countless days and nights talking together."

ON JUNE 24, 1989, Jiang Zemin was introduced to the nation as the new general secretary. The *New York Times* reported that he "looked a bit glum, his brow slightly furrowed," adding, "He may have been reflecting on a disquieting realization: The job he is assuming is a precarious one."

Around the world, China watchers were taken by surprise. If one had made a short list of the expected pretenders to the Red Throne in early 1989, Jiang Zemin's name would not have been on it, and most concluded that his term would be brief. His base, observed a source in Hong Kong, is "his popularity, but in China that's not enough. He has no organizations behind him, like the military or the state security organs." "This is a temporary succession government," a Western diplomat stated. "I don't think anyone expects it to live very long."

Others saw merit in the selection. "This decision leaves people with hope," said one Chinese official. "He doesn't have the blood of Beijing protesters on his hands," noted a foreign diplomat. "At least, he can shake hands with foreign leaders." In a prescient analysis, a China scholar talked of the compromise necessary to move forward. "In terms of balance," he said, "he seems a very good choice—a symbol of openness to the outside but at the same time in tune with the elders."

Others called Jiang "very smooth, very suave, a likable man." A consultant who had met Jiang at a trade exhibition was even more enthusiastic. "I didn't think we had a politician in the United States of that caliber," she said. "He walked in, and it was like the king walking in."

In Beijing the response was tempered. Jiang was considered a "Shanghai man," not a term of endearment. It marked an ironic reversal. Four years earlier the people of Shanghai had labeled him "Beijing's man" when he became their mayor. As he had to do repeatedly throughout his career, Jiang would have to prove himself. This time it would be to the entire country and to the rest of the world.

At first, Jiang toed the official line, declaring that "severe punishment" had to be meted out "to the plotters, organizers, and behind-the-scene commanders who staged the turmoil and rebellion." "For them," he said, "not an iota of forgiveness should be given." At the same time he reached out to intellectuals and encouraged them to speak their minds. Though many publicly decried his appointment, they were privately relieved that it was Jiang Zemin, not Li Peng, who had been promoted.

One writer would later claim that Jiang's detention of Wan Li was his first "contribution" to the crackdown; another, that Jiang's takeover of the *Herald* marked the beginning of the irrational events. The truth seems more prosaic: Jiang was simply doing his job as best he could. By nature and career, Jiang was a cultural traditionalist, a political conservative, and an economic reformer. He was loyal to the Party, and he revered Deng Xiaoping.

FOR JIANG'S FAMILY, NEWS of his elevation came as a relief. In late May they had noticed that he was no longer making public appearances and feared the worst. "It was rare for a Shanghai Party secretary to disappear for that long,"

Jiang Zehui recalled, "especially during this time of student protests and political controversy. We didn't know what was going on." When concerned relatives called, all Wang Yeping could say was "We're safe," adding cryptically,
"Nothing bad has happened." On June 24, when the announcement came,
Jiang's family members were as nonplussed as any Western pundit.

"If Third Brother, as he has said, wasn't prepared," noted Jiang Zehui, "we
certainly weren't! It came as a total shock. My first reaction was that a heavy
burden of history had been dropped on his shoulders.

"We didn't feel extremely happy," she confided, "and we certainly didn't
celebrate. His appointment wasn't worth celebrating. It was just after June 4,
and it wasn't clear where the country was heading. It was a very difficult
time."

Jiang Zehui kept in touch with Jiang's wife, who seemed more resigned
than elated at what fate had just offered up. "She was anxious, concerned
about her husband and their future," said Jiang Zehui. "She didn't say she was
worried, she didn't complain or anything, but I've known her for so long, I
could tell."

Her anxiety was understandable. Since the founding of Communist China,
the anointed successors of Mao Zedong and Deng Xiaoping had an unblem-
ished record of coming to grief. Liu Shaoqi was humiliated and hounded to
death during the Cultural Revolution. Lin Biao was forced to flee and died en
route. Hu Yaobang and Zhao Ziyang were removed dishonorably and remained in disgrace. Only Hua Guofeng did not experience a dire ending—
just an embarrassing one. (Yet there had been no dearth of those hoping to
get the open job; ultimate power is ever enticing.)

The news was a burden for other family members as well. At the time
Jiang Zemin's older son, Mianheng, was a thirty-seven-year-old graduate student in the electrical and computer engineering department at Drexel University in Philadelphia. Although the Cultural Revolution had delayed his
education, Mianheng had succeeded in graduating from Shanghai's prestigious Fudan University, where he earned a degree in radiochemistry. Passing
a national exam, he then took a master's at the Chinese Academy of Sciences
before entering the Ph.D. program at Drexel in 1986.

Mianheng had been accepted in 1985 but could not afford to attend until
the following year when his father's old classmate, Hun Sun, who had immi-
grated to the United States and had become a professor at Drexel, helped
him secure a teaching assistantship. Living on $800 per month, Mianheng,
his wife, and their recently born son lived on the third floor of a dinky row

house. He worked hard and was unassuming. "If you didn't know who he was, you wouldn't have a clue," said Kevin Scoles, one of his advisers. His teachers remember him as a "brilliant researcher."

During the run-up to June 4, Mianheng kept to his studies and away from on-campus rallies. Following June 4, he sought almost total isolation; he did not know what was happening to his father in China but he did know that his filial relationship had become common knowledge at Drexel, certainly among the Chinese students who accosted him with in-your-face verbal threats and hostile phone calls. Mianheng was aware that his father had been in Beijing but he had no idea why. Telephone communications with his family, normally very limited (due to connections and cost in those years), had been cut off for weeks. Perhaps, Mianheng wondered to himself (as he later told friends), his father could be in line for promotion, possibly to the Standing Committee or even premier. Then again, political volatility remained high and anything could happen.

On June 24 Mianheng received an urgent message from the head of his department, Professor Bruce Eisenstein, a distinguished engineer who would later become president of the Institute of Electrical and Electronics Engineers (IEEE), to come to his office at once.

"Have you heard the news from Beijing?" Professor Eisenstein asked.

Mianheng shook his head; he had not. His heart raced: something had happened.

"Your father is the new general secretary of the Communist Party."

"Party chief?" Mianheng said, his face flushing. He, like many Chinese, probably expected Li Peng to get the job; even under normal conditions the natural progression would have been from premier to general secretary, and this seemed especially likely after June 4.

"I have two things to tell you," stated Professor Eisenstein. "First, the FBI and local police have contacted us and offered to protect you twenty-four hours a day. We do not need them—we will protect you. Second, we will continue to treat you like a normal student."

"That's all I'd want," said Mianheng, whose attitude "endeared him to colleagues."

When he returned to his small apartment, the telephone was already ringing. A reporter from the Associated Press wanted to know Mianheng's reaction to his father's appointment, his father's policies, and the violence in Tiananmen. Caught off guard, Mianheng came up with a famously quick-witted response: "My father is my father, and I am me."

Mianheng hoped that his "American-style," personally independent yet cleverly ambiguous remark would end the press inquiries and assure his anonymity, but he received his first lesson in the ways of American media when his exact quote was picked up by major newspapers and immortalized in numerous stories. Burned by his sudden public persona, Mianheng became even more determined to maintain his privacy. He politely refused further interviews. As he explained to one reporter: "I don't want to be popular in the public." When pressed, he added, "I really don't want to talk about myself and my father and my family, so I really hope you can understand my situation."

Worse, some of Mianheng's fellow students, mostly Chinese and irate over June 4, continued to taunt him. He received unpleasant letters. One exclaimed, "What gives you the right to enjoy the freedom of our campus when your father is the dictator of China?" Some fellow students began pressing Drexel to expel him.

To escape the press corps who were badgering him at home and avoid the students who were confronting him at school, Mianheng took shelter with Gu Yuxiu, his father's famous old professor, who was then in his late eighties and living in retirement in Philadelphia after a distinguished career at the University of Pennsylvania. Though Professor Gu and his wife lived in a small, one-bedroom apartment, they gladly shared it with Mianheng and his family during the early difficult days after his father's ascent. Professor Eisenstein, true to his word, protected Mianheng at the university, enabling the younger Jiang to weather the storm, finish his thesis, and obtain his doctorate.

In Beijing, the elder Jiang was facing his own difficulties. In the wake of June 4, economic reform was largely deferred, and political reform was shut down altogether. Most new policies, programs, and ventures now had to be categorized as "socialist" or "capitalist," the turbid way they used to be. Those with the former label were endorsed, and those with the latter rejected. Foreign investment all but dried up. Just as Jiang was attempting to establish a new regime, China was starting to stagnate.

Four or five days after the announcement of his promotion, Jiang called Shen Yongyan.

"Congratulations," Shen said, surprised to hear his old friend's voice. "We're so proud of you." He felt awkward and uncertain about how to address the new leader of the country.

"Don't be so fast to congratulate me," Jiang quipped. *"Yuntou zhuanxiang."*

The funny, self-deprecating expression means something like "I'm confused and disoriented—dizzy—from being whirled around so much."

Shen laughed; his old friend hadn't changed. Years later Shen would hasten to add, "Of course, Jiang is no longer '*Yuntou zhuanxiang.*' "

Jiang was calling Shen not only to chat and relax, as he had done so many times in the past, but because he had something on his mind, something still bothering him.

"Yongyan," he said. "You must continue to work on the book." Jiang was referring to his decades-old translation of his Russian mentor's now-far-outdated monograph on power generation, the project he had resurrected in anticipation of becoming a professor.

"Zemin, you have become general secretary," Shen responded incredulously. "What do you need this old book for?"

"We must *shan shi shan zhong,*" answered Jiang. Start well, complete well. "Although the Soviet gentleman has passed away, I must keep my promise."

From then on Jiang would periodically call Shen to check on the book's progress. He would not relent until the day the publisher sent him copies. The book's introduction, in which he summarized the contents and acknowledged the help of Shen and others, was dated "November 1989," the same month as a milestone event that solidified Jiang's leadership. Apparently, while he was politicking by day, he was writing by night.

The book was finally published in 1990. It had taken thirty years, but he kept his promise. Though technologically irrelevant and a mere curiosity, the book made Jiang proud. The next year, he visited the Soviet Union on his first trip as Party general secretary. His mentor had died, but Jiang made a point of presenting a copy to the man's family. As for the book's modest royalties, he donated them to the Shanghai Children's Foundation; he also purchased copies as gifts for his old automotive colleagues.

Shen Yongyan remembered Jiang's frequent late-night calls in the early days after his ascension. "We'd talk about many things, nothing momentous, often his adapting to the form and frustration of the daily routine of his new life. He was under so much pressure from so many directions, and sometimes, after dinner, he'd just be lonely. He's human like the rest of us; his family was still in Shanghai."

Jiang was sitting all alone in Zhongnanhai, the head offices of the Communist Party and the State Council, literally by himself in the center of power, isolated politically by his high position and isolated personally without family or friends. He said to Shen, "You know, I can't just go around visiting my neighbors here."

At the time Jiang Zemin became the leader of the world's most populous country, here is what was "whirling him around and making him dizzy." China was in a post-Tiananmen depression and ostracized by the international community. The country was awash in bitterness and recriminations, corruption was rampant, the economy was stagnating, and foreign investment had stopped. Virtually all of Jiang's colleagues had more experience in the central government than he had; several thought they should have had his job, and a few continued to think they might yet take it away. Furthermore he was working and living in temporary quarters, a small, unassuming building with an office in the front and a bedroom in the back. And since he had never spent much time in Zhongnanhai before, he had to learn which building was what and who worked or lived where.

Jiang was alone and not entirely at the top. The government was in the control of others. He had no network of senior support. He had no personal staff. He had no relationship with the army, which seemed oblivious to his leadership. And China's elders, some of whom were lukewarm about his appointment, would continue to exercise behind-the-curtain power. Jiang knew that virtually everyone, from the inner circles of Beijing to China scholars abroad, was dismissing him as an interim leader, a placeholder, much like the hapless Hua Guofeng after Mao. He would later say he felt as if he were "standing at the edge of a deep canyon" or "treading on thin ice."

Even Richard Nixon, who generally had a good sense of foreign affairs, did not give Jiang much of a chance. "Li Peng is ruthless, intelligent," the former U.S. president said. "And in a struggle after Deng's death, he would have Jiang Zemin for lunch."

Chapter 11

JULY – DECEMBER 1989

"Men Are Not Saints"

O N   T H E   C O N T E N T I O U S   I S S U E of where to lay blame for the Tiananmen tragedy, Jiang staked out a moderate position. Conservatives said the cause was deviations from Marxism ("the bitter fruit of violating this [Marxist] line," according to one senior leader). "We told you so" was never far from their lips. Led by Premier Li Peng, Beijing mayor Chen Xitong, and others, hardliners called for a vast purge of all associated with the deposed Zhao Ziyang or who had liberal leanings, along with an uncompromising repudiation of their permissive philosophy. Those on the other end of the political spectrum argued that reform had accelerated China's development and that the causes of the disturbances were complex.

As a devout Party loyalist, economic reformer, and former student protester, Jiang sought middle ground, declaring that the quelling of the "counterrevolutionary rebellion has proved the strength" of the Party but also questioning Party organization, ideology, and ethics. He reaffirmed the philosophy of "one country, two systems," reassuring anxious representatives of Hong Kong and Macao. "We practice our socialism and you practice your capitalism," Jiang told them. "Well water does not interfere with river water." At the same time he warned them to respect the Party's policies. "We will not practice socialism in Hong Kong, Macao, and Taiwan," he said. "But you should not transplant capitalism onto the country's mainland."

While he decried laxity in socialist education, Jiang sought contact with the nonsocialist world. "We should boldly learn everything valuable from ancient Chinese education and foreign education," he said at one meeting, but at another conference the same week, he declared: "We must enhance socialist ideology while carrying out to the end the struggle against bourgeois liberalization."

In July, as if responding to the demands of the now-suppressed student movement, the Politburo decided to do "seven things" regarding "matters of universal concern to the masses of people." Topping the list was the eradication of corruption and nepotism within the Party. A dragnet soon snared several "princelings," offspring of high-ranking officials. The message was clear: Jiang Zemin was serious about fighting corruption. (Over the next two years, regulations would be enacted to curtail a wide range of official perquisites: New Year's banquets would be downgraded to tea parties; travel restricted— so no more meetings at resorts; official automobiles put off-limits for personal use—so no more expensive foreign cars; and even year-end bonuses and work-supplied commodities—foodstuffs like eggs, which were considered part of ordinary compensation for ordinary managers—would be cut back.)

Also in July, Jiang made his first trip out of Beijing to inspect the future site of the massive Three Gorges Dam, the world's largest hydroelectric project, which Li Peng championed. When Jiang returned, he visited Li in the hospital, where the premier was recuperating after suffering some kind of post-Tiananmen breakdown. In his personal diary, published soon after he retired in 2002, Li quotes Jiang as comforting him by saying, "Once you have taken the route, let it be. A man tends to fall ill after a long period of stress and fatigue."

"The first time I met Third Brother after his elevation was in August, when I came to Beijing on a business trip," recalled Jiang Zehui. "He asked me to have dinner with him in Zhongnanhai. My son and I went to Qinzhendian, his office—it was his temporary dorm as well. It wasn't very special. The strangest thing about the visit was that it didn't feel strange."

When Jiang Zehui mentioned that the family was planning a grand celebration for the fiftieth anniversary of the martyrdom of their father, Jiang Shangqing, which would take place on August 29, Jiang Zemin dismissed the idea. "This is exactly what students complained about during the turmoil," he said. "We need to cut down these official celebrations."

Go ahead with the commemoration, Jiang told his sister, but observe three guidelines: first, the services should be simple; second, relatives must not accept invitations to banquets; third, relatives must not make any special requests of local officials and not expect any special treatment when they visit. Jiang suggested that his sister present a single basket of flowers.

In early August Jiang began building his political base. Visiting Shanghai, he was accompanied by colleagues Zhu Rongji, Wu Bangguo, and Chen Zhili, all of whom would eventually go to Beijing to assume high positions in the central government. Notably, Jiang made his first appointment at this time, bringing Zeng Qinghong, then Shanghai deputy Party secretary, to Beijing as deputy director (vice minister) of the General Office of the CPC Central Committee, a crucial position of coordination and influence strategically located in the southern section of Zhongnanhai, which is known as "Party Center." Jiang would also appoint his loyal secretary, Jia Ting'an, to head the "Jiang Office," also a vice minister–level position. (Jia had come with Jiang from Shanghai.)

Recruiting Zeng Qinghong was an especially inspired move. A close confidant of Jiang's, he had astute political acumen and an impeccable Party background and personal network. His father had been a military commander, Party leader (he held positions in the Organization Department), and senior minister who was influential in eastern China, particularly in Shanghai, where his protégés included Wang Daohan. His mother had been an early Party worker, one of the few women to survive the Long March, and the director of a Shanghai-based kindergarten that children of senior officials attended. Both for administrative operations and for political strategy, Zeng Qinghong would prove invaluable to Jiang Zemin.

Unrepentant tough talk continued on August 8 when Jiang and Premier Li Peng met thirty-six "heroes in quelling the anti-government riots." Jiang thanked them for safeguarding the Party, the socialist system, and the People's Republic. Yet the next day he reauthorized the sale of foreign newspapers, banned since June, at hotels catering to foreigners.

A week later came one of the most far-reaching triumphs of conservative values when Party cells were reintroduced into government ministries, reversing what Jiang Zemin's deposed predecessor, Zhao Ziyang, had determined to do. Moreover, Jiang backed the collective leadership's decision that required officials to reaffirm their loyalty to the Party. "The aim of political reform is to strengthen and perfect Party leadership," Jiang said, "not to dilute, curtail, or abolish it."

AT THE SAME TIME Jiang signaled that he would not simply adhere to established norms. Li Qiankuan, a well-known film director, had recently finished *The Grand Ceremony of the Founding of the Country*, an epic story of the Communist victory over the Nationalists. It included three major battles and climaxed with Mao Zedong's declaration on the roster above Tiananmen Square of the People's Republic of China.

It was a glorious, politically correct film, except for one problem. Li had chosen to portray Chiang Kai-shek, Mao's classic antagonist, as a normal human being rather than as the one-dimensional thug that mainland film-makers had depicted in the past. Censors refused to release the film unless Li altered the generalissimo's character, making him more brutal. He refused, and the high-profile two-part film was slated for storage.

"Several people asked me bluntly if I harbored 'warm feelings' toward Chiang," Li recalled. "In 1989 that was an accusation."

"China's leadership had just changed," Li continued, "and the government was anxious about the fortieth anniversary of the People's Republic on October 1, 1989. This film was meant to be released for the celebration, but officials differed in their opinions about it. It's always risky for government functionaries to sign off on a controversial film. The safest and easiest thing for them to do is to kill it. Knowing the politics, I became worried, frustrated, morose. I felt like a parent who was watching his child die and was not able to prevent it. My wife is my codirector; we were staying on the lot of the Beijing Film Studio and literally couldn't eat or sleep. We were just depressed. It was summer, and the hot, humid weather made us feel worse."

The Politburo Standing Committee member responsible for media and culture, Li Ruihuan, heard about the film and intervened. Originally a carpenter, Li Ruihuan was popular among artists and intellectuals for his open views and quick wit. He suggested that director Li appeal directly to the new general secretary, Jiang Zemin, whom Li Qiankuan had never met and whose opinions he did not know.

On the afternoon of August 8 a screening was held in Zhongnanhai for Jiang Zemin, other Standing Committee members, and five military leaders. "The survival of my film depended entirely on what would happen," director Li noted later. "Even the day before one senior official had nixed the film's release. . . .

"I was asked to give a fifteen-minute introduction," Li recalled. "My wife was nervous about what I might say. She worried that as a director, I always spoke with authority and demanded obedience, and that, well, I scowled a lot. She kept warning me to sound humble and smile. These people are *really* the leaders of the country, she said, not a bunch of actors costumed up to look that way!"

Li Qiankuan and his wife, Xiao Guiyun, were ushered into the empty screening room. After ten minutes a staffer informed them that the leaders were arriving. Li Ruihuan, who would chair the meeting, came in first and waited for Jiang Zemin. Soon, one after another, the other Standing Committee members entered: General Secretary Jiang Zemin first, followed by Qiao Shi and Yao Yilin; then the army men, including Generals Liu Huaqing and Yang Baibing.

Li Ruihuan introduced the awed film directors to each of the leaders. After brief greetings, all found their seats quickly, as if each knew his place: Standing Committee members in the front row, generals in the back row.

The meeting began when Li Ruihuan walked to the front of the room and in his high-pitched voice said, "Director Li, please explain to General Secretary Jiang and the other leaders how you made this film. What's its status now? Tell us about it."

"As an artist,' said director Li, addressing Jiang and the other dignitaries, "I take up the camera with a passion for my craft and a responsibility for my country. In this film I am committed to be both objective and artistic. About eight years ago, when my wife and I were directing another film about the War of Liberation, old General Tang Zhenlin came and said to our crew, 'We fought terrible hardships to establish our country. Millions of us dedicated our lives and sacrificed our blood for New China. So you artists shouldn't be afraid of challenges in bringing these stories to the screen.' I was touched by the old general's ardor and told him that I looked forward to the day when I could reenact the historic moments, particularly when the Red five-star flag was raised over the pavilion in Tiananmen Square. Gentlemen, this is that day—"

Jiang Zemin interrupted with applause and said, "Great! Great!"

When the director finished, Jiang applauded again and said, "Director Li, please sit here," and pointed to the empty sofa seat next to him in the center of the room. Aware of the strict protocol that ruled seating arrangements, Li demurred.

"I started talking to myself," he recalled with a smile. "I thought, 'Well, I'm a director; I know exactly where I should sit—and it's certainly not there. That seat is definitely not for me. That's the seat for Deng Xiaoping.' So I responded to Jiang, nervously, 'General Secretary, I'm just a director. I will sit on the side.' "

But Jiang stood and motioned more authoritatively to the place beside him. "Here, please," he said again. "If your work requires you to sit here, you should sit here." Jiang was not just being polite: he had reserved that seat because he wanted to ask director Li questions during the screening.

As the film started, Jiang leaned over and whispered, "Who's the actor playing Chiang Kai-shek?"

"It's Sun Feihu," Li answered.

"He really looks like Chiang, doesn't he?"

The director felt no pressure to agree. "Physically, he doesn't look much like Chiang at all. But he captures Chiang's temperament and disposition very well."

Jiang nodded. "Right, right," he said.

When a black and white segment appeared in the film, Jiang asked, "Did you shoot this yourself?"

"No, I used archival footage here, which I integrated into the scenes."

During the next section, a dramatic part, Jiang inquired, "Where did you get this archival material from?"

Li corrected the Party chief again: "No, this part isn't archival at all. I shot the footage myself and used a special technique to make it look old."

Jiang continued to ask questions until he became absorbed in the story. When the film ended with Mao Zedong waving his cap from atop the Tiananmen Pavilion and shouting "Long live the people!" the Party chief patted the director's hand.

"After he patted my hand *twice,* I knew that he liked the film," Li recalled. "Once, I thought, could have been an accident."

Jiang stood, praised Li's filmmaking abilities, and explained some of the innovative techniques that the director had revealed to him during the screening.

"Comrades, I think the film we saw is very interesting," Jiang said to his colleagues. "I also learned some things about filmmaking. Director Li used historical archives. He also shot special footage and merged it cleverly with the archives, real ones and fake ones together—I was fooled. He is obviously a talented director. As for my personal opinion about the film, I would like to hear your views first."

Jiang turned to his uniformed guests. "I never fought any battles and have no military experience," he said. "But I was wise enough to invite these senior generals, who have fought countless battles, to join me for the screening today. I suggest that our revered military leaders give their views before we civilians do."

Many suggestions followed, but none had to do with the character of Chiang Kai-shek. After forty minutes or so, when everyone had had their say, Jiang spoke.

"Comrades, while I was watching the movie, I was thinking that our young generation tends to make horizontal comparisons, across geographies. They compare China with the Western world; they see America and Europe as advanced and Hong Kong and Taiwan as prosperous, and they become envious. Our young people are not good at making vertical comparisons, across time periods. To appreciate how far China has come, one must appreciate how backward we once were and how difficult our road has been. Chairman Mao and other proletarian revolutionaries sacrificed their lives to bring us where we are. On our Red five-star flag there is blood of millions of martyrs."

Jiang turned to director Li. "I'm quite moved by your film," he said, "but what is its theme? Here's a suggestion: 'The establishment of our country did not come easily.' "

"Jiang's statement was the green light," Li recalled. "My film would survive."

It would do more than survive, going on to win the Golden Rooster, China's version of the Academy Award, and to be recognized as one of the most important films in the history of Chinese filmmaking. Known in English as *Birth of New China*, it was China's entry for Best Foreign Film at the 62nd Academy Awards in 1990.

Years later Li Qiankuan remained grateful to Jiang Zemin. "Given the political situation and Jiang's recent appointment as Party general secretary," Li observed, "that he would allocate three and a half hours to watch and discuss the film, and then support my nontraditional portrayal of Chiang Kai-shek, was unprecedented."

THE WORLD OUTSIDE THE screening room remained less upbeat. The country was still reeling from the aftereffects of June 4, and Jiang had to tread carefully between taking action against the protesters and continuing Deng's policy of reform and opening-up. At least twice in September, Deng spoke with senior leaders, including Jiang, about his prospective retirement. On September 26 Jiang faced his first worldwide test when he and five other leaders held a rare news conference. The audience was packed with more than three hundred Chinese and foreign reporters, and only one question was on everyone's mind.

"It was a rebellion," Jiang stated, adding that *rebellion* was a technical term for what had happened. When asked to explain his reluctance to comment on the possibility of executions, he responded, "China must be ruled by law."

He also replied curtly when asked if "the Tiananmen tragedy" could have been avoided. "First, I'd like to correct you in using the word *tragedy*," he said. "We feel it wasn't a tragedy. We hold that it was a counterrevolutionary rebellion aimed at opposing the leadership of the Communist Party and over-throwing the socialist system." This scripted answer conformed to Deng Xiaoping's judgment that the "turmoil that later developed into a counter-revolutionary rebellion" was caused by a convergence of international and domestic trends and was therefore unavoidable.

Jiang characterized the army's action as self-defense and, without hesitation or concern for the foreign press, added that the violence started only when demonstrators attacked tanks and army personnel, leaving the military no choice but to respond. (Images of massive numbers of destroyed army vehicles were being broadcast on national television to justify the commencement of martial law action during the night of June 3, despite the fact that their actual destruction had taken place largely during the day of June 4.)

Commenting on the press conference, which had been scheduled for one and a half hours but lasted almost two, the *Los Angeles Times* wrote that Jiang "showed not the slightest sense of irony" when he criticized foreign reporting of what had happened in Beijing. "There is a proverb," he said: " 'What is false will turn into truth after being repeated one thousand times.' "

Jiang made sure to focus on the future. He stressed that there would be no change to China's strategic goals of economic and political restructuring. He said that the overwhelming majority of the students and other people had become involved in the "turmoil" because of their dissatisfaction with corruption and other social problems. "The young people are our hope and we should educate and unite them," he said.

The new general secretary answered questions about the fate of his predecessor. "Comrade Zhao Ziyang has a longer record in serving the Party, so I think he enjoys a better standard of living than I do," Jiang remarked. "We adopted a down-to-earth attitude to Zhao Ziyang. He did some things beneficial but also erred in implementing specific policies."

Jiang fielded a question from a French reporter about rumors that a female student had been arrested and sent to Sichuan province, where she was raped by a group of farmers. "How will you handle this situation?" the journalist asked.

The question caught Jiang by surprise. He hesitated, then responded, "First, I've never heard about this incident. Second, there are many untrue and absurd reports circulating all the time." A French newspaper commented that Jiang had dealt with the challenge wisely. Though many of the answers at the press conference had been rehearsed, this one was spontaneous. "Answering questions at a press conference is a major challenge for a state leader," Jiang would later tell Shen Yongyan. "It reveals, or exposes, a leader's knowledge and wisdom."

Just prior to the press conference, Jiang paid a well-publicized visit to Yan'an, in Shaanxi province—the terminus of the fabled Long March and the hallowed cradle of Chinese Communism where Mao Zedong and other elders had lived and worked during the war years. At what was in effect a revolutionary shrine, Jiang said, "The Yan'an spirit of self-reliance as well as hard struggle and plain living has not become obsolete."

On the day Jiang arrived in Yan'an, he called Shen Yongyan, explaining that he wanted to come to Yan'an soon after becoming general secretary to reaffirm publicly his Communist commitment. "I complimented him on his good idea," Shen recalled, "but suggested that he shouldn't go along with the official arrangements. Visit poor families in the area, I told him. Jiang said he would do just that, and he asked me to follow the news on the radio. To conclude, Jiang joked that the real reason he was calling was to test how well the telephones worked."

While in Shaanxi, Jiang inspected Xi'an, its capital, where despite a hectic schedule he met several old professors from Jiaotong University. Even with all his new pressures and anxieties, Jiang was animated when remembering their classes. "I should come back to my alma mater more often," Jiang said, "to see my teachers."

ON OCTOBER 1, the fortieth anniversary of New China, brass bands and smiling dancers paraded along Chang'an Avenue and through Tiananmen Square, where four months earlier tanks had rolled and troops had marched. In his first national address as Party general secretary, Jiang described China's "socialist road" and ongoing reforms as "the irreversible tide of history." The building of democracy, he said, must relate to the realities in China and be carried out in an orderly way, step by step, within the orbit of socialism. "In this process," he said, "some of the practices in capitalist countries can serve us as reference, but they must not be copied indiscriminately."

Jiang put forth the conundrum of the times. He stated that reform was of two kinds: one that upheld the "Four Cardinal Principles" of Communism and one that was founded on "bourgeois liberalization" (i.e., Western-style democracy and capitalism). The new general secretary made it clear that he would not waver in his commitment to socialism. He also reflected endemic coservative hostility toward the West, particularly the United States, warning that "international reactionary forces have never given up their fundamental stance of enmity toward and [intent to] overthrow the socialist system."

The Party called on everyone to study Jiang's speech. "We must use it to reach uniform understanding, take uniform action, and together strive for the final victory," stated *People's Daily*. At the same time Jiang reached out to disaffected groups. Concerned that intellectuals were being held responsible for the protests and marginalized, the Party chief urged officials to "respect knowledge, respect the intellectuals," and provide good working conditions for them. Without knowledge, he said, it would be impossible to build socialism.

Several officials of the prior administration were allowed to stay in their positions. Confirming this, the Xinhua News Agency reported that Wen Jiabao met with an Ecuadorian minister. Wen had been director of the CPC General Office under Zhao Ziyang and had famously accompanied the deposed Party chief on his final, ill-fated, emotion-wrought appearance in Tiananmen Square, and so his political survival was no oversight. When Jiang Zemin had been in transition, prior to his formal election and at the apogee of the Tiananmen protests, Wen had handled the sensitive logistics—welcoming Jiang at the airport, accompanying him to meet the elders, preparing living arrangements, and generally helping to get things started. The general secretary-to-be was appreciative, noted Wen's loyal service, and recognized his professionalism, thus catalyzing what would become their long working relationship.

In a little-known move to modernize, Jiang restored a rational approach to decision-making. "After June 4, some believed that 'decisions should be made by the Party,'" recalled Dr. Song Jian, state councilor and chairman of the State Science and Technology Commission (1985–98). "They criticized our efforts to make decision making more scientific and democratic" as somehow reflecting the discredited liberal views of Zhao Ziyang. "To Jiang's credit, he backed our position, after which others felt free to express similar views."

Jiang also announced that the policy of sending students abroad to study would continue. In meeting thirty-one students who had returned from foreign countries, he said that he understood why some overseas Chinese students were "misled by some foreign media, misunderstood what happened in the country during the turmoil earlier this year, and engaged in some extremist acts." They would be welcomed back, he said, once they realized and corrected their mistakes. "Men are not saints," Jiang said, referring to those who protested the military action. "So how can they be free from faults?" During the three-hour session he listened to the students. "I see China's future and hope in you young people," he said.

Even so, China began to feel the impact of the world's repugnance. Tourism and foreign investment fell; diplomatic contacts were curtailed, and aid programs suspended. The once rapidly expanding GNP dropped precipitously. But the more pressure foreigners applied, the more defiant Jiang became. He pointed with pride to Zhu Ziqing, the Yangzhou poet who, following World War II, refused to eat American grain. "The young people of China should take him as a model," Jiang said, "and not bow, act obsequious to, and blindly envy the West." Regarding dissident Chinese students working with foreign media, he had only contempt. "I wonder," he said, "whether the blood of the Chinese nation still flows in their veins?"

JIANG'S ELDER BROTHER, Jiang Zejun, died in the fall of 1989. When he had first become ill a few years earlier, Jiang brought him to Shanghai for medical treatment and he lived with the family. In his last days, Jiang Zejun enjoyed watching his younger brother on television. As a memorial, Jiang Zemin wrote an elegiac poem.

> *I hear, my brother, that today you passed away, and I am deeply saddened. In remembrance, I compose the following poem in the style of Ziyege [fourth-century classic with a sad feeling].*

> *How can your brother escape the sorrow of your passing;*
> *Memories run all the way back and love has no limit.*

> *Remember those days returning home along the lake;*
> *And singing together on the river until the setting sun.*

> *Those days drinking together in Dongquanmen;*
> *And seeking beautiful flowers on the Huai River.*

> *Those days playing music in the mountains and on the waters;*
> *And Grandpa Shixi writing calligraphy until the ink runs dry.*

Dongquanmen is the section of Yangzhou where the Jiang family lived. "Seeking beautiful flowers on the Huai River" refers to twenty-year-old Jiang Zejun's heroism in going to east Anhui province ("Huai River") in 1938 to fight the Japanese invaders; "seeking beautiful flowers" symbolizes seeking a better world.

THOUGH JIANG WAS ESTABLISHING himself as the voice of China, he still had no power base of his own, and Deng Xiaoping feared that the vacuum could lead to instability. Mao Zedong once said famously, "Political power grows out of the barrel of a gun." In China that gun is the People's Liberation Army (PLA), over which the Communist Party has always insisted on maintaining absolute control. As such, the highest level of command of the PLA is the Central Military Commission (CMC), an organ of the Communist Party. Mao had held the position from 1936 until his death in 1976, when he was succeeded by Hua Guofeng. In 1981 Deng Xiaoping, with his history of army honors and the PLA's support, displaced Hua. It was through his control of the military in addition to his power in the Party and respect of the people that Deng was able to compel the ouster of two Party general secretaries, Hu Yaobang in January 1987 and Zhao Ziyang in June 1989.

But Deng now worried that he had set a dangerous precedent. A stable government was essential to realize his vision for China, and he could not leave Jiang vulnerable to a military-backed coup. Deng needed to act while his personal authority was still strong, and he began an uphill campaign to make Jiang Zemin, who had zero military experience, chairman of the CMC at a Party plenum in November.

Some senior leaders, including President Yang Shangkun, did not agree with Deng's choice. Jiang, they said, had no army knowledge; the man had never even fired a gun. He was first an engineer, then a politician. Deng believed, in accord with Communist doctrine, that the first duty of the military was to serve the interests of the Party. From this perspective, it followed that whoever ran the Party should also run the military.

Throughout September and October Deng worked to build his case for Jiang, pointing out that the general secretary had handled student protests in Shanghai better than the military had handled them in Beijing. Gradually Deng convinced key members of the CPC Central Committee, who had the highest respect for the Paramount Leader. (Reportedly, General Zhang Aiping, the former defense minister who had been the comrade-in-arms of Jiang's adoptive father, Jiang Shangqing, gave firm and unwavering support to Jiang Zemin in the early days of his leadership.)

On November 9 Jiang Zemin was elected chairman of the Central Military Commission. He was now head of the two most powerful institutions in the country, the Communist Party and the People's Liberation Army. In name if nothing else, he had control of a military that stood three million strong. Candid and plainspoken, Jiang did not gloss over his nonexistent military record in his acceptance speech. "I said at the previous plenary session that I was not fully prepared when I was elected general secretary of the Central Committee. This time I am not fully prepared, either. I have no experience in military work, and I feel my abilities fall far short of what the position demands. But since the Party has assigned the work to me, I must make every effort to learn about military affairs and familiarize myself as soon as possible with the armed forces and carry out my duty conscientiously and actively."

Although Deng was no longer present at CMC meetings, he was still the behind-the-curtain leader of the country. In a move that would soon have unintended consequences, he arranged that the plenum make two other appointments to the military commission: President Yang Shangkun as CMC first vice chairman, which made him second only to the inexperienced, shaky Jiang Zemin, and General Yang Baibing, Yang Shangkun's overly ambitious younger half-brother, as CMC secretary general, which put him in charge of running daily operations. Yang Baibing was also head of the PLA General Political Department, which controlled army propaganda and could facilitate the promotion of senior officers, including generals. It was because of the power and networking of the two brothers throughout the military that some sarcastically referred to the PLA as Yang Jia Jiang, the Yang Family Army.

Deng had a long comrade-in-arms relationship with Yang Shangkun, who had been a senior army officer since the 1930s. After being purged during the Cultural Revolution, allegedly for eavesdropping on one of Mao's phone conversations, Yang was reinstated by Deng and became an early supporter of his reforms. Deng asked that Yang Shangkun be his personal representative on the CMC, both to demonstrate his continuing involvement and to keep an eye on the untested new chairman. At the same time, the wily Deng had concerns about the noble, respected Yang, who, as the leading senior elder, was regarded as a potential successor to Deng should Deng predecease Yang.

To counteract Yang's influence, Deng arranged for General Liu Huaqing, a former commander of the navy, to be vice chairman of the CMC as well. Analysts saw a rough balance of PLA power between Jiang and Liu on the one hand and the Yang brothers on the other.

Jiang would need all the help he could get, particularly with Yang Baibing, who had a patronizing view of the still green chairman and largely ignored him. He usually did not accompany Jiang on inspections of PLA facilities, a snub that was obvious, and he felt slighted when Jiang didn't give him important assignments. The relationship between the two men grew increasingly tense, which was a gnawing problem for Jiang, since during this period he had little real military power.

Jiang's struggle with the Yang brothers would continue for three years, but before he could confront them, he had to prove himself. His challenge was to modernize an army that was heavy on personnel, light on technology, and short on respect for their new leader. Determined to succeed, Jiang would tour more than one hundred military installations over the next two years, poking into minute aspects of their operations. He studied the lives of ordinary soldiers as well as the strategies of generals and could be seen ambling through barracks and eating army grub. He took special interest in base libraries and insisted that they be stocked with more books.

A story is told how Jiang would practice a militarylike gait the night before reviewing troops. He would march back and forth in his room, pumping his arms precisely and stepping his legs stiffly as he kept a careful eye on the mirror, monitoring posture and expression. Although the story may have been circulated to denigrate Jiang, it epitomized his total commitment to his CMC responsibility. He who underestimated Jiang Zemin would not have the last laugh.

AFTER JUNE 4 PARTY conservatives, led by elder Chen Yun, used their resurgent power to rein in the pace of Deng's reforms, which they assumed were distorting the economy and undermining Communism's ideological purity. Jiang was caught in the middle, appreciating Deng's overall vision but believing in socialist principles and needing the support of conservatives to maintain unity.

Chen believed that the "planned economy is primary, the market economy supplementary" and that deviations in recent years had caused a "mortal wound" to the economy. At the November Party plenum, Chen's views were restored as the Party line and laid out in a thorough, systematic critique of reform. Speaking at the plenum, Jiang asserted that the "greatest lesson" was that the country must not "depart from its national conditions, exceed its national strength, be anxious for success, or have great ups and downs"—ideas consistent with Chen's well-known conservative way of thinking.

In a November seminar with newspaper editors, he took a hard line. "When the mass media depart from Marxism and run counter to the people's interests," Jiang said, "great harm results." Citing the "incidents" of the past spring, he urged the editors to learn from their mistakes. It was their duty, he said, to educate the people in "patriotism, socialism, collectivism, and the spirit of self-reliance and hard struggle." In any country, he told them, there is no such thing as absolute freedom of the press.

Private companies, some of which had supported the student movement with financial aid, were subjected to crippling investigation and public rebuke. Jiang was not a reticent participant in the recidivistic attacks on entrepreneurs. "Self-employed traders and peddlers," he wrote, "cheat, embezzle, bribe, and evade taxation." Under the conservative resurgence, Jiang oversaw the increase of military funding and a reduction in education funding, the kind of policy against which he had protested in 1946. Professors and students at leading universities, particularly in Beijing and Shanghai, were put through reeducation campaigns, which involved physical labor (such as weeding grassy areas on campus) along with political indoctrination.

At year end Jiang visited troops in the Fuzhou Military Region, directly across the straits from Taiwan. In Minxi, a famous revolutionary camp where Mao once held forth, Jiang told Red Army veterans that the "revolutionary ideals" of the Great Helmsman could be achieved by "promoting army ideological work."

"By swearing allegiance to values propagated by Chairman Mao in preliberation years," one Chinese source said, "Jiang is telling today's Party elders and generals that he will always take their interests to heart." Reaching out to the army was starting to work. The PLA's newspaper quoted a Fuzhou-region soldier as saying, "Chairman Jiang has taken time out to see our company. This means he has real feelings for the army." On the same trip Jiang told Party officials, factory managers, and overseas investors that Deng Xiaoping's open-door policy would be accelerated, not delayed. "No matter how the international situation changes," Jiang assured them, "China's reform and open policy will remain unchanged."

The changes to which Jiang was referring were happening in Eastern Europe. In November the Berlin Wall fell, precipitating the collapse of Communism throughout the region. It was said, with some hyperbole, that the anti-Communist revolution took ten years in Poland, ten months in Hungary, ten weeks in East Germany, ten days in Czechoslovakia, and finally, in Romania, ten hours. On Christmas Day the world watched as Romanian dictator Nicolae Ceausescu and his wife, Elena, were executed by a military firing squad, which began shooting even before the order was given.

Ceausescu had been among the first to support the Chinese government's action in Tiananmen Square, and Jiang, who looked back fondly on his so-journ in Romania, had considered him a friend. In Ceausescu's gruesome death, the new general secretary saw a warning.

China's cryogenic relations with America began to thaw, albeit slowly and quietly, in the fall of 1989. United States Ambassador James Lilley began discreetly by reinstating the valuable security relationships that provided intelligence sharing between the two countries and targeted the Soviet Union. Even though he was a "pariah for shielding Fang Lizhi"—the noted astrophysicist and high-profile prodemocracy dissident who had taken refuge in the U.S. Embassy during the military actions in Tiananmen Square—and for representing the country that led the international imposition of sanctions against China, Lilley was able to restart economic activities, such as the sale of Boeing aircraft.

At the time, China desperately sought to obtain U.S. government export approval for a Hughes communication satellite that was supposed to be launched by a Chinese rocket in the spring of 1990. Developing a commercial space launch business was a matter of great importance to the Chinese leadership, both to shore up national prestige and as a lynchpin of their technology development strategy. Ambassador Lilley explained to Washington that "the satellite launch was important to the whole business of opening up China"—he stressed linkage with China's scientific community—and as a result of his intervention, President Bush waived a congressional prohibition in December 1989.

In late October, former President Richard Nixon, honored in China for his pioneering role in reestablishing diplomatic relations with America, came to Beijing to talk bluntly to Chinese leaders. Speaking as an "old friend," Nixon framed his appeal "in terms of reality." A short time later, negotiations began to secure the release of Fang Lizhi and to resume World Bank loans.

On January 10, 1990, Jiang Zemin ordered the end of martial law in Beijing. It was a sign not just of the new year or the new decade but of a whole new era.

Chapter 12

1990 – 1991

"Stability Overrides Everything"

T O THE REST OF THE WORLD, China compared unfavorably to Eastern Europe. When those Communist countries had to decide whether to call in the military or lose power, they all chose the latter, opting against suppressing their citizens in order to prop up their regimes. Several described their decision as "rejecting the Chinese solution." In the Soviet Union, Mikhail Gorbachev was undermining, albeit inadvertently, the authoritarian brand of Marxism in which he himself still believed.

By contrast, China remained true to its Communist roots. "China is surrounded by friendly countries and not by capitalist states," Jiang said at the time. "China was liberated by its own revolutionary army and not by the Soviet Red Army, as had been the case in Eastern Europe." It is an army, Jiang observed, that "has been proven to have substantial fighting power" and "is under the absolute leadership of the Party."

Jiang used the worldwide crisis in Communism to his advantage, solidifying the authority of both the Party and himself. He was cautious about further political reform—a tactical move designed to assuage the fears of senior elders, who blamed such reform for the demise of Communism elsewhere. Jiang also asked the artistic community to "pay attention to the national flavor and style of their works while absorbing good things from foreign cultures," and to create more works that reflect socialist construction and represent the realities of life.

Primarily, though, Jiang reached out to the Party's traditional base of support. In January 1990 he descended a shaft in the Datong coal mine in Shanxi province to bring Spring Festival greetings to the miners and thank them for their hard work. He also visited the miners at home, chatting with everyone.

"If all cadres keep close flesh-and-blood ties with the masses, we will be invincible," he said. In the same month Jiang toured a national athletic training center where he mingled with army teams. After losing a table tennis game with a world-class woman player, Jiang said, "It's not easy to fight a champion."

Just before the Chinese New Year, Jiang invited Shen Yongyan to his home in Zhongnanhai. Shen had come to Beijing to request a loan of 50 million yuan (about $10.6 million) from the People's Bank of China. Timing was critical. First Automotive Works, where Shen had been vice president since 1981, was going through a difficult period and could not pay its workers, which Shen wanted to do before the holiday period. When he explained the situation to Jiang, the general secretary called the governor of the bank, helping to secure the loan.

"I was a little apprehensive as I rode through the fabled deep-red walls of China's center of power," Shen recalled. "Would things be different now, awkward, with my old friend? By then Jiang had been Party general secretary for over six months and was beginning to settle into the position. When I arrived at his home, I barely entered the door when we embraced. Jiang was the same as ever."

Although not feeling well, Jiang's wife, Wang Yeping, also greeted Shen warmly. "I can say this for sure," he said. "She had no lust for power or status; she was hardly euphoric about her husband's newfound position and prestige."

The house where Jiang lived and worked was a small *siheyuan*, a traditional-style four-sided home built around an open courtyard. Modest inside and out, it had once been a residence for guards of the emperor. As Jiang showed him around, Shen noted the simple way in which the family continued to live. Aside from the bedrooms, which included one for Wang Yeping's mother, there was only a small living room, a study, a dining room, and a kitchen. There was a single television set.

Jiang confessed his concern about his wife. "Although I'm the one who became general secretary, she's more nervous than I," he said. "I feel for her: I don't want her getting sick. She says that Party general secretaries end up badly." Although Wang Yeping would never feel at ease in the public eye, she would learn to play her role with poise and grace.

"After the tour, we sat down to a leisurely dinner," Shen continued. "Six dishes and one soup. Wang Yeping ate very little. We had Shaoxin red rice wine—Jiang and I finished one bottle together. He likes wine."

General Secretary Jiang made his first foreign trip in March 1990. The destination was Pyongyang, capital of North Korea, where he greeted "Great Leader" Kim Il-Sung, one of Planet Earth's most totalitarian rulers, in a warm embrace of socialist unity. "I am overjoyed," Jiang said as a mass of forty thousand children shouted slogans of welcome in Chinese and Korean, "to have fulfilled my year-long wish." He then praised "the profound friendship between our two countries."

Held at Kim's urgent request, the discussions focused on "domestic construction and international problems of interest." The two leaders agreed to stick together, no matter what was happening in Eastern Europe, and pledged to maintain socialism in Asia. Though the move reassured China's leaders, Jiang was aware of the fine line he was walking in terms of public opinion at home and abroad. It was a theme that would sound again and again in the early, tentative years of his leadership.

As if to counterbalance the "Great Leader" embrace, Jiang invited thirteen Beijing University students to Zhongnanhai. He shook hands with each as he or she entered Huairen Hall. "I was delighted to receive your letter," he told them. "I planned to write you back, but I thought it better to talk in person. We should exchange our opinions frankly."

After listening to the students speak about topics such as education and the meaning of success, Jiang offered advice that he himself had always followed. "Young people need to combine their own career planning with the needs of the nation," he said. "No one can be useful apart from social, national, and people needs.

"The isolated individual's struggle," he added, "is a dead end."

Once again Jiang showed that he could be progressive while adhering to the Party line.

It was this ability, in part, that won approval for the development of the vast Pudong New Area in eastern Shanghai. When Deng Xiaoping made his annual Chinese New Year's visit to Shanghai in 1990, Wang Daohan, who had responsibility for Pudong's feasibility plan, spoke with him about its urgency. Deng considered the project a priority and was pleased that Jiang was taking responsibility for it. He assigned a secondary role to Li Peng, reaffirming their relative ranks.

Zhao Qizheng, who would become director of Pudong in 1993 (and nicknamed "The Godfather of Pudong"), later explained Jiang's commitment to the New Area. "After Jiang Zemin became mayor of Shanghai," he recalled, "he gave instructions, both strategic and tactical, for the Pudong development plan. After he became general secretary, every time he returned to Shanghai he inspected Pudong. At the 1999 Fortune Forum for international business leaders held in Pudong, President Jiang said, 'Six years ago the Lujiazui area, where we are now, was simple farmland with barely a few houses; today it has become a prosperous financial and trading area with many skyscrapers.' In 2001 Jiang called Pudong 'a microcosm of Shanghai's modernization, and the symbol of Chinese reform and opening-up.' . . .

"In 1997, when he was inspecting Pudong, Jiang was introduced to China's first common utility tunnel," added Zhao Qizheng. "Suddenly he said that he wanted to go underground to see it. People in his party panicked; they explained that the utility tunnel was too narrow and dangerous for a man of his age. 'Please don't go down there,' they implored. 'I was once an engineer,' he answered, 'so I will go down to have a look.' Though not a thin man, he stepped down the steep ladder, walked about fifty meters, and said, 'Very good, I now understand this new advance in city infrastructure construction.' "

IF PUDONG WERE TO attract substantial foreign investment, its laws and structures would have to conform to international standards. But no matter how many characteristics of capitalism such reforms took on, Deng and Jiang continued to view themselves and their policies as socialist in nature. For them, the difference between capitalism and socialism lay not in the presence or absence of markets or state planning but in the public ownership of assets and enterprises and in the ultimate goal of society.

Even so, while conservatives continued to worry that Communism's traditional values were being eroded, Jiang sought to achieve harmony between development and ideology. "Economic development and ideological integrity must not be set against each other," he said. "We must persevere in reform and opening-up, and at the same time we must also resolutely resist the corrosive influence of decadent capitalist ideology. These are two sides to the same coin."

The first anniversary of the Tiananmen tragedy loomed. One month before, on the seventy-first anniversary of the May Fourth Movement, Jiang sought reconciliation by praising China's twenty million "intellectuals." "We should welcome those comrades," he said, "who made some wrong remarks and did some inappropriate things at that time when they were not clear about the truth, but now have seen things in a new light and learned a lesson. As for those comrades who still fail to find new understanding of the issues, we should continue to help them warmheartedly and wait patiently."

Jiang continued to oppose "bourgeois liberalization" and to promote the "hundred flowers" call for open expression of diverse ideas. To Westerners, the two policies were contradictory; to Jiang, they were complementary. Opposing bourgeois liberalization, he asserted, did not mean slowing reform and opening to the outside world. Rather, he explained, it helped ensure their success by maintaining stability.

As for the "hundred flowers," Jiang urged different schools of arts and sciences to contest with one another, but he cautioned that creative and academic freedom must not be used as an excuse to violate the Four Cardinal Principles: the Socialist road, the people's democratic dictatorship, the leadership of the Communist Party, and ideology based on Marxist-Leninist and Mao Zedong Thought. Although to Westerners this constraint put a stringent, even laughable limitation on true academic freedom, Jiang genuinely believed that promoting diverse ideas and preserving Communist control were compatible. Notwithstanding the constraint, he knew that creative competition in the marketplace of ideas empowered social progress and needed to be encouraged.

In the month before the Tiananmen anniversary, Jiang agreed to be interviewed by Barbara Walters on ABC Television. When she inquired about the crackdown, he explained that "the PLA exercised maximum restraint, as proven [he said] by the fact that nearly a thousand military trucks and armored cars, including tanks, were burned at the time," adding, "Had we failed to adopt resolute measures, the entire capital of China would have been thrown into chaos, resulting in a national disaster.

"However, we should learn some lessons from the experience," he continued. "As a Chinese proverb goes, 'A fall into the pit, a gain in your wit.' " Jiang said that in future incidents riot police would use nonlethal weapons to maintain order. He also paid his respects to those PLA soldiers who died in the battle. "We cherish their memory," he said.

"At the same time," he added, "our government at all levels has shown great concern about those people wounded or killed by accident." Referring to the famous photograph of the lone man staring down a long line of tanks on Chang'an Avenue, he said, "That picture is a case in point. How could the tanks have been stopped by a young man? Because they would never roll over him, that's how!"

Walters asked Jiang about Fang Lizhi, who was still hiding in the U.S. Embassy in Beijing almost a year after being targeted as China's most wanted "counterrevolutionary criminal" for his role in the 1989 protests. Jiang asserted that Fang's fate touched the nerve of Chinese sovereignty and dignity. "Fang Lizhi is wanted under Chinese law," Jiang said stiffly. "He was one of the backstage manipulators in the incident of last year. He and his wife were both behind-the-scene plotters.

"There can only be two preconditions for the settlement of the issue," continued Jiang. "First, Fang Lizhi must admit his guilt, and second, the United States should ensure that he will not do anything against the People's Republic of China in the future. Fang Lizhi is a criminal wanted by China, and yet he has fled to a foreign embassy and secured protection there. So how do you think the Chinese feel? We won't return to old times; the Qing dynasty is gone forever! Beginning in 1949, the Chinese people have finally stood up."

Though his words sounded harsh—to Jiang they were patriotic, essential for restoring China's wounded pride—he was actually pointing a way out of the maze by laying down two conditions for Fang's release. The standoff, a stumbling block to both sides, had helped confine China–U.S. relations to the cellar. Jiang wanted a way out, but only a way with sovereignty and dignity.

At the conclusion of the interview, Jiang softened his tone, shifted to English, and reached out to his audience. "Despite the present difficulties in Sino-U.S. relations," he told Walters, "I am convinced that the American people will gradually come to understand what really happened in China last year and support our joint efforts toward the restoration of normal bilateral relations."

On June 4, 1990, the *People's Daily* headline said it all: "Stability Overrides Everything."

WHEN SADDAM HUSSEIN INVADED Kuwait in August 1990, Jiang dedicated several Politburo Standing Committee meetings to assessing the international ramifications. He asked Foreign Minister Qian Qichen to lead the discussions, which focused unsurprisingly on suspicions that the United States was taking advantage of the situation to pursue its "hegemonistic" goal of controlling Persian Gulf oil reserves. Although China ultimately supported United Nations resolutions backed by the United States, it sought to pursue its own interests, which at this time centered on reestablishing China's image as a respected, major power little more than one year after the televised tragedy of Tiananmen.

The swift American victory in Desert Storm early in 1991 shocked Chinese military leaders, who had expected the United States to become bogged down fighting in the unfamiliar desert terrain. Jiang, in particular, took great interest in the startling advances of high-tech weaponry. He was fascinated by the photographs and sought to learn all he could about specific weapons systems. China's armed forces, he realized, were not in the same league. From this time forward, modernizing China's military would become one of Jiang Zemin's primary pursuits.

IN NOVEMBER, ON THE TENTH anniversary of the establishment of the Special Economic Zones, Jiang attended celebrations in Shenzhen and Zhuhai. On the three-hour flight back to Beijing, accompanied by senior officials including Wen Jiabao, Jiang was eager to discuss China's early, limited experiments with the stock market. The idea was controversial—some called it "bourgeois liberalism."

"General Secretary Jiang asked me many questions," recalled Liu Hongru, who would later become the first chairman of the China Securities Regulatory Commission, "and he took many notes."

"Where does the stock market's money come from?" Jiang inquired.

"Ninety-five percent of the money comes from individual investors," Liu stated, hastening to add that the fundamental ownership of the companies did not change "since over sixty percent of the equity still be owned by the State or collective organizations."

"When stock prices go up," Jiang continued, "who makes money, and who suffers losses?"

Liu explained that the pricing of stocks was determined by the market theory of supply and demand. Since only five companies had been selected for China's experiment, too much money was chasing too few stocks. "The demand is very strong, and that's why prices are continuing to go up," Liu said, adding, "This is not realistic."

Jiang also asked about supervision and regulation, specifically what to do when government officials and Party members bought stocks.

At the end of the flight, Liu told Jiang, "No matter what, we should continue our stock market experiment—our reform must not go backward. Please trust me, as an old Party member, I would not carelessly push for privatization. But since mistakes are unavoidable, I hope that we don't punish people or affix political labels. If that happens, no one would be willing to take responsibility."

Jiang agreed to continue the stock market but cautioned that it be carefully studied and not expanded further until China gained more experience.

THROUGHOUT THE YEAR JIANG traversed the country on "inspection tours"—to Hainan province in May, to Tibet in July, to Xinjiang in August, to Liaoning in October, to Guanxi in November. By the beginning of 1991, the year he turned sixty-five, he had circumnavigated much of the nation's frontiers in a high-energy effort to show that the Communist Party was firmly in charge and he was its new leader. He came face to face with the grinding poverty of the country's peasants and looked to improve their conditions. Such poverty, he was told, was due in part to the excessive fees and fines levied by local officials for trumped-up, and in some cases illegal, reasons. The sordid practice became a new target in Jiang's fight against corruption.

Tibet, with its restive minority, had been taken by Communist China's army in 1950 (retaken, many Chinese say). The area had been named the Tibet Autonomous Region in 1965, a move that allowed for the expression of local customs and rites but failed to satisfy the Tibetan people's desire for independence. In March 1989 anti-Chinese demonstrations broke out in Lhasa, Tibet's capital. The local Party secretary, Hu Jintao, imposed martial law. When Jiang visited, the order had been lifted for only ten weeks.

Jiang hoped to leave Tibetans with good feelings about his administration. To aid the local economy, he approved building a new airport and promised to assign more technocrats to the region. At the same time he warned leaders to take sterner measures against "separatists."

Throughout the vast country, but primarily along China's long borders, there are pockets of minorities whose diverse cultures, languages, and religions are seen as a potential threat to political stability. For example, Xinjiang province in the northwest is predominantly Muslim and has its own special needs and problems. Jiang urged all ethnicities to "resolutely fight against division and turmoil," while also granting that "the regional autonomy of minority nationalities should be improved."

In October, continuing his "army work," Jiang boarded an escort vessel of the North China Sea fleet. After inspecting the command room, he said, "Let's go see the kitchen." Everyone advised him against it. "The gangway ladder is too narrow for you," the officers told him, "and the temperature inside the kitchen is too hot. You had better not go." Jiang was undeterred as he climbed down the ladder to visit the kitchen, which was "as small as a birdcage."

Jiang played host at the Asian Games, which were held in August 1990 in Beijing. He called the event an unprecedented sports meet for the continent and said that the games would further the friendship among Asian peoples. Significantly, it was Jiang, not Deng, who lit the symbolic opening-night flame in Tiananmen Square.

Still, after over a year in office, the general secretary had little real power independent of his colleagues. Li Peng ran the State Council and could make decisions without advising him. Other members of the Politburo Standing Committee ran their own spheres of interest, such as Li Ruihuan, who had propaganda and media, and Qiao Shi, who controlled Party organization, discipline, and internal security. And the elders, particular Deng Xiaoping, were actively involved in setting policy and advising on governance.

When Jiang met with foreign dignitaries, he would consult with other senior leaders. When Jiang gave a speech, it would be circulated to all members of the Standing Committee for their comments, and each would have to sign off by affixing his signature. If a member had issues or questions, he would note them directly on the document in his own handwriting and expect an explanation or resolution. If the matter was serious or remained unresolved, he could call a formal meeting of the Standing Committee to adjudicate it.

Such collegiality and the requirement of advice and consent are the operating hallmark of China's collective leadership system—indeed they epitomize the normal practice of how the Party's kind of democracy and checks and balances work at its highest level. Nonetheless, during Jiang's early years in office, he was particularly deferential to his colleagues, more solicitous of their opinions and support than he would be in later years. Though he would always recognize and respect the Party's system of collective leadership, as his power grew Jiang Zemin would increasingly assert his own individuality.

Jiang's early-years strategy was simple. First, he had to protect his position; for this he needed the continuing support of Deng Xiaoping and leading elders Li Xiannian and Chen Yun. Second, he had to establish an independent source of power; he worked this by whirlwind trips to the provinces, reaching out to the military, and appealing to the masses through the media. Third, he had to seize opportunities to promote his own people. But everything hinged on the first step; without that lifeline of elder support, he would be adrift.

Accordingly, Jiang kept in close touch with all three patriarchs, visiting them frequently and seeking their advice. Jiang met frequently with Deng throughout 1990, including in December when China's still–Paramount Leader expressed satisfaction for the previous eighteen months. When Jiang arranged for Wu Bangguo to become Party secretary of Shanghai in 1991, he asked him to pay special attention to the three elders whenever they visited Shanghai. "General Secretary Jiang is an extremely savvy man," said one of Jiang's old Yangzhou schoolmates. "He doesn't call attention to himself as long as the elders are still around."

In Jiang's favor was Deng's mounting frustration with the country's sluggish growth and stagnant reforms. The problem, to Deng, was conservative policies. A Party plenum in December 1990 stressed the "integration of the planned economy with market regulation" and reiterated conservative ideas such as "sustained, stable, and coordinated" development and "acting according to one's capability."

Deng was fed up. With little support in Beijing, he decided to go to Shanghai to give some talks, which were then summarized in four articles that appeared in *Liberation Daily*, the Shanghai Party newspaper, between February and April 1991. The articles written under a pen name but unabashedly reflecting Deng's views, blasted "ossified thinking," ridiculed concerns about whether policies were part of socialism or capitalism, promoted vigorous economic expansion, and admonished Shanghai leaders to "courageously take a risk, boldly use foreign capital." Counterattacks were published in Beijing suggesting that Deng's approach, though not Deng himself, represented "bourgeois liberalization." On March 1, Deng and Jiang met privately at Deng's residence, possibly discussing these matters.

With Deng's support, Jiang focused on the economy. When advising State Council planners who were drafting China's eighth five-year plan, he stressed science and technology, which would become a recurrent theme. The Gulf War demonstrated the importance of high-tech weaponry and reinforced Jiang's belief that electronics were vital to the country's military strength and international competitiveness. As a result, he sought closer links between industry and defense in developing advanced electronics. No one else among China's leaders had better credentials for the new, science-based world of commerce and warfare, an expertise that enabled Jiang to expand his influence.

In February Jiang offered a visiting Soviet leader financial credits so that the impoverished Soviet Union could purchase Chinese goods. It was a propaganda windfall for the Party, substantiating the claim that Chinese-style socialism was superior to Soviet "revisionism." Personally, it was a satisfying turn of events for Jiang, who recalled China's near-total dependence on Soviet aid, and how his own automotive plant had suffered, thirty years earlier, when the Soviets pulled out their advisers.

Jiang was constantly engaged in diplomacy, meeting with innumerable visiting delegations. In just one month, April 1991, he met officials from Britain, Cambodia, Papua New Guinea, Syria, Nigeria, Australia, Tunisia, and the Soviet Union. He also hosted former U.S. president Jimmy Carter and countless Chinese groups.

Still steaming at the glacial pace of reform, Deng Xiaoping arranged for the enterprising Zhu Rongji, then Party secretary of Shanghai, to become vice premier. Zhu's portfolio on the State Council was industry, agriculture, and finance. In spite of their personality differences, Jiang and Zhu had worked well together in Shanghai. An ardent reformer, Zhu would become a strong counterweight to Li Peng and other conservatives. This rebalanced the State Council so that on matters of policy Jiang could now assume a centrist position without actually having to change any of his views.

A few months later, in a quiet move approved by both Deng Xiaoping and Jiang Zemin, three senior officials who had been purged along with Zhao Ziyang—Politburo Standing Committee member Hu Qili and Secretariat members Yan Mingfu and Rui Xingwen (Rui had been Shanghai Party chief when Jiang was mayor)—were rehabilitated (though to lower positions). It was another sign that China was returning to a progressive path.

Moreover, Party hardliners were starting to accept Jiang as the boss. Interviewed by a Mexican newspaper, Li Peng said Jiang had "acquitted himself well in the major leadership position [Party general secretary]," adding, "He is very learned." A few weeks later Vice President Wang Zhen, a staunch conservative, offered the opinion that Jiang "is well-versed in Marxism and Mao Zedong Thought. His faith in Communism is firm, and he has broad knowledge."

Though Jiang spoke of reform, there was little in his economic pronouncements to which conservatives could object. In his July 1, 1991, speech on the seventieth anniversary of the Communist Party, Jiang called for ideological struggle to oppose peaceful evolution, stressed that state-owned enterprises are the "backbone strength" of socialism, and warned that "shaking public ownership of the means of production" would undermine socialism and harm the people.

As THE SECOND ANNIVERSARY of Tiananmen approached, Jiang took a five-day trip to Moscow, the first Party leader to visit the city since Mao Zedong's trip in 1957. The purpose, Jiang said, was "to continue to develop the good-neighborly and friendly relations" with the USSR. After four years of negotiations, the two countries resolved contentious border disputes; they also issued a joint communiqué increasing ties in a variety of fields. Jiang's 1991 trip to Moscow paralleled Gorbachev's 1989 trip to Beijing, the May dates coinciding precisely.

For Jiang, one of the highlights of the trip was his return to the huge automotive plant where thirty-five years earlier he had worked as an intern. In a meeting with management, Jiang thanked the factory for training seven hundred technical personnel for China. Then he dispensed with formalities and using his rusty but functional Russian reminisced with old friends.

One elderly woman showed him a photo of a thirty-year-old Jiang posing with a pretty young Russian girl. "That's me!" said the woman. "Do you remember?" She turned the photo over to point out Jiang's signature on the back. Another worker from the power control room said that most of those with whom Jiang had worked were now retired, but they sent their warm regards. The general secretary, the worker confided to reporters, had been "very popular with women."

Analysts speculated that Jiang's visit would usher in a new era in Sino-Soviet cooperation. They were wrong. No agreement was reached on the sale of Soviet aircraft and military technology to China, and the two countries now had radically different approaches to socialism. More significantly, the Soviet Union would soon cease to exist. When Jiang bade farewell in Moscow, he bade farewell to the old era.

On August 19, 1991, hardline politicians in the Kremlin, desperate to maintain Party supremacy, took Gorbachev captive in an ill-fated, hamhanded coup attempt. Jiang, who was visiting west China's Qinghai province at the time, returned immediately to Beijing. Deng Xiaoping called a meeting the next day, August 20, to assess the still-murky situation in Moscow with Jiang, President Yang Shangkun, Premier Li Peng, and Foreign Minister Qian Qichen. Some Chinese leaders were privately pleased at the resurgence of conservative forces in the Soviet Union, even hailing the coup as a "good deed," but they were aghast just two days later when Boris Yeltsin, backed by overwhelming mass support, pulled the coup plotters back down and broke the back of the Communist Party. Although Gorbachev was reinstated, the Soviet Union never recovered. In a few months, it would implode and disintegrate, a seventy-year experiment in Communism failed and finished.

The lesson was not lost on China's leaders. Over the next several months as the Communist Party was declared illegal and the Soviet Union collapsed, Jiang held high-level meetings to discuss the possible impact on China. As if by reflex, reformist moves were slowed. Even though Deng suggested that

Chinese leaders might be overreacting to foreign events, a new level of caution was indicated.

There was heated debate about "peaceful evolution," the (supposed) insidious plan of the West (particularly America) to overthrow the socialist system in China by subtle social transformation, not overt military action. Arguments raged over whether Deng's reforms were leading the country through a "peaceful evolution" to capitalism.

For his part, Jiang sought underlying reasons for the Soviet demise. Socialism, he concluded, was not one of them. Instead, he attributed the collapse to mishandling the diverse nationalities and ethnic groups within the vast union. He was convinced that the Soviets had placed too much emphasis on political reform and not enough on economic reform—too much *glasnost* (openness) and not enough *perestroika* (restructuring). In China the priorities were reversed. Even conservatives agreed: Only a thriving economy could keep the Party in power.

"We must gradually aim at the separation of the functions of government and enterprise," Jiang said in a speech supporting Deng's reforms. "We must cut down on unnecessary administrative interference in enterprises, so that they can have autonomy in management and be financially self-sufficient." The speech confirmed Jiang's entry into economic policymaking, solidified his centrist position, and indicated his growing power.

In October Kim Il-Sung, North Korea's "Great Leader," arrived in Beijing for a ten-day visit. Taking his guest through China's largest television manufacturing joint venture, Jiang hinted that Kim should consider economic reforms and foreign investment. The ritual cliché that China and North Korea were "as close as lips and teeth" was omitted from official accounts, a move suggesting that China was preparing to establish closer ties with prosperous South Korea. On a side trip Jiang took North Korea's president-for-life to his hometown of Yangzhou to show him the memorial to Shi Kefa, his hero.

JIANG WAS BECOMING acculturated to his position and increasingly comfortable with his status, and he followed established norms of behavior. For example, each summer he continued the tradition of China's senior leaders traveling to Beidaihe, the seaside resort on the Bohai Sea about 200 miles east of Beijing, where along with holiday recreations, beach sports, and personal camaraderie, they held political discussions, set Party policies, made national plans, and came to agreement on sensitive personnel promotions and retirements. According to journalist Jasper Becker, special "air-conditioned trains carrying wives, children, grandchildren, nannies, secretaries, advisers, academic specialists, cooks, drivers, and the entire palace guard arrive at a station cordoned off by armed and helmeted soldiers." The leadership compound of "porticoed mansions . . . that resemble Louisiana houses . . . [were set] within a six-mile stretch of closed-off beach . . . [where] every place in the sun is determined according to Party hierarchy" (the West Beach being reserved for Jiang Zemin, the Politburo Standing Committee, and senior generals).

Yet as a result of position, protocol, and constant public attention, Jiang had come to feel that his life was no longer his own, and he complained about the personal strictures to Shen Yongyan.

"He has no control of his own clothes," Shen observed. "He often has no idea of what he must wear." During one of Shen's visits to Zhongnanhai, an aide interrupted the two men as they were finishing dinner to tell Jiang that he needed to change his clothes for the next function. "I asked if I could tag along," Shen recalled with a smile. "When we walked into Jiang's bedroom, his clothes were already laid out for him. Because he was meeting with workers, he dutifully took off his Western sports jacket and started putting on the high-buttoned Mao jacket. But Jiang's aide, as if a schoolteacher talking to a seven-year-old, said softly but curtly, 'No, you must change your shirt as well.' Even his shoes were chosen for him."

With so many constraints on his freedom, Jiang needed relaxation. He also needed exercise. Every day he tried to have a good walk around Zhongnanhai, after which he would swim in the same pool that Mao Zedong had used.

It was during this period that some of the elegant, traditional Chinese buildings in Zhongnanhai—the former home of emperors and the current seat of power—were renovated and refurbished, particularly those that served as venues for meeting foreign dignitaries. For Jiang Zemin, restoring these intricate exemplars of Chinese civilization was a step toward restoring China as an international leader—a goal seemingly far in the future.

One of the renovated buildings was a teahouse that opened directly onto the South Lake, across which one could see the Great Hall of the People in Tiananmen Square. Jiang Zemin went to this special place on August 15, at the time of the Moon Festival—a sentimental, reflective occasion—to watch the full moon and its reflection on the lake. One can imagine Jiang remembering the poems of his youth as he contemplated the beauty of the scene and the prospects for China.

During his first years in office, Jiang was developing his own style, distinct from those of his predecessors. Under his direction China was entering a period that some have labeled "neoauthoritarianism," a philosophy where a strong central government accelerates economic development while limiting political freedom in order to keep society focused on the all-consuming goal of growth. An instinctive believer in this approach (though not in the label), Jiang tightened controls on the media and strengthened China's internal security forces.

"It took less than a year to assuage my concerns," stated Wang Daohan. "I was surprised how quickly I became confident that Jiang would be able to sustain his position and accomplish his goals. I was greatly relieved! Of course, Deng Xiaoping was still alive and he promised he would provide all needed support."

Jiang did not wield in-your-face authority. Rather, he quietly, methodically worked to establish himself as China's supreme leader. Where he felt he had to be uncompromising, he was resolute. When it came to the plight of the poor, he was compassionate. When it came to the yearnings of intellectuals, he was empathetic. When it came to the struggles of managers and workers, he understood their problems. At one time or another, Jiang Zemin had lived in most of China's worlds. Yet he still relied on the elders, sought consensus, appeased factions, watched rivals, and promoted his people. Jiang Zemin was a man for this season.

Chapter 13

1992

"Bold Explorations and Accelerated Reform"

BEFORE HE DIED, DENG Xiaoping yearned to see China irreversibly on the road to greatness. He was not pleased with the current pace of development, slowed by the conservative tide after Tiananmen. As 1992 began, the eighty-seven-year-old Paramount Leader decided to force matters into the open, and he did it by barnstorming around southern China stumping for reform. His passionate, personal journey would resuscitate China and revitalize Jiang Zemin.

When Deng boarded his special eight-car train at Beijing's central railroad station on the morning of January 17, he was a private citizen, traveling with his wife, Zhuo Lin, and two of his daughters, Deng Rong and Deng Lin. Doctors had advised the increasingly infirm old man not to go, and though Deng continued to be revered as an icon, his actual power and influence had diminished. Even the Chinese press, which had in the past covered Deng's every step, would publish no reports on his grand excursion for almost two months.

Deng had been enjoying his retirement, dining with his large family and playing bridge, a game at which he excelled. It was from this life of leisure, and with failing senses, that Deng Xiaoping emerged one last time to do political battle. For China to take its place among the world's great nations, Deng knew that its economic base would have to expand dramatically, and to breathe new life into the economy, Deng told confidants, he needed to leave Beijing. He chose to head south, to the Special Economic Zones (SEZs) that he had established in Guangdong province, where he expected to find strong support for his reformist ideas. From then on Deng's trip would be known as *Nanxun,* which means "Southern Tour" but connotes something grander, along the lines of "Imperial Inspection Tour of the South."

At his first stop in Wuhan, Deng got right to the point. "Here's what our problem is right now," he said when Hubei provincial leaders met him at the train station (in his private railroad car). "Our leaders look like they're doing something, but they're not doing anything really worthwhile. When I watch television, all I see are meetings and ceremonies. Our leaders must think they're television stars." In a verbal message, sent through the Hubei Party chief, to the Central Committee in Beijing, Deng drew a line in the sand. "Anyone who is against reform," he warned, "will be put out of his office." Deng was contesting for the soul of the Party; this time he was not turning back.

Jiang was shocked. Although long recognizing the need to reform, he believed in socialism's core tenets of state ownership and central planning and he generally agreed with his conservative colleagues that reforms should be measured and unhurried. Now he was conflicted and uncertain: Jiang Zemin was at a crossroads.

Two days later Jiang told officials that the whole Party should "liberate their thoughts" and quicken the steps of reform and the open-door policy. "We have to greatly develop advanced technology and promote economic construction with one heart and one mind." He stressed that it was imperative to "aggressively cut back nonessential meetings and reduce excessive routine functions."

Just days before Deng departed, Jiang had urged Shanghai to "accelerate reform and opening to the outside world" and "take new steps in deepening reforms." A week later he called on Party cadres to be honest and frugal in order to build trust among the masses. "We have to change the working style of the leadership at various levels," he said.

In Shenzhen, a birthplace of China's economic miracle, Deng spoke to an enthusiastic crowd. "The success of Shenzhen clearly proves there was no need to worry whether we are following 'socialism' or 'capitalism.' Only suspicious people raise the question and they are self-defeated. From now on, we should increase foreign investment, form more joint ventures, and take advantage of Western technology and management. Don't worry! Some critics think that we may sink into capitalism sooner or later, but they have no common sense.

"These [foreign joint venture] firms make profits under our law, pay taxes, and provide our workers with jobs and pay," Deng added. "What's wrong with that?" He warned, "If we don't continue to improve people's living standard, if we don't continue to build the economy, there will only be a dead-end road for our Party."

Upon his departure, Deng addressed the Shenzhen Party secretary publicly, saying, "You must speed up development!" It was an astonishing statement. Nowhere else in China was reform moving as fast as it was in Shenzhen. Critics in Beijing often pointed to the city as a case study of what happens when reform moves *too* fast. Now Deng was telling Shenzhen leaders to move even faster. He took up a metaphor used by Mao: "We must not act like women with bound feet," he said.

"Certainly we must watch that we don't deviate to the Right," Deng said at his next stop in Zhuhai. "But deviating to the Left is an even greater danger that we must prevent." He again called for opponents of reform to step down—a remark that cut a wide swath. Some thought Deng was targeting Li Peng, who as premier was in charge of the economy. Others claimed Jiang Zemin was not exempt, even though he had been speaking out vigorously for reform. "Whoever is against reform," Deng repeated, "will be driven out of power."

But Deng was even-handed. "The present central leadership," he said, using the code phrase for Jiang Zemin, "has done a good job . . . Of course," he added, "there are still many problems, but problems exist at any time."

In Guangdong, Deng was met by his old comrade-in-arms, President Yang Shangkun, and his power-minded brother, General Yang Baibing. The Yang brothers came to "escort and protect the emperor [Deng]," backing Deng's stance on reform and hoping to set themselves apart from those in Beijing. Could Deng's frustration mean he might change the central leadership? If such rumors ever materialized, the Yang brothers wanted to be close by.

As Deng's train rolled across southern China, and the Paramount Leader kept speaking out bluntly, the mainland media's silence became problematic. Hong Kong reporters were tailing Deng all along his route, capturing every comment, but not a single item appeared in any mainland paper. Some decision on high had been made to suppress the big news.

Uncertain of where Deng's Southern Tour would lead, no one in Beijing wanted to get trapped in a definitive position. Yet word of his travels and incisive commentary was becoming widespread, and the awkward absence of press was causing senior leadership to lose credibility. (While the Politburo agreed on February 12 to allow a limited dissemination of Deng's remarks to senior officials—hoping that Deng would be satisfied and his ideas contained—the wily patriarch used local papers in Shanghai and Shenzhen to give his views first exposure in the mainland media.) Deng Xiaoping was on a crusade, and many now knew it.

Jiang decided to go public with his support, but he did not abandon his characteristic caution. Not only did he believe that Deng's position was correct, but he also figured that the Paramount Leader would prevail. Pressure was building within the Party to support his call for reform. At the Chinese New Year, Jiang placed a telephone call to Deng, who was in Shanghai, and wished him well. The well-publicized conversation made no reference to Deng's Nanxun, but the timing was not accidental. Nor was Jiang's New Year's speech, when he called for "bold explorations" and "accelerated reforms."

It wasn't enough. Hearsay and rumor swirled that Deng might remove Jiang Zemin as general secretary and Li Peng as premier at the Fourteenth Party Congress in the fall, and replace them, respectively, with Qiao Shi as "core" (Party general secretary, president, and military chairman) and a "steadfast" liberal like Li Ruihuan or Zhu Rongji as premier. (Qiao himself spoke of "some leading comrades" who feign support for reform; he advised them to step down from power.) How close Deng really came to dismissing Jiang during this sensitive time is a matter of speculation, but Deng *was* deadly serious about market reforms, and anyone impeding (or seeming to impede) progress would not last in leadership.

No doubt Jiang was concerned. Irrespective of hearsay and rumor, he knew that Deng's Southern Tour (Nanyun) comments were being interpreted as critical of him. He realized that his skewing to the more conservative views of the elders and his Politburo colleagues in Beijiing was, in the light of Deng's onslaught, no longer the most stable position to hold. Furthermore, down deep Jiang was an economic reformer, even if not with Deng's missionary zeal.

Jiang Zemin decided to take action. Deng's Southern Tour had become a test of his leadership and he was not about to fail it. After strategizing with Zeng Qinghong, who had an exquisite political sense, Jiang reached agreement with Li Peng, an erstwhile rival but now equally vulnerable, to accelerate reform. Over the next few months, they would authorize a slew of papers promoting Deng's speeches, perhaps twenty or more. Jiang had made his decision to back Deng and he was not going to be half-hearted about doing it.

To begin, the Party Central Committee, under Jiang's aegis, prepared a paper that summarized Deng's main ideas. On February 28 "The Notice About Passing On and Studying Comrade Deng's Important Talks" was circulated to Party branches throughout the country. The Central Party School, the citadel of advanced Communist thought, distributed written copies of Deng's talks to two thousand students and faculty. With its network of alumni in key positions throughout the country, the Party School was an ideal vehicle to propagate the new policy.

The final breakthrough came in early March. In a two-day, all-member Politburo meeting, Deng's Nanxun speeches were studied carefully, and in one of its most important decisions ever, the Politburo agreed to endorse his words and ideas.

Although the decision was said to be unanimous, and everyone indeed supported it in public, there were sharp differences hashed out in private. President Yang Shangkun, Deng's longtime friend, began forcefully by advocating that the Party's highest body ratify Deng's reforms. Jiang immediately supported Yang and in a candid and effective talk admitted that he himself had been lax in promoting reform. The more conservative members of the Politburo, realizing that they were now outmaneuvered, sought to limit the damage by arguing that Deng's admonition to "guard against Leftism" applied only to the field of economics.

Nonetheless, from this moment forward Deng's Nanxun commentaries would be considered the "great guidelines" of reform and development in China, the essence of socialist modernization, and the theme of the forthcoming Fourteenth Party Congress. The whole Party and country, the Politburo now asserted, should study seriously Deng Xiaoping's important statements on building socialism with Chinese characteristics.

The next day, March 11, six weeks after Deng Xiaoping's Southern Tour, the official Xinhua News Agency finally reported the fact of its occurrence. It was the lead story. "We must be more daring in opening and reform," read the article. Deng's Nanxun had become the policy of the Party.

Encouraged by the new thinking, intellectuals and army leaders mounted their own campaigns to combat Leftist dogma and oppressiveness. Deng and Jiang loyalists formed investigative teams called "work groups" to expose and eliminate Leftist influences in major newspapers such as *People's Daily* and *Guangming Daily*.

Jiang proclaimed the new vision with zeal, lacing his speeches with quotes from Deng and calling for rapid reform virtually every time he spoke. In May he asked the Politburo to be more enthusiastic about Deng's talks and ideas, and in June he gave a pathbreaking speech to the graduating class of the Central Party School.

In his intensely scrutinized address, Jiang declared that any Party official who criticized or altered Deng's policies "could be sacked at any time." Although Jiang castigated decadent Western values, he criticized Leftism for equating reform with "going down the capitalistic road," and he refuted Maoists for arguing that the central task of the Party was not economic development but "class struggle."

In parts of the speech, Jiang's language was almost identical to that used by Deng during his Southern Tour. Transcripts were circulated throughout the Party and to all units of the armed forces (PLA), and were made required reading for "conscientious study."

The speech hinted at greater change to come. Jiang said that at the Fourteenth Party Congress, to be held in September, the current phrase "socialist commodity economy" would be replaced by the blatantly reformist "socialist market economy." In a culture attuned to slight shifts in wording, the new term was an ideological bombshell. Descriptions of things political were always sensitive and conversions had to be made with caution. After decades of anti-Rightist, capitalist-bashing propaganda, too abrupt a change in language could be disruptive.

How had the bellwether phrase "socialist market economy" come about? Jiang had concluded that a new label was needed for China's new system, and after considering many options he just decided that this was the one he liked best. The word "market" needed to emerge prominently, but it also needed to be consistent with a socialist system.

Three days after Jiang gave his Party School speech, he went to Deng Xiaoping's home to request the Paramount Leader's agreement to use "socialist market economy" as the new banner of reform. Jiang had not consulted Deng prior to the speech. Ever since Deng's Southern Tour (Nanxun), it was up to Jiang to figure it out for himself. In this sense, Deng's Nanxun was indeed a test for Jiang, and his Party School speech was his final exam.

The phrase was a natural for Deng. For years he had been saying that capitalist systems have planning and socialist systems have markets, and that the Party should stop debating theoretical distinctions between capitalism and socialism. Chen Yun and Li Xiannian, also consulted after the speech, agreed as well. Deng then concluded, "If everyone agrees, we have a theme [for the Fourteenth Party Congress]. We don't want to waste time with further debate." Although it would take another year for the phrase "socialist market economy" to become China's official guiding principle, there was no doubt that reform had entered, in the words of a *China Daily* editorial, an "unprecedented new phase."

"Jiang's Party School speech was extremely sensitive," recalled Teng Wensheng, his chief speechwriter. "It was coming just after Deng's Nanxun and had to reflect his reformist ideas, but the Party and the country were not prepared for such new thinking. There was resistance; many different constituencies had to be considered. As such, Jiang set his [oratorical] tone as that of a discussant, not a directive giver. He had to build consensus."

Jiang had set a precedent. In preparing Party leaders for new policy at a Party congress every five years, he would first float the idea in a speech at the Central Party School in the spring, allowing it to be discussed widely, so that when the new policy was formally presented at the Party congress in the fall, it would already be accepted.

Once the Chinese media were permitted to report on Deng's Nanxun, his every step became a political earthquake, his every word a revealed truth. Virtually every report about public affairs contained references to Deng's "Imperial Tour of the South." Mainland writers now gushed over Deng, calling the new round of reform "a warm spring wave that spread over all China, clearing away people's hesitation, anxiety, and doubt." Provinces across China sought new ways to reform. The entire nation was upshifting into the fast lane. From 1992 on China's growth rates would lead the world.

In 1992 China's GDP grew an unprecedented 12.8 percent, a number that far exceeded Li Peng's estimated 6 percent. Though such white-hot growth would bring serous problems, especially inflation and increased corruption, it would turn China into an economic superpower whose modernization and prosperity would astound the world. Had it not been for Deng Xiaoping's Nanxun and its early support by Jiang Zemin, such development might not have happened for years—if at all.

When Deng told audiences to "watch out for the Right, but mainly defend against the Left," he was making an explicit, final break with the Party's rigid, doctrinaire, ultra-Leftist past. Though Deng was rejecting Maoist mass movements with all their ideological strictures, he believed he was enhancing—not rejecting—the original essence of Mao Zedong Thought. From the beginning of Deng's transformations in 1978 to his Southern Tour in 1992, China had continued to debate political ideology, crossing the river of reform, in Deng's metaphor, "stone by stone." After 1992 the debate was over, the path was clear, and the speed was swift.

"I can't imagine what China would be like today," one senior leader said a decade later, "had not Deng Xiaoping made his Nanxun."

JIANG VISITED JAPAN IN APRIL to celebrate the twentieth anniversary of Sino-Japanese diplomatic ties. Promoting economic cooperation with businessmen eager to enter the Chinese market, he visited Matsushita Electric (Panasonic) headquarters in Osaka and put aside a territorial dispute over a group of islands in the East China Sea that the Japanese call Senkaku and the Chinese call Diaoyu. Also included was a meeting with Emperor Akihito for a court luncheon, during which Jiang reiterated an invitation to visit China.

Jiang put his personal stamp on the trip. Remaining true to Chinese values, he insisted on visiting former Prime Minister Kakuei Tanaka (1970–74), who had initiated the new Sino-Japanese relationship. Like Richard Nixon in America, Tanaka had been tainted by scandal in Japan—he was arrested for bribery—but the Chinese continued to honor him even though it was no longer useful to do so. To this day Nixon and Tanaka are remembered in China as great men.

When Jiang arrived at Tanaka's traditional-style home, many of the old man's family were waiting by the door. As Jiang stepped out of his limousine, one of Tanaka's granddaughters offered him a bouquet of flowers. "Welcome," she said in English.

"I've come to your country for a state visit at the time of the twentieth anniversary of the normalization of relations between Japan and China," Jiang told Tanaka. "It's natural for me to think about your historic contribution to the normalization. The Chinese have a saying, 'While you drink, never forget who dug the well.' I come today to thank you and pay my respects to Your Excellency."

Jiang was at ease with the Japanese press. Before his departure he spoke with Japanese reporters about his upcoming travels. When asked about his personal life, he talked about his wife, his children, and their own wives and children, describing them as a happy family. "We have one grandson and one granddaughter," he said, adding with a grin, "This number is in accord with China's family planning policy."

Jiang told the reporters, "I follow the philosophy that whatever my job is, I try to like it and learn things about it. Therefore I now read books on history, science and technology, and world affairs." Jiang said that he enjoys classical music but is not against fast-tempo music such as disco, "which young people like."

Jiang was also interviewed on NHK Television. "What do you do during your spare time?" the interviewer asked.

"I think I have very little spare time. If I have time, I like to read literature."

"May we ask you to write down one of your favorite sayings? Here's the brush."

The camera zoomed in as Jiang wrote two verses on a piece of paper.

"People say you like Chinese classics," said the interviewer as he looked at Jiang's calligraphy. "I think this one is a poem from the Tang dynasty. Would you please explain it?"

"Here's what I wrote," said Jiang. " 'If you wish to have an unobstructed, breathtaking view of a thousand li [about 500 kilometers or 311 miles], you must ascend one more flight of stairs.' The preceding two verses read, 'The setting sun disappears over the mountains, and the Huanghe [Yellow River] flows into the ocean.' "

Six months later Emperor Akihito of Japan made a historic trip to Beijing, the first time a Japanese monarch traveled to the People's Republic of China. At a banquet hosted by Jiang, the emperor made the unprecedented acknowledgment that his country's invasion of China had caused "great sufferings" to the Chinese people.

As COMFORTABLE AS JIANG now appeared in his leadership role, there were rumors suggesting the contrary. Although rumors occur in all political systems, those circulating about China's senior leaders, especially in the West, tend to exaggerate the degree to which political jockeying occupies their time. Personal positioning is always part of political life, but China's national leaders, like America's, spend the vast majority of their time working together to run their country. Although there were often divergences of views on the best way for China to achieve its goals, there was virtual unanimity on what those goals should be.

In mid-1992, however, there was one series of rumors that was substantive and self-sustaining and, for a time, consumed a great deal of Jiang Zemin's energy. President Yang Shangkun, Deng Xiaoping's well-entrenched, long-time friend, and his aggressive half-brother, General Yang Baibing, were expanding their power and posing a threat to Jiang's leadership. (Qiao Shi was likely involved as well.) Using their influence in the army and their relationship with Deng, the Yangs seemed intent on feeding their oversized ambitions. Yang Baibing had recommended the promotion of one hundred new generals, many of whom were close associates and personal friends.

Though Jiang had spent the preceding two years diligently building his relations with the military, his position remained dependent on Deng. Jiang's independent influence on the army, though growing, was still modest.

China scholars, seasoned journalists, and tabloid writers with little regard for truth all told tales of political intrigue, some of which conflicted with one another and all of which government spokesmen labeled fabrications. There were stories of the machinations and maneuverings of the Yang brothers, and of Jiang Zemin's countermeasures, which called upon old friends in high places (including General Zhang Aiping, his martyred father's comrade-in-arms) and relied upon the resourceful perspicacity of Zeng Qinghong, then deputy director of the Party's General Office. Reportedly reaching Deng's son and then Deng himself, Zeng and Jiang warned that the Yang brothers were undermining the cardinal principle that the Party must rule the army. A military coup, they hinted darkly, was not out of the question. Deng was counseled by his chief military adviser, General Liu Huaqing, who at a crucial moment in a private meeting with Deng concurred with Jiang. Senior elder Bo Yibo, whose advice Jiang sought regularly, also supported him.

Shortly before the opening of the Fourteenth Party Congress, when Deng Xiaoping recommended senior personnel for the Central Military Commission, neither Yang Shangkun nor Yang Baibing was on the list. The political battle was over and the outcome unambiguous. Yang Baibing was relieved of all military posts, although, as a face-saving measure and in recognition of his support for Deng, he was given a position in the Politburo. Equally important, Yang Shangkun was removed as vice chairman of the CMC, and although he would remain state president for six more months, he and his brother were out of the military and out of power. Considering the prominence of Yang Shangkun and his long closeness to Deng, and the power of the "Yang Family Army" in the PLA, their removal was a startling victory for Jiang Zemin. It may have been the watershed event in the confirmation of his leadership.

THE FOURTEENTH PARTY CONGRESS, held in October 1992, made three related decisions with far-reaching implications. First, it established as its guiding principle Deng Xiaoping's slogan that the country should "build socialism with Chinese characteristics." Second, it made clear that the country's goal in reforming its economy was to build a "socialist market economy." Third, it asserted that the Party must focus on developing the economy.

The blunt linking of China's defining "socialist" ideology with the capitalist-tinged term "market" carried enormous symbolic significance, yet when Jiang Zemin delivered his keynote political report at the Congress, it was more evenly textured than his speech to the Party School had been four months earlier. On the one hand he said that reform and opening up was "the most clear-cut characteristic of the new historical period" and that Deng Xiaoping's "new revolution" was "aimed at *fundamentally* changing the economic structure rather than patching it up." On the other hand, he sought harmonious equilibrium. "We should proceed from actual conditions, keep development within the limits of our capabilities, and maintain an overall balance," Jiang said. "In our efforts to speed up economic growth, we should avoid the mistakes of the past."

He called for economic expansion of eight or nine percent annually through the year 2000—higher than the six percent target in the current five-year plan drafted by Li Peng, but less than the 10 percent that Deng Xiaoping was advocating. Nevertheless, watching Jiang's address on live television, Deng said, "I should applaud this Report."

By the time the Fourteenth Party Congress concluded, Jiang Zemin had established his preeminence, or, more accurately, Deng Xiaoping had established it for him: first, by energizing Jiang to accelerate market reforms with his Southern Tour (Nanxun) earlier in the year; second, by backing Jiang in his struggle with the Yang brothers over control of the military in the tense months prior to the Congress; and, third, by providing a more reform-minded Politburo Standing Committee, with Vice Premier Zhu Rongji and the forty-nine-year-old Hu Jintao (suddenly the odds-on favorite to become the future leader) replacing conservatives Song Ping and Yao Yilin (both of whom followed the centralized control philosophy of elder Chen Yun, which was opposite that of Deng's market-driven orientation). Jiang was pleased to work with Hu Jintao, who had good relations with both the liberal followers of Hu Yaobang (from the Communist Youth League) and the conservative Song Ping (under whom he had worked in Gansu province following the Cultural Revolution).

In a meaningful change to the process of governance, the Central Advisory Commission, whose members had at least forty years of Party service, was abolished, thus marking Jiang's emergence from the shadow of the elders. Established in 1982, the Commission had provided "political assistance and consultation" to the CPC Central Committee. By eliminating the Commission, Deng curtailed the elders' involvement in politics and increased the prerogatives and flexibility of Jiang and other current leaders.

Though Jiang did not get everything he wanted—his "suggestion" to delegation heads that they direct member voting for a certain mayor's admission to the Central Committee was not followed—the Congress was a great personal triumph. Not only had Jiang beaten back a serious political challenge, but he had also grown in strength and confidence in all areas of his leadership—political, economic, media, military. Reflecting back in late 2003, a year after he would retire as general secretary, Jiang singled out this moment in 1992 as his personal turning point.

Still, politics were complex. The collective leadership of the new Politburo Standing Committee, men of competence, commitment, and long service, augured well for running the country. The seven had common goals, but the very strength of their personalities meant that each had individual ambitions as well as beliefs that could come into conflict with Jiang's leadership. This was particularly true of Li Peng, Qiao Shi, and Li Ruihuan, who were ranked second, third, and fourth respectively. Li Peng was premier and head of the government; Qiao Shi would become chairman of the National People's Congress; and Li Ruihuan would become chairman of the Chinese People's Political Consultative Conference.

Fifth in rank was Jiang's Shanghai colleague Zhu Rongji, who would have almost total control of the economy (and who did not consider consensus building to be part of his mandate). Sixth was Liu Huaqing, who would be the last military officer on the Standing Committee; and seventh was the forty-nine-year-old Hu Jintao, selected by Deng, who was responsible for Party organization and personnel.

Near the end of the Congress, it became clear that as far as Deng Xiaoping was concerned, Jiang Zemin was his successor. The now eighty-eight-year-old Deng, escorted by his daughter, Deng Rong, entered the Great Hall of the People to greet the newly selected senior leaders amid the sea of delegates, but singled out Jiang Zemin in a highly publicized show of support. For twenty minutes Deng walked with Jiang, side by side as if equals, while everyone else, including Li Peng, trailed a few steps behind. It was the ultimate blessing by China's Paramount Leader, and it was broadcast nationally on China Central Television for the entire country to witness. "The Congress was well-organized," Deng said, grasping his successor's hands. "I hope all will continue their efforts."

In spite of this vote of confidence, Jiang's staying power continued to be questioned. Prevailing opinion was that, even with Deng's support, Jiang did not have sufficient strength in the Party and the army. Foreign analysts compared his power base unfavorably with that of Qiao Shi, who some critics assumed was waiting for the right opportunity to challenge Jiang. To make matters worse, Jiang's closest associate, the highly capable Zeng Qinghong, was not elected to the CPC Central Committee. (Nathan and Gilley refute the common assumption that Jiang tried and failed to promote Zeng faster. Zeng preferred "quiet power over formal position" and sought only minimum ranks commensurate with each stage of his careful, planned advancement.)

After the Congress, as if to prove his critics wrong, Jiang acted swiftly to remove generals loyal to the Yang brothers and replace them with modern professionals. In this action he had the backing of Generals Liu Huaqing and Zhang Zhen, with their deep loyalties throughout the PLA. For just this reason, Deng Xiaoping had asked them to serve as CMC vice chairmen, even though both were past retirement age. "With the establishment of the new Central Military Commission [CMC]," Jiang observed, "the quality of the whole leadership has been improved."

Restructuring the CMC was just the start. Many senior officers and even more regional commanders were either retired or reassigned, and career officers loyal to the new leadership were promoted to their positions. One newspaper described the shake-up as "the biggest, widest, and most extensive high-level military reshuffle since the founding of the People's Republic."

To ensure PLA loyalty, political indoctrination was intensified. Numerous articles in military publications affirmed that the army should absolutely follow the Party and its core leader, Jiang Zemin. Only those officers who agreed with this policy would be promoted.

Jiang did not hesitate to consolidate power on all fronts. He became head of three of the Party's "Leading Groups"—Finance and Economics, law enforcement, and Taiwan Affairs—putting him in direct charge of policymaking in those areas. He promoted two associates to the Politburo: Wu Bangguo, the Shanghai Party chief, and Qian Qichen, the foreign minister. He also selected Ding Guangen, a traditional conservative but not a Leftist ideologue, as head of the Publicity (Propaganda) Department. Ding hailed from Jiang's Jiangsu province; he was a bridge-playing partner of Deng Xiaoping and could be counted on to mold the Chinese media in Jiang's image.

IN FOREIGN AFFAIRS JIANG furthered Deng's policy of opening-up. In August 1992 China established diplomatic relations with South Korea, and the next month Jiang hosted a grand reception for South Korean president Roh Tae Woo. North Korea protested the Sino-Korean rapprochement as "incomprehensible, unimaginable, and unacceptable," admonishing China that it should "treasure the militant friendship forged with lives and blood by the two countries." When North Korean strongman Kim Il-Sung came to Beijing a few weeks later, his demand for aid was rebuffed. Instead of the two submarines, five missile destroyers, and eighteen J-8 aircraft that he had requested, he received a mild promise of limited economic and technical help.

The way in which diplomatic relations between China and South Korea were initiated depicts how Jiang Zemin liked to receive information and how he worked with those who reported to him. Trained in the sciences, Jiang respected State Councilor Dr. Song Jian, a distinguished scientist and mathematician who had made significant contributions to China's aerospace program. Soon after becoming general secretary, Jiang told Song, "Whenever you have something that you think I should read, just send it over to my office."

Song complied with Jiang's request by sending him papers, articles, and books. "I'd simply have my secretary walk over and lay it on his desk," Song recalled. "I had no agenda: there was great variety in what I thought interesting or important. On average, I probably sent him something once a month." Though the vast majority of Song's transmissions involved science and technology, there were exceptions.

In the winter of 1990 Dr. Song was contacted by a colleague, Dr. Lee-Jay Cho, an American-educated Korean sociologist who was then director of the prestigious East-West Center at the University of Hawaii. Dr. Cho had a special request: he had been asked by South Korean president Roh Tae Woo to find a confidential, high-level channel to signal his country's interest in establishing economic and political ties with China. Through Dr. Cho, President Roh's initiative was conveyed to Dr. Song, who then delivered it to Jiang in his usual way.

After reading the letter, Jiang decided that the time and circumstances were right, and he commenced the formal diplomatic process by passing it to China's Foreign Ministry. In early 1991 South Korea and China exchanged trade offices, and in mid-1992 they established diplomatic relations.

Wang Daohan, Jiang's old friend and mentor, also had special access. This took on extra significance when he was appointed chairman of the Association for Relations Across the Taiwan Straits, a nongovernmental organization (NGO) that had a parallel organization in Taiwan. The idea was that NGOs could have more flexibility than governments to find new ways of reducing tensions. At Jiang's request, Wang Daohan reported directly to himself.

"I never hide anything from Jiang," said Wang. "I never hesitate to tell him anything—especially if I think that he may not know it. From time to time he also asks for my opinions. We keep in close touch. Every time I'm in Beijing, I go to his home. As old friends, we speak about many things, personal things, just like we did before he became China's leader. Jiang hasn't changed. Sometimes when he encounters conflicts, he tells me about them. He knows he can trust me to give him my honest feelings and to keep the matters confidential. If he asks me something that I don't know, I'll first do research, then tell him whatever I find out."

NEAR THE END OF 1992 Jiang made a decision that changed the course of science and technology in China. According to custom, a national plan for the following year, prepared by Vice Premier Zhu Rongji, would be discussed at a Politburo meeting, over which Jiang Zemin, as general secretary, would preside. As part of the 1993 plan, Dr. Song Jian, who was in charge of science and technology, suggested that China encourage the development of high-tech, entrepreneurial, start-up companies by authorizing the creation of several dozen high-tech industrial parks to house them. Zhu Rongji, however, was adamantly opposed to using start-up companies and industrial parks to drive science and technology—he favored large state-owned enterprises—and his resistance set the stage for a dramatic debate. Vice Premier Zhu and State Councilor Song, who was invited to the Politburo session, would go head to head.

"I had the duty to find ways for science and technology to help the nation achieve its developmental goals," explained Song. "Early on I began to brainstorm some innovative ideas."

The first step was the Sparks Program, which began in the middle 1980s and focused on building rural and township enterprises of low and medium technology. By the early 1990s China was ready for the second step: the development of high-technology enterprises in the cities. Here Song came to believe that the best strategy would be a bold one: establish national-level high-tech industrial parks, with favorable policies to encourage the creation of new, innovative companies. He and his teams developed a detailed plan, modeled after the American high-tech parks that grew up around Boston, San Francisco (Silicon Valley), and Austin. For Zhu Rongji's national plan, Song wrote a carefully crafted paragraph affirming this high-tech entrepreneurial policy and authorizing the high-tech parks. But Zhu disagreed with Song and crossed out the paragraph.

Everyone recognized that without accelerating science and technology China's development would go nowhere. The issue was not whether to do it but how to do it best. Song advocated small, entrepreneurial companies, leveraging China's young scientists. Zhu Rongji promoted large, state-owned enterprises (SOEs), leveraging China's industrial strength.

"I was good friends with Vice Premier Zhu," noted Song, "but on this matter we disagreed sharply. We had no choice but to bring our opposing views to the Politburo."

The meeting lasted three hours, but less than twenty minutes was devoted to the high-tech debate. Zhu Rongji argued that China's large state-owned enterprises, for which he was responsible, should be the place to develop China's advanced science and technology. Not only did SOEs have administrative systems in place, Zhu said, but they also had the critical mass necessary for advanced research and development. "We have so many SOEs," pleaded Zhu. "They can do it!"

"Zhu was totally committed to revitalizing China's SOEs as part of his overall plan for the national economy," explained Song. "It was a tremendous burden, and this drove his analysis."

When Dr. Song Jian spoke, he stated that he represented China's science community, not only his personal position. He argued that SOEs were precisely the *wrong* place to develop new science and technology, since innovation in general was young people's work, and the bureaucracy and static systems of large SOEs would inhibit, not enhance, their creativity.

"In the seniority-based hierarchy of state-owned enterprises, how could young people ever get a chance to do anything original, to challenge accepted ways and norms?" Song asked. "Young people would never be respected, no matter how good their ideas."

Song explained how difficult it was for scientists to work within the confines and strictures of SOEs. "If we're serious about innovative science and technology, we need to break the old mold," Song implored the Politburo. "Why not free China's best and brightest young scientists to create dynamic start-up businesses on their own?"

Premier Li Peng, to whom Song reported and who was a reliable supporter of science and technology, backed Song's new thinking, although Zhu and Song alone carried the debate. As the presiding official, Jiang Zemin did not enter the discussion but listened intently and took a few notes.

Finally Jiang spoke. "I agree with the proposal by Comrade Song Jian," he said. Then he addressed the vice premier. "Lao Zhu [Old Zhu, a term of endearment], you shouldn't so staunchly oppose this idea. Let them give it a try.

Maybe it will work; maybe it will be important. Our most talented young people should by all means carry this on. After some years we can review the program and judge it properly."

It was a typical Jiang meeting, which he managed methodically. He did not inject his opinion but enabled protagonists to present their positions and encouraged participants to speak their minds. He kept the focus on key points, which he wrote down for himself in large, clear characters. At the end he summarized the collective conclusion and went around the room to bring everyone into it.

After the session Song went over to Zhu, smiled, and whispered, "Comrade Rongji, I beat you one to zero on this one!"

"Just go do your business," said Zhu with a twinkle.

Years later Song reflected on this milestone in China's science and technology. "Jiang Zemin has an inclusive, confidence-building style in managing meetings," he said, "and he's skilled in presiding over differences of opinion. He works to achieve harmony and consensus, making everyone feel part of the decision, even if total agreement isn't possible. It was because of this—and my friendship with Zhu—that I could joke with him afterward."

What became known as the Torch Program began with twenty-four national-level, high-tech industrial parks and grew to fifty-three, spawning high-tech companies and new industries. It was the second step in accelerating China's science and technology. The third and final step would have to wait until 1995.

THROUGHOUT HIS TENURE AS China's leader, Jiang relied on old friends, seeking their advice and enjoying their companionship. Every year from 1990 to 1999 he celebrated the Chinese New Year in Shanghai, where he dined and reminisced with older comrades. Former Vice Mayor Ye Gongqi, who was always present, also visited the Jiang home in Zhongnanhai. "We had simple meals," Ye recalled. "Everyday homemade food, about four to five dishes, nothing fancy. Jiang's family members joined us. At the dining table we discussed many things, sometimes frank or personal things." One of these, Ye said, was Jiang's dissatisfaction with his cook's rendition of a favorite dish, *hongshao rou,* pork braised in soy sauce. "Not as good as it was in Shanghai," Jiang grumbled. Ye also revealed that, per Jiang's doctor's advice, he was not supposed to eat fish skin, which his chef dutifully removed before cooking. "Fish doesn't taste good without the skin," the Party chief lamented.

Jiang's house was full of books but not much else. "My children tell me that my furniture is too old," Ye observed; "Jiang's furniture was older than mine."

But if the possessions were modest, the welcome was warm, especially from Jiang's wife, Wang Yeping, who was suffering from cervical vertebrae problems and held her head at a constant tilt. Yet when friends visited, she brought out the tea and fruits herself. When another Shanghai vice mayor died, she invited his widow to her home. As China's First Lady, Wang preferred domestic duties to social glamor.

"She manages family business," observed Jiang Zehui, her sister-in-law. "She took care of family elders for years: my mother, her mother, Third Brother's parents. Now she makes sure the children and grandchildren grow up well. She started shouldering family responsibilities early, since her father, my second maternal uncle, died young. Although she was born into a well-off Shanghai family, she is modest and lives a simple, ordinary life; she doesn't like showing her face in public. I call her San Sao, Third Sister-in-Law."

The couple complemented each other. After a day of endless demands, Jiang Zemin looked forward to his wife's Shanghai-style cooking. His favorite, though, remained the cuisine of Yangzhou.

BY THE END OF 1992 China's economy was starting to overheat, threatening to unleash inflation. Jiang returned to the country's roots, stressing that agriculture and rural work were essential for modernization. He knew that China's stability ultimately depended on its farmers, who account for two-thirds of its vast population. In December he made an unscheduled inspection of Hubei province to speak with local officials and peasants. There were problems in the countryside, and Jiang wanted to hear from the people affected.

"It almost doesn't pay to grow crops," a village Party secretary told him. "Production costs have risen, and sales prices have fallen. Moreover, all kinds of heavy levies have been piled on peasants' backs."

"How would you solve the problem?" Jiang asked.

"The peasants should only pay a tax on their grain," the cadre offered. "The rest of the levies should be paid by the village, increasing peasants' enthusiasm."

At another village Jiang asked why grain prices were so low. "Better productivity yields too much supply," he was told. "The main problem is distribution," someone else said. "Storage," said another; "in the past we stored the grains among the people, but now they have 'new thoughts' [i.e., it's below their dignity] and won't store grains at home."

"Their 'new thoughts' may not be right," Jiang said. "The masses should regard food as their heaven."

In one village he noticed a group of farmhouses and asked his driver to pull over. He and Wen Jiabao, who directed agriculture, got out of their van and walked over to the mud-brick home of Liu Keju, a fifty-one-year-old plasterer.

Jiang extended his hand. Liu said that he had never met any "big officials" before but would gladly give his opinions. "I thank Deng Xiaoping for the freedom of production," he said. "In the past we couldn't earn much money even if we didn't sleep at all, but now that we have autonomy, our life is much better. I wish no change of the system of responsibility that links rewards to output."

"Old Liu," Jiang said, "the state is stable when the farms are stable. The Party's policy of 'Let the people get rich' won't change."

"Then why do we have so many levies and taxes now?" Liu asked.

"What levies?"

"Too many to count," Liu said. "Money spent on dinners and wine alone exceeds ten thousand yuan a year in our village."

"Is it for weddings and funerals?" Jiang asked. "Or entertaining?"

"I'm a plasterer," Liu explained, "so I get to work in different places around here. I see a lot; I see officials from higher levels being wined and dined when they come to our village for meetings and inspections."

Jiang was disheartened. "Only when the peasants are prosperous and free," he told Hubei officials, "can civility and progress be guaranteed in the new century."

In December a conference on rural matters was held in Wuhan and attended by leaders of six provinces. Jiang spoke with the authority of one who had current, firsthand information. To the amusement of no one, he repeated antigovernment catchphrases he had picked up from the peasants. Levies would be restricted to five percent of a district-specific average net income. No more promissory notes would be allowed, Jiang asserted, and the outstanding ones had to be paid off. (Local governments had a way of issuing promissory notes to farmers instead of paying them in cash, since local leaders wanted to use the cash for speculative investments, such as purchasing real estate in faraway coastal boomtowns. In addition to hurting farmers, such speculation fueled inflation.)

LATE IN 1992, WHILE in Shanghai promoting development, especially in Pudong, Jiang said that although China was dedicated to economic growth, it would place equal emphasis on creating a socialist "spiritual civilization." It was an early expression of Jiang's vision to instill values and laud culture, and it would come to mark his leadership.

In foreign policy as well, Jiang used a new slogan. Bill Clinton had just been elected president of the United States, displacing the Beijing-friendly George H.W. Bush after running partly on a get-tough-with-China campaign, and China's leaders were wary of him. Meeting in December with a small delegation from the U.S. House of Representatives, headed by Patricia Schroeder, Jiang first used the sixteen-character slogan that he hoped would characterize U.S.–China relations: "Increase trust, reduce troubles, develop cooperation, and avoid confrontation."

By December 1992 no fewer than twelve editorials had been published by *Liberation Army Daily* in which Jiang Zemin was hailed as the "core of the Party" and the only "commander of the army." His stewardship was called a reflection of the "tradition of the veteran Red Army." Jiang had gained control of China's armed forces at a time when failure to do so could have threatened his position.

Once in charge, he knew what to do. As CMC chairman, Jiang approved the promotion of all senior officers and spoke personally with those being elevated to major general and above. In this way he solidified his authority over the army and established a robust source of national power. The civilian who had once practiced marching in front of a mirror had come a long way.

The year 1992 was a turning point for Jiang Zemin in more than securing his political leadership. It also marked a change in his thinking. Although he had been one of the pioneers of Deng Xiaoping's reforms, Jiang was an active participant in the conservative retrenchment after June 4, 1989 (even as he sought to moderate hardline policies and strike a more centrist position). Now he unambiguously committed to the market economy. Jiang Zemin had held the Party's top title since 1989, but it was not until 1992 that he truly became the leader of the Third Generation.

Graduation photo of Jiang Zemin, mid-1947, a few months before his twenty-first birthday. *(Courtesy of Shanghai Jiaotong University)*

Graduation photo of Jiang Zemin and his classmates in the electrical and machinery (engineering) departments of Shanghai Jiaotong University, mid-1947. Jiang Zemin, wearing dark-rimmed glasses, is third from the right in the third row. His two closest friends are in the top row (center), Wang Huijiong just to the left of the right shutter, Tong Zonghai directly in front of the left shutter. See contemporary pictures of Wang and Tong at the end of the second photo section. *(Courtesy of Tong Zonghai)*

Jiang Zemin (center) with engineers and technicians at the First Automotive Works in Changchun, May 1957. *(Courtesy of Shen Yongyan)*

Jiang Zemin (center, with dark coat and glasses), with members of his Power Plant division at the First Automotive Works in Changchun, early 1960s. *(Courtesy of Shen Yongyan)*

Jiang Zemin (center) with other Chinese apprentices and students in Moscow, 1955 or 1956. *(Courtesy of Shen Yongyan)*

Jiang Zemin at Shanghai Electrical Equipment Research Institute, July 1962. *(Courtesy of Yang Guohui)*

Jiang in Shannon, Ireland, heading a delegation on a United Nations–sponsored world tour of free trade zones, October 29–31, 1980.

As vice chairman of the State Administration Commission on Import and Export Affairs, Jiang explains the new Special Economic Zones in Guangdong and Fujian provinces to the Standing Committee of the National People's Congress, August 21, 1980. *(Xinhua News Agency)*

As minister of Electronics Industry, Jiang shows the revered Chen Yun (seated), a Politburo Standing Committee member, the new integrated-circuit technologies for computer applications, March 3, 1984. *(Xinhua News Agency)*

Jiang in San Francisco (below) with Dr. Liu Chining (head of Hewlett-Packard China), celebrating his promotion from vice minister to minister of Electronics Industry, June 1983. The inscription on the cake reads "Congratulations to Mr. Zemin for your honorable promotion to minister." *(Courtesy of Dr. Liu Chining)*

The new leadership of Shanghai, Party secretary Rui Xingwen (second from left) and Mayor Jiang Zemin (fourth from left) visit the construction site of the new Shanghai railway station, June 27, 1985. *(Xinhua News Agency)*

Mayor Jiang (second from right) shows Vice Premier Wan Li (second from left) a scale model of the new Shanghai railway station, October 1986. Minister of Railways Ding Guangen is on the far right. *(Xinhua News Agency)*

Mayor Jiang accompanies NPC Chairman Peng Zhen on an inspection of Shanghai No. 1 television factory, February 15, 1986. *(Xinhua News Agency)*

Shanghai Party secretary Jiang accompanies Deng Xiaoping during the Chinese New Year in Shanghai, February 10, 1989. *(Xinhua News Agency)*

Jiang meeting with non-Communist parties just prior to the Chinese New Year, February 1988.

Jiang at an exhibition in Shanghai with Zeng Qinghong (behind and to the left of Jiang) and Wang Huning (to the left of Zeng, leaning over), late 1980s.

Mayor Jiang welcomes England's Queen Elizabeth II on her arrival at the Shanghai airport, October 15, 1986. (*Xinhua News Agency*)

An expanded meeting of the Politburo following the military action in Tiananmen Square to build consensus for Jiang Zemin's elevation to general secretary, June 19–21, 1989. Jiang is seated right center (sitting straight up). *(Xinhua News Agency)*

Jiang Zemin, Li Peng, and Qiao Shi (right to left) speaking with Marshall Nie Rongzeng (seated) at the expanded meeting of the Politburo, June 19–21, 1989. *(Xinhua News Agency)*

Jiang Zemin enters the Great Hall of the People just prior to his formal election as the new general secretary of the CPC Central Committee, June 23, 1989. Li Peng is to the left of Jiang, Qiao Shi is behind and between Jiang and Li, and Yao Yilin is behind and to the right of Jiang. *(Xinhua News Agency)*

Party general secretary Jiang (center) with Li Peng (left) and Li Ruihuan (right) at a national propaganda meeting soon after assuming his new position of leadership, July 20, 1989. (*Xinhua News Agency*)

Jiang Zemin (center) with other members of the Politburo Standing Committee taking questions from foreign reporters at his first press conference after becoming Party general secretary, September 26, 1989. From left to right, Li Ruihuan, Song Ping, Qiao Shi, interpreter, Jiang Zemin, Li Peng, and Yao Yilin. (*Xinhua News Agency*)

Jiang walks with Deng Xiaoping on the day he was elected chairman of the Central Military Commission at the Fifth Plenum of the Thirteenth Party Congress, November 9, 1989. Deng's daughter, Deng Rong, is next to him. (*Xinhua News Agency*)

Deng Xiaoping speaks with Jiang Zemin at the Fourteenth Party Congress, October 1992. Just behind are Li Peng (left) and Qiao Shi (right). *(Xinhua News Agency)*

Jiang Zemin and Li Peng with the Central Advisory Commission (elders of the Communist Party with forty or more years of membership), October 19, 1992. Front row, from left to right, Li Peng, Song Renqiong, Jiang Zemin, and Bo Yibo. *(Xinhua News Agency)*

President Jiang delivers the eulogy at Deng Xiaoping's memorial service, February 25, 1997. *(Xinhua News Agency)*

Former president Yang Shangkun congratulates Jiang Zemin on being elected state president at the Eighth National People's Congress, March 27, 1993. *(Xinhua News Agency)*

Senior leaders chat in the VIP room during a break at the Fourth Session of the Seventh CPPCC, March 23, 1991. From left to right, former president Li Xiannian, Li Peng, current president Yang Shangkun, Wan Li (partially hidden), and Jiang Zemin. *(Xinhua News Agency)*

At a Chinese New Year reception in the Great Hall of the People in Beijing, Jiang speaks with Wang Daohan, chairman of the Association for Relations Across the Taiwan Straits, January 30, 1995. *(Xinhua News Agency)*

Former Shanghai mayor Wang Daohan, Jiang Zemin's career-long mentor and friend, being interviewed by the author in Shanghai, June 2001. *(Courtesy of Adam Zhu)*

Jiang meets his old professor, the remarkable ninety-three-year-old Gu Yuxiu, at the United Nations in New York, October 23, 1995. *(Xinhua News Agency)*

Jiang visits a farmer's cave home in Yan'an, the Party's historic revolutionary base, September 9–11, 1989. (*Xinhua News Agency*)

Wishing peasants in Doudian village, near Beijing, a happy Chinese New Year, Party general secretary Jiang, with Wen Jiabao (left) and Zeng Qinghong (center), makes dumplings with a local family, January 22, 1993. (*Xinhua News Agency*)

While inspecting flood-stricken Heilongjiang province, Jiang visits an eighty-year-old peasant in his cave home, September 5, 1998. Wen Jiabao is on the right. (*Xinhua News Agency*)

President Jiang takes his first step onto Hong Kong soil just prior to its historic repatriation to China, June 30, 1997.
(*Xinhua News Agency*)

Grand ceremony of Hong Kong's repatriation to China, with President Jiang (center left) and Prince Charles (center right) leading their delegations, July 1, 1997.
(*Xinhua News Agency*)

President Jiang with Prince Charles at the ceremony of Hong Kong's repatriation to China, July 1, 1997. British Prime Minister Tony Blair is on the right; Chinese Premier Li Peng is on the left.
(*Xinhua News Agency*)

Jiang visits the family of a Boeing employee, Cary Qualls, in Seattle and shows pictures of his grandchildren, November 18, 1993. *(Xinhua News Agency)*

Jiang and his wife, Wang Yeping, at the Yuquanshan resort in Beijing, April 19, 1992. *(Xinhua News Agency)*

Jiang and Wang Yeping visit Colonial Williamsburg in Virginia, October 28, 1997. The eighteenth-century English-style hats are a gift from the Williamsburg Foundation chairman. (*Xinhua News Agency*)

Giving a thumbs-up, Jiang rings the opening bell at the New York Stock Exchange in New York, October 31, 1997. (*Xinhua News Agency*)

Welcoming U.S. President Bill Clinton to Beijing, President Jiang hosts a formal ceremony outside the Great Hall of the People in Tiananmen Square, June 27, 1998.
(*Xinhua News Agency*)

During his state visit to the United States, President Jiang and President Clinton hold a joint press conference at the White House in Washington, D.C., October 29, 1997.
(*Xinhua News Agency*)

Chapter 14

1993

"We Will Show the World That We Are Trustworthy"

ALTHOUGH SOME STILL THOUGHT the Party chief was a transitional figure, this attitude was starting to change. "Jiang Zemin might not be as dumb as most people thought," said A. Doak Barnett, the doyen of American China scholars. "And China's political succession might not be as abrupt and violent as many China experts predicted."

Jiang built on his growing momentum with a series of strategic moves. At a national conference on propaganda, he ordered Deng Xiaoping's speeches publicized, essential for restraining Leftists; he also recruited several media men from Shanghai to work in Beijing. He held a conclave of General Staff officers and regional commanders to plan defense strategies; the deeper agenda was ensuring the army's loyalty after the wave of far-reaching personnel changes.

Unexpectedly, Jiang called Major General Ba Zhongtan, a former commander of the Shanghai garrison, out of retirement to command the People's Armed Police (PAP). Formed in 1982, the PAP's mandate was to safeguard public security and protect Party and government institutions. Fulfilling his 1989 promise, Jiang substantially grew the force, equipping it with riot-control gear including rubber bullets, water cannons, stun guns, tear-gas canisters, body armor, and other nonlethal crowd-control devices. After the Tiananmen tragedy various military units were transferred from army to police jurisdiction, increasing the PAP to about one million servicemen by 1995 and about 1.8 million by 1998. Any new demonstrations would be handled by the PAP, not by the army.

In addition, Jiang quietly but radically expanded the Ministry of State Security, giving it broad powers to maintain public order and ferret out corruption, in addition to its stated roles in espionage and counterespionage. The Ministry's mission required it to monitor (and spy on when needed) ordinary citizens, Party members, government officials, and foreign nationals. It did not go unnoticed that by building up the People's Armed Police and the Ministry of State Security, Jiang was setting up his own independent base of assertive (and potentially intrusive) power that was outside the ring of control maintained by the Beijing Party organization, run by the combative Chen Xitong, and by the PLA general staff, with whom he was still not very close.

Jiang's actions were not uniformly popular. Some began grousing that the general secretary was forming a "Shanghai Faction" (*Shanghai bang*), since some of his appointees had come from his former city. Deng Xiaoping, critics said, feared that factions could split the Party. "New leadership in the new era," Deng liked to say, quoting a Chinese proverb signifying diversity, "must reflect the five lakes and four seas."

Chen Xitong, the Beijing Party boss who may have had designs on Jiang's job, was irate. This was his town, he thought, and he had not been consulted on Ba's appointment to head the PAP, which would now alter the balance of power in the capital. When the two men next met, "the porcelain teacups rattled as Chen banged his fist on the table," recalled one observer. Jiang responded with silence and an aloof stare.

Further asserting his authority over the army in June, Jiang promoted six military leaders to the highest rank of senior general, the first time since 1988 that such an honor had been awarded. The ceremony marked the end of the Yang brothers' military influence; all the men promoted were loyal to Jiang.

IN FEBRUARY JIANG ZEHUI was elected vice chairman of Anhui province's People's Congress. Immediately Jiang called his sister. "Was your position 'arranged' by the provincial government?" he asked bluntly.

"I told him the truth," recalled Jiang Zehui. "Two constituencies worked for my nomination: Hefei's [Anhui's capital] science, technology, and education delegation, since I was president of Anhui Agriculture University; and the Chuzhou City delegation, the rural area where I had worked for over ten years during the Cultural Revolution. Both had confidence that I would represent them effectively. Third Brother was pleased—relieved, too!"

"You must serve the people who placed their trust in you," Jiang advised his sister. "All these years you have been an educator in universities. You don't have a broad understanding of society; you have no knowledge of the legal and legislative process. You should learn law. You must expand your horizons. You should visit grassroots organizations. And always stay close to people from all walks of life.' "

IN MARCH THERE WERE rumors of last-minute Leftist opposition to Jiang becoming state president at the Eighth National People's Congress. A few conservative elders resisted the idea of one person leading State, Party, and Army, but the outcome was never in doubt. Jiang Zemin was elected president of China; out of 2,909 total ballots, only sixty were cast against him or were abstentions. In contrast, when Li Peng was elected to a second term as premier, delegates cast 210 votes against with 120 abstentions, something of a milestone of personal expression in what had traditionally been a rubber-stamp body.

Foreign media busied themselves reading political tea leaves. One Asian news source drew a link between what they called Jiang's "unassuming appearance" and the need to sustain the "leadership's shaky cause." The article implied that since "China's propaganda machine" had "waxed lyrical" about "Jiang's kind nature and common touch," he must be a figurehead without real power. "It is a question of when, and not if, his support disappears," the piece quoted one diplomat as saying. "He could survive a certain time during the transition period after Deng's death, but his ultimate demise is virtually guaranteed by total lack of military power." It would be hard to get it more wrong than that.

The news source, like so many others, underestimated Jiang, who continued to consolidate power in his unobtrusive way. He had recently taken over the Party's Leading Group on Finance and Economics, the government's most important policy-setting organ for economic policy. In July, he appointed Zhu Rongji governor of the People's Bank of China (China's central bank), a risky job with the economy already in overdrive. Determined to institute discipline and controls, Zhu removed Li Peng's people and installed three new vice governors. (Apparently, Li Peng had some kind of serious illness during April 1993; at first denied by press spokesmen, when his absence became obvious, he was said to have a bad cold. Western sources reported that Li suffered a mild heart attack. In any event, he was out of action until June.)

A quiet but equally significant move in Jiang's accretion of control occurred in March when he promoted Zeng Qinghong, his confidant, to be director (full minister) of the General Office of the CPC Central Committee, the administrative hub of the Party. Replacing Wen Jiabao, who had been appointed an alternate member of the Politburo, Zeng was now positioned to use his intimate knowledge of inner Party workings to promote Jiang and his agenda, tightening his grip on power. One news service, evincing no foresight, called it a "minor reshuffle."

AMID THE PRESSURES of the period, Jiang managed to enjoy himself. During an inspection trip to Hainan, he visited the island's university. After giving a lecture, he walked into the library. As students recognized him, they rushed over. "I notice that your school has a statue of Su Dongpo," said Jiang, referring to an eleventh-century poet. "He had great influence on culture in Hainan. Who can recite his poem 'Shuidiaogetou'?" A few students raised their hands, and a proudly smiling Jiang recited a few verses in unison with them.

It was raining, but the weather could not dampen the news that China's president was on campus. Soon hundreds crowded around the famous visitor. "Students should have broad knowledge," Jiang advised. "Literature and art enhance your aesthetic sense and enrich your thoughts and lives. Tolstoy, Shakespeare, Balzac, Dante, Leonardo da Vinci. Don't limit yourselves to your own specialties." Science majors needed to know more humanities, Jiang said, and humanities majors needed to know more science. "If you want to study other countries' advanced knowledge," he added, "you must master foreign languages. When I was a student, we got up at five every morning to recite sixty English words."

Worried that China's leader was running behind schedule, the university president tried to persuade Jiang to leave, but the man who had twice planned to become a professor was having too much fun. "China's future depends on you," Jiang told the crowd. "The competition in the world is mainly the competition for knowledge. As an ancient sage said, 'Everyone is responsible for the fate of a country.'" Jiang left them with the poignant words of Mao Zedong: "The world is both yours and ours, but finally it is yours."

THE BUSINESS WORLD WAS starting to notice China's surging economy. "The numbers are indeed dazzling," the *Asian Wall Street Journal* reported. "In 1976, 80 percent of China's production was directly owned by the state. Now it is about half. The economy is growing at a sizzling 12 percent, easily the fastest in the world. Foreign-exchange reserves are brimming. And the system is delivering the goods to the country's emerging middle class. In 1980 the masses bought 600 washing machines a day; today they're soaking up about 40,000. Thirteen years ago some 10,000 televisions were sold daily; today it's about 70,000. These are facts no skeptic can ignore."

At the same time inflation was spiraling out of control. The cost-of-living index climbed 15 percent for the year, fueled by a 46 percent increase in fixed investments. Jiang called for full-blown measures to prevent "the economy from overheating in order to avert major upheavals and major losses," adding that "small-scale shocks are inevitable."

In June, Jiang went to Deng Xiaoping's home and received his support for instituting tighter microeconomic controls in a plan of austerity. Stressing the importance of "financial work," Deng told Jiang, "No matter what, the government should have complete control of the financial system and of prices in the market; inflation would bring major losses to the people. The yuan [RMB—Chinese currency] should not be devalued too much."

"The frightening specter of runaway inflation was a major challenge for Jiang," recalled Wu Xiaoling, vice governor of the People's Bank of China. "How could we cool the economy and still maintain the momentum of reform? We tackled the root causes of the problem, such as unauthorized fund-raising and too much credit. And Jiang sent Zhu Rongji to serve as governor of the People's Bank—both agreed that local investments had to be curtailed."

"Nineteen ninety-three was a crucial year for President Jiang," explained Leng Rong, vice director of the Party Literature Office, which is responsible for compiling and editing works of the top leaders and important documents of the country and Party. "The overheated economy was a major threat, not only to reform but to social stability, and Jiang had to guide China through its first experience with macroeconomic controls of a market economy. In a planned economy, there is no need for such tools; if the economy is overheating, if there's inflation, you just shut down the factories or change their output. Now China had a new system.

"It was experimental and risky," Leng continued. "When the soft landing was achieved, it demonstrated the superiority of the new system, which was reinforced by the springing up of new products, goods, and services, many of them available to almost everyone by the middle 1990s. This was a major breakthrough for Jiang."

In response to Deng Xiaoping's instructions to "seize the opportunities" for rapid growth, Jiang demurred, citing three problems: corruption, income disparity, and inflation, the first two of which would remain chronic. "Speeding up development must be done on the premise of China's actual conditions of the moment," he said.

Overall, however, Jiang was positioning himself as the prime interpreter of Deng Xiaoping Theory. On the practical side, he took leadership of reforming the economy. On the theoretical side, he arranged a series of seminars promulgating Deng's ideology. On military matters, he told a conclave of army strategists that "Deng's military thinking should be considered the pillar of the People's Liberation Army."

But Deng himself voiced distaste for what he deemed to be a "cult of personality" being raised up around him. He was unhappy with the veneration of Deng Theory, uneasy about exhibitions that eulogized him, and uncomfortable with plans to erect statues of his likeness. "There is no need to say Deng Xiaoping Theory is very great, extremely correct, and exceptionally thorough," he said. "It is neither penetrating nor perfect; in future practice, it will have to be enriched, improved, and revised in some aspects." Deng added, "I am not being humble, just practical."

When Jiang went to Deng's home to celebrate his ninetieth birthday in August 1994, the Paramount Leader complained that many organizations were honoring him with activities. "We should not do that," Deng ordered sharply. He was not just being modest or polite. "They should not be allowed to do that," he repeated.

DURING THE SPRING OF 1993 Jiang organized an elite group of about thirty economists, social scientists, and political theorists. The idea was to allow the group to brainstorm in a protected, isolated hotel in the Yuquan Hills northwest of Beijing. Out of these sessions came fifteen advanced papers, which Jiang hoped would lay a new foundation for reform.

As head of the Party's Leading Group on Finance and Economics, Jiang took the initiative in setting economic policy. He also wanted to reach out to intellectuals and involve them in the process of governing. Finally, by setting the agenda for political and economic theory, Jiang reinforced his position as heir apparent to Deng Xiaoping. It was expected in China that its top political leader should also be its leading political theoretician. Mao had been both, as had Deng. It was time for Jiang Thought to begin to emerge.

Political reform, however, was not on the agenda. Jiang authorized propaganda boss Ding Guangen to tighten control over media and the arts. Press coverage of sensitive topics was limited, and "liberal" film productions scrutinized. Operating under Jiang's directives, Ding instructed the media to focus on "positive developments" and to avoid showing the Party in an unflattering light.

Farewell My Concubine, directed by Chen Kaige and starring Leslie Cheung and Gong Li, winner of the Palme d'Or at the Cannes Film Festival and the most internationally acclaimed Chinese film at the time, was banned in China. Although approved by China's Film Bureau, it was pulled after a private screening for the Politburo, during which some members reportedly walked out. In addition to the film's sexual content (including homosexuality), its main character is seen to suffer as much persecution under Communist rule (during the Cultural Revolution) as under Japanese occupation and the Kuomintang regime. It was as if the director were saying that the three epochs of Chinese history were all equally repugnant.

Nonetheless Jiang continued reaching out to the world. In June he wrote to the International Olympic Committee, reaffirming Beijing's bid to host the 2000 Olympic Games. (The bid would not succeed: America, with other nations, would blackball China in ongoing protest over the violence in Tiananmen Square.)

At about the same time Jiang met with the religious leader of Thailand's Buddhists and showed his erudition by summarizing the two-thousand-year history of Buddhism in China. He asserted that China's Constitution protects "normal religious activities," and he supported exchanges between religious followers from China and overseas.

In April, Jiang empowered Wang Daohan, chairman of the China Association for Relations Across the Taiwan Straits, to meet the urbane Koo Chen-fu, chairman of the purposely parallel Taiwan Foundation for Exchange Across the Taiwan Straits, for highly visible bilateral talks in Singapore. This unprecedented meeting, the highest-level formal contact between China and Taiwan in decades, was enabled by a private communication in 1990 from Taiwanese president Lee Teng-hui to Chinese president Jiang Zemin—mediated by the U.S. ambassador to China, James Lilley—which affirmed that Taiwan would not declare independence.

ON A SIMILAR FRONT, THERE was a flurry of activity over the anticipated return of Hong Kong to China scheduled for 1997. In July 1993 British foreign secretary Douglas Hurd visited China to deal with tensions over democratic reforms championed by Hong Kong governor Chris Patten. After reiterating China's position, Jiang appealed to British and Hong Kong business interests and common sense. The ultimate guarantor of Hong Kong's stability and prosperity, Jiang told Hurd, would be China's huge market. The previous January Jiang had told Hong Kong guests, "We will keep our word and promise. We will show the world that we are trustworthy."

A further sign of China's opening-up was the proliferation of beauty pageants. Once derided as symbols of "bourgeois decadence"—Jiang had been forced to cancel one while running Shanghai in 1988—the contests had sprung up across the country in recent years. At least fifty were now counted. Anything that could be made into a title was: Miss Etiquette, Wine Queen, Air Stewardess. Shenzhen held what it called China's first national pageant in May. The spectacle was a strange mixture of traditional dress, extravagant ballgowns, and T-shirts worn with hot pants.

DURING THE SUMMER, a lapse in American intelligence exposed U.S. government attitudes toward Jiang Zemin. The Chinese containership *Yin He* (Milky Way), en route to the Middle East, was suspected of carrying contraband chemicals to be used in the production of chemical weapons (nerve gas). Motivated by suspicions that China was a habitual violator of nonproliferation agreements and that this specific cargo was destined for Iran, Washington ordered U.S. Navy warships to shadow the vessel and prevent any offloading until it was thoroughly searched.

After strident charges and countercharges, Jiang felt compelled to tell visiting Americans that there were no illegal chemicals on the *Yin He*. As Robert Suettinger, at the time a national intelligence officer specializing in East Asia, reveals, "The message did not get through," even though U.S. Ambassador to China J. Stapleton Roy reported through channels that "Jiang's statements ought to be given credence, since an inspection proving him wrong would be extremely damaging to his reputation." But, according to Suettinger, "Washington was not interested in Jiang Zemin's reputation." Nonproliferation experts in the U.S. intelligence community were running the operation and determined to make a public example of China. They remained certain of their information and chose to disregard Jiang's assertions.

Sensitive negotiations produced agreement for a joint team of Chinese and Saudi Arabians to search the *Yin He*. American experts were not permitted on board but could advise the Saudis. After a full week of examining all 782 containers, a certification was signed, attested to by the Americans, that no prohibited chemicals were on board.

A few weeks later, National Security Adviser Anthony Lake classified China with Iran, Iraq, Burma, and North Korea as "backlash" states, which he defined as those threatening the "circle of democracy." His uncompromising prescription was to "isolate them diplomatically, militarily, economically, and technologically." In China, Lake's speech was read as reconfirming Washington's unalloyed belligerence toward Beijing, "tipping the balance of the debate in China," notes Suettinger, "about what U.S. strategic intentions toward China really were." China's strategic analysts now concluded that the United States had instituted a policy of containment to prevent China's emergence as a world power.

At the same time, Jiang was facing military and hardline criticism over China's "weak reaction" to the *Yin He* incident. He responded with balance, articulating Deng Xiaoping's policy of "not seeking confrontation, not provoking confrontation, [but also] not avoiding confrontation and not fearing confrontation." He sought to maintain Deng's approach of working constructively with the United States, but this was becoming increasingly difficult to do. Sino-American relations were already headed in the wrong direction just as President Jiang was to have his first meeting with President Bill Clinton.

ON NOVEMBER 15, 1993, Jiang boarded China's version of *Air Force One* for the first visit to America by a Chinese leader since the calamity in Tiananmen Square. His destination was Seattle, where he would attend the Asia-Pacific Economic Cooperation (APEC) conference and hold a carefully choreographed summit with President Clinton. Months earlier Jiang told his country's ambassadors and Foreign Ministry officials that China's objective was to "fully restore relations with the United States to pre–June 4, 1989 levels."

Jiang had made the decision to go in spite of opposition on both sides. In America China's critics in Congress thought it wrong for an American president to lend legitimacy to a government that had used military force on student demonstrators. In China it was not forgotten that Clinton, in his 1992 presidential campaign, had criticized his opponent, President George H.W. Bush, for "coddling dictators from Baghdad to Beijing," effectively equating Jiang Zemin with Saddam Hussein.

Jiang's agenda, according to Robert Suettinger, "was complex and nearly impossible. . . . He had to show himself as a tough and determined leader, reflect the growing anger of the collective Chinese leadership at the shabby treatment of China by the United States, defend China's positions (especially on sensitive human rights issues), but at the same time encourage the American leader to take a more balanced, long-term approach to China and establish some personal rapport with him." Congresswoman Nancy Pelosi, who was head of the Congressional Working Group on China, urged Clinton "not to smile or greet Jiang too effusively" when they first met in Seattle.

But the Chinese president had more than diplomacy on his mind. He was eager to showcase the growing Chinese economy and to stump for new investments. Landing in San Francisco for a brief stopover, Jiang encouraged business leaders to think big when it came to China. "I am sure," he said, "that the American business community, with its immense strength and rich experience, will not let opportunities slip through its fingers."

From the Seattle airport Jiang went directly to Boeing. At the vast Everett factory, he praised the aircraft-manufacturing giant for being a pacesetter in improving Sino-U.S. relations. He told three thousand workers that China was Boeing's largest customer outside America, countering the common complaint that China had an unfair trade surplus with the United States. By then, China had committed to purchase or lease 234 Boeing jets at a cost of some $9 billion.

Staying in character, Jiang requested a visit with an ordinary worker's family, and Boeing asked Cary Qualls, a thirty-three-year-old assembler, to host the Chinese leader. When Jiang arrived at the Qualls home, he greeted the family in English, which he continued to use sporadically throughout the visit. "I heard you were the 'Worker of the Month' four times," Jiang said to Qualls. "You must have done a wonderful job." He then peppered his host with questions: Where did he come from? When had he started working at Boeing? How long was his commute? Did the couple own their house?

As Qualls's wife, Melanie, served tea and freshly baked cookies, Jiang presented a large stuffed panda to the couple's daughter. In return, she gave him one of her drawings. "She drew Sleeping Beauty for you," her mother explained. "It's beautiful," Jiang said. "I'll give it to my granddaughter; she loves drawing, too." Jiang reached into his pocket and took out pictures of his grandchildren, which he proudly passed around the room. Before leaving, he gave the family some Chinese mementos, including an embroidered kitten, which he said were gifts for the coming Thanksgiving holiday.

President Jiang's first meeting with President Clinton was not nearly so cordial. Lasting ninety minutes and described by both sides as "positive and constructive," the summit was, in reality, frosty and frustrating. Clinton was described as "somber and stiff," while Jiang was said to be "nervous"—more concerned with the Chinese officials on his side of the table than with the American president and delegation on the other.

After Clinton's welcoming remarks, Jiang took out a prepared document and spent fifteen minutes reading its strongly worded text. It was a lecture, not a discussion. Jiang chastised the United States for failing to understand China's human rights situation and the differences between the two countries. He asserted that nations must not interfere in the internal affairs of other nations. U.S. secretary of state Warren Christopher said that Clinton "came right back and described to Jiang why it was necessary for China to make improvements in the human rights field." What Clinton did not know at the time was that Jiang had been constrained by China's collective leadership.

When Clinton extended China's most-favored-nation (MFN) status earlier in the year, he had said that he would renew it again only if Beijing improved its human rights record. Now he outlined for Jiang five areas where America would require progress: Red Cross access to prisons, release of political prisoners, dialogue with the Dalai Lama on Tibet, investigations into prison-made goods, and freedom for families of dissidents to emigrate.

Jiang did not respond directly. Instead, he pointed out that Asians "give greater emphasis to the rights of the many rather than to the privileges of a few." On the subject of arms proliferation, Jiang expressed his government's irritation with the U.S. sale of F-16 fighter planes to Taiwan, while acknowledging American concerns about Chinese weapons sales to other countries.

Changing the tone, Jiang presented Clinton with a Shanghai-made saxophone and suggested that they play a duet with Jiang on the *erhu*. But even that offer may have arisen from a misunderstanding. A report by Jiang biographer Bruce Gilley suggested that a Chinese translator had inadvertently overheard and misinterpreted a sarcastic aside from Clinton to one of his aides. "I should have brought my saxophone along to get some practice in," the irritated American president was reported to have said. Trying to make sense of the remark, the translator told Jiang, "Mr. Clinton says he would like to play his saxophone for you."

Speaking with the press afterward, Clinton tried to put the best spin on the meeting. "These two countries have been somewhat estranged since Tiananmen Square," he began. "And the very fact that we talked today I think is a positive sign that both of us are interested in trying to resolve our respective problems." Commenting on Jiang's responses, Clinton was circumspect. "I thought we began a dialogue, and that's all I think I should say today."

Jiang acknowledged divergent views of human rights but commented, "I believe that to attach conditions to MFN is a remnant of the cold war and should be discarded. If we acknowledge our diversity, we can respect each other . . . the shared interests between our two sides are far greater than the differences." Jiang added, "Some Americans who censure China on the questions of human rights fix their eyes only on an exceedingly small number of lawbreakers who, having violated China's laws by endangering national security, naturally should be brought to justice. Every country does this."

Seeking positive momentum, Jiang invited Clinton to China. "Mr. Clinton said he looked forward to going in the future," reported Chinese foreign minister Qian Qichen. "He said it was something he had wanted to do since he was a child."

While Clinton and his advisers were unimpressed by the meeting, Jiang won kudos in Beijing for obtaining Clinton's agreement to improve Sino-U.S. relations without conceding anything on human rights or other vital issues. "He was neither haughty nor humble," opined Military Commission vice chairman Zhang Zhen. "The whole Chinese army is proud of and inspired by Comrade Jiang Zemin."

Jiang received a warmer welcome three days later when he flew from Seattle to Cuba, becoming the first Chinese president to visit the Caribbean island since Fidel Castro's revolution in 1959. Castro gave an enthusiastic reception to his fellow Communist head of state, one of the few remaining in their recently diminished world. The visit sent the message, pointedly, that China would conduct an "independent foreign policy." Tellingly, one of Jiang Zemin's favorite lines of poetry comes from the early-twentieth-century writer Lu Xun: "We Chinese have backbone." After quoting the sentence in a 1993 interview, Jiang went on to say: "We shall never yield to unreasonable pressure exerted on us by foreigners."

IN MID-NOVEMBER, THE THIRD Plenary Session of the Fourteenth Party Congress passed "the resolution establishing the socialist market-oriented economy system." Linking "market" with "socialism" was now the official directive of China's economic policy. Appropriately, in the same month Jiang spoke at a study session honoring the publication of Volume III of the selected works of Deng Xiaoping. Its 119 articles elaborated Deng's theory of constructing socialism with Chinese characteristics—the "Marxism of today's China." Jiang hailed the publication as "a major event in the political life of our country and our Party. . . . Coupling Marxism with Chinese reality, it is the guiding flag of the socialist cause and the spiritual pillar of our people's revitalization."

In December Jiang led the Communist Party in celebrating the hundredth anniversary of the birth of Mao Zedong. As part of the centenary honors, China's central archives began to publish Mao Zedong's original manuscripts—inscriptions, letters, drafts of articles, telegrams, annotations, commentaries, reading notes, poems, and classic poems. On the cover of the book, the calligraphy of the characters of the title was written by Jiang Zemin.

"The best way to remember Comrade Mao Zedong," Jiang said in a speech before ten thousand guests in the Great Hall of the People, "is to be guided by [Deng's] theory of building socialism with Chinese characteristics . . . and to keep pushing forward the cause established by Mao and the old generation of proletarian revolutionaries." By explaining Mao Zedong Thought in terms of Deng Xiaoping Theory, Jiang Zemin was, in essence, establishing himself as a guide to their political principles. It was a natural step in the development of his own Jiang Thought.

Chapter 15

1994

"The Outside World Has a Terrible Misunderstanding of China"

GALLOPING INFLATION SPURRED ON by consumer fears and worker unrest dominated Jiang's agenda in 1994. Rumors of grain shortages led to panic buying and food-hoarding frenzies, spiking prices by as much as 50 percent. The national inflation rate, fueled by explosive growth, was 22 percent, the worst since the People's Republic was founded; urban inflation, driven by quick-profit real estate construction, was higher still. Desperate workers demanded living wages, compelling state banks to transfer money to hopeless factories through "stability and unity loans" that had no chance of being paid back. Jiang told bankers that the money was for "workers to buy dumplings for the Chinese New Year." But just in case the dumplings didn't suffice, he also readied riot troops and imposed news blackouts.

"If price controls are released, prices go up," explained economist Li Yining. "That's what happens in a planned economy. It's like pushing a ball into water; if you release your hand, the ball will pop back up."

Jiang visited marketplaces in Beijing and Shanxi province. "Fuel, rice, cooking oil, salt, soy sauce, vinegar, and tea are the seven daily necessities," he said. "A small 'shopping basket' affects social stability; reform and development cannot be separated from stability." At one meat counter Jiang asked about prices, then suspiciously inquired: "Were the prices lowered today because of our visit?"

"To keep prices stable, we must attach the utmost importance to the farming sector," Jiang said while touring a farmers' market in Tianjin. "We must set up vegetable production centers and large pig farms around major cities. We must increase the ratio of investment in agriculture to total investment."

Vice Premier Zhu Rongji instituted a series of unpopular austerity measures—severe restrictions on bank credit and fixed-asset investments— making him the bête noir of the free-wheeling provinces that preferred acting as if they were independent countries with unlimited budgets. In the spring Jiang began traveling the country warning regional officials that they must put the "overall situation of the country" ahead of local interests.

The fix began working, but financially strapped enterprises suffered. Jiang was saddened to learn that his first place of employment, Shanghai Yimin Food Factory, was struggling to survive. In this case Jiang was loath to let the market take its course. Instead he asked Wu Bangguo, Shanghai's Party secretary, to take "active measures to help." "You must not let it fail," Jiang said.

Yet Jiang was convinced that Deng was right: The way to improve China's economy was not to back away from reform but to pursue it more aggressively. He advocated further freeing pricing controls, eliminating command quotas, and imposing new policies on taxation and banking. His goal was to tip the balance from a planned economy to a market economy. His prescription for the economy targeted three questions: How fast can we grow? Can we afford (or tolerate) the consequences? Will we benefit the masses?

THE ARMY NEWSPAPER, *Liberation Army Daily,* ran a story on Jiang's commitment to build the People's Armed Police into an "important armed force" for "maintaining social stability." Describing their antiriot training, Jiang said, "This kind of competency is what we should have, especially in large cities. . . .

"It is impossible to build our economy without a stable and united social environment," he continued. "We must always heighten our vigilance against some foreign forces that infiltrate our country and carry out subversive activities. We must resolutely nip in the bud every symptom that endangers social stability. This is the duty of the PAP."

Mindful of the need to focus on the army, Jiang promoted nineteen senior PLA officers to the rank of general, including the head of the unit that guarded Zhongnanhai, the leadership compound in central Beijing. With characteristic energy, he engaged military personnel at all levels. On virtually every trip to the provinces, he toured a local army base, met with senior staff, and chatted with soldiers. He walked through barracks and hospitals and assessed the quality of clothing and food. Checking canteens on military bases was almost a ritual for Jiang, who added one yuan per day per person to the PLA's food budget. He also increased army salaries 20 percent above those of local officials of comparable rank, knowing that it was easier for civilians to earn extra money on the side.

During army inspections Jiang always wore an olive-green Mao jacket. He was not an army veteran like Mao or Deng, so it would have been presumptuous for him to wear a PLA uniform. On the other hand, his customary suit and tie were too Western and too distant from the world of military men. Jiang's visits were always reported in army publications and usually in the national news.

Jiang made it a priority to visit National Defense University, the country's leading military institute of higher learning, three or four times a year. He liked lecturing to students, mingling with officers, and dining with instructors. He attended as many PLA functions as possible—both formal ceremonies such as promotions and social events such as concerts and benefits. In his spare time he learned everything he could about military matters. He did not rely on summaries but read military documents in their entirety, relishing technical details. In the early 1990s he probably spent more time with military papers than with Party papers.

In August Jiang received an army stamp of approval in an article that General Zhang Zhen, CMC vice chairman, wrote for the Party magazine *Qiushi (Seeking Truth)*. Praising Jiang for paying "a great deal of attention to the inheritance and glorification of the fine tradition of the army," General Zhang saluted him as a worthy successor to Deng and Mao. It was a significant endorsement because Zhang had the widest network and most credibility among senior officers.

Jiang did not try to micromanage the army. "Respect professional soldiers handling professional work" was his motto. Whenever General Zhang proposed a slate of personnel requests, Jiang would approve it quickly. The understanding was that Jiang would give PLA officers unprecedented autonomy in running the army in return for their support of his leadership. For Jiang to maintain power and implement his policies, he knew he had no choice.

AS THE FIFTH ANNIVERSARY of Tiananmen drew near, Jiang offered up the controversial idea that "a bad thing has been turned into a good thing." He stated, "As a result, our reform and opening program has forged ahead with steadier, better, and even quicker steps." The foreign media excoriated Jiang for what seemed to be his rationalization of the use of lethal force. Yet a decade later many intellectuals and business leaders, even those who had participated in the 1989 demonstrations, would admit, however reluctantly, the truth of what Jiang had said earlier. Political stability had, in fact, accelerated economic resurgence.

Jiang also made the aggressive claim that U.S. president Bill Clinton's China policy sought to convert the country into a "vassal" of the West. It was an unusually harsh characterization, but it gave Jiang the nationalistic credence to deliver blunt criticisms to his own people, including an unflinching warning to the Party's Central Commission for Discipline Inspection. There were only two dangers, he said, that could spell doom for the Communist Party—if China's economy could not be kept in good shape or if corruption continued to get worse.

To seek economic balance, the Party decided that the wealthiest regions of the country should assist the poorest. With this goal in mind, Jiang inspected Guangdong and Fujian provinces, two of the fastest-growing regions in the world. While in Fujian, he reaffirmed that state-owned enterprises are "the core of our national economy," but he seemed defensive when adding, "And they still play a leading role in our development of the socialist market economy." Rebuking those pushing for more rapid privatization, he continued, "We should not lose confidence in state-owned enterprises and consider them burdens to the country."

Sometime during the summer of 1994, according to gossip emanating from the British Foreign Office, Jiang Zemin "threw a fit," complicating efforts to reestablish Sino-British relations. At issue was Hong Kong. The rules for repatriating the island had been clearly set, but Britain, according to Jiang, was now trying to change the colony's political structure just three years before the date it was to be returned. Britain's sudden interest in granting democracy to Hong Kong, after 150 years of its own imperialist rule, seemed hypocritical. To Jiang, it was also patronizing.

When discussing Sino-U.S. relations with visiting U.S. secretary of state Warren Christopher, Jiang used the expression "The fat man didn't get that way with just one bite." The *Far Eastern Economic Review* tried to parse the enigmatic phrase: "Was it an appeal for a step-by-step improvement in Sino-U.S. relations from their current nadir? Or a dismissive comparison of America's mere two hundred years on the world stage to China's four thousand years?"

TO ASSIST HIM DURING challenging times, President Jiang had a staff of competent, dedicated professionals. His key political administrator and adviser was rising star Zeng Qinghong, director of the CPC (Party) General Office; and his key personal assistant was longtime secretary Jia Ting'an, who was appointed deputy director of the CMC (military) General Office. In China's system of governance, the "General Office" is the nerve center that controls daily activities, enables communications, processes documents, convenes meetings, commissions reports, formulates policy options, and conveys orders to subordinate bodies. Jiang Zemin now had two of his closest associates at the crossroads of the flow of information and at the center of the conduct of operations for both the Party and the army, the two most powerful organizations in China.

Zeng Peiyan, a longtime associate of Jiang, focused on domestic policy and ran operations for the Party's Leading Group on Finance and Economics. Tall, austere, and intellectual, with a businessman's intensity and a scholar's precision, Zeng stressed rigor in analysis and consistency in policy. For presentations and reports, he was always well prepared with clear structure and reasoned arguments backed by arrays of statistics. Although Zeng Peiyan and Zeng Qinghong were not related, the two were labeled, in the internal argot, "Jiang's Two Zengs."

You Xigui, a professional secret service officer, managed President Jiang's personal security. The craggy-faced You, who had worked in Beijing since before the Cultural Revolution, favored rugged PLA attire and tolerated no nonsense.

Jiang's speechwriter and key researcher was Teng Wensheng, a natural intellectual with a broad background in Party ideology and thought. Teng was born in 1940 into a mid-level peasant family in Hunan province. "We had food to eat, clothes to wear," Teng said, "but my grandparents never went to school and couldn't read." He benefited from a Communist program that provided scholarships for poor kids to attend school. Further Party-provided aid enabled Teng to attend People's University in Beijing, where he majored in Party history. Following his graduation in 1964, he was one of five people selected in a nationwide talent search to work at the Marxist-Leninist Thought Academy, whose chairman was Chen Boda, a Maoist-Leftist propagandist who in two years would call for "sweeping away all monsters and demons," thereby helping to ignite the Cultural Revolution. After two months, Teng was moved to *Red Flag (Hong Qi)*, the Party's primary magazine, whose editor in chief was also Chen Boda. Fortunately, the two deputy editors were Hu Shen and Deng Liqun, both of whom would figure prominently in advancing Teng's career.

For five years during the Cultural Revolution, from 1969 to 1974, Teng Wensheng along with all other intellectuals at *Red Flag* were sent to a May Seventh Cadre School in the countryside of Hebei province to farm rice. Deng Liqun was labeled a "capitalist roader"—ironic considering his later views—and sent to the same school. As fate would have it, since Deng believed that he would never return from this Mao-inspired domestic exile, he had taken all his books with him, and since their Red Guard–like chaperones were often lax, Teng was able to read extensively from Deng's classic literature collection.

During these agrarian years, Teng became good friends with Hu Shen, a first-rate scholar not yet thirty years old who could recite 5,000 poems. They could hardly keep from growing close because Teng and Hu shared the same Kang bed, which had hot coals underneath to provide heat. "Whenever we went to town to take a bath," Teng recalled, "Hu would write a poem." In 1973, Hu was called to Beijing to serve on a team drafting a speech for Zhou Enlai (coordinated by Deng Xiaoping since Zhou's health was poor). In late 1974, Hu was asked to write a history book, *From the Opium Wars to the May 4th Movement,* and he requested that Teng come to Beijing to help.

After Deng Xiaoping took power, Teng Wensheng joined the Political Research Office, which was first under the CPC General Office and then the Party Secretariat (rejoining Deng Liqun, then its vice minister and later its minister). From 1980 to 1987, Teng helped draft special documents and speeches, including Deng Xiaoping's crucial August 18, 1980, address to the full Politburo on political reform. "I was privileged to join Deng Liqun and hear Deng Xiaoping's personal ideas on this vital speech," Teng recalled.

In 1987 General Secretary Zhao Ziyang did not think that the Secretariat Research Office reflected his liberal political philosophy, and he replaced it with the Political Structure Reform Office, headed by Bao Tong (who would become the most senior official imprisoned after the Tiananmen crackdown and a prolific political writer after his release). Due to obvious differences with Zhao Ziyang and Bao Tong, Teng Wensheng was not hired by the new office, but went to work for Bo Yibo, who was executive vice chairman of the Central Advisory Commission. "I was annoyed with Hong Kong news reports," remembered Teng. "They wrote 'Teng Wensheng laid off' as if I were an unemployed scholar, broke and needing a shave." When the new CPC Policy Research Office was founded in mid-June 1989, after June 4 but before Jiang Zemin was formally acclaimed general secretary on June 24, Teng became its vice minister. He would become minister and director of the office in 1997.

"I had first met Jiang Zemin in 1985," Teng remembered, "when he was minister of electronics. At the time, I was propaganda head of the Party Rectification Office and we had come to the electronics ministry to hear a report on their political progress. I noted how sharp Jiang looked. He was scholarly, ministerial, very comfortable in his position—and had a full head of hair."

During his thirteen years working for Jiang, from 1989 to 2002, Teng was tireless, especially on foreign trips, where he organized materials and prepared talks. A practical man with a round face, Teng was praised by subordinates as down to earth and humble, a boss who was concerned about their welfare. When complimented on his extraordinary work for the president, Teng demurred: "I just handle some details, take some notes," he said. Teng was not pleased that some Hong Kong publications had "exaggerated my role and contribution" as a "top aide" to Jiang. "I'm not that important," he said with a smile. "Those stories are not even close to truth. I'm not a big scholar, just an ordinary intellectual." Though self-deprecating, Teng was justifiably proud of his special contribution to the history of China's reform.

IN SEPTEMBER JIANG TRAVELED to Russia, Ukraine, and France, state visits planned to build goodwill. He signed a variety of nonaggression pacts and trade agreements. In Russia his summit with President Boris Yeltsin "put the seal on a constructive partnership" between the two giant countries, meaning that they agreed not to counteract each other but stopped well short of a bilateral alliance. Standing down nuclear missiles targeting each other, adopting a no-first-strike policy, and settling noisome border disputes symbolized the confidence the two sides were building.

While in Russia, Jiang visited Tolstoy's home, where his off-the-cuff literary analysis of the great writer's masterpieces surprised the Russian guides. He also visited the Mir mission control center and spoke to cosmonauts onboard the orbiting space station. Jiang lauded the success of their emergency manual docking of a supply ship after automatic operations failed.

In France Jiang had occasion to discuss his concept of democracy. "The outside world has a terrible misunderstanding of China," he told the first secretary of France's Socialist Party. "They think China doesn't want democracy. In fact, the Chinese people struggled for more than a hundred years for China's independence, protection of people's basic rights, and realization of democracy . . . There is no such thing as a stereotyped democracy, nor is it possible to have such a thing. Today, China carries out political reform precisely for the purpose of developing and perfecting a socialist democracy suited to its national conditions."

Perhaps the most notable feature of Jiang's journey was the presence of his wife, Wang Yeping. It was the first time she accompanied him on a high-profile tour, and only the second time in the history of Communist China that the leader of the country had taken his wife on a state visit abroad.

At the time Wang Yeping was described in a Hong Kong publication as "introverted, lenient, kind, and hospitable." Retiring by nature, according to the article, "she is persistent and serious when doing things, often keeps quiet, leads a plain life, wears ordinary clothing, and does not use cosmetics." Complementing her gregarious husband, she liked "peaceful and quiet days." She stayed in touch with old friends and colleagues in science and technology, using these contacts to update Jiang on the latest advances at home and abroad.

"Being useful when one is old" was one of Wang Yeping's mottos, though her neck problems caused pain and interfered with her normal activities. She considered it a "burden" to accompany her husband because, she said, her "strength falls short of her will." She never liked "appearing in the limelight." Being a public figure, she said, was just not part of her personality.

Unfortunately, being a public figure was just what the changing times demanded of her. The Chinese Foreign Ministry had begun to realize the importance of projecting a positive picture of the country's leaders in the international media. One way to humanize China's image was for its leaders to travel with their wives. Mikhail Gorbachev was the first Soviet leader to travel with his wife, Raisa, and her stylish presence helped alter the world's impression of a reforming Soviet Union.

In China Premier Li Peng had taken his charismatic wife, Zhu Lin, on foreign tours, enhancing his stature as a diplomat. "Li Peng has not the slightest traces of male chauvinism," revealed Zhu Lin, an executive in the power industry. "Whenever he was free, he would lend a helping hand in household chores, either when he was an ordinary official or later a minister or even after he became the premier." This description of Li Peng's domestic duties clearly clashed with his post-Tiananmen image.

When Jiang's plane landed in Moscow on the first leg of his European trip, he may have been more anxious about how his wife would react to the official affairs and crowds of reporters than about how the Russians would deal with border disputes and nuclear weapons. For ten days in Russia, Ukraine, and France, Wang Yeping played the role of China's First Lady with dignity and aplomb. She never enjoyed it, but she performed her job well. Despite her physical discomfort and emotional stress—she endured constant, excruciating pain throughout a state banquet in Paris that lasted for more than three hours—she pluckily maintained a visible presence at Jiang's side. Her husband was pleased, not only for China's image, but also because he genuinely enjoyed seeing his wife, who had put up with so many hardships over the years, being honored on the international stage.

With the 1994 trip came a change in media policy. An internal Party directive ordered China's news organizations to "properly report on the relevant activities by Comrade Jiang Zemin's wife during the visit abroad." Customarily, the press stayed away from the personal lives of senior leaders. Even a flattering article that violated the privacy policy for Party and state leaders could get the writer fired.

THE PARTY PLENUM IN late September 1994, on "Party Construction," made decisions on reforming the process of promotions, including the use of democratic selection tools such as surveys. The plenum was also when the transition from Deng Xiaoping to Jiang Zemin was discussed. Although no formal document was prepared, Deng had been indicating to family, staff, and associates that he was becoming less active in politics. About six weeks later, on November 11, he informed those close to him that he would no longer be involved in political issues or decision-making. He cautioned that leaders should be very circumspect about decision-making, and at his advanced age he feared he could make mistakes. It was time, Deng said, for the new generation of leaders, with Jiang Zemin at its core, to take full responsibility for China.

On the afternoon of October 1, National Day in China, Deng Xiaoping was driven to the Diaoyutai State Guesthouse in Beijing, where he was helped out of his car and lowered into a wheelchair. The previous February, he had made his final public appearance at the dedication of a bridge in Shanghai, where he showed unmistakable signs of advanced age. Since then he had not attended any official functions, and rumors of his death had been circulating with increasing frequency. But the Paramount Leader still had something to say. That night he hosted a dinner to honor a group of retired Party leaders. It was the first time the ninety-year-old Deng met colleagues while sitting in a wheelchair. The last published photograph of Deng showed him watching the National Day fireworks. Though the image portrayed Deng as vacuous and uninvolved, what he told his colleagues was lucid and far-sighted.

Deng requested that one of the attendees, Bo Yibo, an "Immortal Elder," disseminate Deng's dinner comments. "Here's the problem I'm always thinking how to solve," Deng told Bo. "Inside the Party, in China and overseas, my personal role and influence are considered extremely significant, even indispensable. This is not a good thing. One day when I really die, this may cause shocks to the Party and the state. I hope that in a short period of time the central and provincial leading bodies will unify their thinking and make a firm determination to unite closely around the Central Party with Comrade Jiang Zemin at its core."

Bo Yibo wrote in *People's Daily* that the transition from Deng to Jiang had the same historical importance as the establishment of New China in 1949, which made Mao Zedong the country's First Generation leader, and the beginning of reform in 1978, which recognized Deng Xiaoping as the leader of the Second Generation. "We must uphold Jiang Zemin as the only core," Bo stated. On Deng's wishes, the general secretary was being anointed as his successor.

At about this time Jiang brought Shanghai Party secretary Wu Bangguo to Beijing as a member of the Secretariat, which ran the day-to-day affairs of the Party and had broad powers. As such, Wu would assist Hu Jintao with Party work. Savvy observers predicted that the fifty-three-year-old Wu, who had been appointed to the Politburo in 1992, along with two other Politburo members, Hu Jintao and Wen Jiabao, would be leaders of the next generation. Wu Bangguo and Hu Jintao had both studied at Qinghua University and joined the Party at the same time. They were said to be well acquainted, to "cherish the same ideals," and to follow the same path.

Huang Ju, the Shanghai mayor and new Party secretary who had been close to Jiang since the late 1980s, was appointed to the twenty-one-member Politburo as a replacement for the former Party secretary of Tianjin, who had died of cancer the year before. Custom might have directed that the vacancy be filled by a new representative from Tianjin, rather than another from Shanghai. In addition, Li Ruihuan, a Politburo Standing Committee member, had been the mayor and Party secretary of Tianjin, and so the Politburo vote that was now going to an associate of Jiang might have ordinarily gone to one of his. It was unlikely that Jiang could have made this move without approval from Deng Xiaoping, who supported the general secretary's need to form a dominant group in China's highest decision-making body as soon as possible. Deng could die at any moment, and before that happened both men wanted to secure Jiang's position as successor.

IN NOVEMBER PRESIDENT JIANG flew to Indonesia to attend his second APEC summit and to hold his second meeting with President Clinton. The atmosphere in Jakarta was decidedly less tense than it had been in Seattle, and the two leaders discussed a broad range of issues, including human rights, Beijing's missile- and nuclear-technology transfers to Pakistan and "rogue states," and North Korea's nuclear development. The Chinese leader said there were "no differences" between Beijing and Washington on the Korean issue.

Clinton cautioned that "further progress on human rights would be very important to further progress in our overall relationship." Jiang replied that China wanted to extend human rights within its society, but not at the expense of stability, which had to remain its highest priority. He underscored that China's sovereignty could not be violated when it came to any issues, including human rights.

Clinton acknowledged the cultural differences between the countries but said that he would pursue "without apology" his goal to influence human rights policies among Asian countries. "Everywhere people aspire to be treated with dignity, to give voice to their opinions, to have a say in choosing their leaders," he had said in an address at Georgetown University before departing. "I don't think we have to choose between increasing trade and fostering human rights and open societies."

President Jiang proposed five principles to build a new constructive relationship between China and the United States: having a long-term perspective, respecting each other's national conditions while maintaining a spirit of friendship, making full use of the advantages of both economies, cooperating on international affairs, and increasing high-level contacts. The principles were general, not specific (which always eases agreement), and Jiang again unfurled his sixteen-character maxim for improving bilateral relations.

Notwithstanding his duties, Jiang found time to indulge his passion for science. In late 1994, when inspecting Tianjin, he interrupted his schedule to visit Nankai University because he wanted to understand something in fundamental physics. While giving Jiang some technical papers, a professor asked him, "Can you really read these when you're so busy?" "Yes," Jiang answered. "It's part of my job as well as my interest. Modern science is developing so rapidly that I must study to keep up with it."

Jiang wandered into the library and talked with students from the Chinese literature department. He amazed them by reciting Wang Bo's poem "Ode to Tengwangge Pavilion" and Su Shi's "To the Tune of Mid-Autumn." As Jiang said farewell, he told the students: "I envy you with such a nice school; I'd really like to study here."

"President Jiang's scientific training and long experience as an engineer have made him especially good at logic," said Zhao Qizheng, minister of the State Council Information Office and an associate of Jiang since the middle 1980s in Shanghai. "He is also knowledgeable about many areas of science. My degree is in nuclear physics. I am very confident talking about science in front of others, but very cautious in front of President Jiang."

In December Jiang decided that it was time for Politburo members to attend a lecture on law, particularly on international trade and China's bid to enter the World Trade Organization. The lecturer was a distinguished professor from Shanghai, Chao Jianmin, and for China's senior leaders it was like the first day of law school (only here the professor was more nervous than the students). Zeng Qinghong, who arranged the session, escorted Chao into President Jiang's formal red-carpeted conference room, the fabled decision-making center for all China. As they circumnavigated the huge oval table with its thirty-two chairs, Zeng encouraged Chao: "Speak freely; be brave; tell us what you really think. You should treat us like your students."

Jiang spoke first, introducing Chao and issuing a firm directive: Everyone must understand the law, believe the law, follow the law, and use the law to manage the state. Chao gave a spirited and engaging lecture, interweaving real-world examples and cases with governing theory and principles. He did not avoid China's problems. The wholesale stealing of intellectual property, he said, not only infuriated foreign companies but undermined Chinese creativity. Unbridled smuggling, he explained, was enabled by excessively high tariffs. At this point Jiang cut in and asked, "Did officials from MOFTEC [Ministry of Foreign Trade and Economic Cooperation] come?" On seeing a hand rise, Jiang said, "You should listen carefully and study these ideas well."

After the lecture an exhausted Chao took some time collecting his books and belongings. Not until one of Jiang's assistants whispered, "The President is waiting for you," did Chao realize that Jiang had been standing patiently by the door. "Thank you, professor," Jiang said. "We've learned a great deal from you today; you have improved our mental agility."

Jiang closed the year 1994 with culture, declaring that promoting China's national arts was important for educating the broad masses, especially youngsters, and for inspiring the national spirit. He called for better art schools and colleges, more attention to folk art, and improved living conditions for artists. He also extolled traditional Chinese art forms. On December 20 a month-long Peking Opera festival opened in Beijing. In the audience was Jiang Zemin.

Chapter 16

1 9 9 5

"Spiritual Civilization"

J IANG ZEMIN WAS COMING into his own. On New Year's Day, with four hundred dignitaries gathered in the Great Hall of the People for a tea party, he spoke on "spiritual civilization," which sought a balance between the individualism of the market economy and the collectivism of socialist ideology. There was nothing religious about Jiang's "spiritual" prescription for an ideal Chinese society. Rather, it was to be a blending of Marxist philosophy and traditional Chinese culture, uplifting ethics and reestablishing morality in an increasing mercantile and materialistic world.

"Spiritual civilization" was also meant to restore the Party's credibility and authority during the country's tumultuous transformation, and to enable Jiang to become China's leading political theorist. The expression—which was first put forward by Deng Xiaoping at the end of 1979, though it would remain marginalized until Jiang revitalized it—would set the political agenda over the next two years.

Torrid growth, essential to be sure, was part of the problem. For example, in the provinces local officials found themselves caught between the central government, which demanded that inflation be controlled, and their own constituents, who clamored for even greater growth. For economic reform to succeed, Beijing needed cooperation, integration, and long-term planning.

Mao (almost always) and Deng (usually) could issue decrees and expect virtually everyone to follow them. Not Jiang. He had to build consensus. His way was to bring the appropriate leaders together and float the new policy, then allow discussions, encourage modifications, and make the new policy official only when he and his staff were highly confident of its acceptance and success.

Meeting with provincial leaders (Party secretaries and governors) was often part of Jiang's process of governance. It was not uncommon in such sessions, however, for provincial leaders to express total support for the central government's policy, but then find some reason why their particular province was sufficiently unique or had special difficulties so that the policy should not be implemented there.

This time, though, the economy was sufficiently overheated that Jiang was determined to corral local leaders. At a conference of provincial governors at the end of 1994, he along with Li Peng and Zhu Rongji had denounced local protectionism. Jiang set the tone by asking a governor, "What's the price of a *jin* [a little over a pound] of eggs?" in his province. The governor answered, "A little more than three yuan." Zhu Rongji broke in: "I don't think so," he said. "I was there a few days ago; the price was over five yuan."

The incident provided a taste of things to come. Jiang required each governor to report his province's inflation and growth rates for 1994 as well as to forecast rates for 1995. Everyone gave an inflation rate that was no higher than the growth rate—claims that no one believed. The figures given were not only implausible, they were impossible—since for the country as a whole inflation well exceeded growth.

Jiang fumed. At one point he pounded the table. Provincial Party secretaries and governors who had failed to support the central government were criticized by name. He said that if they lacked sincerity they could be dismissed. That evening Jiang asked his staff to write a tough commentary for *People's Daily* admonishing the regions to "defend consciously the authority of the center." Jiang and Zhu called in each governor for a personal interview. They asked for a vow of allegiance to Beijing and its austerity policies, leaving the problem of how to deal with local reaction to the governors themselves. Nonetheless, the vast majority of such meetings were harmonious; they were always part of Jiang Zemin's style of leadership.

A MASSIVE RESHUFFLING OF provincial leaders would occur after Deng's death, and Jiang and his team worked to move their people into position. Not surprisingly, it was around this time that the term *Shanghai Faction,* which had been used for years among senior officials, entered common parlance. A Party official told of a meeting he had attended with Jiang's team. "Some people say we have a Shanghai Faction in the central leadership," Jiang reportedly told the attendees. "They are very wrong in saying this." But after a pause he added, "Many people have worked in Shanghai. Those of you who have worked there and are here today, please raise your hands." Not a small number shot into the air.

Jiang also arranged for his recently promoted associate, Wu Bangguo, to be given jurisdiction over areas of finance, taxation, and macroeconomic policy, a move that would result in Wu becoming vice premier. The promotion was noteworthy in that Wu's experience was on the Party side, not the government, and people read his elevation as another signal that Jiang was extending his own authority.

With the media Jiang was less subtle. Early in the year a document known as "Twelve Rules Governing Journalism" was circulated as part of the plan to buttress ideology. The rules included a prohibition against foreign investments in Chinese newspapers and against Chinese reporters writing articles for foreign publications. Important news was to be released in a centralized manner, that is to say, through the official Xinhua News Agency, and not interpreted locally. Interviews with important people would require prior approval, and news coverage for payment was banned. The press should "give a hand but not make trouble," Jiang said, adding they ought "to pool together resources but not sow discord."

At a propaganda conference, Jiang enumerated a "twenty-point directive" on what should and should not be reported in the media. Examples of the latter, according to Jiang, were "negative phenomena" such as worker demonstrations and other conflicts between the government and the people. Examples of the former were stories that portrayed "unity and stability," which he considered vital for molding public opinion in the "new era," a euphemism for the period that would follow the death of Deng Xiaoping.

At the Chinese New Year Jiang laid out an Eight-Point Proposal that would set Taiwan policy for years to come. Entitled "Continue to Fight for the Accomplishment of the Great Cause of Reunification of the Motherland," the speech alternately promised economic prosperity and threatened military action.

"There are only two ways to settle the Taiwan question," Jiang said. "One is by peaceful means, and the other is by nonpeaceful means. . . .

"Reunification," he went on to assure his listeners, "does not mean that the mainland will swallow up Taiwan, nor does it mean that Taiwan will swallow up the mainland."

He promised that foreign investments in Taiwan and the nongovernmental exchanges between Taiwan and other countries would not be affected and that the island would enjoy legislative and independent judicial power. It would also be allowed to retain its armed forces and administer its party, government, and military systems on its own. Jiang also said that the mainland would not station troops or send administrative personnel there but that Taiwanese would be allowed to hold positions in the central government. Above all, he declared that the principle of "one China" was inviolable and non-negotiable.

The speech, which many speculated had been the brainchild of Wang Daohan, did not please most people. Foreign critics dismissed it for not offering anything new, while hardliners in China bashed it for being soft and weak. Not a single high-level general offered early support. China remained obsessed with Taiwan, which it considered a renegade province, the last vestige of 150 years of foreign intrigue to divide the motherland.

Meanwhile in Taiwan, a number of recently published books exploited growing tensions with China. One of them offered a battle-by-battle scenario of a potential Chinese invasion of Taiwan. On being given a copy, Jiang remained nonchalant. "There are lots of books like this on the market in Taiwan," he said. "I have not read any of them." Then he added, "I am the chairman of the Central Military Commission, and I am not aware of such plans. So how could they exist?"

REGARDING CORRUPTION, JIANG'S ACTIONS divided opinion. In February 1995 Zhou Beifang, the head of the Hong Kong branch of the huge Capital Iron and Steel Corporation, was arrested on charges of "major economic crimes." Zhou was a business partner of one of Deng Xiaoping's sons, and his father was a close friend of the Paramount Leader himself. To some, the news signaled that Jiang was serious about fighting corruption. To others, the arrest seemed more a case of the central government trying to control independent enterprises than a real effort to stamp out corruption. "It's a kind of old political tactic," said an observer in Hong Kong, quoting a Chinese proverb. "'Killing the chicken to scare the monkey.' It's a warning to local authorities to obey the central government."

In one of his more inspired personnel moves, President Jiang recruited Wang Huning, a brilliant political economist and former head of Fudan University's Department of International Politics, to head the political section of the Party's Policy Research Office, where China's grand visions and specific directives, both domestic and diplomatic, were developed. Jiang had first met Professor Wang in the middle 1980s, when Jiang was mayor of Shanghai and

Wang was just being appointed, at thirty-one, the youngest-ever associate professor at Fudan. When Jiang came to Beijing as the surprise general secretary in 1989, he was said to be carrying an exposition on corruption written by Wang. A trenchant essayist, Wang argued that a strong central authority was essential to effect reform.

Only forty years old in 1995, Wang Huning was a prodigious translator of Western books and ideas, and he would become Jiang Zemin's man for scholarly policymaking and theory development. Intense, tall, and with the sharp-eyed look of an intellectual, Wang would often be with the Chinese leader, sharing private dinners at the Jiang home and spending parts of summers at Beidaihe, where, along with policy discussions Wang watched American films such as Steven Spielberg's *Schindler's List* and Martin Scorsese's *The Last Temptation of Christ*.

Wang recognized the "soft power" of national culture to accomplish political goals in foreign affairs. "If one nation-state is able to make its power appear reasonable in the eyes of another people," he wrote, "then its desires will encounter less resistance. If the culture and ideology of one nation-state are attractive, other people will voluntarily follow it." When Jiang Zemin harbored concern that the "cultural imperialism" of the West, particularly the United States, could diminish China's sovereignty, he found strong intellectual support in Wang Huning.

Jiang's daily routine became a media item during the National People's Congress in March. "When I'm in Beijing," he said, "I'm usually circulating around Zhongnanhai, or I go to the Great Hall of the People, attend military meetings in the Jingxi Hotel, or engage in state activities at Diaoyutai [State Guesthouse]. I never have an opportunity to visit the Wangfujing department store or the Yansha [Lufthansa] shopping center. First, I'm too busy with my official work. Second, I don't want to disturb the people."

Jiang noted that as a student, he never learned how to swim, though he had tried. He got his chance, as it were, during the Cultural Revolution. Being "set aside" as a "capitalist roader" meant that he had plenty of time to practice in Wuhan's East Lake. Swimming was now his primary exercise, Jiang said, and he got in six hundred meters almost every day.

ON AN INSPECTION TOUR of Jiangxi province in late March, General Secretary Jiang made a special trip to the place where the ashes of former General Secretary Hu Yaobang were buried. During the visit Hu's widow asked Jiang to erect a monument to her husband and inscribe it with the words "Being

Frank, Open-hearted, Selfless, and with a Clear Conscience." Jiang immediately agreed. Hu was thrifty, Jiang said, yet had no savings—evidence of his moral purity. "Hu was bright and valuable for the Party," he wrote to the widow.

Whether the pilgrimage was the product of good planning or lucky timing, it would help Jiang move against the corrupt Beijing Faction, which was led by an antagonist, Chen Xitong, the Beijing Party chief. When fighting corruption, Jiang could now do so wearing the mantle of the esteemed Hu Yaobang, whose death had triggered the student movement of 1989. In addition, by reaching out to Hu's followers in the Communist Youth League, Jiang broadened his base of support.

Chen Yun, the leading conservative elder, died on April 12, further signifying the passing of the older generation. Now that Deng had won the "death race" between the two, some said that China's market reforms were more secure. But with an increasingly strong Jiang Zemin as general secretary, those reforms were no longer in doubt in any event.

That same week, in the remote hill country outside Beijing, the city's executive vice mayor, Wang Baoshen, shot himself in the head. Wang had been under scrutiny for corruption stemming from his instructions to a bank to lend one billion yuan (about $120 million) to a private telecommunications company.

Xinhua reported the disturbing news only on its English-language service. Otherwise the story was not covered domestically, fueling suspicions of a major scandal. Rumors flew that Beijing Party chief Chen Xitong and his associates were embroiled in Wang Baoshen's illegal activities—Wang had been known as "Chen's Money Box."

Even though he was only a city leader, Chen Xitong was one of the more powerful men in China, and he never really accepted Jiang's leadership. Over the years he had made various attempts to undermine the general secretary's authority; as late as September 1994 Chen was brazenly challenging Jiang's position. "The core is not bestowed," he said in Beijing, an incendiary comment. "The core is something you have to live up to, you have to rely on everyone to support you." According to China watcher Willy Wo-Lap Lam, Jiang "hid his anger well" over the years and "exercised a high degree of patience and tact."

Stories about the greed and arrogance of Chen and his cronies were commonplace in Beijing. His administration was egregiously corrupt; bribe-taking was rampant. "Access" had a price; approvals cost more. Funds raised to support the city's bid for the 2000 Olympics had vanished; the vice mayor in charge of construction funneled the most profitable projects to his brother's company; and even taxi drivers told of municipal funds being used to maintain mistresses and prostitutes.

It couldn't last. An investment scandal involving $380 million in the distant city of Wuxi was traced back to Beijing's Capital Iron and Steel enterprise, part of Chen Xitong's empire. Corruption investigators had been watching the company's illegal money-raising scam since 1992. In 1994, after collecting incriminating evidence, they began closing in. When the link to Chen was confirmed, and the magnitude of the corruption was revealed, Zeng Qinghong assumed responsibility for the case.

Chen did not go down without a fight. Following the suicide of Wang Baoshen, he spoke out against corruption. "Wang's problem was his own," he said, blaming the vice mayor's actions on "the evil ways of capitalism." Moreover, Chen tried to placate Jiang. In speeches after the suicide, he highlighted Jiang Zemin's name several times. Before then it had been his practice to mention it only once every other speech, the bare minimum according to informal Party custom.

At the end of April 1995 Chen Xitong was dismissed from office. In 1997 he would be sentenced to twelve years in prison for accepting bribes and misusing public funds, and his name would become a synonym for corruption. *Xitong* is a homonym for the Chinese word meaning "system," and the "Chen system" came to signify the kind of blatant official corruption that Jiang was trying to eradicate.

How Jiang brought about Chen's well-deserved downfall is an inside example of his political acumen. In one way or another, he and Zeng Qinghong secured agreement from every relevant leader, from seven Party elders to Politburo colleagues Li Peng and Qiao Shi to the family of the ailing Deng Xiaoping. Qiao's protégé, Wei Jianxing, had overall responsibility for the corruption investigation and was the prime candidate to replace Chen as Beijing Party chief.

In Beijing few mourned Chen, who was notorious for an extravagant lifestyle of villas, swimming pools, mistresses, guard dogs, and unlimited expense accounts. "People would be dancing in the streets," joked one former student protester, "if the government allowed demonstrations."

When Jiang announced Chen's dismissal at a closed-door gathering of the Beijing leadership, he had to balance the need for discipline and rooting out corruption with the desire to encourage and rejuvenate officials who were disoriented, discouraged, and fearful. "It was the hardest speech I had ever written," recalled Teng Wensheng.

The ouster was viewed as a triumph for Jiang and enhanced his image as a corruption fighter. It sent a message to other officials with secrets to hide. "Cadres who lead corrupt lives and fool around with women will not be promoted," Jiang said soon after Chen's arrest, warning that any officials who suffered from the five weaknesses—lust for power, money, women, fame, and exploiting their connections (*guanxi*) for immoral gain—could lose their jobs. Yet Jiang did not gloat. "The Central Committee took charge of the cases of Wang and Chen, receiving a positive response both inside and outside the Party," he said in his bland public comment on the case. "As a result, the anticorruption effort is now being carried out more extensively."

MAY 1995 WAS A MONTH for history, art, and science. Japanese prime minister Tomiichi Murayama arrived in Beijing to reaffirm the "future-oriented" relations between the two former foes. For Jiang Zemin, who had been evicted from his middle school by the invading Japanese, it was a moment of personal closure when the prime minister paid a solemn, apologetic visit to the Marco Polo Bridge just outside Beijing, the site of the 1937 clash that triggered war between Japan and China.

Also in May Jiang visited Zhu Jizhan, a master of traditional Chinese painting, on his 105th birthday. A few weeks later he gave a speech about artists and writers, whom he called "engineers of the souls of mankind." In the speech, entitled "Dedicate the Most Beautiful Spiritual Nourishment to the People," Jiang exhorted all artists to "carry forward and spread national art and enhance the national spirit," to "love the motherland," and to "make constant innovations." He warned them, too, to "consciously resist money-worship, individualism, and other unhealthy practices; to never lower the quality of artistic work or even lower their moral quality to pander to the low tastes of some people, thus debasing themselves." The creative tension was one of Jiang's enduring themes.

For the annual conference on science and technology, the largest of its kind, Dr. Song Jian, chairman of the State Science and Technology Commission, was responsible for suggesting the agenda and helping prepare President Jiang's speech. Months earlier Song had sensed that China was ready for the third and final step in elevating science and technology to a core national strategy. The Sparks Program for developing rural and township enterprises was a decade-long success (step one), and the Torch Program to start new high-tech companies was showing progress (step two). What was needed now, Song concluded, was to institutionalize the strategy.

"Following my arrangement with President Jiang," recalled Song, "I sent

关于~~建立~~ 确立 科教兴国战略中央的信

泽民同志：

　　按中央决定，五月下旬(5月25—29日)召开科技大会。我们组织专家为您起草了一篇讲话(草案)，中办将进一步修改，最后报您审定。

　　起草间，广泛征询了科技界的意见。比较集中的是：这次大会应为今后十年指出战略方向，动员全国科技界，为实现"三步走"战略目标而奋身奋斗。都希望这次会议要有时代特征，有新意，都赞成大会主题定为落实小平同志"科技是第一生产力"，落实您提出的关于"科技生产力要有一个新的解放和大的发展"的方针。

　　大家恳切期望您的讲话中明确使用"科教兴国战略"的表述。众云理由如下：

　　所有发达国家走向工业化时，都实现了此种发展战略转变。美国在起草《宪法》(1778年)时注重科技为本；德国十九世纪初靠科技起家；日本明治维新(1860年)倡科教兴国，二战后改为技术立国；南韩技术立国成功；彼得大帝(1672—1752，康熙同代人)私访欧洲后，立志科技而兴起；中国辛亥后，全国上下呼号"德赛升堂"。可见，科技兴国是近200年来各国共同成功经历。

　　中国，1978年科技大会后，特别是小平同志提出"科技是第一生产力"后，全国上下纷起响应。大部分省、市以"科技兴省、兴市、兴县"为方针，动员全民学科学、用科学。很多产业部门也早就提出"科技兴化"、"科技兴石(化)"等方针。"科技兴农"在农村近家喻户晓。故"科教兴国"已是呼之欲出，为大势所趋，约定俗成。

　　另外，大家希望，您的讲话应高屋建瓴，对今后十年的科技方针全面阐述，使之成为跨世纪的纲领性文件。起草小组正是按科技界这个愿望努力了三个多月，结果似仍不完全满意，寄希望于政研室能予改进。率陈民意，不当处，望指正。

　　附《讲话(草案)》一份，请阅知。

宋健

1995年3月14日凌晨

The original letter that Dr. Song Jian, state councilor and chairman of the State Science and Technology Commission, sent to President Jiang Zemin that led to the establishment of the national strategy "Revitalize the Country Through Science and Education," March 14, 1995.

him a letter, dated March 14, 1995, that proposed 'the establishment of a national strategy for revitalizing the nation through science, technology, and education.' "

As a result, Jiang had the Politburo Standing Committee discuss and approve the proposal, and at the May conference he announced the grand national strategy to "Revitalize the Country Through Science and Education." In his speech, after explaining that creativity needed to be nurtured for scientific advancement, Jiang stressed the right kind of education. China's traditional system of "exam-oriented education," he said, needed to be modified and upgraded to "quality-oriented education."

IN JUNE, ON AN INSPECTION tour of Jilin province, Jiang and his wife visited the First Automotive Works in Changchun, where they met Shen Yongyan, who observed that life at the top was not easy for the Jiang family. Wang Yeping confided in Shen that their house was hardly a home. Her husband had constant meetings and other engagements, which often ran until late at night. Wang's mother, who was living with them, was deteriorating from old age. At dinner she would ask for an extra pair of chopsticks. "They didn't know for whom that fourth pair was meant," Shen said, "though they speculated that it might be for her long-deceased husband, who she said would sometimes 'join us from the window or door.' "

Wang noted that the couple's two sons and their families did not visit as often as she would like because they didn't want to be perceived as taking advantage of their father's position. They want to be successful in their own right, she said. Wang Yeping also felt the constant stress of her husband's job and told Shen about the files that she sometimes saw lying around his office. The documents, which she did not read, reported mostly negative news. "Explosions here, rioting there," she said, "murders, corruption, terrorism—little that was nice." It was just the normal burden of leaders, but seeing it depressed her, causing her health to deteriorate further. "She really wanted her husband to retire soon," Shen remembered.

Public appearances continued to pose difficulty for her; even the smallest motions were painful. "When you take your wife on state visits in foreign countries," Shen told Jiang privately, "you always seem to hold her arm and drag her along. On television that looks a little awkward."

"What should I do? If I don't help her along," Jiang responded plaintively, "it'd be hard for her to move."

Wang told Shen that after her traumatic experience at the French state dinner, during which she had to suffer in silence, she would try to avoid foreign travel in the future. Certainly, she said, she did not want to attend any more banquets, unless protocol absolutely demanded it of her. Still, she soldiered on, gamely fulfilling required responsibilities. "It's remarkable how tough she's become," Shen observed.

During the visit Shen Yongyan gathered a few of Jiang's former colleagues, and the group sang Peking Opera for hours. "I recorded the session," Shen recalled, "and gave Jiang the tape. He loved it. He hung on to that tape as if it were a state secret! Twice now I've arranged this Peking Opera program for him. It was the highlight of the trip—and his best way to relax."

SUCH LIGHT-HEARTED MOMENTS WERE not frequent. In early June relations between China and America soured when Taiwanese president Lee Teng-hui spoke at his alma mater, Cornell University, in upstate New York. He was the first Taiwanese head of state ever to visit the United States, and the fact that he had been given permission to enter the country infuriated the mainland government. Even though Lee's trip was characterized as a "private visit," it seemed to represent a step toward Taiwanese independence, and a fundamental change in U.S. policy. Lee Teng-hui appeared to be planting the seeds for the emergence of "two Chinas" or "one China, one Taiwan," an incendiary notion that Jiang considered a frontal assault on Chinese sovereignty. Just before leaving for America, Lee had reviewed military exercises, an act that did not seem coincidental.

Jiang was personally offended by what he felt was deception on the part of the American president. Only weeks before in Moscow, at the fiftieth anniversary celebration of the end of World War II, the two leaders had conversed about Taiwan. According to Jiang, Clinton had promised that he would never allow Lee to visit. "The U.S. government adheres to the 'one China' policy," Jiang quoted Clinton as saying, "and insists on maintaining relations with Taiwan on a nonofficial basis." Several days after his return to the States, Clinton personally approved Lee's visit.

"U.S. political figures do not keep their promises," Jiang said in a meeting with Foreign Ministry officials. "Even the president of a great, powerful nation can tell a lie in your presence. We lack an adequate understanding of the U.S. political situation and political figures, so we are easily taken in."

In a sense Jiang's analysis was correct. His government had an absolute authority that Clinton's did not. Under pressure from Congress, which voted 396 to 0 in the House and 97 to 1 in the Senate to allow Lee's visit, the Clinton administration changed its policy. Yet the fact remained that the American president had made a promise he did not keep. China had been insulted, and Jiang was irate. Virtually every time he spoke, whether in public speeches to domestic audiences or private comments to foreign leaders, he called U.S. policy toward China "confusing and arrogant." "The United States will have to pay a price," he said, for "seriously infringing on China's sovereignty."

In confidential talks with senior military officers, Jiang hinted at the possibility of military action. "The Taiwan independence movement is getting out of hand," he said. "And we cannot let this go on. We must heighten our guard and strengthen our resources and combat-readiness." A picture of Jiang with PLA naval units in the Yellow Sea evoked images of a parallel photo of Mao forty years earlier. He was under pressure from the army to be even more aggressive, for a time receiving eight hundred irate letters a day from officers protesting Lee Teng-hui's visit to the United States. "We would rather rebuild Taiwan from scratch," one missive stated, "than let it be taken by somebody else." During this period Jiang confided to friends that he sometimes couldn't sleep well.

China withdrew its ambassador to the United States and canceled meetings with American officials on weapons proliferation. In July Jiang went to Germany, and at the Mercedes-Benz factory in Stuttgart, he awarded a prized automotive joint venture to Daimler Benz instead of to an American auto company. In Munich and Bonn the Chinese president delighted his hosts by proclaiming that relations between China and Germany were enjoying "an all-around boom."

Although Clinton attempted to repair relations with a private letter to Jiang, the Chinese president believed that Lee Teng-hui's U.S. visit was a test of his leadership, a challenge on the part of America and Taiwan to probe his capacity to manage a crisis. Taking an uncompromising stand was the only answer, Jiang concluded, that would both restrain foreign foes from further aggression and convince domestic critics he could protect the country's interests.

Though the aging Deng Xiaoping was slipping in and out of a semicomatose state, he revived long enough to issue a directive. "Handle Sino-U.S. ties and cross-strait relations rationally," he stated. A later report quoted Deng as saying, "We must never let Taiwan run away." The combination, neatly balanced, was what Jiang needed. Whatever he did would now be viewed as carrying out Deng's orders.

Between July 21 and July 26 the Chinese military launched six M-9 surface-to-surface ballistic missiles into a test range only eighty miles north of Taiwan. On one day Taiwan's stock market fell 4.2 percent. A second round of war games, which involved naval exercises in the East China Sea, commenced in late August and triggered a similar stock market drop. Disturbingly, China's Foreign Ministry spokesman did not even know about the second missile-launching exercise until Xinhua issued a press release.

By early September the situation stabilized, with political analysts calling Jiang "the big winner" and Taiwan "a potential loser." The Chinese president had shown that he was not afraid to take action. In October Jiang observed a joint navy–marine–air force live-fire war game with missile destroyers, frigates, and a fleet of submarines. At sea onboard a command ship watching missiles and torpedoes hitting their targets, he stated that "the new situation sets new and higher requirements for building the navy," which must be "quickened," he stressed, "to promote the accomplishment of national reunification." Two months earlier Jiang did his part to help ameliorate relations with the United States by freeing jailed human rights activist Harry Wu, a concession that did not compromise China's sovereignty or pride.

It was President Jiang's custom when he traveled to a foreign country to visit the staff of the Chinese embassy. Speaking informally at the embassy in Germany, he was more patriarch than president. "No matter what you do," he advised, "you should become a little indifferent to fame, money, and status. A person, just like a nation, will become hopeless if he or it worships material wealth and does not have a sense of the spiritual." Jiang quoted a poem by Lu Fangweng: "People driven by fame and profit are like oxen driven by fire; a wandering gull flies over rivers and lakes [and is more content]."

At China's embassy in Hungary, Jiang took Confucius—whom he called "a great educator in ancient China"—as his guide to promote self-study. Jiang quoted favorite sayings of the Chinese sage: "Real knowledge is to know the extent of one's ignorance"; and "The essence of knowledge is, having it, to apply it; not having it, to confess your ignorance."

"It does no good to pretend to be knowledgeable," Jiang said at China's embassy in Finland. "I always try to learn something new wherever I go. Knowledge is infinite, but life is short. The more you study, the higher your spiritual station; the higher your spiritual station, the happier you are."

At a Party meeting on September 28 Jiang deepened his development of political theory. In homage to Mao Zedong's famous 1956 speech "On the Ten Major Relationships," he gave an address on China's Twelve Relationships, which explored tensions between opposing social and economic forces. Among these were reform versus stability, speed versus efficiency, economic growth versus the environment, eastern versus western regions, market mechanisms versus macro controls, public versus private sectors, opening to the world versus self-reliance, central versus local authorities, strengthening defense versus economic development, and materialism versus ideological and cultural progress.

Years later the talk was remembered. "It is my personal belief," said Zeng Peiyan, then minister of the State Development Planning Commission, "that President Jiang's Twelve Relationships speech still guides us. He contributed to two major transformations. He helped guide China from a planned economy to a socialist market economy and from uncontrolled growth to an efficient plan that optimizes resources."

On the seemingly interminable, intractable problem of state-owned enterprises (SOEs), Jiang made progress. Working with Vice Premier Zhu Rongji, he developed a formula for "grasping hold of large-scale enterprises and letting go of the small ones." The largest ten thousand or so SOEs would be propped up with bank loans and investments, while hundreds of thousands of smaller enterprises would be allowed to be privatized in one way or another. It was a policy that enabled the government to maintain public ownership and thus remain socialist, but also allow economic reform to progress and the economy to prosper. It was good policy, but it wasn't good enough.

IN A SIGN THAT RELATIONS between China and the United States were not mended, a minor diplomatic crisis erupted over Jiang's trip to the United Nations, which was marking its fiftieth anniversary on October 24 with a celebration that would include the largest gathering of world leaders in history. In the months leading up to the gala event, American and Chinese officials had struggled with the question of whether Clinton would extend an invitation to Jiang for a formal state visit while he was in America.

The Chinese wanted to be accorded the honor, but the Americans hesitated, suggesting that Jiang make a "working visit" instead, a far less glamorous occasion. President Clinton could not risk further criticism from an already hostile Republican-controlled Congress or from highly vocal human rights activists.

Eventually Jiang agreed to "a working summit" with Clinton, but Foreign Minister Qian Qichen accused the United States of lacking the "political will" to receive the Chinese president with full state honors. Jiang refused to go to Washington as a point of pride, and the meeting was scheduled for New York instead.

At the United Nations each world leader was given five minutes to speak to the General Assembly. Jiang used his time to defend the rights of sovereign nations against the world's superpowers. Though he mentioned no name, it was clear that he was referring to the United States. "Certain big powers, often under the cover of 'freedom,' 'democracy,' and 'human rights,' set out to encroach upon the sovereignty of other countries," he said. "Those who fabricate excuses to infringe upon other countries' sovereignty and interfere in their internal affairs will, in the end, eat their own bitter fruit."

Aggressive as President Jiang's speech may have been, his much-anticipated visit with President Clinton turned out surprisingly well. That afternoon at New York's Lincoln Center for the Performing Arts, the leaders of China and America entered a formal reception hall, exchanged a few pleasantries, and sat down to endure the kaleidoscopic flashes of cameras prior to their discussions. First Chinese reporters and then, separately, White House correspondents had their photo ops.

According to the schedule, a private talk between the two presidents, attended by only a few aides, would last thirty minutes. After that a larger conference was set for another thirty minutes. However, the atmosphere during the private talk was so positive that it lasted ninety minutes.

Though the usual subjects—China's WTO bid, human rights, Taiwan—were touched upon, the meeting focused on the small, concrete steps that the two countries needed to make to resume high-level contacts and exchanges. Jiang suggested joint efforts to combat international crime, drug trafficking, and terrorism, and cooperating to improve the environment, points that he took from Clinton's United Nations address. Clinton reaffirmed Washington's commitment to the "one China" policy and promised that visits by Taiwanese officials to the United States would be "rare" and "private" in nature.

According to Robert Suettinger, the American scribe at the meeting, "Jiang spoke confidently and without notes, making eye contact with Clinton and seeking to engage him personally in a genuine dialogue. He addressed controversial issues directly, occasionally easing the atmosphere with mildly humorous asides, some in English." It was the first time that the two presidents had relaxed in each other's presence and their "dialogue was not entirely an exchange of scripted talking points." Clinton commented afterward that "it was the first time he had begun to understand and appreciate Jiang as a politician."

Jiang's true personality had shone through when he and Clinton had run into each other two days earlier at the UN. The Chinese president asked his counterpart, "How's your saxophone playing?" The two leaders were observed laughing together.

While in New York, Jiang invited his old math professor, Gu Yuxiu, then living in Philadelphia, to come to New York as his guest at a UN banquet. Honoring his teacher gave Jiang personal pleasure, but asking the ninety-three-year-old sage, who had been one of China's most distinguished academics, to come to New York, rather than he himself going to Philadelphia, bothered Jiang. This was not the Chinese way. Though his duties as China's head of state precluded him from traveling, he continued to feel uneasy. Two years later, when he would again visit the United States, redressing this lapse of respect would be high on Jiang Zemin's agenda.

JIANG CONTINUED TO BREAK new ground in China's foreign policy. In November he made a historic trip to South Korea, the first Chinese head of state ever to do so. Expanding economic ties and initiatives for peace on the peninsula were the primary items on the agenda. In his address to the Korean National Assembly, Jiang praised the two countries' common culture and vowed that China's military strength was "purely defensive." Significantly, a Chinese spokesman indicated that the clause in the nation's 1961 friendship treaty with North Korea, which committed China to North Korea's side in the case of war, should no longer be regarded as effective.

On one issue there was total agreement between China and South Korea—outrage over Japan's alleged unrepentant arrogance. A Japanese official had recently told reporters that Japan "did some good" during its 1910–45 colonial rule of Korea, and his subsequent resignation did not assuage the outpouring of anger. Jiang warned against the revival of Japanese militarism. "Neighboring countries," he said sharply, "should make Tokyo learn its history accurately."

JIANG'S YEAR WAS FRAMED by films. In February he invited director Xie Jin to Zhongnanhai to discuss Xie's plan to produce an epic film, *Opium Wars*, that would be released at the time of Hong Kong's return to China in 1997. (Hong Kong had been ceded to the British after the First Opium War in 1842.) In December Jiang celebrated the ninetieth anniversary of filmmaking in China by greeting two hundred film producers, directors, and actors. When he saw familiar faces, he became animated and spoke of their films from the 1930s—he said he could still sing many of the songs on their soundtracks. Jiang mentioned several foreign films that he watched after World War II, particularly *Casablanca* and *Roman Holiday.*

As DENG XIAOPING CONTINUED to fade, public symbols of the transition to Jiang Zemin began to appear. A number of posters went up depicting Jiang and Deng together in various poses. One showed images of Jiang in a business suit and Deng in a Mao jacket, both men smiling and clapping. Another, in traditional watercolor style, depicted the two men standing, Jiang slightly behind Deng, hands clasped in a reverential manner. Still another, entitled "Glad and at Ease," had Jiang looking down at Deng, who was standing with a cane—a portrait that Xinhua called "both political and artistic." Li Qi, the state artist who had painted official portraits of both Mao and Deng, was commissioned to do one of Jiang Zemin "mixing with the masses." The artist said, "I shall try to capture in paint not only the charm of the great general secretary, but also the harmony that Comrade Zemin shares with ordinary Chinese people."

Chapter 17

1 9 9 6

"Talk More About Politics"

IN ENGLISH, JIANG ZEMIN's new phrase "talk more about politics" sounds funny. This is because the word *politics,* as in "playing politics," carries the slightly negative connotation of a field of opportunists, glad-handers willing to say or do almost anything in order to get elected to office or schemers conniving to enhance their personal positions in organizations by the calculated manipulation of superiors.

To Jiang, politics was a lofty ideal, expressing the high calling of Communism's vision of a cultured, well-off society that encourages both moral and material advancement. Politics was the mechanism to improve the vitality of the Party and the rectitude of its members, and as such it was a subject of honor and value.

"By politics," Jiang told a Party plenum in late 1995, "I mean political direction, political stand, political viewpoints, political discipline, political perception, and political sensitivity . . . Can we afford not to pay attention to politics, or can we afford to lower our guard and stop fighting when hostile forces in the West want to 'Westernize' and 'divide' us, and impose their 'democracy' and 'freedom' on us?"

In unveiling his national "talk more about politics" campaign, Jiang was focusing on building the Party as he prepared to succeed Deng Xiaoping. The phrase "talk more about politics" *(jiang zhengzhi)* could also be translated as "pay attention to politics" or "stress politics." Although it sounded superficially similar to Mao's exhortation to "emphasize politics" *(tuchu zhengzhi),* there was a vast difference between the two.

While Mao encouraged class struggle of the proletariat, Jiang promoted high-minded integrity of the Party. Mao's enemies were capitalism, feudalism, and, especially during the Cultural Revolution, "old" Chinese culture.

Jiang's foes were corruption, disunity, and ideological malaise. Mao sought to sever the links between modern society and what he believed to be certain stultifying aspects of "old" Chinese values in order to construct a "new socialist order." Jiang sought to revivify Chinese values and integrate them with socialism to enhance the country's moral fortitude and thereby create, as he put it, a "spiritual civilization." Finally, Mao wanted to overthrow the old ways by instilling revolutionary fervor, while Jiang wanted to protect the current system by preventing internal decay. Jiang's vision of an ideal Chinese society was his lifetime dream, and a prime directive of the "talk more about politics" campaign was to study Jiang's speeches.

In January Jiang gave his most conservative talk in years. Speaking to propaganda officials from every province and wearing a Mao suit, he condemned "the cultural trash poisoning the people." "We cannot sacrifice culture and ideology," he said, "merely for a short period of economic development," warning that any ideologically suspect publications would face a "severe crackdown."

Jiang unveiled his ideas for developing China's "spiritual civilization," along with its "material civilization." The way to achieve "spiritual civilization," he believed, was to "talk more about politics." The combination of the two campaigns formed the coalescing core of Jiang Thought, which he proffered as the guideline for building a modern, well-off society. While Jiang always put economic development ("material civilization") first and thus followed Deng, he also constructed the parallel line of moral, social, and cultural development ("spiritual civilization"), which would both build on Deng Theory and begin to distinguish him from his predecessor. "While we put economic construction as the core task," he said, "this does not mean that other types of work are not important."

Jiang's campaign appealed to traditional Communists who fretted that China's headlong pursuit of material advancement had eroded its Marxist ideals. Later Jiang would arrange for Party committees and Marxist ideology to play a more central role in schools, farms, and factories. For the army, twenty thousand officers would be trained to give study sessions on the teachings of Mao and Deng in light of Jiang's theories.

"General Secretary Jiang brought out the idea of 'spiritual civilization' at a critical moment," noted Vice Minister Leng Rong, a Party historian and expert on Deng Xiaoping Theory. "China was aggressively developing a market economy with its natural focus on competition, and morality and ethics were suffering. Jiang took the reins and spoke of a new balance between the material and the moral, that a 'spiritual civilization' should be weighted equally with 'material civilization.' This was a bold move since many assumed that all China need do was dive headlong into the market economy without restraint or reflection."

Jiang's "spiritual civilization" helped deal with the new uncertainty about classes. The old Communist ideal was the sacrificing, selfless worker, but this model no longer worked in a competitive, knowledge-based market economy. Such self-sacrifice, if followed literally, could even be counterproductive to China's development.

"So who, in the market economy, is an ideal Communist?" was a question asked by Party intellectuals. The new model, everyone agreed, must be different from the one of the past. "But people still need a coherent set of social rules and ethical guidelines to maintain a stable and civil society," noted Leng Rong.

"China was faced with an onslaught of Western ideas and values, which came along with the market economy," Leng continued. "We have a saying that the more potent Western culture 'punches' Chinese culture, almost in the sense of Samuel Huntington's 'clash of civilizations.' With globalization, China could either close back up and keep its culture for a while, or continue its opening-up, which was essential for continued development, and find a new way to protect its cultural integrity."

Jiang sensed this strong need to bolster Chinese culture. If traditional belief systems were to be shattered at a time when China's huge population was experiencing dramatic change, the social fabric of the country could unravel. He worried that Occidental culture was so strong that, riding the powerful Westerly winds of the market economy, it could change China fundamentally. Only a China that was "culturally coherent," said Leng Rong of Jiang's vision, could in the long run "sustain itself as an independent country." To maintain its development and assure its autonomous existence, China needed a culture of its own—and not one that was defined solely in negative terms about the West.

It was for this purpose that Jiang had introduced his concept of "spiritual civilization." As someone who eagerly learned and benefited from other cultures, all the while maintaining, admiring, and promoting his own country's traditional values, Jiang Zemin himself was the embodiment of his own philosophy.

In the past, the Communist Party had used the term *morality* as a hammer to conform people's ideological beliefs into whatever was the then-current political norm. This is not how Jiang Zemin used it. To Jiang, *morality* represented the purest form of Chinese civilization, the word conveying a series of high-minded ideals in family, patriotism, education, social order, science and technology, music, art and literature, honesty, hard work, and even etiquette.

JIANG HELD HIS OWN family to the highest standards. In early 1996 Jiang Zehui became president of the Chinese Academy of Forestry. For a year she had hesitated in accepting the offer. "I was worried that my taking the post might reflect negatively on Third Brother," she said. "People might think I got the job because of him."

"You are a scientist," Jiang had said to his undecided sibling, "so being president of the Academy is not like becoming a minister of a central government ministry. You are being recognized for your achievements, but you should make up your own mind. Remember, forestry is your specialty."

"After hearing him out," said Jiang Zehui, "I decided to accept the Academy's offer, and in March my husband and I moved to Beijing. Once here my brother again counseled me to 'continue studying and learning and strive to achieve great things.' "

"Scientific research is a good thing," Jiang told his sister. "But as president of the Academy, being an outstanding scientist is not enough. You should broaden your knowledge; for example, learn about China's long-term development strategy."

"He reminds me of this all the time," added Jiang Zehui.

"I know Jiang Zehui very well," said Ye Gongqi, a former vice mayor of Shanghai. "She dare not request any personal favor from her brother. President Jiang likes the famous saying, 'If the upper beams aren't straight, the lower ones will be slanted. If the middle beams aren't straight, the whole house will collapse.' This means when those above behave unworthily, those below will do the same, and as a result the whole Party and the country will suffer."

"We have an unwritten rule," said Jiang Zemin's sister: "No one should bother him for family matters. We don't want to disturb his work or give him trouble. During holidays, of course, he invites us to his home, where we all get together. Mostly Third Brother and I talk on the telephone.

"My brother was the leader of our family long before he became a government official," she continued, "and he bore much responsibility. He knew what was going on with each family member, including his or her education, life, and work. After he moved to the central government, his wife, Third Sister-in-law Wang Yeping, handled all the family issues. My brother now focuses on the next generation of the Big Jiang Family. As long as they love studying, such as science, foreign languages, or cultural pursuits, or are doing legitimate business, he feels happy for them. Our family, like many others, suffered so much—Third Brother and I often talk about our hardships, and he'll sigh deeply."

Jiang is especially enamored of his grandchildren and has found it difficult not to show off their pictures to friends and first-time acquaintances. They live with their parents in Shanghai and come to Beijing during vacations and holidays, much to the delight of Grandma and Grandpa. "My grandchildren are now in primary school," Jiang told *Time* magazine in 1997, "and one thing that I frequently warn myself is that I should not indulge them too much."

THE CONFRONTATION WITH TAIWAN, inflamed the previous summer, was heating up again as the PLA transferred the main force of its First Army to Fujian province, just across the Straits, in preparation for military exercises. The original plan had been to move the entire First Army, but CMC chairman Jiang rejected the proposal, explaining that "too much action" would cause adverse consequences. After vigorous arguments, a compromise was reached. Only two divisions would be transferred. Spy satellites estimated the force at around 150,000.

Though Jiang had managed to reduce the size of the operation, he was not in absolute control of it. General Zhang Wannian had garnered authority to conduct live-ammunition maneuvers with minimal real-time oversight from the Politburo. A new military command structure, integrating sea fleets and air forces of the military regions, was assigned the "historic mission of the reunification of the motherland." Called the PLA Command Center on Taiwan, its commander-in-chief was General Zhang.

On March 8 three M-9 ground-to-ground missiles with a range of 350 miles were fired at one-hour intervals from a railway in Fujian. The designated target area lay forty-seven miles west of the southern Taiwanese port city of Kaohsiung. A few hours later China's military leaders vowed to increase pressure in the "struggle" for reunification. At the National People's Congress, which convened that day, Jiang reiterated his commitment to "the peaceful-unification, one country–two systems policy," but he also stressed that China would "absolutely not permit any force, in any way, to change Taiwan's status as an inalienable part of China."

The timing of the nine-day military exercise was not accidental. The action ended just three days before Taiwan's presidential elections, which were held on March 23. Though the island claimed to be a republic (a claim rejected by China), the Kuomintang party had ruled the country since the end of the civil war. That dominance was coming to an end; the 1996 Taiwan election was called the first free national election on Chinese soil. To the Communists, the introduction of "democratic elections" was part of a conspiracy to further the cause of Taiwanese independence. Even worse, the despised Lee Teng-hui, who was referred to by mainland media as "a sinner of a thousand iniquities," was expected to win. It was the worst crisis since China had shelled the off-shore islands of Quemoy and Matsu in the 1950s.

By establishing a northern and southern target zone for its missiles, the Chinese military engineered a virtual blockade of Taiwan, cutting off its sea and air lanes for about two weeks. Freedom of navigation in the Taiwan Straits was disrupted, and the reliability of the island's economy, entirely dependent on international commerce, was shaken.

The United States could not allow the challenge to pass without response. The Seventh Fleet's USS *Independence* carrier battle group, with one hundred Tomahawk cruise missiles and more than fifty state-of-the-art aircraft, plus a flotilla of advanced warships and a nuclear submarine, began patrolling the northern end of the Straits. U.S. defense secretary William Perry revealed that a guided-missile destroyer, cruiser, and reconnaissance aircraft were keeping watch. President Clinton labeled China's actions "provocative and reckless." On March 10, in an overt escalation, the United States dispatched a second carrier battle group, the nuclear-powered *USS Nimitz* with ninety operational aircraft, to the vicinity.

As tensions rose, almost forty American warships entered the theater of operations, a force whose firepower far exceeded that of China's three naval fleets combined. With eloquent understatement, U.S. secretary of state Warren Christopher said that the ships had come only to observe and "cool tempers" and to "be helpful if they need to be."

Chinese leaders, including President Jiang, were incensed by the U.S. presence. Although hawks argued for eight triggering events, any one of which would elicit a Chinese attack on Taiwan, Jiang agreed to only two: foreign intervention or invasion, and a declaration of Taiwanese independence. Neither of these happened, and after the election of Lee Teng-hui, the crisis subsided. The Politburo agreed to give Lee several months to show where he stood on the "one China" imperative. For its part, Taiwan hinted at compromise, reducing talk of its campaign to join world bodies and agreeing to consider direct transportation links with the mainland.

Speaking with Japanese politicians a month later, Jiang volunteered that he had been the one to order that the missile tests continue even as the U.S. armada entered the Taiwan Straits. Had rumors of the Chinese military acting independently struck a nerve?

"Why were foreign aircraft carriers dispatched in response to military drills within our own territory?" Jiang asked with noticeable agitation. He offered a justification of China's "military drill" as necessary to demonstrate "our position on Taiwan's independence and foreign interference." Jiang then apologized for losing his temper. "I spoke a little loudly today," he said. "I did not do so on purpose. Thinking of the past, I unconsciously become emotional."

The power of domestic politics to influence foreign policy was epitomized during this period when Jiang Zemin's two rivals in the Politburo Standing Committee, Qiao Shi and Li Ruihuan, voiced tougher, harder-line positions on Taiwan, implicitly criticizing Jiang's weaker, softer approach—even though, according to foreign commentators, both Qiao and Li were supposed to be more liberal and reformist than Jiang. Using jingoistic nationalism to advance personal careers was nothing new among national leaders vying for power anywhere, but Qiao Shi's and Li Ruihuan's stringency on the matter brought into focus the subtle, multidimensional moves that Jiang had to make to keep China's Taiwan policy finely balanced.

Jiang greatly desired reunification but had no desire for escalated tensions with Taiwan or the United States—yet he needed to convince his country, and his military, that he was resolute. Former U.S. secretary of state Henry Kissinger, who met with Jiang during this time, remembered that the Chinese leader "wanted to get the confrontation behind him in a way compatible with Chinese self-respect." Kissinger expressed great admiration for Jiang, with whom he had a long and frank relationship. "In the 1996 crisis," he noted, "President Jiang chose a very Chinese way of letting me know that events wouldn't spin out of control. I said to him that when I saw Chairman Mao, he said that China can afford to wait a hundred more years to resolve the Taiwan situation. I asked President Jiang, 'Well, is that still true?' The president answered, 'No, it's no longer true. That was twenty-four years ago; now we can only wait seventy-six more years. . . .'

"Nonetheless," Kissinger added, "President Jiang staked out a strong position on Taiwan."

WITH THE TAIWAN CRISIS receding, politics again took center stage. Jiang assumed responsibility for personnel issues in the run-up to the critical Fifteenth Party Congress, scheduled for the fall of 1997, though he shared decision-making authority with other members of the Politburo Standing Committee. His office, led by Zeng Qinghong, began preparing lists of candidates for the Politburo and Secretariat. At the same time Qiao Shi began making plans of his own.

In April the third-ranking Qiao embarked on a diplomatic tour of Ukraine,

Russia, Cuba, and Canada. In a break with custom, he made no reference in his speeches and interviews to "the Party leadership with Jiang Zemin as its core." Instead, he spoke about the future of the National People's Congress, of which he was chairman. It was, he said, China's most representative body of "people power" and, as such, must "develop systems and legal codes to consolidate democracy." Qiao hinted that the State Council and even the army should "report to the NPC and accept its supervision." He asserted that the best way for political reform to proceed was to expand NPC powers, a move that would also happen to expand his own powers. Qiao was distinguishing himself from Jiang and he was doing so in a very public forum.

Jiang Zemin seemed to counteract these tactics by adopting a more centrist position, perhaps advised to do so by Wang Daohan. By this time Wang was spending more time in Beijing helping his old friend prepare for the expected succession. Jiang might stop by Wang's home for an impromptu visit. So great were his respect for the man and his trust in his opinions that once Jiang waited nearly two hours for Wang to return home. Prior to a trip that Wang took to America, Jiang personally called a delegation leader to ensure that his octogenarian counselor would get sufficient rest during the journey.

With Wang's advice, Jiang infused his primary political maxim, "talk more about politics," with a more expansive message, instructing *People's Daily* to write that the main point of the slogan was "to provide a forceful guarantee for economic construction and social development." The phrase echoed Deng's decree to take "economic construction as the core," and it reassured reformists that there would be no return to the "old road of talking empty politics and using politics to break up everything."

In June Jiang told senior propaganda and news officials that certain Leftist polemics "confuse people's thoughts." He reconfirmed that Deng's policy of reform would not change. "The direction of our ship has been fixed," Jiang said, "and it will not be altered." He also telephoned the editor of the Party journal, *Seeking Truth*, to congratulate him for an anti-Leftist commentary that he had written for *People's Daily.*

A series of nationalistic articles in the authoritative *Economic Daily* criticized the expanding influence of foreign investment in China, implicitly challenging the entire policy of opening up. In a remarkably blunt public rebuttal a month later, *People's Daily* published a high-profile commentary that defended foreign joint ventures by detailing how they brought management and technology in addition to capital. Although the Party mouthpiece admitted there were always problems, it asserted China "shouldn't give up eating for fear of choking." The extraordinary public duel between two leading newspapers suggested high-level differences among senior leaders, likely Li Peng and Zhu Rongji on the Left and the Right respectively (with Jiang in the center but coming down far closer to Zhu).

For his part, Wang Daohan turned to his large network of contemporaries, many of them retired generals and Party elders with whom he had served in the army. He solicited their advice and encouraged their support for Jiang Zemin.

FOR TWO WEEKS IN MAY President Jiang paid a state visit to six African countries—Kenya, Egypt, Ethiopia, Mali, Namibia, and Zimbabwe—and signed more than twenty agreements on economic, technical, and cultural cooperation. In Ethiopia he addressed leaders at the headquarters of the Organization of African Unity on "Sino-African Friendship." All six countries reaffirmed their support for China's position on Taiwan.

On a trip to Henan province in June, Jiang followed a route similar to the one taken by Mao Zedong when he had inspected China's first "people's communes" there in the late 1950s. Jiang spoke with peasants and local officials in a manner that observers found reminiscent of Mao. The symbolism was not obscure, and the media coverage was not restrained. A sporty, smiling Jiang wearing an open shirt and a casual red scarf, surrounded by similarly clad schoolchildren, all clapping euphorically, had an unmistakable similarity to a 1959 picture of Mao in his Hunan hometown.

In the same month, Jiang met with Anthony Lake, national security adviser to President Clinton, who brought along a litany of standard-fare "talking points"—trade, human rights, Taiwan (especially after recent tensions). But instead of tackling these painstaking issues, the Chinese leader seemed more taken by the aquatic connection of their names, "Lake" and "Jiang" (meaning "river"), the philology of which he explored in "idiomatic English." By proceeding to ruminate on "computer chip technology, Chinese poetry, and philosophy," Jiang was doing more than manifesting good spirits (or acting "quirky and strange," as some who countenance only diplomatic formalities have remarked); it was his way of signaling to the erudite Lake, a professor and scholar as well as foreign policy careerist, that all was going reasonably well with U.S.–China relations, at least at the moment. Looking at his staff and shrugging, Lake put away his talking points. (In another meeting in July, Jiang told Lake that Deng Xiaoping had entrusted to him the responsibility for managing U.S.–China relations. No date was given for the prior handoff, but Robert Suettinger, who was at the meeting, estimated it to have been early 1994.)

In late June Jiang embarked on a six-nation trip to Spain, Norway, Romania, Uzbekistan, Kyrgyzstan, and Kazakhstan. The Central Asian leg focused on national security. China's Xinjiang province had been the target of attacks by Muslim separatists, and Beijing believed that the terrorists were being aided and possibly masterminded by coreligionists from across the almost three thousand kilometers of rugged, difficult-to-monitor borders.

For newspapers and critics, however, the most noteworthy moment of the president's trip concerned a less weighty matter. At a welcoming ceremony in Madrid, the Chinese leader was caught on camera very publicly combing his hair, while standing next to a rather baffled-looking King Juan Carlos. The awkward photo hit the front pages of Spanish newspapers and was picked up by the international press. It was not the first time Jiang had been framed grooming himself in public. It had happened in 1993 at the National People's Congress and again in 1995 at the fiftieth anniversary of the United Nations. Media merriment at the expense of the Chinese leader did not amuse the country's Foreign Ministry.

In spite of his mild-mannered vanity, Jiang was not afraid to laugh at his own physical appearance. At about 210 pounds, he was thirty to fifty pounds above his ideal weight, and he was known to quip that it would be hard to "move" him from office. Later in the year, he evinced more of his self-deprecating humor on a visit to an army base in Guangdong province. While reviewing the troops, he tried to sit down on a folding stool, misbalanced himself, and fell to the ground. The retinue of officials and soldiers watched anxiously, worried about how their leader would react. Jiang put them at ease. He should have thought to sit on the ground to begin with, he told them, because then there would be no place to fall. The crowd burst into laughter. Poking fun at oneself, which Deng could do on occasion but which would have ruined Mao's self-inflated image, is a good trait in a national leader.

At the same time Jiang was sensitive to charges that he was building his own cult of personality. For his seventieth birthday on August 17, he instructed his staff not to plan any elaborate celebrations.

EIGHT WEEKS EARLIER, around the time of the seventy-fifth anniversary of the founding of the Chinese Communist Party, Jiang introduced his theory of Seven Major Distinctions. A passionate defense of socialist ideology, the Distinctions explored the differences between Marxism and non-Marxism; socialism and the "corrupt thoughts of capitalism"; a civilized, healthy lifestyle and a "negative, decadent lifestyle"; and a multisector economy centered on public ownership and wholesale privatization.

Jiang refuted accusations that he was returning to Maoism by blaming foreign critics for misrepresenting his ideas. In his speech celebrating the CPC's seventy-fifth anniversary (which focused on building a high-quality Party team), Jiang stated: "Some newspapers and magazines outside China have distorted the facts to claim that China has returned to the past practice of taking class struggle as the key link. We will absolutely not initiate mass movements." Corroborating his consistency with Deng, Jiang authorized increased media coverage of Deng Xiaoping Theory, including publication of three books. One theme was that although Deng had laid out the principles of reform for the Special Economic Zones, it was only under Jiang's leadership that the SEZs flourished. Another was that Deng's self-admitted "mistake" of not opening up Shanghai ten years earlier justified current policies favoring the metropolis.

Although some have read in Jiang's acts a reach for authoritarian power, the truth was that he did not even dominate the Politburo's Standing Committee. He had expanded the Committee's mandate from the broad, policy-setting body that it had been under Mao and Deng to a more hands-on, operational role, but Jiang was still only one among seven, and a majority vote still decided all issues. "We are a working collective," Jiang said on more than one occasion. "As a leader of this working committee, I have only one vote, with no special powers."

Jiang continued his unrelenting efforts to strengthen the power of the Party. In particular, he expanded the General Office of the Party's Central Committee, which was run by his chief aide, Zeng Qinghong. Under Zeng's leadership, the department's main staff more than doubled to some 350 members, and its reach extended to economics, corruption, domestic security, and intelligence.

Zeng also created a first-rate think tank of leading scholars and academics to advise on policy and further Jiang's cause, lauding them as "the Party's assistants and strategists." It was an ambitious move that caused a backlash among certain cadres who were already jealous of Zeng's competence and achievements. But with Jiang's support, Zeng Qinghong continued his work. In the same vein, Jiang increased the policymaking authority of the various Leading Groups within the Party, including those on Foreign Affairs, Ideology and Propaganda, and Finance and Economics, the last of which was occasionally at odds with the State Council.

In the midst of his strategizing, Jiang did not forget the importance of reaching out to the Chinese masses. Just prior to a Party plenum in late September, he took a five-day trip through seven poor provinces along the fifteen-hundred-mile Beijing-to-Kowloon (Hong Kong) railroad. Seeking better understanding of the problems of poverty, Jiang visited peasant families, spoke with local officials, and showed the sympathy that had endeared him to many people during his career. "Solving the problem of shelter and food for our peasants in the villages," he said, "affects the long-term balance and stability of our economic and social development."

Taking a pre–Party conclave excursion was a favorite Jiang technique. He would then walk into a high-level meeting with the freshest, press-the-flesh, dirt-real data. When Jiang Zemin would meet with colleagues, who among them could claim to have more recently touched the face of China's poor?

Jiang also toured old revolutionary bases along the route, including remote mountain villages where the weary Red Army had rested during the celebrated Long March. Later that fall he marked the sixtieth anniversary of that epic journey by calling it "a world-shaking heroic poem for the Chinese nation." For the moment he used the historic setting to call for a "synthesis of the old revolutionary spirit with the development of a socialist market economy." By linking his antipoverty drive with renewed revolutionary zeal, Jiang was giving practical voice to his "talk more about politics" campaign.

In early October Jiang's status as a political theorist received another boost when the Party plenum approved his vision of "constructing a spiritual civilization." Formally called "The Resolution on Socialist Spiritual Civilization," the new agenda for China emphasized "ethical thinking," "education and scientific culture," and "positive morality." It was founded on the three pillars of Jiang Thought: socialism, patriotism, and collectivism. "At no time," Jiang stated, "should we sacrifice spiritual civilization in return for temporary economic development."

Western media feared a return to Communist orthodoxy, but Jiang's references to Marxism–Leninism and Mao Zedong Thought were more a homage to China's Communist roots than a renewed embrace of its archaic ideology. Jiang sought to integrate Communism's core values into a fresh, vibrant, high-tech, high-culture China in order to invigorate society, not impede it. This was no throwback to Mao's mass movements; actually, it was almost the reverse.

Political economist Laurence Brahm called Jiang's spiritual civilization "a positive bid to construct a new ideological platform" that would facilitate, not retard, essential but sensitive reforms in state-owned enterprises, the heart of socialism. More personally, the codification of spiritual civilization, according to China analyst Willy Wo-Lap Lam, "served to establish Jiang Zemin as the philosopher-king of the Chinese Communist Party."

BUILDING A SPIRITUAL CIVILIZATION was not all philosophy and lofty ideology. In 1996 China instituted its "Strike Hard" campaign against crime. According to Amnesty International, 4,469 people were put to death by the state, far more than the rest of the world put together. Most death sentences were carried out swiftly after sentencing, and many publicly in front of crowds, with the condemned paraded to open fields or courtyards. Typically, they were executed with a bullet to the back of the head.

The Chinese government defends its right to "strike against serious criminals such as drug traffickers" and to publicize the executions as a deterrent to others. What surprises foreigners is that a large majority of the Chinese people support capital punishment, believing, along with their government, that collective rights exceed individual rights. This attitude pervades all aspects of human rights issues in China.

A GALVANIZING NEW BOOK called *China Can Say No,* written by five young Chinese intellectuals and published in May 1996, declared that it was time for China to stand up for its rights. "A great conspiracy directed at China from the 'free world' is being formulated," the book asserted. The plot, allegedly masterminded by the United States, sought to "contain" China by attacking its policies on human rights, copyright protection, and Taiwan. The authors, who included a poet, a professor, and two journalists, accused America of deliberately undermining Chinese culture through films that glorified violence and individualism. The implication, reflecting a sea change in public opinion, was that the Chinese government was too naïve, too accommodating, or too preoccupied with economic growth to deal with the American threat.

At about the same time Jiang and Clinton announced their intention to make state visits to each other's countries in 1997 and 1998. Although disagreements remained, relations between the two governments had improved. Now it was the Chinese people, not their leaders, who were growing more anti-American.

Closer to home, Jiang took a goodwill tour of South Asia in November. In the Philippines he agreed to shelve territorial disputes in the South China Sea and concentrate on joint development. Ever the good-natured ham, he danced the cha-cha and sang a duet of "Love Me Tender" with President Fidel Ramos during a festive soirée on the presidential yacht. Westerners who could not describe even one of Jiang's policies now knew that the Chinese leader enjoyed the ballads of Elvis Presley.

His stop in India made Jiang the first Chinese president ever to visit his country's historic rival, a symbolic event that "charmed" the Indian people. The objective was to build mutual trust between the wary neighbors—the two most populous nations on earth—and to work toward resolving their long-standing border dispute, which had triggered a shooting war in 1962. "One has to climb higher," Jiang said, using an oft-quoted poem, "if one aspires to see farther."

In Pakistan, China's traditional ally, Jiang played peacemaker, urging all countries in South Asia to "set aside disputes for the time being and concentrate on development and cooperation." It was a testament to China's national importance and Jiang's personal credibility that he could visit Pakistan and India on the same trip, which was called "one of the most successful diplomatic swings through Asia by a Chinese leader in many years." Back home, Jiang was praised for enhancing China's status as a "great Asian power," a perception that enhanced his own status as well.

An even larger story was the repatriation of Hong Kong, now little more than six months away. In December Jiang met with shipping magnate Tung Chee-hwa, the newly appointed chief executive-designate of the Hong Kong Special Administrative Region (SAR). Tung's appointment was no secret; he had become the leading candidate the year before when, at a preparatory meeting, Jiang singled him out to shake his hand.

Reaction to Tung was mixed. The business community saw him as a positive sign that Beijing viewed Hong Kong as an "economic flagship." The promoters of democracy were more cautious. Tung may have been a Hong Kong resident of nearly thirty years' standing, but it was not clear where his allegiance lay. In 1986 Tung's business had been bailed out by a $120 million loan backed by the Chinese government.

"During the hundred and fifty years of British rule, every Hong Kong governor was appointed by British royalty, and they never consulted the Hong Kong people," Jiang said, congratulating Tung on his new position. "You are the first Chinese chief executive. . . .

" 'One country, two systems' is our fixed state policy, and not an expedient measure," Jiang added. "We won't intervene in affairs that are under the jurisdiction of the [Hong Kong] SAR."

IN DECEMBER JIANG SPOKE to another group who were inherently wary of government influence, giving a major address on art and literature at a convention of three thousand of the country's leading writers and artists. In his talk he struggled to balance desires for intellectual freedom with need for social stability. As a state leader, he feared the chaos that dissenting views could cause; as a devotee of poetry and literature, he knew that art should not be constrained; and as a patriot, he deplored how Chinese culture could be swamped by Western influences.

"It is impossible for literature and the arts to be separated from politics," Jiang told the audience, "especially when facing the pressure of the dominant position of Western countries and dealing with the infiltration of Western ideology." He warned against "all kinds of decadent cultural influences of capitalism and the exploiting classes" and urged Party cells to "improve" their supervision of literature and the arts.

Jiang struggled to harmonize the natural contradiction between creativity and stability. "On the one hand," he said, "we should point out that literature creation greatly requires writers and artists to give play to their personal creativity, and the question of what and how to write can only be probed and gradually resolved by writers and artists themselves in their artistic practice.

"On the other hand," he added, "we should also urge literary workers who hold themselves responsible for the people to unswervingly adapt to the needs of the vast numbers of the masses . . . pay close attention to the social effects of their own works in a serious and responsible manner, and provide the people with the best spiritual food."

It was an ardent effort to synthesize ideas that are naturally repellent: artists and writers could have all the creative freedom they wanted, provided that their work had Party approval. The incongruity was blatant. Still, Jiang had not had to address the issue at all. He could have offered pleasing words of welcome, a little inspiration, and been done with it. Instead, he chose to give a speech that revealed his own inner conflict. Though he could not grant writers unimpeded freedom, he still could show his love and respect for them. One of Jiang's old friends was Ba Jin, the great Chinese novelist, whom he knew from Shanghai. The Chinese president also performed with artists; at the convention he stepped up on stage and sang along with famous singers.

Even if one disagrees with his positions, one cannot doubt that Jiang Zemin is a lover of literature who struggles mightily with China's restrictive social policy, and that his campaign to instill "spiritual civilization" in China, irrespective of political objectives, emerged from the deep well of his internal resources.

Jiang was less torn when it came to Western influence on Chinese culture. "If we lose the ability to create our own things, blindly worship things foreign, and copy indiscriminately the capitalist value outlook of the West," he said, "we will end up imitating every move of others and eventually turning into a dependency of others. . . .

"Only a literature with ideological and cultural independence can head for the world in a dignified pose," he concluded, "and can stand towering like a giant in the world's family of cultures."

Jiang had already taken steps to counteract Western influence. In 1996 the government banned four thousand product and company names that "sounded Western." He also authorized $12 million to construct a library of modern Chinese literature, making the decision in spite of the current austerity. Jiang derived personal satisfaction from media reports on the library. "Jiang," Xinhua commented, "has written an important chapter in the country's literary heritage."

As 1996 ended, Jiang looked ahead to the Fifteenth Party Congress scheduled for the following fall. He expected to accomplish much during the next twelve months but never imagined that it would become one of the most important years in his life.

Part Three

Emergence

1997–1999

Chapter 18

J A N U A R Y – S E P T E M B E R   **1 9 9 7**

"How Can We Improve Their Lives?"

O N N E W Y E A R ' S D A Y 1997 China Central Television (CCTV) began broadcasting a twelve-part documentary series on the life of Deng Xiaoping. Produced by CCTV in cooperation with the Party Literature Office, which is responsible for the biographies and legacies of China's senior leaders, and featuring interviews with President Jiang and the Deng family, the series had been in production for four years and few missed the meaning of its airing now. The ninety-two-year-old patriarch was near death. His house had been converted into a sort of intensive care facility, and it was there that Deng lay, surrounded by an around-the-clock staff of doctors and nurses. In the advanced stages of Parkinson's disease, he was starting to lose consciousness.

Deng Xiaoping was China's Paramount Leader, and with his imminent passing, Jiang Zemin was about to become his successor, the country's undisputed leader. The timing was fortuitous: The economy was strong; inflation was tamed; society was stable; and the international scene was reasonably quiet.

Speaking with those preparing documents for the Fifteenth Party Congress, an event that took place only every five years, the general secretary made his opening gambit. "We must not treat every word that Deng said," Jiang stated, "as though every sentence were gospel truth." On its surface, this statement was nothing unusual—it could apply to anyone, even Marx or Mao—but Jiang was showing his grasp of history.

Upon taking charge after the death of Mao Zedong, Hua Guofeng had adopted the stultifying Two Whatevers policy: Whatever Mao decided we uphold; whatever Mao instructed we do. By decreeing stagnancy, Hua accelerated his own downfall. With that in mind, Jiang knew better than to deify Deng, a move that would succeed only in diminishing himself.

To achieve greatness, Jiang had to differentiate himself from Deng, extending him but not contradicting him. The key would be to develop areas that Deng Theory did not cover, so that Jiang's political theory could be viewed as distinct from Deng's without opposing it. Four such areas were described in a book published in late 1996 (as an overt rebuttal to Leftist criticism) titled *Having a Heart-to-Heart Talk with the General Secretary.* First was dealing with the overheated economy by dampening inflation. Second was Jiang's overarching theory of "spiritual civilization," which sought to balance the increasing materialism and decadence in society with an emphasis on morality and culture. Third was promoting science and technology as an engine of growth for the twenty-first century. Finally, Jiang envisioned a "Greater Chinese Civilization" that would promote unity and cooperation among the mainland, Hong Kong, and Taiwan.

Each of these grand ideas implied an addition to or extension of Deng Theory. A good example was Deng's famous statement "Socialism does not mean being poor," which Jiang enriched, according to the thrust of his own philosophy, by adding a second clause: "Socialism does not mean being poor; nor does it mean being culturally deprived." It was a neat sentence: the first clause pure Deng, the second pure Jiang. In building on Deng, Jiang was helped by the fact that, in the wake of Tiananmen, Deng had admitted to erring in the neglect of ideological education, a statement that Jiang's staff circulated among the inner Party.

As HIS CONDITION DETERIORATED—the inveterate smoker had developed a lung infection—Deng Xiaoping was transferred to the PLA 301 General Hospital. Jiang visited a few times, sitting near his bed in the hospital's special wing reserved for senior leaders. Just before the Chinese New Year in early February, Deng asked Jiang to pass his best wishes to the people for a happy holiday; he said he hoped that "the two major events of the year—the repatriation of Hong Kong and the Fifteenth Party Congress—would be successful under the leadership of the CPC with Jiang Zemin at its core." It may have been their last conversation. On February 19, at 9:08 P.M., the long-expected event occurred. Deng Xiaoping, Paramount Leader of China for more than two extraordinary decades, was dead.

One hour later, on a floor below where Deng's body lay, Jiang convened an emergency meeting of the Politburo Standing Committee. Unlike the confusion that had erupted when Mao Zedong died, there was no uncertainty and little anxiety. Everything had been choreographed in advance. At 2:42 A.M., about five and a half hours after his death, Deng's passing was announced to the public. The official announcement said only that death had been caused by respiratory failure and that a formal funeral committee of 459 members had been formed with Jiang Zemin as chairman. Significantly, there were no vice chairmen.

Foreign analysts speculated about all kinds of putative behind-the-scenes maneuverings, which government spokesmen dismissed as fabricated and insiders called exaggerated. Were the Yang brothers, out of power since 1992, touring southern provinces to drum up support? Was Qiao Shi contemplating an alliance with followers of the deposed Zhao Ziyang? Why was there only an "intriguing silence" from Party elders Wan Li and Bo Yibo? But in spite of the assumed political tension, Beijing remained calm. There were no outbursts of hysteria such as those that had occurred after the death of Mao Zedong and no mass demonstrations like the ones that had followed the death of Hu Yaobang. Financial markets remained stable, unaffected by the news. For seven years Deng had been preparing the country for this moment. In that time Chinese society had matured, and for the departed leader, there could have been no greater tribute than the general equanimity with which his demise was accepted.

In the following days the political situation clarified quickly. The People's Liberation Army and the People's Armed Police made declarations of support for Jiang. So did three senior generals. Jiang's investment in army work was paying a good dividend, proving the wisdom of Deng's advice to his successor, "Out of five working days, spend four with the top brass."

To consolidate a winning position and unify the country, Jiang reached out to a broad base of key officials, exemplified by the long list of appointees to Deng's funeral committee. Even Yang Baibing, whom Jiang had ousted in 1992, was given a high position, thus showing respect to Yang's brother, former president Yang Shangkun. The seventy-seven-year-old Hua Guofeng, Mao's successor whom Deng had replaced, was also included. But the reconciliation was not all-inclusive. Extremes of Right and Left were not represented: Zhao Ziyang, the deposed liberal Party chief, and the octogenarian hardline ideologue Deng Liqun were missing from the funeral, though both had reportedly asked to attend.

On the morning of February 24 President Jiang led a host of senior officials in a long, slow processional around Deng's casket at the PLA 301 Hospital. As they marched, the distance between Jiang and Li Peng, the second in line, was noticeably greater than the distance between any of the other participants. To symbol-conscious China, it was a clear statement of Jiang's preeminence. Wearing white flower boutonnieres in the lapels of their black funeral suits, the officials bowed reverently three times before the casket and then offered their condolences to the Deng family, who had asked that no elaborate ceremony be held. Jiang and other senior leaders accompanied Deng's remains to Babaoshan Revolutionary Cemetery in western Beijing, where they were cremated. Along the route, thousands lined up to bid farewell to their beloved Paramount Leader.

CCTV broadcasted the events nationwide, along with images of Deng, and repeatedly played audio clips of him praising Jiang. "The choice of Jiang Zemin is correct," the public heard their just-departed Paramount Leader say over and over and over again.

At a solemn memorial service in the Great Hall of the People, before ten thousand of the country's elite, Jiang lavishly praised his predecessor's "glorious fighting life," his achievements and legacies. "We deeply mourn Comrade Deng Xiaoping," he said. "The Chinese people love Comrade Deng Xiaoping, thank Comrade Deng Xiaoping, mourn for Comrade Deng Xiaoping, and cherish the memory of Comrade Deng Xiaoping because he devoted his lifelong energies to the Chinese people, performed immortal feats for the independence and liberation of the Chinese nation." Five times during the fifty-minute oration, Jiang paused to wipe his eyes with a handkerchief.

His tears became the subject of debate. Critics called them part of a calculated display, but they underestimated Jiang's personal feelings for Deng. In addition, as a devoted patriot, he felt genuine reverence for the man who had quite literally spent his life making China strong. For the hundreds of millions of rapt Chinese who watched the understated memorial on television, the president was expressing their own emotions and, in the process, winning their hearts.

In his most unambiguously reformist speech in almost eight years of leadership, Jiang vowed to move forward with Deng's style of economic reforms. "We must take the deepening of reform," he said, "as the key to further advancing our entire cause." He then called for a "multifaceted, multidimensional open-door policy" that would access "all the advanced fruits of civilization" from foreign countries, irrespective of their social systems. Jiang did refer to the need to balance material gain with his vision of "spiritual civilization," but this was a day for reform, not ideology.

Jiang seemed to be setting a standard for himself when he quoted Deng as stating that officials have but two approaches to their work: "One is to act as a bureaucrat [protecting personal position at all costs], the other is to work [taking action and risk with bold initiatives]." The general secretary was already deep into the process of preparing his groundbreaking political report for the Fifteenth Party Congress.

Even in death Deng differentiated himself from Mao, whose embalmed and meticulously maintained corpse lies perpetually in state in Tiananmen Square. According to his wishes, after Deng was cremated in the short private ceremony, his ashes were scattered from an airplane into the Yellow Sea. The event was seen on television as cameramen recorded the tears of Deng's widow, Zhuo Lin, and other members of the family. Zhuo Lin was shown crouching next to Hu Jintao, who was helping to escort the remains for their final disposition. Together the pair emptied the funeral urn into the waves below.

Two days after the memorial service, General Fu Quanyou ordered all PLA soldiers and People's Armed Police to study the president's eulogy. To avoid any ambiguity, General Fu instructed officers to "maintain absolute and complete unity with the Communist Party Central with Jiang Zemin at the core." A *People's Daily* editorial on February 25 used the phrase "Central Committee with Jiang Zemin at the core" nine times.

Then on March 1, a week and a half after Deng's death, Qiao Shi voiced his support for Jiang's leadership at the opening of the National People's Congress. "We should carry forward Deng Xiaoping's goals," he told the 2,808 delegates, "and more closely unite around the Party Central Committee with Jiang Zemin as its core." Although Qiao had spoken publicly at least five times in the last ten days, it was the first time he had mentioned Jiang by name. In his NPC closing speech, Qiao repeated his recognition of Jiang as the "core" of the new leadership. He also advanced his ideas for increasing the power of the legislature and for creating a "system of laws" that even Party officials would have to obey.

General Liu Huaqing, the most senior CMC vice chairman and Deng's personal representative, pledged his allegiance to Jiang and praised his "military thoughts." General Liu's support was significant because some assumed that he had been a critic of Jiang. Everyone, at least for the moment, was rallying around Jiang Zemin.

The detail-oriented Jiang had left little to chance. Soon after he had received word from doctors that Deng was nearing death, he began meeting privately with Politburo members and Party elders to outline the future administration of the Party and the government. Deng had instructed that he would not tolerate power struggles "as long as I am alive," but that left open what might surface after his death.

BY THE EARLY SPRING OF 1997, reform had become the major theme of the Fifteenth Party Congress, driven in part by the increasingly urgent need to solve the problem of deteriorating state-owned enterprises (SOEs). The debate centered on the issue of "ownership," and whether the Party should endorse the controversial idea of converting SOEs into shareholding companies— that is, allowing institutions and individuals, not only the state, to own the means of production. To some conservatives, the move seemed uncomfortably close to privatization, the antipode of Communism.

To Westerners unaccustomed to epic struggles over political ideology, the issue of "ownership" may seem obvious, arcane, or even frivolous. But in China, the question of who should own what was complex, prominent, and very serious. Political ideology is like religious conviction in that both are belief systems and as such generate uncompromising dogmas and white-hot emotions. To some true believers, the Communist Party broadening its position on the ownership of enterprises would be like the Catholic Church loosening its doctrine on the virginity of Mary.

The dramatic, indeed radical, shift in the idea of ownership came about as the result of a long and intricate process of inner-Party mechanics, led but not dominated by General Secretary Jiang. It featured careful study and analysis, honest argument and debate, some maneuvering and frustration, and on occasion, ad hominem accusations and personal animus. The change in the ideology of ownership was a defining moment in China's two-decades-long process of reform.

The Leftists charged that the new reforms would be leading China "down the capitalist road." Nor did they spare the recently deceased Deng Xiaoping in their assault. Led by ideologue Deng Liqun—known as "Little Deng," to differentiate him from Deng Xiaoping—hardliners sought to reassess Deng's reforms in the light of Communist orthodoxy. Deng Liqun blamed the epidemic of corruption—which the former propaganda boss claimed was "at least several times worse than in the days of the Kuomintang"—on market reforms. The Leftist logic implied that if Deng could err so glaringly on the economy, he could have also erred in his selection of Jiang Zemin.

In April Jiang sought unity among senior leaders and called a meeting of the full Politburo. "When I was asked to take up the position of Party general secretary," he told those assembled, "I thought there must be other cadres who had better ability or higher seniority." At that moment General Wang Ruilin, the closest aide of Deng Xiaoping, interrupted him. "General Secretary, you are being too self-deprecating," he said. "We all know it was Comrade Xiaoping who made the arrangements." Whether or not the exchange was scripted, the impact was the same: Jiang Zemin had the backing of the Deng Faction. Critics scoffed that Jiang was so unsure of his position that he needed an obvious show of support.

Jiang also asserted preeminence for the Party, a position that ran contrary to Qiao Shi's. "If the *zhengquan*—or Party-and-state power—is not in the hands of the Party," Jiang reiterated, "economic development and other accomplishments will come to naught." By supporting both Deng's reforms and Party preeminence, Jiang was positioning himself in the center of the political spectrum. It was a vantage point from which he could fend off attacks from both Left and Right and impel the nation forward.

In a breakthrough address to a graduating class of the Central Party School, Jiang went public with the fresh ideas that he intended to present at the upcoming Party congress. At more than twelve thousand words, the talk was considered sufficiently important that almost all of China's top leaders were in attendance. It turned out to be a milestone in the contemporary history of reform.

The address focused on how to revitalize China's moribund state-owned enterprises, which employed more than 100 million urban workers and, aggregated together, were losing money. Enterprises were competing for permission to declare bankruptcy, since that was the only way to get government aid for their workers.

But Jiang worried that too many bankruptcies, in the absence of an effective social security system, could swell unemployment and threaten stability. He preferred a strategy, promoted by Zhu Rongji, in which healthy enterprises "merged" or "acquired" sick ones, for which the government would offer almost $25 billion in incentives. In many cases, a successful company would be forced to absorb a failing one in a desperate effort to protect jobs. (What happened, of course, was that by coercing such antimarket interventions, the sick firm would often infect the healthy one, bringing down both.) Although the economy looked promising in early 1997, the continuing decline of SOEs told of deep underlying problems.

In his highly anticipated address, Jiang floated the idea of converting a portion of SOEs to a shareholding system, a concept that seemed at odds with a core tenet of classic socialism. He got around this by explaining that the socialist principle of "public ownership" did not necessarily mean "state ownership."

Socialism could be maintained, Jiang argued, through a broad range of diverse "owners," such as cooperatives, collectives, worker groups, local and regional governments, other SOEs, and to a lesser degree, private firms and individuals, and foreign capital.

He also backed such financial market ideas as company mergers and stock exchange listings to help revitalize state industries. Ultimately, Jiang claimed, better management and the more efficient allocation of capital would produce more goods and services for the overall benefit of the masses, thus reaching the ultimate ends of socialism even through nontraditional means.

New and diverse forms of ownership had begun to sprout in the late 1980s. By the mid-1990s private business was the fastest-growing sector in China. Many economists now believed that conversion into shareholding companies offered the only hope for troubled SOEs. This meant that Party policy would have to change if it were to keep up with economic reality. In 1997 under Jiang's leadership, it would do just that.

Since the fall of 1996 a team of forty experts had been working under Wen Jiabao, along with Zeng Qinghong, to draft Jiang's political report for the Fifteenth Party Congress. One member of the team was Lu Baifu, deputy director of the Development Research Center of the State Council.

"I lived the history of China's reform," Lu asserted. "I was there from the beginning under Deng Xiaoping in 1978, and I was privileged to have worked with President Jiang during 1997. I was there for all the breakthroughs. To appreciate what Jiang has accomplished, one must understand the background. China's reform is a story without precedent. . . .

"There were three difficult periods in the modern history of reform," Lu explained. "The first was at the beginning, in 1978–1980. The second was after June 4 [1989] until 1992. The third was in preparation for the Fifteenth Party Congress in 1997."

The first wave of reforms was agricultural in nature and gave responsibility for production back to individual farmers. The second focused on cities and saw the lifting of price controls. Though the movement slowed after Tiananmen Square, it was revived in 1992 by Deng's Southern Tour (Nanxun).

But then, after five years of growth, the country came to a crossroads. Its choice of direction would be codified at the Fifteenth Party Congress by Jiang's political report, which would set the agenda for the next five years. "The collective process of drafting and editing the report," recalled Lu, "was intense."

"There were two basic questions that General Secretary Jiang had to consider," Lu stated. "First, should ownership of Chinese enterprises be restricted to the state? Or could there be multiple kinds of owners, representing various social sectors? More controversially, should China permit privatization, as Eastern Europe did?

"The second question," Lu continued, "was whether the strategy of an enterprise would change if the state was the sole owner, a majority owner, or a minority owner. All of this may sound theoretical, but please understand, in China, theory meant ideology, which was the foundation on which our social and political system had been built. This is why arguments over ownership were so passionate. In a real sense, the whole system was at stake."

The general population joined the debate, sending thousands of letters on the subject to the Party's Central Committee. Small business owners implored that restrictions be loosened, while conservatives contended that state ownership was required by a socialist system. "Jiang focused on this ownership controversy with utmost seriousness," Lu recalled. During the sensitive period—late 1996 to early 1997—Jiang met with scholars and officials, read magazines and letters, heard oral testimony, and received summaries of technical documents. He reread some of the classic works of Marx and Lenin and reviewed the history of Chinese reform since 1978.

Jiang came to conclude that reform was best implemented gradually. "He used clever psychology to win over some of the opposition," observed Lu. "I was in a meeting where Jiang noted that in one of Lenin's works—it happened to be on grain taxes—the Communist icon said that he now saw how policy had to be formulated according to the real situation. Lenin said, 'Marxists believe that revolutionaries should not bind their hands and feet by theory.' Elaborating on Lenin, Jiang said, 'Reality should dictate; dogma has no place.' Jiang wanted to find in the Communist classics—the works of Marx, Engels, and Lenin—antecedents for China's reforms. In this way, he could move the country forward and still keep the Party united."

Before 1997 the governing principle of China's economy was that the private sector would "supplement" the state sector. Jiang now recommended that the private sector be classified as an "important component" of the economy, along with the state. The state, Jiang asserted, should withdraw from certain sectors, such as retail and light manufacturing, while retaining control of key industries, such as natural resources and infrastructure. Like many of China's economists, Jiang had come to believe that shareholding was the best hope for SOEs.

Jiang's speech at the Central Party School was the first time that he aired these views. "In Chinese, we say *chuifenghui*," Lu explained. "To 'blow a wind,' to send a message ["trial balloon"], to see how people react to it."

IN MAY THE FRONT PAGE of *People's Daily* carried an article by Li Peng and an interview with Qiao Shi, neither of which mentioned Jiang Zemin as the "core" of the leadership, an obvious omission. Qiao, who did not even mention the Party, said that "according to the Constitution of China, all power in the country belongs to the people, and the people exercise state power through the National People's Congress and local people's congresses at various levels."

Jiang had his own priorities. In early 1998, Li Peng would have to relinquish the premiership after serving the statutory maximum of two terms, and since he was too young to be asked to retire, the only protocol-appropriate posts were the National People's Congress (NPC) chairmanship and the State presidency. If Qiao Shi still occupied the former, Jiang would be forced to cede the latter, which he was loath to do. Not only was Li Peng's post-Tiananmen image hardly helpful for Chinese diplomacy, but Jiang believed that he himself was the country's best senior statesman and he intended to focus on international affairs for the final five years of his leadership. (Li Peng's complete retirement was not an option since his political strength remained robust and his departure would invite renewed calls to "reverse the verdict" on Tiananmen, the consequences of which would be, Jiang felt, destabilizing and unforeseeable.)

Now was a historic moment. Empowered by its remarkable economic surge, China, after centuries of subjugation, would reemerge as a great power, and President Jiang was determined that he be the one to bring it about. He also happened to like the pomp and ceremony of the head-of-state position.

A political contest was shaping up, and the Fifteenth Party Congress in the fall would see its outcome. If Jiang could deal with Qiao, his power would be unassailable. Knowing this, Jiang Zemin began the process of encouraging, or compelling, Qiao Shi to retire.

AS SPRING TURNED INTO summer, there was a more exciting transition to think about. For 925 days a huge "countdown board" in Tiananmen Square had been ticking off the seconds to July 1, 1997, when Hong Kong would be repatriated to China. The historic event had been anticipated for decades.

On June 30 President Jiang became the first leader of the People's Republic of China to set foot on the island of Hong Kong. As he descended the steps of his Air China 747, he seemed to hesitate just as his foot reached the final rung, as if to savor the moment. The next instant he was engulfed by enthusiastic welcomers holding flowers and raising flags.

At 6:15 P.M. a sunset ceremony marked the end of British rule. Ten thousand guests watched a farewell pageant featuring military bands and dancing. Hong Kong's governor, Chris Patten, gave his final speech, but neither President Jiang nor Hong Kong chief-executive-designate Tung Chee-hwa was there to hear it. (In the last years of Britain's 150-year rule, Patten had moved Hong Kong toward becoming an elected democracy, a policy that Beijing condemned as hypocritical.)

The formal handover ceremony took place on the fifth floor of the Hong Kong Convention and Exhibition Center. With its swooping circular roofs, said to capture "the rhythm and delicacy of a seabird's wing," the striking edifice extended into Victoria Harbor and housed the world's tallest glass wall, which framed a sweeping view of Hong Kong's famed waterfront.

At 9:15 P.M. an elaborate banquet was served to an array of Chinese, British, and other foreign dignitaries. Joining President Jiang were Britain's Prince Charles and U.S. secretary of state Madeleine Albright. Two hours later four thousand guests arrived for the official ceremony, ushered to their seats as British and Chinese bands played patriotic music. As if to underscore the equality of the occasion, huge British and Chinese flags hung in parallel behind the massive stage.

At ten minutes to midnight Prince Charles delivered a brief farewell message. "We shall not forget you," His Royal Highness said. "And we shall watch with the closest interest as you embark on this new era of your remarkable history." It was a pointed if somewhat self-righteous warning. The prince's own government had refused to grant refugee status to the islanders over whom it had ruled for a century and a half. After he spoke, the Union Jack and the Hong Kong flag were lowered as a British military band played, for the last time, "God Save the Queen."

They were replaced, a moment after midnight, by the Chinese flag with its five yellow stars on a red background, and the regional flag of the Hong Kong SAR, which features a type of local orchid known as a Bauhinia. As the two flags rose, a Chinese military band played "March of the Volunteers." In Tiananmen Square 100,000 chosen people, the largest gathering since the 1989 protests, watched the occasion on television. As the Chinese flag reached the top of the flagpole eight seconds after midnight, the precise time determined during elaborate negotiations, joyous pandemonium broke out on the streets as people screamed, jumped and danced, waving Chinese and

Hong Kong flags. One hundred and fifty-six years of colonial humiliation had come to an end. It was the dawning of a new era.

At 12:04 A.M. President Jiang addressed the audience at the Convention Center. "This is both a festival for the Chinese nation," he said in his deeply resonant voice, "and a victory for the universal cause of peace and justice." He then reaffirmed his commitment to Deng Xiaoping's principle of "one country, two systems," asserting that day-to-day life in Hong Kong would change very little. When the president finished speaking, Prince Charles and Governor Chris Patten, according to agreement and protocol, excused themselves and headed straight for the British Royal yacht *Britannia*, which, as soon as they boarded, sailed off into the dark night of the South China Sea.

A few minutes later British prime minister Tony Blair and U.S. secretary of state Madeleine Albright also left the ceremony. They were boycotting the inauguration of the Hong Kong SAR to protest the fact that the provisional legislature had been chosen by a committee selected in Beijing and was replacing one that had been elected by the people of Hong Kong.

At the swearing-in ceremony Jiang sat in the front row, next to Deng Xiaoping's widow, Zhuo Lin. When Hong Kong chief executive Tung Chee-hwa mentioned Deng's "one country, two systems" principle in his inaugural speech, Jiang asked Zhuo Lin to rise and accept a thundering ovation from the huge audience. It was the president's way of paying homage to Deng, who was directly responsible for the historic moment. Not only had Deng coined the phrase as a way to bridge the ideological chasm, but when negotiations with Britain first began in 1982, he had also insisted on nothing less than China's full sovereignty over Hong Kong.

Earlier in June Tung Chee-hwa had commented on the handover. "Freedom is not unimportant," he said. "But the West just doesn't understand Chinese culture. It is time to reaffirm who we are. Individual rights are not as important as order in our society. That is how we are."

On the evening of July 1, two million people lined Victoria Harbor to watch a light and sound spectacular, one of the most elaborate in history. The Chinese fireworks, with their massive aerial patterns and interweaving layers of exploding lights, dwarfed the British display of the previous night. It was a fitting way to symbolize repatriation. After all, fireworks had been invented by the Chinese in the heyday of their own imperial majesty. The $13 million cost, covered by private donors, purchased, among other extravaganzas, a flotilla of twenty barges, each carrying a huge light display that flashed the words to a medley of songs so that the multitudes on shore could join the mass sing-along.

Jiang Zemin and Li Peng were determined to celebrate Hong Kong's return with the citizens of Beijing as well. Before noon on July 1 they hurried back to the capital, where later that day, at a ceremony in Beijing Workers Stadium, a stately and proud Jiang, vigorous despite the punishing schedule, addressed 62,000 guests. His theme was ending a "century of humiliation" by Western imperialism. What he had referred to as "vicissitudes" when speaking in Hong Kong, he now called "national disgrace." The future, he promised, would be different.

"A major cause for the backwardness that China suffered after the industrial revolution in the West," Jiang stated, "was the unwise closed-door policy adopted by the then feudal rulers, who, unaspiring as they were, forfeited China of its ability to advance with the times and to resist the imperialist aggression, leaving it many records of national betrayal and humiliation. . . ."

"To lift themselves out of poverty and backwardness, a rotten legacy of history," Jiang continued, "it is imperative for the emancipated Chinese people to concentrate on economic development and conduct extensive economic, trade, scientific, technological, and cultural exchanges and cooperation with all other countries in the world."

The glorious events and soaring rhetoric could not help but link the triumphant return of Hong Kong to the solidifying leadership of Jiang Zemin.

Political wranglings in preparation for the Fifteenth Party Congress quickly returned to center stage. With Jiang's May speech at the Central Party School, economic issues had been decided. The internal struggle was now all about personnel, not policy.

At the end of July the Beijing leadership departed for its annual summer trek to Beidaihe. The seaside retreat enabled senior officials to get away from their daily routine and talk informally about decisions that would drive the country for the next year. Although the excursion took place every summer, it had added significance every fifth year when it came just prior to a Party congress.

In an unusual Xinhua press release with a Beidaihe dateline, Premier Li Peng voiced strong support for Jiang. "The Chinese leadership with Jiang Zemin as the core is powerful and united," Li said in a meeting with former Japanese prime minister Morihiro Hosakawa, and he called for a rallying of support behind Jiang. Many observers would now assume the opposite, of course—that it was precisely the *disunity* among senior leaders that had prompted the premier's remarks.

The Beidaihe meetings hit gridlock. There was expected consensus on economic policy but little on key personnel. Nonetheless, Jiang seemed confident. "It may not be a bad thing," he mused, "that discussions over personnel issues go on until just before the congress opens." If nothing else, the discord confirmed that the Chinese government was not a dictatorship.

In mid-August a flurry of newspaper articles praising Jiang's economic policies were juxtaposed with his essays and speeches on morality and ethics. Sometimes these were published alongside similar works by Mao Zedong and Deng Xiaoping, drawing the not-unintended parallel.

Jiang gained another advantage with the appointment of his close associate, Jia Qinglin, as Beijing Party secretary. A former power engineer like Jiang, Jia had a natural affinity for the general secretary; both men had spent twenty years in the First Ministry of Machine-Building Industry. When Jiang was director of the ministry's Foreign Affairs Bureau, Jia was general manager of the ministry's major export enterprise, and they had frequent contact. As they became friends as well as colleagues, Jiang Zemin would come to rely on Jia Qinglin and reciprocally, through trying circumstances, protect and promote his hard-working friend.

Just prior to the opening of the Fifteenth Party Congress, according to custom, the last plenum of the Fourteenth Party Congress was held. This was no rubber-stamp meeting, and it exemplified how the system of "inner-Party democracy" was actually supposed to work. Some three hundred full and alternate members of the Party's Central Committee would have to make vital decisions that had not been worked out in advance. In one demonstration of unity, the plenum recommended that Deng Xiaoping Theory be inscribed in the Party Constitution and thus elevated to the same status as Mao Zedong Thought—even though, as many recognized, some of Deng Theory contradicted some of Mao Thought.

Capitalizing on Deng's enshrinement, Jiang's aides had taken to referring to Deng as "the chief architect of reform" and to their own boss as "the chief engineer of reform." A nice play on the Party chief's original profession, the message was that, as Deng's legitimate successor, Jiang was building the economy in accord with the patriarch's blueprint. On one issue there was no doubt: General Secretary Jiang Zemin would remain the "core" of the Party's leadership.

Three days before the Congress opened Chen Xitong, the disgraced former mayor and Party chief of Beijing, was expelled from the Party and charged with masterminding the huge corruption scandal. Observers deduced that Jiang Zemin, who remained adamant in fighting corruption, was feeling politically secure.

The political electricity energized factions on both extremes to seek influence over the Party congress. Supporters of Leftist ideologue Deng Liqun circulated his harsh critiques of the liberalizing economic reforms, while proponents of deposed liberal Party chief Zhao Ziyang issued an open letter asking that he be freed after eight years of house arrest. A few days later another letter, purportedly written by Zhao Ziyang himself, was circulated around Beijing. Seeking redress of the verdict on Tiananmen Square, the document claimed that it was "baseless" to label "the 1989 pro-democracy movement as a counterrevolutionary rebellion." That the deposed Zhao felt free to express such dissenting opinions, even while confined, was one sign among many of how much the government had changed since the authoritarian days of Mao.

SEPTEMBER 12 MARKED THE opening ceremony of the Fifteenth Party Congress. Seated in the Great Hall of the People were 2,048 regular delegates and sixty specially invited delegates (senior Party members and retired leaders). As CCTV broadcasted the event live, Jiang delivered his political report. At two and a half hours long, it was the most far-reaching speech of his career, and it called for reform and restructuring while reaffirming the country's core values and mores. With this report Jiang set the agenda for Chinese policy into the twenty-first century.

Under the umbrella of Deng Theory, Jiang articulated an ardently reformist position. China should judge every policy, he stated, "by the fundamental criteria of whether it is favorable for promoting the growth of the productive forces in a socialist society, for increasing the overall strength of the socialist state, and for raising the people's living standards." These were known as the Three Favorables, which Deng Xiaoping had coined during his Southern Tour (Nanxun) in early 1992.

Jiang also highlighted the importance of orthodoxy. "We must never discard Marxism-Leninism and Mao Zedong Thought," he reassured his partisan audience. "If we did, we would lose our foundation." At the same time he asserted that Marxism, like any science, needed to change as time and circumstances advanced. He also explained that China was in "a primary stage of socialism," a period in which it would remain for a long time to come. (The common estimate was a comfortable hundred years, at least.) During this stage, Jiang said, the country had to use market forces to develop and industrialize. "This is a historical stage over which we cannot jump."

He reiterated his call for steadiness in the face of change. "It is of the utmost importance to balance reform, development, and stability," Jiang said, "and to maintain a stable political environment and public order." Without stability, he added, "nothing could be achieved."

In terms of specific reforms, Jiang focused on restructuring state-owned enterprises—estimated to number about 370,000—into shareholding companies. He also showed appreciation for the importance of capital and financial market tools such as mergers and acquisitions. "Any form of ownership that meets the criteria of the Three Favorables," Jiang said, "can and should be utilized to serve socialism." He then called for "removing the fetters of the irrational ownership structure on the productive forces and bringing about a situation featuring multiple forms" of ownership. Although he said that "public ownership" should always dominate China's economy, he enlarged the meaning of the term to include many different forms, including collectives and even shareholding companies. This expanded definition alone was an ideological breakthrough.

"President Jiang rid the Party of the ideological obstacles to different kinds of ownership," said Leng Rong, vice minister of the Party's Literature Office. "What he did not do was to give up Marxism or socialism. In fact, he strengthened the Party by providing a modern understanding of Marxism and socialism—which is why we talk about a 'socialist market economy with Chinese characteristics.' "

In his political report Jiang made a clear separation between government and business, enabling state-owned enterprises to become viable marketplace competitors. "The government should not directly interfere in the operation of enterprises," he cautioned. "And enterprises have to be restrained by the owner and should not harm the owner's equity." From now on, market forces would dominate.

Jiang spoke of three critical moments for "emancipating the mind": Deng Xiaoping's "Seek truth from facts" triumph over Hua Guofeng's Mao-worshipping "Two Whatevers" in 1978; Deng's Southern Tour (Nanxun) that revitalized reform in 1992; and the "new period" in which reform of ownership would restructure the economy.

At the same time, the government warned provincial leaders not to go too far or too fast with privatization. Another way of maintaining socialism was by selecting about a thousand leading SOEs for continuing government support.

The idea was to raise their status to that of world-class conglomerates that could compete with the likes of General Electric, Mitsui, and Siemens.

While the primary thrust of the political report was economic, Jiang also repeated the Party's commitment to reform the political structure, improve the administrative system, and strengthen the legal system. This included extending the scope of democracy at the grassroots level. At the same time he made sure to reject Western-style democratic systems. To some surprise, Jiang pledged that China would reduce its armed forces by half a million over the next three years. He also assured delegates that the Party would continue fighting corruption.

Jiang's speech was hailed as a breakthrough in reform, for which he was quick to share credit. The political report, he told the closing session, "is the crystallization of wisdom of the collective leadership and whole Party."

Immediately following the Congress, the Party Central Committee convened its first plenum. It was time, once and for all, to select the Politburo and its powerful Standing Committee. In years past the election had been a hand-clapping affirmation of backroom decisions made months before by Deng Xiaoping, Chen Yun, and other elders. This time the lack of agreement among senior leaders meant that no one knew for sure what the precise outcome would be. Party insiders called it a "leap forward" in "inner-Party democracy."

Though Jiang had called for unity in his political report, it was clear that while he could request it, he could not coerce it. Selecting senior personnel was not a matter that he, or any one person, could control. There would be competitive elections of sorts, with secret ballots. Central Committee members could nominate up to six or seven candidates for the Politburo in addition to the official shortlist. Then the new Politburo, with twenty-one members and a similar secret procedure, would select appointees from among their own for the Standing Committee.

Jiang Zemin retained his number-one rank, followed by Li Peng. Zhu Rongji jumped two ranks to number three, while Li Ruihuan remained at number four. They were followed by rising star Hu Jintao, who was being groomed to be the next general secretary; Wei Jianxing, an ally of Qiao Shi; and finally Li Lanqing, a compromise candidate who had been Tianjin's deputy mayor under Li Ruihuan.

The new lineup had two omissions, one startling, one shocking. Startling was the fact that there was no military representative on the Standing Committee. This was read as a sign of Jiang's tighter control of the army. In his view, the military should be a professional force backing the prevailing political order, not a political faction in its own right. The military downgrade symbolized a break with China's politically rigid past when the army held the key to power, and it reconfirmed Jiang's increasingly confident leadership.

The shock was that Qiao Shi, number three in the Party, was out of power. The news first broke the day before when Qiao's name did not appear on the Central Committee list. This meant, unambiguously, that he had retired. No explanation was offered for what seemed like an abrupt exit. Certainly Qiao had never even hinted about retirement, and among many delegates to the National People's Congress he was popular. Now he was history.

Not only delegates were caught off guard. On CCTV's primetime news, viewers across the country saw Qiao Shi—a very familiar face whose every meeting and move were featured nightly—casting his vote for the new Central Committee, right after Jiang Zemin and Li Peng. But on CCTV's repeat of the same newscast three hours later, Qiao's appearance was edited out.

What had happened to Qiao? There is general agreement that age was the technical factor in effecting Qiao's retirement, and that Jiang was both the prime mover and the chief beneficiary of it. The Party, it was said, was "fortified and enriched" by a combination of experience and youth. One elder made the difference. A surprise speaker at a late-summer Politburo meeting, Bo Yibo suggested that "we set the age of seventy as the cutoff age and that everyone who is above this age should retire, excepting of course Comrade Jiang Zemin. Even though this is a collective leadership, we still need a leader, a core. Jiang Zemin is that core." (Jiang had a good relationship with Bo Yibo; ever since his early days as general secretary he had sought Bo's guidance and often visited the senior elder at home.)

The rule would be set with arithmetic precision so that it would catch Qiao but not Jiang, the "core" leader whose continued presence was required for stability. The cutoff date was June 1997: anyone who had turned "over seventy"—in other words, seventy-one—before July would have to retire. Jiang Zemin's seventy-first birthday had passed in August, but that date was two months after the artificial deadline. As of June, Qiao Shi was already seventy-two.

China has always given great weight to the opinion of its elders, and the advice of the founding elders of the People's Republic was held in particularly high esteem. Qiao Shi could not contest the revered Bo Yibo, one of the "Immortals." With no other option that would also allow him to maintain his dignity, he offered his resignation. As a matter of respect, Jiang agreed to appoint Qiao's close associate Wei Jianxing to the Politburo Standing Committee. In any event, Qiao retired and did so with honor, though the cover story that retirement was entirely his own idea was not credible.

On September 30 China watchers noted television footage of Jiang Zemin and Qiao Shi "chatting and toasting each other" at a National Day banquet in the Great Hall of the People. The unlikely pair sat at the same table and wore broad smiles. "Inner-Party democracy," though messy, had worked. The two would meet again a few weeks later, and again warmly, when senior officials lined up to bid farewell to Jiang before his high-profile trip to the United States. In the new era, even tense rivalries were handled with decorum.

Jiang succeeded in enabling several of his close associates to be voted into the Central Committee, especially his confidant and chief administrator Zeng Qinghong and State Education Party chief Chen Zhili, where they joined, among others, domestic policy advisor Zeng Peiyan and speechwriter-researcher Teng Wensheng. Zeng Qinghong was also appointed to the Party's Secretariat, where he would oversee day-to-day Party operations. Adept at solving complex political questions and effecting critical compromises, Zeng was also named as an alternative member of the Politburo even though until now he had not even been a member of the Central Committee.

Having achieved great success at the Congress, Jiang began planning for the future. At an early meeting of the new Politburo, he signaled that he would be supporting Hu Jintao to be his successor as general secretary at the next Party Congress. "We are getting on in years," Jiang said, "and should delegate more authority to younger members." He then gestured toward Hu. "Comrade Jintao, as well as other capable young cadres, will win new achievements for the Party," he said. "We of the Third Generation should do more in paving the way for the young and minimizing their obstacles." Like Deng Xiaoping before him, Jiang Zemin was planning a peaceful transition. As ever, stability was his top priority.

IN MAY 1997 REPORTER Andrea Koppel interviewed President Jiang on CNN and asked, "When you wake up in the morning, what weighs heaviest on your mind?"

"Everyone has different personal habits," Jiang replied. "I usually go to bed quite late, and the biggest question when it comes to domestic affairs that bears on my mind, is how to provide enough food and clothing to the 1.2 billion Chinese people. How can we improve their lives? Speaking from the perspective of human rights, that is their right to subsistence. It would be difficult for a country which does not face the same kinds of conditions that we do to imagine . . . I am always thinking, how to enable part of the people, part of the regions, to get rich first, and then to finally achieve the objective of common prosperity. This is always the most important task for us. Although I majored in electrical engineering and I once studied higher mathematics, I still find it quite difficult to solve this equation."

Regarding his schedule, Jiang said that he stays up late, "often until midnight . . . pondering over questions." In the morning he must "brush up for a lot of functions," so he has to be "very quick."

Speaking with *Time* magazine, Jiang said, "Some nights I cannot get to sleep; for instance, when natural disasters occur. Despite modern science and technology, we still depend mainly on the weather for agriculture. I owe a lot of special thanks to my wife. She tends to persuade me that, after all, I have to eat and try to get some sleep because the next day I have to continue working."

In the same interview Jiang discussed his personal interests. "I am the president of the People's Republic of China," he said, "but I am also an ordinary citizen, and I have my own interests and hobbies. For instance, I read Tang dynasty poems, Song dynasty lyrics, and Yuan dynasty verses, and some of Dante, Shakespeare, Balzac, Tolstoy, and Mark Twain. All of these give me great enjoyment. I also like to listen to Mozart, Beethoven, Schubert, Strauss, Tchaikovsky . . . I believe all fields of art are linked with one another."

"When Third Brother calls the family, it is usually late at night," confided Jiang Zehui. "The only personal time he has is at night. He always tells me that he has 'endless things to learn.' In addition to newspapers, books, and journals, when foreigners come, he must read about their countries' culture, history, economy, and current affairs. He watches the CCTV *National News* and often CCTV's *Focus* [investigative] program—and if he sees a report that bothers him, he'll call up the local officials. If my brother has time, he enjoys literary and art programs."

An example of how Jiang reacts to problems he discovers on television occurred in the spring of 1998 when he saw a report on how four hundred primary school students in Shandong province became sick after ingesting iodine-calcium tablets of poor quality. Not waiting for morning, he telephoned officials of the Public Health Ministry, who informed him that the deputy head of the local epidemic prevention department had sold the defective tablets for personal gain. Furious, Jiang called Wu Guangzheng, then Shandong Party secretary. "By no means should officials be allowed to com-mit evil after being blinded by money and material gain," he said. "Severe punishment must be meted out to those criminals." In addition to demanding justice, Jiang worked to ensure that such events not be repeated. This story does not illustrate freedom of the press, but it does portray the incipient power of the Chinese media to monitor and watchdog government.

"Jiang usually calls me at night, after 10:30 P.M.," confirmed Shen Yongyan, one of the president's closest friends for over almost fifty years. "He calls to relax, to calm his nerves, to get away from all the high-pressure things that beset him. We talk about all sorts of subjects, speaking for about twenty to thirty minutes, that's all. . . ."

"Probably he's nervous that if we talked too long I might ask him for personal favors," Shen said, chuckling. "He's told me that if I need something vital for myself, like in a medical emergency, he would try to help, but that I can't worry about others. Many people know that Jiang and I have a close relationship. Our friends have real problems, such as injustice in the courts or unfair treatment by the local government. But I can't do anything for them." Sometimes Jiang called Shen during the day, and their staffs would hear laughter emanating from their respective offices. "I am from Beijing," he would respond when secretaries inquired who was calling. "My last name is Jiang."

"Since our relationship goes back so long," Shen explained, "Jiang and I talk about personal, family issues. On rare occasions I've brought to him my own problems. However, even if I follow his advice—even if I get his signature in support—there is no guarantee of solution. One time I did exactly what he instructed in dealing with a matter I thought unfair that involved the city, but I still ended up a failure. When I later told Jiang that his advice had not worked, he simply said, 'Well, that's local protectionism. What can I do?' There are practical limits to even his power. He has been general secretary for years; he may be the most experienced head of state in the world; yet there are many things he cannot control in China. But this I know: Jiang Zemin is my real friend."

Sometime during 1997 President Jiang called his scientific adviser, Dr. Song Jian, with an unusual request. He had just read Song's article on the chronology of ancient China and he was taken by one particular quote, a prescription for China written in 1922 by the philosopher-mathematician Bertrand Russell, who had spent the previous year lecturing at Peking (now Beijing) University. "It will be necessary for the genuinely progressive people throughout the country [China]," Russell wrote, "to unite in a strongly disciplined society, arriving at collective decisions and enforcing support of those decisions upon all its members."

Jiang requested ten copies of Russell's original book *The Problem of China*, which Song arranged to be delivered. "President Jiang has evinced deep insight into Chinese society," commented Song. "He foresees that if China would adapt Western-style democracy, there would be no force concentrated enough, and no force powerful enough, to keep the country united and assure its continued development. Full democracy is a worthy goal for China as it is for other countries, but China cannot yet afford it."

Chapter 19

OCTOBER – DECEMBER 1997

"My Ears Still Work Very Well"

ON OCTOBER 26 PRESIDENT JIANG embarked on an eight-day landmark visit to the United States. Although he had met President Clinton on four prior occasions, this trip marked the first formal head-of-state summit between the two leaders. Aware that the American media had been growing wary of China of late—perhaps it needed a new adversary after the demise of the Soviet Union—Jiang told his staff to plan a full-blown state visit. Not all of it should be serious, either. It was time, Jiang decided, to show America the new face of China.

The visit generated controversy even before he arrived. Special interest groups, primarily those representing Taiwan and Tibet, were planning to protest Jiang's appearances. Human rights activists vowed to dog the Chinese president at his every stop—Hawaii, Washington, Philadelphia, New York, Boston, and Los Angeles.

Jiang was up for the challenge. If he wanted to reach Americans, he would have to run the gauntlet of American ways. But he would be prepared. His senior advisers, led by Zeng Qinghong and Wang Huning, mobilized China's best policy analysts to compile briefing books on all manner of topics from diplomacy, trade, and areas of contention (such as human rights, Taiwan, and Tibet), to information about individual people, American history, and places on the itinerary. Months before the visit researchers were dispatched to Washington and New York to ascertain where Jiang should go, with whom he should meet, what themes he should stress, how to generate positive media coverage, and what progress could be made in bilateral relations.

In China anti-American rhetoric was dialed down. Several months earlier the Party's Propaganda Department began the remaking of America: Newspapers changed their style; radio and television changed their tune; books critical of the United States were spirited off the shelves; new books on the United States were monitored; and speeches by strident academics were squelched.

In a pre-trip interview with the *Washington Post* on the outskirts of Shanghai, Jiang gave American readers a taste of what to expect. His people had requested that the newspaper known for investigative reporting submit its questions in advance. As a result, Jiang's responses were scripted, a constraint that seemed more frustrating to him than it did to his interviewers, so he would often launch into extemporaneous banter, lacing his comments with phrases of English and lines from Chinese poems and proverbs. When the journalists tested the rules by posing unannounced follow-up questions, Jiang was eager to answer them.

Then, dropping the choreographed format altogether, Jiang offered in passable English that he would be glad to expand their informal talk as long as his words would be considered "off record." After over an hour of candid interaction, in which he was "animated, cheerful, and friendly," Jiang said he would let his aides decide if some of these comments could be published. The *Post* reported that "permission was subsequently given to use the most interesting of them."

One of these, a point that Jiang made about Tibet, made reference to the Gettysburg Address. "Lincoln was a remarkable leader, particularly in liberating the slaves in America," Jiang said. "When it comes to slavery in China, most of China got rid of slavery long ago, except in Tibet, where it was not until the Dalai Lama left that we eliminated serfdom . . . The impression I get is that you [Americans] are undoubtedly opposed to slavery, yet you support the Dalai Lama."

He continued in this vein, expressing his opinions in a way that drew on his knowledge of Western history and ideas. On human rights he expanded on the idea of Albert Einstein's "theory of relativity," which, he said, "I believe can also be applied to the political field." "Both democracy and human rights are relative concepts and not absolute and general. . . . One country's human rights situation cannot be separated from the actual conditions of that country . . . Undoubtedly, there can be discussion on the human rights issue, but I hope that the West understands that our primary issue is to ensure that all Chinese people have adequate access to food and clothing."

Regarding Taiwan, Jiang spoke of reading *Gone With the Wind* and seeing a television series on the U.S. Civil War, then asked rhetorically: "The purpose of your Civil War was to unite America together, yet on the issue of

Taiwan some of your people support separating Taiwan and China and cannot understand how strongly 1.2 billion people feel about reunification of their motherland. This makes people think that standards you apply to others are not the same as those you apply to yourselves."

In order to give Jiang's state visit optimal opportunity for success, both presidents offered the kind of symbolic gestures that are the nonverbal language of diplomacy. Considering the political climate in Washington, where Clinton had been under great political pressure, including allegations of illegal Chinese funding for the Democratic Party, these symbols were necessary. Addressing the United States' trade deficit with China, the Chinese government announced major purchases of American products, including thirty aircraft from Boeing said to be worth about $1.7 billion. Earlier in October Jiang had invited U.S. ambassador James Sasser and his wife for a private dinner in Zhongnanhai, a special gesture to an American envoy.

In late October the Asian financial crisis hit with tsunami force. Beginning in Thailand where debts were enormous and expectations euphoric, economic fear spread rapidly and threatened to upset the financial world order. The Hong Kong stock market shed nearly one quarter of its entire value in four days—the worst drubbing ever—and the Hong Kong dollar was threatened by speculators. Chinese leaders worried that they might have to call upon the mainland's $130 billion in foreign reserves to prop it up. President Jiang was not about to face the charge that Beijing "was a weaker steward of Hong Kong's prosperity than the recently departed British." Yet just three days away from departing for America, Jiang continued with his long-anticipated plans.

On October 25, the day before he would leave for the United States, Jiang announced that China had agreed to sign the International Covenant on Economic, Social, and Cultural Rights, which recognizes "the inherent dignity" and "the equal and inalienable rights of all members of the human family," thus obligating China to protect its citizens from discrimination. China's Xinhua News Agency published a rare admission. "There are still violations of human rights in social life," Xinhua wrote, seeking to blunt expected American criticism. "As a developing country limited by natural conditions, China cannot avoid certain problems in promoting the people's economic, social, and cultural rights."

On Sunday, October 26, 1997, at just past 9:00 a.m., Jiang's Air China 747-400 touched down at Hickam Air Force Base, near Pearl Harbor on the island of Oahu in Hawaii. Along with the president were his wife, Wang Yeping, and about eighty Chinese officials, security staff, and journalists, including Jiang's close associates: Qian Qichen, vice premier and minister of foreign affairs; Zeng Qinghong, special assistant and senior Party administrator; Zeng Peiyan, minister of the State Planning Development Commission and domestic policy adviser; and Teng Wensheng, research director and speechwriter.

President Jiang was welcomed with full formal honors, which China had made a requirement for the trip. A long red carpet was rolled out; Jiang reviewed a military honor guard; and a twenty-one-gun salute boomed out from U.S. Army 105mm howitzers, whose thunderous explosions shook the air base and rumbled across the nearby bay.

A hundred people waved American and Chinese flags and shouted, "Welcome! Welcome!" (*Huanying Huanying*) in both English and Chinese. Referring to China's recognition of the increasingly vibrant Chinese American community, a third-generation Chinese American real estate lawyer said, "They realize that we can be useful in building support for better relations with the United States."

Hawaii was the ideal place for Jiang to begin his American odyssey, with its beautiful weather, large Asian population, and low level of protests. Pearl Harbor, a deeply symbolic place, highlighted past, powerful bonds between China and the United States, when they had united in common cause during World War II.

After a brief ceremony on the airfield, where Jiang praised Hawaii as "a shining pearl in the Pacific," and "an important bridge for contacts between the Chinese and American people," a police-led motorcade took him to Pearl Harbor. There, in a solemn ceremony, Jiang dropped a lei in the harbor and placed a wreath of white carnations at a marble wall inscribed with the names of the 1,177 American servicemen killed onboard the USS *Arizona* during the Japanese attack. Although Jiang did not speak, the symbolism was clear: If China and America were allies once before, they could certainly be friends and partners now.

In his *Washington Post* interview, Jiang had discussed the relevance of this historic moment. "Lessons from that incident cannot and should not be forgotten," he said. "The Second World War brought many countries in the world great disaster. Peace and development are the main themes of our world today. However, the world is still far from tranquil. The supreme interest of China is peace and nation building."

Speaking at a luncheon hosted by Honolulu mayor Jeremy Harris, who had just returned from China, Jiang noted that "Dr. Sun Yat-sen, the forerunner of China's democratic revolution, set up China's first revolutionary organization—Revive China Society—in Honolulu." He recounted his visit to the *Arizona* National Memorial, "where I acquired more firsthand knowledge of the Pearl Harbor incident that shocked the world," and he recalled how "the Chinese and American peoples fought shoulder to shoulder against fascist aggression." While a small group of fifty pro-Taiwan protesters gathered outside, Jiang ate beef tenderloin, cooked rare, and sautéed *opakapaka*, a Hawaiian pink snapper.

Enjoying an exhibition of a hundred students from a hula dancing school, Jiang volunteered for a brief lesson in making the undulating movements, a scene that elicited applause and cheers from the two hundred guests. "He's got great rhythm," the troupe's director said.

Later that afternoon Jiang took a very public swim on Waikiki Beach. Surrounded by a flotilla of fifteen bodyguards—burly U.S. Secret Service agents swimming in tandem with wiry Chinese agents—he struck out for open water, going a surprising three hundred feet offshore. "Aloha, Jiang Zemin," John Pomfret wrote in the *Washington Post.* "Snapping on a bold red-and-white bathing cap and a bodacious pair of blue paisley swimming trunks, hiked up high over his paunch, the owlish world leader waddled into the salubrious waters of the Pacific Ocean on Sunday afternoon. He swam. And swam. And swam. In fact, Jiang, at 71, stayed in the water for almost an hour . . . His paddling seemed modeled somewhat on the breaststroke. His head bobbed up and down with rhythmic regularity."

Back on shore Jiang was a little breathless, a little shaky, but he got his land legs back and beamed with pride over his athletic achievement. "Very good," he exclaimed as he dried himself on the beach. "I feel very excellent." When asked by reporters if he was enjoying Hawaii, he bellowed in English, "I like it!" Later that day, he explained why he maintains a rigorous swimming schedule. "I will not surrender myself to old age," he said. "You have to be young in spirit to maintain your vigor."

Jiang then joked, "I am swimming very slowly." Perhaps he was recalling the outrageous claims made by Party propagandists adulating Mao's legendary Yangtze River swim by the Wuhan Bridge in the summer of 1966. They reported that the seventy-two-year-old chairman had swum some fifteen kilometers in sixty-five minutes, a time severalfold faster than the world record. The wild claim elicited guffaws from foreigners and fears from educated Chinese, who took it as another sign that their country, caught in a cult of personality and on the verge of the Cultural Revolution, was descending into national madness. Jiang Zemin, it should be noted, swam for about as long as Mao, although his distance covered was a rather more modest single kilometer.

Was Jiang's ocean trek planned as an engaging way to introduce him to America? Or intended for back-home consumption to show a vigorous, healthy leader, with allusions to Mao? The truth is neither: Jiang swam because he wanted the exercise. He hardly ever missed a day in his Zhongnanhai lap pool, and he knew this might be his last opportunity to swim for the remainder of the hectic trip.

Jiang's entourage seemed decidedly less knowledgeable about the sport. Zeng Qinghong marched into the surf still wearing his sunglasses. "Flopping about like a bespectacled dolphin," wrote the *Washington Post*, "Zeng did not shed his shades even when he showcased a few butterfly strokes." Not to be outdone, Deputy Foreign Minister Li Zhaoxing, "looking as dignified as a Buddhist sage, waded gingerly into the drink. He was followed by China's ambassador to the United States, Li Daoyu, who was accompanied by a bodyguard who swam without removing his socks."

As Jiang's tour continued on to Colonial Williamsburg in Virginia, where Jiang could indulge his interest in American history, the Asian economy continued to deflate, pulling the U.S. stock market down with it. On October 27, while Jiang was flying high above the American continent, it was "Black Monday" on Wall Street: the Dow Jones Industrial Average plunged 554 points, the largest point drop in history. It was bad luck for Jiang: The mood of America was literally sinking beneath him.

Nevertheless Jiang played tourist in Colonial Williamsburg, where he soaked up cram-course historical lessons, met actors playing patriot Patrick Henry and founding father Thomas Jefferson, and donned an eighteenth-century, gold-trimmed tricorn hat for photo ops. Wang Yeping, looking heartier than she had when disembarking in Hawaii, was presented with a colonial white bonnet, bedecked with ribbons, while a hundred feet away a few sign-holding activists were largely ignored.

Jiang faced a minor setback when Virginia governor George Allen asked his wife, Susan, who was mayor of Williamsburg, to host a luncheon in his stead. Allen claimed to be campaigning for a fellow Republican, which was true, but no one believed it to be the reason for his absence. Simply put, meeting the Chinese leader carried too much political risk. At the lunch Jiang was subjected to a polite but pointed lesson on democracy by Mayor Susan

Allen. She spoke of "the universal human principles upon which America is built—freedom, liberty, and representative democracy."

In his toast Jiang graciously thanked Allen for her "heart-warming remarks," then showed he had done his homework. "Williamsburg once made important contributions to the struggle of the American people against colonialism and for national independence," he said, and "seven signatories to the Declaration of Independence, including Thomas Jefferson, who drafted the document, were all graduates of the College [of William and Mary in Williamsburg]."

IN LATE AFTERNOON IT was on to the main event. Landing at Andrews Air Force Base outside Washington, D.C., after the hundred-mile hop, Jiang and his wife were greeted by Vice President Al Gore and a military honor guard in a ceremony that marked their official arrival. Transported by a twenty-car motorcade, Jiang arrived at Blair House, the official residence of foreign dignitaries.

After hardly enough time to freshen up—certainly none to rest—Jiang greeted officials from the Chinese embassy, then later, at about 9:15 P.M., went to the White House at the invitation of President Clinton for, in the words of a spokeswoman, an "intimate, personal, and nonofficial" talk. Clinton's idea was to "break the ice" before their formal summit the next morning. In a conversation described as "broad and philosophical" by U.S. officials, Jiang and Clinton spoke about issues of mutual concern, including trade and human rights. One concrete piece of business was to ratify an agreement to install a dedicated "hotline" telephone to facilitate communication in times of crisis.

Jiang's evening visit to the White House included a fifteen-minute tour of the presidential residence. The highlight came when Clinton showed Jiang a manuscript of the Gettysburg Address, one of five known copies written in Lincoln's own hand. The Chinese leader lit up when he saw the original penning of the words that he had memorized as a child and quoted ever since— and he began reading them aloud.

The ice was broken. Jiang's reverence and enthusiasm for this valued piece of Americana sparked a connection between the two leaders that had been missing in past encounters. "That facilitated the most probing and candid discussion of the human rights issue in their five meetings," said one U.S. official on the tour. "It was a genuine conversation." While "the disagreement was rather profound," he added, "it was not angry."

In his autobiography President Clinton recalled the informal night encounter: "After almost five years of working with him, I was impressed with Jiang's political skills, his desire to integrate China into the world community, and the economic growth that had accelerated under his leadership and that of his prime minister [sic], Zhu Rongji, but I was still concerned about China's continued suppression of basic freedoms and its imprisonment of political dissidents. I asked Jiang to release some dissidents and told him that in order for the United States and China to have a long-term partnership, our relationship had to have room for fair, honest disagreement."

According to Clinton, when Jiang said that he agreed, the two leaders began to debate the axial question that China's critics cannot avoid: How much change and freedom could China accommodate without risking internal chaos?

The two presidents talked until 11:00 P.M., at which time Jiang departed for a much-needed night's rest. For his part, Clinton went to bed "thinking that China would be forced by the imperatives of modern society to become more open, and that in the new century it was more likely that our nations would be partners than adversaries." Clinton would later conclude that Jiang "had done well" on his American trip.

OCTOBER 29 WAS the day of high ceremony, with the long-anticipated Jiang-Clinton summit meeting at the White House in the morning, a joint news conference in the afternoon, and a gala state dinner in the evening. At the summit the president of the world's most populous country and the president of the world's most powerful country would discuss, and hopefully reach agreement on, a wide range of issues in the areas of security, economics, environment, and law enforcement.

At 10:15 A.M., the opening ceremony was held on the South Lawn of the White House. As befit a head of state, it included a twenty-one-gun salute and President Jiang's inspection of the honor guard. President Clinton, formal yet warm, expressed admiration for the "progress China has made in such a short time." Addressing Jiang, he said, "Your reforms have lifted millions from poverty . . . The Chinese people enjoy today a better standard of living than at any time in China's history." Clinton complimented Jiang for laying a wreath at Pearl Harbor and "paying tribute to the alliance between our peoples that brought victory in World War II," and he said that "our great nations must join our strength again."

Confident and poised, President Jiang said, "The shared interests between China and the United States have increased rather than decreased; our potential for cooperation has expanded rather than diminished," and he called for "cooperation in various fields and proper handling of differences between our countries." Jiang concluded by saying, "Let us, the Chinese and Americans, join hands and, together with people around the world, work hard to bring about a new century of peace, stability, and prosperity."

The Chinese leader wore a black suit and "a shiny tie the color of a salmon," while the American leader, also in a dark suit, was "wearing a black tie with a white diamond pattern." Yet when they appeared at their joint news conference later that afternoon, their ties seemed to match. Clinton's was the same; Jiang must have dashed back to Blair House and changed into one that was almost identical to Clinton's. A cute gesture, but did it also signal Jiang's desire to bring China and America closer?

During the ceremony, which included a fife-and-drum rendition of "Yankee Doodle Dandy," Hillary Rodham Clinton watched over Wang Yeping. Having been alerted that she was somewhat infirm, Mrs. Clinton gestured that Wang sit, helped her to her chair, and then put her at ease by sitting down next to her whenever she needed to rest.

During the formal part of the summit, which lasted from about 10:30 A.M. to 3:15 P.M.—with a break for lunch hosted by Vice President Gore—Clinton and Jiang spent some of the time in private conversation. Though the summit would pass in a spirit of goodwill, there were delicate issues to cover. One was the matter of China's alleged involvement in funding congressional campaigns, a controversy that had been brewing since spring. Jiang assured Clinton that China had done nothing illegal and that he would make sure that Chinese officials cooperated in the investigation. He then asked Clinton to ensure China's admission to the World Trade Organization by the end of 1998. The American president could only promise to do his best without asking member states to bend the rules.

On other matters there was greater accord. At Clinton's suggestion, the two leaders agreed that Treasury secretary Robert Rubin and Executive Vice Premier Zhu Rongji should work together to "promote financial stability in Asia." Rubin had just led a delegation to Beijing in September, when he met with Jiang for the first time. "We didn't know what we'd find," recalled Rubin. "I, like most Western officials, knew and respected Zhu Rongji but really didn't know President Jiang. I was impressed, surprised actually, with the depth of his commitment to market reform. He had a powerful vision, shaped, he said, by his international travels. He was engaging and interesting; we had a real conversation." Upon meeting Rubin, Jiang quipped, "The Treasury Department is always the most important in any country. Meeting a Treasury secretary makes you think you will become rich."

Though Clinton and Jiang differed sharply over human rights, each leader achieved his primary goal for the summit. Clinton obtained China's commitment to work with the United States in constructing a network of political, military, and economic ties, which was part of a larger effort to turn "strategic competitors" into "strategic partners." Jiang got the United States to reiterate its "one China" policy, expand "China–U.S. trade and economic ties, and support China's WTO accession." More significant was the fact that Jiang was being honored with a formal state visit, recognition that in the eyes of the United States government, China was finally emerging from the long, dark shadow of Tiananmen Square. It would give Jiang, when he returned to Beijing, the enhanced stature of a global leader. On a personal level, though separated by culture, age, and hardline political pressures in both countries, the two presidents, for the first time, established a genuinely good rapport.

American foreign policy officials called the summit "enormously successful." National Security Adviser Sandy Berger offered the opinion that Jiang and Clinton expressed "greater ease of communication, less stiffness, less polemics in how they talk" than they had at their four previous encounters. "I think that there has developed over these five meetings a bond," said another American official with direct access. "I think when Jiang talks about 'my friend Bill Clinton' and [now] having met with him five times, he's doing more than going through the motions."

During the negotiations the Chinese were hard-nosed and in spots intransigent, yet American officials who participated in the summit came away with a new respect for Jiang Zemin. A spirit of candor seemed to exist. "There has been an evolution from their first, highly scripted meeting in Seattle in 1993," said one official. "Jiang is much more willing to leave his talking points to speak clearly and directly." Specifics aside, the smooth process of the summit itself was reason enough to call it a success.

Even the presence of protesters didn't dampen enthusiasm. Gathered in Lafayette Park across Pennsylvania Avenue from the White House, they were an eclectic crowd about two thousand strong—pro-Taiwan supporters, Tibetans, Inner Mongolians, anti-abortionists, anti–child labor activists, environmentalists, religious missionaries, union leaders, liberal Democrats, Buddhist monks in burgundy robes, and Chinese Americans wearing cartoon Clinton masks. As the demonstrators made as much noise as they could, a string of speakers condemned China for human rights abuses. Different banners were held aloft; several said, "Free Wei Jingsheng," a well-known Chinese dissident. The protesters also sported two huge puppets resembling Jiang and Clinton and made them dance together. On hand were celebrities Richard Gere and Bianca Jagger, while a phalanx of police on horseback and motorcycles, in cars and on foot, restricted the protesters to a far area of the park.

At the joint press conference Jiang alluded to the protesters with grace. "I have been immersed in an atmosphere of friendship from the American people," he said, adding, "However, sometimes noises came into my ears.

"According to Chinese philosophy," Jiang continued, "Confucius said, isn't it a pleasure to have friends coming from afar? And naturally, I am also aware that in the United States, different views can be expressed, and this is a reflection of democracy. And therefore I would like to quote a Chinese saying, which goes, 'Seeing it once is better than hearing about it a hundred times.' I've also gotten my real understanding about this during my current trip. However, I don't believe this will have any negative impact on our effort to approach each other."

The eagerly awaited press conference, held in midafternoon in the Old Executive Office Building before hundreds of reporters and cameramen, combined formal diplomacy, media sensitivity, and—to the delight of attendees—spirited, spontaneous exchanges. President Clinton began by listing items discussed at their just-concluded summit: security dialogues and military exchanges; cooperation on North Korea's "dangerous nuclear program"; Taiwan; proliferation of weapons of mass destruction; fighting international organized crime, drug trafficking, and alien smuggling; cooperation on "rule of law" programs; economic growth; China's WTO bid; environmental protection; and human rights and religious freedom. Praising "China's extraordinary human resources that will lift it to its rightful destiny of leadership and widely held prosperity in the twenty-first century," Clinton said, "the United States welcomes China's emergence as a full and constructive partner in the community of nations."

President Jiang accentuated "the principles of mutual respect, noninterference in each other's internal affairs, equality and mutual benefit, and seeking common ground while putting aside differences." He described enhanced contact between China and America, such as regular summits, consultations between officials, exchanges between the armed forces, and cooperation in "economic, scientific, and technological, cultural, educational, and law enforcement fields."

After finishing his opening statement, Jiang said, "Now, questions are welcome," and he pointed to a questioner, without noticing that Clinton had just done the same thing. After a moment of amused confusion, the two national leaders clowned a bit, before Clinton deferred to his guest's selection.

The temperature on that mid-fall day rose considerably with a high-impact question about "the shootings in Tiananmen Square . . . [that caused] many Americans to view China as an oppressive country that crushes human rights." After setting the stage aflame, the reporter launched a verbal projectile at each president. To Jiang, he said, "Do you have any regrets about Tiananmen?" To Clinton, he said, "Are you prepared to lift any of the Tiananmen sanctions, and if not, why not?"

Jiang went first, laying out his oft-told, carefully scripted explanation that what he called "the political disturbance" had "seriously disrupted social stability and jeopardized state security." He defended the "necessary measures" the Chinese government had to take "to ensure that our country enjoys stability and that our reform and opening-up proceeds smoothly."

Clinton responded with "a very different view of the meaning of the events at Tiananmen Square," asserting that a "continuing reluctance to tolerate political dissent has kept China from politically developing the level of support in the rest of the world that otherwise would have been developed." He noted the lifting of sanctions on peaceful nuclear energy, with other areas to be "reviewed on a case-by-case basis."

Jiang was ready to counter. Shaking his right index finger at the audience, diplomatically not at Clinton, he said, in English, "I would like to speak a few words, in addition, to this question." Anchoring his argument on the differences between China and America—"different historic and cultural traditions, different levels of economic development, and different values"—Jiang averred, "It is just natural for our two countries to hold different views on some issues . . . the concepts of democracy and human rights and of freedoms are relative and specific ones, and they are to be determined by the specific national situation of different countries."

"I just have to say one other thing," Clinton continued, eliciting laughter from the audience eager for the two world leaders to prolong their free-style debate. "First of all," he said, "the United States recognizes that on so many issues China is on the right side of history, and we welcome it. But on this issue we believe the policy of the government is on the wrong side of history." Then Clinton went personal: "I think it would amaze many of our Chinese guests to see some of the things that have been written and said about me, my family, our government, our policies," concluding, "and yet after all this time, I'm still standing here and our country is stronger."

Though the press tried to play up the remarks as evidence of tension, Jiang treated the matter as a mere difference of opinion. Beaming throughout the press conference, Jiang was obviously enjoying himself. He repeatedly broke into English, addressing one questioner as "yellow-dress lady."

"I don't suspect that President Jiang has ever been subjected to a press conference like that," commented Sandy Berger. "I think that's good, and I think that's healthy." Other officials were relieved that, although Jiang made it clear that he had heard the protesters, he never displayed anger at any of the questions. "It showed some acceptance of our traditions," said one.

Certainly all feelings were cheery at the state dinner that night. An invitation was the hottest ticket in years. Not in recent memory had there been an A-list like this one. If anyone doubted the importance of China, the 234 dinner guests, almost every one a luminary, proved otherwise.

From government, there were former President Jimmy Carter, Lady Bird Johnson, five secretaries of state (Madeleine Albright and her predecessors— Henry Kissinger, George Shultz, James Baker, and Alexander Haig), Treasury secretary Robert Rubin, Federal Reserve chairman Alan Greenspan, and every senior congressional leader.

From business, there were no less than thirty CEOs, including Jack Welch of General Electric, Maurice Greenberg of AIG, Michael Eisner of Disney, Steven Jobs of Apple Computer, and Steven Spielberg of DreamWorks. "I'm not here as a businessman," observed Spielberg, one of the most successful film directors ever. "In a sense, I feel like I'm Forrest Gump eavesdropping on a moment in history."

From the media came more glitterati, including CBS's Dan Rather, NBC's Tom Brokaw, and ABC's Diane Sawyer. One reporter's choice for the "odd couple of the evening award" was Madeleine Albright and her escort, the actor Patrick Stewart, who played the bald, vigorous Captain Picard on *Star Trek: The Next Generation.*

Prominent Chinese-Americans attending were cellist Yo-Yo Ma, AIDS scientist David Ho, Washington governor Gary Locke, and novelist Amy Tan, who mused that she "had a lot of mixed feelings" about Chinese policy but wouldn't have missed the dinner. "I don't think that strides and improvements in human relationships and human conditions come from standing on the outside and chest-beating," she said.

In keeping with the time of year, Hillary Rodham Clinton decorated the room in autumnal tones of apricot and gold. As for her dress, she was "swathed in prom-princess lavender satin" designed for her by Chinese-American fashion designer Vera Wang, one of the guests, while Wang Yeping wore a "deep purple velvet tunic over a slit midnight blue dress."

The formalities began at 9:00 P.M. Standing next to each other, the two presidents made quite the pair. Clinton wore an elegant black tuxedo; Jiang an elegant, dark blue Mao suit. The image of "elegant yet different" exemplified Jiang Zemin's vision for China.

The two leaders offered toasts of friendship. Clinton made reference to the *I Ching* (Book of Changes), and Jiang quoted Henry Wadsworth Longfellow: "But to act that each tomorrow finds us farther than today," the Chinese president recited. "Act, act, in the living present."

In his formal address President Clinton noted his visitor's extraordinary life: "Mr. President," he said, "in your lifetime you have witnessed the sweep of a remarkable century, both in China and abroad. And in your different occupations you have lived a rich sampling of the human enterprise." The American president then paid his respects to Chinese history: "Long before the United States was even born," he said, "China was a stronghold of creativity, knowledge, and wealth. From the printing China invented to the poetry it produced, from medicine and mathematics to the magnetic compass and humanistic philosophies, many of China's earliest gifts still enrich our lives today."

After a toast and applause, President Jiang called China and America "two great nations" that "have a major responsibility for the future of the world." As for "differences that cannot be resolved for the time being," he advised they be "put aside while concentrating on seeking common ground." As for "broad common interests," he listed "the maintenance of world peace and security, the promotion of global economic growth and prosperity, and the protection of the living environment of mankind."

Another toast, and it was on to dinner, which, according to the *Washington Post,* consisted of mingled "Asian and American flavors for the ultimate surf-and-turf feast. Lobster was poached in lime leaves and lemongrass and pressed into a timbale with corn-leek relish for starters, while the pepper-crusted Oregon beef in the entree came from Asian cattle bred with American angus. Marzipan panda bears and mandarin tea tartlets accented . . . dessert of orange sherbet swirled into giant chocolate oranges."

After dinner a fleet of overgrown golf carts whisked the luminous guests to a large tent on the White House's South Lawn, which had been transformed into a prefabricated concert hall, bedecked with crystal chandeliers and simulated French windows. As they arrived, military violinists serenaded them with a medley of songs such as "It Ain't Necessarily So." Then on the makeshift stage the National Symphony Orchestra performed a half-hour program of American music that featured Leonard Bernstein's "Overture to *Candide,*" an abridged version of George Gershwin's "An American in Paris," and Aaron Copland's hand-clapping "Hoedown."

The classiest state dinner of the decade came to a close when Clinton wished Jiang farewell with a quip about his malfunctioning vocal cords—"I'm about to lose my voice, aren't you glad?"—and a look ahead to Clinton's coming visit to Beijing next year. Jiang, speaking in English, maintained the musical theme. "In Hawaii, I played Hawaiian guitar," he said. "But I know you play very good sax." It was almost midnight, and for China's seventy-one-year-old leader, tomorrow would be a very long day.

AFTER THE GRANDEUR OF THE NIGHT before, the morning after began with a grueling breakfast encounter with fifty members of Congress, including many of its harshest, most vociferous China critics. Beforehand an insufficiently rested Jiang met privately with the four leaders of the House and Senate: Republicans Trent Lott and Newt Gingrich, and Democrats Tom Daschle and Richard Gephardt. After the thirty-minute meeting, held in Gingrich's office, the four men took Jiang to the Capitol Rotunda, the imposing circular atrium that connects the House and Senate chambers. During the tour Jiang was treated to an impromptu history lesson from Gingrich, a former history professor who never lost his penchant for teaching.

At the ninety-minute breakfast, Jiang's dining companions hit all the hot buttons—human rights, religious freedom, weapons proliferation, and allegations of harvesting human organs from executed prisoners. Jiang defended China against all the charges and voiced the hope that "more Congress members will visit China." "We can now claim," he said, "that never before has Chinese society been as prosperous and open as today," adding that his government intended to "expand democracy . . . and build a socialist country under the rule of law."

Not satisfied, the congressional leaders countered with their own assertions. "You cannot have economic freedom without political freedom," Gingrich lectured Jiang in the same unendearing, oppressive tone that had come to irritate many of his colleagues. "And you cannot have political freedom without religious freedom. You cannot have a system that is half-totalitarian and half-free. It will not survive." Senator Lott told Jiang that it was "almost impossible for our country to improve relations with those aiding Iran." Dick

Armey handed Jiang a list of thirty Chinese citizens who, he said, were being persecuted for their religious convictions, and he asked that they be released.

Jiang did not rise to the bait, and the congressional leaders found new respect for the first Chinese leader to sit among them. "A number of senators and House members really put it to him," noted Democrat Howard L. Berman. Though Jiang's answers "were not satisfactory," he admired Jiang's resilience. "To his credit, he did not get defensive, he did not storm out." Nancy Pelosi, who would become House Democratic Minority Leader in 2002, said Jiang "was evasive but engaging."

Jiang handled himself in much the same way in an 11:30 A.M. television interview with Jim Lehrer for the PBS *NewsHour.* Lehrer suggested that Jiang's news conference with Clinton had been perceived by the American press as "an unprecedented blunt exchange, almost a debate between the two leaders of the two most powerful nations in the world." "Is that how you saw it?" he asked Jiang.

"I believe yesterday's press conference gave us an opportunity to express our views freely," Jiang replied. "Being good friends means that each should treat the other with all sincerity and not hide any views." In English, he added, "Do you agree with that?"

Lehrer persisted: "But that's how you saw that yesterday, as a healthy exchange?"

"My answer is yes," said Jiang without hesitation. "I don't think that it hurt the relationship . . . As far as the Chinese side is concerned, we have all along believed that we need to work to seek common ground while putting aside differences."

"Does it disturb you to be questioned as much as you have about human rights?" Lehrer asked.

"I'm not disturbed at all," Jiang answered. "China does not feel that it has done anything wrong in the field of human rights. China has a tradition of five thousand years, and different countries have different histories and cultures . . . I have already felt that I am welcomed by majority of the American people here."

It was a polished performance. Jiang had prepared responses crafted for the most controversial issues. He hinted that change would eventually come to China, only asking that his country be allowed to decide when and how.

The *Washington Post* and the *New York Times* ran unusually upbeat stories on the Jiang-Clinton summit, then noted the Chinese media's selective coverage. The *Post* article, "This Just In: Gosh, Everything's Swell in China, Presidential Visit to U.S. Is Unsullied . . . and Unreported," stated that "there were no unflattering photos or articles" that day. The *Times* article, "At Home, Rosy News for Jiang's Trip," said that China's media, remarkably uniform in emphasizing the pomp and symbols, "extolled the happy moments of the trip and glossed over less pleasant tidings." While the Western press gave wide coverage to Jiang's hour-long swim in Hawaii, it was not reported in the Chinese press. Someone high up must have killed the story, apparently deciding that paddling in the Pacific would not strike the proper tone at home.

At 1:10 P.M. Jiang spoke at a special forum of six foreign affairs associations. He claimed that "ancient Chinese came up with such plain ideas as democracy and the rule of law as 'people being essential to a state while their governance follows prescribed laws.' " He traced the history of a China transitioning from a "people suffering humiliation and bullying" to "national independence and liberation though strenuous struggles," and he looked forward to "the Chinese people succeeding, through hard work, in building a strong and prosperous country." Promising to "only promote world peace and stability rather than pose a threat to anyone," Jiang vowed that "China will never seek hegemony even after it becomes a developed country in the future."

On Tibet, it was Jiang's turn to give a history lesson, highlighting its oppressive feudal system that had existed before China's takeover. Regardless of whether that system justified China's domination, it was a point that many Americans ignored or had not even bothered to learn. Jiang described pre-China Tibet as "a theocracy with a heavy stint of slavery," adding, "The serfs, bond servants to their masters, had no human rights whatsoever." He avowed that China's "democratic reform" had "emancipated some one million serfs and slaves through peaceful means," and he compared it to "the liberation of black slaves in American history."

Irrespective of issues, Chinese resent Western hypocrisy on Tibet. It is no secret that Europe and America have also used armed force against less powerful regions. In addition, Western criticism is particularly grating because of the high-handed manner in which it is often delivered. At a private Beijing dinner hosted earlier by Jiang for American leaders, including Henry Kissinger and AIG chairman Maurice Greenberg, one guest became rudely vocal about Tibet, pestering the Chinese president with hostile questions. Since the man was not satisfied with his host's response, he continued his harangue, making everyone uncomfortable. Suddenly Jiang stood up. The Americans waited anxiously, worried that he had taken offense and was about to storm out. Instead, Jiang took a deep breath and belted out the traditional American folk song "Home on the Range." It was a charming way to put an ill-mannered dinner guest in his place.

FROM WASHINGTON, JIANG AND his large entourage departed in midafternoon for Philadelphia, where he could spend only about four hours en route to New York. But those hours were packed: speeches at two universities, meetings with local officials and three university presidents, a symbolic visit to Independence Hall, and personal visits with an old friend and an esteemed teacher. Philadelphia reporters reflected the surprise that Americans felt on seeing the Chinese leader. "The city got a taste of the unexpected from Jiang," they wrote. "A more Americanized, personable, and English-savvy pol than many of those invited for three tightly controlled events were expecting."

First stop was Drexel University in west Philadelphia, where Jiang's oldest son, Mianheng, had graduated with a Ph.D. in computer and electrical engineering six years earlier. Drexel president Constantine Papadakis, who would praise Jiang fulsomely, put out the invitation to the "dad of a Drexel alumnus" as soon as Jiang's American tour was announced.

Moments before the presidential motorcade approached the university, police commandeered three empty buses and positioned them along the curb in front of demonstrators. A reporter overheard a policeman say, "Zemin's people didn't want him to see any of the protesters."

"The Chinese asked us to move all the demonstrators so they would be out of the president's view," said Mayor Edward Rendell, who accompanied Jiang during his time in Philadelphia. "We tried to explain to them as patiently as possible that we couldn't force them off of public streets."

Just before 5:30 P.M. Jiang, accompanied by 140 people in his troupe, arrived at Drexel's nine-hundred-seat auditorium, which was jammed with elected officials and corporate leaders (who had just participated in a seminar on doing business in China). Hundreds more, faculty and students, were standing wherever they could. Among the dignitaries onstage with President Jiang was Pennsylvania governor Tom Ridge.

Jiang charmed the audience. Away from heated political debates in a friendly academic setting, he relaxed. "I have to express my heartfelt thanks to the principals of Drexel University and all the professors, especially those who educated my son," he said in English to the delight of the crowd. "I want to give them thanks for the technical lesson for having given him the honor of receiving a Ph.D. degree.

"At home," he continued, "we have now a Ph.D. degree, but I have only a bachelor's degree." The crowd cheered.

Congressman Curt Weldon presented an orange and white Philadelphia Flyers jersey to the guest of honor. Emblazoned on the back was the name JIANG. The Chinese president was now an honorary member of an NHL team.

Grinning broadly, Jiang rose, tugged a sleeve of the jersey as if to check it out, and then grabbed the microphone. He said that his grandson, whom he adored, had lived for three years in Philadelphia with his father, Mianheng, and would love the shirt. "He liked the football very much," Jiang said in English, eliciting laughter and applause at his appreciation of American sports, which clearly needed some fine-tuning.

One of Jiang's former classmates at Shanghai Jiaotong University, Hun H. Sun, was a professor at Drexel and had mentored Jiang Mianheng when he was a student there. Split by China's disruptive modern history, Sun, the scion of a family that had been among the richest in China before the Japanese invasion, had gone to America in the 1950s for graduate work, while Jiang joined the underground Communist Party.

"I ran away," Sun observed pensively, "and he stayed and took over China."

Unlike most people with his background, Sun's father, Sun Yufong, had chosen not to flee the Communists but instead tried to work with them to re-build the country. At first the elder Sun was given the title "people's capital-ist," but during the Cultural Revolution he was severely persecuted for his "bad class background." Robbed of his possessions, stripped of his dignity, and denied medical care, he died. Four ancient Chinese scrolls, worth mil-lions of dollars and confiscated by the Communists, are now on display in a Shanghai museum, where they are labeled "donations" from Sun Yufong.

His son, an American for fifty years, never returned to his native land, even turning down a personal invitation to visit from Jiang Zemin himself. "I have mixed feelings about it all," Professor Sun reflected. "I lost my father to the system. But I have a lot of hope for President Jiang."

At Drexel, the professor apologized to the president, saying that because of "personal difficulties," he was not able to accept the invitation. "I com-pletely understand," Jiang replied warmly.

While in Philadelphia, Jiang paid a special visit to his former professor, the now ninety-five-year-old Gu Yuxiu. Gu had conformed to the Western order-ing of names and used a different system of transliterating the Chinese, so that he was now known as Yu Hsiu Ku. Overriding objections from security agents, Jiang insisted on visiting Professor Ku at home, reflecting Confucian respect for his teacher.

When Jiang and his wife arrived at Ku's modest apartment behind Philadelphia's Academy of Music for a half hour of home-cooked food and reminiscences, his demeanor changed instantly from senior leader to deferential student. The almost mystical transformation of the man who had stood up to fifty hostile congresspeople that very morning would have disoriented Westerners, but it did not faze the Chinese at all. Anything less would have been at variance with their tradition.

"It was remarkable to see the president of China together with Professor Ku," noted Li Zhaoxing, then China's vice foreign minister. "Jiang Zemin was modest and well behaved, just like any ordinary student in the audience of his esteemed teacher."

Jiang gave Ku a book on Chinese culture and noticed that a poem he himself had written hung proudly on the wall of Ku's study. It read: "Emphasizing education and paying respect for one's teacher, / Remembering one's youth when studying hard, / Calculus plays a critical role, / An old man contributes much to his motherland." The poem embodied the fifty-year bond between student and teacher, and looking at it afresh, Jiang said to Ku, "Emphasis on education and respect for one's teacher are traditional virtues of China. Having the chance to visit you, I feel very excited." Like his revolutionary father before him, Jiang believed that traditional values had an important place in the modern world.

Professor Ku and his family, including his wife, three children, and many grandchildren, treated China's president and his wife, Wang Yeping, to dishes of hometown Shanghai food, including lotus soup and steamed dumplings with red bean. Jiang recalled that Professor Ku never brought teaching materials to class, lecturing entirely from memory. Reciprocating, Ku remembered how young Jiang Zemin sat in his front row, looking so serious and taking copious notes.

After dinner Jiang rose to leave. "As a professor of electromechanical engineering, a playwright and a poet," he said to Ku, "you are really extraordinary."

Asked whether finding himself in the spotlight with Jiang after so many years of relative anonymity felt strange, Ku answered in a whispery voice: "No. Because it is the Chinese way, it seems very strange to an American audience."

Ku summarized his remarkable relationships: Because he had been a friend of Zhou Enlai, he explained, he was then a friend of Zhou's successor, Deng Xiaoping—and thus a friend of Deng's successor, Jiang Zemin, who, coincidentally, had also been his math student. Similarly, having been an adviser to Chiang Kai-shek, Ku had had the confidence of every Nationalist government in Taiwan.

But Professor Ku noted that Jiang Zemin had visited for purely personal reasons; there was no political agenda. "He wanted to come here and relax," said Ku. "Just the two of us. But he listened to my advice, and he's going to think about it. I think all other things are minor compared to world peace. And universities are for world peace, right? . . .

"I am nonpolitical," he added. "I do have my ideas, but only as a retired professor. I just enjoy life. I don't try to influence anybody."

On occasion over the previous decade Ku had written to Jiang on matters of politics and international affairs. Jiang had never responded, Ku said, "because of security reasons." But in 1990 Ku wrote to Jiang advising that it would be in China's best interest to allow the dissident leader, Fang Lizhi, who had taken refuge in the American embassy in Beijing since June 1989, to leave the country. Shortly afterward the professor received an unexpected call from his former student. "He said to me two words," Ku recalled. " 'Watch television.' " Turning on CNN, Ku saw the news that Fang Lizhi was being released.

"When I became ambassador to the United States in 1998," recalled Li Zhaoxing, "I visited Professor Ku. He was a fascinating man and was proud to have corresponded with President Jiang. When Ku went to Oklahoma, President Jiang asked our consul general in Houston to visit him."

When Professor Ku died in 2002, Jiang Zemin felt a deep sadness, the passing of the old era. He telephoned Ku's wife to offer his sympathies and sent a wreath of flowers, saying that Ku's "noble spirit" would inspire generations of Chinese. In his formal letter of condolence, President Jiang wrote that Professor Ku was "a teacher of all ages," noting that he was an "assiduous life-long learner, paid close attention to the motherland's reunification, and had offered his suggestions on the matter."

"President Jiang's attitude toward Professor Ku was not an isolated case," Li Zhaoxing commented. "He bestows high respect on older comrades who have retired. Earlier in 1997, when President Jiang visited Shanghai, he invited a group of retired officials, not the current ones, to a private banquet. This reflects his commitment to Chinese tradition. I've heard Jiang say that people should treat each other without snobbery, that they should learn from each other no matter what their status, and that those who have retired have much wisdom to teach us."

With limited time and more to do, Jiang was driven to the University of Pennsylvania Museum of Archaeology and Anthropology, where, after taking a quick tour of the Chinese collection, he gave a short speech praising Penn's Wharton School of Business for developing management courses for Chinese officials and executives. Jiang told how his reunion with Professor Ku "reminded me of our university life, which is the golden age of one's life—and one cannot but cherish it so much." He quoted a Chinese poem: "You never know where you will meet your old friend in your long life."

Then it was on to Independence Hall, where Jiang's motorcade had to drive up an unlit pedestrian path to avoid a rowdy crowd of two hundred demonstrators lying in wait. But they made such a ruckus—screaming through bullhorns and banging without rhythm on cheap drums—that Jiang's visit to the Liberty Bell had to be canceled. With little time allocated for sightseeing, the delegation went directly to the Assembly Room, where a guide explained its glorious history, while Jiang sat at the oak desk where the Declaration of Independence had been signed in 1776.

It is not hard to explain why President Jiang's visit to Independence Hall, the birthplace of American democracy, agitated critics. To those who assumed that China was a vast totalitarian state, like the repressive regimes of North Korea, Iraq, and Cuba, the outrage was understandable. Said one reporter, "To the demonstrators, it seemed incongruous for the head of the world's largest authoritarian government to bask in the historical richness of a place known for the establishment of democracy."

The harder question is why Jiang, after the grand ceremony in Washington, would subject himself to such abuse. Worse, his visit also invited the ridicule of critics back home, who would accuse him of worshipping American values. Slammed in both America and China, there was no political upside here.

A good assumption is that Jiang Zemin visited Independence Hall just because he wanted to. In his youth he had studied Thomas Jefferson's thoughts and deeds. During the Japanese occupation the words "life, liberty, and the pursuit of happiness" had given him hope and inspiration—and it meant a great deal to literally see the physical embodiment of those ideals. Jiang felt a kinship with the American revolutionaries who had driven out the same British colonialists who had also taken Hong Kong from China. The revolutionaries had acted out of patriotism, and perhaps more than anything else,

Jiang considered himself a patriot. His visit to Independence Hall was not political gesture; it was personal pursuit.

PROTESTS ASIDE, JIANG HAD been warmly welcomed in Philadelphia, but his
next stop, New York, provided a very different reception. The only senior
leader who was willing to meet him, for a 7:30 A.M. breakfast, was former
President George H. W. Bush, who had been chief of the U.S. Liaison
Office in Beijing in the 1970s. The leading local politicians—Governor
George Pataki, Mayor Rudolph Giuliani, and Senators Daniel Patrick
Moynihan and Alfonse D'Amato—all declined. They either cited "schedul-
ing conflicts" or refused in outright protest. Guiliani, eyeing higher office,
had "grave concerns about China's human rights policies," while Pataki's
spokesperson cited "the upcoming election," even though the governor was
not running.

Nonetheless Jiang managed to spread the word about China's growth.
His first stop was the New York Stock Exchange, where, standing on the
balcony that overlooked the trading floor, he was given the honor of ringing
the opening bell. The balcony itself was draped with the American and
Chinese flags, and the symbolism was rich: Though the two countries
might disagree on any number of issues, they were in perfect accord on the
positive aspects of the free market system, including the need to raise capital. And if anyone doubted that Communism had been modernized, much
to Jiang Zemin's credit, one need only note that the same bright red five-
star flag that Chinese human-wave soldiers had held when storming American positions in the Korean War was now giving blessing to the New York
Stock Exchange, on which the shares of seventeen Chinese companies
were trading.

New York Stock Exchange president Richard Grasso presented Jiang with
a bull-and-bear sculpture, representing strong and weak markets. Not to be
outgifted, Jiang gave Grasso a green flying horse, saying in English, "I hope
that your market will be as vibrant as a flying horse."

The story is told that U.S. ambassador James Sasser, when visiting Presi-
dent Jiang one day, was surprised to find him reading a biography of Franklin
Delano Roosevelt. Jiang wondered whether he could learn from the way
Roosevelt dealt with stock market speculators, a problem in China's early-
stage, cowboy-capitalism market economy. Sasser noted, half seriously, that
Roosevelt had taken a major stock manipulator, Joseph P. Kennedy, father of
President John Kennedy, and made him head of the Securities and Exchange

Commission. Jiang retorted that that would be a good idea for China "if only I could figure out who the biggest stock manipulators are."

From Wall Street in lower Manhattan, it was on to IBM headquarters in Armonk, a suburb just north of the city. There CEO Lou Gestner greeted the president in Chinese. *"Lao pengyou,"* he said, *"ni hao!"*—Old friend, how are you?

With eight joint ventures in China, IBM's good relations with the government were a necessity, not a nicety, a point reinforced by Gerstner's references to his long friendship and many meetings with Jiang. As for Jiang, he had something else in mind. A former minister of electronics and a lifelong technology buff, he was eager to see the latest computer products. A Chinese-American IBM scientist, whose father had been an officer in Chiang Kai-shek's Kuomintang army, gave the tour in Mandarin.

The ostensible reason for visiting technology companies was to assess possible applications in China, but in truth Jiang just loved this stuff. He was fascinated by three futuristic devices in particular: a credit card–like device that enabled the transmission of data between two people during a handshake by using the body's natural conductivity; a system called "kiosk banking" that facilitated financial transactions on the Internet; and a supercomputer for forecasting the weather. In making his inquiries, Jiang used English terms, such as "integrated circuits . . . prototype . . . chip," evincing more technical understanding than virtually any American politician.

"I am of your profession," Jiang told his hosts, "but it's a pity I've not been engaged in it for many years."

Back at his hotel, the famed Waldorf-Astoria on Park Avenue, Jiang met three hundred members of New York's Chinese community. He told the gathering that as a youth, he read many books about the West and studied the languages. "You can read a hundred books on a subject," he said, "but you get so much more by seeing it, even if just once." Jiang then posed for pictures before departing to soak up more technology.

Crossing the Hudson River, he visited AT&T and Lucent Technologies in New Jersey. At AT&T he inspected network operations, and at Lucent he put on protective clothing—white gown, disposable booties, gloves, and a hood-like mask—to enter a sealed "clean room" where the most advanced microchips were being fabricated.

"I certainly didn't understand President Jiang's technical questions, nor did many of the Americans," recalled Foreign Minister Li Zhaoxing, who was on the tour. "But Jiang was really enjoying himself talking to the scientists; he loves high tech."

Jiang was equally enthusiastic that evening at a dinner held in his honor at the Waldorf by the U.S.–China Chamber of Commerce and the U.S.–China Business Council, which led the lobby in Washington promoting permanent normal trade relations (PNTR) for China. Two hundred top business executives paid a thousand dollars a head for the privilege of learning how China could make their big companies even bigger. In the nineteenth century poor Chinese laborers had come to America—Gold Mountain, as they called it— to seek their fortunes. Now prosperous American businessmen were heading in the other direction to do the same. Already the United States had 23,000 projects in China with a contractual value of over $36 billion and had become the second largest investor in China.

This was Jiang's world. These CEOs were courting him, not he them— they had the money, but he had the market. He was relaxed and radiant, working the crowd, pumping hands, and preaching business. There would be no questions tonight of human rights or harvested organs.

After describing the substantial opportunities for U.S. business in his country, Jiang made a savvy political point, criticizing the fact that China's most favored nation trading status (which the United States gives to all but the most inimical regimes) still came under annual review. The instability created by such uncertainty, Jiang told his audience, meant that "American entrepreneurs doing business or making investments in China always feel the sword of Damocles hanging over their heads." Instability: to CEOs, it is among the greatest of evils.

Jiang left his audience on a high note, promising, with rising energy in his voice, to "continue to open our markets steadily." He concluded by quoting Franklin D. Roosevelt: "The only limit to our realization of tomorrow will be our doubts of today. Let us move forward with strong and active faith."

When Jiang finished speaking, the audience gave him a standing ovation. He beamed, and as he raised his glass for a collective toast, he singled out Henry Kissinger with whom to clink glasses.

EARLY ON NOVEMBER 1 Jiang and his party took off for Boston, where he was scheduled to give a high-profile speech at Harvard. Senior U.S. and Chinese officials had urged him not to go for fear of the extremely hostile public spectacle that his visit was sure to incite, but Jiang rejected their advice. Harvard was the pinnacle of the academic world, as much a temple of American achievement as Wall Street. He had heard about the university's intellectual grandeur his entire life, and he wanted to see it for himself. It was a gutsy decision: To Harvard he would go.

The warnings were well founded. Five thousand people took to the streets of Cambridge, the largest demonstrations since the Vietnam War, braving the chilling rain to shout insults at the Chinese president and chant slogans demanding democracy for China and independence for Tibet and Taiwan. This was expected. What was not expected was that, among the demonstrators, more than twelve hundred were marching in *support* of Jiang, shouting their own slogans and waving Chinese and American flags. The pro-Jiang marchers wore badges, distributed by the Greater Boston Area Chinese Association, saying "Welcome President Jiang" in Chinese characters.

There was an eerie balance between the two sides, since the hardcore anti-Jiang protesters numbered only about fifteen hundred. In the battle for sonic supremacy, however, there was no contest. People seem to shout louder when they are against something than when they are for it.

In most locations members of the opposing camps stood in the same crowd, cheek by jowl, making it difficult to figure out who was on which side. Mini-debates broke out, but under the watchful eye of hundreds of police officers there was no violence. At one location human rights activists and Tibetan exiles shouted, "Free Tibet, free Taiwan," while a group of mainlanders sang China's national anthem and shouted back, "One China, only one China." To confuse matters further, some of the protesters had conflicting agendas. For example, some pro-democracy Chinese activists had no interest in granting "China's Tibet" its independence.

The only people allowed beyond police barricades were prearranged groups known to be friendly, such as children from the Chinese School of Cambridge who, just before Jiang's cavalcade appeared, emerged from a cafeteria waving bouquets of flowers and dancing in traditional Chinese costumes. As the fleet of black limousines arrived on campus, Jiang came within yards of demonstrators, his closest encounter with this alien species. Huge black and white banners exclaiming "Free Tibet" intruded on his field of sight, and high-pitched Chinese dissidents, yelling in Mandarin, filled his ears with their electronically amplified words: "Down with one-party dictatorship," "Down with Jiang," "Jiang Zemin go home!"

But massive red banners praising Jiang and patriotic Chinese flags were also visible, creating a kaleidoscope of chaotic American democracy. Those able to read Chinese characters needed a scorecard to sort out the different factions and their placards. "I think it is a surprise for the media that there are as many supporters as opponents," said a Harvard medical student.

Well before 11:00 A.M., the scheduled start time, Sanders Theater, Harvard's largest lecture hall, was packed. An overflow audience of more than a thousand—consisting of selected scholars and Asian specialists, a few journalists, and other Harvard faculty, students, and staff chosen by lottery—was waiting. To accommodate the strong interest, Jiang's speech would be broadcast on closed-circuit television to other on-campus venues, with audio provided in Mandarin and English.

Harvard president Neil Rudenstine welcomed President Jiang by noting that Harvard had a long tradition of China studies but that he would be the first Chinese leader to speak there. For Jiang, this speech was the big one, and he was ready for it.

Jiang began, as he normally did, with some specifics of place. "Harvard was among the first American universities to accept Chinese students," he said. "The Chinese educational, scientific, and cultural communities have all along maintained academic exchanges with this university." He then went into his working premise, explaining, as he often did to Westerners, that one could not properly judge his country until one understood it. "To promote the development of China-U.S. relations," he stressed, "China needs to know the United States better, and vice versa.

"To know China better," he continued, "one may approach it from different angles. China is a country with five thousand years of civilization. Therefore it is important to approach China from a historical and cultural perspective." In this context Jiang recalled his first lesson in high-school calculus. "My teacher quoted a line from Zhuang Zi, a Chinese philosopher [who lived] over twenty-five hundred years ago, which reads, 'Cut away half of a rod and keep on halving what is left, and there will be no end to that process.' This gave me a vivid concept of limits."

Calculus? Limits? What other national leader had ever referred to the essence of calculus—the nature of the "limit"—in a major speech? Other leaders had studied calculus, but Jiang was so fascinated by it, philosophically, that it informed the nature of his thinking. It was the springboard from which he could launch an intellectual history of ancient China.

Interesting in their own right, Jiang's descriptions evinced the depth of his love for Chinese culture, a passion that formed the foundation of both his patriotism and his political philosophy. He spoke of ancient Chinese astronomy that integrated the universe and humanity; various schools of philosophical thought; the contributions of Chinese mathematics, music, and medicine;

then on to silk-weaving, porcelain-making, metallurgy, and shipbuilding; and finally China's "four great inventions of paper-making, gunpowder, printing, and compass" that "changed the face of the world."

Jiang used the prismatic composition of light as a metaphor to support his political theme: "Sunlight," he said, "is composed of seven colors; so is our world full of colors and splendor. Every country and every nation has its own historical and cultural traditions, strong points and advantages. We should respect and learn from each other." His challenge to Westerners was to view China not through their own perspective but with an understanding of China's unique culture and history. To "help you to know China," Jiang offered four "observations."

First, the tradition of solidarity and unity. ("The Chinese nation is a big family composed of fifty-six nationalities.") Second, the tradition of maintaining independence. ("After one hundred years of struggle, China has stood up again as a giant.") Third, the peace-loving tradition. ("We will never impose upon others the kind of sufferings we once experienced.") Fourth, the tradition of constantly striving for self-perfection. ("Ancient Chinese philosophers proposed the following doctrine: 'As Heaven maintains vigor through movement, a gentleman should constantly strive for self-perfection.' " This idea, he said, spurs "the Chinese people to work hard for reform and renovation.")

In an overt rejoinder to President Clinton, who had said China was on "the wrong side of history," Jiang asserted that China's policies are "all based on both reality and history." Jiang switched to English for the final quarter of his speech, praising America for its "pragmatic attitude and creative spirit" and noting that "in our cause to further open up and achieve modernization, we have spared no efforts in learning from all the fine cultural achievements of the American people."

Jiang concluded by drawing a parallel with American culture. "I highly appreciate the motto on the gates of your university," he told the overflowing audience. "It reads: 'Enter to grow in wisdom' and 'Depart to serve better thy country and thy kind.' Young people in China also have a motto: 'Keep the motherland in heart, and serve the people with heart and soul.' I hope that in the cause of building their own countries and promoting world peace and development, younger generations of China and the United States will understand each other better, learn from each other, enhance the friendship, and strive for a better future."

Throughout his forty-five-minute speech, Jiang had some competition. Outside the theater demonstrators maintained a steady of chorus of screams and rants, so that inside the theater the muffled sounds of their bullhorns provided a sustained level of background noise. Jiang seemed unbothered by the low-level ruckus, although at times the volume of his deep voice seemed to increase.

China's president also had to ignore a Taiwan-born Harvard professor who, after removing his sweater, stood with his back to the stage in a T-shirt that read, in English and Chinese, "Taiwan is not part of China: Two countries, two systems." In similar style, several students stood wearing T-shirts that said "Free Tibet."

After his speech Jiang agreed to submit to a question-and-answer session, an event that his handlers had wanted to avoid. Jiang told his staff that he wasn't worried about going "unprotected" and gave the Q&A the green light. The university did make concessions in that the questions were set beforehand, though they were not shown to the Chinese delegation in advance, and that the entire Q&A session would be limited to fifteen minutes. Rather than risking protests or diatribes from the audience, a committee of four Harvard scholars—led by Ezra Vogel, director of the Fairbank Center for East Asian Research, and Bill Kovach, curator of the Nieman Foundation for Journalism—had solicited questions from the Harvard community. The committee selected questions it thought best hit issues that Jiang could avoid in press interviews back home.

Vogel read the questions aloud, but not before warning that they would be tough to answer. "We hope," he said to the riveted audience, "that President Jiang will remember that Harvard is a place where democracy works." The first question came from the Joint Committee for Protesting Jiang Zemin's Visit to Harvard.

"Jiang Zemin asked the West not to engage in confrontation but dialogue," the question said. "However, why does he refuse dialogue with his own people? Why did the Chinese government order tanks in Tiananmen Square on June 4, 1989, and confront the Chinese people?"

Jiang responded by describing the diversity of China, the difficulties of running such a large country, and the various channels leaders use to learn about people's views. Then, as if continuing this same line of reasoning, he made a remark that surprised his audience and became the next day's headlines. "It goes without saying," he said, "that, naturally, we may have shortcomings and even make some mistakes in our work. However, we have been working on a constant basis to further improve our work."

Was Jiang hinting that China's actions in Tiananmen might have been "mistakes"? Though he did not criticize the government, his remark in the context of the question seemed an unprecedented break from the canned rhetoric of the past.

After a straightforward question and answer on Tibet, Jiang agreed to take another question from the floor. "This is completely unrehearsed," Vogel told the packed house, "and I hope that some of you will think of a question."

A man in the balcony jumped up to demand information about imprisoned dissident Wei Jingsheng, but Vogel shouted the protester down. "I did not recognize you," he said. "Would you please sit down!" Then he said, "President Jiang Zemin has said that he would like to hear, first of all, from an American. This is for an American audience." Vogel then called on a woman in the back of the hall who turned out to be a reporter from *Newsweek*. She asked the Chinese leader for his reaction to the shouting, chanting protesters outside the lecture hall.

"I do have my understanding about the general concept of democracy," Jiang began, warming to the question. "However, during my current trip to the United States, starting from Hawaii, I felt more specific understanding of the American democracy, more specific than I learned from books. Although I am already seventy-one years old, my ears still work very well, so when I was delivering my speech, I did hear the sound from the loudspeakers [bullhorns] outside. However, I believe the only approach for me is to speak even louder than it."

Even before Jiang's answer was translated, the Chinese-speaking members of the audience erupted with laughter and applause. When the answer was translated, the English speakers joined in. The audience, cheering on the whole, loved it.

Professor Vogel spoke for many when he praised Jiang's appearance and concluded by telling a little secret. Just before arriving, Jiang had confessed to Ambassador Sasser that he felt like he "was coming to a big examination at Harvard." Vogel added, "I think we can say that he happily passed his examination." In the words of one reporter, "Jiang joked about, but was not dismissive of, the U.S. system of liberties." For President Jiang, it was a pitch-perfect note to strike.

But it was Jiang's comments about Tiananmen Square that engendered the most commentary. Jiang had used the words "mistakes" and "shortcomings" with subtlety, allowing for different interpretations. To those in China, Jiang meant that, in general, mistakes and errors are unavoidable in the work of government. To foreigners, the juxtaposition of contrite words with Tiananmen was refreshing. "It's something a Chinese leader has never said," said Merle Goldman, a China expert at Boston University.

In grading his performance, China experts in the audience gave President Jiang high marks. Joseph Fewsmith, a professor at Boston University, noted, "He was clearly relaxed, enjoying the moment, as when he took the question about his reaction to the protests outside. He handled it like an American politician, deflecting it with humor." Boston College's Robert Ross observed, "It was the first time a Chinese leader voluntarily subjected himself to a week of questioning without the respect normally given to leaders of China. Now he can go back and say to his colleagues, 'Not only can I submit to questioning, I can handle it and defend our values at the same time.'"

Jiang lunched with two hundred Boston business leaders, an event that was attended by Acting Governor Paul Cellucci and Mayor Thomas Menino, neither of whom exhibited any of the reluctance that their New York counterparts had in meeting the Chinese president. Cellucci said that the state was determined to do more business in China, particularly in telecommunications, biotechnology, and engineering.

Breaking away from his prepared text, Jiang made some asides in English, joking that he had been talking too quickly for his translator. "I would like to save you time, you know," he said as the audience laughed. He had the audience breaking into applause as he recalled his visit to the area fourteen years before (when he was electronics vice minister). "I went to the Wayside Inn," Jiang ad-libbed, referring to a restaurant in the Boston suburb of Sudbury. "Delicious beef tips."

JIANG'S FINAL STOP WAS Los Angeles, where he landed not much before midnight. From his room at the Beverly Hills Hilton he called Shen Yongyan to share his excitement. "Jiang asked me if I had seen his speech at Harvard," Shen remembered. "He was very proud of that speech. He said that his entire U.S. trip was turning out much better than he had expected."

On Sunday morning, November 2, Jiang began his one day in southern California at Hughes Electronics Corporation, where he learned about satellite communications equipment being manufactured for China. Later, at a General Motors plant, he sat in a Buick Regal, which GM would begin to manufacture in the Pudong New Area of Shanghai the following year. The old engineer was captivated by four high-tech automobiles, GM's cars of the future, and was eager to slip behind the wheel of the prototype "SSC Intelligent Vehicle," a computer-laden van that employed onboard radar to avoid accidents and that could tap into a satellite signal to unlock its doors should the driver lose the key.

Then it was back to the Hilton for a lunch with 750 of southern California's elite, which drew from the worlds of business, entertainment, and politics. Before joining the expectant guests, President Jiang met privately with California governor Pete Wilson and Los Angeles mayor Richard Riordan to discuss business and trade. Los Angeles was no New York, and it laid down a red carpet of official welcome, reflecting California's economic dependence on China.

At the gala midday affair, Jiang mingled with an eclectic California group that included media tycoon Rupert Murdoch, former Secretary of State Warren Christopher, futurist thinker Alvin Toffler, and dancer Cyd Charisse. Business leaders from southern California technology companies, banks, and media organizations formed the core of the attendees.

By now protesters were a familiar sight, but in Los Angeles they had style. The scene resembled Mardi Gras. It was almost as if the demonstration were a form of performance art or a Hollywood Does Protests comedy routine. The thousand or so protesters were a menagerie. One "all-American" man was dressed in pedal pushers with red and white stripes on his right leg and stars on a blue background on his left leg, while a woman representing Death wore a black dress, a black veil, and black face paint. One group demanding that Taiwan get into the United Nations stood across Wilshire Boulevard from another group demanding that America get out. Placard-holders surrounded the hotel, excoriating a hodgepodge of ills, from organ harvesting in China to motorcycle helmet laws in America. A producer of films on Tibet hired a pair of actors dressed as Chinese police to march around a real Tibetan nun and monk, their hands tied up and their faces smeared with movie-makeup blood. The police uniforms, the not-well-known producer said as he played to the local news cameras, were from Richard Gere's new anti-Chinese movie, *Red Corner.*

Throughout lunch Jiang was vivacious and engaging, hardly the "wooden and bland" statue that some had expected. He had Governor Wilson on his right and Mayor Riordan on his left, and he chatted them both up, turning this way and that. The USC Trojan Marching Band, well rehearsed, gave a rousing performance of the Chinese national anthem, while the assembled capitalist elite marched in step, as it were, with the soaring revolutionary melody and the Communist-inspired words that call upon all who would not be slaves to "rise up."

In welcoming President Jiang, Governor Pete Wilson called California "the state built with Chinese muscle [constructing the railroads] in the nineteenth century and with Chinese genius in the high-tech world of the twentieth century." The Republican governor, who had recently been on a trade mission to China, alluded to democratic values as Jiang, sitting on the dais, remained pleasantly attentive. "The great elixir of individual freedom," Wilson said, "is the best prescription to accelerate and multiply your success in achieving your goal" of building China.

For the last major address of his U.S. trip, Jiang promised his Los Angeles audience that a growing friendship between his country and their city would bring economic, scientific, and technological benefits to both sides. "China has become the second-largest trading partner of Los Angeles," he said, noting that "nineteen California cities are twinned with Chinese cities."

Speaking English for the last half of his twenty-minute speech, Jiang told of his admiration for Los Angeles, which he had visited twice before, the first time being in 1980 when he had been part of an early reform commission. "It has taken me seventeen years to realize the beauty of this world-renowned city," Jiang ad-libbed. He concluded by quoting a well-known Chinese proverb: "A ten-thousand-mile journey begins with the first step."

"He's playing to the business community here," said China scholar Richard Baum of UCLA. "He played to the diplomatic and press community in Washington, the academic community at Harvard, the historic community in Virginia, and the business community here and in New York. He's touched all the bases."

After the luncheon Jiang held a private meeting with senior American evangelist Billy Graham. The topic was religious freedom in China, a source of much protest. "Twenty years ago hardly one church was open in all of China," said Graham in a statement following the meeting. "Today there are tens of thousands, and we should be very grateful for that."

Jiang had been scheduled to leave Los Angeles that afternoon, but he extended his visit by a day in order to attend an enthusiastic banquet that evening with some nine hundred leaders of the Chinese-American community. Held downtown at the Biltmore Hotel, the event reflected the Chinese government's desire to court the increasingly influential community as a way to improve relations with the United States and to thwart lobbying efforts by Taiwan.

In his informal remarks to the high-energy crowd, Jiang gave a thumbs-up to his state visit, predicted a bright future for U.S.–China relations, and fore-

cast that "in the twenty-first century, China will be built into a strong, democratic, culturally advanced . . . country." Inspired by his reception, Jiang sang
a few bars of his favorite Peking Opera, much to the delight of his audience,
who gave him a standing ovation. " 'A bright moon in the sky,' " a grinning
Jiang crooned, as he launched into the Chinese opera *Zhuofangcao,* while
still wearing on his neck the welcoming garland of flowers. He then conducted a brief, rousing performance of "Ode to the Motherland." Adding to
the fun, the Mandarin-speaking Jiang had Cantonese-speaking members of
the crowd "laughing out loud as he practiced his Cantonese."

Jiang did not avoid Taiwan, the most divisive issue in the Chinese-American
community, which in southern California alone had grown to 400,000. In recent years emigration from the mainland had changed its political bent. The
pro-Taiwan faction, which had been in the majority for years, was now being
surpassed by those who supported Beijing. Referencing the recent repatriation of Hong Kong, Jiang said, "The Taiwan question will also be eventually
resolved. To achieve the reunification of the motherland is the common aspi-
ration of the entire Chinese people, including the compatriots now living
overseas." Loud applause followed.

The next morning President Jiang boarded his retrofitted Air China jet-
liner for his triumphant return to Beijing. In his departing letter to President Clinton, Jiang said, "I have been personally touched by the profound
friendship of the American people toward the Chinese people. Such
friendship serves as a powerful driving force for the growth of China–U.S.
relations."

"Jiang Zemin established himself as a diplomatic heavyweight," UCLA
professor Richard Baum said of the U.S. tour. "This was a major coming-out
for him—not just here but back home with his audience in China."

It was the crowning moment in an already glorious year. Jiang had won
unimpeded leadership at the Fifteenth Party Congress, and then had to deliver the goods. To those who thought him to be stiff as a personality and a
bumbler in foreign affairs, Jiang demonstrated that he had a sense of humor,
could handle tough crowds of congressmen and reporters, was able to charm
audiences and win adherents, and most important, could manage complex bilateral relations with the United States.

Jiang's journey was a rite of passage for a leader who, prior to his American
trip, had proven that he could *become* China's leader but had yet to prove that
he could *be* China's leader. Now he had shown that he could handle delicate
diplomacy, business boosterism, nettlesome protests, and intrusive media.

"This is Jiang's year," said Wang Chi, a professor of Chinese studies at Georgetown University. "He wanted the help of the American government to build up his image," Wang said, "and he got it."

LESS THAN TWO WEEKS LATER China released Wei Jingsheng, its most eminent political prisoner, from a labor camp and put him on a flight to Detroit. The Xinhua announcement, made four hours after the plane had departed, was terse. "Wei Jingsheng has been released on parole for medical treatment because of his illness," it read. "Wei has gone abroad for medical treatment."

The timing of the release was not coincidental. Jiang was both signaling China's self-confidence and rewarding Clinton for the success of the summit. Armed with this tangible benefit, the American president would have more power to advance their common goal of improving China–U.S. relations. Both countries had played the diplomatic game tactfully—the United States by not backing China into a face-losing corner with public pressure, and China by holding up its end of the unspoken bargain.

"We are very pleased with the release," a White House spokesman said on the matter of Wei Jingsheng, "and we look forward to having him in the United States for treatment." Asked whether the release had been arranged during the summit, the official replied carefully. "Obviously the release of dissidents was something we discussed," he said, "but I don't want to characterize the reason for his release right now."

Two months later, in a further follow-up to the summit, Jiang assured U.S. secretary of defense William Cohen, who was in Beijing, that China had stopped all sales of antiship cruise missiles to Iran and would not provide any "over-the-horizon" technology to upgrade the ones the Iranians already had.

AT THE END OF NOVEMBER President Jiang attended the APEC conference in Vancouver, but the trip became a state visit to Canada. Although some protests were mounted, Canada treated Jiang with special regard. Strengthening Canada's already excellent relations with China was one of Prime Minister Jean Chretien's top foreign policy objectives. By increasing trade with Asia, he hoped to decrease Canada's dependence on America.

Jiang appeared delighted to be back in North America. "Sporting a leather bomber jacket and a proud smile," read a Reuters account of his appearance, "Jiang confirmed he was finally a man at ease in the international spotlight." Later on his Canadian tour, Jiang made another sartorial statement by donning a white Stetson hat, mirroring Deng Xiaoping's 1979 act of assuming the rough-and-ready image of an American cowboy, the personification of rugged individualism sure to appeal to audiences in North America and back home in China.

But despite Jiang's personal successes, the summits did little to help Asia's troubled economy. Before long the currency fluctuations and plummeting stock markets began to have a serious impact on China. On December 14 Jiang traveled to Kuala Lumpur for an East Asian summit. He promised his country's cooperation in stabilizing currency volatility and helping ASEAN nations reform their economies, and he pledged $1 billion to the International Monetary Fund's plan to rescue Thailand, the epicenter of the financial earthquake.

Two days later he made an even more important vow, promising not to devalue the yuan or subsidize China's exports. The news came as a great relief to countries that had feared devaluation of the Chinese currency. Such a move would have helped China maintain its competitive export position relative to other nations, but it would have escalated the crisis by causing "domino effect" devaluations throughout the region. "If China had 'broken peg' [devalued], it could have destabilized everything," commented former U.S. Treasury secretary Robert Rubin, himself a hero in the Herculean multiyear effort to restore financial stability. "China withstood the pressure; they acted responsibly."

Jiang also tried to dispel any suspicions of ulterior motives or ultimate ambitions. "China will never seek hegemony," he said. "China will forever be a good neighbor, a good partner, and a good friend with ASEAN countries."

CHINA HAD UNDERGONE MOMENTOUS changes in 1997. With the death of Deng Xiaoping and the orderly transfer of power to Jiang Zemin, an old era had ended. With the repatriation of Hong Kong to the motherland, innovations in blending market economics with socialist theory, Jiang's consolidation of power and undisputed preeminence, and his high-profile state visit to the United States, a new and promising era had begun.

According to *Time* magazine, Jiang's "remarkable performance" forced "a worldwide re-evaluation" of the man and his mission. Arnold Kantor, a former U.S. diplomat, remarked: "One shouldn't be fooled. Jiang is enormously smart and capable, but his persona is unpretentious and folksy, almost intentionally disarming."

Chapter 20

"Reform in China Has Now Entered the Assault Stage"

P RESIDENT JIANG LOOKED TO 1998 as a time to consolidate gains and focus on the economy, yet the year began with a seemingly minor but highly symbolic effort to encourage good manners. Initiated with a front-page commentary in *People's Daily* ("On Stressing Decorum") that quoted Confucius, Deng Xiaoping, and Jiang Zemin, the campaign admonished people to speak more civilly with one another. More than an etiquette lesson, it revealed much about China's leader and the direction in which he wanted to take his nation.

"Our country has always been known as 'a land of propriety,' " the commentary read. "Stressing civility and decorum is a fine tradition of our nation." It then made reference to the Confucian code of ethics, the standard of ancient Chinese gentility, and blamed the Cultural Revolution for the breakdown in contemporary manners. The ultra-Leftists had come to equate behaving with civility, decorum, and according to law as "bad things," the article informed its readers. Having good manners became tantamount, in the distorted views of these radicals, to espousing feudalist, capitalist, and revisionist ideals. In short, a polite person was a bourgeois person. It was a twisted, old-line Communist view of traditional Chinese culture, and *People's Daily* made clear that it was not one with which Jiang Zemin at all or ever agreed.

"The fine moral heritage of ancient times and the fine achievements of other countries in building civility and decorum," the article opined, had been "blindly negated" due to "the long-lasting influence of Left ideology." Decorum, it continued, "is not just a formality. It is an indispensable, important component of the effort to build socialist spiritual civilization."

It was as if Jiang had written the commentary himself. By equating good manners with good socialism, Jiang avowed the importance of traditional Chinese culture, which had been in danger of being lost under rigid-rule Communism. A return to past ideals, he believed, would "enable our country to stand like a giant among all nations of the world with a highly civilized spiritual outlook." It was a legacy that the Party general secretary, with only five years remaining in office, dearly wanted to bequeath to his country.

A communitarian exemplar of such decorum, indeed of Jiang Zemin's utopian exhortation to create a spiritual civilization, was established in Zhangjiagang country in the president's home province of Jiangsu. Rules and norms of behavior were codified in the *Civilized Citizen's Study Book,* and all citizens were required not only to memorize and follow them, but also to post them on the walls of their homes and offices. The book prescribed "six musts," which included advice on how to speak correctly and apologize properly, and proscribed ten "must nots," which banned offensive language, lewd acts, boisterous quarreling, flouting of traffic laws, and other uncivilized conduct. It also gave instruction in personal hygiene, such as washing one's hands before eating or after visiting the toilet, taking regular baths, trimming one's nails, and not spitting. What's more, Zhangjiagang had spotless, odor-free public lavatories, a sea change in China.

THE NINTH SESSION OF the National People's Congress (NPC) opened on March 5. As usual, personnel changes took center stage. As had been determined by the Party congress the previous fall, Zhu Rongji would become premier and Li Peng NPC chairman. Equally anticipated was the emergence of Hu Jintao, who at fifty-four was the youngest member of the Politburo Standing Committee, as Jiang Zemin's choice for state vice president. It was another sign that Hu was the leading candidate to succeed Jiang.

Working in Hu's favor were, as Jiang outlined to the CPC Central Committee, his "lofty morality and high prestige." Hu enjoyed strong support from Party members and had the backing of non-Communist parties and ethnic minorities as well. Significantly, Jiang told the Central Committee, the new vice president "must not be a controversial figure and he must not be tinged with factionalism." Recounting his numerous trips abroad, the president observed that he had often felt that he was of a different generation than most Western leaders. The leaders of those nations were young, he said, attuned to new knowledge, and physically vigorous. Jiang admitted that his own stamina occasionally failed him in their presence. It would soon be time for a change.

Jiang also expected Hu's appointment to alter international perceptions of China. "People overseas pay great attention to a change of government," Jiang said. "But probably no one has thought that we would choose Hu Jintao. People do not believe that we would promote a young man to assume the post of state vice president. What will people say? Let's wait for their verdict."

On March 16, as expected, Jiang was elected to a second five-year term as China's president and head of state. The vote was a strong 97.8 percent of the votes cast by the deputies. Hu Jintao, the new vice president, received 96.4 percent. In addition to having the president's support, Hu was popular among younger officials. A Party leader since his days as head of the Communist Youth League, he was personable as well as intelligent. Using his legendary, near-flawless memory, he won over delegates by remembering their names and details about their families. Party elders appreciated Hu's modesty and respect. Like Jiang himself, Hu was seen as another Zhou Enlai, the beloved late premier; the hundredth anniversary of his birth had been celebrated with great fanfare the month before.

Zhou Enlai, according to Jiang, combined "firmness of principle with flexibility of strategy," stressing that "correct ideas could succeed only after much waiting and many setbacks. And much painstaking and accurate work had to be done before the truth could be specified and widely accepted." For Jiang Zemin, Zhou Enlai was a modern role model.

Jiang wanted to expand the powers of Hu's office, making him the country's first active vice president. Having come to know U.S. vice president Al Gore during the past year, Jiang wanted China's vice president to play a similar role. Jiang hoped that Hu might chair certain task forces, meet foreign leaders, and generally be considered a likely successor.

Jiang also proposed that at some point Hu should become a vice chairman of the Central Military Commission. For his entire political career, Hu had worked on the Party side, where he had built a solid reputation, but he had no army experience, a handicap with which Jiang could empathize. With this appointment, Hu would have ample time and opportunity to learn about the military. Jiang insisted that such an appointment, at the right time, would ensure "the Party's absolute leadership over the Army."

"There is no need to speed up the process," Jiang later in the year told senior PLA officers, some of whom continued to resist appointing civilians to the CMC. "However, it will also not do to drag our feet." (Hu's appointment would come in 1999.) Jiang also gave Hu opportunities to represent China in meetings with international leaders and to travel abroad, a move that was carefully highlighted. "Chinese diplomats," confided one source, "have subtly explained to foreign governments about the special status of Hu."

The most immediate impact of the National People's Congress was Zhu Rongji's promotion to premier. A staunchly pro-market reformer with a reputation for an "iron face" and fierce temper, Zhu was determined to restructure the Chinese bureaucracy and enhance the efficiency of state-owned enterprises. In a major streamlining, at least eleven ministries and ministry-level bodies—relics of central planning that were hampering market-oriented reforms—were eliminated, merged, or spun off into holding companies. Some 33,000 positions were eliminated, a number that could rise as high as half a million once the cuts hit the provincial and local governments. In addition, Zhu promised to reform taxation, reorganize the grain-marketing system, privatize housing, and restructure the banking system. He set the national growth rate target at eight percent, an aggressive goal in a year when the Asian financial crisis was shrinking other economies in the region.

At a news conference following his appointment, Premier Zhu made a bold pledge, vowing to convert the majority of China's large SOEs into profit-making ventures within three years. It seemed like an unattainable goal, but Zhu was unconcerned with the political fallout of failure. "No matter whether there is a minefield ahead of me," he asserted, "or whether there is a deep ravine in front of me, I will bravely forge ahead, will not turn back, and will do my best until my last breath."

The relationship between Jiang Zemin and Zhu Rongji, forged in Shanghai, was dynamic if not often harmonious. It was a testimony to Jiang's management acumen that he did not hesitate to promote Zhu and leverage his extraordinary skills, even given the premier's unpredictability, occasional impetuousness, and inexhaustible capacity to rub people the wrong way. Though Zhu would run the economy operationally, Jiang would maintain control of its primary policies. This meant that, from the beginning, limits would be set on Zhu's prerogatives. Accordingly, Jiang kept his position as head of the Party's Leading Group on Finance and Economics, the highest authoritative body for policymaking in these areas. Zhu remained one of two vice heads. In this way Jiang retained authority over such major decisions as interest rates, loans to large enterprises, and economic relations with America.

Jiang also maintained control over international relations. He felt that his greatest contribution would come in diplomacy, and he was eager to build this legacy. Unlike premiers in the past, Zhu Rongji would not be taking a leading role in foreign affairs. In any case, it was clear to both men where

Zhu's responsibilities lay. "Reform in China has now entered the 'assault' stage," Jiang noted, and he knew that there was no one better to lead the attack than the new premier.

President Jiang and Premier Zhu had their differences, in policy as well as in personality. To Zhu, far-reaching economic reform was the top priority, and he wanted to make it happen as quickly as possible, saying that acute pain was better than chronic suffering. Jiang, on the other hand, worried that shock therapy could destabilize China as it had Russia and other Eastern European countries.

The foreign media tried to make much of the alleged competition between Jiang and Zhu. "It remains to be seen," said one report, "whether they will throw their lot in together, or scheme against each other, with the winner using the loser as a scapegoat." But the reality was that Zhu's ascent was made possible by Jiang's support. The two men had different personalities but a common mission: to transform China into a world power.

Jiang was also pleased to elevate several former subordinates to cabinet-level positions in the new government. In the past, promotions of those associated with the so-called Shanghai Faction had generated controversy. This time the reaction was muted, even positive. Analysts believed that a well-executed "soft landing of the economy" and relative insulation from Asia's financial crisis had won praise for the current leadership.

Premier Zhu began to implement his plan. He concentrated power in the State Economic and Trade Commission (SETC), a superministry that Zhu had been developing since 1991 as a way to detach archaic industrial ministries from government control and make their state-owned enterprises more responsive to market forces.

The SETC's mandate was not to try to run these industries, as had the now-defunct ministries, but rather to use market information and industrial policy to avoid duplication and waste. The underlying SOEs were restructured as independent legal entities so that they could operate autonomously in the marketplace.

The SETC chairman was Sheng Huaren, former head of Sinopec, China's largest petrochemical company, with about $40 billion in annual revenues and almost one million employees. "State-owned enterprises are the pillars of China's economy and the central point of the reforms of Deng Xiaoping and Jiang Zemin," Sheng later reflected. "Yet there were no precedents, no models. All was exploration. The big step came when these SOEs became responsible for their own profit and loss. We found that we needed a great deal of work in the areas of law (such as well-defined property rights), management independent of government, and a scientific system of decision-making. All this was new and, to many, daunting."

Sheng's first test was to try to fulfill Zhu's ambitious goal of making the majority of large SOEs profitable. "We weren't frightened," Sheng recalled, "but recognized the arduous task. We gave the three-year period various names, such as 'Reform and Difficult Relief Period' and 'Hard Battle Times.'"

Sheng recalled how he and his staff accompanied Jiang Zemin on six long inspection trips of SOEs, during which he gained insight into the president's management style. "We visited those provinces with highest concentrations of SOEs," he said. "Inner Mongolia, Sichuan, Shaanxi, Xian, Shandong, Hubei, Liaoning—some more than once. President Jiang spends a great deal of time reading and studying reports, but he is the first to admit that you must see problems with your own eyes and talk to the people involved. There is no substitute, he says, for being there."

Jiang was concerned about the social and political aspects of SOEs as well as the economic ones, and he was up for the grueling schedule. Inspecting the factories by day and traveling the roads by night, he worked intensively with Sheng and his team. During their journeys the group had many long talks, which often resulted in changes in policy. "For example," Sheng said, "by seeing the overbuilt factories and redundant labor, we realized that we had to downsize, which meant that we had to allow some insolvent, loss-making factories to go bankrupt. As for the laid-off workers, it would be the government's responsibility to take care of them. We had to find ways to safeguard their basic subsistence and plan their resettlement and retraining."

Although two levels of command separated the men, Jiang did not hesitate to call Sheng directly to discuss any issue. At the same time the president was careful to respect the chain of authority, usually informing Sheng's superiors, Premier Zhu Rongji and Vice Premier Wu Bangguo, whenever he planned to go around them (or had already done so).

"I'll tell you a secret," Li Zhaoxing, minister of foreign affairs, confided. "President Jiang has the personal telephone numbers—office, home, cell— of each director general of every department in the Foreign Ministry and all of our senior diplomats in our foreign embassies. He likes to get information directly, not filtered. He wants to speak with the most knowlegeable person, even if that person turns out to be very young. He has no compunction about calling anyone.

"As you can imagine," Li continued, "President Jiang's calls are legendary in the Foreign Ministry. Our diplomatic personnel really strive to know their areas, because they never know when President Jiang may be on the phone!"

A BOOK THAT DISCUSSED internal Party struggles over ideology, reform, and corruption—all issues high on Jiang Zemin's list of priorities—was published in the spring of 1998. Called *Crossed Swords* and written by two senior writers at *People's Daily*, it described the twenty-year battle between reform and Leftism in China. Coming down hard on what was but was not called remnant Maoism, *Crossed Swords* spotlighted what it saw as the successful destruction of three negative "cult" influences: the "cult of personality," which was destroyed by Deng Xiaoping's 1978 directive that practice is the sole criterion of truth; the "cult of the planned economy," which was torn down by Deng's 1992 Southern Tour; and the "cult of ownership," eliminated at the Fifteenth Party Congress in 1997. The book, which became a best-seller, clearly supported Jiang and was designed as a counterattack on Leftists. It also showed the general public a rare glimpse of the very real differences of opinion that existed within the Party.

Around the same time Jiang attended a special screening of the blockbuster movie *Titanic*, which had opened in the United States that past December. He emerged full of praise. "You should not imagine that there is no ideological education in capitalist countries," Jiang said to some NPC delegates. "*Titanic* speaks of wealth and love, the relationship between rich and poor, and vividly describes how people react to disaster."

The distribution of major Hollywood movies in China was still in its experimental phase, having begun only three years before. The number of imports was limited to just ten per year, both to protect China's shaky domestic film industry and to avoid the accusation of allowing in too much "Western pollution." After the president's enthusiastic review of *Titanic*, the subtitled film was hastily shown to senior officials on a large screen in Zhongnanhai and then to enthusiastic, record-breaking audiences.

"I don't mean to publicize capitalism," Jiang defended his enjoyment of the movie. "But as the saying goes, 'Know the enemy and know yourself,' and you can fight a hundred battles with no danger of defeat."

IN JUNE PRESIDENT BILL CLINTON would be arriving in the ancient Chinese capital of Xi'an for the start of a nine-day summit trip. As China made preparations for the highly anticipated event, some disturbing news came out of

South Asia. On May 11 the Indian government conducted three nuclear tests. Two days later, two more. Pakistan responded with several nuclear tests of its own, the first in its history. Both series of explosions surprised American intelligence, and while India and Pakistan were widely condemned internationally, they were celebrated by jingoistic masses at home. As one of its reasons for testing its weapons, India cited the danger posed by China.

Speaking to *Newsweek* on the eve of Clinton's visit, Jiang was perplexed by the Indian justification. "In November 1996 I paid a successful visit to India," he said. "I was accorded a very friendly reception by the government and people of India. That visit has left me with very good memories. I was very surprised that they conducted the nuclear tests. I was even more surprised that they cited China as a reason for their nuclear testing. I really don't know what kind of threat China poses."

Thoughts of nuclear weapons were put aside, however, as Jiang geared up for the parallel summit. It would be the first visit of a sitting American president in nine years, and Jiang felt that it symbolized the reemergence of his country into the community of major nations. Clinton's China trip, his longest overseas tour as president, would be a special one: he was not stopping in any other country. Such exclusivity was a tribute to China's importance, and both sides were eager to make things go smoothly.

Though it was cordial, the summit meeting itself lasted only two hours, during which the two presidents agreed to delete preprogrammed targets from their nuclear missiles, while setting aside Beijing's demand that the two nations also eschew first strikes. Though it was a largely symbolic gesture—retargeting a missile takes less than thirty minutes—Jiang said that the agreement "shows the whole world that China and the United States are cooperative partners instead of adversaries." In light of the recent South Asian nuclear tests, it also sent a message to the world. Where China might once have been considered unstable, it was now an active participant in securing world peace.

More significant than the actual meeting, the Clinton-Jiang joint press conference was broadcast live and uncensored to the Chinese public. Nothing was off limits, including a discussion of Tiananmen Square. For the first time ever the Chinese people heard criticism of the crackdown. It came from Clinton, of course, but it was startling all the same.

"For all of our agreements," Clinton said, "we still disagree about the meaning of what happened then." As a serious Jiang looked on, the American president continued, "I believe, and the American people believe, that the use of force and the tragic loss of life was wrong."

Jiang stuck to the official line that the use of force had been necessary for maintaining the stability and security of the country. Even so, it was a genuine debate aired in public and a historic moment for China. For the rest of the world, it was yet another sign that the Middle Kingdom was maturing into a responsible leading nation.

To Clinton, "the main point of the press conference was the debate itself." He noted, "It was the first time the Chinese people had ever seen their leader actually debate issues like human rights and religious liberty with a foreign head of state," adding that "Jiang had grown more confident in his ability to deal with such issues in public and he trusted me to disagree in a respectful way, as well as to stress our common interests."

The press conference was also a gift from one president to another. At one point Jiang told the journalists, "I am president of the People's Republic of China; I need to protect the interest of the Chinese people. Mr. Clinton is the president of the United States, and in the same way, he needs to protect the interest of the American people."

When Jiang later rehashed the moment in a phone conversation with Shen Yongyan, he explained his underlying motives. "I specifically spoke those sentences," he said, "because I wanted to help Clinton deal with his domestic political pressure." Jiang knew that by agreeing to a live broadcast of the press conference, which dealt with such controversial issues as Tiananmen and Tibet, he was signaling America that Clinton's efforts to befriend China were paying off. It was Jiang's way of thanking the American president for his commitment.

At the state dinner that night, Jiang developed the theme of China's new openness, and Clinton marveled at China's phenomenal growth. Clinton quoted a Chinese proverb: "Be not afraid of growing slowly; be only afraid of standing still."

There were other similarities between the two leaders, both of whom were known to enjoy the limelight. After dinner Jiang asked the conductor of the military band, which had been entertaining the room all evening, if he had a saxophone.

"President Clinton can play one or two songs for you," Jiang explained. But there was no saxophone to be had. Instead, the conductor asked if the Chinese leader wanted to conduct the band. Clinton egged him on. "You can do it, Mr. President," he said. "Go for it."

Jiang did not need much egging. He took the baton and, whipping it to and fro, led the musicians in a rousing rendition of "Ode to the Motherland," as the Chinese dinner guests sang along. Then it was Clinton's turn to conduct the band through a partial version of John Philip Sousa's "Hands Across the Sea." The military band shouted "Wonderful!" while the high-powered audience laughed and clapped throughout. The conductor regained control to play a rendition of Joni Mitchell's "Chelsea Morning," the song that had inspired the Clintons to name their daughter Chelsea, who was accompanying her parents on the trip. Then it was Jiang's turn to perform again, playing "Turkey in the Straw" on the *erhu.*

On June 29 Clinton gave a speech and answered questions at Beijing University, in much the same way as Jiang had done at Harvard. Once again the Chinese leader instructed that the entire session be broadcast live nationwide. The student audience did not hold back, questioning democracy and human rights in America, criticizing military sales to Taiwan, and challenging Clinton's philosophy on individual versus collective rights. They also asked how he would feel if there were demonstrations outside the lecture hall as there had been when Jiang spoke at Harvard.

That evening President and Mrs. Clinton were the guests of President Jiang and Madame Wang at a private dinner at their official residence in Zhongnanhai. "The more time I spent with Jiang, the more I liked him," Clinton wrote in his autobiography (in the context of this dinner). "He was intriguing, funny, and fiercely proud, but always willing to listen to different points of view. Even though I didn't always agree with him, I became convinced that he believed he was changing China as fast as he could, and in the right direction."

Speaking at a press conference in Hong Kong five days later, Clinton lauded Jiang: "I have a very high regard for his abilities. . . . He's a man of extraordinary intellect, very high energy, a lot of vigor. . . . He has vision. He can visualize. He can imagine a future that is different than the present."

China's new bilateral relations with the United States represented a major shift in the government's five-decades-long diplomatic policy. If China continued on its course to became a global leader, Jiang would accomplish something that neither Mao nor Deng had ever done. "In the days of Mao and Deng, China was mainly seen as a leader of the Third World," said one source. "Jiang aides are arguing that, thanks to his leadership, China has achieved a global status equivalent to a major first-world power."

Jiang was also having a positive impact on the foreign media. "There is much progress that critics ignore," wrote the *Los Angeles Times,* while *USA Today* ran a column by its founder, Al Neuharth, saying that much of what the U.S. media wrote about China was "simply not factual or fair." Even the stoutly anti-Communist *Wall Street Journal* published a front-page story describing the Chinese people as living far better, with more freedom and less control, than in the past, and it noted that in spite of all these encouraging strides, "China can't silence its American critics." A *New York Times* editorial noticed "signs of unexpected openness" in China and concluded that the country had changed. This new awareness on the part of the U.S. media was a milestone—and a personal tribute to President Jiang.

Chapter 21

J U L Y – D E C E M B E R   1 9 9 8

"I, as a Witness of History . . ."

WHEN JIANG ARRIVED IN Hong Kong to celebrate the first anniversary of the territory's return to Chinese rule, and to open the sprawling Hong Kong International Airport, he did not disappoint his admirers. "Hong Kong's return to her motherland is the accomplishment of the millennium in the history of China," Jiang told the crowd of local leaders and mainland officials. He also averred that the "one country, two systems" principle had been fully implemented. "Hong Kong people manage Hong Kong," he said, an assertion that had been confirmed by a Reuters report earlier that spring. "British officials make no secret of their delight at how China has handled the immediate post-handover period," the wire story read. "They say Beijing has stuck to the letter of its agreement not to meddle in the territory's affairs." Maintaining Hong Kong's autonomy had always been Jiang's objective. China had far more to gain by supporting the island's prosperity than by trying to control it.

On the trip Jiang behaved more like a politician campaigning for office than the head of an authoritarian government. At a senior citizens center he chatted with residents about mahjongg strategy in fluent Shanghainese, then switched to Cantonese to greet crowds at a local shopping center. As people pressed to meet him, he seemed a bit overwhelmed but recovered with a quip in the local tongue. "I want to shake hands with every one of you," he said, "but I know from experience, if I shake hands with this one, but not with that one, it is no good—*mm hou!*" Despite the heavy security and insistent fans, he also managed to converse with a little girl. Jiang told her that though he understood Cantonese, he could not speak it well. China was not yet a democracy, but its engaging president had a knack for making it seem like one.

Jiang dressed for each venue. At the shopping center he wore a white shirt with an open neck and a tan windbreaker. At a naval base inspection on Stone-cutters Island, he sported a green military-style uniform as he marched down a red carpet. "Your presence has great symbolic meaning," Jiang told four hundred troops stationed there. "It shows that the Chinese people have stood up."

On the trip Wang Yeping was subjected to the kind of scrutiny normally reserved for the spouses of Western leaders. Occasionally disparaged for her lack of style, Wang scored a victory of sorts when a local fashion designer named Flora Cheong-Leen complimented her understated suits. "Her clothing has to be mature and conservative," said Cheong-Leen approvingly. But William Tang, another Hong Kong designer, called her look dated. "People believe Mrs. Jiang is a good wife and mother and don't criticize how she dresses because she was never in the limelight at all," he said. "If she didn't step out of her house, that would be fine. But the problem is she is now representing China beside her husband, and it's necessary for her to change her image a bit."

Flora Cheong-Leen had the opposite opinion. "Mrs. Jiang is a traditional woman who is subtle and shy," she remarked. "Bear in mind that women from the mainland do not like to make themselves outstanding by fashion." She offered general fashion advice: "Make yourself and other people feel comfortable. Do not let the fashion overshadow your character."

BACK HOME A NEW crisis was brewing, this one involving the People's Liberation Army. Since the middle 1980s China's military had become increasingly involved in commercial activities. Begun innocently enough to supplement declining budgetary allocations, the army's business interests had taken on a life of their own, evolving into a vast network of thousands of loosely connected enterprises and companies, which included hotels, nightclubs, karaoke bars, golf courses, airlines, pharmaceutical companies, cellular phone networks, cosmetics suppliers, stock brokerages, and electronics firms. The military even owned two of the twelve teams in the country's new professional basketball league. As many as a million enlisted soldiers—almost a third of China's armed forces—and 70 percent of all PLA's facilities were said to be involved.

Worse, military-related enterprises engaged in smuggling that was said to be costing China between $12 billion and $25 billion per year. In some cities companies associated with the army or the police distributed illegal satellite TV dishes. In a country notorious for counterfeiting music, movies, and software, rogue elements of the PLA were also major bootleggers.

To Jiang, the PLA's business interests were an ominous development for two reasons: they shifted the army's focus away from defense, and they increased the army's independence of civilian control. At best the army's commercial ventures were a conflict of interest that bred corruption. At worst they were illegal and insidiously corrosive of defense-of-the-nation resolve. But were they also untouchable? As much as Jiang Zemin despised military moneymaking, he had to choose the time and place to do battle. He had to make sure that he had the support of the leadership of the PLA and the People's Armed Police before issuing the order that all forces under their command divest themselves of nonmilitary commercial interests. In July 1998 Jiang was ready. At a joint meeting of the PLA and PAP high command, Jiang Zemin, acting in his capacity as chairman of the Central Military Commission, gave that order.

"Companies operated by units under the military and armed police forces," he stated officially, "must earnestly conduct housecleaning, and shall without exception no longer engage in commercial activities, effective immediately." Going further, Jiang asked the armed forces to set an example for the rest of society.

Following Jiang's pronouncement, General Fu Quanyou, chief of the General Staff, called on "every unit and every cadre" to implement their chairman's new decree "without conditions." Jiang told General Xiong Guankai, the deputy chief of the General Staff and chief of military intelligence, "An army under the threat of corruption will not be best able to defend the country."

The decision bucked entrenched power. It took, General Xiong noted, "vision, bravery, and guts." Many influential people stood to lose a great deal from the policy change. Jiang had worked for years to build support and loyalty within the military, and now he spent some of that credibility capital to make his move. "Since the army is a military organization that is used to obeying orders rapidly," observed General Xiong, "President Jiang's policy could be implemented much faster than it could in the Party or the government. With such anticorruption progress in the army, an example was set to move further and faster against corruption in the other sectors."

But logic and probity do not guarantee success. Some senior generals were concerned that the military could not withstand any more "shocks" and that "accounting and inspection" regimens would upset army morale, preparedness, and military construction. Some on the Politburo were said to harbor doubts about the decision because they feared that any disorder in the military could be catastrophic. So Jiang maneuvered a tactical retreat that still allowed him the larger victory. He continued to insist on separating the military from commerce, but he withdrew his request for investigations into past activities. By the end of the year, the government and the military would largely come to terms on the separation.

EVEN AS JIANG WAS negotiating with the military, he was called upon to take active command of it. In July massive flooding of the Yangtze River, the worst since 1954, required a substantial mobilization of personnel to provide disaster relief. The campaign involved some 300,000 PLA soldiers, including one hundred generals, five million militiamen, and eight million local officials, workers, and peasants. "With all routes flooded," explained Information Minister Zhao Qizheng, "the logistics of transporting and coordinating such a large-scale antiflood army to arrive at a certain place at a certain time was no different than that of a shooting war. In terms of human life, the battle that Jiang Zemin commanded against the flood was even greater."

By mid-August the death toll passed two thousand, with 240 million people displaced by the rampaging waters. The destruction of agriculture and industry was incalculable. Jiang went to the front lines to encourage the flood fighters and praise the PLA. "We are going to win the final battle!" he exhorted the soldiers. "Are you confident of doing that?" "Yes, we are," they roared back.

Epidemics broke out in flood-ravaged areas. On inspecting heavily damaged Hunan province in south-central China, Jiang placed priority on building adequate shelter for displaced families before the onset of winter. "We must ensure victims have adequate food, clean drinking water, and clothing," he said. "They must have adequate shelter and access to immediate medical care."

In early September Jiang postponed state visits to Japan and Russia. As the president continued visiting inundated regions, the death toll passed three thousand. More than fifty million acres were flooded, five million homes were destroyed, and economic losses reached $20 billion. Jiang attempted to boost morale by praising the efforts of the people and calling their struggle a vindication of the Party, the socialist system, and the PLA. "The victory," he said, "has also signified that the Chinese nation possesses the glorious tradition of constantly striving to improve itself and of waging hard struggle, and that the Chinese nation is a great nation with strong cohesiveness."

The great flood brought out both the engineer and the poet in Jiang. He waxed eloquent on Chinese glory and recounted individual acts of heroism; he also gave technical instructions on disaster relief and future flood prevention, describing the rebuilding of homes and the construction of water conservation facilities.

ON SEPTEMBER 14 Yang Shangkun, former president of China and one of China's "Immortal" revolutionary leaders, died at the age of ninety-two. Though Jiang had had issues with him and his brother years earlier (the "Yang Family Army"), the president insisted on visiting Yang in the hospital even at the height of the flood crisis. Although "Glorious Yang" had requested a simple funeral, he was given a state funeral, led by President Jiang.

The weekend before, Jiang reached out to the nation's filmmakers, inviting fifteen prominent directors and actors, including Li Qiankuan and Sun Daolin, to Zhongnanhai. The purpose was to discuss the future of China's film industry. It was also Jiang Zemin's idea of a good time.

"Jiang knew our names," recalled director Li. "Some of us he knew personally. Jiang loved art and respected artists. We could talk to him like an old friend, not a state leader. He was very warm."

According to protocol, the propaganda minister, Ding Guangen, was supposed to chair the discussion. But he hardly said a word. In meetings that Jiang enjoyed, he didn't want a moderator, much less need one. "I am pleased to exchange views about our film industry," Jiang said casually, "Some of you I have not seen for quite some time."

There was no agenda except, as Jiang put it, "just to chat during the weekend." Everyone joined in. "We talked passionately about filmmaking in China," said director Li. "We were artists, not politicians. We didn't feel any pressure sitting next to state leaders. We were honest and open in voicing our opinions."

When Tian Hua, a former actress who ran an acting college, requested more authentic army props for her students who were making military films, the Party chief smiled. "Tian Hua," he said, "you have the best sense of timing. Sitting here is our General Chi Haotian, minister of defense. He can help you out."

As the general protested laughingly, Jiang continued. "Take advantage! Tian Hua," he urged the actress, "General Chi can't get away. Just tell him everything that you need: uniforms, equipment, production support, bases for your students to get military experience. Just tell him!"

Similarly, Jiang offered aid to Sun Daolin, who, nearing eighty, was intent on finishing an epic film about the making of the first railroad in China in the hardscrabble years of the late nineteenth and early twentieth centuries. But he was having no success; potential investors said that his movie was not commercial. At the meeting with Jiang, the elderly director burst into tears, saying, "It is so difficult to produce themed films that commend our national heroes and praise patriotism." After hearing the story, Jiang turned to Ding Guangen—the propaganda minister was a former minister of railways—and asked him to look into the matter. The Ministry of Railways funded the film.

When the film *Zhan Tianyou* (named for the man who devoted his life to building China's railroads) premiered three years later, Jiang commented that it vividly depicted the "admirable character of noble-minded people" who struggled for the "rejuvenation of the Chinese nation," and that it projected a "patriotic spirit." He said the film was of "great significance for encouraging the general public, especially the young generation."

At the meeting with filmmakers Jiang also heard controversy. A young writer named Wang did not hesitate to promote his radical views. Recently the minister of culture, Sun Jiazheng, had given a speech criticizing the view that all Chinese films should be about real-life heroes or social role models. Artists, he said, should be selective in choosing their subjects and pay more attention to those with artistic appeal. Sun's key point, a welcome one, was that Chinese filmmakers should make all types of films rather than feel constrained by ideology. Young Wang voiced his disagreement with Minister Sun, who sat a few feet away. (Wang's own screenplay, *Lei Feng's Diary*, was based on the apparently true story of an altruistic soldier who had died young and became a lionized, Leftist role model during Mao's 1960s.)

"It is not true that we have too many hero films," the writer exclaimed. "On the contrary, there are too few heroes on our screens today. We need more heroes. We should mobilize all our resources, and justly and forcefully exalt our heroes."

Minister Sun was not pleased by Wang's viewpoint or his vehemence. But that a young firebrand could criticize the publicly stated policy of a senior official, in front of Jiang Zemin, without fear of repercussion was in itself progress.

During the discussions none of the other leaders, such as Ding Guangen or Zeng Qinghong, said much. They all followed the lead of their boss in learning to listen to artists. At the end Jiang stood and made a kind of closing statement.

"I am so happy to see that our old artists are enthusiastic and determined, and that our young ones are coming up to surpass the veterans. We should advocate a 'hundred flowers' to grow and bloom. If there were only one kind of flower, our film industry would be impoverished. We must allow many diverse kinds of flowers to be planted, nurtured, and appreciated. Only then will our world be more beautiful."

The two-hour discussion concluded by Jiang saying, "Well, let's have lunch together."

Everyone followed China's president into a nearby dining room, where name cards assigned seats around a long rectangular table. Lunch was light and healthy, with about ten simple courses. As the meal drew to a close, Zeng Qinghong spoke up. "This is such a creative gathering," Zeng said with a sly grin. "We shouldn't just focus on food. Artists should perform!"

Zeng saw that his boss was in good spirits, so he invited him to recite a poem. Never shy about taking the stage, Jiang did so—in Russian. The Chinese president then turned to Sun Daolin. "I liked your dubbing for Shakespeare's *Hamlet,*" Jiang said. "Your 'To-be-or-not-to-be' soliloquy was wonderful." Zeng Qinghong interjected, "Daolin, please try some Hamlet for us." When he was finished, Jiang applauded loudly, and then one after another everyone performed. Even Vice Minister Zhao Shi sang a piece from a Peking Opera. "I had known her for many years," remembered director Li, "and I had never seen her perform like that."

Actress Tian Hua recited a poem, and when she finished, Zeng Qinghong said, "Director Li sings very well, particularly those folk songs from northern Shaanxi province." Li Tieying, a Politburo member, agreed, "Yes, sure. I can even smell vinegar in his singing." (People from northern Shaanxi love vinegar). Then, Jiang said, "Director Li, I have never heard you sing before. Please try one."

The always effervescent Li stood and belted out the folk tune "Xin Tian You" with great flourish. When he finished, Jiang said, "Director Li is not only a great filmmaker, he is also an outstanding singer. Honestly, this is not an easy piece; its wide range and register are very challenging. Great job!"

Jiang showed off his white Yamaha piano, which had an electronic memory that stored the music that had been played on it previously. "It's my favorite," said Jiang. "The piano can automatically replay the whole piece, just the way you performed it."

To no one's surprise, Jiang sat down and started playing, and Zeng Qing-hong, orchestrating, asked the guests to sing along. "Director Li," Zeng said, picking the least bashful of the already outgoing group, "our general secretary is playing; you should be singing."

Jiang played "An Evening in a Suburb of Moscow," an old Russian love song. Director Li invited a young actress, Yu Hui, to start the singing with him. Others joined in, and Jiang accompanied the group. Li and Jiang sang some duets together, and then Li played the piano and Jiang sang. The Chinese leader invited the noted composer Wang Liping to play a popular song, "The Ocean Is My Home." Everyone knew the lyrics and sang together— especially Jiang, who seemed devoid of artistic inhibitions. After the singing, Jiang posed for photos with each artist.

The party did not break up until a staff member came to take the guests on a tour of Zhongnanhai, with its magnificent architecture and marvelous paintings. "I wish you good health and happiness forever," Jiang said as he made a point to shake the hand of every guest. "I look forward to seeing your films."

"Jiang calls artists 'engineers of the soul,' " said director Li afterward. "He desires Chinese artists to do more than just keep up with advanced culture in the world; he wants them to pioneer and extend it. 'Outdated ideology,' Jiang said, 'must not restrain Chinese artists, who must catch up with China's rapid reform and opening-up.' Though we all recognize that there are certain limits in Chinese society, these too are changing. Jiang loves to be with artists; I have been to his home many times."

Only weeks earlier director Li had been discussing the proposed China Film Museum with Tian Congming, minister of the State Administration of Radio, Film, and Television (SARFT). Tian said the idea had first come from Premier Zhou Enlai in 1958, but because of the Cultural Revolution the project had gone into long hibernation. It was not revived until the 1980s, but then the austerity campaigns put it on ice again. Tian told Li, "If we keep delaying, we'll never have a national film museum."

Director Li responded with characteristic energy: "Chinese filmmaking has a rich history of almost a hundred years. It's a shame we don't already have a museum." Minister Tian confided that if SARFT presented the project through official channels, it would likely be killed as too expensive.

"Well, let me help then," Li exclaimed. "Let our artists take charge this time. We won't go through the bureaucracy. We'll go to the president directly." Li knew of Jiang's personal interest in promoting China's film industry; the

Chinese leader had made a point of visiting China's main movie studios in Beijing, Shanghai, and Changchun.

The next day Li Qiankuan drafted a letter to Jiang Zemin and invited other noted artists to cosign with him, getting about twenty to affix their names with his. "For almost a hundred years," Li wrote, "China has been, and continues to be, a major film producer in the world in terms of the number of annual productions. As such, we should build a national film museum, which would be important for the Chinese film industry and for us artists as well." Li concluded by requesting Jiang's "personal support for the project" to "dissolve all the red tape and get the project started."

Within three days Jiang Zemin forwarded director Li's letter to the office of propaganda chief Ding Guangen. "Please ask Guangen to study the project and take care of it," Jiang wrote directly on the letter, adding, "Please inform me of the final decision. August 21, 1998, Jiang Zemin."

Although Jiang did not order that the museum be approved, nor even say that he supported it, his instructions applied optimal "light pressure" to urge the project forward. The matter was not significant enough for Jiang to expend his always-limited political capital by mandating it irrespective of the opinions of others, but his concluding remark—"Please inform me of the final decision"—made any sentient official realize that Jiang Zemin wanted the museum built. "In China," remarked director Li, "we all know what that phrase means."

Jiang's "light pressure" encouraged other senior leaders to switch on green lights. A large plot of land, ten thousand *mou* (1,640 acres), was set aside near Beijing's Capital International Airport, and by late 2005, on the hundredth anniversary of the Chinese film industry, the China Film Museum, a landmark building, is expected to open.

JIANG COULD BE EQUALLY gracious with those who might be considered his adversaries. In mid-October, he held a milestone meeting in Beijing with Koo Chen-fu, who, as chairman of the Taiwan-based Straits Exchange Foundation, was Wang Daohan's counterpart in exploring relations between the two governments. It marked the first official contact between mainland China and Taiwan in five years, and the highest level of discussions since 1949.

Although the men had their disagreements—Koo reportedly told Jiang, "Only when the mainland has achieved democracy can the two sides of the Taiwan Straits talk about reunification"—they discussed a wide range of topics, from Chinese opera and poetry to Darwin's theory of evolution. Jiang even entertained his startled visitor with a short rendition of Taiwan's national anthem.

"The ice is broken," Koo said. "We hope it's melting."

Jiang's visit to Russia, which had been delayed by the devastating floods, took place in November. He and Russian president Boris Yeltsin, who was in the hospital with pneumonia, issued a joint communiqué that for "the first time in the history of relations between the countries, the demarcated line on the eastern and western sectors of the Sino-Russian border had been accurately marked in the field."

The next day Jiang spoke in the "Science City" of Novosibirsk in Siberia. Complimenting Russia on its "wealth of achievements in scientific research," he said that he hoped the "difficulties now encountered by the Russian scientific and technological community are temporary ones," and he briefed the sophisticated audience on science in China.

Jiang had decided to give his speech entirely in Russian even though senior Chinese officials had thought the idea unwise. The Chinese ambassador in Moscow advised the president to give his introduction in Russian and the rest of his speech in Chinese, so that it could be translated professionally. The request was futile; the president chose to give the complete speech in Russian, and it did not go well. While its content was fine, its form was not.

Jiang began to sweat as he struggled with unfamiliar words and complex phrases, and the audience, reflecting his unease, became uncomfortable. Those who thought that Jiang Zemin would thereafter retreat to traditional protocol did not know the man. Giving speeches in the language of the country he was visiting was a personal passion: it was how he showed his hosts his appreciation of their culture and it was how he pushed himself to continue to learn.

From Novosibirsk Jiang flew to Tokyo for the start of a historic six-day state trip to Japan, the first ever by a Chinese head of state. Although he had been to Japan several times before, this was his first visit as president, which was meant to mark the twentieth anniversary of the signing of the China-Japan Peace and Friendship Treaty.

Much had changed in the intervening years. Japan was now China's largest trading partner, and China was Tokyo's second-largest. China was also the biggest recipient of Japanese aid. Even so, relations between the former enemies remained testy. Before the visit Beijing demanded that Japan make a formal apology during Jiang's stay for the atrocities that were committed during World War II. Meanwhile a small but powerful right-wing minority in Japan was blocking any attempt to "dishonor" the "Imperial Army"—notwithstanding the fact that in the process of bayoneting babies, raping women, and poisoning civilians, the "Imperial Army" had already succeeded in bringing dishonor upon itself.

The issue at hand was subtler than its outline would suggest. In 1995, on the fiftieth anniversary of the end of World War II, Japanese prime minister Tomiichi Murayama had already expressed "deep remorse and a heartfelt apology" for the "tremendous damage and suffering" inflicted on "the people of many countries, particularly those of Asian nations" through Japan's wartime "colonial rule and aggression." But just before Jiang's visit, Prime Minister Keizo Obuchi had apologized overtly and abjectly to the Korean people, expressing his government's "remorseful repentance." Now China wanted the same strength of apology.

To the Japanese, however, there was a fundamental difference between its actions against Korea and against China. Korea had been a Japanese colony for thirty-five years, between 1910 and 1945. In China the Japanese had not been colonizers but merely occupiers, and then only for the eight years between 1937 and 1945. To the Chinese, who had lost upward of twenty million people during that period, such a distinction was rude and insulting.

On his arrival Jiang issued a statement saying there was a need to "seriously summarize the experiences of the history of China-Japan relations" for the "development of bilateral friendship and cooperation toward the future." At an unofficial dinner hosted by Prime Minister Obuchi that first night, the conversation was about grandchildren and the arts. Jiang joked that because the temperature in Tokyo was much higher than it had been in Russia—and because of the sake—he was able to warm up and regain his strength.

Meanwhile Japanese and Chinese officials announced glumly that President Jiang and Prime Minister Obuchi would not sign a joint declaration after their summit meeting. The cancellation of the signing ceremony reflected the apparently unbridgeable gap between Japan and China over the wording of Japan's apology. The controversy would color Jiang's entire visit.

Tokyo suggested a compromise in which Obuchi would offer a stronger *oral* apology to Jiang during their summit meeting in addition to the weaker expression of "remorse" in their written joint declaration. But Chinese foreign minister Tang Jiaxuan was not sure that the Chinese president would accept the compromise. Jiang Zemin, Tang told his Japanese counterparts, "belonged to a different generation." After all, Japan's occupation had played a crucial role in his patriotic development. Though each side denied the significance of the setback, both countries were embarrassed by Japan's latest failure to say "sorry" to China for its wartime aggression and brutality.

Nonetheless, Jiang continued to express his pleasure at being in Japan— he presented the emperor and empress with a pair of crested ibises, a rare red bird with a total world population of just 137. Yet tension was simmering just below the protocol-placid surface, and during the formal two-hour summit meeting, it broke loose.

After Prime Minister Obuchi's pre-set oral apology, President Jiang embarked on a twenty-five-minute lecture on Sino-Japanese relations, saying that he disagreed with the prevailing Japanese view that "there is no more need to talk about the history between the two countries." Rather, the Chinese leader contended, "straightforward discussions of historical issues will strengthen the partnership" and "will pave the way for the future." He told the prime minister that the Chinese people had suffered more terribly under Japan than they ever had under European powers.

Late that night the troubled joint communiqué was finally issued after a five-hour delay. Its statement of remorse fell far short of China's requests. As one Japanese Foreign Ministry official observed, "Both sides were not ready to resolve the history issue . . . to leave it behind and to see only the future."

The Chinese also found fault with Obuchi's oral apology. The prime minister had used the word *owabi*—carefully chosen, no doubt by committee—to express his sentiments. To the Chinese, *owabi* was an informal word, equivalent to *dao qian* in Chinese, which is a general expression of apology used in everyday language, even for minor inconveniences, such as bumping into another person. The Chinese preferred that the Japanese use the word *shazai*, equivalent to the Chinese *xie zui*, which is used to apologize for serious offenses or crimes. Each side had refused to budge, though Japanese officials claimed there was no difference between *owabi* and *shazai*.

Though the rest of the trip went smoothly, with agreements on economic development and the "one China" policy, the dispute had left its mark. At every turn Jiang seemed intent on reminding the Japanese of the importance of history, citing a Chinese saying, "Without forgetting the past, make a lesson for the future." He continued his lecture at a court banquet hosted by Emperor Akihito and Empress Michiko, as well as later at the official state dinner given by the prime minister. "In the fifty years from the end of the last century to the middle of this one," he told the slightly discomfited guests, "Japan's militarists waged wars of aggression against China on many occasions. They brought enormous damage to the Chinese people and also left bitter lessons for the Japanese people . . . Only if China and Japan draw lessons from history will it be possible to prevent the recurrence of tragedies and to develop long-term friendship."

The Japanese were surprised by the Chinese leader's doggedness in pursuing the issue. Jiang said, "I, as a witness of history, personally experienced the anguish of seeing the country's [China's] territory being annexed and the nation's very survival hanging in the balance. We have the responsibility to teach this chapter of history to the younger generation."

Japanese officials were said to have "visibly paled" when Jiang rehearsed Japan's wartime militarism in the presence of the emperor and empress. Apparently, Japan's Foreign Ministry had grave enough concerns that ministry officials had approached their Chinese counterparts about striking a deal. If the Chinese president agreed to stop talking history, the Japanese might agree to certain concessions. Without even inquiring as to what those concessions might be, the Chinese side refused. Persuading Jiang Zemin to "stop talking history" was not a task that any Chinese official wanted to tackle.

Such intransigence, even truculence, seemed out of character for the normally polite, politically moderate Jiang, and cynics suggested that he needed to spout anti-Japanese rhetoric in order to appease conservative factions in the Party and army. That was nonsense: his criticisms of Japan stemmed purely from principle. The Japanese had a responsibility to apologize without reservation, he believed, and the fact that they hedged proved all the more why they must do so. On this particular issue Jiang Zemin was not going to back down. He was willing to embrace the future, but only if the past was properly settled.

ON DOMESTIC MATTERS, JIANG also faced challenges. In a year in which the region had faced financial crisis and China had experienced some of the worst flooding in its history, the economy had failed to grow at Zhu Rongji's projected eight percent. It was, in fact, growing at 7.8 percent, a remarkable achievement given Zhu's estimate that the floods alone had deducted one full percent, but this fact did not satisfy his critics, many of whom were unhappy with his cost-cutting measures, anticorruption crusade, and intimidating personality. At a joint Party–State Council economic conference, some officials made sarcastic remarks targeting Zhu. "Has it not been said that Zhu Rongji best understands economics?" went a typical comment. "Have you no responsibility if the economy starts sliding down the moment you become premier?"

Jiang spoke in Zhu's defense, but on the day the conference ended *People's Daily* published three commentaries on Jiang Zemin's "two guarantees," which were to "guarantee the basic livelihood and re-employment of workers laid off by state-owned enterprises, and full and timely payment of old-age pensions for retired personnel." At least one of Zhu's subordinates thought that these editorials were designed to diminish the premier, since Jiang's "two guarantees" would be fulfilled in contrast to Zhu's failing to deliver his one "guarantee" of an eight percent growth rate.

December 18 marked the twentieth anniversary of the Third Plenary Session of the Eleventh Party Congress, the auspicious commencement of Deng Xiaoping's economic reforms that Jiang Zemin was now leading. "It was a historic decision that determined modern China's fate," Jiang said in commemoration. "There is no doubt that reforms and opening-up have become the most striking characteristic of China in the new era."

Chapter 22

1 9 9 9

"All Sorts of Feelings Well Up in Me"

THE LAST YEAR OF the twentieth century began badly. On New Year's Day fifty disgruntled workers, many of whom had been laid off, appeared outside of Zhongnanhai and staged an illegal protest. They claimed to have been cheated by a brokerage company affiliated with the military, which had defaulted on payments in a multimillion-dollar stock market scam. On the same day an exiled dissident announced that a group of writers planned to form a Chinese Labor Party in defiance of the law banning opposition parties. The announcement came soon after three dissidents were handed long jail sentences for trying to establish the China Democracy Party. Jiang said that subversive activities would be "nipped in the bud" and that China would never tolerate Western-style democracy. Government enforcers followed up by outlawing any material that "endangered social order"; in the ensuing dragnet, police swept newspapers, publishing houses, television and film studios, and software companies.

On the international front, in addition to constant tensions over Taiwan and human rights, China found itself with a noisome new problem. In the United States, a Republican congressman named Christopher Cox confirmed rumors of a still-classified report claiming that China had been engaged in the active, systematic, and continuous theft of secret military technology. The report alleged that two American corporations—Hughes Electronics and Loral Space and Communications—had supplied rocket guidance technology to China. Cox, who was chairman of the special investigative committee, hinted of darker revelations yet to come.

A Chinese spokesman responded on New Year's Day, calling the committee findings "sheer fabrication" and a "distortion of China's peaceful use of space technology." He accused the report of "deliberately undermining China–U.S. relations."

The day also happened to be the twentieth anniversary of the reestablishment of diplomatic ties between the United States and China. While President Jiang and President Clinton exchanged official pleasantries, commending strides in bilateral relations, the reality was colder.

A New Year's Day that was supposed to be cheerful ended in gloom. In a matter of hours Jiang was beset with three of China's thorniest problems: the unintended consequences of economic reform, the precarious balance between social stability and individual freedom, and the country's delicate relations with America. Within months each would explode around him.

ON MARCH 25, PRESIDENT JIANG became China's first head of state to visit Switzerland, but when he was greeted in Berne by hundreds of protesters, many of whom were exiled Tibetans waving slogan-festooned balloons and chanting "We want dialogue," he became incensed. Lashing out against his hosts for allowing such demonstrations in the very place where he was supposed to be received with full military honors, an indignant Jiang told Swiss President Ruth Dreifuss, "You have lost a friend."

Snubbing the ceremony and keeping Dreifuss and her cabinet ministers waiting outside in the federal square for thirty minutes, Jiang castigated Switzerland for its "disorder" and admonished the government to provide "minimum politeness" for its foreign guests. As Jiang saw it, China itself was being insulted and its dignity diminished.

ON APRIL 25 A STARTLING, bewildering challenge came from what seemed to be nowhere. Without warning, more than ten thousand practitioners of a bizarre religious sect called Falun Gong materialized in Beijing and surrounded Zhongnanhai, the seat of power in the People's Republic. Buses had entered the capital in the predawn hours carrying protesters, some from as far away as Zhejiang province, eight hundred miles to the south. Throughout the day even more sect members filled the city's sidewalks, five and six deep, sitting silently, many in meditation.

Falun Gong, which literally means "the Practice of the Wheel of the Dharma," was first preached in 1992 in Changchun, where Jiang once worked at the automotive factory. The sect's founder, Li Hongzhi, a middle-aged former grain clerk and soldier, claimed to be a master of the ancient art of *qigong*, which professes to use breathing and meditation to channel energy and improve one's health. Li, who now lives in America but remains Falun Gong's absolute leader, combined concepts from *qigong*, Buddhism, and Taoism with his own mystical theories to form what he proclaimed to be an "advanced system of cultivation and practice" leading toward enlightenment.

The practice of Falun Gong includes five sets of exercises, performed to Chinese music, involving lotus postures and hand movements. As such, it is sometimes billed as an exercise system, though it is actually a quasi-religious cult that engages in meditative behaviors and occultlike rituals. According to sect lore, the *falun* or "dharma wheel" is a rotating, high-energy body; Li described it as a miniature of the cosmos, and he professed to install it telekinetically into the abdomens of practitioners as a way to collect cosmic forces and expel bad karma. Some followers claimed to feel the wheel whirling in their bellies, and devotees were told to harness this power, rather than use medicines, to cure disease. With its syncretic belief system of quack health claims, psychic fantasies, and amalgamated philosophical-theological ramblings, Falun Gong is like an Asian version of what might result from a three-way megamerger of L. Ron Hubbard's Scientology, Mary Baker Eddy's Christian Science, and Madame Blavatsky's Theosophical Society—a New Age cult, if you will, with Chinese characteristics.

The movement spread through word of mouth, and in just a few years its membership climbed into the millions. By early 1999 foreign reports suggested that there might be as many as seventy million people practicing Falun Gong all over China; a government count put the number of confirmed believers at about two million. Though it was called "the largest voluntary organization in China, larger even than the Communist Party," the sect was still marginal. Prior to the April 25 demonstration, some senior leaders had never even heard of it.

"How could it be?" Jiang exclaimed to Shen Yongyan, "that in one night the Falun Gong just appeared? Did they come from under the ground? Where was our Ministry of Public Security? Where was our Ministry of State Security?"

Sect leaders asserted that the eerie gathering was not a political protest but a petition for the release of forty-five practitioners who had been detained by police in Tianjin for besieging the office of a magazine that had published what they felt was a slanderous article. The explanation did not reassure the government—any large, unauthorized gathering was cause for alarm.

Jiang blamed Luo Gan, the Politburo member responsible for internal security, for the lapse in intelligence. But in spite of their concern, China's leaders made no immediate comment on the incident, and it went unreported by the state-controlled media for two days.

Meanwhile officials from the State Council Appeal Office, a bureau that handles public complaints, met with the practitioners. "The government isn't opposed to *qigong*," one senior leader reportedly said, "but you can't gather like this. You must go." A resolution was reached, and the practitioners dispersed quietly. For the moment, the crisis seemed over. But senior leaders were astounded to learn of Party cadres among the demonstrators, even an official from State Security.

Through Shen Yongyan, Jiang learned of another sect member. "I told Jiang," Shen recalled, "about a female vice president at our automotive plant, a graduate of the prestigious Shanghai Finance and Economics Institute, who practiced Falun Gong. She had hypertension, and because she refused medical treatment, she died of a cerebral hemorrhage. Jiang knew the woman and was dumbfounded."

"How can so many intellectuals practice Falun Gong?" Jiang asked Shen. "What can these people be thinking?"

From the outset Jiang was more suspicious of the sect than were his colleagues—more sensitive to its underlying motives, more agitated by its supernatural pretensions, and perhaps more prescient of what harm it could do. His position was uncompromising. On that first night he wrote a blistering letter to senior leaders. Denouncing Falun Gong as "a cult," he asked, "Is there a 'mastermind' plotting and directing behind the scenes?" He speculated about foreign influences and expressed "deep regret" over the Party's sad ideological state.

"I can't believe Marxism cannot triumph over Falun Gong," he wrote.

Jiang attributed the sect's growth to negligence on the part of Party officials in charge of ideological and cadre work. He berated the security ministries for not knowing about the huge demonstration in advance. "Who says that there was no inkling that Falun Gong believers were gathering at Zhongnanhai?" Jiang asked at an urgent Politburo meeting the next day as he brandished printouts from Falun Gong websites announcing their convergence on Zhongnanhai. "Comrades, how frightening this is!"

Jiang's hard-nosed attitude may have been at odds with that of other senior leaders, who advised a more textured approach. For the time being, though, action against Falun Gong would have to wait. While Jiang pondered what to do at home, two incidents occurred abroad. Both involved the United States, and neither was nice.

THE FIRST WAS THE bombing of the Chinese embassy in Belgrade by American-led NATO forces in early May. As Chinese leaders sought an appropriate response, students across the country took to the streets. To all who remembered Tiananmen Square a decade before, it seemed ironic that Chinese protesters were now lambasting their leaders for being pro-American. The matter required careful strategy, one that would appease a furious public without alienating an apologetic America. For weeks President Jiang walked a thin line, trying to defuse the tension.

The task was not made easier by the release on May 25 in Washington of what became known as the Cox Report, which contained incendiary charges that China had been relentlessly stealing the most sensitive U.S military secrets, particularly nuclear weapon designs and missile guidance systems. Coming just after the embassy bombing, the timing of the release could not have been worse.

"The People's Republic of China (PRC)," the Cox Report stated, "has stolen design information on the United States' most advanced thermonuclear weapons . . . including the W-88, a miniaturized, tapered warhead, the most sophisticated nuclear weapon the United States has ever built." The stolen material was said to contain classified details on seven thermonuclear warheads, every one deployed in the U.S. ballistic missile arsenal. "PRC penetration of our national weapons laboratories spans at least the past several decades and almost certainly continues today." Worse, China's protracted espionage was alleged to represent official policy and an imperialist agenda. "The PRC seeks foreign military technology as part of its efforts to place the PRC at the forefront of nations and to enable the PRC to fulfill its international agenda.

"The PRC's long-run geopolitical goals include incorporating Taiwan into the PRC and becoming the primary power in Asia," the Cox Report asserted. "The PRC has not ruled out using force against Taiwan, and its thefts of U.S. technology have enhanced its military capabilities for any such use of force. The PRC has also asserted territorial claims against other Southeast Asian nations and Japan, and has used its military forces as leverage in asserting these claims." Ominously, the report concluded that "these PRC goals conflict with current U.S. interests in Asia and the Pacific, and the possibility of a U.S.-PRC confrontation cannot be dismissed." China was also accused of handing over information to anti-American regimes, including Iran and North Korea. Six weeks earlier a *New York Times* story had claimed that China had *twice* stolen U.S. nuclear secrets, originally in the 1980s, and when those designs did not work, Chinese agents came back in 1995 for another round of thefts.

Throughout the crisis Jiang remained silent, but other Chinese officials responded with indignation. In April Zhu Rongji denied the allegations: "I can also state in a very responsible manner here that neither I nor President Jiang Zemin know anything about that, and we too also once asked the senior military leaders in China, and they told us they didn't have any knowledge of that." Information Minister Zhao Qizheng decried the "great slander against the Chinese nation," blaming it on "typical racial prejudice." In light of the American hysteria surrounding Wen Ho Lee, where in a firestorm of media he was accused and virtually convicted of nuclear espionage, the charge could not be easily dismissed.

When the *New York Times* broke the story in March, it said that the culprit was a Chinese-American scientist inside Los Alamos National Laboratories who "stuck out like a sore thumb." The subsequent investigation and Lee's harsh incarceration exposed a troubling degree of Sinophobia. The sixty-year-old nuclear physicist, against whom espionage charges were ultimately dropped, was held for 278 days in solitary confinement and not allowed to speak with his family in his native tongue. In the end Lee pleaded guilty to mishandling nuclear secrets and was fined $100. The presiding judge in his case considered the government's treatment of the scientist so abusive that in an official statement to the court he offered an unusual formal apology to Lee and delivered a stinging rebuke to the government.

In his May press conference Minister Zhao asserted that China was perfectly capable of developing its own weapons technology as evidenced by its atom, hydrogen, and neutron bombs, that the reputedly stolen information on U.S. nuclear warheads was readily available on the Internet, and that the report offered no substantive evidence of theft. Zhao noted numerous Chinese achievements in aerospace and weaponry that had been accomplished without the help of outsiders. It seemed that the Chinese were just as offended by the idea that they needed foreign assistance to make technological advances as they were by the charge that they were thieves.

Distrust emanated from both sides. Along with the embassy bombing three weeks earlier, the Cox Report defined a new low point in Sino-American relations, which had held such promise just the year before. Thanks to two successful summit meetings between Jiang and Clinton, the nations had started to use the term "strategic partner" in reference to each other. They now reverted to the old phrase, "strategic competitor." Internal memos in both Beijing and Washington even surfaced a more threatening descriptor: "archenemy."

As events unfolded, Jiang did not make a single public statement on espionage until September 2000, when he was forced to do so during his interview with Mike Wallace on *60 Minutes*. Although every major nation spies on virtually all of its adversaries and potential adversaries (and occasionally a few of its friends), no national leader ever wants to get caught up in discussing such matters; "plausible deniability" is always the operative catchphrase. Also, Jiang was too preoccupied with domestic affairs to enter into useless finger-pointing, especially as hardliners in each country seized the opportunity to gain political advantage.

Ironically, the Cox Report's accusations could work to China's advantage. By showcasing the country's enhanced nuclear weapons capability and advanced missile technology, the revelations bolstered China's reputation as a military power. Clearly, that was not what Congressman Cox had in mind.

THOUGH JIANG KEPT SILENT, the sudden eruptions at home and abroad took a physical toll. He was noticeably fatigued; his eyes drooped, and his gait was less jaunty. His policies of reform and opening-up were at stake. Only through economic development, he repeated in virtually every speech, could China be truly strong. Even military strength required economic strength, which in turn required trade, investment, and technology—all of which were impossible, Jiang argued, without decent relations with the United States. In one speech he used a principle from his original discipline, engineering, to encourage China's citizenry to convert the "energy" of its "justifiable rage" into the "glorious work" of building the country.

Analysts monitoring China's internal power struggle tracked the government's attitude toward membership in the World Trade Organization, which had been put on hold since the embassy bombing. Zhu Rongji stated that the stalled WTO talks would not resume immediately. He quoted Jiang as telling President Clinton, "It is not the time yet for talks; the atmosphere is not good." Jiang's response reflected his long-term approach to getting what he wanted. "Stick to principles," one of his favorite aphorisms reads; "refrain from impatience, proceed in a gradual and orderly way, and success will come when conditions are ripe."

In March 1999 the National People's Congress voted to amend the Constitution to embed Deng Xiaoping Theory as the state's guiding ideology, officially codifying what previously had been only assumed. By getting Deng's principles formally inscribed, Jiang was securing the legal foundation for implementing his own reforms. By allying with Deng, Jiang could safely pronounce that the Communists of today are not the Communists of yesteryear, just as the "socialist market economy with Chinese characteristics" is not the kind of straitjacket socialism the world used to know. About this there was no dissension among China's active senior leaders, all of whom followed Deng more closely than they did Marx or Mao. "Old wine in new bottles" was not what was happening in China; the bottles did not change, but the wine inside tasted very different.

Jiang had been a true believer in socialism. As a student protester, he had marched under the Communist banner, confronting foreign domination and decrying domestic decrepitude; as an adult, he had helped drive out the corrupt Kuomintang regime, restore Chinese dignity, and build the New China. Jiang was so committed to the core tenets of Communism that, early in his tenure as general secretary, he informed a group of senior leaders, "I don't like private businessmen."

What had set off Jiang's ire was an upbeat report about a displaced worker, a middle-aged manager who had been laid off from an ailing state-owned enterprise. Lacking any means to sustain his family, the man was forced onto the streets to hawk cheap knickknacks. Whether the accidental entrepreneur was lucky or smart, his tiny business became so successful so quickly—he hired other laid-off workers and expanded to several locations—that to celebrate his commercial triumph, he threw a big party, to which he invited his former colleagues who were barely hanging on at the ever-declining government factory. "If we don't stop these business owners," Jiang warned in an internal meeting around 1990, "they will put an end to socialism."

Years later, at an informal get-together of state leaders, Jiang walked over to an attendee of that decade-old meeting and admitted that he had been wrong: "What I said back then about private business was not correct. Experience has proven that China needs entrepreneurs and business owners; they are part of our socialist system for building our economy and society." Jiang continued: "At heart, I'm an engineer, not an ideologue. Systems work or they don't work. If they don't, you fix them; if they do, you keep them. Private business works. All that matters is what's good for China."

ON JULY 7 LEE Teng-hui, president of the Republic of China, the official name of Taiwan, said on German radio that the two governments, mainland

China and Taiwan, enjoyed a "special state-to-state" relationship that was "nearly a decade old." On July 20 Lee expanded his disruptive statement.

"It is not a relationship between one legitimate government and one renegade group," Lee said. "Or a 'one China' internal relationship between one central government and one local government. 'One China' does not currently exist and can emerge only after a democratic reunification. Therefore for mainland China to regard Taiwan as a 'renegade province' shows complete ignorance of historical and legal facts on the part of Beijing."

To mainland Chinese, the separation of Taiwan was a symbol of weakness and a legacy of colonialism. A common perception was that the United States supported Taiwan and sold it weapons in order to thwart China's emergence as a great power. Most Chinese believed that for their country to be truly great, it would have to be made truly whole. To Jiang Zemin, only when China is completely unified, only when Taiwan is returned to the motherland, will "China finally be at peace for the first time since the Opium Wars," as journalist Jasper Becker put it. Recognizing that the emotions of even most overseas Chinese resonate with Jiang's impassioned yearning for this national unity, Becker drew the analogy to "the belief in medieval Europe that all members of society should belong to the one true [Catholic] Church." Hong Kong had returned in 1997; Macao was due back at the end of 1999. For mainlanders, Taiwan was the missing piece.

Progress between China and Taiwan came to a halt. Wang Daohan, president of Beijing's Association for Relations Across the Taiwan Straits, had been scheduled to go to Taiwan in the fall. The trip was canceled. *People's Daily* accused Taiwanese authorities of overestimating their own strength and plotting secretly to advance the separatist cause, and it likened Lee Teng-hui to "an insect trying to dig up a tree."

Jiang used even stronger words. He was not, he said, "someone who likes war, but 1.2 billion Chinese people are concerned about what happens in Taiwan." Time and again he had made clear his government's policy: Taiwan and the mainland were one country operating under two systems with the ultimate aim of peaceful reunification. No other interpretation would be tolerated. The military threat was implicit. Again, Jiang's rhetoric had to maintain that fine balance between not antagonizing the international community while at the same time reassuring hardliners at home.

MEANWHILE JIANG STILL HAD the problem of Falun Gong, and he still rejected strategies of moderation. To him, the sect's slogan of "truthfulness, benevolence, and forbearance" was deceptive and cunning, and it threatened to usurp Communism's moral authority. In this sense Falun Gong was a sort of counterfeit form of Communism, a movement of the masses that offered oddly similar inspirations and promises but was dangerous and destructive. The argument was not unlike the one that Western religions had used in their early tirades against Communism, arguing that Marxism, with its false visions of an earthly utopia, was a counterfeit form of religion.

In a May memo, shortly after the NATO attack in Belgrade, Jiang had wryly observed, "If Falun Gong masters can foresee everything, why didn't they predict the bombing of our embassy?" But his sense of humor regarding the cult was short-lived; the matter was now the highest national concern. On July 19 Jiang called a meeting of the Politburo Standing Committee, and three days later the Ministry of Public Security issued an edict: The Falun Gong was "an unlawful organization that has to be outlawed."

Lest anyone misunderstand the terms *unlawful* and *outlawed,* the decree listed a litany of Falun Gong activities that were now illegal: promotions, publicity, demonstrations, gatherings. Party members were forbidden to participate on penalty of expulsion. An arrest warrant was issued for sect founder Li Hongzhi, who was accused of spreading "superstition and malicious fallacies to deceive people, resulting in the deaths of many practitioners." Hundreds of Falun Gong members were hustled into custody.

In suppressing the enigmatically popular cult, the Chinese government adopted some of the terminology of the anticult movement in the West. It put out a report on "spiritual poisoning" that accused the cult not only of being covertly political but also of engaging in such criminal activities as tax evasion, drug dealing, smuggling, assassination, and kidnapping. It also called the Falun Gong "a menace to freedom of religion and social stability." With unintended irony, the report quoted psychologist Margaret Singer—an expert on mind manipulation, coercive persuasion, and recruitment techniques—whose original work had examined the brainwashing techniques used against American prisoners of war in Korea.

The Falun Gong response had its own flavor of the absurd. Its spokespeople fabricated quotes for Jiang, conjuring up words such as "No measures are too excessive to exterminate Falun Gong; those who are beaten to death will be counted as suicides." They also charged that Jiang was afraid of Falun Gong because *he* was superstitious and believed that the Chinese embassy had been bombed by the Falun Gong founder "using supernormal powers" in order to disrupt Jiang's plan to implement the crackdown.

Silly accusations aside, the government considered the cult a serious threat to its stability, which had already been shaken by economic turmoil and international incidents. In August the Communist Party linked the campaign against Falun Gong with ongoing efforts to reinvigorate itself with Marxist and socialist ideology. *People's Daily* called on Party members to study a new book with a long title: *Marx, Engels, Lenin, Stalin, Mao Zedong, Deng Xiaoping and Jiang Zemin Discuss Materialism and Atheism.* As Party chief, Jiang had embarked on a "Party Rectification" drive that sought to reaffirm its ideological base even while China deepened its commitment to a market economy. His "Three Stresses" campaign, which was first aimed at thwarting corruption and recapturing Marxist values, was refocused and integrated with the nationwide effort to eradicate Falun Gong.

MEANWHILE, JIANG SOUGHT PROGRESS on economic matters. In April 1999 Premier Zhu Rongji made his ill-fated trip to Washington, planning to reach agreement on China's entry into the WTO. In preparation, Jiang and Zhu argued internally that accession would increase foreign investment, stimulate good Chinese companies to be more competitive, and force inefficient state-owned enterprises to either meet the demands of market or go mercifully out of business. Jiang even sought to open China's sensitive telecommunications market, which he called "stiff and ossified," adding that "it has a bureaucratic style, it goes for industry monopolization, it makes enormous profits but has no concept of providing services. Foreign capital must be brought in." Zhu told the Politburo, "We have been negotiating for thirteen years . . . Black hair was turned white. It is time to conclude the negotiations."

Conservatives warned that a flood of foreign competition, required by WTO rules, would put millions of workers out of their jobs and onto the streets, catalyzing social unrest. In addition, foreigners would soon dominate key industries, such as finance and retail.

This debate had simmered for years, but it now intensified in the context of Zhu's American mission. Party leaders tagged the trip "high risk" since U.S. politics had "poisoned the atmosphere" with vitriolic "China-bashing" of everything from trade to spying. Another problem, as providence would have it, was that U.S.-led NATO forces had just begun to bomb Yugoslavia, heating up anti-American sentiments in China.

Jiang did not disagree with his colleagues but argued that considering "the overall situation of our national interests, the visit should proceed as planned." Since "we must continue to deal with the United States," Jiang said, "there is no need to arouse various misunderstandings . . . by terminating the visit."

Had he not arrived at such an inopportune moment, Zhu Rongji, with his engagingly direct style, would have been a hit in America. Unfortunately, after offering greater concessions on opening China's markets than many in his country thought wise, and after laying all his political capital on the table in one big bet to strike a deal, Zhu watched while his best offer to get China into the WTO was spurned by President Clinton.

Clinton "quickly realized his error," according to Joseph Fewsmith, and "called Premier Zhu in New York on April 13 to make a commitment to get China into the WTO by the end of the year," but the damage had been done. Nationalistic politics in Beijing, animated and energized by Clinton's mistake, was taking over, and it was assaulting Zhu and buffeting Jiang.

"We had reached agreement when Zhu was in Washington," noted former Treasury secretary Robert Rubin, "but we thought we'd have a better chance with Congress if we'd wait a few weeks to get out of the spotlight. But somehow, to our collective embarrassment, our agreement was leaked on the Internet—we never did figure out how the leak happened, and we certainly didn't anticipate the reaction in China to the delay in formalizing the agreement. Later in the year, though, Jiang and Clinton had their breakthrough."

Rubin was right, but in the meantime the Chinese were furious that their concessions were made public and assumed that the Americans had done it deliberately. Fewsmith states that "the posting was widely seen in China as a way to publicly hold the Chinese government's feet to the fire, an action bound to evoke a hostile response." After all, the embarrassing disclosure was put up on the official website of the Office of the United States Trade Representative.

The unauthorized seventeen-page "Sino-U.S. Joint Statement" was instantly translated and distributed to China's senior leaders. Worse, according to Fewsmith, "the posting allowed public opinion to play a role in China. Large enterprises and provinces that would be affected by China's entry began to calculate the impact on themselves. With the posting, the Chinese government lost control of the flow of information."

"The reaction was as strong as a force-six earthquake," reported an insider close to Zhu. "Rumors flew thick and fast in Zhongnanhai, and people ignorant of the true facts [thinking Zhu had approved its release] even said, 'How can Lao Zhu have done such a thing?'" Internet articles and student demonstrators labeled him a "traitor" and made ugly comparisons to Japan's schemes to subjugate China and reduce it to a colony. Zhu himself said, "The Americans look down on us Chinese. This is politics, not child's play." When the American bombs hit the Chinese embassy three weeks later, the anti-American fervor weakened Zhu further.

Critics within the Chinese government suggested that the real "traitor" was Jiang Zemin, said Joseph Fewsmith. "It was after all Jiang who encouraged a closer relationship with the United States, who pushed for China's entry into the WTO, and who was slow to react to the U.S.–NATO action in Kosovo. These voices stemmed largely from the military. This is not to say that the entire People's Liberation Army was critical, but simply that there is a very nationalistic wing within it. And with the U.S. bombing of the Chinese embassy in Belgrade, these voices became both strident and difficult to ignore. Jiang was, in the immediate aftermath of the embassy bombing, in a very difficult situation." The combined opposition of broad nationalism (popular, intellectual, military), sef-protecting bureaucracies, Leftist ideologues, and political rivals became a potent force that almost blocked Jiang's strategic vision for China.

If Jiang Zemin were a dictator, as many Americans imagined him to be, he would not have cared. He could have supported Zhu whether his colleagues liked it or not, and if not, they would have ceased being his colleagues. But in the Party system of "centralized democracy," a vote of the Politburo Standing Committee could overrule Jiang—and Li Peng was particularly pointed in criticizing Zhu. For one, Li accused Zhu of disloyalty because he [Zhu] publicly stated that he had not wanted to go to the United States but had done so at the request of Jiang, thus appearing to redirect blame for the unsuccessful trip onto Jiang, an indiscretion that reportedly disappointed Jiang.

Officials wondered: What would the general secretary do?

Jiang could have jettisoned Zhu. Zhu's was the face that had been lost, and Zhu's was the face that some wanted banished. By making him a scapegoat, Jiang could have strengthened himself, but this he did not do. While Zhu remained low-key for about three months (amid rumors that he had quit or been sacked), Jiang assumed a more nationalistic posture in internal meetings by directing "harsh rhetoric" toward the United States. He evoked Mao's phrase that "U.S. imperialism will not die" and advocated "biding time while nurturing grievances." He also modified the premier's responsibilities in conducting WTO negotiations and in reforming state-owned enterprises.

Each seeking the best for China, Jiang and Zhu had begun to differ on the future of failing SOEs. Zhu believed that, for the most part, they could not function in a market-driven economy, but for Jiang the integrity of China as a socialist state was tied to their continuing existence. Instead of just reducing the state's share of SOE ownership, as Zhu advocated, Jiang focused on the political benefits of maintaining SOEs; he talked more about their importance to Party leadership and social stability and less about their bottom-line deficits and antiquated structures. By redefining Zhu's role, Jiang achieved three political objectives with one political move: he effected a temporary strategic retreat on China's WTO entry; he became more active in setting SOE policy; and he protected the vulnerable Zhu from additional attacks. (Reportedly during Zhu Rongji's low point during the summer, when he was beset on all sides, Jiang's wife, Wang Yeping, met with him and encouraged him to "struggle on.")

In August Jiang renewed his call for deeper reforms, giving the signal that China was ready to resume talks on joining the WTO. Coming soon after Party leaders had returned from their working vacation at Beidaihe, the speech suggested that Jiang had enabled Zhu Rongji to regain ground in their ongoing battle with those who would go slower with reform. Jiang confounded his critics by reaffirming his support for Zhu and for their mutual policy of reconciling with the United States and pursuing China's WTO entry.

On September 7 "technical level" WTO talks resumed; it was the first time that American and Chinese trade negotiators had met since the embassy bombing four months earlier. At the APEC summit in New Zealand two days later, Jiang Zemin and Bill Clinton held a two-hour discussion, described as "very productive, very friendly, and quite comprehensive," though Jiang lectured Clinton on Taiwan and gave him as a gift a book denouncing Falun Gong, which some American officials took to be in bad taste. Clinton asked U.S. trade representative Charlene Barshefsky to resume negotiations with Chinese trade minister Shi Guangsheng "as early as Sunday" and said that his goal was to reach agreement on China's WTO bid by the end of the year.

China-U.S. relations were back on track, despite continued tension over Taiwan. "The Taiwan problem has always been the most prominent issue in China-U.S. relations," Jiang said. "There have always been some forces in the United States who want to cripple the reunification of China."

In August two Chinese PLA officers were executed for selling military secrets to Taiwan. Their traitorous disclosures were about China's army exercises and missile testing in 1995 and 1996, which were intended as retaliation for Taiwan President Lee Teng-hui's visit to the United States in 1995 and to influence the high-stakes elections in 1996 in which Lee was nonetheless re-elected. Jiang was reportedly so enraged by this act of treason that he would not commute the death sentence. He was also said to freeze pay raises for the army.

IN THE MIDST OF controversy and crisis came a day of celebration to which Jiang had been looking forward throughout the frenzied, tempestuous year. October 1, 1999, marked the fiftieth anniversary of the founding of the People's Republic of China. Spectacular displays and solemn ceremonies took place in a magnificently refurbished Tiananmen Square. The highlight was a massive parade, presided over by the president, who gave a congratulatory speech to the nation.

It was the largest parade in Chinese history. Lion dancers prowled the pavement, and immense dragons of gold, orange, and pink—each supported by twenty-four men—snaked through the streets. Jets flew overhead, tanks rumbled along the avenue, and thousands of uniformed soldiers marched in perfect unison. Innumerable other marchers, wearing brightly colored scarves and waving Chinese flags, chanted fifty sanctioned slogans—one for each year of Communist rule—while more than ninety elaborate floats honored Chinese achievements, such as those in science and technology. Three floats were dedicated to China's supreme leaders: Mao Zedong, Deng Xiaoping, and Jiang Zemin. Tellingly, almost every public portrait of Jiang showed him standing slightly lower and to the front of Deng and Mao.

The festivities were the president's grand vision and he himself had helped shape their expansive nature, but the grandeur had not come without debate over costs and benefits. Jiang was not conflicted, nor would he be denied. He insisted on showcasing China's resurgence in what was also the tenth anniversary year of his own rise to power.

"In celebrating the [PRC's] fiftieth anniversary," Jiang said at a Politburo meeting, "we should mainly calculate political accounts and not let ourselves be tied down to calculating economic accounts." He also authorized substantial new projects in conjunction with the celebration, including sixty-seven major infrastructure projects in Beijing involving highways, subway stations, and theaters.

As Jiang watched the massive parade standing erect high above the open roof of a black limousine, his solitary, regal presence personified his stature and vision. He wore a gray Mao suit, a style originally developed by Sun Yat-sen to be modern without being Western. The image was no accident: it looked almost exactly like the one of Deng Xiaoping during the historic 1984 parade that marked the first flourishing of China's reawakening. As Deng had done, Jiang spoke to the multitudes through three microphones mounted on the car's roof: "Hello, comrades! . . .

"Our great motherland has traversed a course of five thousand years," he proclaimed. "In this long history the Chinese nation has, with its own wisdom, ingenuity, and outstanding creativeness, made an indelible contribution to world civilization. In the new millennium, it will contribute even more to world civilization with splendid new achievements . . . China will surely emerge as a prosperous, strong, democratic, and culturally advanced modern socialist country in the east of the world."

There was no doubt that day as to who was leading the nation to this exalted state. "Long live the great People's Republic of China!" Jiang proclaimed. "Long live the great Communist Party of China! Long live the great Chinese people!"

IN LATE OCTOBER PRESIDENT Jiang embarked on a landmark trip to Britain, where he stayed in Buckingham Palace and was feted by Queen Elizabeth II. To the melodic strains of their respective national anthems, Jiang was welcomed by the queen, Prime Minister Tony Blair, and other dignitaries in a formal rite at Horse Guards Parade, London's largest open space. All were then driven in horse-drawn carriages along the Mall, the tree-lined royal avenue leading to Buckingham Palace.

The next day a moment occurred that symbolized Jiang's lofty goal of China's integration into the world community. In the morning, he and his wife, Wang Yeping, were taken to Greenwich Observatory in east London. Jiang examined the exhibits while walking through the astronomical station and instrument hall. He came to a standstill in front of a special telescope called a Transit Circle. It is here, through the instrument's crosshairs, that the prime meridian, or longitude 0°, is defined. Every place on Earth is measured in terms of its angle east or west of this line—just as the equator divides the Northern and Southern Hemispheres. Jiang stood astride the famous line so that, for a moment, the leader of the largest population on the planet had one foot in the Eastern Hemisphere and one foot in the Western.

Returning home, Jiang continued trying to bridge the two worlds. On November 7 he talked to President Clinton about the progress of trade negotiations. He was impressed by Clinton's willingness to make concessions, such as raising quotas on China's textile exports to America. After consulting with Premier Zhu, Jiang concluded that Beijing should "speed up the accession process" if the WTO's negative impact on China's economy could be contained.

After six days of grueling negotiations and intense personal effort by the top leaders of both countries, Jiang announced, with great fanfare, an end to long-standing trade disputes with the United States. The agreement, which he called "of profound realistic and historic significance," would be the linchpin in China's admission to the WTO.

At a reception in Beijing honoring the U.S. delegation headed by Charlene Barshefsky, Jiang was optimistic and eloquent. The agreement, he said, would be "a driving force that will contribute to the development and prosperity of a global economy." According to Barshefsky, "President Jiang views and handles the bilateral negotiations for China's WTO entry from a strategic perspective."

It was a major victory in Jiang's overall plan of Da Guo Zhanlue, which literally means "Big Country Strategy." By forging diplomatic partnerships with the major powers, principally the United States, he believed that China would be on an equal footing in shaping the new world order.

Jiang had faced enormous domestic pressure that was resisting China's WTO entry—including Li Peng's constant opposition (representing China's vast bureaucracy and state-owned sector)—and yet he did what he believed was best for his country's growth and strength. According to Joseph Fewsmith, "Although Premier Zhu Rongji bore the brunt of public criticism, President Jiang Zemin similarly came under attack by nationalistic opposition leaders for 'selling out the country' and being soft on the United States." Jiang then had to devote significant time and effort to "defending himself and rebuilding support for joining the WTO." Fewsmith said, "The agreement on China's entry into the WTO will rank with President Nixon's 1972 visit to Beijing and President Carter's extension of diplomatic recognition to China as a major step in bringing China into the world." Writing soon after the historic WTO agreement had been reached, Fewsmith observed that "the big winner appears to be Jiang Zemin. Jiang has spent the last two years trying to solidify China's relations with the major powers of the world, and this agreement will allow him to say—correctly—that China has now been recognized as one of the great powers."

As if representing China's hopes for the future, on November 20 the nation that invented the rocket a millennium earlier successfully launched the first test flight of a spacecraft designed to carry Chinese astronauts, known as *taikonauts*, into Earth orbit. The vehicle was named *Shenzhou (Divine Ship)* by Jiang Zemin himself. It seemed a play on a classical Chinese term for the country, which literally translates into "divine land," and it captured the pride that the people felt for their achievement.

Abandoning the tight secrecy of the past, Xinhua released a colorful account of the *Shenzhou* flight, describing the feelings and tensions at the launch site, in the Beijing spaceflight command center, and onboard the four monitoring ships at sea. The question of allocation of scarce national resources, which some could argue might be better spent on, say, rural education or welfare for laid-off workers, almost never came up. The Chinese people voiced virtually unanimous support for *Shenzhou*. It was about national pride, for which no price was too high. According to Jiang, who authorized the manned space program in 1992 (cumulative costs were said to be a little over $2 billion through 2003), it was also about stimulating China's science and technology, and the military value of orbital flight.

Three days later a delighted President Jiang inspected the recovered *Shenzhou* capsule as it was opened in Beijing, and he met with the technical personnel who had directed the space flight. He encouraged them to make even greater contributions to high technology in China and to strengthen the country's defense capabilities.

AT THE SAME TIME less glorious aspects of Chinese society were also being scrutinized. On December 16 China's auditor-general announced that hundreds of government offices, banks, and state-owned companies had reported misappropriated funds during the course of the year. While some of these cases were due to a lack of market expertise, many involved corruption.

In China as elsewhere, corruption is a drag on the economy and a scourge on society. Because corruption distorts economic decisions and undermines the rule of law, both of which are essential for a stable, prosperous society, it cannot be tolerated. Jiang had fought corruption, in one form or another, throughout his career. In addition to being corrosively immoral, he believed it to be the largest stumbling block preventing China from reaching its full potential as a great nation.

As Jiang escalated the campaign against corruption, powerful men were arrested. The head of China's most popular cigarette producer, the so-called tobacco king, was sentenced to life imprisonment for embezzling $3.5 million. A vice minister of public security, the most senior official responsible for antismuggling enforcement, was arrested "on suspicion of complicity with smugglers." And the deputy governor of Jiangxi province, who had amassed $650,000 by demanding ninety separate bribes, became the highest-ranking official to be executed since 1949.

Jiang played a "key role" in the capital decision. "For such a flagrant criminal," commented *People's Daily*, reflecting Jiang's views, "only the death penalty is sufficient to safeguard national law, satisfy popular indignation, rectify the Party work style, and fight against corruption," adding that "in socialist China there is no special citizen in the eyes of the law, no special Party member in the eyes of Party discipline, and no one can escape the punishment of the law if he has broken the law, no matter how high his position or how powerful he is."

The most egregious corruption case erupted in the port city of Xiamen; it involved untold billions of dollars in smuggling and would become China's biggest scandal in fifty years. The smuggled items ranged from petroleum to shoes, with luxury cars, on which 100 percent tariffs were levied, being particularly attractive merchandise. Multiple branches of the Party, government, and military cooperated with the Yuan Hua company, which at the peak of its crimes supplied a deviously large part of China's retail petroleum market.

The scandal was hushed up for months, and when Jiang found out, he was enraged. His anger grew when the head of the Discipline Commission explained that the investigation had been stalled because the ringleader had powerful patrons or *hou tai* on his side.

"Now I'm your *hou tai*," Jiang said. "And no one's higher than me!" Nonetheless the Xiamen case would drag on for years, ultimately affecting someone close to Jiang.

Jiang's ally in fighting corruption, Zhu Rongji, instructed investigators to "grab the big and release the small." Those who took small bribes were given immunity if they agreed to cooperate and turn in the big bosses. A kind of witness protection program was established to protect informants, a rare offer in China's justice system. "I have a hundred coffins," Zhu said famously. "Ninety-nine for corrupt officials and one for myself."

In his July 1 speech celebrating the seventy-eighth anniversary of the Communist Party, Jiang criticized negative attitudes and tendencies. "Some comrades' confidence about the final victory over capitalism by socialism and the future of the construction of socialism with Chinese characteristics has been weakened," he said. "Some, pursuing personal interests, have drifted with the money-worshipping tide and even grabbed state property by taking advantage of their official positions."

In an attempt to curb corruption, Jiang reinforced conflict-of-interest policy. Family members of high-ranking officials could not run businesses within the administrative scope of their parents or spouses, and they would be forbidden to receive money or gifts by taking advantage of their influence.

Jiang did not simply want to reform the worst elements of the Party; he wanted to make sweeping changes to all of it—a worthy goal, and an unenviable task. One of his weapons was a Party-wide rectification or reeducation campaign called the Three Stresses—"stress study, stress politics, stress healthy trends"—which was designed to improve the quality of Party members and the efficacy of Party organizations. "Party construction," as Jiang called the process of strengthening the Party, was always one of his primary concerns, and he pursued it vigorously, with both theoretical ideas and operational programs.

Launched in December 1998 as a nationwide effort to reinvigorate the Party, the Three Stresses campaign was conducted intensely throughout 1999. It required officials to renew their ideological studies and reconstitute their moral correctness through day-long sessions of rigorous criticism, self-criticism, and education, which "stressed" political theory, political consciousness, and proper conduct. The campaign was managed by Vice President Hu Jintao, who was president of the Central Party School, and coordinated by Zeng Qinghong, who was appointed director of the Party's powerful Organization Department in March. Jiang was pleased with what Hu and Zeng, leaders of the next generation with a common goal, accomplished.

For Jiang Zemin, a year that should have been upbeat and hopeful had been buffeted by crises and controversies. Now, as it drew to a close, optimism was rising again. He had managed to weather extraordinary storms. A quiet coda to 1999 was written in mid-December, when America and China reached agreement over compensation for the April bombing of the Chinese embassy in Belgrade.

National pride was sparked anew on December 20 when China welcomed Macao back to the family fold. At a formal ceremony, Jiang spoke grandly about the former Portuguese colony's future. In Beijing thirty thousand people gathered in Tiananmen Square to mark the repatriation, which became official at midnight. All eyes focused on the giant countdown board that had been ticking off the seconds until Macao's return. Amid brilliant displays of fireworks, singers performed and traditional dragon and lion dances were staged. The events were televised so that the whole country could share in the patriotic excitement.

It was the turn of a new century and the beginning of the next millennium, and China reveled in celebratory rites and festivities. At China's Millennium Monument, the starkly modern edifice that combines celestial forms and patriotic symbols to commemorate fifty centuries of Chinese civilization and to inspire the national spirit, President Jiang Zemin, dressed in black, emerged from a lineup of similarly attired senior leaders to give a short, soaring speech that glorified China's historic reemergence. Then he dramatically led the countdown of the final ten seconds to the new millennium.

At the New Year's concert in the Great Hall of the People, two Chinese chorales, two symphony orchestras, and dozens of musicians performed Western musical and operatic pieces along with modern Chinese compositions. Along a lengthy stretch of the Great Wall, ten thousand people holding blazing torches were arranged in the shape of a dragon, the enduring symbol of Chinese civilization, to greet the new millennium. When the New Year's bell tolled, two thousand just-married couples embraced nationwide.

In his New Year's speech, President Jiang spoke not only of China's goals and visions but of those of all humankind. "The people of all countries of the world," he said, "regardless of their nationalities and faiths, are elated over the arrival of this historic moment."

Even within the context of unity, however, he made it clear that China's future would be self-determined. "The Chinese nation," he promised, "will be rejuvenated due to the motherland's complete reunification and the establishment of a prosperous, strong, democratic, culturally advanced, and modern socialist country."

In spite of his confident tone, however, realizing such a vision would be difficult. The past year had demonstrated what a tightrope Jiang walked in almost every aspect of Chinese life. Yet he still believed that only the Party could maintain economic momentum and provide material prosperity, revitalize Chinese culture and civilization, and look after the interests of all the people.

On New Year's Day President Jiang went to the Working People's Palace of Culture, adjacent to Tiananmen Square, to hear a concert performed on the nation's newest and largest set of bells, the Chinese Bells of Harmony, which were modeled on the 2,400-year-old Zenghouyi Bells. Consisting of 108 finely crafted pieces, the chimes were said to resonate with the spirits of the people. On the bottom row of the biggest bell was an inscription by Jiang, which read, "May the Chinese Bells of Harmony be preserved for thousands of years."

No doubt one of Jiang's own New Year's wishes was to leave a similar legacy of culture and beauty, along with peace and prosperity, to the country in his care. Though there were many problems to solve, Jiang could look back on his decade of leadership with a good deal of satisfaction. Standards of living had risen dramatically. Poverty was at its lowest level, and literacy was at its highest. The economy was growing and society was stable. Hong Kong and Macao had returned to the motherland. The country was respected in international affairs. And the Chinese people could approach the future, for the first time in centuries, with confidence and optimism.

THOUGH JIANG FOCUSED ON the future, he never forgot the past. Cell phones and computers may have linked China with the rest of the world, but the country's heritage continued to make it unique. Appropriately, Jiang chose to commemorate the old century and commence the new one with his Big Family. "Let's gather together," he told his younger sister, Jiang Zehui, in late December. He asked her to invite relatives and close friends for dinner at his home. Since the last member of his father's generation had died, Jiang had become the leader of his family, and this was his perennial duty.

Though his own sons were away, Jiang was delighted when two dozen people arrived at his Zhongnanhai home. Along with Jiang Zehui and her family, there were the sons of another sister and their families, members of an uncle's family, and several old friends.

To start things off, Jiang Zemin recounted the history of China in the twentieth century, telling both the personal story of the Jiang family and the larger saga of the country's trials and triumphs. When he finished, he called over the young people and asked them to translate into English what he had just said. He asked them questions in English and Chinese. If his questions were in Chinese, they were required to translate the questions into English first and then answer them in English. If his questions were in English, they would simply continue in English. The man who was almost a professor loved to play teacher. Giving "English tests" was great family fun, and he was pleased that the younger generation was fluent and equally pleased that he could still keep up with them.

Dinner was about to be served when Jiang Zemin made a startling request: Everyone, young and old, now had to speak English. It was the international language of the twenty-first century, and it was to be the dinner conversation language at the Jiang family celebration. If one thinks, as many Westerners still do, that China is an insular, repressive, xenophobic, totalitarian dictatorship like Cuba, North Korea, or the former Iraq, or a "strategic competitor" (potential enemy) of the United States like the Soviet Union during the cold war, then just try to imagine Fidel Castro, Kim Jong-Il, Saddam Hussein, or Nikita Khrushchev taking on a dinnertime role as the family teacher of English.

The meal was a homey affair, featuring Yangzhou food, which relies more on the original flavors and colors of ingredients than on oily sauces. Along with various kinds of dumplings and other dishes, there were the president's favorite "Lion's Head" meatballs, made of pork and stewed with cabbage. After the meal came the *lian huan,* or family party.

"My brother seemed happy and relaxed," noted Jiang Zehui, "perhaps the happiest I'd seen him. It had been a long time since we had enjoyed a *lian huan* together. My son, who works at China Central Television [as an editor], was the host."

Everyone performed. The songs ran the gamut from operas and old folk songs to contemporary hits. "Of course," Jiang Zehui remembered, smiling, "Third Brother did most of the singing." That was not because he was the leader of the country, or even of the family, but because he knew the most songs. "He loves singing songs from diverse cultures," she said.

The Chinese president, here family patriarch, sang Peking Opera, patriotic tunes from the anti-Japanese war period such as "Yellow River Chorus," Russian songs from the 1950s, and American songs from the 1930s that he had learned in college. He performed *dao qing* from Yangzhou, a kind of traditional folk art that requires the performer to sing a folk tale and play a simple instrument (like a guitar) at the same time.

No matter what he selected, whether it was the Spanish "Pigeon" or the Italian "O Sole Mio," Jiang sang in the song's original language. "The entire group sang along when we could," recalled Jiang Zehui, "but most of the time my brother went solo." As his sister put it, "He was very *jin xing*"—enjoying himself immensely. "I think he knew how rare it was to get so many of us together," she said, "and he was pleased that the younger generation was growing up to be successful members of society."

Before dinner, while Jiang was describing China's modern history, he became pensive. "It was not easy for our parents' generation," he told his family. "They sacrificed a great deal for the construction of New China so that we might have a better life. We are now entering into a new century, and we are thankful to them that our country has become peaceful and prosperous."

He then softly added, "Tonight, I am really *gan kai wan qian.*"

Gan kai wan qian is a Chinese idiom that even interpreters have difficulty explaining. Taken separately, the words mean "feelings" *(gan)*, "sighing" *(kai)*, "ten thousand" *(wan)*, "thousand(s)" *(qian)*. The "ten thousand thousands" *(wan qian)* suggests an inestimably large number and thereby expresses enormity. The "feelings, sighing" *(gan kai)* pairing conveys deep emotion. But when the four words are strung together, a kaleidoscope of connotations emerges, none of which is resident in the literal meanings of the independent words. They combine to suggest warmth and nostalgia prompted by a triggering event. One possible English translation is "flooded with feelings," but it is not quite there, since *gan kai wan qian* implies a two-step process. It is a Proustian notion: Something has to happen first in order to unleash these warm torrents of nostalgic emotion.

It had been a tumultuous century. It had been a tumultuous year. Looking back on how far his country had come, with family and friends gathered around him, Jiang could not help but feel bittersweet pride in the past and cautious optimism for the future. Another translation of *gan kai wan qian* might be "all sorts of feelings well up in me," which was exactly how China's leader felt on the eve of the new millennium.

Part Four

Vision

2000–2004

Chapter 23

J A N U A R Y – J U N E 2 0 0 0

"We Recognize and Respect the Unique
Sensitivities and Sensibilities of Scientists"

IN THE YEAR LINKING the two millennia, President Jiang would stress
three principal themes: the revitalization of the country through science
and education, the development of China's "Great West," and the introduction of a new change-making philosophy for the Communist Party called
Three Represents.

In his New Year's speech, Jiang spoke of peace and harmony in an increasingly global society. At the same time, just in case and mindful of his duties as
chairman of the Central Military Commission, he reorganized China's armed
forces to "strengthen [their] quality and win high-tech wars." For fifty years
each of the three branches of the armed forces—army, navy, air force—had
relied on its own independent, top-to-bottom support system. Now the entire
military would share one integrated system, enabling the People's Liberation
Army to react faster and to operate with higher efficiency. Jiang had been
working on the new structure for some time, and it was initiated on January 1.

In February Jiang signed a decree modernizing military headquarters at all
levels, the objectives being to fight the high-tech battles of the new century,
improve the effectiveness of command operations, give priority to ideological
education, and uphold the cardinal rule that the army must follow the Party.
He also added a new "CMC chairman's office" in the PLA's imposing ultra-
modern headquarters on Chang'an Avenue, directly west of Tiananmen
Square. Called the August 1 Building to honor Army Day, the gleaming
edifice was a far cry from the military's humble beginnings, when its rough-
hewn guerrilla fighters lived in caves. The chairman's office, outfitted with the
latest telecommunications equipment, was a huge suite that took up much of
a whole floor. For Jiang Zemin, it wasn't for show.

IN JANUARY THE STATE Development Planning Commission, run by Minister Zeng Peiyan, announced for the first time since China's Communist revolution in 1949 that "private enterprises should be put on an equal footing with state-owned enterprises." Zeng said that the government would eliminate all restrictive and discriminatory regulations in taxes, land use, business start-up, and import and export that were "not friendly toward private investment and private economic development." Private firms might also have access to China's stock markets.

Jiang continued fighting for greater accountability within the Party. "The more we do in reform and opening-up and in developing a socialist market economy," he said to the graft-busting Central Commission for Discipline Inspection, "the stricter we should be in running the Party well." "The Party leads everything," he continued, "workers, peasants, the military, academic circles, and business circles . . . If the Party is always firmly and forcefully governed, the nation definitely will be correctly and effectively governed." He stressed that Party committees at all levels should perfect a "responsibility system" that would be held accountable when problems arose. The selection and promotion of officials must follow strict rules, he said, and moral quality must be considered in the process.

Onlookers took note when President Jiang was seen accompanying Jia Qinglin, the Beijing Party chief, on a tour of the capital and praising him for his "splendid work" as Beijing mayor. Jia had been Party chief of Fujian province during the massive Xiamen smuggling operations, then under intense investigation. Though he himself was not involved, his wife reportedly was, and Jia's career was imperiled. Some officials believed that Jia should bear responsibility for the scandal, and most observers assumed that Jiang Zemin would retreat from his plan for the Party to promote Jia to the Politburo Standing Committee in 2002. But by identifying himself with Jia in this overt act of support, Jiang helped his beleaguered friend, who some said was being treated unfairly by political opponents.

Commenting on an increasing swirl of rumors, Li Peng, chairman of the National People's Congress, spoke for his colleagues. "Now there is talk again in the Party and overseas about the leadership at the Sixteenth Party Congress," he said in an address. "There are many versions of the talk, but they are all hearsay." Then he added, "No persons and small groups can impose their wills on the collective leadership."

As a CRITICAL PART of China's long-term strategic plan, Jiang sought to transform the growth-poor, resource-rich western areas of the country into prosperous economic zones. The future of China's reform, he repeatedly said—indeed, the future of China itself—was dependent on the successful development of the Great West, home to many of China's fifty-five ethnic minorities. Over the years, as the economy in coastal regions had become stronger, the disparity between east and west had become larger. "For President Jiang," observed Planning Minister Zeng Peiyan, "creating regional balance in China's development was an important guiding principle. He worried that geographic imbalance could affect national unity and social stability."

Although Deng Xiaoping had called attention to the problem in 1988 and Jiang had been concerned about it for years, he held off initiating any programs until 1999 because he had to be sure that the economies of coastal regions had become self-sustaining before the central government could turn its attention elsewhere. Now, finally, it was time for the Great West.

Jiang called for the country to be "daring" and "resolute" in building the region, which consisted of ten provinces and autonomous regions, including the Chongqing municipality. Covering some 56 percent of China's territory, the Great West accounted for 50 percent of the country's mineral deposits. Economists stated that if China's west did not catch up with its east, the country's goal of becoming a mid-level developed nation by the middle of the twenty-first century could not be achieved. Jiang admonished the wealthier coastal provinces to provide financial, technological, and managerial assistance to the poorer, western ones. "The development of the west," he assured them, "will also bring new market opportunities to the east." He endorsed a kind of big brother system in which China's most successful cities would partner with needy provinces: to begin, Shanghai with Xinjiang and Shenzhen with Guizhou.

At the National People's Congress Jiang explained his strategy to a delegation from Qinghai province. Top priority, he asserted, was cultivating talent. To that end, he pushed for policies that would "actively bring in outstanding talented people from all parts of China and also those returning from abroad, and also fully exploit the role of local talent." He encouraged authorities to create better working and living conditions and provide economic incentives to attract and retain professionals.

Jiang counseled patience. Though he envisioned initial success in five to ten years, he cautioned, "The whole country must profoundly understand that the great development of western China is a grand strategy for a hundred and a thousand years." Developing China's Great West was now a high priority; though accomplishing the vast endeavor would take, in Jiang's words, "the sustained efforts of many generations," the initiative would become one of his prime achievements.

"Moving from slogans to action," noted Zeng Peiyan, "was exhilarating— especially after years of dreaming about it." For example, the Qinghai-Tibet Railroad, a visionary plan first put forward in the 1950s, had never been implemented because of inadequate technology and funding. Jiang resurrected the idea, saying that the railroad was necessary to spur economic development, establish communications between east and west, and improve the living standards of the minority ethnic groups in the regions. (The plan was not without its foreign critics, who suspected that China's primary motivation for undertaking the hugely expensive project was military, part of a long-term strategy to dominate South Asia.)

But massive growth meant unusual problems. Jiang was especially concerned about the environment and indigenous minorities, so he asked Zeng Peiyan to visit the United States to learn from the American experience in developing its West.

JIANG BELIEVED THAT ECONOMIC practice and political theory were partners, that China's development needed both policy and ideology to be real world, up to date, and enabling. As such, he was ready to float a new idea.

On an inspection tour of Guangdong province in late February 2000, he was speaking in Gaozhou, a small, underdeveloped city where he focused on the complaints of peasants. Jiang assured them of Party support. "Handling China's affairs well depends on our Party's ideology, style, organization, discipline, combatworthiness, and leadership ability," he told six hundred village and township officials. "As long as our Party always remains the loyal representative of the development needs of China's advanced productive forces, the forward direction of China's advanced culture, and the fundamental interests of the large majority of the Chinese people, it will stand invincible forever . . . and lead the people onward."

It was a threefold dictum—advanced productive forces, advanced culture, fundamental interests of the people—and this was Jiang's first expression of it. It had no name, did not make the headlines, seemed simple and casually mentioned. Yet this articulation was neither simple nor casual: Jiang Zemin's words were few, but their impact would be profound.

A few days later, in Guangzhou, Jiang reiterated the threefold message at a meeting on Party building. Although Xinhua buried the sentence in its report and the new philosophy still had no name, it would soon dominate political discourse.

In early March *People's Daily* published a high-profile commentary that marked the first national exposure of Jiang's campaign to modernize the Party through what the article labeled, for the first time, Three Represents. "All the struggles carried out by our Party are, in the final analysis, aimed at liberating and developing productive forces," *People's Daily* declared, adding that "any move to surpass the present historical development stage by indiscriminately copying and applying to today's practice a number of characteristics and practices of socialism at its mature stage will all the same hinder the development of productive forces." The meaning, turgid and mind-numbing to Westerners, was riveting to many Chinese. In essence, the Party mouthpiece was saying that it was permissible to abandon, for the foreseeable future, any idealistic principles of socialism that did not work in today's world. Moreover, it warned, some aspects of "mature-stage" socialism may actually "hinder" progress.

"President Jiang's Three Represents speech in 2000 was just like Deng Xiaoping's Nanxun [Southern Tour] speeches in 1992," said Li Changchun, the Guangdong Party secretary who, within three years, would come to run ideology and media in China. "A tremendous driving force."

"Wang Huning and I wrote the Gaozhou speech," said Teng Wensheng, as he described the public origin of Three Represents. "Just before President Jiang's trip to the South, he called me to his office. He had obviously given the concept serious thought. 'Marxism has so many theories out there,' Jiang said, 'Marxism, Leninism, dialectical materialism, historical materialism—we need something applicable to the realities of contemporary China that makes sense and is easy to remember.' " Jiang told Teng that his new theory "didn't have to explain everything."

"In Jiang's first presentations, the theory was very preliminary," explained Teng. "Over time it would mature."

Jiang knew that to lead China's global, knowledge-based economy, he had to modernize the Party's ideology, and Three Represents was the mechanism by which he would do it. But for China's leader, the theory of the Three Represents, which he developed in concert with Zeng Qinghong and Wang Huning, meant even more. It was to be his legacy to a country that was already making the transition toward new leadership. In fact, it was during this period that he made clear his support for Hu Jintao as his successor. In a high-level Party meeting, Jiang lauded Hu for his "ideological resoluteness," particularly with respect to his leadership of the Three Stresses campaign.

To most non-Chinese, Jiang's Three Represents appears as yet another dense thicket of Communist rhetoric, more Big Brother brainwashing of the cadres. Even the designated name, *Represents,* sounds syntactically odd in English. Yet in Chinese it has coherence and subtlety. The phrase is a literal translation of *san ge daibiao:* for Represents, Jiang is using the common Chinese word *daibiao,* which is the same term used to describe, say, the Beijing "representative" of a foreign company (*san* means "three" and *ge* is a grammatical marker). Jiang's intent was that although Communism, in its industrial age formulation, was not viable as a contemporary economic system, the Communist Party, by "representing" these three powerful principles, would be modernizing Marxism, advancing with the times, and securing its place at the vanguard of society. The Party, as Jiang always asserted, had to come first. "Success in running things well in China," he said, "hinges on our Party."

JIANG ALSO WORKED TO modernize education. Recently a series of school-related cases of violence had gripped the nation's leaders. In one, a middle school student killed his mother with a hammer "because he could not bear his position in class and the pressure from his parents." In another, two young students hacked a fellow student to death. And in a case of parental rage, a father "took some people to beat up the class teacher because the student had not been assessed 'three good' [marks] and made a Young Pioneers team leader."

Jiang called these reports "really shocking" and advocated a broader concept of education, one that did not focus on academic achievement to the exclusion of other skills. He called on schools to reduce homework, to teach courses that would create "a spirit of innovation," and to move from "exam-driven education" to "quality education." He also spoke about the importance of creating "well-rounded individuals" with improved "moral, intellectual, and fitness levels."

Referring to old stories about students tying their hair to ceiling beams to keep from falling asleep and prodding themselves awake with awls, Jiang continued, "We cannot shut up young students in books and rooms all day; we must let them take part in some social practice to broaden their vision and enhance their social experience."

Jiang's ideas provoked controversy as well as praise. Education in China had a long tradition, and many were wary of change.

IN MATTERS OF CONTROVERSY, Jiang had his own, sometimes poetic way. Speaking informally with the press during the annual session of the National People's Congress, Jiang was asked by a Taiwanese reporter whether a war with Taiwan would be a case of "burning beanstalks to cook beans," an allusion to fratricidal strife from a poem of the Wei dynasty.

"This phrase of yours is taken from the verse of Cao Zhi," Jiang responded smoothly. "They were boiling beans over a fire made of beanstalks," he said, reciting the fifth-century verse by heart. "Came a plaintive voice from the pot, 'O, why, sprung from the selfsame root, what need each the other fry?' . . .

"If fratricidal strife arises because some people promote Taiwan independence," Jiang continued, "it is of their own making that we are frying each other. We 'sprang from the selfsame root'—from one China. Why should anyone promote Taiwan independence?"

The room erupted in applause, but a few days later on March 18 the former mayor of Taipei, Chen Shui-bian, was elected president of Taiwan in an upset victory. After more than fifty years of one-party rule, the Kuomintang was out of power. Even though Taiwan was not generally recognized as an independent state, it had become a majority-rule democracy. The themes of the onetime dissident lawyer's campaign were to develop Taiwan into a high-tech "green silicon island," promote lasting peace in the Taiwan Straits, and uphold the Taiwanese spirit. Chen was also the first Taiwanese leader to aggressively advocate independence.

Beijing was agitated. Although the Kuomintang and the Communists had been enemies for more than seventy years, they had one vital belief in common. Both held as a fundamental tenet that there was only "one China" and that the mainland and Taiwan were part of that same country. Although they disagreed violently as to which of them represented China's legitimate government, while the Kuomintang was in power, Beijing did not have to worry about a declaration of Taiwanese independence. The election of Chen Shui-bian and the coming to power of the Democratic Progressive Party, whose platform was committed to independence, changed the situation overnight. From now on the two sides would have to tread carefully to avoid irreparable error.

Before Chen's election Premier Zhu Rongji had warned, "If Taiwan's voters make an impulsive choice, they may never have a chance to regret it."

After the election Zhu was no less blunt, saying, "We will never hold any negotiations" with any people or parties "that advocate Taiwan independence."

Though believing the same, Jiang was more politic. "Anything can be discussed so long as dialogue and negotiations across the Taiwan Straits are conducted on one basis, namely, the recognition of the 'one China' principle," the president said, although he backed his colleague by adding, "Premier Zhu Rongji made our stand and viewpoint very clear." Overall Jiang's message was one of reconciliation: "The election in the Taiwan region is over. We said before and still hold today that whoever comes to power in Taiwan is welcome to the mainland for talks, and we may also go to Taiwan."

Behind the scenes, however, Jiang reportedly took a tougher stance, assigning General Cao Gangchuan, a missile expert, to take charge of military policy relating to Taiwan. "If we were to take military action," Jiang reportedly said, "it should be sooner rather than later."

Although the president noted that Chen had received less than 40 percent of the votes—which he interpreted to mean that at least 60 percent of Taiwanese voters did not support independence—he worried about the future: "With a Democratic Progressive Party politician as president," Jiang said, "the percentage of Taiwan residents favoring independence may grow considerably." In an internal speech, he castigated Taiwan's pro-independence politicians as "slavish worshippers of the United States." "Many Taiwan politicians say yes to whatever the U.S. tells them," he complained. "But whatever the mainland suggests, they always say no."

IN APRIL JIANG ZEMIN embarked on a groundbreaking trip to Israel, Palestine, Turkey, Greece, and South Africa. The tour signified how far China had come in the world since Jiang had become its president. No Chinese head of state had ever visited Israel before; indeed, China had been a perennial supporter of Yasser Arafat's Palestine. The fact that Jiang was stopping in both places reflected China's maturing diplomacy and its new prestige in international affairs.

The Israelis welcomed Jiang warmly, and he in turn praised their long history and rich culture, comparing their glory and their sorrow to that of his own people. Speaking to the Knesset, the Israeli parliament, Jiang noted that "friendly relations between the Chinese and Jewish nations can be traced back to ancient times." He continued, "More than thirteen hundred years ago the ancestors of our two time-honored and great nations began their exchanges through the famous Silk Road and forged our profound friendship. During World War II Jewish people suffered cruel persecution by the Nazi fascists. Tens of thousands of Jewish refugees sought asylum in China [when no other country would take them]. Although the Chinese people were also suffering through a very difficult period, they still stretched out their friendly hands to the Jewish people, receiving and treating them in a kind-hearted way."

For many first-time visitors to Israel, a symbolic, early stop is Yad Vashem, the Holocaust memorial in Jerusalem dedicated to the six million Jews exterminated by the Nazis during World War II. It is here that one feels the driving emotion of Israel to never again allow the Jewish people to fall victim to virtual extinction, and it was here that Jiang Zemin, who knows all too well the inhuman brutality of national subjugation, sensed their monumental, ineffable suffering. Upon seeing a picture of a Jewish child being killed by Nazi soldiers, the Chinese ambassador to Israel, who accompanied Jiang on the visit, said that she had seen a similar photo at the Museum of Chinese Revolution History, where the child was Chinese and the soldiers Japanese.

That afternoon Jiang met with Israeli prime minister Ehud Barak. Amid friendly talk of economic cooperation, there was a source of tension. Although Israel had agreed to sell China an early-warning airborne surveillance system called Phalcon (to be installed in Russian-supplied aircraft), it was now being pressured by the United States to cancel the sale. When Barak met with Jiang in Jerusalem, it was less than twenty-four hours after the Israeli prime minister had met with President Bill Clinton in Washington. Expressing his strong displeasure, Clinton had warned that the $250 million deal, which over time could grow to $2 billion, might imperil U.S. aid to Israel, estimated at nearly $3 billion per year (most of which was defense related). The concern of U.S. lawmakers was that Israel's highly sophisticated system, which tracked multiple enemy aircraft simultaneously, could enhance China's capability to attack Taiwan or harm U.S. personnel if there were ever a conflict between America and China.

Israel was angered by the American stance. The sale of the Phalcon system did not involve the transfer of any American technology and therefore did not break any American law. An Israeli official called the U.S. pressure a "steamroller" and accused the U.S. of applying one standard to Israel and a different one to Britain and France, which had also sought the Chinese contract, only to be beaten out by Israel.

Barak assured Jiang that Israel would not cave in to pressure, but in early July the one Middle Eastern democracy did just that and canceled the Phalcon sale. To Jiang, the incident was a flagrant example of American interference in China's affairs, and he felt that he had been blindsided, if not deceived, by Barak. At the UN Millennial Summit in New York in September, Jiang would refuse to meet with the Israeli prime minister.

But on that warm April evening in Jerusalem, President Jiang was honored at a state dinner hosted by Prime Minister Barak, who encouraged Israeli participation in China's high-tech industries and the development of its immense western region. In his speech, the Chinese leader dismissed the so-called clash of civilizations theory, saying that "in our view, all civilizations in history were created by people and are the common assets of all mankind."

As usual, Jiang looked for lessons in his surroundings. At the Zohar Agriculture Research Center he wandered around in a short-sleeve shirt and sun-shielding cap, inspecting biotech-bred high-grade fruits and vegetables. Deliberately situated in the scorching Negev Desert south of the Dead Sea, the Center had exceptionally poor natural conditions consisting of a dry, burning-hot climate and highly saline soil. Yet the Center's world-class Israeli agritechnology had enabled nearby regions to make modern agriculture an important industry.

Jiang asked many questions, largely in English, about the Center's technologies, cultivating processes, and even marketing. He inquired about temperature control in the canopies, soil reclamation, seed amelioration, and whether the flavor of the muskmelons was influenced by the soil. Fascinated, he praised the researchers for their achievements in such a harsh environment.

"The land and soil conditions in China's western region, such as in Gansu and Qinghai provinces, are similar to what you have here," Jiang told the Israeli scientists. "Your techniques of growing fruits and vegetables, including muskmelon and green pepper, are well worth studying by Chinese farmers."

Continuing his high-tech tour, Jiang visited several world-class companies, including ECI Telecom, a telecommunications leader that had installed fiber optic networks in most of China's provinces, including the longest fiber optic backbone network in the world that stretched 4,500 miles across rugged terrain in Inner Mongolia. For over a decade most international calls originating from China had been processed through ECI equipment. During his visit to their facilities, Jiang spoke with his office in China using ECI's Internet Protocol Telephony equipment.

In accord with the precise parallel plan, President Jiang then crossed over the blood-contested boundary and met with Palestinian president Yasser Arafat. Jiang reiterated his theme of friendship and peace, taking up, as it were, the mantle of an even-handed, high-minded mediator. At a special session of the Palestine Legislative Council in Bethlehem, Arafat seconded the goodwill, calling China "a faithful friend who never failed us or stopped supporting us for a single moment." In return, Jiang declared his country's continued belief in the Palestinian cause. "We wish that the people in this region will soon 'turn their swords into plowshares' and jointly build a beautiful future," he said. "The Chinese people will always be the trusted friends of the Palestinian people." After his speech, which was interrupted frequently by applause, Jiang wrote a message in the Council's visitors' book: "I wish Palestine an even more beautiful tomorrow!"

The president also made sure to enjoy himself. Visiting the Dead Sea, the lowest spot on earth, he took a leisurely float in its mineral-rich waters. Surrounded by aides and wearing a blue swim cap and goggles, Jiang spent fifteen minutes floating on his back in the salty, oily water, which is known for its legendary therapeutic powers. "Fantastic, fantastic," he said when he emerged, wrapping himself in a green robe.

Reflecting back three years later, Jiang expressed sorrow. "In April 2000 I visited Israel and Palestine," he said. "I spoke with many Israeli families and was touched by their situation. I finally came to understand why so many Jewish people have won Nobel prizes. I also spent a night with Arafat and the Palestinian leadership. The situation seemed hopeful then. Look at the region today [late 2003]. It has become bleak and desolate, a ruined place. No one wants to visit anymore."

In Turkey Jiang again referred to the old Silk Road that had facilitated the exchange of materials and ideas between East and West. It had also given rise to the Muslim minorities in China's western provinces, which Beijing considered potential threats to its national security. Receiving assurances from Turkey, a Muslim country, that it recognized China's sovereignty over those peoples was an achievement. As if underscoring this point, the Turkish speaker of parliament said that "under the leadership of President Jiang, China has become a bulwark of stability."

BACK AT HOME, JIANG gave a major speech in which, for the first time, he put Three Represents at the top of his public agenda. Speaking at a Party Construction Work Forum, Jiang called Three Represents "the essence of

the existence of our Party, the foundation of our ruling power, and the foun-
tainhead of our strength."

Notwithstanding Jiang's intensity, Three Represents still had opponents,
and the battle over its significance would have long-range consequences.
Amid rumors of leaked documents, internal investigations, and discussion of
"six kinds of errors" made by those who rejected Three Represents, critics
charged that Jiang's intention was to substitute his own Three Represents for
Deng Xiaoping Theory as the guiding ideology for the Party and army. The
charge was misleading, perhaps deliberately so, in that Jiang planned to extend Deng Theory, not replace it. What was truly being replaced, though no
one would come out and say it, was nineteenth-century Marxism and Maoistic
class struggle.

In response to resistance to Three Represents, the Party began to promote
the theory more aggressively. At various meetings of Party secretaries and
media people, Vice President Hu Jintao defended the idea with confidence
and vigor, saying, "Comrade Jiang Zemin's theory of Three Represents is a
development of Comrade Deng Xiaoping's theory on building a socialist road
with Chinese characteristics. We must overcome the interference caused by
all kinds of Leftist and Rightist thoughts."

IN MAY PRESIDENT JIANG hosted Philippine president Joseph Estrada on a
state visit to Beijing, and the two leaders agreed to resolve conflicting territorial claims in the South China Sea that had strained ties between their two
countries. The dispute was over a swath of islets and shoals known as the
Spratly Islands, which, exemplifying how complicated borders can be in Asia,
were also encumbered by overlapping claims from Brunei, Malaysia, Taiwan,
and Vietnam.

"During my meeting with President Jiang," Estrada said, "he reassured me
that China does not pose a threat to the Philippines."

More interesting to the Philippine media, the two presidents "sealed their
friendship not with a kiss but with a song." The usually staid, protocol-driven
banquets in the Great Hall of the People turned into a moment of bonding
between Jiang and Estrada, who had been a well-known actor before he entered public service.

The animated evening began when a Chinese musical group surprised
Estrada by playing "Kahit na Magtiis," the popular Filipino song about bearing the sufferings that have come one's way. Learning that the Philippine
president had written the song himself, Jiang good-naturedly goaded him

into singing it, then reciprocated by singing "O Sole Mio" and some Chinese and English songs. The Philippine delegation loved it.

On another positive note, the U.S. House of Representatives passed legislation authorizing permanent normal trade relations (PNTR) with China. In months of rancorous debate, those who opposed the legislation usually cited China's human rights abuses, but their underlying motivation was more often pressure from American labor unions, which feared cheaper labor costs overseas. Supporters of the bill argued that by opening China's domestic market to American products, American values would be exported as well. President Clinton had made PNTR a major initiative of his final year in office, but he needed Republican support to pass the bill, which was opposed by many in his own labor-oriented Democratic Party. Texas Republican Bill Archer, chairman of the House Ways and Means Committee, called the PNTR bill "the most important vote that we cast in our congressional careers."

The legislation then went to the Senate, where its passage was virtually assured, thus ending the twenty-year-old annual review of China's trade status and reinforcing U.S. support for China's entry into the WTO. By separating the issues of trade and human rights, the United States seemed finally to appreciate the Chinese sense of diplomacy, a move that would likely enhance American influence in the region, not diminish it, as PNTR opponents claimed.

A few days later Jiang telephoned Clinton to thank him for his support, but he also noted that Congress had added conditions that China could not afford to accept. Jiang remarked that Beijing-Washington ties "on the whole, have been steadily improving and developing," and the two leaders again agreed to cooperate in promoting the nonproliferation of nuclear weapons and the stabilization of the Korean peninsula. Clinton advised Jiang to seek face-to-face dialogue with Taiwan's new leader, Chen Shui-bian, while Jiang reminded Clinton that "properly" handling the Taiwan issue was the key to further improving bilateral relations.

On North Korea Jiang was caught in a conundrum. If North Korea did not reform its economy, it could collapse, creating untold collateral damage to China. At the same time China was North Korea's longtime ally and Jiang felt compelled to support the existing regime, led by strongman Kim Jong-Il, who had become North Korea's "Dear Leader" after the death of his father, Kim Il-Sung, North Korea's "Great Leader." Not only was loyalty at stake, but also credibility, since decades of Chinese propaganda had promoted the North Korean cause.

Privately, Jiang attempted to reason with Kim during a secret visit to Beijing, his first in seventeen years. Less than a month later Kim Jong-Il and President Kim Dae Jung of South Korea held the first inter-Korean summit in fifty-five years. Jiang may have catalyzed the pathbreaking event. In letters to the two leaders, the Chinese leader called them statesmen of "vision and wisdom" for their decision to meet. "I heartily rejoice at the complete success of the North-South summit and hereby extend my warm congratulations," he wrote to the North Korean leader. He expressed similar delight to Kim Dae Jung. Calling the meeting of "historic significance," Jiang said that China always supported peaceful reunification through dialogue and negotiation.

One sore spot in China's relations with America was Iran. In exchange for Iranian rejection of Muslim separatists, as well as for securing a stable source of imported oil for China's growing energy needs, Jiang's government had years before agreed to transfer to Iran some weapons technology, including antiship and antiaircraft missiles, as well as to develop a joint program for short-range ballistic missiles.

America declared that China's military assistance to Iran, which it labeled a state sponsor of international terrorism, was an obstacle to improving ties. Although China had curtailed its military assistance to Iran after 1997, in June Iranian president Seyyed Mohammad Khatami came to Beijing, where he was welcomed by President Jiang; Khatami's visit focused on trade but may also have led to renewed military aid.

REACHING OUT ACROSS the decades, Jiang sent flowers and a congratulatory telegram to Kuomintang General Zhang Xueliang in honor of his one hundredth birthday. Zhang was known for his role in bringing the Communists and the Kuomintang together in common cause against Japan, when he and another Nationalist general arrested their leader, Chiang Kai-shek, in an effort to force him to stop the civil war with the Communists and instead join them to fight the Japanese. Chiang was released unharmed after negotiations in which Zhou Enlai played a crucial role. General Zhang was later imprisoned by Chiang Kai-shek for his treason and spent decades under house arrest in Taiwan. Sixty-four years earlier the ten-year-old Jiang Zemin had written about (and lauded) the event as part of his secondary school entrance exams.

While Jiang was praising Zhang for his "distinguished and patriotic service," newly elected Taiwanese president Chen Shui-bian, who had just assumed office on May 20, was sending his own congratulatory message to the elderly general. Honored by both Communists and Nationalists, Zhang, then living in Hawaii, was perhaps a symbol of how the two sides could come together for common cause.

FOR JIANG, SCIENCE AND technology were a lifelong passion, and they became his driving force for accelerating China's development, including its military. Early in 2000 Jiang asked Dr. Song Jian to summarize "the history of social and industrial progress created by modern science." Jiang wanted to understand how scientific discoveries generate new products, new industries, and new areas of knowledge; for example, how quantum theory led to lasers, powerful medical diagnostics, and startling breakthroughs in astronomy and cosmology. In subsequent speeches Jiang noted that four scientific theories had revolutionized the world—relativity, quantum physics, genetics, and information science—not only expanding human knowledge but also having "a profound influence on political, economic, and cultural lives."

In June, at the closing ceremony of the annual combined conference of the prestigious Chinese Academy of Sciences and Chinese Academy of Engineering, President Jiang set a goal for China to be among the top ten nations in science and technology by 2010. "We have learned from the ups and downs in Chinese civilization," Jiang said, "that only development is the solid truth." Jiang encouraged China's science leaders to seek innovation in knowledge as well as in technology. "The nature of science is innovation," Jiang asserted, and he began to speak about Three Innovations—in economic structure, science and technology, and political theory—and for a time it seemed to be an emerging new element in his philosophy.

"President Jiang has two core developmental strategies," observed Planning Minister Zeng Peiyan. "The first is 'revitalizing China with science and education.' The second is sustainable development. To accomplish both, Jiang nurtured scientific creativity." In a preface for a series of science books, Jiang encouraged everyone to play a role in the process. "All of society must take part in advancing China through science education," he wrote.

Jiang Zemin received a mark of distinction when his long interview was featured in *Science* magazine, the leading professional scientific publication in the United States. He was also invited to write a guest editorial. To the man who had once hoped to become a professor of engineering, it was a milestone. No other national leader had been accepted by *Science* in quite this way.

"We recognize and respect the unique sensitivities and sensibilities of scientists," Jiang wrote in his *Science* editorial; "we understand that scientific creativity is the very source and lifeline of a knowledge-based economy."

In his interview, which was published in June, Jiang sounded two themes: China's strategy to rejuvenate the country through science, technology, and education, and China's contributions to the international science community. After detailing the rise and fall of scientific achievement in Chinese history, Jiang expressed his hope that the nation's glory days were not only in the past.

"My point is that, on the one hand, the Chinese people have every reason to be proud of their ancient tradition of civilization, but on the other hand, we should not stop learning—not even for a single day—from all the fine traditions of the world," he said. "Confucius once said, 'Whenever there are three people walking together, one of them is bound to be able to teach me something.' And Confucius also said that 'to say you know only if you know and to say you don't know when you don't, that is knowledge.' "

After discussing the excitement of basic research, the promise and danger of the Internet, and his own background as an engineer-turned-politician, Jiang concluded the interview on a wistful note. "One thing that I am rather envious of," he said, "is that Clinton, Chirac, Blair, and Schroeder are all of a younger age." It seemed the dawn of a promising new era, and Jiang knew that his time as a leader of it was limited.

Still, he was determined to keep pace. In August, at the Beidaihe seashore resort, he met with six world-renowned scientists, all foreign academicians of the Chinese Academy of Sciences, five of whom were Nobel laureates.

"Busy as he is, President Jiang makes time to meet with scientists and educators, and he makes friends with them, too," remarked Minister Zeng Peiyan. "He pays attention to leading-edge science and technology and recommends that those of us close to him do the same. Often he understands a scientific issue not just qualitatively, in its general sense, but quantitatively, with specific depth. When he has questions, we can't answer them; we have to call experts."

Even so, Jiang was not ashamed to admit to being in over his head from time to time. "I'm already of such an age that grandchildren ask me to help them with their schoolwork," he said, telling how one had asked for his help with an arithmetic problem. After quickly solving it using algebra, he was embarrassed to hear the child announce, "It is wrong." Jiang noted that he had then had to fall back on working out the problem numerically. "That almost beat me," he admitted. "It was not so easy."

The symbolism of the anecdote was not lost. "We must," Jiang said, "without the slightest hesitation, promote more younger cadres to key posts in the Party and the government."

Chapter 24

July – December 2000

"Chinese Spy or Not?"

JIANG HAD A KEEN interest in Russia. He had trained there in the 1950s and always loved its literature. As his own time was coming to a close, he was curious to see how the new Russian president, Vladimir Putin, would fare at the beginning of his.

On July 18 Putin paid his first visit to China. There had been indications that the "strategic partnership" between Russia and China, which Boris Yeltsin had promoted so heavily, was less important to the country's new leader. Jiang's staff had worked for weeks preparing agreements to be signed by the two presidents.

The most pointed agreement was a joint rejection of the American plan to develop a missile defense system. Accusing the United States of "striving for unilateral superiority" in military and security matters, the text said that this violation of the Anti-Ballistic Missile Treaty would lead to a new arms race and "a reversal of the positive trends in world politics that emerged after the Cold War."

Speaking to journalists, Jiang and Putin were careful not to suggest that China and Russia were establishing an anti-U.S. alliance. "I can describe my talks with President Putin as a pivotal conversation that inherits from the past and opens a new chapter for the future," Jiang said. Putin was even more effusive: "He speaks and sings in Russian, knows Russian poems and history. I must say I was amazed. It is good that people like him, who know and like Russia, are leading China now. Given this situation, I hope our cooperation will not be limited to economic and military sectors but will grow in the cultural field, too."

A statement from the talks asserted that the growing friendship between Russia and China "promotes the formation of a multipolar world and a new just, rational, international order." "Multipolar" was the code word meaning a world not dominated by the United States, but China's effort to align itself with Russia was primarily intended to prevent America from implementing its missile defense system, rather than to develop any permanent alliance. In the long term, Jiang knew that if the United States were to be contained in Asia, China would have to go it alone against the world's "peerless super-power."

IN EARLY SEPTEMBER 2000 the Millennium Summit was held at UN Head-quarters in New York with more than 150 heads of state in attendance, mak-ing it the largest gathering of world leaders in history. President Jiang's short address focused on safeguarding peace, promoting economic development, establishing a new world order, and strengthening the role of the UN.

Aside from the grand ceremonies, three unusual things emerged from Jiang's trip: a photograph, a cultural exhibition, and a very high-profile inter-view. Regarding the photo, a dramatic shot that was published widely, Jiang explained, "At the summit I invited the leaders of the other four permanent members of the UN Security Council—President Clinton, President Putin, Prime Minister Blair, and President Chirac—to come to my hotel. When we posed for a group photo, we all clasped hands. It was spontaneous—and I happened to have been standing in the center."

When a visitor weightily suggested that this photo symbolized China's reemergence into the center of world affairs (reflecting the Chinese word for China, Zhongguo, or "Middle Kingdom"), Jiang demurred. "I think," he joked, "it was because I was the oldest."

To coincide with Jiang's visit, Information Minister Zhao Qizheng pro-posed that China present a cultural extravaganza. Jiang approved, and Zhao organized a three-week exhibition called "Experience Chinese Culture in the United States, 2000," which included concerts of traditional Chinese music and a magnificent display of art and fashion at New York's Javits Center. The exhibition featured a 280-piece collection of Chinese paintings and sculpture, but clearly the crowd favorite was the fashion shows—full stages of folk and traditional garments followed by avant-garde offerings from chic designers. Pencil-thin Chinese supermodels showed off startling contemporary gowns, while clusters of elaborate and exotic costumes portrayed China's numerous minority groups.

Jiang wrote, "Through this window, people in the United States may have a glimpse of China's splendid and uninterrupted civilization of thousands of years as well as the Chinese people's new cultural creations and attainments based on the fine cultural traditions of their ancestors."

Even critics called the Chinese president's trip "unusually well-planned." But one more public event was needed, and Jiang made a bold and unprecedented move by inviting the notoriously hard-hitting Mike Wallace to interview him for CBS's *60 Minutes,* America's highest-rated television newsmagazine. There would be no restrictions on Wallace's questions. Jiang's advisers were nervous.

As the interview was edited, Jiang began by reminiscing in English about the first time he and Wallace met, back in 1986, when he had been mayor of Shanghai. He added, still in English, "I hope to convey through your program my best wishes to the American people."

In addition to general queries about human rights and totalitarian rule, Wallace bored in on specific sensitive areas. On the embassy bombing in Belgrade, Jiang maneuvered deftly between not alienating the American public and not contradicting Chinese policy.

"Do you still think today the United States intentionally bombed the Chinese embassy in Belgrade?" Wallace asked.

"I can only put it the other way round," Jiang replied, evading the trap. "The United States is a country that possesses technology at a very high level. Therefore, up to the present, the U.S. explanation of 'bombing by mistake' is not convincing."

At the same time, he alluded to his own government's role, not in instigating the protests that followed, as many Americans believed, but in controlling them. "We guided the anger of over 1.2 billion people onto the track of reason," Jiang said, repeating his words to President Clinton at the time of the bombing. "This was not at all easy." Then he added diplomatically, "It is mainly because you represent the Americans, and I represent the Chinese— I'm afraid that it will not be easy at all for us to come to the same understanding of this incident."

Calling for a "constructive strategic partnership" between China and the United States, Jiang used a meteorological metaphor to portray the ups and downs of Sino-American relations: "Of course, like natural phenomena, sometimes there is wind and rain, sometimes it is cloudy, sometimes the sky is even covered with dark clouds, and sometimes it changes from cloudy to fair."

Turning up the heat, Wallace asked Jiang if he agreed with a Chinese newspaper that described the United States as a threat to world peace.

"I do not like to use too much harsh language," Jiang said after expressing his desire to enhance "mutual friendship and understanding." He then explained, "You have developed your economy so much and you have developed your science and technology so much that you are in a kind of relatively high and advantageous position. As a result, you often may take an attitude of not treating other countries very equally. I would like to speak frankly and sincerely . . . the United States perhaps often overestimates itself. What I mean is those in power in the United States are perhaps tinged with hegemony and power politics."

Since Jiang so admired Lincoln's Gettysburg Address, Wallace asked Jiang, why didn't Lincoln's ideal government "of the people, by the people, for the people" apply to China? Why didn't China allow free elections of its national leaders?

Jiang said that what Lincoln described had not yet been realized even in the United States but "still remains the goal of American leaders today." He then added, "I am also an elected leader, though we have a different electoral system. Each country should have its own system, because our two countries have different cultures and historic traditions, and different levels of education and economic development."

Wallace tried to unnerve Jiang with what he thought was a derogatory Chinese metaphor about Jiang's well-disguised sharpness: "One of the reasons for your success is 'hiding needles in cotton,' as described by some people. Is this the secret of your success?"

Jiang answered, "In China, hiding needles in cotton is a very positive expression to praise others. Such an assessment was given to our former leader, Deng Xiaoping. I cannot be compared with him. However, I can say I am quite a decisive character. This is certain. Eleven years have passed since I became the general secretary, and I have stuck to the faith that I will always do my best to work for our country and motherland. Perhaps my diligent work has earned me the assessment you mentioned."

Wallace used humor in an attempt to score points. When Jiang said, "I have a lot of friends among the leaders of both parties, Republican and Democrat," Wallace retorted, "So you give money to both their campaigns?"

Jiang turned serious. "Are you just joking? We have never done such things. I have read the campaign platforms of both parties, and whoever becomes president will be friendly [to China] because this is in the strategic interests of the whole world." When Wallace thrust with "That's spoken as a true politician; there's no candor in it," Jiang parried with "I don't think that *politician* is a very nice word." Later he remarked in accented but understandable English that he was counseled "not to pay attention to the unfriendly remarks candidates might make about China during the campaigns, because once elected they will be friendly," adding, "I only hope that's true."

There were moments of tension. When Wallace accused Jiang of being a dictator, the Chinese leader retorted, "Your way of describing what things are like in China is as absurd as what the *Arabian Nights* may sound like." As anyone who understood Chinese politics knew, Jiang had to abide by the decisions of the majority of his high-ego colleagues on the Politburo Standing Committee. That China was not a democracy in the Western sense was clear, but neither was it a dictatorship.

One awkward but riveting moment occurred when Wallace asked Jiang about Wen Ho Lee, the Chinese-American nuclear scientist accused of spying for China.

"You seem defensive for the first time in this interview," Wallace said. "I sense this is a difficult subject for you."

"No," said Jiang in English, "not difficult for me. This is your feeling." Then he turned the question around on the interviewer. "What do you think?" Jiang asked.

"I'm not supposed to think," Wallace answered.

Jiang began to smile. "Chinese spy or not?" he said.

"What do I think?"

Jiang smiled even more broadly. "That's right."

Wallace sat in silence. In the outside world, doubt was already being cast on the case, which would end with an apology to Lee and a rebuke to the government.

"You will consider carefully," Jiang said.

"I am considering carefully," Wallace replied. "You stopped me."

Still speaking English, Jiang continued: "This is the first time I discover your face [having] difficulty to answer the question."

"Yes, that's true," Wallace admitted. "I probably shouldn't answer it."

By the time the show aired, Wallace had edited in a wry voiceover. "If there was any time to change the subject," he intoned, "this was it."

Wallace's next choice of topic was Tiananmen Square, a move designed to put Jiang on the defensive. But when he caught Wallace off guard with his response, he did the same to some colleagues in Beijing.

"In the 1989 disturbances we truly understood the passion of students who were calling for greater democracy and freedom," he said. "In fact, we have always been working to improve our system of democracy."

It was the first time that a senior Chinese leader still in office had publicly expressed any sort of sympathy for the students. By using the ambiguous term "disturbances," Jiang was distancing himself from the more negative, inflammatory descriptions—such as "counterrevolution," "riot," and "turmoil"—that had prevailed previously. And by referring to "our system of democracy," the president was implying that while China's definition of democracy might not coincide with America's, that did not mean that some form of it did not (or should not) exist.

Wallace asked about the never-identified protester who had halted a column of tanks with his outstretched hand and paper shopping bag. That iconic photo, wired around the world, had become the enduring image of Tiananmen.

"I don't know where he is now," Jiang responded. "Looking at the picture, I know he definitely had his own ideas."

When Wallace pressed the issue, Jiang replied sharply. "I know what you are driving at," he said, "but what I want to emphasize is that we fully respect every citizen's right to fully express his wishes and desires. But I do not favor any flagrant opposition to government actions during an emergency. The tank stopped and did not run the young man down." Jiang observed that the man had not been arrested, but he left ambiguous whether he had ever been identified.

In his short, direct, even poignant statements about Tiananmen, Jiang was giving notice that the unfortunate events of June 4, 1989, should no longer be a stumbling block among people of goodwill. His apparent willingness to address the issue in a fresh way was a small step in the long process of healing the still-open wound.

Jiang endeared himself to his audience by taking on the unlikely role, for a leader of 1.2 billion people, of David to Wallace's Goliath. Viewers loved it when Wallace complained that Jiang's answers were too long, and the president shot back that his answers were the same length as Wallace's questions. If Wallace wanted shorter answers, Jiang quipped, he should ask shorter questions!

Avuncular and plainspoken, with black glasses framing expressive eyes, the Chinese president seemed to be enjoying himself, even when the probes went deep. Never one to turn his back on a captive audience, he serenaded

Wallace with "Song of Graduation," a protest song from his youth. He was also eager to employ his far-from-perfect English without self-consciousness. Nor did he hide his pride and pleasure in being able to recite Lincoln's Gettysburg Address.

Going one on one with Mike Wallace was daring and dangerous—surely surprising for a Chinese leader. Jiang was exposed to a fusillade of verbal indignities, but it was precisely his vulnerability, and his presence under stress, that made for such good television. Jiang struck the right tone—engaging, down to earth, open, unpretentious, and never ducking a question. He made himself likable, and America liked him.

In this one appearance, Jiang reached millions of people, more than any Chinese leader ever had, and by showing that he was a personable, approachable, even vulnerable human being, Jiang caused some viewers to question their doctrinaire image of China, long stereotyped by the American media as a rigid, oppressive dictatorship antagonistic to the United States. The *Washington Post* called Jiang Zemin's *60 Minutes* interview the "Pick of the Week" of all American television programs. Some called it the single best presentation of China ever made to the American public.

Perhaps the highest accolade came from media maven Bill Clinton. Chatting with Jiang before lunch at the UN, where heads of state had gathered for the Millennium Summit, Clinton praised his performance. "I see you've taken American television by storm," he said. "Mike Wallace is so mean to all the rest of us. He's purring like a little child [with you]. I saw it; it was great." Clinton smiled and added, "I'm so jealous."

Jiang and Clinton met again, more formally, at the Waldorf-Astoria Hotel. Clinton agreed that the new Taiwanese leader had retrogressed on the "one China" stance. When asked about China's repression of religion, Jiang insisted that China was not repressive. Reaching back into history, he reminded Clinton that Christianity in China carried a lot of "baggage" due to its association with Western "humiliations." He said that Christianity had come along with foreign incursions into China, which he compared unfavorably to the introduction of Buddhism and Islam.

After meeting with Clinton, President Jiang lunched with three hundred of New York's A-list personalities, including Henry Kissinger, New Jersey governor Christine Whitman, and numerous business leaders. Jiang was relaxed and gregarious as he worked the room, clinking glasses and renewing friendships. He delivered his forty-five-minute speech, which focused on China's domestic progress and human rights, entirely in English—better, the host joked, than

Clinton could have done in Chinese. Speaking of Clinton, normally the center of attention, one wondered how he felt leaving the Waldorf that day, knowing that New York's high and mighty had come to dine with Jiang Zemin, not him.

The next evening Jiang came to Lincoln Center to attend a concert by the China National Traditional Orchestra. At a packed preconcert reception, Jiang saw an old friend, real estate tycoon Nina Kung Wang, chairwoman of Hong Kong's largest private company, who stood out in the crowd of dark-suited corporate executives in her royal blue, classical Chinese dress. The controversial pig-tailed Wang, who has been called the richest woman in Asia, began peppering Jiang with comments about education in China, one of her many charitable projects. In the bustle, Jiang's only response was to notice her new hairstyle.

While in New York, Jiang told six hundred overseas Chinese that he would step down from his positions as Party general secretary and state president at the end of his current terms. "I would like to ride on the wind," he said, a phrase that echoed the desire of a Song dynasty poet named Su Shi to retire from public service. Jiang mused that he would like to again enjoy the freedom he had lost while being a state leader. He did not mention his third post as chairman of the Central Military Commission.

Yet at a meeting of non-Communist parties in Beijing, Li Ruihuan declared that no final decisions on future Party leadership had been made. "Quite a few people inside and outside the Party and inside the military hope that Jiang will remain in office and concentrate more energy on Party building, the development of Party theory, and army building," he said. "They also hope that Zhu Rongji will retain his post as premier in order to advance state enterprise and financial reforms more satisfactorily."

A FEW WEEKS LATER, as if in counterpoint to his stellar performance on 60 Minutes, Jiang lost his temper at a press conference in Beijing. The incident occurred when he was asked by a Hong Kong reporter whether his support for Tung Chee-hwa's second term as Hong Kong chief executive constituted an "imperial order."

Thrusting his finger into the air and turning red, Jiang ranted at the man. "You cannot create an uproar and then claim it is big news," Jiang said, referring to Beijing's apparent endorsement of Tung's reelection. "Don't think you can start criticizing me that I have 'secretly appointed' Mr. Tung just to get a big story [for yourself]. . . .

"I do not say he is the 'imperial choice,' " Jiang continued, obviously angry at the loaded phrase. "There is no such thinking at all. You can't say we have any 'imperial order' and then criticize me [for your own expression].

"You media need to brush up your general knowledge level," Jiang added, continuing to jab his fingers as if the reporters were errant students in need of a lecture. "Got it? You [Hong Kong] guys are only good at one thing. You go to every corner of the world [to cover stories] and can run faster than Western reporters.

"But the questions you keep asking are too simple and sometimes naïve. Understand it or not? Got it? I'm sorry I have to tell you this in the capacity of an elder person. I am not a journalist, but I must tell you the truth about life."

Jiang had a proverb. "There is a Chinese saying," he said, " 'Keeping quiet would make a man rich.' But since you are so warm about [interested in] this matter, it would not be good if I didn't say anything. I can always say 'no comment,' but you all will be unhappy." Overtly frustrated, Jiang admitted, "I've fought 100 battles already; I've seen a lot."

Though the West would view the story as an amusing anecdote, in Hong Kong, where the local population lived in suspicion of Beijing, it would be labeled "the most striking news story of the year."

In the course of the brief brouhaha, the Chinese president compared the Hong Kong journalistic corps unfavorably to Mike Wallace, who, Jiang said, had challenged him but had maintained a good spirit. They had talked freely, laughed, and even joked, he said. Mike Wallace, the standard of decorum? Was this the first time in the octogenarian's long career that he had been "accused" of being fair? Would Jiang's respectful review hurt Wallace's rapier reputation?

A spokesman for Wallace said the *60 Minutes* veteran had seen a transcript of Jiang's comments and took them as a "compliment." The spokesman said, "If anyone thinks something else, they only have to look at the interview . . . It is pretty clear we asked all the tough questions. You can still ask a leader tough questions and keep normal relations."

Not everyone thought Jiang's encounter with Wallace went well. Back in Beijing, some high-level officials complained that it was inappropriate and unseemly for Jiang, as China's head of state, to be "exposed" to the brusque, goading assault of Wallace's questioning, to suffer such "indignities." They felt it was not a small matter and they criticized Jiang for having done it and his people for having arranged it. They were unhappy, too, about Jiang's independent, unauthorized comments about Tiananmen Square. Others, perhaps those with more international appreciation (and less identified with

June 4, 1989), were pleased and proud of how well their president had handled the tough American media. They argued that Jiang's openness and warmth under pressure, and the clarity and directness of his responses, enhanced his likability and credibility, and that the impression he made on millions of Americans improved China's national image more than had any other public relations event in memory. The American press was nearly unanimous in supporting the latter view.

Li Peng, who had ordered martial law in Tiananmen eleven years earlier, was taken aback that Jiang had "understood" the "passion of students." " 'The Party leadership several years ago reached the consensus that the Party's verdict on the June 4 events should remain intact,' " one source quoted Li as saying, " 'Moreover, the official assessment can only be changed after a decision collectively made by members of the Politburo Standing Committee.' "

Procedurally, Li Peng was correct. It is a cardinal principle of China's collective leadership system that major policy decisions must be approved by the Party's senior leadership, and Li exploited the fact that Jiang was caught committing this bureaucratic shortcut. At a meeting of the Politburo Standing Committee, Li effected a resolution that called for a strongly worded assertion, on behalf of the CPC Central Committee, that the Party's past judgment on Tiananmen was not only correct, it was also inviolate. He wanted to make as sure as possible that, come what might, the judgment on Tiananmen could not be reversed.

A directive was sent out to all senior-level ministers and provincial leaders affirming the correctness of the original judgment of the events of Tiananmen and now making it permanent. To support the decision, a four-hour videotape was prepared that purported to prove the ulterior motivation of the students to foment turmoil and overthrow the government in the "counterrevolutionary" movement. When Xinhua published the transcript of Jiang's *60 Minutes* interview, his comments on June 4 were removed, as was the exchange over whether the U.S. bombing of the Chinese embassy was an accident.

Also extirpated were his pensive, self-deprecating reflections on assuming national office in 1989: "I was not prepared to become the leader of all China. I hoped that a more capable and appropriate person could be considered. In the end, Deng Xiaoping and other leaders of the older generation thought that I was appropriate," Jiang concluded. "I can only bend my back to the task to my dying day."

IN THE XIAMEN SMUGGLING CASE, the largest in Chinese history, China wrangled with Canada over extraditing the criminal ringleader, since Canada did not extradite suspects to countries where they might be executed. Zhu Rongji, who spearheaded the investigation, voiced frustration at the slow pace. "Regarding this case," he said impetuously, "even if President Jiang Zemin is involved, we would pursue it up to his level." To Zhu's chagrin, it would be an oft-quoted sentence.

In September Chen Kejie, a former NPC vice chairman, was executed for taking bribes—the highest Party official ever to be put to death for his crimes. Jiang had faced high-level pressure to commute Chen's sentence, but his resolute refusal boosted his popularity with the people. Jiang believed that only harsh punishment ("striking hard"), along with education and system reform, could root out corruption. In October auditors announced that they had discovered $11 billion in mismanaged funds in Chinese government offices and businesses. The battle against corruption seemed never-ending.

Jiang sought solace by calling Shen Yongyan. If Jiang wanted to relax after a grinding day, he picked the wrong time and the wrong friend, because what he got was more grinding. "China is facing hard issues," Shen began. Jiang asked him to elaborate and then listened patiently while he did.

Shen summarized what he said were China's four primary problems. First, hopeless corruption. Second, worsening unemployment. Third, strange and ugly social phenomena. Fourth, disparity between rich and poor. Shen had been thinking about these four problems for a year and was waiting for the right time to present them.

Jiang requested examples, and Shen started with the third category. "When I was visiting Hainan province," he told Jiang, "I needed a haircut. My friends told me that over half of the barbershops and beauty salons were actually whorehouses, the hairstyling being just a front, a cover-up for prostitution. I was told, when you go to a beauty salon, check if there are private rooms. If there are, get out."

Jiang, who hears these kinds of stories all the time, agreed with Shen on his first three categories of problems, but as to the last—the increasing gap between rich and poor—he took issue. "When Deng Xiaoping initially decided to let one segment of the population get rich first," he said, "everyone knew that income disparity would be a natural byproduct—it was inevitable. But our expectation was that entrepreneurs, by creating new products and starting new businesses, would lift up the entire population by providing more jobs with better pay and by offering an increasing variety of goods and services that would be available to everyone. It is government's role to take care of the less fortunate, to redistribute income, to find a better balance between rich and poor, and to stop illegal moneymaking. The system is hardly perfect, but it does work. I don't know what's better—certainly not the old way where nobody had anything."

A PLEASANT TOPIC ON Jiang's agenda in September was the Olympic Games, which were being held in Sydney, Australia. When Chinese athletes returned home with twenty-eight gold medals—the best results in Chinese history and the third best in the world—the president exulted. "The people across the country are filled with joy," Jiang told the medal winners. "You have shown the great confidence and strength of the Chinese nation to stand on its own feet among the world of nations."

Jiang was referring to more than just medals. Earlier in September he had sent a formal letter to the International Olympic Committee endorsing Beijing's bid to host the 2008 Olympic Games. "With the support of the Chinese government and all of the Chinese people," he wrote, "I firmly believe that Beijing will make extraordinary efforts and definitely will make the 2008 Olympic Games high-standard ones."

Almost as a defining characteristic, Jiang had always been a patriot, and his desire that China host the Olympics was another expression of his nationalistic pride. That fall two other incidents spoke to the same sentiment. Both centered on China's civilization; one was about the past but involved the future; the other was about the future but involved the past.

In November Chinese scholars announced with great fanfare that scientific dating of ancient artifacts had pushed back the earliest Chinese dynasties more than a thousand years into the third millenium B.C., putting ancient China in the same chronological era as ancient Egypt. Called the Xia-Shang-Zhou Chronology Project (named for the three earliest dynasties), the five-year research effort focused on discerning the timelines of these dynasties and involved two hundred scholars in archaeology, ancient inscriptions, astronomical history, and early manuscripts. The founding date for the Xia dynasty was set at 2070 B.C., although later reports would have it even earlier, at around 2200 B.C. Not surprisingly, Chinese media trumpeted the news.

No sooner had the announcement been made, however, than other scholars, largely foreign, began questioning both the science and the motivation. Accusing the Chinese of rushing toward a forced and perhaps predetermined conclusion, foreign critics charged mainland scholars with giving "an illusion of consensus" and, worse, outright chauvinism. "It's much more a political and nationalistic urge than a scholarly one," asserted an American historian. It did Chinese credibility no good when one scholar felt compelled to credit "the superiority of socialism to develop a multidisciplinary approach" as a reason for the Chronology Project's success.

Other foreign scholars defended their Chinese colleagues, praising the intense commitment to study ancient history and accusing the accusers of having "vested interests" in their own chronological reconstructions. An academic donnybrook ensued. The Chinese media, predictably, were incensed.

In the summer of 2000 an article had criticized the project as "providing fuel for a potentially dangerous form of nationalism in China" and targeted the project leader, Dr. Song Jian, who, it claimed, had "suggested the project as a way of mining the country's past to shore up its present leadership." Song, a former state councilor, had authorized the Chronology Project in 1995.

In actuality, Song was a true scientist, perhaps the only one among China's senior leaders. He had made contributions to the fields of cybernetics, control theory, and applied mathematics and was considered the founder of the country's environmental movement. In explaining his reason for initiating the Chronology Project, Song wrote, "A history without chronology is not history at all. It can only be called rumor or myth."

"Don't worry about the criticism," Jiang Zemin counseled the always-elegant Song Jian. "Just do good research." The Chinese president stressed, "We will be faithful to the highest level of scholarship," and he issued a proscription: "Neither the Party nor the government should comment on this project. The Chronology is purely scientific."

The second controversial project was the new China National Grand Theater or Beijing Opera House, a futuristic design planned for a site just west of the Great Hall of the People next to Tiananmen Square. Designed by a French architect, Paul Andreu, the basic shape was an enormous, gleaming egglike dome 220 meters long, 150 meters wide, and 49 meters high, all of it floating on an artificial lake. The theater's unusual roof, made of a glass and titanium composite material, would have two visually distinctive sections. It was a startling design, appearing as if a gigantic droplet of water had welled up from the center of the lake or a UFO had landed on its surface. The edifice would house a 2,416-seat opera hall, a 2,017-seat concert hall, and a

1,040-seat auditorium for dramas. Visitors would enter through a transparent tunnel under the lake, which would be surrounded with grass and trees. Opera fan Jiang Zemin, who wanted to make a bold statement about China's modernity, had backed the unexpected winning design.

The scheduled completion date was late 2002, just as Jiang's term of leadership would be coming to a close. But in June 2000 more than a hundred Chinese architects petitioned the government to stop construction of the Grand Theater, which was said to cost between $300 million and $400 million. "If this opera house is built," the petition read, "we will be blamed for years to come and will become the laughingstock of international public opinion, while the reputation of our government will be ruined." In addition to objecting to the high cost, the architects argued that the arresting modern design was incongruous with the traditional style of nearby structures. Admirers called the unusual structure a "pearl." To detractors, it was an "alien egg," hatched, as it were, "within the sight-lines of the Great Hall of the People, Tiananmen Square, and the Forbidden City, the country's most enduring monuments."

The government announced that rumors of the construction being stopped were "nonsense," but after three petitions of architectural outrage, construction was stopped cold. The outcry suspended the project for over a year. The Politburo Standing Committee held several meetings on the matter, and in the end Jiang himself made the final decision to allow the National Theater to go forward. In the fall of 2001 construction was restarted, with completion targeted for the end of 2004.

From the southern tip of Zhongnanhai, where Jiang Zemin liked to view the moon and its reflection on the South Lake, one could look across the waters and see the breathtaking edifice rising. Abutting the Great Hall of the People, the National Grand Theater symbolized China's new thinking—pioneering, contemporary innovation anchored in enduring history and tradition.

THROUGHOUT HIS CAREER JIANG has had a passion for information, for accessing raw data. As an engineer, he dealt with problems. If a power plant shut down, what were the readings? If a production line was not operating efficiently, what were the bottlenecks? As a political leader, he also dealt with problems. For example, how would China's entry into the WTO affect environmental pollution? What were the forecasts? What was the experience of other countries?

As state president, Party general secretary, and CMC chairman, Jiang had multiple channels for receiving information. In addition, his personal office had numerous sources of input and advice, including the country's leading research institutes, think tanks, and academic institutions. But for Jiang Zemin, even all this was not enough.

Jiang likes fresh perspectives, those devoid of political spin and personal concerns, and he likes going outside of official channels and around the system to get them. Jiang reaches out to people he trusts, such as his longtime confidant Wang Huijiong.

A wiry man with a quick mind and a fast tongue, Professor Wang is a senior researcher at the prestigious Development Research Center of the State Council, China's top think tank for policy analysis. He is well traveled and astute, yet down to earth and unassuming, with interests that have included economic development, sustainability, energy policy, finance policy, urban poverty, technology transfer, and U.S. relations. Trained as a systems engineer, Wang studies these kinds of complex issues methodically and holistically, an approach that resonates well with Jiang. Wang is fluent in English and sensitive to Western ways; he has consulted for the World Bank, and his two daughters, the older a computer engineer, the younger an intellectual property attorney, live and work near Washington, D.C. Although he is in his late seventies, Wang attends up to ten international conferences a year.

"When I learn important new things, especially from outside China, I send the information directly to President Jiang," said Wang. "Since few people know that Jiang is my friend, no one tries to impress me. I get him the facts; what he does with them is his business." . . .

"Jiang gets my unrestrained opinions on all subjects," Wang, a natural intellectual, went on. "I have nothing to gain, no agenda to promote, no position I'm seeking. We're old, old friends. I give him an honest assessment— the facts as they really are—particularly about Western ways and thinking. I distinguish between fact and opinion, but I do not give him political advice. I've never been involved in politics; I'm an academic. . . .

"A scholar can be frank," Wang continued. "Top leadership must deal with emotions and unanticipated reactions. Jiang needs just-in-time information, the latest developments; he must get multiple points of view."

"I sometimes telephone Professor Wang to ask him questions," Jiang told friends. "The topics are usually in economics, perhaps about sustainable development and the environment, but they could be about almost anything." Jiang is proud of his deep-thinking, self-effacing friend, and he has told his Politburo colleagues about "my classmate, Wang Huijiong."

When Jiang invites Wang to his home, usually in the early evening, it's often just the two of them enjoying long talks that last through dinners of simple Yangzhou-style food. "When Jiang and I get together," said Wang, "we're just old friends relaxing; our discussions range very freely. He differs from other senior leaders in that he has broad interests in culture, history, science, and social science. He doesn't dwell on the past. He particularly likes science and philosophy. Sometimes we joke about important topics, the way longtime friends do in private; of course we realize that serious subjects are really serious, but nonetheless a joke once in while can give a fresh perspective."

Wang smiled as he described a meal: "We eat with chopsticks, of course. Sometimes, if a grain of rice falls onto the table, President Jiang uses his chopsticks to pick that grain up and redeposit it in the bowl. 'We must respect the hard work of our farmers,' he says."

Another person whom Jiang occasionally asks for advice is Dr. Song Jian, who for more than ten years was head of all science and technology in China. "I enjoy speaking with President Jiang because he has such a thirst to explore new ideas," said Song. "He calls me with specific questions, or just to discuss some topic. Once he asked why the world exists in three dimensions. I went to his office and for an hour discussed Riemannian [non-Euclidean] geometry and N-dimensional space! There aren't many world leaders interested in such subjects. Later, speaking to a group of mathematicians, Jiang joked, 'You people think in many dimensions; I still have to live in only three.' "

"President Jiang will ring me at home after 10:00 P.M.," continued Song. "I am never surprised to receive his call. Recently, he asked about the divergent physics of Newton and Einstein, and how quantum mechanics relates to each."

Once Jiang posed what sounded like a chicken-and-egg question. "'Which comes first,'" he inquired of Song, "'theory or practice?' There are different opinions on this, I know: whether theory guides practice to make it more efficient, or practice develops theory to make it more real."

"Actually, it's a profound question," commented Song. "Jiang was thinking practically, as an engineer, but I needed to research the subject." Although Song took the question in a scientific context, Jiang may also have had political theory on his mind.

"I told President Jiang that I agree with modern philosophy," concluded Song, weeks later. "Practice comes before theory: real world data is what we use to induce our theories, which are then tested against new data to confirm or refute them. The process is called 'induction,' where science develops general principles to explain observed instances. So although theory and practice work together, practice does come first."

Jiang thought for a moment, then agreed, pleased to see how seemingly paradoxical questions can be answered.

"Often when we attend a social or political function together," added Song, "he'll come over to me and ask, 'Have you heard any new theories? Don't keep me in ignorance!' Jiang, it seems, is interested in hot science the way some people are interested in hot gossip.

"It has been so invigorating for scientists and intellectuals under President Jiang," explained Song. "Foreigners can't imagine what it was like living through decades of anti-intellectualism, especially during the Cultural Revolution. We heard absurd slogans, such as 'Don't read books; the more books you read, the more stupid you become,' and 'Mother is close; father is close; Mao is closer.' President Jiang has been a source of enlightenment. That is why the scientific community has been among his strongest supporters—particularly for his theory of Three Represents, which promotes 'advanced productive forces.' "

If one knows a man by his friends, Wang Huijiong and Song Jian bear fine witness for Jiang Zemin.

Another old friend is Henry Kissinger. "When we've met over the years," Kissinger reflected, "President Jiang has explained his perception of China's domestic evolution, without particularly asking for my comments. He said that if there were chaos in China, the country could never develop its socialist market economy and there would be unpredictable international fallout. President Jiang would always listen intently to whatever I had to say, without agreeing or disagreeing, and then on occasion, he might later do something akin to what I had suggested."

The friendship between Jiang Zemin and Tong Zonghai, Jiang's college roommate and the person who found him his first job, has remained unaltered for over half a century. Due to difficult times, Jiang and Tong had no contact for years after they separated in 1948. They met briefly around 1952 in Beijing, when Jiang was visiting on business. "Jiang came to the Ministry of Energy Industry, where I was working with Soviet engineers," said Tong. "We embraced and caught up with our lives and families. We wanted to have dinner together, but neither of us could afford a restaurant. . . .

"President Jiang is just like he always was," Tong remarked. "When we meet, we talk about old friends and comrades—like Li Enyu—where they are, what happened to them. I tell him things he might not know, and he tells me things I surely don't know. For example, Jiang told me what he learned about the Nanjing antidrug campaign of 1943, how the underground Communists exploited the conflict between the Japanese and the Chinese puppet government to build their own power. I had absolutely no clue that the Communist Party was using and taking advantage of the campaign until Jiang told me. He didn't know back then, either; we participated in the demonstrations out of conviction and passion, simply because we believed that it was the right thing to do for our country. After fifty years we marveled how dangerous that march had been; it would have meant nothing for the Japanese military police to shoot us. . . .

"That antidrug campaign was a turning point in our lives," explained Tong. "We could finally express our feelings; our social awareness expanded, our student ties strengthened. Without movements like this, it would have been impossible for students to join forces and fight the Kuomintang in the civil war. Jiang has always been skilled in getting comrades to work together. I had several photographs of Jiang and me from our student days, such as our graduation pictures together, but because the baccalaureate robes we wore were labeled 'foreign' by radical leftists, during the Cultural Revolution they destroyed all but one."

Chapter 25

JANUARY – JULY 2001

"My Life Was Closely Associated with Almost Three-Quarters of the Last Century"

PRESIDENT JIANG LIKED TO WELCOME the New Year by broadcasting greetings around the world in different languages. He recorded short, cheerful messages in English, Russian, Japanese, Spanish, and perhaps others that were broadcast on China Central Television's international channel and on China Radio International. Jiang believed in the power of speaking with people in their native tongue, and he was sensitive to the nuances in something as simple as New Year's good wishes Therefore he was not happy when, rehearsing his lines at home in Zhongnanhai, he saw the Italian greeting scroll across the TelePrompTer. To his dismay, the words, chosen by others, seemed canned and generic.

Jiang headed for his library, where he leafed through several Italian books, mouthing words and testing out phrases, searching for an appropriate way to articulate his feelings. In the end, he chose to recite a traditional poem.

Throughout his career Jiang often used poetry to make points, express emotions, and highlight culture. At one point he exchanged poems with French president Jacques Chirac, copying them out in his own calligraphy. *People's Daily* published two four-line poems written by Jiang for the 1998 National People's Congress to express his hopes for a better future. He used the awakening of spring after a severe winter as a metaphor for China's emergence from its protracted problems.

> *The sun peeps out from snow-clad willows by the ice-covered river,*
> *Jadelike trees and flowers fete my eyes with spring.*
> *The scene, like a heavenly painting painstakingly drawn by nature,*
> *Tells that everything in the world comes from hard work.*

As 2001 DAWNED, the issue of Tiananmen Square was again in the news with the publication of *The Tiananmen Papers,* which purported to be the inside story, based on purloined Party documents, of the machinations at the top of the Communist Party during the 1989 protests. The vividly detailed, day-by-day revelation of events leading up to June 4 made headlines in the foreign press. One charge was that Jiang Zemin had gained "supreme power" through "a constitutionally irregular procedure," the revelation of which, the editors claimed, would "undercut" his authority, a prognostication not borne out by subsequent events. Ironically, the publication may have resuscitated the political fortunes of Li Peng, who, it was reported, took the offensive, asserting that the book was part of an "international conspiracy" to overthrow the Party.

An official Chinese spokesman rejected the work as fake, repeating that the Party and the government "had already made a correct conclusion about the political disturbances that took place in Beijing . . . and that the conclusion would not change."

In February, Jiang convened a Central Committee Work Conference, where in addition to discussing his new vision for the Communist Party (Three Represents), each member of the Politburo Standing Committee gave a public affirmation of support for ("reveal his attitude" on) two sensitive policies: Jiang's campaign to eradicate the Falun Gong cult, for which Party and public interest had been lagging; and the "correctness of the Party's verdict" on the events of June 4, 1989, which related to the publication of *The Tiananmen Papers.* Each senior leader declared that had it not been for the government's resolute actions against the demonstrators, stability could not have been ensured and China's economy would not have flourished.

Yet a more balanced view of the terrible events in Tiananmen Square also seemed to be emerging. Time had provided perspective, even among former student protesters themselves.

FOR JIANG ZEMIN, JANUARY's highlight was a special reception that he hosted in Zhongnanhai for about twenty of his old classmates and their spouses. It fulfilled a promise made seven years earlier, when he had told Wang Huijiong that he had could not attend a similar reunion in Beijing. "Please convey my apologies to our classmates," Jiang said to Wang. "Tell them that my position makes it very difficult, but I promise to attend a future reunion."

Over the years Jiang would occasionally lament that he still had not made it to any of the reunions. "Our old friends must think it's because of my 'high position' that I choose not to attend," Jiang told Wang. "This is not the case; it's just that every time I've been occupied with some event or circumstance. But I must keep my promise."

At 3:00 P.M. on the first Saturday of the year, the reunion was held. It lasted until 9:00 P.M., when government cars took everyone home. The old friends sang songs together, including "One Day When We Were Young." Jiang and his wife posed for pictures with each classmate and spouse. "In Chinese traditional morality, keeping one's promise is an important virtue," Wang commented.

When one classmate died several months later, Jiang called the man's wife to offer his condolences, even though he had only met her at the reunion. Wang later told Jiang of a seriously infirm classmate who had never married and was without relatives; he had been confined to a nursing home in far-off Yunnan province. Jiang called local officials and requested that they improve his care, even though he remembered only the man's name, not his face. "That was so typical of Jiang," said Wang.

DRAWING FROM THE SAME deep well of Chinese tradition, Jiang called for "ethics and morality" to be on the same plane as law in governing China, and he spoke of a "rule of virtue." "In the governing of a nation," he told a national conference of propaganda officials, "the rule of law and adherence to ethics have always been complementary and supplementary."

Jiang's reference to ethics as a balance to law—with its distinctive overtones of Confucian philosophy—seemed a switch in direction and fascinated intellectuals. For decades, China's ancient teachings had been condemned by orthodox Communists as "feudal." Though Jiang's words were intriguingly vague, people speculated that he was seeking to create a new hybrid system of Confucian moral philosophy and Marxist political theory.

Some saw the move as a way of countering the odd appeal of Falun Gong, whose members were exploiting the vacuum in Marxist belief to promote their own fanciful notions. But scholars flocked to Jiang's new thinking, seeing it not only as a basis for sound moral guidelines in a time of social dislocation but also as a wedge to pry open the door to China's rich philosophical heritage that the Cultural Revolution had slammed shut.

"This man is no longer living under the shadow of his predecessors—Mao Zedong or Deng Xiaoping or whomever," said one researcher, who observed that Jiang was the first Party leader to import elements of Confucianism into Communism.

As part of his efforts to revitalize the Party, Jiang noted that most government officials who had grown up during the time of the Cultural Revolution had not received any kind of moral education. At the same time Jiang blamed the terrible errors in Party history on flawed implementation rather than on Communism's basic formulation. To rectify both, he set in motion an initiative to introduce Confucian classics into mainstream thinking. A flurry of seminars and forums sprang up on "running the country with virtue" along with "governing the country according to law."

When meeting with the leader of Japan's opposition Social Democratic Party, Jiang mentioned that the Communist Party was "seriously studying" whether to lift a ban on admitting private business owners as members. He speculated half-seriously that if all the managers and entrepreneurs ended up joining other parties, the Communist Party would be "stripped of cash." "We do not hesitate to change our theories in accordance with current conditions," he said. These seemingly offhand comments would herald one of the major themes of 2001.

IN ANOTHER SIGN OF changing times, a seventeen-member evaluation delegation from the International Olympic Committee (IOC) began a final inspection visit of Beijing as part of the competition to determine the host city for the 2008 Olympic Games. The Chinese city was the odds-on favorite, but the government was determined not to leave anything to chance. Resentment still smoldered from losing the 2000 Olympics.

A massive $20 billion infrastructure and environmental cleanup campaign was initiated, called "one of the greatest building projects undertaken in China since construction of the Great Wall." Bright signs and trendy slogans—"New Beijing, Great Olympics"—sprung up throughout the city. Taxi drivers were taught crash-course English.

President Jiang welcomed the IOC delegation, led by Hein Verbruggen, to Zhongnanhai, where they met in a resplendent room of intricate Chinese design. "This meeting with the highest rank of government in your country serves to underline the commitment by the Chinese government to the Beijing bid," Verbruggen told Jiang as he wished the city good luck in the July 13 decision.

On their last day, the IOC delegation took a morning tour of China Central Television—to assess whether it could handle the massive telecommunications requirements of mounting an Olympics—and had an afternoon farewell visit with President Jiang. Welcoming the IOC to CCTV was its young, innovative president, Zhao Huayong, who was bringing vigor and new thinking to the massive state-owned broadcaster. With the IOC properly impressed, Zhao could finally relax, knowing that his role in China's monumental Olympic drive was over.

That evening Zhao Huayong was sitting in his fifteenth-floor office, watching CCTV's half hour-long *National News (Xin Wen Lian Bo)*, the most important television show in China. With a first run at 7:00 P.M. and a repeat at 10:00 P.M. every evening, it had an audience of hundreds of millions and garnered a disproportionate share of CCTV's $700 million of annual advertising revenue, increasingly critical in a market economy to which CCTV was having to adapt. More critically, *National News* was watched regularly and carefully by China's senior leaders—who did not always agree among themselves on what should or should not be broadcast. Given its impact, Zhao Huayong scrutinized the show every day, monitoring it like a field marshal.

It was precisely 7:20 P.M. when his red phone rang. It was the hotline reserved for senior leaders. In China, hotlines to the media are as significant as those to the military, and when the red phone rings, its presence fills the room. Though Dan Rather would hardly fret over a call from the White House, this is China, and Zhao took the call with trepidation.

"Is this Zhao Huayong?" a slightly officious voice asked, and after receiving a slightly shaky yes in response, delivered the news: "The general secretary would like to speak with you."

A news producer before he became a media executive, Zhao had spent innumerable hours with Jiang Zemin over the years covering his activities, and he had formed an almost personal relationship with the country's leader. But when the hotline rings, previous encounters evaporate. All that matters is "Why?"

"Hello. Is this Zhao Huayong?" said the voice most familiar.

"Good evening, General Secretary. It's me," Zhao responded, doing his best not to betray apprehension. "I've just seen you on *National News;* you looked good in the Olympic meeting." As always, CCTV's lead story was about the comings and goings of Jiang Zemin, the country's leader. There was rarely an exception to this unwritten rule.

Jiang was not distracted by the compliment. "Thank you, but did you notice any problem?"

"No . . . General Secretary, I'm sorry, but I didn't notice anything unusual." Zhao flushed. There must have been something seriously wrong with the ultrasensitive show. "We made mistakes? Right, General Secretary?"

"I'm probably the only person who might notice," Jiang said, "but I had *two* meetings today in the same meeting hall—one should have been reported and the other should not have been. My meeting with the Olympic delegation was appropriate for *National News,* and your coverage was quite good. The footage showing me greeting and shaking hands with delegates was accurate. But the subsequent footage, showing us sitting and speaking, was not. My other meeting was with a longtime personal friend. He happens to be a senior electronics executive—I've known him since my days as electronics minister—but we were speaking only as friends, not for official business. Although your voice-over narration about the Olympic visit continued to be correct, the footage got mixed up, and you erroneously broadcast what was supposed to be a private meeting with my old friend."

"I am terribly sorry; this is a serious error." Zhao was speaking faster. "I will immediately investigate, find out what happened, and report to you as soon as possible. We will punish those responsible and make sure it never happens again."

"It's really my fault," Jiang responded warmly. "I shouldn't have had two meetings with foreigners in the same hall. Foreigners look as much alike to us as they say we look alike to them."

Zhao could almost feel Jiang smiling, but he knew not to make light of any such slip-up. "This is a serious error," he repeated. "I will investigate right away."

"Even though we can say it's my fault," Jiang continued, "you should analyze what caused the problem. It may seem like a small matter, and I doubt the Olympic delegation would take notice, but such a mistake reflects on our professionalism and diligence and should not happen."

"Yes! Yes! What you said is absolutely right."

"I'm an engineer. Everyone makes mistakes, but an engineer must analyze what caused the mistake. Was it a random accident, negligence, or a systemic problem in the line of production? These are different conditions requiring different responses. If the problem is in production, then it is a problem to fix. Please don't be hard on yourself or your people. But make sure you get the right footage for the 10:00 P.M. show."

"I'll give you a full report after I go down to the News Center."

"Call me back after you investigate. I'll be waiting."

Jiang had two interests here, one professional, one personal. As China's senior leader, he knew that mistakes on CCTV's highly sensitive *National News,* though small this time, had their own way of becoming disruptive; and as an inveterate engineer, he was actually curious how such a mix-up could have occurred.

Zhao called the News Center. "There's been a serious problem on *National News,*" he said. "I'm coming down. Nobody move!"

When Zhao entered the screen-filled room, he observed what could have passed for a time-freeze scene from a science fiction film. Indeed, no one had moved; faces were reddened or ashen, the only sounds labored breath.

"Get me tonight's program!" ordered Zhao. "The general secretary had two meetings; I want all the footage." Zhao did not explain; this was the time to solve the problem, not to discuss it. "And get the camera crew here."

Engaging his news-producing experience, Zhao quickly discovered what had happened. There had been no communication between the camera crews and the editors, nothing written, nothing oral. The crews had rushed back from Jiang's 4:00 P.M. meeting—caught in Beijing's notorious traffic, they hadn't arrived until after 6:00 P.M.—and when they delivered the video-tape to the anxious editors, who were not on the shoot, the editors just rushed to the cutting room to assemble the footage in order to meet the hard dead-line for the 7:00 P.M. broadcast.

The camera crews, instructed to follow President Jiang unless told other-wise, had done their job by taping his two meetings. However, since the footage of each meeting was brief and not properly labeled—they were on the same day, in the same place, and with the same person (President Jiang)—a mix-up had occurred in the editing room. Zhao saw how easy it was for the editors to have blended the two meetings together, time con-straints being what they were and foreigners looking as they did. After rap-idly but carefully substituting the proper pictures, Zhao screened the corrected frames a number of times and had the camera crews confirm their accuracy to make absolutely sure that this time there was no mistake. At last satisfied, Zhao ordered the revised film to be shown on CCTV's hourly news headlines at 9:00 P.M. as well as on the full *National News* re-peat at 10:00 P.M.

At 8:25 P.M. Zhao was back at his desk preparing to call the country's leader. He took a very deep breath before picking up the phone.

"This is Zhao Huayong from CCTV," he said somberly. "I've been in-structed to report to the general secretary."

"One moment," said a woman with what seemed to be a knowing chuckle. Within seconds Jiang was on the phone.

"Hello, General Secretary. We found the problem. It was our fault, but it has been corrected, and the revised story with the proper footage will be the lead on the 9:00 P.M. o'clock headlines as well as on *National News* at 10:00 P.M. We made a serious mistake, and we are ready to accept the consequences."

"You are so efficient, Huayong, I'm quite impressed. But remember, I'm still an engineer, and I'd still like to know what caused the problem."

Zhao proceeded to give a detailed description of the system failure.

"I suspected as much," Jiang replied with professional satisfaction. "Having worked on production lines for as long as I did gives you a sense of such failures. Television production is no different from automobile production: Good communication all along the line is essential. Have a clear plan so that you don't make the same mistake again."

Zhao thanked Jiang and was prepared to hang up in order not to take up more of the senior leader's time. But Jiang kept talking, now more personally. He began telling Zhao of his long friendship with the electronics executive whose television appearance had triggered the trouble. As the conversation continued, touching on various subjects, Zhao began to relax, feeling as if he were having an evening chat with a relative or mentor.

Finally, after some twenty minutes, Jiang concluded by returning to the original topic. "You know it really was my fault," he said. "I confused the crew by meeting the two groups in the same place."

"No, General Secretary, it was our fault. It was a failure of the system. I accept personal responsibility and will accept punishment; I will also punish those responsible."

"Please don't do that," Jiang enjoined Zhao. "Your reporters, crews, and editors work very hard. Just encourage them to be diligent and to strive constantly to improve themselves. You know, I didn't call the relevant departments [to whom Zhao and CCTV report]; I wanted to bring this matter to a conclusion just between you and me."

Zhao Huayong would later reflect on his behind-the-scenes drama: "It was an emotional roller-coaster ride, barely more than an hour from start to finish. And I appreciate why General Secretary Jiang spent time talking to me about nonbusiness subjects at the end. He wanted to calm me down after the harrowing experience, restore my confidence. Just imagine: the president of our country instructing and comforting me, even preventing me from overreacting in punishing my people. I was very touched and will remember this for the rest of my life."

IN LATE MARCH FOUR editors of the *Washington Post* interviewed President Jiang in Zhongnanhai. After a formal session of anticipated questions and prepared answers, the Chinese leader shifted to his favorite give-and-take style, speaking at times in colloquial English, teasing his interlocutors and cracking jokes.

Calling him "charming and good-humored," one *Post* editor observed that Jiang seemed genuinely puzzled by their interest in the case of a China-born American researcher who had been detained on security-related charges, and by U.S. interest generally in human rights in China. "I have a very big question in my mind," Jiang stated. "The United States is the most developed country in the world, in terms of its economy, its high tech. Its military is also very strong. You have a lot of things to occupy yourselves with. Why should it be that you frequently take an interest in cases such as these?"

In a lighter part of the interview, Jiang admitted feeling tense when being questioned by reporters. "Leaders of any country will feel a headache when they meet with foreign journalists," Jiang stated. "The president of the United States is also no exception. I personally observed that, too."

Jiang kidded his visitors about their youth. "I think today we can see the difference in age is very obvious," Jiang said. "Of course, you are much more energetic than I am. But I have to say I am probably more experienced in life. This is not out of pride. It's a practical fact." With no exaggeration Jiang said, "My life was closely associated with almost three-quarters of the last century."

To provoke Jiang to assess the strange appeal of Falun Gong, one reporter asked whether the Chinese people, "having lost faith in Communism, were searching for something to believe in."

Jiang acknowledged that perhaps some Chinese have given up Communism; then, switching to his patchy but passionate English, he said, "But I still trust it." Professing steadfast belief in the political philosophy that he had first embraced as a student, he sounded a poignant note. "When I was young," Jiang mused, "I thought Communism would come very quickly, but now I don't feel like this."

The issue continued to preoccupy Jiang. Bringing it up at a private meeting in late 2003, he said, "Years ago, when we joined the Communist revolution, we believed that the socialist system should take over the world, that it would be good for the world. Today, while we still have strong faith in

Marxism, our thoughts about 'taking over the world' have changed. The world has changed; the times have changed. . . .

"I often think about history," Jiang reflected. "I'm seventy-seven years old now, and I have experienced diverse and dramatic times. I truly believe that all types of social systems should be able to coexist in peace."

WHILE JIANG WAS THINKING grandly, an incident occurred that reminded everyone how easily such peace could be disrupted. On April 1, 2001, a Sunday, a U.S. Navy EP-3E Aries II surveillance plane took off on a routine patrol to gather electronic data off the coast of China. With an eavesdropping range of 200 to 460 miles, the craft's equipment enabled the crew to intercept a variety of Chinese electronic communications, which were of potential interest to U.S. military intelligence.

For decades U.S. aircraft like the EP-3E, often operating out of Japan, had flown surveillance missions along China's borders, their activities monitored closely by the Chinese military. According to custom, when an American spy plane flew its route, which was always over international waters, Chinese fighters would scramble and trail the intruder from a safe distance. It was part of the game: Each side did what it could to learn about the other, but each also abided by generally accepted, if unwritten, rules of aerial conduct. Recently, however, the American military had become concerned because, as sources later put it, the Chinese intercepts had become aggressive.

On this particular occasion two PLA F-8 fighter jets took off to track the lumbering, unarmed EP-3E. One of the Chinese jets was piloted by a veteran named Wang Wei, a pilot with a reputation: The Chinese called him fearless; the Americans called him reckless.

There was a collision. Though the cause was disputed, the effect was not: The American plane was crippled; the Chinese plane was lost. Supported by the testimony of the pilot of their second plane, the Chinese proclaimed that the larger, four-engine U.S. spy plane had veered, suddenly and deliberately, into the smaller Chinese jet, shredding the F-8's tail with its propellers. According to the testimony of the American crew, the Chinese pilot was a "dangerous daredevil" who had twice brought his faster aircraft within feet of the EP-3E. On the third fly-by, he struck the American propeller with fatal results.

Whichever story was true, the ending was the same: The Chinese plane disintegrated and went down into the South China Sea. Although Wang Wei was seen descending with an open parachute, no sign of him was found, and he was presumed to have perished. The American aircraft sustained damage to a wing and engine, declared an emergency, and landed, without permission, at the nearest airstrip—on China's Hainan Island. Never before in the history of the U.S. military had there been such a collision or emergency landing, certainly not one that left a $100 million spy plane in the control of the Chinese military. Everything about the tragedy was contested, including where it had occurred.

The next day the recently inaugurated American president, George W. Bush, demanded immediate U.S. access to the plane and requested that it be returned "without further tampering." Washington asserted that the plane enjoyed "sovereign immunity" and the Chinese should not board it. On April 3 President Jiang blamed the United States for the incident and, sensing a hardening of popular opinion, demanded an apology.

Behind the scenes, Jiang was more concerned about the fate of the missing pilot than about the international turmoil. Former Ambassador to the U.S. Li Zhaoxing (later foreign minister) remembered Jiang's many questions at an emergency meeting after the incident: "Do we have the exact coordinates of the crash?" "Can we confirm that his parachute opened?" "What life-preserving equipment does he have?" "How much food and water does he carry?" "What, precisely, did the other pilot say?" "Did he *really* see the parachute?" Jiang directed every available Chinese vessel, military and civilian, to aid in the search. At its peak the massive rescue operation involved around fifty ships, seven hundred fishing vessels, and more than seventy planes. Jiang also inquired into the welfare of the American crew and was relieved to learn that the twenty-four members had landed safely. "At that first meeting," Li Zhaoxing recalled, "the only thing on President Jiang's mind was human beings, Chinese and American."

In response to the heated rhetoric from Beijing, a White House spokesperson commented that Washington had no plans to issue an apology, since it had "done nothing wrong." "I have heard some suggestions of an apology," said Secretary of State Colin Powell. "But we have nothing to apologize for. We had an emergency." American officials began referring to its crew as being "detained" by the Chinese government.

The accident came at an awkward time for Jiang. He was about to depart for Latin America, where he was seeking political support as well as promoting trade. The annual human rights resolution condemning China was about to be submitted to the UN; the new Bush administration was taking a harder line toward Beijing than had Clinton's; and Beijing's bid to host the 2008 Olympics would soon be put to a vote.

In the first break in the hostile atmosphere, U.S. diplomats were permitted to see the plane's crew and reported them to be in good health. The next day, in a parallel show of goodwill, Colin Powell expressed "regret" for the loss of

Wang Wei, the missing pilot. The Chinese Foreign Ministry conceded that the actual collision had occurred outside Chinese air space but pointed out that afterward the U.S. plane penetrated Chinese territory illegally. In his most conciliatory statement yet, President Bush expressed his own "regret" over the loss, but stopped short of making an apology. "Our prayers," he said, "go out to the pilot and his family."

CONFIDENT THAT THE INCIDENT was not likely to escalate, President Jiang departed on schedule for his twelve-day Latin American tour. Accompanied by Chinese businessmen, he was continuing his campaign to court smaller countries to balance "American hegemony." Mentioning the spy plane standoff only twice during the entire trip, Jiang was determined to learn more about Latin America and build new relationships for China in the American hemisphere. He visited six countries—Chile, Argentina, Uruguay, Brazil, Cuba, and Venezuela—and in every one he talked trade and investment, signing about twenty agreements and impressing his hosts with his visions of economic opportunities.

Jiang did his homework. In Chile he asked detailed questions about wine-making in the local grape-growing foothills of the Andes Mountains, and he delighted his audience by delivering a forty-minute speech entirely in Spanish. He had begun learning Spanish following his visit to Spain in 1996 and had secretly studied the new language in preparation for this trip.

"I prepared intensely for two months," Jiang recalled, "My teacher was head of the Spanish section in the Foreign Ministry—he later became our ambassador to Mexico. To heighten the surprise, I began my speech in English and said I would try to speak some Spanish—and then proceeded to give the rest of the speech in Spanish.

"I joked that since my Spanish was crude, I would distribute a printed copy of my speech. But I would only do so, I told the audience, at the end of my speech, so that everyone would have to listen while I spoke."

Jiang was serious as well. The United States would soon be seeking to censure China before the UN Human Rights Commission. U.S. officials said the timing, set long in advance, had nothing to do with the spy plane matter. Sponsored by a Western nation nearly every year since 1989, the 2001 resolution, like the nine before it, criticized China's "severe measures" restricting its citizens' freedom of religion, assembly, and speech. It also urged Beijing to "preserve and protect the distinct cultural, ethnic, linguistic, and religious identity of Tibetans and others."

But every time the resolution had been introduced, China managed to avoid censure through a wily strategy of trade deals and backroom lobbying of the swing votes on the fifty-three member commission. It was no coincidence that five of the six countries on Jiang's trip were members. "He's signing trade and investment agreements everywhere he's going," said a human rights expert of President Jiang. "This is the same approach China uses every year [to defeat the resolution], and it always works."

Jiang concluded his Latin American travels by receiving a dramatic pledge from Venezuelan president Hugo Chavez that his country would back China on the UN vote and support Beijing's bid to host the 2008 Olympics. Jiang joked that Venezuela was his last stop, because, according to China's culinary customs, one leaves "the best dish for last." But joking aside, Venezuela's strong support lit up Jiang's entire trip, impressing his always-skeptical colleagues back in China. Jiang showed his gratitude by laying a wreath at the mausoleum of Simón Bolívar, praising Venezuela's "liberator" and "father of the country." He also lunched with Julio Iglesias, the Spanish superstar singer—arranged as a surprise by President Chavez—and before long the two presidents were singing backup to Iglesias's megahits. On April 19, twelve days after leaving China in the heat of the spy plane confrontation, Jiang flew home—and right back into its repercussions.

SEARCHING FOR THE SMOOTHEST way out of the crisis, Jiang had devised a high-road analogy: "I have visited many countries and seen that it is normal for people to ask forgiveness or say 'excuse me' when they collide in the street," he said on arrival in Chile. "But the American planes come to the border of our country and do not ask forgiveness. Is this behavior acceptable?"

Public sentiment in China was growing more hostile, limiting Jiang's options. Two reactions, picked at random from the streets of Beijing by an American news source, exemplified the mass anger. "Chairman Mao would have fought to make the Americans apologize," said a middle-aged man. "Jiang Zemin is too weak," agreed a young woman; "he doesn't dare fart unless America agrees!"

It was an echo of the outcry that had occurred two years earlier after the embassy bombing. Once again President Jiang was being pressured and tested by both sides. Every day of "detention" of the American crew was another black mark against Jiang in world opinion, while the lack of a U.S. apology made him seem ever weaker to his own people. In Argentina Jiang stated that China "never gives in to any outside pressure on issues of principle related to China's state sovereignty and territorial integrity." Abroad, critics wondered whether Beijing's bid for the 2008 Olympics was now in jeopardy. "The Chinese must have realized," one Western diplomat later observed, "just how close they were to a complete international breakdown."

Jiang stood strong, maintaining his measured approach. "Given the important roles of our countries," he commented in both Argentina and Uruguay, "I think we should find an adequate solution to this problem." At the same time *People's Daily* began preparing the public for the crisis's end. Recognizing the wounded pride and national frustration, the Party mouthpiece echoed Jiang's philosophy, saying, "Turn patriotic enthusiasm into strength to build a powerful nation."

The most difficult phase of the confrontation ended when diplomats worked semantic miracles to enable Beijing to claim that Washington's double use of the word "sorry" in its official letter offered sufficient face-giving apology for the accident. Stating that both President George Bush and Secretary of State Colin Powell had expressed "sincere regret" over the missing Chinese pilot, the letter also said that the U.S. was "very sorry" for entering China's air space without permission and admitted that the landing in Hainan did not have verbal clearance.

In a clever ploy, the final wording of the letter—which required hours of haggling—was negotiated entirely in English, an unusual procedure. By reaching agreement solely on an English text, the Chinese had more flexibility in providing their own translation. "We wrote a letter that is factually accurate," said an American diplomat. "It was also a letter that the Chinese felt they could use . . . it allowed a little more wiggle room." The next day Beijing announced that the Americans would be released on "humanitarian grounds." It would take until July 4 (no symbolism intended) before the navy plane, which the Americans would be forced to disassemble into boxable pieces, could be brought back to the United States. There it would be reassembled, equipped with upgraded electronics, and returned to service somewhere in the world.

Though the West, in general, appreciated Jiang's handling of the crisis, many Chinese did not, and they berated their leader for backing down. Disbelief and resignation, punctuated by indignation and outrage, flooded Chinese-language websites, some of which crashed under the onslaught of messages. One e-mail offered this analogy: "If someone peeps at your wife when she is having a bath and your son goes out to drive that person away but instead he is beaten to death, what would you do?" Another argued: "In releasing the Americans, it would appear that we are weak and fear them." Exercising more free speech than Westerners think exists in China, more than a few Chinese called for President Jiang to resign.

On April 14 the Chinese media curtailed its outpouring of anti-U.S. rhetoric. Apart from a few human-interest stories about the pilot's family and articles claiming broad public support for Beijing's decision to release the spy plane's crew, there were few mentions of the episode and no vitriol. Again, the situation was reminiscent of 1999. The people were welcome to vent their rage, but only within a controlled context and only for a limited amount of time.

Columnist Nicholas Kristof, for several years a Beijing-based reporter, called America lucky that "Jiang Zemin used his influence to tamp down Chinese populist anti-Americanism." He speculated that another kind of Chinese leader, "trying to arouse public anger [one who would seek to accrete personal power by feeding the people's jingoistic appetites], might have put the American spy plane crew on trial and executed the captain."

WHILE CHINA WAS TAKING extraordinary measures to rescue one of its citizens, it was systematically executing thousands of others. The moves, however disparate, were not inconsistent. Wang Wei was a national hero, protecting his country; those condemned to death were criminals, undermining their country.

In April 2001, the government commenced a new round of its Strike Hard campaign against serious crimes, a draconian policy applauded by an overwhelming majority of the Chinese people. According to Amnesty International, in the first three months more people were executed in China than in all other countries of the world combined for the previous three years. Between 1990 and 2000, the period of Jiang Zemin's leadership, Amnesty documented almost 20,000 executions, a figure government sources call "exaggerated" and critics claim is far below the actual number.

Driving the Strike Hard campaign was mounting concern about social unrest, including crimes previously unknown in Communist China, such as bank robberies carried out by armed gangsters. According to *People's Daily*, Strike Hard focused on violent crimes: "explosions, murders, robbery, kidnapping, poisoning; gang crimes and crimes with Mafia features; thefts and other crimes that affect the public security."

"No government wants to use the death penalty more than it has to," said Liu Hainian, a professor at the Chinese Academy of Social Sciences' Law Institute. "The government wants to reduce the use of the death penalty . . . but it has to fit with China's reality. We cannot cause harm to people's lives and property by reducing the use of the death penalty."

JIANG BEGAN FOCUSING ON the Internet, a medium of enormous power and challenge toward which he had mixed feelings. His two sons, who were living with their wives and children in Shanghai, worked in information technology. Jiang urged the nation to develop information and network laws, as well as technologies, to help China prosper in the Internet era. The chief concern, Jiang noted, was the rampant spread of "superstitious, pornographic, violent and other harmful information and Internet crimes."

In June Jiang combined three of his passions—art, science, and education—by visiting an international exhibition of seven hundred works of art, contributed by thirty-two universities, that used science as themes or inspiration. Jiang noted that the paintings, sculptures, and calligraphies, most of which related to scientific discoveries, would both give aesthetic pleasure and enhance scientific understanding.

At the China Association for Science and Technology in the same month, Jiang praised the "scientific spirit" as "the soul of the people's appreciation for science and culture," which, among other benefits, established "a correct world outlook, life outlook, and values outlook." "Many prominent problems," Jiang said, "are caused by the absence of a scientific spirit."

Jiang frequently provided personal support for high-level scientific conferences. Sometimes he would give the keynote address; often he would meet with foreign scientists who attended—at, for example, an international nanotechnology forum in July and a strategy session on the human genome project in August. Jiang knew that his participation would require media coverage, which would increase interest in the topic, thus promoting his grand strategy to "revitalize China through science and education." The public good was not his only motivation, however; he also liked mingling with scientists and discussing the latest discoveries and theories. To Jiang Zemin, leading-edge science was great fun.

IN LATE JUNE, THE Three Tenors—Luciano Pavarotti, Placido Domingo, and José Carreras—performed in a gala concert before an elite audience of thirty thousand in the Forbidden City and hundreds of millions on television. The magnificent Imperial Palace shone with blazing lights, and Tiananmen Square became a massive parking lot for hundreds of luxury cars, as elegant women in evening dresses and gentlemen in tuxedos arrived in an unending stream.

The next day Jiang invited Pavarotti, Domingo, and Carreras to lunch and congratulated them on their "powerful performance," which he called "a showcase of the cream of Western opera combined with the glory of Chinese ancient and modern civilization." Predictably, the quartet began to sing in various combinations. "The president sang a duet with me of 'O Sole Mio,' " said Pavarotti. "I think it was very good. I would like to say it was romantic, absolutely."

When a reporter asked Pavarotti how Jiang would fare as an opera singer, the Italian superstar smiled. "You want me to be diplomatic?" Thinking for a moment, he said, "If this man can express himself with the soul and the willpower that he has, even in singing, he certainly would be a big star." Then he added, "Probably he needs to practice."

Jiang greeted Pavarotti, as he greeted many dignitaries, in the gracious elegance of Zhongnanhai's main reception hall (Han Yuan Dian), where the splendor of traditional Chinese architecture exemplifies the grandeur of Chinese civilization. Inside are three semicircular rings of armchairs, about two dozen or so all together. The primary guest is seated to Jiang's right, in the center of the inner ring, while young women in long, luminescent-red Chinese gowns keep teacups filled and hot. Young men, likely security agents but not in uniform, sit unobtrusively along the back walls. Jiang is always prepared with personal facts about his guest(s), information he uses to create a warm atmosphere.

A tour of the idyllic grounds—formerly the private domain of China's emperors—is often a feature of presidential audiences. For special guests, like President Clinton or Pavarotti, the tour guide is You Xigui, the head of the Central Garrison Bureau (Zhongnanhai security) and Jiang's personal bodyguard. For a military man, General You knows a great deal about the art, architecture, and history of Zhongnanhai's marvelous structures, giving out all manner of details of dates, numbers, and events.

Lest a visitor get the wrong idea about the fact-filled You, he hastens to explain that being a tour guide is not his real job. "*This* is my real job," he asserts, giving his hidden hip pocket multiple slaps without much of a grin. The sound of heavy metal reveals he packs a hidden weapon, likely a fearsome one. "Terrorists are scared of Mr. You," whispers a senior official close to Jiang. No one doubts it.

JULY 1 MARKED THE EIGHTIETH anniversary of the founding of the Communist Party of China, and great expectations were in the air. Each city had its own form of celebration. In Zhejiang province, the birthplace of the Party, there were cultural events and tours; in Shanghai, concerts of revolutionary and patriotic music; and in Beijing, an exhibition of relics, including the first red flag raised over Tiananmen Square.

The anniversary was also commemorated with an eighteen-hour television marathon that featured a major address by the general secretary. Speaking before a live audience of ten thousand, Jiang praised the Party for China's resurgence after a century of degradation, hailed the past two decades of social and economic reform, and pointed to his new theory of Three Represents as key to the Party's future. But hidden in an otherwise unsurprising speech were a few electrifying sentences.

The thrust of Jiang's message, which ran about fifteen thousand words in English translation, was that the Party should adapt the principles of Marxism to current conditions in China. After rehearsing Communist history, Jiang gently criticized dogmatic attitudes. Then he dropped his bombshell.

Telling Party officials to give up "outdated notions" about Communism, Jiang declared that reform had created "new social strata" of entrepreneurs, technical personnel, managerial staff, freelance professionals, and the self-employed in the "nonpublic sector," and that most people in the private sector are engaged in "honest labor and work," obey the law, and contribute to society. In order to maintain the momentum of reform, he argued, these new social strata should be welcomed as members of the Communist Party. These people, he asserted, "are also working for building socialism with Chinese characteristics." With classic subtlety, Jiang packaged the startling new policy in what seemed to be a traditional political box: "It is also necessary to accept those outstanding elements from other sectors of the society who have subscribed to the Party's program and Constitution, worked for the Party's line and program wholeheartedly, and proved to meet the requirements for Party membership through a long period of tests."

Entrepreneurs and technical personnel, he pointed out, are the driving force behind China's "advanced productive forces," the first of his Three Represents. If such people continue to be banned from Party membership, he said, the Party cannot truly claim to be leading the nation. He had maneuvered around the historically loaded term *capitalist* by inventing a new label for this class of potential Party members in which private business owners, along with others, would be included. They were now to be known as the "new social strata."

"Our fundamental objective in building socialism is to ensure our people prosperity and well-being," Jiang said. "With economic development, our people will live a better life and their personal property will increase gradually. In view of this, it is not advisable to judge a person's political orientation simply by whether he or she owns property or how much property he or she owns. But rather, we should judge him or her mainly by his or her political awareness, moral integrity and performance, by how he or she has acquired the property, and how it has been disposed of and used, and by his or her actual contribution to the cause of building socialism with Chinese characteristics."

Later that day Jiang called Shen Yongyan in Changchun. "What did you think of my speech?" he asked, after some family small talk.

"You gave a good speech," said Shen. "I didn't see any problem with it."

"Then you didn't listen too carefully," said Jiang. "Many people are against it."

"Why?"

"The controversy centers on whether we should allow private business owners to join the Party."

It was the first practical application of Jiang's Three Represents, and it was a stunner. Realizing that Jiang's speech was proclaiming a fundamental change in the essence of the Communist Party, Leftists erupted. One of the first public objections came from Ma Bin, a former vice director of the Development Research Center and a Party member since 1935. Agitated by Jiang's speech, Ma Bin prepared a principled refutation and sought sympathetic former officials to join with him. Recruiting thirteen of the like-minded, including prototypical hardliner Deng Liqun—who was in the process of drafting his own letter—Ma Bin published the Letter of Fourteen. It was distributed samizdat-fashion in Beijing and circulated widely on the Internet.

As Ma Bin saw it, his short letter struck to the heart of the issue. "Comrade Jiang Zemin openly called for admission of owners of private enterprises to membership of the Party," he wrote, claiming that "the proposition that capitalists, who personify Capital, should be allowed to join the Party, has immediately caused enormous confusion in the minds of Party members." Ma Bin called Jiang's move "a blatant attempt to manipulate opinions of Party members and set the stage for foisting this erroneous position on the Party congress by invoking the need to uphold Party unity." Ma Bin, who had studied metallurgy in the Soviet Union, boldly set forth his accusation: "This constitutes political misconduct unprecedented in the history of our Party."

Writing in the name of "a group of old Communist Party members," Ma

Bin laid down his challenge: "We hereby solemnly declare that we firmly and without reservation oppose the proposition that private business owners be allowed to join the Party. We believe that Comrade Jiang Zemin's position in this regard is entirely wrong." The letter then listed the old-line catechism of nineteenth-century Communism. Arguing that the "admission of capitalists to membership of a Communist Party is unheard of in Marxist theory or practice that has emerged since the *Communist Manifesto* was first published," Ma stated, "This in no way constitutes a 'creative renewal' of Marxism, but rather, an outright negation of its basic principles." He then added the rhetorical question "How could a capitalist, as a member of the exploiting class, be expected to devote his or her whole lifetime to struggle for the realization of Communism?" and he concluded, "Comrade Jiang Zemin's views do not make any sense in this respect."

As it turned out, Ma's efforts to recruit fellow travelers to cosign his open letter proved difficult. As one example, when he approached a leading scientist, the exchange revealed how strongly China's science community supported Jiang Zemin's Three Represents. Professor Bi Dachuan was a mathematician and defense expert, who, having suffered grievously during the Cultural Revolution, was known to be outspoken and hard to intimidate. Bi Dachuan and Ma Bin were old friends.

"Look what's happening to China under current policies," said Ma, beginning his appeal. "Falun Gong!"

"They're absurd," retorted Bi. "Gangsters!"

"They're frustrated laid-off workers, suffering under 'reform,' " Ma continued, criticizing Three Represents. "Workers no longer have a right to a job as they once did under traditional socialism."

"Burdening and bankrupting companies with overstaffed workers just sets China further and further behind the West," said Bi, now seriously. "The only products China could sell on world markets 'under traditional socialism' were bamboo baskets and poor shoes. Now we sell computers and launch satellites."

"China is becoming an imperialist country!" exclaimed Ma.

"I'd love to be an imperialist country," Bi responded, joking to make the economic point. "The last time our embassy was bombed, all we could throw back was eggs."

Reflecting on his two-hour debate with Ma Bin, Professor Bi said, "He's a lovely idealist but completely wrong on this one. Jiang's Three Represents are liberation for China's development. That's why the entire scientific community backs him. This is the first time that scientists and engineers—the 'vanguard' of 'advanced productive forces'—are recognized for our enormous contribution to China."

Now that Ma Bin had gone public criticizing Jiang, and had done so vehemently and not without skill, what would become of him? "His colleagues in the Development Research Center were worried about their old friend," said Professor Wang Huijiong, Jiang's longtime friend, who also worked in the same high-powered think tank. "They asked me, 'Will President Jiang take action against Ma Bin?' I told them no, he would not."

"Whatever happened to Ma Bin?" Jiang Zemin asked Wang Huijiong the next time they spoke. "He may be a little conservative, but he's not thinking right about this issue. Ma Bin is a good person; some people must have influenced him."

"Jiang respected Ma Bin because of his dedication to the Party and the country, and for his knowledge and rectitude," commented Wang. "The president went out of his way to protect Ma Bin, who is still active. Foreigners don't appreciate how democratic China has become."

The most dangerous Leftist challenge to Jiang Zemin's modernizing vision for the Party came a few days later, in the form of a public petition spearheaded by Deng Liqun, the eighty-six-year-old Marxist ideologue and former propaganda chief. Since 1997 he had become increasingly militant in challenging Jiang's leadership. With true-believer fervor, Deng Liqun denounced the general secretary's plan in a ten-thousand-character letter. Distributed widely on the Internet, Deng's manifesto galvanized old-line Communists, incensed progressive Party members, and generally provided grist for political mills of all colors.

"Whom does he represent?" asked Deng Liqun, referring to the Party general secretary. "Jiang's speech represents the 0.3 percent of the population who are private business people. According to the definition of Mao Zedong, our Party should represent the 95 percent of the people who are the masses and revolutionary cadres. So Jiang has become an 'enemy of the people' and should be condemned and punished by the Party and the people."

Deng's petition, which was also signed by sixteen other hardcore Marxists, characterized Jiang's move as an "extremely serious political mistake." Deng accused Jiang of currying favor with Western media by presenting China as an increasingly capitalistic country. He then quoted Jiang's own words against him, referring to a 1989 Party ruling forbidding private businessmen from joining the Party.

"Entrepreneurs of privately owned business cannot join the Party," Jiang had said at the time. "I agree with this position. Our Party is the pioneer of the proletarian class. If we allow persons who do not want to give up exploitation and live by exploitation to join the Party, what kind of Party on earth would we want to construct?"

Deng Liqun's letter also attacked the entrepreneurs themselves, calling them "tax dodgers and tax evaders who paid barely 10 percent of what they really owed," who promoted "many nonregulative and illegal business behaviors," and who were a "hotbed" of corruption. "They send officials one chicken in order to get back one cow," he charged. Business owners, Deng wrote, were increasing the "wealth gap" in China, since "the great disparity between the poor and the rich is primarily embodied in the ownership of property."

Teng Wensheng, who drafted the speech for Jiang, had a different view. "President Jiang's eightieth anniversary speech offers a fully mature and complete understanding of Three Represents," Teng commented. "Chinese experience has proved that having only a state-owned sector doesn't work, can't work. We should encourage other sectors to coexist."

Explaining the controversial decision to allow business owners to join the Party, Teng dealt with reality. "We have Party members 'jumping into the sea' [going into business]," he noted. "They are upright citizens, earn their money lawfully, pay their taxes, and accept the Party Constitution. Why not let similar people join the Party? If it works in one direction, why not the other?

"But this is only my opinion," Teng added. "As for Deng Liqun [Teng's old boss and Cultural Revolution campmate], I can't convince him. Let him take time to figure it all out."

Though most Party officials applauded Jiang's reforms, Deng Liqun and his traditional Leftists enjoyed support in certain circles. Some mid- and lower-level Party officials, who felt threatened by social change and unhappy about erosion of personal power, backed Deng, albeit often in secret.

Jiang argued that unless his changes were made, the Party would wither. That would mean no socialism in any form. A *China Daily* editorial said that by modernizing the Party, Jiang was enabling it to avoid the terminal fate of its sister parties in the former Soviet Union and Eastern Europe, adding, "To imagine a China without the Communist Party is nightmarish."

Notwithstanding the severe criticism from the die-hard Left, Jiang's speech enjoyed wide support in the Party. In the days following, every member of the Politburo endorsed it. Analyzing its political context, Professor

Joseph Fewsmith concluded that the speech "received strong support within the Party and represents far more than the general secretary's personal views . . . [and] was intended to convey a program of wide-ranging political reform, albeit not one of [Western-style] democratization." Heir apparent Hu Jintao noted that General Secretary Jiang had thought about the speech for a long time and had expended a great deal of energy on it. Jiang's conclusions, Hu said, were based on both China's domestic conditions and the "historical lessons concerning the rise and fall, successes and failures of some political parties in the world"—an overt allusion to the collapse of socialism in the Soviet Union and Eastern Europe.

JIANG WAS NONE TOO pleased by Deng Liqun's brazen attacks and commissioned a counteroffensive. Propaganda boss Ding Guangen made personal visits to media outlets, imploring them to follow the new Party line and guard against being used to promote "deviant" ideas. The government also shut down two Leftist publications, a monthly and a weekly.

Jiang continued to avow adherence to Marxism, while pointing out the dangers of dogma. "We should view Marxism as a science that develops along with the development of reality," he said. "There is no limitation for practice, nor for ideological emancipation." He added, "The only correct attitude toward Marxism is to develop it while adhering to it, and to adhere to it while developing it."

None of these tactics deterred the Leftists. Using the Internet, they generated intense debate, the very fact of which, if they had thought about it, should have convinced them that China was changing and the Party would have to change with it.

ON JULY 13, 2001, in Moscow the IOC would announce the host city of the 2008 Summer Olympic Games. In Beijing it was Friday night, and an estimated 400,000 expectant Beijingers gathered in Tiananmen Square, hoping to celebrate victory. At the appointed moment CCTV, which had been broadcasting from Moscow for most of the day, flashed the message WE HAVE WON in triumphant red characters across the screen. In Tiananmen the news appeared on a huge scoreboard. A roar of excitement rumbled through the square and from there across the entire city.

In a brief speech, a beaming President Jiang, as euphoric as the rest of his countrymen, thanked the IOC, the people of China, and all who supported

Beijing's bid, and he called on everyone to make the Olympic Games a great success. He then returned to the balcony of Tiananmen Gate to rejoice with the huge crowds in the square below.

As people celebrated by throwing flowers, waving flags, and banging on drums and gongs, cars zoomed along Beijing's main thoroughfares honking incessantly. "This is a year of triple happiness for China," many said, referring to the Party's eightieth anniversary, the country's upcoming entry into the World Trade Organization, and now the successful Olympic bid.

As China rejoiced, world leaders called to congratulate its president. Western analysts wrote that Beijing's victory marked a high point in Jiang Zemin's tenure. Winning the Olympics had increased his stature both at home and abroad.

Less than twenty-four hours later the government announced that a Chinese-American professor who had been detained for four months would be released. Technically convicted of espionage in a five-hour trial, Li Shaomin was now ordered to leave the country. Speculation had been rife that Li would be released *before* the Olympic vote in order to mitigate criticism of China's human rights record, which had been seen as a potential threat to the bid, but the release had not occurred. No amount of public pressure had swayed the Chinese government. Not even President Bush had been able to persuade Jiang to intervene. But now that the Olympic bid had been won, a proud China seemed pleased to comply. National pride trumps international demands.

In a happy coincidence, two days after the Olympic announcement in Moscow, Jiang paid a visit to the same city, sealing his good relations with Russian president Putin by signing a new friendship treaty and purchasing military equipment. The highlight of the trip was Jiang's address at Moscow University, a massive campus that boasted twenty miles of corridors. Before an audience of a thousand students and dignitaries, which included President Putin, Jiang delivered a forty-minute speech "The Beautiful Future of China-Russian Relations" entirely in Russian. This time his Russian went well; Jiang had been studying the language.

Jiang said that every time he visited Russia, he felt as if he were "returning home." When he mentioned such famous Russians as Pushkin, Tolstoy, and Tchaikovsky, while speaking of Russia's long history and splendid culture, the crowd cheered. After Jiang had finished, Putin came to the podium and said that there were no major impediments, not even language barriers, between the two countries.

That Jiang should be in Russia at this time—so soon after Beijing's Olympic victory—was a triumph for both the man and his country. For years the Soviet Union had been a mentor to China in its journey toward Communism, but the two countries had since gone their separate ways. Russia had sped into a market economy and a quasi-Western-style democracy, while China had chosen a more cautious approach, adopting reforms in graduated steps and always with an eye toward maintaining stability. Its people had not experienced the kind of political and press freedoms the Russians had; nor, however, had they suffered its consequences.

TRAVELING IN ANHUI PROVINCE in late April, Jiang had visited Mount Huang (Huangshan, or Yellow Mountain), called "the loveliest mountain in China," where he felt inspired to compose a simple four-line poem in classical Chinese. Huangshan is to the Chinese something like the Grand Tetons are to Americans; generations of painters, poets, scholars, and warriors had come to praise its splendor and be inspired by its grandeur.

In his poem, entitled "Random Thoughts on Climbing Mount Huang," Jiang told of his rapture after ascending the mountain and musing on its "lofty crags and rosy mists." He ruminated that "our country appears as if a beautiful painting and brings me joy," and that he "took up my dreamy pen to describe the exotic sights." As he did, "the day broke through the rolling clouds and the sky was red for ten thousand miles."

Red clouds and distances of great length must have been on his mind, since similar images embellished the poem that he had presented to Fidel Castro two weeks earlier during his Latin American tour. The red clouds, at least, seemed to express his lifelong feelings about the prevalence of the spirit of Communism.

Chapter 26

AUGUST – DECEMBER 2001

"The Knowledge in Our World Is Rich and Vast, and the Mysteries of the Universe Are Infinite"

HOUGH CHINA HAD IMPLEMENTED striking economic and social reforms over the course of Jiang's tenure, the country was indisputably not a Western-style democracy. The question was when political reform would come. In an interview with *New York Times* journalists, including foreign affairs columnist Thomas Friedman and Beijing bureau chief Erik Eckholm, that very question was posed.

"It has always been our objective to develop socialist democracy," Jiang claimed. "We suggested a long time ago that without democracy, there would be no socialism, let alone socialist modernization." He then defined "socialist democracy" as the state that exists when "people are masters of the country, their society, and their own destiny." He reminded his interviewers of China's "thousands of years of feudalistic autocracy," and said that only after the founding of New China did "the political status of the Chinese people" undergo a "great leap forward" and "fundamental change." Without this awareness, Jiang said, "it would be impossible to have a fundamentally correct understanding of the essence of China's political system."

Continuing, Jiang asserted that it was imperative for China which he called a multiethnic developing country, to have strong political leadership in order to rally its 1.2 billion people behind the cause of modernization. "Otherwise the country would fall apart like a heap of loose sand," he said, justifying in this way the slow pace of political reform.

"There's one thing I have to make very clear," he said. "It is impossible for democracy here to be exactly the same as democracy practiced in the Western world, as would be preferred by people in the West. . . .

"I am seventy-five years old now," he reflected. "I lived for three-fourths of the last century, and I can tell you with certainty: Should China apply the parliamentary democracy of the Western world, the only result would be that 1.2 billion Chinese people would not have enough food to eat. The result would be great chaos, and should that happen, it would not be conducive to world peace and stability."

Many of the questions had a provocative edge. Jiang was asked whether the U.S. plan to develop a missile defense system was a threat to China. "You have only twenty or twenty-five missiles able to hit the United States," the questioner asked. "If we put a shield up, you're out of business."

"To be frank," Jiang responded, "it seems that you know how many missiles we have better than I do. I have to say that I have doubts about whether the figure you give is the correct one or not. But let me be clear about one thing. The reason we possess weapons is not for offensive purposes. They are all for our own defense. So we would keep an appropriate number of weapons to meet our defense needs."

When Jiang addressed the next question—"Why would you open a workers' party to capitalists?"—it was clear that he had answered it many times before. "I believe I can be a very good professor in a university, giving lectures about this," Jiang said. "Because what we insist on doing is a combination of the fundamental tenets of Marxism applied to the real conditions in China. But we have to know that Marx and Engels lived more than 150 years ago. The *Communist Manifesto* was published 153 years ago. It is impossible to apply every single word or sentence they wrote at that time to today's reality."

Asked whether he surfs the Web, Jiang said, "My grandson is much more technically proficient than I am. As an electrical engineer, it is not a problem for me to surf on the Net. But I have to admit that it is quite difficult for me to work with the mouse. . . ."

"People think we are here for a vacation," Jiang told his guests, referring to the heavily guarded Beidaihe compound of light yellow two-story manors befitting a beachside resort. "But actually it's impossible to take a break, even for a single day.

"But there is one thing that I have to do every day. I have gone swimming each of my eleven days here already, no matter what the weather conditions."

In giving interviews, Jiang practiced what he preached. "The president stresses to Chinese officials that they should stay in touch with foreign media," said Information Minister Zhao Qizheng. "He says we should express our ideas in ways that foreigners can understand. We should present facts about China and allow overseas correspondents to draw their own conclusions. President Jiang believes information facilitates understanding. That's why he attaches great importance to the Internet; the rapid development of China's Internet came from his push."

Jiang said he, like a million Americans, liked to read the *New York Times* every morning, which reflected both his facility with written English and his cosmopolitan perspective of the world. The irony that the *Times*'s website, along with other news-oriented websites, was routinely (but not consistently) blocked by China's cyberpolice was a source of discomfort to him. It is a policy he promotes publicly and defends privately, but he does neither joyously, because the policy handicaps China's development. There is nothing Jiang wants more than for Chinese scientists, scholars, artists, and executives to excel, and he knows that by restricting their access to information, the government is limiting their capacity to compete. It is the tension between a stable, controlled society and a volatile, vibrant one. It is a conundrum for China's leaders that will not go away.

THE AUGUST DAYS THAT followed were among the most serene for the Chinese leader. Ensconced in his beach house, Jiang looked forward to China's entry into the WTO. Other than modest political activities, no major events seemed on the horizon. Jiang spent his time reading briefing books and a few tomes on economics and foreign affairs. He also continued his study of foreign languages. At Beidaihe that summer, he brought along several language experts so he could practice his linguistic skills. "If you can't communicate with another person because of differences in language," Jiang said, "how can you exchange ideas or reach agreement?"

Jiang also preached what he practiced. He was acutely aware of the language capabilities of his colleagues, and he was never neutral about assessing them or bashful about critiquing them. He greatly admired those who could speak foreign languages, especially English, and he chided, even goaded, those who could not.

When he met with a foreigner, protocol required that Jiang use a translator, normally assigned from the Foreign Ministry. But when the official meeting was over, especially when there was a lunch or dinner involved, Jiang switched to English (or Russian) and enjoyed the natural interaction. If certain members of his government or staff were not able to follow, he chided them to learn with good-natured public pressure. "Of all the people here," Jiang would say with a smile, "only Mr. X and Mr. Z cannot understand us [speaking English]." Even Jiang's driver could not escape. "I've had to start studying English again," the driver said, "or else I'd be embarrassed whenever I drive the president."

The reverse was true as well. Once in a meeting with senior staff, he noticed that an associate who had studied in the United States had not spoken. "Lao Y, you speak marvelous English," Jiang said. "Why aren't you using it today?" The Chinese leader then joked, "Maybe you worry that you would embarrass me by comparison?"

"President Jiang's facility with foreign languages is well known," said Information Minister Zhao. "He likes learning new vocabulary words in different languages and discussing the subtleties of their meaning with native speakers. He is constantly advising those around him—even low-level assistants—to become more facile with other languages, particularly English. He also corrects our mispronunciation or misuse of foreign words. Once when we were talking about which nuclear reactor was the safest, I mispronounced *r* in the word *pressure,* using a guttural sound. Jiang corrected my pronunciation and asked me why I made the mistake. I said because my first foreign language was German."

Jiang considered his capacity to communicate in the language of the country he was visiting to be part of his diplomatic mission. He tried to study English every day and had a number of tutors at the ready. Before each of his international trips, Jiang would push himself, as if he were a student cramming for an exam, to extend his knowledge of the relevant languages.

"I am a courageous person when it comes to speaking foreign languages," he said, not revealing a state secret. "I don't feel embarrassed at all, even when I make mistakes. To learn, you must speak. Don't worry, talk!"

For pure pleasure, Jiang read science and poetry, almost always late at night. When he was at Beidaihe, where his load of official functions was lighter, he could indulge. By granting freedom of time and separation of place, the seaside resort facilitated reflection and deeper thinking. Jiang kept in touch with friends, often discussing matters far afield. One night in mid-August he wrote a letter to Professor Wang Huijiong as part of their ongoing discussions on the history and evolution of science.

Writing in his own hand, Jiang set down his thoughts. "The knowledge in our world is rich and vast, and the mysteries of the universe are infinite. The knowledge and mysteries that one uses throughout life to seek and probe are rather limited. Philosophers [scholars], ancient and modern, Chinese and foreign, have accumulated many treasure houses of knowledge; however, there is still a long way to knowledge of the infinite universe. There is no limit. The universe is changing constantly, but the changes follow objective laws and patterns. Human wisdom may enable us to discover many of these laws and patterns so that we may expand the areas of our understanding, such as the findings of Palindrome Pythagorean Numbers and the Golden Section. [Jiang's letter was triggered by two unusual articles that Professor Wang had sent to him on these subjects.] We should treasure the limited time of our lives and continuously discover new areas of knowledge. Confucius said incisively, 'Study first, then you will know what you don't know.' "

Although Jiang was a committed Marxist and as such an avowed atheist, he pondered the profound issues of human existence. His fascination with the mysteries of knowledge, the universe, and the human mind had overtones of the spiritual, not in the common religious sense of praying and worshipping but as expressing wonder and awe for the majesty of Nature.

Jiang's letter centered on palindromes, which literally means "running back again" and are sequences of letters, characters, or numbers that read the same way in both directions. In English, the challenge is to create visually identical strings of letters that have the same understandable (non-nonsense) meaning when read forward and backward. Simple examples are "Madam, I'm Adam" or "Draw, O Coward," which read and mean the same left to right or right to left.

Since the Chinese language uses ideogrammatic characters instead of an alphabet, and the sequence of how the characters are ordered determines the grammar as well as the meaning (or lack of meaning), Chinese palindromes are difficult to construct because both the grammar and the meaning are changed, often radically, when characters are read in reverse. A simple example is *"shang hai zi lai shui,"* which means "Shanghai tap water," and *"shui lai zi hai shang,"* which means "water comes from the ocean." The challenge for Chinese palindromic poets is to create elegant, artistic poems, however similar or different in sense and feel, when read from either end.

In other words, while English palindromes strive to make sentences whose meaning must be precisely the same in both directions (since the letters are identical reading either way), Chinese palindromes have a far richer opportunity to express complex, interrelated ideas and emotions when its two separate readings emerge from the same set of characters. Jiang gave two such examples in his night letter. "Once upon a time," he wrote, "there was a restaurant named Nature House (Tian Ran Ju), and inside a pair of antithetical couplets were hung:

Ke shang tian ran ju
Ju ran tian shang ke

When the first line of the couplet is read in reverse, it is the second line."
The diverse meaning of the two verses—which Jiang did not explain in his letter because it is self-evident to any Chinese reader—goes something like this:

A guest visits tianran ju [literally, "a house in nature"]
By surprise [he] becomes a guest in heaven

Literally,

Guest [ke] goes to [shang] Nature [tian ran] House [ju]
Unexpectedly [ju ran], Heaven [tian shang] guest [ke].

Jiang then gives a more complex example of a four-line palindrome poem written by a Song dynasty poet. There are, in fact, two poems in the one verse, each the palindrome of the other. It is a special example because the meanings are surprisingly similar, though with a different feeling. The straightforward reading has a wistful, bittersweet tone.

Fine, fraying grasses beside tranquil beaches
Clouds deserting slowly to distant mountains
The sign's rolled up, the tavern's empty, the day's forever
Birds cry, flowers fall, spring passes away.

In the inverted version of the poem, the meaning is largely the same, although the pleading seems more insistent. It is a remarkable feat for a Chinese palindrome to preserve the meaning when all the characters are read in reverse order.

Dying spring, falling flowers, crying birds
Forever day, empty tavern, rolled up sign
Mountains afar clouds desert slowly
Tranquil beaches, fraying grasses, alas.

中共中央办公厅

世界的知识是浩瀚的，宇宙的奥秘
是无穷的，任何人毕其生去探索追求
这些知识奥秘，也总是极其有限的。
古今中外的哲人已化结果（积累）知识宝
库，但高于无穷尽的宇宙，还相距甚远，
永无止境。宇宙千变万化，但高于存在
的客观规律。人类的智慧可以逐步认其
中若干规律，犹同义勾股、黄金分割、主石
析折屈已知的领域。我们要珍惜生命
的有限时间，去不断开拓去知识的新领域
孔老夫子说学而精释，学、然后知不足

Jiang Zemin's personal letter to Professor Wang Huijiong, his old classmate and lifelong friend, as part of their ongoing discussions on the history of science. It is written on the stationery of the General Office of the CPC Central Committee, Beidaihe, August 12, 2001. *(Courtesy of Wang Huijiong)*

中 共 中 央 办 公 厅 P1

回文勾股数

(一)从前有一字餐馆 名叫天然居

里面挂着一副著名的对联

客上天然居

居然天上客

上联倒过来成下联。回文典型例子。

(二)唐朝陈子高诗句

纤纤乳草春滩、冉冉云归远山。

帘卷堂空日永、鸟啼花落春残。

中共中央办公厅 P2

把色首特例过来，从岗后一字经前须减

残春莨花竞鸟，永日室室卷帘。

山远归云再么，渐平草乱纤么。

(三)音乐中亦有数似回文观象 杨振宁

教授在一九七二年南开大学作了对称与物理

的学术报告时，质子之巴赫的一小段优

美的乐曲，将其乐谱按相反顺序弹出去

演奏出来，就成为另一段风格迥异的音乐

江泽民 二〇〇一年八月十二晚

WHEN THE AIRPLANES HIT the World Trade Center and the Pentagon on September 11, Jiang was transfixed by the terrible sight. His first reaction was to reach out to President Bush and the American people.

The next day Bush called to thank Jiang and to say that he looked forward to working together with all leaders of the world community to crack down on international terrorism. He told Jiang that he hoped that their two countries would strengthen their cooperation on the UN Security Council.

While Jiang was unambivalent in his condemnation of the terrorist attack and sincere in his offer of support, many in China did not share his point of view. Chatter on the Internet revealed a populace far less sympathetic to America than its leader. Years of frustration over intrusive U.S. power, exacerbated by the 1999 embassy bombing and recent spy plane collision, had spawned an anti-American sentiment, held by many, that the United States "had it coming." Although most people expressed sympathy for the dead, they argued that America, by acting as "the world's policeman," had to "share at least part of the blame."

Jiang, who did not share this belief, launched a diplomatic initiative. He wanted to make sure that China participated in the international debate on how to respond to the assault. In the process, he would protect his country's own vital interests. His flurry of calls focused on the leaders of the other three members of the Security Council: Russia, France, and Great Britain. Jiang told his counterparts that terrorism was a threat to world peace and had become a public scourge. He stressed that it was "very necessary and very urgent to have international cooperation."

Thinking strategically, Jiang sought to counterbalance the stern American response that he knew would be forthcoming. He laid out China's position, stating that any military actions against terrorism should have "conclusive evidence and specific targets," make sure that innocent people were not harmed, comply with the principles of international law, and respect the role of the UN Security Council. All actions, Jiang said, should safeguard world peace.

Jiang believed that foreign intervention across international borders was fundamentally wrong. Certainly China did not want precedents to be set that could, under some circumstances, be used against its own territory. He was also concerned that a prolonged international crisis could undermine China's economy, which required a high level of growth to stay ahead of massive unemployment, and he feared that a war on terrorism had the potential to expand American power even further. Any extension of U.S. armed forces would not be in China's long-term interests, particularly if American troops took up long-term residence near China's borders.

On the domestic front, Jiang worried about restive Muslim populations in troubled Xinjiang province. He wondered whether terrorists there might be plotting similar acts of violence; he ordered a review of security regulations and asked that more stringent procedures be enforced. The government restricted diplomats from visiting sensitive regions of Xinjiang; suspicious Muslim groups were put under heightened surveillance; and flights to Middle Eastern countries were curtailed.

China's support for American actions was not unconditional. In return for not opposing military action in Afghanistan, China expected something—specifically, a change in the American attitude toward the way China handled its own terrorist threat in Xinjiang and Tibet. "There can be no double standard" was China's refrain about the fight against terrorism.

At the 2001 APEC forum held in Shanghai in October, Jiang Zemin met George Bush under conditions that, two months earlier, no one could have thought possible. Bush's entire presidency had been transformed by the horrific attacks, and the war on terrorism would be his focus hereafter. In a tectonic shift of the geopolitical landscape, traditional rivalries were reassessed in light of a frightening new world where fanatical, anarchic, shadowy enemies stalk modern societies, killing indiscriminately while imagining they do God service. No longer would Bush be describing China as a "strategic competitor," the phrase made famous during his 2000 election campaign.

Speaking with reporters en route to Shanghai, Bush said he hoped to develop a personal relationship with Jiang. "I look forward to meeting him," Bush said, "so he can see that I'm a sincere person when I say that I want to have good relations; that I understand there will be moments where we agree and moments where we disagree, but we'll work to have good relations." Bush and Jiang had spoken by telephone three times—twice since the September 11 attacks—but Bush said that was not enough.

Just the previous April Bush had kicked open a hornets' nest by mentioning that he would defend Taiwan if China attacked it, naïvely removing a deliberate ambiguity that had long informed U.S. policy toward mainland-Taiwan relations. Now, suddenly more seasoned, the American president said, "I support a 'one China' policy," adding, "and I look forward to reaffirming that with Jiang Zemin."

At a press conference following his first meeting with the Chinese leader, Bush praised Jiang and his government for their immediate response to the attacks of September 11. "There was no hesitation," Bush said, "there was no doubt that they would stand with the United States and our people during this terrible time. . . .

"Two great nations will rarely agree on everything," Bush added. "I understand that. But I assured the president that we'll always deal with our differences in a spirit of mutual respect. We seek a relationship that is candid, constructive, and cooperative."

As if to underscore that point, neither leader dwelled on traditional points of friction. Bush did not mention human rights, and Jiang offered only a brief comment about Taiwan. Still, although the two presidents declared themselves partners in the war on terrorism, there were moments of subtle differences. Jiang sidestepped a question on whether Beijing supported the strikes against Afghanistan, and he reiterated the importance of clearly defining targets in order to "avoid innocent casualties." For his part Bush noted pointedly, "The war on terrorism must never be an excuse to persecute minorities," an unmistakable reference to China's Muslim and Tibetan populations.

Body language suggested a newfound friendship. At one point Jiang held Bush by the elbow as the American leader whispered an aside. Reciprocating, Bush casually put his arm around Jiang as the two turned and left for a lunch of shark's fin soup, pan-fried lobster, and steak. They appeared to be enjoying each other's company, though at times Bush seemed more relieved than elated. There was no doubt that both leaders, who had been through a rollercoaster year in their relationship, were making an extra effort to appear comfortable with each other.

In the rush of events following September 11, the new relationship between China and the United States was not fully appreciated by the American public. The *Washington Post* noted, "Public prickliness has disappeared as the government of Jiang Zemin has supported the U.S. campaign against terrorism and even the bombing in Afghanistan—the first time China has supported a U.S. military action since the end of the Cold War." Most Chinese, though they still harbored resentment over the embassy bombing and spy plane collision, agreed that Jiang's move to support the United States in the fight against international terrorism was, according to the *South China Morning Post*, "Beijing's wisest decision in a decade."

The APEC summit, which concluded with a gala party and massive fireworks display over Shanghai's Huangpu River, symbolized China's progressive emergence as a vital and respected member of the international community. It was a triumphant moment for Jiang Zemin.

At a press conference just after APEC, a CNN reporter, speaking in English, asked Jiang about his personal future. "Now you just hosted a major summit, a quite successful one," the journalist said. "Could it be your valedictory, your big performance, before, if, you choose to retire next year from your leadership position? Will you retire? If not, why should you have another term next year?"

Nervous laughter rippled through the audience. In China reporters just don't ask those kinds of questions of their leaders. Before answering, Jiang hesitated and turned to his interpreter for clarification. The interpreter's words were accidentally audible. "The question he just asked," the interpreter told the president, "was whether the successful hosting of this year's APEC leaders meeting means a valedictory speech before you retire next year."

"Aha," said Jiang, smiling broadly, "I didn't catch your main point." Laughter again filled the hall. "What you are interested in is my retirement next year. Is that so? What is it? First of all, will I retire next year? On this point, I will tell you frankly, this will have to be handled according to the stipulation of our country's laws."

One interesting though underreported feature of the APEC forum was that whenever Jiang chaired a meeting, he did so in English. Singapore's prime minister observed that Jiang, whose diction he commended, became more at ease with the language as the week went by, "setting a sterling example" for the children of China. Following Jiang's lead, media briefings by Chinese officials were also conducted in English, an attempt to increase China's influence abroad and encourage the study of English at home.

Jiang also made technology a priority of the summit, spending a good deal of time with a fellow attendee, Microsoft founder Bill Gates. Accompanying the president was his technology-savvy son, Dr. Jiang Mianheng, who sought to combine the best of American and Chinese ways of thinking in order to create a new value system for the advancement of science in China. In the drive to modernize the country's information technology (IT) industry, China watchers enjoyed speculating whether the son was "his father's disciple or his guru."

Dr. Jiang had returned to China in 1992. Following his graduation from Drexel, he had worked at Hewlett-Packard in northern California for about a year, formulating strategies for the Asia-Pacific region and taking business courses at a local university. (As Jiang Zehui tells it, one of the reasons Mianheng moved back to China was because Jiang Zemin wanted his grandson, who was about to begin school, to receive a traditional Chinese education.)

Jiang Mianheng joined the Shanghai Institute of Metallurgy, where he managed the spinoff and financial success of a for-profit technology company. Two years later, leveraging his rapidly developing business skills, he founded an investment company for the Shanghai municipal government that sought to commercialize science and consolidate local companies so that they could face international competition after China's entry into the World Trade Organization. He later became vice president of the prestigious Chinese Academy of Sciences, where, among other responsibilities, he was deputy commander of the *Shenzhou* manned spacecraft program. Dr. Jiang has told friends that his dream is to develop a self-sustainable model for scientific research in China, and perhaps to return to scientific research himself in his original field of high-temperature superconductivity.

Meanwhile, Jiang Zemin had become fascinated by what economist Joseph Schumpeter had termed the "creative destruction" model of the American market, and he had worked to break up the state-run, highly bureaucratic telecommunications monopoly, China Telecom. Jiang was particularly impressed by America's IT surge during the 1990s and had come to believe that the competition, even the chaos, in America's rapidly evolving IT market was a primary reason for its success.

In seeking to apply the model to China, Jiang had to wrestle with the minister of information, who resisted breaking up China Telecom and opening the market to foreign investors. But the president had persisted, and a month after APEC it was confirmed that China Telecom would be split into two competing companies. Over time Chinese consumers stood to benefit from the new competition.

Jiang's younger son by two years, Miankang, was also in IT. After graduating from Shanghai's Second Institute of Technology, a continuing education college, he began employment at the same Shanghai Electrical Equipment Research Institute where his parents had worked more than two decades earlier. Miankang received on-the-job training in Germany at Siemens, the multinational electronics corporation, then returned to Shanghai where he worked for the municipality on information systems.

"Mianheng and Miankang have excellent work styles," commented Jiang

Zehui, their aunt. "They are technically astute, decent, and honest. Mianheng is more outgoing; Miankang is more reserved and calm. Third Brother and Third Sister-in-law are very proud of them."

ON NOVEMBER 10 THE World Trade Organization, meeting in Qatar, unanimously approved China's accession, thus culminating its fifteen-year quest to join the global body. Jiang said that China, "as a member of the WTO, will strike a carefully thought-out balance between honoring its commitments and enjoying its rights."

In mid-December Jiang took part in a three-day National Work Conference on Religious Affairs, which was convened to develop the country's policy on religion for the new century. It was the highest-level meeting ever held about religion in China, and all seven members of the Politburo Standing Committee were in attendance. In his speech Jiang recognized the relevance of religion, acknowledging its contributions to social stability and warning against underrating its role in world affairs. He encouraged participants to "make socialism and religion adapt to each other."

"Asking religions to adapt to socialism doesn't mean we want religious workers and believers to give up their faith," the Chinese leader stated. "Instead, we ask them to embrace our socialist system, the leadership of the Communist Party, follow the country's rules and regulations . . . and contribute to ethnic and national unity." Jiang praised the "broad believing masses" for their support of the nation and highlighted the social function of religion, such as in disaster relief.

But he also warned that no one would be allowed to "abuse religion" in order to sabotage the Party, socialism, or national security—an overt reference to Falun Gong and other unauthorized religions—and he cautioned against "infiltration of foreign forces cloaked in the mantle of religion."

In short, Jiang was promising freedom of religion so long as those religions were under the authority of the state. New rules, instituted at the conference, allowed churches and other religious organizations to register directly with the state as independent entities, rather than as part of one of the official "patriotic" religions. In this manner, various groups among China's "underground" churches could gain a form of official recognition—and avoid punishment—without having to subsume their identities to a religious group with which they did not identify. On the other hand, those choosing not to register could find themselves subject to even more constraints.

As a rational man of science, Jiang had been mystified by the appeal of religion, with all its presumptions and superstitions. He had subscribed to the classic Marxist prediction about religion. "As a social phenomenon," he said a year earlier, "religion has a long history and will continue to exist for a long time under socialism. The ultimate withering away of religion, to be certain, will be a long historical process, probably longer than that of the class and state."

Jiang had expected that religion's influence would gradually diminish. Instead, he now saw, the opposite had happened. Religion had grown more potent as a social force even as educational levels had increased—not simply in China but all over the world. Accordingly, Jiang revised his thinking, particularly after the sudden rise of Falun Gong in 1999. Religion was not of diminishing importance, as he had once believed, but rather a power that needed to be controlled and focused.

Government estimates put China's religious adherents at about 100 million, whereas nongovernment estimates put the number at 200 million or more. Part of Jiang's rationale for the Communist Party to continue to be the ruling Party was that it must "represent" the "overwhelming majority" of the people—the last of the Three Represents. To be consistent, then, the Party could hardly disregard ten percent or more of the population. Most believers—whether they were Buddhists, Catholics, Protestants, Muslims, or Taoists—were also loyal citizens. As such, Jiang concluded, they too were contributing to building the country.

Balanced as it was, this new view of religion was attacked by both extremes of the political spectrum. Left-wing purists saw any accommodation with religion as yet another example of Jiang's anti-Marx revisionism, which they felt was eviscerating the Party's core beliefs. Radical rightists criticized Jiang for not going further and removing virtually all restraints on religious freedom.

Jiang was not deterred. Since his philosophy was evolving into one that sought "to rule the country by virtue," he felt religion could become a more central element of society—a radical change in his thinking. In fact, Jiang now asserted that religion could not be isolated from politics. Visiting a Buddhist temple that fall, he even asked the senior monks for their ideas on channeling "young people's interest in religion," which he thought could support both his vision for a moral and civil society and his desire to repulse destructive elements such as Falun Gong.

Jiang spoke to one of the Buddhist masters about an episode of meditation in his own life, which Jiang called a "fateful encounter." "I once practiced the kind of meditation about which you just talked," Jiang recalled. "It was during a very difficult period, in the late 1950s—there was the Big Steel-Making Movement [Mao's disastrous Great Leap Forward]. I had severe gastric disease [working at First Automotive Works] and practiced meditative sitting for three months—it seemed to have cured my ailment. Meditation can lead one to serenity; it is very marvelous indeed."

IN DECEMBER JIANG VISITED Dr. Qian Xuesen, China's rocket pioneer, at his home in Beijing. It was Qian's ninetieth birthday, and sitting by the revered scientist's bed, the Chinese president exchanged ideas on how science and technology could contribute more to the country's reform and modernization. Jiang reiterated his pledge to protect "the creative spirit, initiative and enthusiasm of scientists."

A year before, on his eighty-ninth birthday, Qian had reflected on Jiang's Three Represents. He talked about why senior leaders should be "equipped with modern scientific and cultural knowledge" as well as with political skills. He called Jiang "a true Marxist" in that Marxism is always advancing. Qian said that Jiang's "high quality" understanding of both science and politics had enabled him to develop the "integrative" principles of Three Represents, which, according to Qian, "are not pure politics, nor pure science, but the product of the organic integration of science and politics. . . . Look at the whole world," Qian added rhetorically. "Which country is developing better than China?"

Qian gave his sense of Jiang: "He has a good foundation in science and technology, and a broad range of interests. He loves to study. Every time we met, we talked about science and technology. I remember in 1989 when he was just transferred to Beijing . . . he showed strong interest in systems engineering, so I gave him my book *On Systems Engineering* on the spot. Subsequently, he employed its principles in his speeches."

In 1991 Qian received a call, out of the blue, from Jiang. He said: "Comrade Xuesen, nowadays physicists are talking about superstring theory. Could you please explain it?" Qian sent Jiang his article addressing abstract philosophical issues in modern physics.

"Although he is occupied with myriad state affairs," the legendary Dr. Qian observed, "General Secretary Jiang still manages to find time to study these state-of-the-art theories. He invites all kinds of experts to Zhongnanhai to lecture to senior leaders about science, technology, economics, and law." In early 1995 Qian sent Jiang an elaborate paper entitled "We Should Study

How to Greet the Twenty-first Century," and two weeks later Jiang drove to Qian's home, by himself, for an animated three-hour discussion about China's long-term development.

IN MID-DECEMBER President Jiang addressed the largest gathering of writers and artists since 1996 and proclaimed that "a great renaissance of the Chinese nation requires not only material advancement but also cultural advancement." He positioned culture as central to the grand rivalry among civilizations. "In today's world the hot competition for integrated national power includes not merely economic strength, technological strength, or strength in national defense," Jiang said to three thousand of China's cultural elite. "It also includes competitiveness in cultural areas.

"It is impossible for literature and the arts to be separated from politics," Jiang stated as his primary theme, "especially when facing the pressure of the dominant position of Western countries and dealing with the infiltration of Western ideology." Jiang warned that the fate of the nation depended on whether China's culture would be strong enough to overcome the "infiltration of corrupt thinking of foreign culture" that was being carried into China along with Western products and services.

Jiang was not without support for his nationalistic views of culture. Beginning in the middle 1990s, many Chinese artists and public intellectuals had begun to swing their incisive, often vitriolic critique away from their own government and toward the West. Even film director Zhang Yimou, whose *Raise the Red Lantern* was banned in China, shifted his target to Western media. "The West has for a long time politicized Chinese films," he complained to reporters. "If they are not antigovernment, they are considered just progovernment propaganda."

In describing "literature and art" as "the flame of the people's spirit," Jiang Zemin expressed his abiding love for China's rich culture. "The spirit of the Chinese people," he intoned, "is not merely felt in the historical process of struggle . . . It is also reflected in the outstanding works of literature and art that the Chinese people have produced during the past several thousand years and in the spiritual creative activities of all the outstanding literary figures and artists in China." Artists, Jiang said, have an "historic mission" to "create excellent works that stand without shame before our times, our socialist motherland, and our people," and he listed the areas in which they work—"literature, drama, film, television, music, dance, visual arts, photography, calligraphy, folk art or acrobatics, or folk literature and arts, or even literature and arts for the masses."

Torn between an intellectual's love of art and a patriot's concern for stability, Jiang was concerned that some intellectuals had used Western-germinated ideas to undermine loyalty to the Party. "Artworks and literary pieces that stay away from the masses are pretentious works," he said. "Literary and art workers should adhere to the truth, oppose falsehood, glorify beauty and goodness, fight evil, advocate science, and combat foolishness."

Jiang called on China's artists and writers to join in his ideological vision of Three Represents. "Constructing advanced culture will contribute to developing the country's advanced production forces," he said, adding that China had to strive to make this "advanced culture" more attractive and inspiring to people everywhere. By showing how advanced culture supports advanced productive forces, and how both bring great benefits to the people, Jiang neatly integrated all three of the Three Represents. It was his last ideological speech before 2002, the year when the Sixteenth Party Congress would determine both China's future and Jiang's legacy.

In a side story at the congress, many of the high-profile delegates who had come to Beijing were put up at Lao Dong Tower, a dilapidated facility with noises that made sleep all but impossible. The living conditions were so bad, the delegates complained, they would be unable to rest and therefore unable to contribute to the conference.

For some reason, a member of Jiang's staff came to the hotel, and after he noticed the deplorable conditions, he reported to the president what he had seen. Jiang was chagrined that artistic leaders were being mistreated, and he instructed that all delegates staying in poor hotels be moved to proper ones. That evening two hundred were transported to Beijing Hotel's renovated east wing. When they arrived, the hotel staff were standing at the entrance, welcoming them. "We were moved that President Jiang would deal with such trivial things," said Li Qiankuan, the film director. "It showed his special concern for artists and writers."

As 2001 DREW TO a close, talk in Beijing focused on the run-up to the Sixteenth Party Congress, scheduled for the fall. The question on everyone's mind was whether Jiang Zemin would retire from one, two, or all three of his leadership positions.

Jiang himself had three objectives for the Party congress. First, he wanted to achieve formal recognition of his Three Represents by its inscription into the Party's Constitution, a move that would include allowing the new elite of society, including private business owners, to join the Party. Second, he hoped the Party would confirm the ascension of certain close associates into the Politburo Standing Committee and key governmental positions. Third, he was being encouraged to maintain a role of real power; this might include retaining his post as chairman of the Central Military Commission or passing a high-level Party resolution requiring him to be consulted on important matters of state.

The assumption was that Jiang would have to give in on a number of his wishes, particularly on getting his associates into top jobs. "It looks like Jiang will have to sue for compromise with the other factions," said a Western diplomat in Beijing. "If he wants to score big in the area of theory, such as revising the Party charter, Jiang may have to accept that one or two of his protégés won't make the Standing Committee."

Certainly Jiang lacked the political clout of his powerful predecessors, Mao and Deng, and had to rely instead on "negotiation, consensus building, and compromise." Said one political analyst, "Jiang Zemin can only win about 60 percent of his political battles, while in comparison Deng Xiaoping won about 90 percent and Mao Zedong won 100 percent." But there were still a number of months to go, and Jiang Zemin had a number of things to do.

Chapter 27

January – June 2002

"Study Three Represents; Practice Three Represents"

S TAKES SWELLED IN 2002, as did the rumors, which is what happens when the process of succession is conducted behind a Chinese wall of secrecy. The year would determine the direction of the Party, the future of China, and the legacy of Jiang Zemin, and considering the high stakes, political circles in China, as well as observers and critics abroad, all seemed in thrall to the latest happenings and speculations. The Sixteenth Party Congress, coming at some still-unknown date in the fall, would sum up Jiang's thirteen-year record, set ongoing ideology and guidelines, and most important, confirm the new generation of leaders. In China personalities dominate policies, and the lineup of those in charge would be the best predictor of the shape of the country for years to come.

Foreign critics sometimes paint a one-dimensional portrait of Chinese politics. In peering behind the veil, they focus on friction, stressing internal rivalries and political battles, and thus make it appear, inadvertently or on purpose, as if such contentiousness and belligerence are the chief operating mode of China's leaders. Reports in Western and Hong Kong media can seem more the work of political cartoonists than political journalists. In China, as in other countries, political leaders do jockey for position and disagree, often vehemently, on matters of policy. But since the Cultural Revolution, with the exception of the period leading up to June 4, 1989, those who govern have largely worked well with one another. The vast majority of their time and energy is devoted to running the country, and the political disputations that occur are more nuanced in substance and compressed in time than the often-caricatured renderings would suggest. As Professor Frederick Teiwes states, "Jiang Zemin's period of 'core' is notable for its lack of 'power struggles,' notwithstanding the efforts of outside observers to divine such conflicts."

China's senior leaders, particularly Jiang Zemin, the current Party general secretary, and Hu Jintao, the coming Party general secretary, were committed to making the transition as smooth and seamless as possible. China was a respected country now, its economy integrated with the world's, and signs of instability would be damaging and intolerable.

Nonetheless rumors were frequent and, to those who enjoy such hearsay, endlessly entertaining. The primary rumors concerned possible positions for Jiang Zemin following the Party Congress and the lineup of senior leaders on the Politburo Standing Committee. One media favorite was a presumed competition, even struggle, between Hu Jintao and Zeng Qinghong, the latter closely associated with Jiang. Another was whether Li Ruihuan, whose views were considered more liberal than Jiang's and who was still below seventy years old, would continue on the Standing Committee. Still others sought to divine who would get which plum job in the Party and the government. In the end, most of the rumors circled back to one: What would be Jiang's Zemin's role and real power after the Party Congress?

Early in the year PLA chief of General Staff Fu Quanyou gave the possibility of Jiang's continuing role some foundation. Speaking at an expanded Party committee meeting, he asserted that the Chinese military should obey Jiang, "no matter when, where, and under what circumstances." General Fu's statement, published in *Liberation Army Daily*, was judged to be a pledge of allegiance to one person rather than to the office. It was also a measure of the respect that Jiang, whose ties with the military had been minimal at his start, had managed to win.

The relationship that observers watched most closely was the one between Hu Jintao and Zeng Qinghong. While it was a virtual certainty that Hu, who was smart, stable, and personable, and enjoyed almost unanimous support, would become general secretary, Zeng's role was less clear, though it would likely involve Party leadership. Confirming evidence came when Hu chaired, and Zeng cochaired, the committee responsible for selecting and vetting candidates for the next CPC Central Committee. Though there was natural tension between Hu seeking appointees from his so-called Communist Youth League Faction and Zeng seeking those aligned with Jiang's so-called Shanghai Faction, the two future leaders sought symmetry and harmony and seemed to get on well together. In fact, such natural tension, more normal than in previous generations, provided China's governance with a rudimentary type of checks-and-balance-system. "Zeng mostly substantiated Hu's views," said a source. "They in fact complemented each other."

JANUARY SEEMED TO HAVE a Middle Eastern flavor—President Jiang welcomed Jordanian King Abdullah, Egyptian president Hosni Mubarak, and Afghan interim leader Hamid Karzai. Abdullah urged China to help "break the cycle of violence" in the Middle East; Jiang told Egyptian media that after September 11 "unstable elements" were increasing and China and Arab countries were both confronted with more "novel issues and new challenges"; and after Jiang thanked Karzai for his stand against terrorism, particularly against Xinjiang separatists, and pledged China's support for Afghanistan's reconstruction, the Chinese president quipped, "I heard yesterday that your costume has taken the lead in world fashion."

In the same month a story broke in the international press that was so bizarre it seemed a rejected first draft of a made-for-television movie script. As the story went, Chinese military intelligence agents, not the sort who normally go about leaking secrets, revealed that twenty-seven sophisticated bugging devices had been discovered in the official aircraft of the Chinese president, a Boeing 767 that was about to be put into service.

Jiang said nothing publicly, and the reaction from official Chinese sources was strangely mute. Apparently the authorities had known about the bugs for months but had not even lodged a complaint with their American counterparts until the sensational story appeared in the *Financial Times* and the *Washington Post*. Still, China remained oddly taciturn on the matter, and no story or accusation appeared in the Chinese media.

White House officials braced for a sharp and vociferous response, but it never came. Analysts like Willy Wo-Lap Lam attributed Beijing's "subdued reaction" to a signal of "eagerness to improve ties with America despite the perennial irritants." American diplomats gave the Chinese credit for being more circumspect when dealing with problems. "I don't know if I'd be so vain as to say the Chinese learned from events of last April," said Admiral Joseph Prueher, who was the U.S. ambassador to Beijing at the time of the spy plane collision. "But I think there is now a desire to prevent every event from becoming a crisis and to handle conflict in a less volatile way."

Deepening the mystery, the fenced-in plane had been guarded around the clock during the remodeling process by twenty PLA agents of an elite unit of the Chinese air force, who worked in teams alongside U.S agents. The security arrangements, which allowed continuous and unimpeded surveillance by the Chinese agents, were designed to prevent precisely what had seemingly occurred.

Over the ensuing weeks a host of rumors fed the story. As for who did the bugging, there were conjectures of millions of dollars gone missing and rivalries high within the Chinese government. A bewildered Li Peng had to endure the wild and absurd allegation in the *Washington Times* that he was behind the bugging, which reputable China analysts said was "100 percent preposterous" and represented "a new low even for a paper known for its China bashing."

As to why China's response was so subdued, one view held that if the Chinese reacted to the bugging with restraint, Bush might feel obligated to return the favor when he arrived in China for his upcoming summit with Jiang. And as to why the leak occurred at this time, there was unfounded speculation that Chinese hardliners sought to disrupt China–U.S. relations before the summit or to weaken Jiang personally by creating a public scandal about a luxury aircraft.

The mystery lingered. The fact that the curious event did not disrupt relations suggested that whatever really happened, it was mutually agreed at the highest levels in Beijing and Washington that the problem should be contained. If this were not the case, the story would have grown. Instead, after a few newspaper articles, it quietly died, just as George W. Bush was departing for China.

THE AMERICAN PRESIDENT ARRIVED on February 21, a date chosen because it marked the thirtieth anniversary of Richard Nixon's pathbreaking trip in 1972, which reopened China–U.S. relations after nearly a quarter of a century of bitter estrangement. From the start George Bush seemed determined to differentiate himself from his predecessor. In contrast to the ebullient Clinton, Bush was more subdued, focusing only on the task at hand.

"We want to talk more in just over thirty hours than Clinton managed in a week," one White House official said. "For us, that will be symbolic enough . . . what better way can there be to set the tone for the next thirty years."

It was also a marked change from Bush's first trip to China in the late 1970s, when his father, George H.W. Bush, had been the U.S. senior envoy in Beijing. On that visit the then thirty-year-old George W. had partaken liberally of the local brew and had tried with unknown success to date several local women. Some things, however, remained the same. Back then, Washington and Beijing had shared intelligence in the cold war against the Soviet Union. This time the common enemy was international terrorism, and the long-dormant cooperation between Chinese and American intelligence services was being reestablished.

After the attacks on September 11, Chinese security officials had surprised their American counterparts by handing over a treasure trove of information on international terrorist groups in two publicized meetings and subsequent undisclosed ones. Jiang raised no objection to the arrival of U.S. forces in Central Asia, and the Chinese military, at the request of America, moved listening stations to the border with Afghanistan in order to monitor Taliban and al-Qaeda communications. How shocked the old cold warriors would have been!

"The United States is not China's enemy now," one Chinese scholar concluded, "and probably never will be." In a high-level briefing for senior officials, the scholar offered China a stark choice: the United States or Osama bin Laden. "We chose the United States," he confided to the *Washington Post*, explaining that while "some Chinese intellectuals and officials reacted gleefully to the attacks," President Jiang realized that China's long-term interests lay with Washington. In return, the United States seemed willing, at least momentarily, to table its own anxieties about a "China threat" in order to focus on the immediate dangers presented by radical Islam.

To Jiang, China's cooperation with America had a larger arch, more about his country's long-overdue international emergence than about a parochial battle against a common foe. In Mao's time, China's foreign policy had been reflexively based on its revolutionary ethos and its self-claimed leadership of the third world. But recent circumstances—from its economic surge to its successful Olympic bid—were bringing the country closer to America and Europe, the "first world," than to its traditional allies.

Bush and Jiang appeared comfortable together. After informal talks and the formal summit, both men expressed satisfaction with the encounters at their joint press conference. Bush thanked the Chinese government for its strong support following the terrorist attacks and called for more areas of cooperation, such as new energy technology, reducing greenhouse gas emissions, and fighting AIDS. The two sides should share not only information, Bush added, but also hope. Jiang noted that both parties had agreed to "reinforce high-level strategic dialogues and contacts at different levels," particularly economic, trade, scientific, and technological.

A pointed question about religious freedom in China sounded rude by Chinese standards. Appending it to a predictable question about missile defense, an ABC News reporter asked, "President Jiang, if I may, with respect, could you explain to Americans who may not understand your reasoning why your government restricts the practice of religious faith? In particular, why has your government imprisoned more than fifty bishops of the Roman Catholic Church?"

President Jiang and Wang Yeping are greeted by U.S. President George W. Bush and his wife, Laura, at the entrance of the Bush ranch in Crawford, Texas, October 25, 2002. *(Xinhua News Agency)*

President Bush takes President Jiang for a tour of the Bush ranch in his pickup truck, October 25, 2002. Their wives are in the backseat. *(Xinhua News Agency)*

President Jiang and President Bush at the APEC meeting in Shanghai in October 2001, about one month after the terrorist attacks on September 11. *(Xinhua News Agency)*

Jiang meets the six-year-old eleventh Panchen Lama, January 12, 1996. A spiritual leader of the Tibetan Buddhists, he was selected as the reincarnated Panchen Lama in 1995 in accordance with religious custom. Li Ruihuan is at the center, Luo Gan back and to the right. (*Xinhua News Agency*)

President Jiang welcomes Russian president Vladimir Putin to Shanghai for a summit meeting of the six-country "Shanghai Cooperation Organization," which focuses on security issues in central Asia, June 14, 2001. (*Xinhua News Agency*)

During his visit to Japan, President Jiang inscribes his calligraphy of a famous Chinese verse, *Deng Gao Wang Yuan* ("Ascend high to see far"), November 28, 1998. (*Xinhua News Agency*)

The heads of state of the five permanent members of the United Nations Security Council meet in New York, September 9, 2000. From left to right, U.K. Prime Minister Tony Blair, U.S. President Bill Clinton, Chinese President Jiang Zemin, French President Jacques Chirac, and Russian President Vladimir Putin. *(Xinhua News Agency)*

President Jiang meets American business leaders at Lincoln Center in New York prior to a concert by the China National Traditional Orchestra, September 9, 2000. From left to right, Information Minister Zhao Qizheng, President Jiang, Culture Minister Sun Jiazheng, Disney International President Michael Johnson, Chinachem Chairwoman Nina Kung Wang, Robert Lawrence Kuhn (author), New York Life International Chairman Gary Benanav. *(Xinhua News Agency)*

President Jiang with former U.S. Secretary of State Henry Kissinger in Zhongnanhai, June 5, 1998. *(Xinhua News Agency)*

Jiang speaking with Professor Wang Jiafu, senior fellow of the Law Institute of the Chinese Academy of Social Sciences, after his lecture for senior leaders in Zhongnanhai, "Legal System Development in the Socialist Market Economy," January 20, 1995. Li Peng is on the right, Zeng Qinghong on the far left. *(Xinhua News Agency)*

President Jiang reviews the military on Chang'an Avenue during the massive parade celebrating the fiftieth anniversary of the founding of the People's Republic of China, October 1, 1999. *(Xinhua News Agency)*

CMC Chairman Jiang inspects the Navy cruise missile ship *Harbin*, October 1995. *(Xinhua News Agency)*

President Jiang (below) pays his respects to the families of the Chinese citizens killed or injured in the U.S.–NATO bombing of the Chinese embassy in Belgrade, Yugoslavia, May 13, 1999. *(Xinhua News Agency)*

Jiang consoles the wife and six-year-old son of pilot Wang Wei, "Guard of China's Sea and Air" (below). Wei was lost and presumed dead after his PLA fighter jet collided with a U.S. Navy spy plane, April 20, 2001. *(Xinhua News Agency)*

Jiang escorts Professor Xie Xide, a noted physicist and former president of Fudan University, Shanghai, mid-1990s. You Xigui, the president's bodyguard and head of Zhongnanhai security, is in the center.

Jiang visits Dr. Qian Xuesen, the revered father of China's aerospace programs, in Dr. Qian's home, December 8, 1999. Executive Vice Premier Li Lanqing is on the right. *(Xinhua News Agency)*

Jiang visits a chemistry research institute with State Councilor Dr. Song Jian (center), chairman of the State Science and Technology Commission, January 8, 1992.
(Xinhua News Agency)

CMC Chairman Jiang awards Yang Liwei, China's first taikonaut, a Space Hero commendation following his successful orbital flight, November 7, 2003 (a year after Jiang retired as general secretary). *(Xinhua News Agency)*

At the Aerospace Technology Research and Experiment Center in Beijing, President Jiang inspects the *Shenzhou I* spacecraft, just after its first test flight, November 24, 1999. Vice President Hu Jintao is in the center. *(Xinhua News Agency)*

Jiang inspects flooded areas with Vice Premier Tian Jiyun (left) and Wen Jiabao (right), then director of the CPC General Office, July 9, 1991. *(Xinhua News Agency)*

Jiang inspects the flooded apartment of a factory worker in Suzhou, Jiangsu province, July 9, 1991. *(Xinhua News Agency)*

Jiang and North Korean president Kim Il-Sung visit the memorial of Shi Kefa, a national hero, in Yangzhou, Jiang's hometown, October 12, 1991. *(Xinhua News Agency)*

President Jiang is welcomed in Havana by Cuban President Fidel Castro, April 12, 2001. *(Xinhua News Agency)*

President Jiang learns the latest in agritechnology at the Zohar Agriculture Research Center in Israel's Negev desert, April 14, 2000. Israeli President Ezer Weizman is second from the right. *(Xinhua News Agency)*

On his state visit to Israel, President Jiang visits the Yad Vashem Holocaust Museum in Jerusalem, April 13, 2000. *(Xinhua News Agency)*

At the end of a concert honoring People's Liberation Army soldiers for their heroic relief work during the Great Flood, CMC Chairman Jiang comes onstage to sing with the performers the popular patriotic song "Ode to the Motherland," October 8, 1998. (*Xinhua News Agency*)

During his visit to the Chinese embassy in Moscow, Jiang conducts an impromptu chorus of members of the China–Soviet Union Friendship Association, May 16, 1991. (*Xinhua News Agency*)

At a concert during a national conference of artists, Jiang comes onstage to join with noted singers, December 20, 1996. (*Xinhua News Agency*)

Jiang meets with the Three Tenors on June 24, 2001, the day after their high-profile concert in the Forbidden City. From left to right, Executive Vice Premier Li Lanqing, José Carreras, Plácido Domingo, President Jiang, and Luciano Pavarotti. *(Xinhua News Agency)*

Jiang and other state leaders attend a New Year's Gala by PLA artists, January 18, 1993. From left to right, Wan Li, Zeng Qinghong (behind), Jiang Zemin, Li Peng, Li Ruihuan, Hu Jintao, and Ding Guangen. *(Xinhua News Agency)*

Jiang plays table tennis with champions during his visit to the China National Table Tennis Team Training Center, January 28, 1990. *(Xinhua News Agency)*

Newly elected General Secretary Hu Jintao stands with former General Secretary Jiang Zemin at the close of the Sixteenth Party Congress, November 15, 2002. *(Xinhua News Agency)*

President Jiang with Premier Zhu Rongji (right) and Vice President Hu Jintao (left) at the Fourth Session of the Ninth People's Congress at the Great Hall of the People, March 5, 2001. *(Xinhua News Agency)*

Secretary General Jiang chairs a regular meeting of the Politburo Standing Committee in its standard setting in Zhongnanhai, February 4, 2002. This particular meeting was on poverty relief programs. From left to right (in rank-assigned seats), Li Lanqing, Hu Jintao, Zhu Rongji, Jiang Zemin, Li Peng, Li Ruihuan, and Wei Jianxing. *(Xinhua News Agency)*

At a tree-planting ceremony in Beijing, Jiang Zemin walks with the nine members of the new Politburo Standing Committee, April 3, 2004. From left to right (in rank-assigned spots), Li Changchun, Huang Ju, Jia Qinglin, Wu Bangguo, CPC General Secretary and Chinese President Hu Jintao, CMC Chairman Jiang Zemin, Wen Jiabao, Zeng Qinghong, Wu Guanzheng, and Luo Gan. *(Xinhua News Agency)*

Jiang is interviewed by Barbara Walters for ABC News in Beijing, May 2, 1990. *(Xinhua News Agency)*

Jiang is interviewed by Mike Wallace for CBS's *60 Minutes* at the Beidaihe summer resort, August 15, 2000. *(Xinhua News Agency)*

Jiang Zehui, Jiang Zemin's sister and president of the Chinese Academy of Forestry, with the author during our interview in Beijing, December 2001. *(Courtesy of Adam Zhu)*

Professor Wang Huijiong, Jiang Zemin's university classmate and lifelong friend, being interviewed by the author in Beijing, December 2001. *(Courtesy of Adam Zhu)*

Tong Zonghai, Jiang Zemin's university roommate, being interviewed by the author in Changsha, December 2001. *(Courtesy of Adam Zhu)*

Shen Yongyan, Jiang Zemin's longtime friend from First Automotive Works, with the author during our interview in Changchun, September 2002. *(Courtesy of Adam Zhu)*

Bush discussed missile defense first, giving Jiang time to prepare his answer. When Bush finished, a Chinese reporter (from CCTV) asked a new question, ostensibly taking Jiang off the hook.

The very next question, another multipart query from an American journalist, returned to the religious question: "With respect, sir, we are eager to hear your response to the original question about the arrest of Catholic bishops in your country and attention to religious groups in general."

Again Bush jumped in and answered his part about China's role in the anti-terror campaign, and again a Chinese reporter saved Jiang by breaking in to ask two softball questions about Taiwan and whether China would become a future threat.

Jiang gave his prepared answers, then hesitated, and said, "Now I am very willing to answer the question posed to me by the U.S. correspondent."

He must have been contemplating the religion inquiry even as he was answering other questions, wondering which would look worse, a response sure not to satisfy or no response at all. As he compared options, it probably came to him that ducking the same question twice was making him appear defensive and China guilty. His evasion, he realized, would be reported in the foreign press, maybe as the lead.

Jiang had lost the initiative and needed to regain it. Breaking into English with a touch of self-deprecation—a savvy shift of mood—he said, "President Bush, he has much more experience than I. When it comes to meeting the press, I think President Bush is much more experienced. I will do my best to answer your question." Jiang continued in Chinese: "In the first question, you mentioned that some Catholic Church people have been detained. I wish to explain that since the founding of China, all the Chinese Constitutions have specified freedom for religious beliefs. There are many religions in China, for example Catholicism and Protestantism. . . . Then we have Islam and a Chinese religion called Taoism [Jiang repeated Taoism in English]. The Constitution has specified freedom for all these religions."

Jiang then explained his own beliefs. "Although I am not a religious believer," he said, "I am very interested and have read the scriptures of various religions; for example, the Bible, the Koran, and China's Buddhist scriptures, the *Vajracchedika-sutra*. I frequently have discussions with religious leaders in China. We sometimes hold gatherings to celebrate the New Year or during holiday seasons. Regardless of their religions, the common ground is that all believers must abide by the laws of China. Anyone who violates Chinese law will not be pardoned simply because he or she is a believer of a certain religion. On this point, even as state president, I am afraid I also have no right to interfere in judicial affairs."

Observers credited Jiang for saving the day—and his image—by not avoiding or sloughing off the sensitive question, but in spite of smiles and handshakes, points of contention remained. "The United States shares interests with China," Bush observed, "but we also have some disagreements. We believe that we can discuss our differences with mutual understanding and respect."

Chief among these was China's weapons sales to Iran, Iraq, and North Korea—the three nations that Bush, just the month before, had claimed formed an "axis of evil." American officials were particularly disturbed about China's assistance to the Iraqi military, including work done by Chinese companies to lay a fiber optic cable used in Iraq's radar defenses.

A few days later, however, a Foreign Ministry spokesman would declare that China was ready to accommodate the United States on arms nonproliferation issues. The implication was that Beijing had decided to align with Washington at the expense of alienating those countries like Iraq, Iran, and other anti-America states with which China had once bonded.

But Jiang signaled that there was a limit to this newfound closeness by drawing back when asked about the potential use of force against Iraq. "During the talks," Jiang said, "I conveyed my views to President Bush that we hope he will treasure peace."

Any such differences were forgotten once the workday was over. At the welcoming banquet that evening, Jiang called over an accordion player and serenaded Bush with his favorite "O Sole Mio." At the press conference he had deferred to Bush's greater experience; at the banquet Jiang was the unopposed star. Observers reported that he "stole the show." A spry seventy-five, the Chinese leader took to the dance floor, first with Laura Bush, then with Sarah Randt, wife of U.S. ambassador Clark Randt, and finally with National Security Adviser Condoleezza Rice. Jiang got on especially well with Rice, who is also fluent in Russian.

"He was kicking up his heels and singing songs," White House spokesman Ari Fleischer reported. "It really was just a delightful touch." Asked whether Bush had danced, Fleischer replied, "In order to avert an international incident of the highest order, President Bush showed judgment, discretion, and valor and observed the dancing from the seated position. International incident avoided."

In spite of the diplomatic politesse and genuine goodwill that seemed to exist, a seasoned Jiang Zemin sought a multipolar world. As soon as Bush departed, he called Pakistani president Musharraf, Russian president Putin, and French president Chirac, three of his country's more traditional allies, to report on his meeting.

IN FEBRUARY PRESIDENT JIANG spoke at a three-day National Financial Work Conference, which dealt with China's shaky financial industry. Attending the conference, which was a full year in planning, were virtually the entire leadership of the Party and government. Wu Xiaoling, vice governor of the People's Bank of China, called Jiang's keynote address "a trenchant, in-depth presentation." It had taken months to prepare and three hours to deliver.

"President Jiang took an historical approach," explained Governor Wu. "He referred to the old days in Shanghai. When loans could not be paid back, he said, some bankers became so distraught, they would jump into the Pu River. Jiang asked, 'How many bankers today have jumped into the Pu—or any other—River because of bad debts?' The president's point was obviously not to encourage suicide but to get the financial system to take seriously the concepts of credit, loans, and debt. He took examples from different cultures; regarding 'supervision,' he discussed the Bubbles Act of 1720 in England. . . ."

"Jiang's perspective," she continued, "enabled even nonprofessionals to understand how the financial sector functions as part of a modern economy—the creation of money, control of credit, development of banks, global integration, plus the experience of countries that descended into chaos. Jiang asserted that China's banks must become true commercial banks. That would be the best way, he said, to allocate resources efficiently. He called for a 'proper credit culture' and 'good faith' among enterprises that borrow. . . ."

"Beyond finance," observed Governor Wu, "this example shows how President Jiang loves to learn, how he pushes himself to gain new knowledge."

At a seminar on the WTO, which China had entered just two months before, Jiang exhorted business and government to "control the initiative amid fierce international competition." Calling China's performance in the WTO "a real test of our learning capacity," he stressed "our problem-solving, competition, decision-making, and innovative capabilities." He used a metaphor from his favorite form of exercise. "In our effort to modernize," he said, "we must go swimming in the great ocean of the global marketplace. We must swim—and swim hard—and do everything we can to enhance our ability to struggle with wind and waves."

ON THE NIGHT OF MARCH 5 the signals of eight state-run cable TV channels in Changchun were hijacked by Falun Gong. In the place of normal broadcasts came forty-five minutes of footage that claimed to be "a truth clarification video" revealing "the state-sponsored persecution of Falun Gong practitioners in China."

"Ten minutes after the Falun Gong attack ended, at 9:10 P.M., Jiang called me," remembered Shen Yongyan, who still lived in Changchun. "I could tell there was trouble," said Shen. "No chitchat."

"Falun Gong practitioners are broadcasting on Changchun's cable system!" an obviously agitated Jiang said. "Who is your city's Party secretary or mayor?"

"I'll find him," Shen responded. He placed an emergency call to the mayor but could get only his assistant, since the mayor was in Beijing attending the National People's Congress. "I don't care what time it is!" Shen told the assistant, who was uncomfortable calling his boss. "I must speak with him now!"

The assistant transferred Shen to the mayor's cell phone, and he delivered the unpleasant news. "The mayor was very upset," recalled Shen. "He told me that he too had just learned what had happened, but that one of the attackers was caught."

Shen called Jiang to report what he had learned. "Your information was correct," Shen said. "Changchun's cable system was attacked. Prime time, everyone saw the Falun Gong programs, the city's abuzz. The mayor said one attacker was arrested."

"Why is he talking about the 'arrested one'?" asked Jiang. "How many got away?

As it happened, many senior officials from Jilin province were already in Beijing attending the NPC. According to Falun Gong propaganda, Jiang called these officials in and ordered a crackdown "without mercy."

WITH HIS APRIL TRIP to Libya and Iran, President Jiang sharply distinguished China's foreign policy from that of America. Libya, characterized by the United States as a "rogue nation," had been implicated in the destruction of Pan Am flight 103 over Scotland in 1988, which killed all 259 people aboard. Iran was a direct supporter of the Hizbollah guerrillas and maintained an unceasing diatribe against the United States.

Jiang's visit had two motivations. One was his central strategy to create a "multipolar" world to counterbalance American power. The other was oil. China's industrial growth had generated an insatiable thirst for liquid energy. A net importer since 1996, China had been eyeing new supplies of oil in Nigeria, Tunisia, Libya, and Iran—Muslim nations where Western oil companies were not entrenched—and he used the trip to showcase China as an emerging ally of the Muslim world.

While in Tripoli—he was the first Chinese leader ever to visit Libya—Jiang attended the signing of an oil pact. In Tehran he took a moment from oil negotiations to make his bluntest anti-American statement in months. In a meeting with Iranian hardline cleric Akbar Hashemi-Rafsanjani, the Chinese president said, "Beijing's policy is against strategies of force and the U.S. military presence in Central Asia and the Middle East region."

But Iran wasn't all geopolitics. Visiting the tomb of the fourteenth-century poet Hafez, a master of Iranian literature known for his spiritual romanticism, Jiang wrote, "Poems are a bridge to exchange the thoughts of people." Then, amid the ruins of Persepolis, once the center of Darius I's vast Persian Empire, Jiang wrote in the visitors' book, "Iran is an ancient and civilized country and it is the heir to magnificent civilizations."

JUST PRIOR TO HIS TRIP Jiang had the thrill of watching the successful launch of China's third unmanned spacecraft, *Shenzhou III*, at the Jiuquan Satellite Launch Center in Gansu province. He said that since the decision to develop the manned space program ten years earlier, China had built indigenous state-of-the art space systems—vehicle, launch site, monitoring network—and trained astronauts and support personnel. Proud that the entire operation was managed by Chinese experts, Jiang said the achievement demonstrated "the Chinese people's spirit of constantly striving to become stronger," encouraged "the Chinese people's national dignity and cohesion," and enhanced the "national might," including the modernization of national defense.

In April Jiang promoted the social sciences, which in China had taken a far backseat to the natural sciences. Touring People's University in Beijing, he said, "Having essential knowledge of philosophy and social sciences is very important for helping people gain a correct understanding of complicated social phenomena and elevate their moral quality and spiritual vista."

Jiang repeated the theme at the Chinese Academy of Social Sciences' twenty-fifth anniversary in July, when he attended a forum with experts on history of science, law, economic forecasting, integrating liberal arts with science, and the relationship between basic and applied research. Jiang listened attentively and took notes; he loved this type of academic analysis. In his speech he called for "vigorous efforts" to step up research in "philosophy, economics, political science, international politics and economics, jurisprudence, history, ethnology, journalism, demography, sociology, literature, linguistics, and archaeology."

All the while his campaign to promote Three Represents was waxing more intense. In April CCTV announced that it would broadcast a series of major programs entitled *Guide for Implementing Three Represents*. Each episode was introduced with the same graphic image—a rising sun, Tiananmen Square, followed by Jiang Zemin speaking, which then faded into a red flag waving across the screen. The four Chinese characters for the words *Three Represents (San Ge Dai Biao)* appeared in large font, followed by the soaring architecture of the Millennium Monument in Beijing with multicolored balloons being released into the air. Each episode concluded with "Study Three Represents; Practice Three Represents," which was also flashed periodically during the program in the lower left-hand corner of the screen.

Although Three Represents was a genuine advance in ideology, heavy-footed propaganda risked turning innovation into parody. Yet in China the propaganda campaign gave out another message, confirmed by constant reinforcement: Not only was the philosophy important, but Jiang's power in the run-up to the Sixteenth Party Congress remained undiminished.

Further evidence of the latter came on May 31. Instead of rooting for the Chinese side at the World Cup games in South Korea—it was the first time China had qualified in forty-four years (but Jiang was never much of a soccer fan)—the Chinese leader chose to give a graduation speech at the Central Party School. As in 1992 and 1997, Jiang's address in this venue was a harbinger of his forthcoming political report at the Party Congress in the fall, which would set the agenda for the next five years. Given to a closed audience of several hundred top-level officials, the speech reaffirmed the status of Three Represents as the tool for modernizing the Party in the new century.

One turn of phrase caught people's attention: Jiang described the current structure of ownership as "irrational." He was right, of course. Public ownership was so confused that often no one really knew who owned what. The result was that in many enterprises there was no concerned or active owner, which meant that management was accountable to no one. Jiang knew this uncertainty had to change.

Jiang also said that "building socialist political civilization is an important goal of socialist modernization." This was the first time the notion of "political civilization" was put forward officially, and it signified that political reform, even if gradual, was now on the agenda. A mainland scholar predicted that political life would shift slowly from absolute obedience toward a more democratic, law-based mode. "This will be a long, painful process," the scholar warned, "and we must be prepared to pay a considerable price for it."

Jiang did not ignore the still-controversial subject of private business owners joining the Party. He used the term "new dynamics" (*xindongli*) to describe how the Party's old and new members could work together toward a common goal. When reports of Jiang's Party School speech appeared in the press, several sections, including this one, were left out, a sign that the issues remained unresolved and probably contentious.

In June Jiang attended a Eurasian security summit in Kazakhstan and assumed the role of peacemaker. The summit focused almost exclusively on reducing potentially catastrophic tensions between India and Pakistan, which had been triggered by militant Islamic attacks in the disputed province of Kashmir and had brought about fearsome nuclear threats in recent weeks.

Indian prime minister Atal Bihari Vajpayee said he would not meet with his counterpart, Pakistani president Pervez Musharraf, until Pakistan took action to curb what India called cross-border terrorist attacks. It fell to Jiang Zemin to act as mediator. It was a novel role for China, reflecting the country's new prestige.

Jiang was determined to be evenhanded, which he knew would be challenging as far as India was concerned. For four decades China had backed Pakistan—helping develop all three Pakistani nuclear plants and supplying missiles and missile technology—in part as a strategic counterweight to India, with which China had fought a bloody border war in 1962. Now China's burgeoning economy was far more important than arcane disputes over slivers of uninhabitable mountains. As Jiang had said on many occasions, China needed peace and stability to continue its growth and modernization.

Jiang issued a public call for negotiations to resolve the immediate crisis. At the same time Chinese diplomats made the same point in New Delhi, Islamabad, and Beijing, while coordinating with Washington and Moscow. In a joint effort Jiang and Russian president Putin each held individual meetings with the two disputants. Encounters with the Pakistani side were naturally more cordial for the Chinese president, but Jiang was careful to strike a balanced note with the Indian prime minister.

Jiang began the meeting by recalling his goodwill visit to India in 1996, reminding the Indian leader of his invitation to visit China, and by noting that "our agreements are far greater than our differences." He then came to the point. "Relations between India and Pakistan have remained tense," Jiang said, "and we are all concerned. As a Chinese saying goes, 'Peace brings benefits to the two sides, and fighting causes destruction to both sides.' Many issues in the world are left over from history, and they are very complicated. We sincerely hope that India and Pakistan will properly solve their existing problems through dialogue and negotiations." India was pleased that, despite Pakistani pleas, China did not lecture New Delhi on what it should do to ease the military standoff.

President Jiang also took time to pay his respects to smaller countries. After the summit he toured Latvia, Estonia, Lithuania, and Iceland. Although none was of consequence to China, Jiang treated each with graciousness and esteem. He was acting not only out of self-interest—he was always seeking support on Taiwan and human rights issues—but also from a sense of history. When Chinese media reported one of Jiang's diplomatic encounters, it hardly mattered whether he was meeting the leader of a small country or a great power, the extent of coverage was usually similar. Westerners found this egalitarianism odd, but China was making up for centuries of inconsequence. To Jiang, treating small countries with diplomatic dignity was yet another affirmation of China's new position in world affairs.

In the family, Jiang's sister Jiang Zehui, who was president of the Chinese Academy of Forestry, won an environmental protection prize for her "ecology first" work in China. When she told Jiang of the honor, she reminded him how he had encouraged her, decades ago, even though she had been rejected by her first-choice schools and could not pursue her desired fields, to become first-rate in her assigned profession.

Earlier she had given him a large, technical book that summarized her scientific research on wood development, particularly bamboo and rattan. "Wow, Zehui," President Jiang said, holding the heavy tome and flipping through its hundreds of microphotographs, "your book is much thicker than mine!"

"But your book [*Jiang Zemin on Science and Technology*]," replied Jiang Zehui, a little embarrassed, "is about your theory of national development through science and technology. My book is only about wood science—it cannot be mentioned in the same breath with yours."

"I am so proud of you," he said.

Chapter 28

JULY – OCTOBER 2002

"A Gentleman Gets Along with Others But Does Not Necessarily Agree with Them"

POLITICAL SPECULATION INCREASED AS the Sixteenth Party Congress approached: Were petitions being circulated among provincial leaders and army generals asking Jiang Zemin to retain his positions? Many higher-level officials looked to Jiang to ensure continuing stability while Hu Jintao, the much-respected new leader, gained experience. They believed that Jiang's wisdom was essential in light of the "complicated and changeable world situation"—particularly Chen Shui-bian moving Taiwan toward independence—and the volatile array of domestic issues, such as industrial restructuring and unemployment.

Jiang's strongest support came from military officers, many of whom hoped he would continue to exercise leadership over the army. It was gratifying to Jiang, who as a civilian had become chairman of the Central Military Commission having no military experience but plenty of doubters. Officers believed that the army's drive for modernization—spearheaded by science and technology, Jiang's specialty—could not be separated from his command.

None of this was intended as criticism of Hu Jintao. Hu was admired, sophisticated, and honest. He was also telegenic, a big plus in a media-dominated world. His expertise was in the Party, which in some people's opinion was necessary but not sufficient for him to assume all the reins of power, including the CMC, all at once and at such a sensitive time.

On matters of state, many wanted to see China represented on the world stage by a younger, more dynamic personality, along the lines of a Bill Clinton, George Bush, or Tony Blair. Jiang himself had argued for such a change, and here Hu was ideal. Some wanted Jiang to step down as general secretary because they disagreed with his ideology and domestic policies. Those on the extreme Left thought Jiang had betrayed Communist ideals; those on the extreme Right believed he was perpetuating autocratic rule.

Finally, there was a large contingent that simply wanted China to evolve into a more open and stable society, a "normal" country as it were, and to this end they sought a smooth and harmonious transition of power, something that had yet to occur in the turbulent fifty-three-year history of the People's Republic. Again, Jiang agreed with this view.

There was never a "battle" between Jiang Zemin and Hu Jintao, as some foreign critics suggested, though there was normal, intense give and take in setting mutually acceptable terms and conditions, primarily regarding personnel. The general secretary had long supported Hu's well-planned rise. At the same time Jiang believed that the country's welfare would benefit by his maintaining, for a while, operational control over the army, and by his continuing advice on Party development, domestic policy, and foreign affairs.

A front-page commentary in *People's Daily* stated that in order "to emphasize unity," Party officials should be guided by Jiang Zemin as the "core of the Party leadership." Though the phrase was standard fare, the context and the timing suggested special significance. Would Jiang maintain his "core" designation beyond the Sixteenth Party Congress? The piece, published just as senior leaders were convening in Beidaihe for critical summer deliberations, also noted that "in order to emphasize stability, the Party had to treasure the existing excellent situation," a reference to the broad success of Jiang's thirteen-year leadership.

The media highlighted Jiang's prowess as a military leader, taking advantage of the timing. August 1 marked Army Day, the seventy-fifth anniversary of the People's Liberation Army, and in a synchronized display the three most influential entities—PLA-run *Liberation Army Daily,* Xinhua News Agency, and *People's Daily*—all published stories and editorials lavishing praise on Jiang for his contributions to the army.

Liberation Army Daily used a full-color insert to promise "eternal loyalty" to the Party leadership under Jiang. The five-thousand-word Xinhua article characterized Jiang's thirteen years as CMC chairman as "a grand journey" that "carried forward the cause of the older generation and broke new ground." There was little doubt that military leaders were encouraging Jiang Zemin to stay on.

Then in the midst of these final maneuverings, senior leaders were hit with a blunt challenge from Taiwanese president Chen Shui-bian, who issued a provocative theory of "each side, one country," a nonsubtle move toward de facto independence. Analysts agreed that Chen's remark would force "those who wanted to push at Beidaihe for Jiang's total retirement to back off, at least for the moment."

In late August it was announced that the Party Congress would begin on November 8, later than usual. There was speculation that the date had been chosen to allow Jiang, who had been invited by President Bush to his ranch in October, to retain his official positions for the visit. This indicated that Jiang would be retiring.

Yet there were conflicting reports out of Beidaihe whether Jiang would retain power and influence over postcongress China irrespective of what official positions he would hold. A "tacit understanding" was reportedly reached that there would be three "no changes," all of which benefited Jiang: no change in the Third Generation leadership (the new leaders would not be considered, as had been expected, the Fourth Generation); no change in the "core" (Hu Jintao would not be called the "core," as had Mao, Deng, and Jiang); and no change in the army's supreme command.

It now seemed that Jiang's apparent bid to remain Party chief had been more a strategy than a goal. All the rumors, which had been fueled by the intense campaign promoting Three Represents, were likely a reflection of this effort to secure his ideological and personal legacy and to promote key associates onto the Politburo Standing Committee, the source of real power. Jiang was bargaining as much for his policies as for himself; they had brought China success, and he wanted to make sure they would continue.

All along, the CMC chairmanship was probably the only position Jiang truly wanted to retain, and there were now reasons to think that he would prevail. The military leadership had come out strongly in his support, and the escalating tensions with Taiwan worked in his favor. Jiang had been dealing with Taiwan for over a decade and had faced down similar threats in 1995, 1996, and 1999. Everyone agreed that Jiang was needed to handle cross-strait relations, considering the likely American intervention if a crisis erupted. Hu Jintao, CMC vice chairman only since 1999, had limited experience with these complexities. Left unsaid was a subliminal concern that only Jiang Zemin could control the military.

"He staked out an impossible position so he could appear to be making concessions when he agreed to step down," said a Party source. "In exchange for that, Jiang wants a place in the Party Constitution and his allies on the Politburo. He looks like he's going to succeed."

WHILE JIANG WAS IN BEIDAIHE preoccupied with all manner of sensitive, inner-Party negotiations, he received a note from his dear friend Wang Huijiong. Wang said that he had just been diagnosed with prostate cancer and would be going in for immediate surgery.

"I wrote to President Jiang just to let him know that I might not be available if he called me," Wang said, not two months later. "I never expected him to respond, certainly not from Beidaihe in the midst of discussions affecting the nation, but the next day he did exactly that. I was really surprised. He asked me not to do anything until he consulted with China's leading doctors."

That same day Jiang personally called one top specialist, who suggested that, considering Wang's condition and age, an alternative treatment was the current standard of care. The problem was that the side effect would be a loss of sexual function.

"My wife and I are quite old," noted Wang, "so this was not a serious issue considering the life-threatening nature of the cancer. Yet Jiang felt obliged to call my wife and explain the situation to her. It may seem strange that anyone, especially the president of the country, would call my wife on such a personal matter, but we are very close lifelong friends. Remember, he was at my wedding, as I was at his."

IN MID-AUGUST JIANG took time out to meet Stephen Hawking, one of the world's leading physicists, who was in Beijing attending a conference on string theory, which dealt with the deepest structure of matter and energy. The wheelchair-bound Hawking, who spoke through a synthesizer, used quantum theory and general relativity to discern black holes, which sit in the center of galaxies and are so dense that not even light can escape their gravity—just the kind of awesome science that fascinated Jiang. During a meeting with Hawking and others, Jiang voiced respect for the unique sensitivity of scientists and said that their discoveries would promote social productivity. Hawking predicted that China would become a major scientific power within fifty years.

The next day Jiang presented the 2002 Fields Medal—the equivalent of a Nobel Prize in math—at the International Congress of Mathematicians (ICM). Convened every four years, the congress attracted 4,270 mathematicians from 101 countries. It was a tribute to the growth of science in China that ICM 2002 was held in Beijing.

At the end of August Jiang and Hu Jintao attended a time-urgent conference of propaganda chiefs and media bosses. Jiang admonished them to enhance public confidence that the Party ensured stability and unity as well as promoted growth and development. Unemployment and corruption were a volatile mixture, and Jiang wanted to head off any public protest before it began. Calling for a "sound atmosphere," he wanted no disturbances prior to the November Congress. Media chiefs were told not to report any conflicting views within the Party—no so-called "noises"—or anything negative in society. The difficulties of laid-off workers were, for the moment, off limits.

Following the propaganda conference, in an awkward effort to follow orders and enforce stability, Chinese authorities blocked access to Google, the Internet's most popular search engine. (A Google search of "Jiang Zemin" brings up one or more vituperative Falun Gong sites somewhere on the first page and, at times, a link to a silly animated game entitled "Slap the Evil Dictator.") A few weeks later, buckling under a chorus of complaints, censors removed the blocks but restricted access to proxy servers, limiting information on Google for all but the cleverest Chinese hackers. Between May and October 40 percent of China's 200,000 Internet cafés were closed down.

In a more telling development, state media generally stopped coupling Jiang's name with Three Represents. In other words, it was no longer "the important thinking of General Secretary Jiang Zemin's Three Represents" or "Comrade Jiang Zemin's important Three Represents thinking." Hereafter, official pronouncements read simply "the important thinking of the Three Represents," with Jiang Zemin's name no longer attached.

For Jiang, this was a case of good news, bad news. The bad news was that Jiang Thought, using his name, would not achieve the same status as Mao Zedong Thought and Deng Xiaoping Theory. The good news was that, by decoupling Jiang's name from his philosophy, senior leadership was agreeing that Three Represents had broad support and would likely be elevated into the Party Constitution.

Speaking at the Central Party School in early September, Hu Jintao evinced strong unity by calling Jiang's May 31 speech at the same school "another important Marxist document" and "an important political, ideological and theoretical preparation for the Sixteenth Party Congress," adding that study of Jiang's new instructions deepened understanding of Three Represents.

ON SEPTEMBER 5, the *New York Times* broke a blockbuster story entitled "China's Leader Won't Hold On, Anonymous Author Says." "Despite ram-

pant speculation to the contrary," the article asserted, "a new account of Beijing's secretive politics says that China's President Jiang Zemin has decided to
give up all of his top posts." The apparent revelation had been published
in *China's New Rulers*, an English-language abridgement of a Chinese-
language book called *Fourth Generation (Disidai)*, which claimed to be
based on inner-Party dossiers. The editors were Andrew J. Nathan of Columbia University, an expert on Chinese politics, and Bruce Gilley, a respected
journalist and Jiang biographer. Nathan called the Chinese account "highly
credible, though impossible to verify fully."

The *Times* publicized the startling material: "The report says that trial balloons this year suggesting that Jiang, 76, should retain one or more of his top
offices failed to win the support of other senior leaders. It says Jiang will step
down as Communist Party chief in November and as China's president next
March, handing power to the 59-year-old heir apparent, Hu Jintao.

"The report asserts that Jiang's advisers have convinced him that in the interests of party unity and his own legacy he must also sign over to Hu his third
title, chairman of the Central Military Commission," the story continued.
"That transfer, the report says, is to take place during the meeting of parliament next March [2003], and Jiang is unlikely to wield major informal power
in the years that follow, contradicting a common view here that Jiang is an-
gling to keep the military title to prolong his influence."

In short, Jiang Zemin was out. Totally out. "The Propaganda Department
was merely giving Jiang a resounding send-off," the respected authors concluded, as if the praise for his tenure and theories was like a gold watch presented to a corporate manager on the occasion of his complete retirement.

"For all his apparent dominance and self-promotion," the same authors
wrote in *The New York Review of Books*, "Jiang Zemin was relatively weak
when compared with Mao and Deng. Both of these men named their successors (several times, in fact). Jiang was not able to dictate unilaterally who
would get a single seat on the Politburo." In their prediction, they allowed
only three Jiang allies—Wu Bangguo at number four, Zeng Qinghong at
number six, and possibly Li Changchun at number seven—on the seven-
member Politburo Standing Committee.

Although the high-voltage story was picked up by the world's press, the
Jiang camp did not react publicly. One insider confided at the time that the
news was not a surprise; then he added that it was also not correct. "You can
be sure," he stated cryptically, "the era following the Sixteenth Party Congress will also be characterized by the name of Jiang Zemin."

An independent source in Beijing, speaking with the *Straits Times* (Singapore), seemed to confirm this view. "The two scholars' confidential reports, if authentic, were based on outdated information," he said, probably from the 2001 Beidaihe retreat, and much had changed since then.

In any event, true or not, the book seemed to support the prospects of Li Ruihuan at the expense of Jiang Zemin in the belief that this was a way to encourage Western-style liberalism in China—the assumption being that by engaging foreign opinion it could influence the political transition. If nothing else, the now international speculation surrounding China's internal affairs confirmed the extent to which the country had become an important player on the world stage.

WHILE COUNTING DOWN TO the Congress, Jiang was also preparing for his trip to the Bush ranch in Crawford, Texas. The invitation showed that the Chinese leader, though of an older generation, had reached a level of camaraderie with the American president in the same league as Tony Blair and Vladimir Putin. This would be Jiang's final visit to the United States as head of state, and he wanted things to go well.

Information Minister Zhao Qizheng announced that China would dedicate a bronze statue of U.S. Captain James R. Fox Jr., whose plane had crashed on a World War II mission in support of China against the Japanese. Fox had been flying the supply route from northeast India over the famous "Hump" of the Himalayan Mountains to China when he was killed. According to Zhao, the inscription on the statue had been written by Jiang himself: "Resting here is an American pilot, who valiantly dedicated his life helping China win the War of Resistance against Japanese Aggression. The Chinese people will forever remember his name, James R. Fox Jr."

In addition, five agreements were to be signed with American companies just prior to Jiang's arrival in the United States. China also strengthened export control over military technologies and freed a Tibetan nun who had been sentenced to nineteen years in prison for inciting so-called counterrevolutionary activities. China–U.S. relations had taken a turn for the better, a trend attributed to the aftereffects of September 11.

When it came to North Korea, its longtime ally, China took a position of principled neutrality. But less than a week before Jiang's trip to America, North Korea announced with impunity that it had been actively developing a nuclear weapons program. Beijing denied that it had aided Pyongyang, claimed not to have even known about the clandestine program, and urged all parties to resolve the issue peacefully through negotiations.

On the American side, the invitation to the ranch was an affirmation of respect. By hosting Jiang and his wife at his private residence, Bush was honoring the Chinese leader both as an important leader of a major power and as a friend.

"It will be a prestigious event," said China scholar Kenneth Lieberthal, who noted that "China's new-found weight in regional and global affairs" had produced "a more subtle and mature foreign policy." Bush, he said, "is right to reward it with a day of personal hospitality at the ranch."

Landing in Chicago in late October, President Jiang was welcomed on a red carpet at O'Hare International Airport by Mayor Richard Daley, a U.S. Navy brass band, political and business leaders, and a thousand members of the city's Chinese community. Ever the engineer, Jiang was more impressed by the fact that O'Hare had *seven* runways. Alluding to the two runways at Beijing's Capital International Airport, Jiang said that China would construct two more prior to the 2008 Olympic Games.

About five hundred demonstrators, largely Falun Gong practitioners from other areas, gathered outside downtown Chicago's Ritz-Carlton Hotel, chosen for Jiang's stay because its twelfth-floor lobby would be far above the chanting crowds. Since his meetings were all held in the hotel, Jiang did not venture out during most of his twenty-four hours in the city. "It's important the trip comes off safely," said a Chinese official. "It's Jiang's closing performance."

After a banquet with business leaders, Jiang greeted staff of the Chinese consulate, overseas Chinese students, and members of Chicago's Chinese community. But the jet-lagged Chinese leader, who said that he had been unable to sleep and felt dizzy, canceled his scheduled speech.

The next day in Houston a revitalized Jiang toured NASA's Johnson Space Center, mission control of the U.S. manned space program, and then drove one hundred miles northwest to College Station, where he paid his respects to "an old friend of the Chinese people"—the highest praise he could bestow—by giving an address at the George H.W. Bush Presidential Library on the campus of Texas A&M University.

Speaking in English to six hundred guests, including the former President Bush and Chinese superstar basketball player Yao Ming, Jiang used his favorite phrasing for relating the two nations: "China is the largest developing country," he said, while "the United States is the largest developed country." It was China's policy, Jiang said, to seek consensus but not uniformity in the conduct of its foreign relations. Regarding divergences, there was nothing strange about that. He cited Confucius, who two thousand years ago said, "A gentleman gets along with others but does not necessarily agree with them," explaining that "harmony without sameness is an important principle in the development of all social affairs and in guiding people's conduct."

Jiang listed the "grave challenges" that mankind faced: terrorism, the spread of weapons of mass destruction, regional conflict, and environmental deterioration. On all these he put China and America on the same side. Both countries are victims of terrorism, he said. "In the antiterrorism struggle, the Chinese people have always stood together with the American people . . . [making] joint efforts to crack down on terrorism as an international scourge." Jiang called for similar joint efforts to prevent "the spread of weapons of mass destruction and to maintain peace and stability on the Korean Peninsula, in South Asia [India and Pakistan], and the Middle East," which he called major issues for all people who seek world peace and stability.

Jiang concluded by offering a vision. Portraying two economies that were complementary, he spoke of the vast potential for bilateral cooperation in trade, energy, environment, science and technology, and education, and he called for a "constructive, cooperative relationship" between China and America.

Then came the point of the trip: an informal summit with George Bush on his sixteen-hundred-acre Prairie Chapel ranch in the heart of Texas, eighteen miles southwest of Waco, about halfway between Austin and Dallas. Getting an early start to the long day, Jiang flew from Houston to Waco, but taking a back road for the drive from the airport to avoid protesters, the motorcade arrived thirty minutes late.

A gracious George and Laura Bush met Jiang and his wife at the entrance. "Welcome to the ranch, our cozy home," said Bush. "Laura and I are very pleased to host you and Madame Wang Yeping."

When the two couples, dressed casually and looking like old friends, were seen together in a photo that graced the front pages of newspapers throughout the world, people commented on how poised Wang Yeping appeared and how far she had come since her early days as China's First Lady.

During the four-hour visit, which featured a private meeting between the two presidents, Jiang noted that "over the past year, our cooperation has expanded and our mutual trust has deepened." He focused on the long term, on the "broad and important common interests" shared by China and America. It was as if he wanted to solidify his positions before he retired.

There were differences between the two leaders as always, but this time they revolved around new issues. On Iraq, the United States was becoming increasingly bellicose about the danger posed by rogue nations; Jiang said that he hoped that all issues could be worked out through the UN. On North Korea, Jiang claimed to be "completely in the dark" about the nuclear weapons program of China's longtime ally, but he added that "China has all along been a supporter of a nuclear-free Korean peninsula and wants peace and stability there." Other subjects included human rights, religious freedom, and military exchanges.

After the talks Bush and Jiang joined their wives for a Texas-style barbecue—southern fried catfish, barbecued brisket, and pork ribs, accompanied by ranch-style beans, black-eyed-pea salad, and potato salad with jalapeño peppers, and topped off with pecan pie. The two couples then piled into George Bush's white Ford pickup truck, men in the front, women in the back, and, looking like a couple of old-time rancher families, drove off for a quick inspection of the spread.

The Crawford summit drew only perfunctory notice from the U.S. press, which had been more fascinated by Jiang's previous visits. Now there were other attention-grabbing stories in the headlines. The day before the Washington-area snipers had been caught. That day Minnesota senator Paul Wellstone was killed in a plane crash. In a Moscow theater Chechen separatists were still holding seven hundred hostages. And Iraq was looming large. Once China and the United States became friends, with due credit to Jiang's strategy of constructive partnership, their relationship was no longer front-page news.

From Texas, Jiang headed to Los Cabos, Mexico, to attend the tenth annual summit of the twenty-one-member APEC forum, where terrorism haunted the proceedings in the wake of deadly attacks on the Indonesian island of Bali, in the Philippines, and in Moscow. Jiang took the role of elder statesman and, despite the dark mood, did so with confidence. Speaking like a veteran free trade advocate, he urged member nations to "rein in trade protectionism." He also urged them to stand together in the fight against terrorism.

For all his talk of building ties, there was one country with which Jiang Zemin had difficulty reconciling. Relations with Japan had been strained by repeated visits by Prime Minister Junichiro Koizumi to Tokyo's Yasukuni Shrine, which honored Japanese war criminals along with its war dead and was regarded as the spiritual center of Japanese militarism. Koizumi had promised not to go back to the controversial Shrine after his 2001 visit there had caused an uproar in China, but just two months earlier, under pressure from nationalistic groups in Japan, he did exactly that. Jiang was angry; this was no small matter. Meeting with Koizumi in Mexico, Jiang raised the issue three times during one forty-five-minute encounter. Asking Koizumi to "stop offending China," Jiang said the issue "touches the sentiments of 1.3 billion Chinese people."

Koizumi sought to smooth over the problem, but Jiang would not be mollified. Not once did he refer to plans for the Japanese leader to visit China. Drawing a "sharp line" between ordinary Japanese people who were victimized in the war and the militarists who started it, Jiang offered Koizumi blunt advice: "So it's better not to make visits to Yasukuni again, never again."

Departing Mexico for Beijing, Jiang stopped briefly in San Francisco for refueling. To accommodate his schedule, a luncheon with local dignitaries was held at the airport. Jiang praised the sisterly ties between Shanghai and San Francisco, calling such city-to-city contacts vital for country-to-country relations, and he concluded by saying, "This afternoon I will take the friendship of the American people back to China."

Though rushed, Jiang still had time for song. After lunch he led the singing, cajoling Mayor Willie Brown and Senator Dianne Feinstein to join him.

On the very day Jiang departed for America, the Party announced that Jia Qinglin, the Party secretary of Beijing, and Huang Ju, the Party secretary of Shanghai—both of whom were close to Jiang—would be stepping down from their current posts and joining the Party's "central leadership." Suddenly the two men were odds-on favorites to be elected to the Politburo Standing Committee at the close of the upcoming Party Congress. Though speculation of all kinds had abounded, the likely elevation of Jia and Huang was the first unmistakable sign that the critics had been wrong and that Jiang Zemin would not be given a "resounding send-off." (Twice Jiang had been thwarted from bringing Huang Ju to Beijing, even though he had been a Politburo member since 1994, a double failure that was hardly a good mark for a "dictator.")

Two days later Zeng Qinghong, Jiang's longtime adviser and administrator, resigned from his position as head of the Party's Organization Department. This move was also widely interpreted as presaging his elevation to the Politburo Standing Committee, an unusual (but expected) jump given that Zeng was only an alternate, rather than a full member, of the Politburo.

The timing of the announcements was notable because Jiang was out of the country when they occurred. The message was that the transition was going so smoothly that the general secretary did not even need to be present. At the same time Zeng Qinghong did not accompany his boss on the trip. Before this the two had often been traveling companions on major State visits. Though some speculated that the decision for Zeng to remain in Beijing was a precaution against anything becoming undone in Jiang's absence, the more likely reason was that this period marked Zeng's personal transition from adviser-administrator to senior leader in his own right and there was much to do before the Congress.

One of the bellwether appointments was that of Liu Yunshan as the new head of the Party's Publicity Department—"propaganda minister"—the position responsible for all media in China. Liu was a professional, which meant the Party was staying the course set by Jiang Zemin and supported by Hu Jintao, one that would maintain stability vigorously and increase freedoms gradually.

Jiang's appointment of senior Party officials just prior to handing over Party leadership to Hu Jintao may seem comparable to an outgoing President Clinton appointing senior cabinet officials that an incoming President Bush had to accept. It is not. The analogy breaks down since the Chinese political system has only one Party, and the transfer of power between Jiang and Hu was negotiated out in detail as an "inner-Party" matter in a kind of comprehensive transition package. A better analogy would then seem to be if Bill Clinton voluntarily agreed to transfer his presidency to his vice president, Al Gore, even though he was not required by law to do so, and as part of the deal, Clinton proposed, and Gore accepted, that several of Clinton's associates would be given cabinet posts in Gore's administration.

But even this comparison would not be accurate, because in the Chinese system of executive governance, the process of appointing senior Party leaders resides with the Party's Central Committee, not the Party general secretary, whereas in the American system, the chief executive, the president, has absolute authority to appoint whomever he likes (subject, in some cases, to confirmation by the U.S. Senate). Since the CPC Central Committee selects all high-level personnel, it is common for officials to serve under multiple leaders. For example, Dr. Song Jian was chairman of the State Science and Technology Commission under three Party general secretaries (Hu Yaobang, Zhao Ziyang, and Jiang Zemin) and two premiers (Zhao Ziyang and Li Peng); he also served under Premier Zhu Rongji as president of the Chinese Academy of Engineering. Technically, the National People's Congress appoints the senior government officials, headed by the premier who recommends to the NPC his slate of ministers, although top-level decisions are normally pre-determined by the Party.

Supporting evidence for those who believed that Jiang would step down fully were reports of a comfortable retirement home being built for him in the Luwan District of Shanghai, near good restaurants, fashionable stores, and chic art galleries. It was also close to the historic site where the first congress of the Chinese Communist Party had been held in 1921. What better location could there be; he would have the amenities of contemporary China, rooted in revolutionary history, in the city that Jiang and his wife loved so much. Certainly Wang Yeping hoped that the couple would return to Shanghai and live out the rest of their lives in peace. Jiang was expected to spend at least half of his time in Shanghai.

Then on October 25 the press reported that Li Ruihuan, number four in the Party, whom some foreign media had crowned as Jiang's chief rival, would be leaving political life. The departure of Li Ruihuan—who at sixty-eight years old was still two years below the cut-off age of seventy—must have been disconcerting to those who had thought (or hoped) that he would become number two in the Party and diminish Jiang's influence.

What happened, it was now clear, was the opposite: Jiang had never been more influential. As they had done throughout his career, people were still underestimating the man—even with so much evidence to the contrary.

Chapter 29

NOVEMBER – DECEMBER 2002

"I Hope That Comrades Will Be United as One"

O N FRIDAY MORNING, November 8, more than two thousand official delegates, joined by dozens of special delegates and a few hundred guests, convened in the Great Hall of the People for the start of the Sixteenth Party Congress. After the national anthem and a brief welcome by Li Peng, the session began with the keynote political (or work) report, which would be presented by the general secretary, Jiang Zemin.

Preparations for the Sixteenth Party Congress had been separated into three areas: the political report; amendments to the Constitution; and personnel. Each area was handled by a different group, with no knowledge of the others' activities, and each group reported to Hu Jintao, who was in charge of the preparatory committee and reported to Jiang Zemin. The construction of the political report, a long and elaborate process that took over a year and involved a team of thirty drafters, was coordinated for Jiang by Hu. The recursive and formal process was designed to engage the Party's collective leadership and produce an authoritative consensus document. In theory, the sixty-eight-page report encapsulated the Party's unified view of the past and vision for the future; in reality, it also reflected Jiang's personal perspectives. He was intimately involved in its creation, particularly at the commencement, setting the agenda, and at the conclusion, adding his ideas and sense.

Jiang first met with the thirty experts who would be drafting his report in January 2002, about ten months before the Party Congress. Hu Jintao was chairman of the drafting committee, and Teng Wensheng, director of the Party's Policy Research Office, played the coordinating role. The thirty drafters represented three core interest groups: key ministries and commissions (such as the State Development Planning Commission and the State Economic and Trade Commission), the Party's research areas (Policy Research Office, Literature Office, and Central Party School), and provincial Party secretaries.

"I remember clearly the first official session with General Secretary Jiang," said Jin Chongji, president of the China History Society and China's official biographer of Mao Zedong and Zhou Enlai. (Jin Chongji was involved in the entire process of preparing the political report.) "We convened in Zhongnanhai on January 14; the session lasted about two and a half hours. Although the drafters had been meeting in different groups for a few months already, this was the first time that General Secretary Jiang addressed the group.

"Jiang started by reiterating the significance of the Sixteenth Party Congress and the key tasks to be accomplished in the political report," continued Jin Chongji. "He laid out the major topics—a review of the past five years since the Fifteenth Party Congress in 1997, and the tasks required to implement Three Represents, which he saw as vital for modernizing the Party. He gave us the primary theme: building a well-off society. He listed some ideas for economic reform, political reform, and cultural development, and of course he stressed Party building. Jiang described his sense of a world rapidly changing, particularly in science and technology, which, he said, accelerates the economy, alters military strategy, affects society, and generates a whole new way of thinking. China must evaluate itself in relation to other countries, Jiang emphasized, which brought us back to developing China's 'advanced productive forces and culture' [two of the Three Represents]. Jiang's thinking had great consistency over the years, and we could see this political report as its summation."

The drafting committee had been established about twelve weeks earlier, on October 26, 2001, more than a year, as it would turn out, prior to the Sixteenth Party Congress. Its first meeting, held in Zhongnanhai, was chaired by Hu Jintao at the request of Jiang Zemin. The committee was divided into eight subgroups to conduct research, which included on-location investigations in sixteen provinces.

"We wanted to know what was on the minds of provincial Party leaders and lower-level officials," said Jin Chongji, who is also vice minister of the Party Literature Office. "We also wanted to find out what the masses wanted. Each of the eight subgroups held about ten in-depth discussions with gatherings of people from all walks of life—political leaders, scholars, scientists, farmers, workers, managers. That's eighty group discussions in total, each lasting two to three hours. We spent two weeks outside of Beijing doing the initial research, returning in mid-November. Each of the eight subgroups prepared its own report, which we then consolidated into one comprehensive report that reflected our best collective thinking on the major issues in the provinces. We had our first research document by mid-December, which Jiang read in preparation for his formal meeting with the drafting committee on January 14."

Subsequent to Jiang's presentation and following his guidelines, the thirty drafters, divided into groups by topic, prepared a detailed outline of the political report. When they reached agreement on the outline about a month later, Hu Jintao took it to the Politburo Standing Committee, which approved it in late February along with suggestions from each member. At that point, the full group of thirty drafters closeted themselves in an off-site location in the Yuquan mountains in northwest Beijing.

"Our first task was to integrate all the comments from each of the seven members of the Politburo Standing Committee, which we did in one large session," noted Jin Chongji, who was among the group. "Teng Wensheng pulled it together into a cogent synopsis. The revised outline was distributed to the full twenty-three-member Politburo [including alternate members], whose feedback was then integrated as well."

Sometime in April consensus was reached on the detailed outline. Then came the first draft. "We wrote quickly," said Jin Chongji. "We followed the same process. First we sent drafts to the seven Standing Committee members, and when we had integrated their comments, we distributed the revised drafts to the full Politburo. Throughout the multi-month process, Hu Jintao held many meetings with the drafters. He was the link with Jiang, reporting progress and bringing back his comments. . . .

"On May 31 General Secretary Jiang released many of the key ideas to a larger audience by speaking at the Central Party School," continued Jin Chongji. "A summary of the speech was published in *People's Daily,* and the exposure enabled us to receive feedback from broad groups of Party officials."

On July 26 a draft of the political report was distributed to 3,100 Party officials in 178 ministries, departments, and areas. Each of these units was required to hold a formal discussion about the report and write up its feedback in detail, with word-specific suggestions, in an official document to be sent to the drafting committee. (As China scholar H. Lyman Miller observed, "If Party congress delegates look bored and sleepy as the general secretary delivers it [the political report] aloud, it is, in part at least, because they have seen its text before—and, in the case of some delegates, several times before.")

"The 178 units had one week to respond," said Jin Chongji. "They were instructed that providing thoughtful feedback was, for the moment, their highest priority (except for genuine emergencies). Feedback was expected to include line-by-line comments or suggested edits."

Gathering up all 178 commentaries, the entire drafting committee traveled to Beidaihe on the sea, where they had the monumental task of assessing the voluminous amount of feedback just received, then redacting the next draft by making careful, consensus-approved edits. This was the time when Jiang Zemin, Hu Jintao, and all the senior leaders were on their annual summer stay at the beach resort. The drafters needed the proximity, since many sensitive decisions had to be made, even down to the choice of single words.

"Imagine the complexity," exclaimed Jin Chongji. "We could have 178 different suggestions for each idea, each line, each word! Worse, the large number of suggestions could often contradict one another. Of course, we didn't actually have 178 ideas for every word, but we often had dozens of ideas and comments on critical sections."

To make the final decisions, the thirty drafters were divided into five teams of six experts, each team handling a specific category: overall or comprehensive; economic; political; cultural; and Party building. Major issues were brought before all thirty drafters, who met regularly as a group.

"Each team had a leader," said Jin Chongji, "and when a difficult decision had to be made, it was taken to Hu Jintao, who kept Jiang Zemin informed."

A revised draft was prepared and again circulated to the Standing Committee and the Politburo, and again each member's comments were considered and collated in preparing yet another revision. By the end of August it was time for final decisions and the last draft, and this was when Jiang Zemin became intimately involved.

"Between August 30 and September 17 Jiang focused on the report, devoting eight full days to scrutinizing and finalizing it," reported Jin Chongji. "He wanted firsthand opinions and met with various interest groups representing the ministries, the military, and the provinces. Then on September 18 he convened a working meeting with the drafting committee, his second formal meeting with all the drafters.

"It was an intense, highly detailed session," Jin Chongji explained. "Jiang added eight specific points, which we integrated into the text. For example, he asked that we make the part on national defense a separate section in order to highlight its importance. He said we should not permit state-owned assets to be managed by rural areas below the level of cities. In one of his more interesting comments, he said that he wanted to communicate a 'sense of insecurity' in the document, which he said reflected the real world. Jiang stressed this point. 'Don't think the good times will last forever,' he said. 'China is facing great challenges, including torrid foreign competition. We have to maintain a strategic focus and treasure unity.' Jiang asked us to modify the report's second-to-last paragraph to emphasis this insecurity, which we did.

"But even after all that," Jin Chongji added, "Jiang never stopped thinking about the report. During his trip to the United States in October, he continued to discuss it with Zeng Peiyan, Teng Wensheng, and Wang Huning, who were along. When he returned, Jiang added one sentence, which dealt with the proper process and right structure for urbanization."

The final political report was then officially presented at the Seventh Plenary Session of the Fifteenth Party Central Committee. (By protocol, the political report to one Party congress is delivered on behalf of the previous Party congress.) The editing process was relentless: a few changes were made in the Seventh Plenary, which met on November 3–5, only days before the Sixteenth Party Congress opened on November 8, the day Jiang Zemin read the report.

The political report was entitled "Build a Well-Off Society in an All-Round Way and Create a New Situation in Building Socialism with Chinese Characteristics." It summarized how China's thirteen-year leader saw China and envisioned the Party, and it reflected his contribution to both.

DRESSED IN A FORMAL DARK suit accented by a red polka-dot tie, Jiang Zemin delivered his address live on television and radio to hundreds of millions of citizens across the country. A record-breaking 1,375 Chinese and foreign reporters were in Beijing covering the event.

Jiang's voice was deep and distinctive, with a growling strength that was at once charismatic and comforting, and his delivery was marked by his signature cadence and rhythm. This was the oration of a leader confident in his domain.

Most of the speech followed a predictable pattern, but even small differences in language could mean major changes in policy. As officials sifted through customary Party phrases that maintained historical continuity and ideological integrity, they were on watch for subtle shifts of wording and phrasing—different stresses—that would convey different meanings.

Jiang began what was essentially his valediction by recounting the achievements that China had made since he had been named general secretary in 1989, a period in which China's national strength had risen dramatically while its society enjoyed long-term stability. There was no doubt that in virtually every aspect of life, the Chinese people were better off now than they had been then.

"We have gone through one trial after another and removed all kinds of obstacles," Jiang said, "thus ensuring that our reform, opening-up, and modernization drive have been forging ahead in the correct direction like a ship braving surging waves."

To no one's surprise, Jiang highlighted Three Represents as the operating mandate to renew the Party and set the future course for China. Calling the new theory "crucial to persist in advancing with the times," he said that Three Represents was a "powerful theoretical weapon" for strengthening the Party and developing socialism, adding that it would be "the guiding principle that the Party must uphold for a long period of time."

Significantly, Jiang also called Three Represents "the crystallization of the collective wisdom of the Party." Almost every time Three Represents was mentioned, the phrase "the important thinking of," not Jiang's name, was used to introduce it. That was the trade-off. By abandoning the notion that it was his own personal theory, Jiang was raising the philosophy to the highest level of importance.

Jiang had described Three Represents many times before, of course, but this time was different. This was the political report to the Party Congress, which meant that he had triumphed.

In promoting his theory, Jiang stressed that Party leaders had to "consciously free our thinking and understanding from the shackles of outdated concepts, practice, and systems, from our erroneous understanding of Marxist dogmatist theories." At the same time he rooted Three Represents in Marxism by stating that it was derived from Marxist methodology and fulfilled the Marxist imperative of "liberating and developing productive forces."

With this line of reasoning, Jiang was leading up to his most controversial initiative—the admission of entrepreneurs and private business owners into the Communist Party. He reaffirmed the importance of the working class and then implied that businessmen constituted a new stratum of this class. They were, in short, "all builders of the cause of socialism with Chinese characteristics."

Jiang believed that the core of Marxism was less about the differences between owners and workers than about an ultimate goal and a defining methodology. That ultimate goal was still an idyllic Communism, but for society to reach it, the defining methodology would have to "advance with the times." The Party had seemingly reinvented itself just in time—or more accurately, Jiang Zemin had reengineered it.

Entrepreneurs and private business owners, Jiang said, should be "encouraged," "protected," and "commended." To those who sensed the subtleties of the wording, it was an outright endorsement. Jiang had prevailed in pushing through this groundbreaking reform. China's prosperity was now increasingly dependent on private enterprise.

Jiang was making the Party more pluralistic, and as such more modern and energetic. Only by "the spirit of reform" and by injecting "new vitality" into its organization, he believed, could the Party retain its "vanguard" position in leading the country. "It is necessary to implement the important thinking of Three Represents," he said to thundering applause, "so that our Party always advances with the times and shares weal and woe with the people."

With Three Represents now recognized as the Party's guiding thought, Jiang turned his political report to the future and set China's overall goal for the next twenty years as the creation of a "well-off society" whose 1.3 billion citizens could enjoy a higher standard of living. The Chinese word that was being translated as "well off" was *xiaokang,* which does not mean "well off" as a native English speaker would understand the term. *Xiaokang* literally means "small well-being," which scholars defined as less affluent than "well off" but better than "free from want." Jiang desired all China to become a "midlevel developed nation," on a level with a country like Portugal, by the year 2050 and, as part of this plan, to quadruple its GDP from its 2000 level by 2020.

Steps in the process included using science to create sustainable development, advancing information technology, and encouraging China's "nonpublic sector" (as private companies were euphemistically called). Jiang said: "We must give full scope to the important role of the nonpublic sector of self-employed, private, and other forms of ownership of the economy in stimulating economic growth, creating more jobs, and activating the market."

Private had now been used openly. Though buried in the sentence, the formerly scorned word was nonetheless present, positive and official. Furthermore, Jiang asserted that privately owned firms should not be at a disadvantage with respect to financing, investment, taxation, land use, market access, and foreign trade, and he pledged more legal protection for private property.

As long as public ownership still had the dominant role, he believed, the government could increase its support for the "nonpublic" sector, which would keep the economy growing at its high rate. Jiang did not define *public ownership* or *dominant role,* two terms with increasingly loose definitions in Chinese political life.

Jiang then confirmed what had already happened and virtually everyone accepted: the abrogation of the utopian Communist principle "to each according to his needs." China, he said, "should establish the principle that labor, capital, technology, managerial expertise, and other production factors participate in the distribution of income in accordance with their contributions." At the same time Jiang sought a new balance of fairness in income levels, resisting both extreme differences and forced equality or, as he put it, "guarding against an excessive disparity in income while opposing egalitarianism."

Political reform was a different matter. Jiang eschewed "Western-style democracy" for China even as he called for academic and political openness. "We must always proceed from our national conditions," he said. "We should never copy any models of the political system of the West." Political reform, Jiang offered, would come by strengthening the rule of law, standardizing systems and procedures, and battling corruption, not by multiparty representative democracy or national-level elections.

The final section of Jiang's political report was devoted to Party construction—strengthening the Party. To the retiring general secretary, this was the foundation upon which everything else was built. Jiang stressed "democratic centralism," which meant using the principles of democracy to guide the appointment of central leaders and the principle of centralism to guide the development of democracy in the country. Directly related, Jiang said, was "inner-Party democracy," which he called "the life of the Party."

He called for expanding pilot projects of "Party congresses with regular annual conferences" (as opposed to every five years) or standing congresses in more cities and counties, and for empowering these congresses with oversight of leading officials. His far-reaching purpose was to break the unchallengeable, monopolistic power of local Party secretaries and oligarchic standing committees (usually composed of eleven members at the county level) by subjecting Party leaders to the permanent, decentralized supervision of Party congresses.

Jiang hoped that these structural changes would drive down corruption. "If we do not resolutely crack down on corruption," he warned, "the flesh and blood ties between the Party and the people will suffer a great deal, the Party will be in danger of losing its ruling position, and it is possible the Party could be headed for self-destruction."

Another core Jiang goal was cultural progress. He called upon his fellow citizens "to make our culture the best among the world cultures," and he sought to instill a "great national spirit," which he believed was essential to preserve China's national integrity. For Jiang, promoting Chinese culture was a patriotic duty.

Military preparedness and foreign affairs, particularly Taiwan, were also matters of high patriotism. Jiang stressed "the military strategic principle of active defense" and called for "leapfrog developments" through science and technology and the pervasive use of information technology. He also reiterated that "the Party's absolute leadership over the army is the eternal soul of the army," and insisted that "there must be no wavering in upholding the fundamental principle and system that the Party leads the people's army." (Earlier in his leadership Jiang had been sufficiently concerned about avoiding coups d'etats that he commissioned research on how such military takeovers happened in developing countries.)

General Secretary Jiang concluded with his overarching vision for China: "Comprehensively building a well-off society, accelerating socialist modernization, enabling socialist China to develop and become wealthy and strong, and making great contributions to human progress are the historical missions that our Party must shoulder bravely."

AFTER THE POLITICAL REPORT, the next order of business was personnel— namely, who would be running the country. On November 13 a secret vote was taken to elect the new Central Committee, the Party's core ruling body that would select all the highest leaders. None of the members of the current Politburo Standing Committee, save Hu Jintao, was listed on the ballot. The issue that had inspired countless speculations was now finally resolved. Six of the seven members of the Standing Committee, including Jiang Zemin and the younger Li Ruihuan, were retiring. The *Washington Post* put it bluntly: "Jiang's victory over Li Ruihuan was a sign of his political influence, which has been underrated time and again."

The next day, the congress's last, the confirmatory vote took place. Delegates marked large red ballots to elect Central Committee members and pink ballots for alternate members. Of the 356 full and alternate members, 180 were being elected for the first time. The average age was 55.4; over 20 percent were under 50. Virtually everyone—98.6 percent—was college educated. There were 27 women, and 35 members from ethnic minorities.

When the results were announced, the delegates in the Great Hall of the People burst into spontaneous applause, a sign of respect for the retiring leaders, especially Jiang. Xinhua praised "the breadth of their political vision and sterling integrity." The delegates were also recognizing that history was being made: China had undergone its first peaceful transition of nonfeudal power.

After the voting the Congress ratified the far-reaching changes outlined in Jiang's political report by passing a resolution to amend the Party Constitution. One of these changes altered the opening sentence of the Party's statement of beliefs, expanding the mission of the Party from being "the vanguard of the working class" to being "the vanguard both of the Chinese working class and the Chinese people and the Chinese nation." This codified what had been an accepted truism for some time: The Communist Party had been transformed from a "revolutionary party" engaged in "class struggle" into a ruling party whose primary role was the development of the nation.

Immediately following came a new passage that invoked the principles embodied in Three Represents as the Party's guiding philosophy. In the next paragraph—the second of the Constitution—Three Represents was mentioned in the same sentence as its well-known predecessors. "The Communist Party of China," the line read, "takes Marxism-Leninism, Mao Zedong Thought, Deng Xiaoping Theory, and the important thought of Three Represents as its guide to action." Jiang's Zemin's path-changing theory was now enshrined, albeit without his name attached, in the Party Constitution.

"If Jiang's thinking is written into the Party's basic guidelines," Wu Guoguang, a Hong Kong political scientist, had predicted, "that will make him a paramount authority."

It seemed fitting, then, that when the vote was called to amend the Party Constitution, Jiang was the one presiding over the sea of delegates. Seated with other senior leaders on the large stage, he called for the tally: "Those who vote for the item, please raise your hands."

As hands shot up throughout the Great Hall, all eyes were on the front row as delegates tried to gauge the reaction of the Party's most senior leaders. No one expected anyone to vote against the resolution, of course, but more subtle reactions—a facial expression or how a hand was raised—were scrutinized.

Zhu Rongji looked stern, but people dismissed this as insignificant; he always looked stern. More notable was the fact that every elder raised his hand instantly, save two: the ninety-seven-year old Bo Yibo, whose lack of responsiveness was justified by his physical frailty, and Qiao Shi, Jiang's old rival, who had reluctantly retired at the previous Party Congress five years before.

During the vote Qiao's hand remained conspicuously in his lap while everyone else's was held high. But just as the count was coming to an end, and the delegates were about to lower their arms, Qiao, as the *South China Morning Post* described it, "waved his hand briefly then quickly put it down." It was the closest thing to dissent.

"Those who vote against the item, please raise their hands," Jiang said.

From several locations around the periphery of the hall, staff voices shouted one after another: "None, none, none."

"Does anyone abstain from the vote?" Jiang asked.

Again came the rapid-fire words: "None, none, none."

"This item is passed unanimously," Jiang declared.

With a look that seemed to express more relief than triumph, Jiang leaned over to Li Peng and said something, then did the same to Li Ruihuan. Whatever debate or strife may have occurred in private, there was nothing but courtesy and decorum on display in public. When Jiang came to the podium for his last time as general secretary, the partisan crowd erupted with applause. He said a few words before the singing of the Internationale. With that, the Party congress was adjourned, and Jiang Zemin walked off the stage.

THE NEXT MORNING WAS COLD AND WINDY, but the harsh weather could not dampen the excitement. Shortly before noon the new members of the Standing Committee of the Politburo of the Communist Party, China's new generation of leaders, were introduced to the world. They filed into an ornate room packed with reporters and cameramen, emerging single file in order of rank from behind a dragon-adorned screen, thus ending months of speculation.

First to appear, as expected, was Hu Jintao, the popular new general secretary. Second, a bit of a surprise to some, was Wu Bangguo, Jiang's colleague from Shanghai who would become chairman of the National People's Congress the following March. Third was Wen Jiabao, virtually assured to become the next premier. Another surprise came in the form of Jia Qinglin, one of Jiang's closest friends, who at fourth was ranked higher than expected and tipped to become chairman of the Chinese People's Political Consultative Conference. Fifth was Zeng Qinghong, Jiang's longtime adviser and administrator, who was slated to manage the Secretariat. Another close Jiang associate was in sixth position, Huang Ju, who was expected to become executive vice premier. Seventh was Wu Guanzheng, the new head of the anticorruption Central Commission for Discipline Inspection. Eighth was yet another close Jiang associate, Li Changchun, who would oversee ideology, propaganda, and media; and ninth was Luo Gan, Li Peng's longtime associate, who would run law enforcement, internal security, and intelligence.

In the short ceremony, a confident Hu Jintao, smiling and waving—and still (by a month) in his fifties—gave a gracious inaugural speech in which he introduced his colleagues to the world's press. Speaking without notes, Hu was the only one to talk. "We will certainly uphold the great trust that the Party has placed in us, and the expectations of all the country's people," Hu said, as he pledged continuity with the policies of his predecessor.

The lineup of the Standing Committee was not as straightforward as it seemed. Though Zeng Qinghong was number five in the official rankings, he was widely recognized as the de facto number two, by virtue of the fact that he was closest to the former general secretary and, along with Hu, had the widest network in the Party. The reason for his place was protocol, since in addition to the general secretary and the premier, the heads of the two representative bodies, the legislative (NPC) and the consultative (CPPCC), had to be accorded the higher rank. Zeng's role of running Party operations, while a position of more actual power, was technically ranked lower.

For Jiang, watching the rise of his protégés was more than evidence of his continuing power. It was a deeply gratifying personal moment; he was pleased to see his closest associates achieve success. With Zeng Qinghong, Jia Qinglin, Huang Ju, Wu Bangguo, and Li Changchun all on the Standing Committee of the Politburo, it was a very good day for Jiang Zemin.

While Western media pointed out that these five of the nine were especially close to Jiang, they did not appreciate the depth of Jiang's relationship with the other four, particularly the new general secretary, Hu Jintao. The fact that Jiang Zemin had long-standing relationships with all nine members of the new Politburo Standing Committee meant there would be more unity and cohesiveness in the future than had existed in the past.

Every leader of the new generation was an engineer. All had been educated in science and technology, and, as engineers, they were experienced in finding real-world solutions to real-world problems. Literally and figuratively, they all spoke the same language. Nicholas Kristof noted that "the average IQ in the Politburo Standing Committee in Beijing is almost certainly higher than the average IQ in the American president's cabinet." (Kristof also said that China's new leaders tended to be "colorless, cautious bureaucrats" in addition to being very intelligent, which hardly seems a bad thing for those running a country of 1.3 billion people in rapid transition.) It was one of Jiang Zemin's more enduring contributions—a government run by pragmatic professionals of the future rather than ideological zealots of the past.

Asked why most American political leaders tend to have legal backgrounds while most Chinese political leaders tend to have engineering backgrounds, Jiang said that he had thought about this difference. "In our times," he explained, "China was oppressed by backwardness and poverty, and many patriotic young people sought to help our nation through science and industrial development. I came from a cultural family, and while I liked science, I loved literature. But I believed, as did many of my generation, that only through science and technology could we save China. That's why we chose to become engineers. I studied engineering because I wanted to build my country. Many of today's leaders felt the same way."

There was one final encomium for Jiang. With the overwhelming support of the PLA, and a large majority of the Party and the country, he retained the chairmanship of the Central Military Commission.

It was, as they say in sports, an "upset." Thwarting expert predictions, Jiang would now emerge stronger after the Sixteenth Party Congress than he had been before. Between 1989, when he was appointed general secretary, and 2002, when he retired from that position, the only vote on the seven-member Standing Committee that he could reliably control was his own. Now he had at least five of the nine.

Even the most learned of observers thought that the experts got it "almost right." Journalist and China historian Jonathan Mirsky called the original prediction of Nathan and Gilley "daringly but not wholly successful." Of the seven members they had predicted for the new Standing Committee, they had hit six, a seemingly superb call in the clandestine world of Chinese politics, even though the six was out of nine, not seven.

A deeper look, however, reveals that while naming names was certainly daring, the core of their conclusion—its thrust and import—was wholly *un*successful. That the authors were correct in listing six of the Standing Committee members was less consequential than the three mistakes they made: With Li Ruihuan, Jiang's main challenger, *out*, and with Jia Qinglin and Huang Ju, Jiang's close friends, *in*, the entire balance of power had shifted. The exclusion of Li and the inclusion of Jia and Huang was politically cataclysmic, and it changed the character of China's new leadership completely. The exchange ratified and reinforced what would now surely be the continuing power and influence of Jiang. Prognostication is risky business; prognosticating against Jiang Zemin especially so.

In the second, dramatically revised edition of their fascinating, revelation-filled book (*China's New Rulers*, published a year later), Nathan and Gilley explain how the "respective fates" of Jiang Zemin (would he retire completely?) and Li Ruihuan (would he remain on the Standing Committee?) would have "profound implications": "Whether they both stayed or both retired, or one stayed and the other retired would materially affect the new leadership and the course it would take." The authors report that Li Ruihuan's status was discussed, openly for the first time, at a Politburo Standing Committee meeting on October 17, and that Li appeared to have "decided beforehand to retire." Jiang said that a "complete transition" was "important, necessary, and urgent," Li affirmed that he would "not join the new Central Committee" (and therefore be ineligible for the Politburo), and while there was tense talk of rumors, the atmosphere was relaxed. Read together, the first and second editions of *China's New Rulers* give special insight into Chinese politics and the experts who study it.

The test for the experts was to assess the relative power and influence of Jiang Zemin following the Sixteenth Party Congress. That was the main issue, and that was what many did not get right. What they had heard as the retirement bell for Jiang turned out to signal the beginning of an era that would be founded on his philosophy. It was the difference between a Jiang Zemin who was out of the game, a venerated but passé retired Party elder, and a Jiang Zemin who had set the rules and was continuing to coach the players. Depending on his health and unforeseen events, Jiang would likely influence policy for five years, until at least the Seventeenth Party Congress in 2007. With the enshrinement of his Three Represents, his long relationship with Hu Jintao, and the control of the Party by his protégés, the age of Jiang Zemin had truly begun.

The lead article in the *South China Morning Post* proclaimed as much. "A new era has begun in China," it read. "But it is not that of Vice President Hu Jintao, who has taken over the top post in the Communist Party. Rather, it is a new era of President Jiang Zemin, who has just stepped down as the Party's general secretary."

Hu Jintao's stylish acceptance speech to the CPC Central Committee lent support to that view. In it he pledged to "seek instruction and listen to the views" of his predecessor on important matters. Hu was speaking to a closed-door conclave of Party leaders, and his words were intended to remain confidential, but they were leaked to the media by at least two officials who had received formal briefings on the talk. According to them, Hu's dignified words were stronger than what might have been expected of a new leader paying respects to a former leader. In addition, by briefing upper-echelon Party officials, the new leadership was explicitly acknowledging Jiang's status as the most senior leader and sage of the new generation.

By formal arrangement, it was agreed that Jiang should be consulted on all matters of state importance. Similarly, just after the new Politburo was appointed, its twenty-five members made a pact that, for at least two years, they would refer deadlocks and disputes among themselves to Jiang Zemin for what would be, in essence, binding arbitration.

China watchers expressed "something close to awe at the way in which Jiang had maneuvered to dominate the proceedings of the week-long Congress" and the personnel appointments that had emerged from it. "Well okay, he's not general secretary, but he has got everything else he could possibly want," commented a Western diplomat. "He's given nothing away. He got rid of a key enemy. He's stuffed the new Standing Committee with his people. And he is the only member of the Third Generation to keep a top job." Though exaggerated for effect—Li Ruihuan was more a "political rival" than a "key enemy" and Jiang's "people" in the new Standing Committee were all highly experienced and competent—the thrust of the comment highlighting Jiang Zemin's political triumph was a fair assessment of what had just happened.

JIANG, LIKE DENG XIAOPING before him, would now be operating "behind the curtain," as it were, holding the levers of military power and guiding his political heirs who were running the Party. Of Jiang's three leadership positions, the CMC chairmanship was, in some ways, the most important. It gave him control of the army and therefore strong influence on foreign policy and domestic security. It enjoyed the most secrecy and had no term limits.

Commentators speculated that Jiang might give up his military post at the National People's Congress in March 2003, but insiders knew that he would be staying on longer. Meeting with a U.S. government delegation one week after the Party Congress, Jiang was asked if he planned to retain the chairmanship for the long term. He chose his words carefully: "At the strong request of the comrades in the CMC, I continue to serve as CMC chairman." He did not elaborate, he did not give his personal opinion, and he did not answer the question. One of his aides, though, mentioned that Jiang could remain on as CMC chairman "at least three years."

There was concern that Jiang's continuing on as CMC chairman might trigger an outcry from the international community. No one wanted China to be labeled a dictatorship, even in exaggeration. U.S. reaction would set the precedent, and it came a few weeks later when President Bush sent Jiang a congratulatory message.

"I always value working with you and working to build up even closer relations between the people of the two countries and to promote world peace and prosperity," Bush wrote. "I am looking forward to cooperating with you further during your continued assumption of the post of the chairman of the Central Military Commission." The American leader's precise language was sending a clear signal of acceptance.

The strange delay between Jiang's appointment as CMC chairman on November 15 and Bush's letter, the contents of which were reported on December 13, suggests some stirrings beneath the surface. At the very least the delay was caused by a need for U.S. experts to assess Jiang's likely longevity in the position. Going further, one may speculate that Bush's letter, which was no doubt welcomed by Jiang and his advisers, could have been a subtle but deliberate intervention to support Jiang in the political process (payback, perhaps, for Jiang's support following September 11).

With the pieces in place, Jiang no longer spoke much about retirement. Silence was his strategy; the brass would do his talking. Three senior generals, Fu Quanyou, Yu Yongbo, and Xiong Guankai, made statements declaring, as General Yu said, "the critical importance of his [Jiang] serving another term in maintaining the stability of the military and of the whole country." The worldly wise General Xiong stated, "From generals to soldiers, personnel throughout the armed forces strongly desire that Chairman Jiang remain in office."

As for the new general secretary, he, like Jiang, was pleased with the smooth transition. Hu was perceptive; he was also three years younger than Jiang had been on becoming general secretary. His long-term success would require inner harmony as well as outer unity, and, according to reports, it was Hu Jintao who recommended to the new Politburo, of which Jiang was not a member, that Jiang remain as CMC chairman. Not everyone was thrilled that Jiang was staying on, of course, but most agreed that it enhanced stability during the transition.

Hu had found a near-perfect opening balance. Even his statement to the Central Committee hit the right tone: He would "seek instruction and listen to the views" of Jiang. The words were a mark of respect, not of subservience. "Seeking instruction isn't the same as seeking orders; it suggests respectfully seeking out a teacher," noted one Party official. "I think Hu understands that his situation is delicate and he doesn't want to offend Jiang. An offended leader can create trouble." A smooth-working relationship between Hu and Jiang would virtually assure amity, if not always unity, on the Standing Committee.

"For at least two or three years," predicted a Party scholar, "the relationship between Hu and Jiang will be like that between Jiang and Deng in the past."

THAT AFTERNOON JIANG AND Hu appeared together in the Banquet Hall in the Great Hall of the People, where they circumnavigated the large space together, shaking hands with many of the two thousand delegates and chatting briefly, while cameras memorialized the historic and celebratory scene. It was a memorable moment for China, the peaceful passing of power from one generation to the next with praise and appreciation. The country was developing not only its economy but also its system of governance. Many Party elders were present, including Jiang's old mentor Gu Mu as well as former rivals Qiao Shi and Yang Baibing, who joined together in the spirit of the occasion.

"I hope that comrades will be united as one, work hard, and make new contributions to the cause of the Party and the people!" Jiang exhorted the crowd. The sustained applause reflected gratitude for all that he had accomplished for China. The next day Jiang's proclamations were emblazoned in red ink on the front page of *People's Daily*.

Hu Jintao praised the Third Generation leadership "with Jiang Zemin at the core" for leading "the whole Party and the people of all ethnic groups throughout the country" in overcoming "all kinds of obstacles" on the road to modernization, adding, "We'll bear in mind that which Jiang Zemin has entrusted to us."

Embedded within the mutual accolades was a revealing difference in how Jiang and Hu referred to each other. Hu, said Jiang, was "the general secretary" of the Party Central Committee. Jiang, said Hu, was "the core" of the Third Generation leadership. The difference was not semantic and not subtle. While Hu Jintao was indeed the new Party chief, he was not, as yet, "the core" of the Fourth Generation. In negotiating the transition, this was a major matter on which Jiang and Hu had come to agreement.

In fact, the Fourth Generation had not yet even come into existence. Perhaps Jiang and Hu had their own timetable. Perhaps the Fourth Generation, whenever it came, would have no core or a multiple core. Perhaps the Fourth Generation would not emerge during Jiang Zemin's sentient lifetime. Hu Jintao was most definitely the general secretary of the Party, but he was most definitely not, at least at this time, its "core."

There had been speculation that even the notion of generational leadership would be abandoned altogether. In late summer veteran China watcher Willy Wo-Lap Lam had noted that the formula for Jiang's partial retirement would include, as an essential element, "shelving the idea of a transition from the Third Generation to the Fourth Generation leadership."

"Jiang's supporters want the very concept of the Fourth Generation mothballed," said one source to Lam. "Thus heavyweights such as Hu and Wen will be looked upon only as younger Third Generation cadres—and Jiang remains the core of the Third Generation." This would enable Jiang to continue to be the key decision-maker on all matters of importance, foreign or domestic.

To that end, as Deng Xiaoping had been called Paramount Leader, Jiang would need a term to define his unique status. In the amendment to the Party Constitution that enshrined Three Represents, a new designation was introduced to describe Jiang: "chief representative." It was a designation that, for historical continuity, the Constitution retroactively (and posthumously) assigned to both Mao Zedong and Deng Xiaoping during the periods of their preeminence.

In the re-creation, Mao had remained "chief representative" for fifty-five years, from the founding of the Party in 1921 until his death in 1976, while Deng had qualified for it only for eleven years, from when he assumed undisputed power and began reforms in 1978 until 1989, when Jiang was appointed general secretary. How long would Jiang hold the title? As one commentator put it: "General secretaries can come and go, but this does not happen to either the core or the chief representative."

The appellation was a remarkable culmination of Jiang's long career. Derided as a lightweight, no more than an interim placeholder, when he was first appointed in 1989, Jiang was now formally recognized in the Party Constitution as the "chief representative" of his generation, virtually on a par with Mao Zedong and Deng Xiaoping.

Thus seven elements confirmed Jiang Zemin's enhanced patriarchic position:

- the composition of the Standing Committee, all nine members of which were Jiang's associates and five of them his closest associates
- his ten-year working relationship with Hu Jintao
- the directives of the Central Committee, the agreement of the Politburo, and Hu Jintao's recognition that Jiang would be consulted on major matters
- his reelection as chairman of the Central Military Commission

- the enshrinement of his Three Represents in the Party Constitution
- the absence of a Fourth Generation and a new "core" of the Party (at least for now)
- his recognition as "chief representative"

How could so many people have gotten Jiang so wrong for so long? Said one news source—getting it right—"As long as people continue underestimating him, he stands a good chance of surprising them again."

IN THE PERIOD FOLLOWING the Party Congress, Jiang dominated public life. On most nights his meetings led the news. In China the nuances of protocol are analyzed to a degree not known in the West. Chinese newspaper readers and television viewers always take note of the way the activities of leaders are reported, scrutinizing every detail, especially the order in which people appear on screen. Although Jiang was no longer general secretary, he was still state president for the next few months, and CMC chairman for an undetermined period. Following protocol, the media still regarded him as the preeminent personality and listed him first in the formal rankings. With all colleagues now retired, Jiang Zemin was the only one left standing.

Was Hu bothered by this? Surely not. Hu was respectful, not reticent, and pleased to see Jiang, sixteen years his senior and the country's longtime steward, savor his valediction.

For his part, Jiang went back to work, focusing on countries important to China's future. Chief among them was Russia. Jiang hoped that establishing a new Sino-Russian partnership would serve as a counterweight to "American hegemony." In early December, President Putin arrived in Beijing, where high on the agenda were terrorism and North Korea. Something else was helping to cement relations between the two giant countries—something not mentioned publicly: China was buying prodigious amounts of Russian military hardware.

Maintaining a busy schedule in December, President Jiang met with a host of visiting dignitaries: Hewlett-Packard CEO Carly Fiorina, to talk technology; a U.S. delegation headed by Representative Henry Hyde, to discuss Taiwan; the speaker of the Iranian parliament, to discuss trade; Bangladeshi prime minister Khaleda Zia, to strategize development; German chancellor Gerhard Schröder, to plan exchanges; Kazakhstan president Nursultan Nazarbayev, to fight the "three forces" (religious extremism, ethnic separatism, and terrorism); and Hong Kong chief executive Tung Chee-hwa and Macao chief executive Edmund Ho Hau Wah, to receive their annual reports.

Behind the scenes, two of Jiang's trusted advisers received new jobs, a bell-wether event underreported in the foreign press. Though their names rarely appeared in the media, Wang Huning and Teng Wensheng, who usually traveled with the president, had made meaningful contributions for years, and now their roles would be repositioned. Wang, who had been vice director of the Party Policy Research Office, became its director, replacing Teng. Teng, who was also Jiang's lead speechwriter, became director of the Party Literature Office.

"I was with President Jiang on his trip to visit President Bush in Crawford, Texas, in October 2002," recalled Teng. "He spoke with me and said he needed to make some changes." Though he had been a witness to history Teng never kept a diary, but he did write poetry. "Sometimes when I was on foreign trips with President Jiang I would compose classical Chinese poems," Teng confided, adding, "I've not shown them to anyone; they're all in a drawer."

Since the Policy Research Office was the Party's think tank for its goals and strategies and the Literature Office was the Party's guardian of its history and legacy, Wang and Teng, both of whom were elected to the CPC Central Committee, would provide continuity between the two general secretaries. There could be no clearer confirmation of the policy and ideology coherence between Jiang Zemin and Hu Jintao than the Party positions of Wang Huning and Teng Wensheng.

Wang was still in his forties and fluent in English. His core tenets included relevant ideology to energize Party building, a strong central authority to maintain stability, bureaucratic cuts to enhance efficiency, and an engaged foreign policy of "big power diplomacy." As for political reform, Wang called it "the self-perfection of socialism" and believed that democracy is best developed in an environment of political and social order.

When Wang Huning attended meetings that President Jiang held with foreign visitors, Wang might be the one, at the end of the meeting, to bring over to Jiang the gift he would offer, according to custom, to these visitors. While Westerners might mistakenly make light of this seemingly secretarial function, the act reveals the intimacy of the relationship between Jiang and Wang. Foreign media speculated that Wang Huning could emerge as an intellectual leader of the Fifth Generation, whose era will probably begin in 2012. When a foreigner mentioned that he had learned from Wang's work, the quick-on-the-uptake strategist responded with a deadpanned quip: "Maybe I should charge you for it." It augurs well for China, and for the world, that someone with a good sense of humor (and well-read) is so close to leadership.

IN EARLY DECEMBER Hu Jintao and Zeng Qinghong, who had recently been named to Hu's former position as head of the Central Party School, made a very public pilgrimage together to Xibaipo in Hebei province. It was there that the Party's revolutionary leaders had established their base in 1947 and led the northern campaign against the Kuomintang. Symbolizing both their Party commitment and their personal rapport, the trip was a solemn, reflective commencement of their terms as senior leaders, though it did not go unnoticed that it also sought to squelch rumors of rivalry that had dogged them for years.

The *People's Daily* article about the Hu-and-Zeng journey was overshadowed by the accompanying photograph. There on the front page were Hu and Zeng touring the revolutionary museum, standing side by side, as if they were partners in history—comrades with evident camaraderie. The picture sent another message, too. Wearing nondescript overcoats, Hu and Zeng seemed to personify Mao Zedong's Xibaipo-given dictum that Party members should be "modest, prudent, and self-disciplined."

The appearance of partnership, though staged, was not feigned. While Hu and Zeng had their moments jockeying over personnel appointments, and would no doubt continue to do so, that was very much a normal political process common to most countries. In the end, as colleagues and friends, men of goodwill rally together. So it was with Hu Jintao and Zeng Qinghong.

As early as June 2002 Zeng had sat next to Hu at a high-profile Party meeting, which none of the other incumbent leaders attended. Their appearance together signaled not only agreement to their ascension—"as clear a sign of consensus as white smoke from the Vatican" (according to Nathan and Gilley)—but also their commitment to work together.

Hu and Zeng had similar views on most issues. They both believed in the preeminence of the Party, and they had supported Jiang's programs in Party building, such as the Three Stresses campaign. They also had similar outlooks on aggressive economic reform, gradual political reform, and maintaining good relations with the United States.

Early on the new leadership reached out to the poor and needy, those left behind by China's dynamic but lopsided economic boom. At a mid-December meeting of the new Standing Committee, Hu Jintao requested more emergency relief for impoverished households and prodded Party officials to go out among the masses, "particularly in areas where difficulties, problems, and contradictions abound." Doing just that, Wen Jiabao, the premier-designate, took his first postcongress trip to Guizhou province, one of China's poorest, where he spoke with peasants and sent a signal that concern for the disadvantaged would be a hallmark of the new administration. Wen's trip also reflected his partnership with Hu Jintao, who had been Party secretary of Guizhou.

At the same time, social stability remained paramount. The appointment of Zhou Yongkang, a longtime friend of Zeng Qinghong from their days in the petroleum industry, as the head of China's 1.6-million-member police force marked the first time in 25 years that a minister of Public Security was a Politburo member. Social discipline, it seemed, would be strengthened not slackened. When Luo Gan retires in 2007 as head of internal security, Zhou Yongkang could be his replacement.

Near the end of December Zhou Xiaochuan, the former chairman of China Securities Regulatory Commission, was appointed governor of the People's (Central) Bank of China, the top financial job in the country. The erudite Zhou, with a Ph.D. in systems engineering from Tsinghua University, promised to bring new professionalism to China's financial system. Jiang was pleased to follow Zhou Xiaochuan's success. Zhou's father, Zhou Jiannan, had been the machine-building minister who, in 1962, had given Jiang the seemingly impossible job of converting the automotive power plant from coal to crude oil in three months, a task that Jiang, for the rest of his life, would call his proudest achievement. Zhou Jiannan, who died in 1995, had been so impressed with Jiang that he helped arrange his promotion.

THIS WAS A GOOD TIME for Jiang Zemin. He was no longer enmeshed in political struggles, and he was enjoying his newly elevated status as chief representative. Foreigners who met him privately in the weeks after the Party congress remarked that he took pride in having engineered a smooth transfer of power to Hu Jintao without eruption of factional rivalries or disputes. As one observer noted, "The implication of such statements is that, contrary to rumor, Jiang has no plans to back Zeng at Hu's expense, or to run a rival power center from his position as head of the military."

About a year later Jiang reflected back: "Comrade Hu Jintao is sixteen years younger than me, and I am very pleased that he has taken over responsibilities. He has worked on the Politburo Standing Committee for over ten years, and to some extent, I may say that it was ten years ago that I set my eyes on him [*kanzhong;* literally, targeted, settled on him]."

In a fitting finale to the year, Jiang reveled in Chinese culture and technology. On December 30 he watched a Peking Opera in which four generations of performers presented traditional and new works; and the next evening he welcomed the New Year by attending a huge joint concert of the Beijing Symphony Orchestra and the British Royal Philharmonic Orchestra. Earlier on the same day *Shenzhou IV,* China's manned spacecraft, rocketed into orbit for its final test flight prior to the anticipated launching of China's first astronaut in 2003. Jiang sent a message of congratulations for "an historic achievement," which he called "a great victory" for China.

Chapter 30

2003 – September 2004

"We Chinese Are All Very Happy About It"

I N J A N U A R Y, T W O M O N T H S before he would give up China's presidency, Jiang was consumed by the urgent crises in Iraq and North Korea. Iraq, in particular, was headed toward a war that Jiang wanted to avoid, a stance that was shared by Russia, Germany, and most vociferously, France. It did not go unnoticed that each of the four countries, particularly France and Russia, had extensive commercial interests in Iraq and billions of dollars of unpaid debts owed to them.

While Chinese enterprises had infrastructure work in Iraq, including an $80 million telecommunications contract, this was not the reason Jiang sought to prevent hostilities. Far more important was the issue of oil. As a net importer of energy, China wished no interruption to the world supply. In addition, war could set back global commerce, to which China's high-growth economy was tied. A U.S. victory would also expand the presence of American power, something that China, with its diverse interests, was anxious to avoid. More insidious, if America succeeded in freeing Iraq, it could set a precedent for transnational intervention to effect changes in regimes. As a matter of principle, Jiang was against any violation of national sovereignty.

At the same time he maintained his distance from the other powers that were opposing the United States. Jiang stressed that UN arms inspections should be enhanced, not ended, but he also asserted that Iraq "had an obligation to make further explanations and clarifications." His strategy reflected China's increasing sophistication in international diplomacy. He neither reacted with knee-jerk opposition to the American agenda, nor automatically sided with China's traditional allies. Jiang managed to take a position for peace and stay above the fray without alienating any party.

"We've got no dogs in this hunt," said one Chinese official.

In late February Secretary of State Colin Powell arrived in Beijing to confer with Chinese leaders about the looming crises. Meeting in the afternoon with President Jiang, after a morning session with General Secretary Hu Jintao, Powell told Jiang that Sino-U.S. relations had entered a new phase, citing increased trade, consultation on crises, and cooperation in the fight against terrorism.

Jiang agreed that bilateral relations had improved over the past year, with "more common interests and wider areas of cooperation." He made sure, however, to put Taiwan front and center. To Jiang, although Iraq and North Korea were troubling, Taiwan was crucial, and he emphasized yet again that the "proper handling of the Taiwan issue" was vital for "future progress in Sino-US relations." Considering China's acquiescence to U.S. initiatives on Iraq, North Korea, and terrorism, or at least its not thwarting them, Jiang expected something from the United States in return, such as a reduction in arms sales to Taiwan or more sensitivity to China's interests.

China was said to have pulled back some of its four hundred short-range missiles stationed in Fujian province facing Taiwan (a claim questioned by American sources). The move, under Jiang's control, suggested growing confidence that Beijing's position relative to Taiwan's would improve, not deteriorate, over time—economically, as Taiwan's commerce became increasingly dependent on the mainland; politically, in the (hoped-for) weakening of support for its pro-independence politicians; and militarily, since the mainland could afford to outspend Taiwan on modern equipment.

Two days after Jiang met with Colin Powell, he hosted Fidel Castro, the self-appointed lifelong ruler of Cuba. Expressing "socialist solidarity" as well as personal friendship, Jiang pledged that China would strengthen its ties with Cuba, and he personified his commitment by accompanying Castro on a visit to Nanjing.

There may have been a time when cozying up to Castro seemed a way to counterbalance the United States's "unipolar" world order, but if so that time had passed. Castro was a political anachronism, an economic liability, and in the West, a media buffoon. Jiang had brought China to great country status, and his support for Castro's totalitarian, impoverishing rule seemed, at least to most Westerners, awkward and self-diminishing. Yet Castro was a popular figure among many Chinese; the bearded Cuban was a swashbuckling, romantic revolutionary, gutsy enough to have stood up to the United States and resilient enough to have survived sanctions for decades. Jiang, like others, found him personally charming.

Two days after meeting Castro, Jiang welcomed Microsoft chairman Bill Gates. From speaking with Castro about raw sugar imports and kidney bean exports, Jiang switched to information technology and the sharing of source code. It was an interesting week: Fidel Castro sandwiched between Colin Powell and Bill Gates. That was how President Jiang spelled "almost retired."

Regarding North Korea, Jiang telephoned George Bush in January and February to register China's opposition to Pyongyang's brazen, in-your-face decision to pull out of the nuclear nonproliferation treaty, and to reiterate that the Korean peninsula should be nuclear free. Although the world's attention was focused on Iraq, the situation in North Korea posed a far greater threat to China. Jiang's censure of Kim Jong-Il's efforts to arm his regime with nuclear weapons stirred debate at home. While some Chinese blamed Pyongyang for the current crisis, others criticized Beijing for abandoning its erstwhile ally and viewed Jiang's position as too accommodating to U.S. interests.

But China's influence on North Korea was less than met the eye. For decades North Korea had played Russia and China against each other. "If Kim tells Jiang he is going to test a nuclear weapon unless Jiang gives him more aid, what do we do? We give him more aid. We don't have a choice," said one Chinese analyst who had dealt with Pyongyang. "We have some influence, but not the kind of relationship where we can tell Kim what to do. If we tell him to do something, he doesn't listen. If we threaten him, he listens even less. If Jiang called him, he might hang up."

Kim's erratic and dangerous behavior threatened to destabilize the entire region. If North Korea got the bomb, Japan might feel pressure to do likewise. Worse for China, it might give the United States an excuse to position warheads on Taiwan. Then what? On the other hand, if Kim Jong-Il's regime collapsed, China would be faced with a massive refugee influx as well as the embarrassment of watching its as-close-as-lips-and-teeth socialist sister state fall apart. From China's perspective, maintaining an ambiguous status quo was preferable to risking either extreme. If that option were not available, China would have to decide between its past and its future. It was another reason why China counted on Jiang Zemin.

ECONOMICALLY, JIANG COULD TAKE pride in the legacy he was leaving. When much of the rest of the world was mired in stagnation or decline, he was providing his successors with robust growth—8 percent in 2002, followed by a blistering 9.1 percent in 2003. The attitude of China's citizens was also a source of satisfaction. The nation seemed to be a haven of order in an increasingly uncertain and chaotic world. "China is definitely the best place to be right now, what with our fast-growing economy and strong public security," said one scientist who had been educated in the United States. "Nobody's going to try any terrorism here."

Jiang could now look to the future. A few days before the concurrent sessions of the Tenth National People's Congress and the Chinese People's Political Consultative Conference in the first week of March, the list of deputies was approved. Of the members of the old Politburo Standing Committee, only Jiang Zemin and Hu Jintao were reelected for another five years, Jiang in the NPC Shanghai delegation and Hu in the one from Tibet. For Jiang to keep his seat, while his contemporaries were losing theirs, was yet another sign, in sign-conscious China, that he would play a continuing and active role in the affairs of state, even as he was about to hand over the presidency to Hu.

At the Tenth NPC's first session, Li Peng took his final bow, presiding over his last official act of public service after a long and controversial career. The same day Zhu Rongji also bade farewell to public life in the form of an extended report that reviewed his government's achievements over the past five years and set forth proposals for the future. The enthusiastic reception from delegates was largely in recognition of Zhu's personal integrity in the face of social and political pressures.

Jiang was relaxed. Meeting with the Shanghai delegation, he noticed the light skin of a farming official. "You are the chairman of the agriculture commission," Jiang said. "You should have a darker complexion. Why do you look like a pale-faced scholar?"

IN THE SAME WEEK HE was to give up his presidency, Jiang was pulled deeper into the crises over North Korea and Iraq. The Chinese media were saturated with reports of his many late-night calls with world leaders, even as his days were filled by attending the legislative sessions. On March 10 Jiang spoke with President Bush about North Korea. "The form of dialogue is not the most important matter," Jiang said. "The key is whether both sides have sincerity, whether the dialogue has substantial content and result, whether it is favorable to denuclearization, whether it can solve the matters which the United States and the DPRK [North Korea] care about, and whether it can safeguard the peace and stability of the peninsula." He had engineered a subtle breakthrough by indicating that China would not oppose the U.S. position that discussions with North Korea must be multilateral. Prior to this, China and Russia had taken North Korea's side in the matter, urging bilateral talks only with the United States.

On Iraq, there was less agreement. Stressing national security, Bush pressed for military action, while Jiang argued for continued inspections. Maintaining his balance, Jiang conceded that "Iraq must comprehensively, strictly, and thoroughly carry out the UN Security Council's resolution and cannot possess weapons of mass destruction."

THE MAIN ELECTIONS OF CHINA'S new leaders were held in the National People's Congress on March 15. Though the results had been predetermined, there was still an air of anticipation. A full generation had passed since the last sweeping change of senior leadership. While Chinese folk music played in the Great Hall of the People, delegates cast their secret ballots.

In quick order, Wu Bangguo was elected NPC chairman; Hu Jintao, president; Jiang Zemin, CMC chairman; and Zeng Qinghong, vice president. Jiang, whose decade as president was now over, jumped up to shake Hu's hand. They exchanged quiet words as the nearly three thousand delegates applauded in unison.

Hu Jintao lived up to his reputation as a "top vote-getter" by garnering approval from an overwhelming 2,939 delegates, with only four in opposition and three abstentions. After thirteen years in power, Jiang did less well, with an approval rate of 92.5 percent. A moment later Zeng Qinghong, also considered an incumbent, received 87.5 percent. Observers said that during the vote on his reelection Jiang seemed a little nervous, fidgeting in plain sight. That Jiang Zemin could be seen as a normal human being personified how open China had become.

For Jiang and Zeng, who had held and administered power for over a decade, the number of nonapproval votes was neither surprising nor terribly meaningful. As the implementer of policies and enforcer of rules, Zeng was expected to register a lower score on the popularity meter. The voting reflected similar behavioral patterns that drive opposing parties in the West to exchange power in a cyclical fashion.

After the elections Hu bowed three times, and Jiang smiled and waved to the crowd. Upon leaving the hall, Jiang walked confidently, steps ahead of Hu, Li Peng, and Zhu Rongji, as vigorous and in command as ever.

The next day the popular Wen Jiabao was elected premier, garnering over 99 percent of the votes. The day after that Premier Wen unveiled his twenty-eight-member cabinet, the team that would run the government for the next five years. Of the four vice premiers, three were especially close to Jiang, including longtime associates Huang Ju as executive vice premier and Zeng Peiyan in charge of the economy and industry.

On March 18, at the NPC's final session, newly elected President Hu Jintao and NPC chairman Wu Bangguo delivered brief inaugural addresses. Hu pledged that he would faithfully assume the powers and perform the functions as prescribed by the Constitution. "I would never let down all the deputies and people of all nationalities throughout the country," Hu said.

President Hu praised his predecessor for his able leadership and distinguished service. He said that Jiang Zemin displayed "political courage of keeping up with the times, and a work style of exerting himself to make the country prosperous;" and "has won the wholehearted love and esteem" of the entire country as well as "general acclaim from the international community." Hu also stated, graciously: "The important thought of Three Represents, which has been created by Jiang Zemin upon pooling the wisdom of the entire Party, is of great and far-reaching guiding significance to the development of all undertakings in China. We would like to extend hereby our heartfelt gratitude and highest regards to Jiang Zemin!"

It was now being reported that Jiang would retain his two parallel CMC chairmanships—one with the Party and the other with the state—for their full five-year terms, which would end in 2007 and 2008 respectively. Jiang revealed his motivation for staying on to Shanghai delegates, explaining that Party elders felt Hu Jintao was "too inexperienced" in military matters and wanted someone to "keep control" *(yazhen)*. "I explained this concept to foreign friends," the outgoing president said. "But no matter how the interpreter translated it, they did not understand the term. At last I made it plain. I said, 'I stay to help Hu Jintao.' "

"I think the relationship between Hu and Jiang is in some ways like that of a father and son, where the father gives the son a certain independence but there is also dominance," said one Party newspaper editor. "But conflicts will appear because to survive Hu must make his mark with policy breakthroughs that may harm Jiang's policies and interests." As China matures, all this is quite natural.

Months later Jiang ruminated about the transition. "Historically," he told a group of associates, "regardless of the times and types of societies, leadership changes almost always came with fights, struggles, and sharp contentions, and sometimes worse. Now the whole world has witnessed that we in China have smoothly, quietly, and peacefully transferred our power to the new generation. We Chinese are all very happy about it."

THE DAY AFTER THE NPC ended, the United States launched a precision-bombing strike against "leadership targets" in Iraq, commencing its war. The next afternoon the Chinese Foreign Ministry issued a "strong appeal" to the "relevant countries to stop military action." It was a perfunctory statement, made without fervor. While China shared many of the same interests as the French-Russian-German opposition, Jiang knew that it was not in his country's interest to antagonize America.

At the beginning of the war, Chinese newspapers presented a highly skewed view, highlighting U.S. errors, mistakes, problems, and losses, and repeating the ludicrous assertions of the fabled Iraqi minister of information. A Chinese reader would have thought the U.S.–U.K. forces were already stuck in a Vietnam-like quagmire.

Media in China was always a sensitive area, and Hu Jintao had fresh, controversial ideas about how it should change. He decided that the press should report each time the Politburo met, another step in making governance more transparent. Hu told media officials that television news allocated too much time to top officials attending meetings and going on routine tours. He called for more "real news content" and stories of human interest, and less coverage of the mundane comings and goings of senior leaders, which he criticized internally as "wasting time." Hu made light of the customary requirement of listing every leader in attendance, with special care taken to get their rank order correct. Lest such ideas be "misinterpreted," the Propaganda Department issued a directive to newspapers not to "misunderstand and distort the meaning of Hu's statements" about the press.

A changing attitude toward the media was evident in the coverage of two crises in early 2003. The first was defused quickly: When explosions occurred at China's most prestigious universities, Tsinghua and Beijing, panic was averted by rapid and complete news reports. *People's Daily* agreed that media "transparency played the greatest role in stopping the spread of rumors and avoiding panic."

There would be no such luck in the second crisis.

WHEN A FRIGHTENING NEW epidemic, Severe Acute Respiratory Syndrome (SARS), broke out in late 2002, state-run media ignored the threat and, when that became impossible, downplayed it. Originating in Guangdong province, the disease first spread to adjacent Hong Kong and then jumped north to Beijing. News of the contagion was suppressed until February 9, and then again after February 25, in order to prevent the unpleasant tidings from affecting the legislative (NPC) and consultative (CPPCC) sessions in early March.

Though SARS cases were multiplying, China's newspapers described the situation as being "under control," "diminishing," and "no longer a threat." Some Western critics charged that the government seemed more interested in stopping the flow of information than in preventing the spread of the disease. Some Chinese media accused their Western counterparts of exaggerating the problem in order to embarrass China.

On April 4 the minister of public health, Zhang Wenkang, claimed in a widely reported news conference that the epidemic in Beijing had been "effectively controlled." In his television talk, he assured the public that there were only twelve cases of SARS in the capital. Many people knew better, and some refused to remain silent about it. Several, including a former chief of surgery, went public with their revelations, giving the whistle-blowing scoop to Western media.

Beijing was awash in rumor, and travelers en masse canceled their trips to China. Soon public pressure at home and abroad forced the authorities to change their policy. On April 17 Hu Jintao ordered that the government "should never cover up the spread of SARS." Hu and Premier Wen Jiabao demanded that China's medical establishment tell the truth and that China's media establishment report the facts. They warned that any officials who misled the public would be punished severely.

A news conference, hastily scheduled for April 20, was to be conducted by the minister of health, Zhang Wenkang, and the mayor of Beijing, Meng Xuenong. Neither showed up. Instead the executive vice minister of health, Gao Qiang, appeared with an aide. The number of SARS cases in Beijing, he revealed, was *eight times higher* than had previously been stated—346, not 37. As for the missing minister of health and mayor of Beijing, a terse statement issued by Xinhua explained why they were not in attendance: They had been fired.

Analysts were dumbfounded. The minister of health was an associate and friend of Jiang Zemin from Shanghai, where he had held a senior position in a medical university; Jiang himself had brought him to Beijing. The mayor of Beijing was a Communist Youth League compatriot of Hu Jintao; he was a rising star, barely three months on the job. But where the legitimacy of the government—and by extension, the stability of the country—was at stake, the current and former Party chiefs stood in agreement. Sacrifices had to be made, and neither personal relationships nor factional alliances could interfere. Hu and Jiang, in parallel, came to the same conclusion.

In truth, culpability could not be contained by blaming individual officials; it was the system that sought to preserve order at all costs. Most likely there had been near unanimity among China's senior leaders, who, not realizing the severity of the disease, agreed to downplay it so as not to cause panic domestically or cast aspersions on China internationally, particularly during the sensitive period of power transition and the national congresses.

If SARS had not spread beyond China, the strategy might have worked, but the Chinese government was overwhelmed by its own reforms. In the new, open era, the highly contagious disease traveled swiftly between countries. By not warning its neighbors, China had inadvertently allowed the epidemic to spread, exposing people beyond its borders to illness and possible death.

Literally overnight SARS stories monopolized China's newspapers and became the main topic of conversation. Though the accounts were now depressing, people felt, ironically, more encouraged. For the first time Chinese readers felt they were getting the truth.

The government seemed willing to admit its responsibility. "Zhang Wenkang and Meng Xuenong Are Sacked for Negligence" ran one headline. In the article the head of the Party's Organizational Department, He Guoqiang, gave a frank assessment of what had happened. "To strengthen the prevention and control of SARS in Beijing and ensure the stability of the capital," he said, "the central leadership decided to adjust the leadership of the Beijing municipal government." That these words were published openly was called by the *New York Times* "a rare, blunt and very public admission of failure if not deception."

In spite of the new optimism, SARS's deadly toll was still mounting. Each day brought fresh cases and more fatalities. China's capital was enveloped with anxiety. Schools were closed; students were advised to learn at home using the Internet. College students were confined to their campuses. Some hospitals were quarantined, while others refused to admit patients suspected of being infected. People stockpiled groceries and holed up in their homes. Others fled the city. The normally bustling metropolis was virtually abandoned as restaurants, theaters, and discos were shuttered.

"We should not complain, but rise to the challenge," Premier Wen said. To show solidarity, he lunched with quarantined students at Beijing University and bowed before medical workers to express gratitude for their sacrifices.

During the crisis Jiang Zemin maintained a silence that some called puzzling and others said showed respect for President Hu's new responsibility. Critics worked overtime, speculating that SARS had become a political as well as a medical battle, and that the future strength of President Hu and Premier Wen would depend on their success or failure in containing the epidemic.

Jiang made his first public statement on SARS in a late April meeting with the Indian defense minister. Speaking in Shanghai, where he had been staying, Jiang told his guest that "the disease posed a serious threat to the health and lives of the people," adding that the leadership was "highly responsible for the people, and they had taken measures to prevent the spread of the disease and had asked local governments to make it a priority."

By using his discussion with a foreigner as the context for his first statement on SARS, Jiang was sending a softer message than if he had made a direct pronouncement on the subject. At around the same time, acting as chairman of the Central Military Commission, he ordered the PLA to dispatch twelve hundred medical professionals to support Beijing's fight against the disease.

As SARS spread, China's media grew bolder. On April 30 *Southern Metropolitan Daily,* the most popular newspaper in Guangdong, advocated a "breakthrough" in how the government dealt with crises and information.

As awful as it was, SARS was a media breakthrough, a step toward a more open and free China. Early proof came on May 2, when the media reported that a mechanical failure had destroyed a Chinese Navy submarine, killing all seventy seamen on board. It was exceedingly unusual for the government-controlled press to report military disasters, especially during the festive period of May Day week.

On the same day Jiang, as CMC chairman, sent condolences to family members of the dead sailors, expressing sorrow over the "big loss," portraying the crew as "the good children of the people and loyal defenders of the motherland." Jiang and Hu Jintao met relatives of the dead sailors, the first time the two men had appeared together since the SARS outbreak. In every public report of CMC meetings, Hu Jintao, though Party general secretary and state president, was listed as "vice chairman," according to protocol a respectful second to his elder, Chairman Jiang Zemin.

Equally telling of the changing media was the decision by China Central Television to carry the U.S. war against Iraq, live and uncensored, on its flagship Channel 1. For the first time in its history, CCTV was broadcasting real-time feeds from Fox News and CNN, taking the raw footage straight, including that from the embedded reporters, and providing real-time translations.

The Xinhua News Agency delivered up-to-the-minute stories from breaking battlefield news to diplomatic activities. In a market economy with multiple news sources, Xinhua had no choice. If it didn't start offering truth and reasonable balance, audiences would turn elsewhere. Saddam Hussein's brutality, the mass graves, and the extreme repression were reported—hardly the old way to describe an anti-American trading partner of China. The unprecedented coverage of the Iraq war gave millions of Chinese a broader and more nuanced view of the world than they had ever before been allowed to see.

Another sign of a changing China occurred on April 20, the same day as the jolting news conference on SARS, when a "confident, healthy" young lady, Wu Wei, won the title of Miss China, besting two thousand contestants in a high-profile beauty pageant. All major newspapers featured the story, pictures and all.

IN MID-APRIL IT WAS announced that North Korea would meet the United States over a conference table in Beijing, with China as a full participant in discussions of its nuclear weapons program. The agreement was a testament to Jiang's diplomatic prowess. By voicing the face-saving idea that the dialogue format was "not important," Jiang had provided a way for both sides to ease into negotiations without compromising their positions. The reason the United States had compromised, a spokesman admitted, was that "China had taken such a major role in setting up" the trilateral talks.

The first meetings were not promising. "We've got nukes," the North Korean leader said bluntly. "We can't dismantle them—it's up to you whether we do a physical demonstration or transfer them. Now what are you going to do about it?"

In its official statement, China said the talks had helped promote mutual understanding, though privately the Chinese were "in disbelief" over the North Korean revelations. "This is a major slap in the face to China, which had really stuck its neck out to make these talks happen," said a Chinese authority. "China will absolutely not accept this. It's a nightmare for our national security . . . China will never allow a nuclear weapon in North Korea."

The symbolism was unmistakable. In the half century since the Korean War, Jiang's China had become a fair arbiter of most international disputes, shifting its position, as it were, around the negotiating table. Its stance told the world that the country now had more in common with America, its old foe, than with North Korea, its old ally. But it was not so much America that China had come to support as world peace. Stability, abroad as well as at home, was the hallmark of Jiang Zemin.

Jiang was proud that China was playing a key role in resolving the stand-off but frustrated that Americans by and large blamed China for the problem. He could abruptly switch subjects just to ask American visitors about the issue. When one responder offered the simple if naïve observation, "Many Americans think North Korea is a vassal state of China and so it is China's problem to solve," Jiang reacted as if by reflex.

"That is not true!" he exclaimed, visibly exasperated. "As a matter of fact, North Korea does not obey China. If we say something, they do not automatically agree. This is what I told President Bush. North Korea is very independent in its decision-making. They are a separate country. Of course, China has friendly relations with our bordering country." Jiang concluded by musing that "many things in this world are rather complicated."

Similarly, Jiang would give visitors his opinion on Iraq—even if they didn't ask. Reviewing his "many conversations with world leaders" and tossing off precise dates of the war's chronology, Jiang admitted he was "stunned" by America's rapid victory. However, he added, the postwar fighting "makes me revise my thinking." Enumerating American casualties of the previous week—"one helicopter shot down with the loss of sixteen lives, then another with six killed"—Jiang concluded, "Solving the Iraq problem is not going to be quick or easy."

From there it was a natural transition to perhaps his major foreign policy theme. "In dealing with issues in today's world," Jiang stated, "the United States should not practice unilateralism. China, along with most European countries, believes that the world should be multipolar. The trend of multipolarization is becoming irresistible."

In addition to foreign policy, Jiang was engaged in his now singular role as chairman of the Central Military Commission, a responsibility he took with utmost seriousness. He attended almost every meeting—an impossibility when he had held multiple posts—and focused on furthering military reform, particularly the PLA's high-tech capabilities.

At the end of April, in the heat of the SARS battle, the Politburo met "to discuss the launching of a new round of study and implementation of Three Represents theory." Directed by Party chief Hu Jintao, the effort was "aimed at helping the entire Party to gain an in-depth understanding of the necessity, essence, and historical role of Three Represents." The Politburo meeting also dealt with the economic impact of SARS and called on all localities and departments not to lose focus on the "central task of economic construction" and to "continuously move forward with economic work while going all out to combat the SARS epidemic."

Although critics savaged Jiang for promoting Three Represents and "economic construction" at a time of national medical emergency, he was determined that China not become bogged down in fear and self-doubt, and he exercised his power to make sure it did not happen. If the economy were allowed to falter, far greater harm would afflict the nation, and many more people would suffer.

Remarkably, within a few months China would eradicate SARS and reenergize its economy. It was a moment to savor. Jiang had come to power in the wake of a domestic upheaval that had threatened to topple China's government. He had now retired, albeit not totally, in the midst of several crises that seemed not to defeat the government but to challenge it to grow. There was every sign that it would.

In his July 1, 2003, speech on the eighty-second anniversary of the Communist Party, President Hu Jintao surprised observers by focusing on the "thorough implementation of the important ideology of Three Represents," which he said was "linked to all aspects of the work of the Party and government" and "linked to the great goal of building a well-off society." Critics had expected Hu to use the occasion to begin to set forth his own political reform agenda, to distance himself from his predecessor. His unmitigated support for Jiang's most identifiable mark was proof that the so-called rift between them was overblown or misread and that, yet again, Jiang Zemin had been underestimated.

President Hu was beginning to articulate his own vision, but he intended that it extend, not supplant, Jiang's. Hu was younger, more pragmatic, more in tune with contemporary times, similar in sense and style to the new generation of international leaders like British prime minister Tony Blair. Hu liked getting out among the people, hearing them, helping them, understanding them. It was as if he were running a very contemporary, almost Western political campaign. When Hu began speaking of "three close to's"—close to reality, close to life, close to the masses—critics cast it in opposition to Jiang's more theoretical Three Represents. It was not. Hu saw his domestic mandate as operational and evolutionary, such as aiding the poor and advancing inner-Party democracy, and he continued to support China's overarching goals and strategies set by Jiang.

Hu promoted a new approach to China's growth called the "scientific development concept," which sought to modify high reliance on gross domestic product (GDP) expansion as a national goal (which could be skewed by high-cost "image" projects) and to look more to a "people-centered," "all-round" approach that, according to Hu, "strives to take a civilized development path characterized by the development of production, a well-off life, and a good ecological environment." Internationally, Hu projected confidence and dignity, personifying a country that had already become a great and respected nation.

For his new life in "retirement," Jiang maintained two residences, his modest courtyard house in Zhongnanhai and a newly built home in Shanghai. As usual, he had his daily swim of six hundred meters—which, he said, he might like to extend. For China's most senior retirees like Li Peng and Zhu Rongji as well as Jiang, the government provided, free for life, a suite of services that included an office, a personal secretary and assistants, a chef, an assistant chef, a fully stocked kitchen in accord with personal tastes, sufficient housekeepers, a car and driver, and more than a dozen security guards. In addition, they had free use of the Diaoyutai State Guesthouse for government-related guests or entertainment, plus free travel within China including guesthouses in every one of the provinces.

"They'll enjoy the *jibie* perks—benefits accorded to their last rank—until they die," explained Laurence Brahm, a Beijing-based commentator. "But what they won't have is what American leaders do—the ability to go out and collect huge fees from speaking engagements." Retired leaders in China are expected to "lead quiet lives" and not to "make public statements and influence policy." Nor should they seek personal enrichment. Becoming a professional celebrity, like former President Bill Clinton, and earning immense compensation for writing books, lecturing, and serving on corporate boards, is not appropriate for a Party elder.

But a retired Jiang Zemin, who had led China into a remarkable new era with vision and grit, would not have to depend on speaking engagements or book contracts to maintain his voice. All he would need to do was pick up the phone. Although there were rumors that a few Party elders wrote letters urging Jiang to step down as CMC chairman, and some others did not think it proper for him to retain the position, most people agreed that Jiang Zemin would continue to exercise "considerable influence" for years and that such continuity was good for the country.

"I hope he can organize some of his writings," Jiang Zehui suggested. "My personal interest would be understanding, from a country leader's perspective, how science and technology can facilitate national development. Of course, he is still so busy and his interests are so broad and rich, I don't know whether he will have time."

Jiang Zemin was a man at ease. "Now that I have no official government or Party position," he said, "I have no pressure [*yishen qing;* literally, "whole body [is] light"].

He enjoyed strong support from his inner staff, each of whom had been well positioned in a strategic job. The appointment of Jia Ting'an, his long-time secretary, as director of the powerful CMC General Office indicated that his influence was not diminishing.

Jiang maintained a rigorous approach to giving directives. When he asked one minister to determine whether a foreigner should visit a certain place, the minister assumed that it was a declarative command.

"I will take him as soon as possible," the minister responded.

"That's *not* what I said," Jiang corrected him. "I did not say Mr. X *should* go. I said you determine *whether* Mr. X should go."

When speaking among themselves, Jiang's closest associates may refer to him as "Big Brother" (Da Ge), not in an Orwellian sense of watching and controlling their lives but in an intimate family sense of warmth, affection, and respect. "Should we tell Da Ge [about the problem]?" one member of Jiang's inner circle may ask another.

The former president continued to greet foreign dignitaries in Zhongnanhai's elegant and classically ornate reception halls—the Indian prime minister and the French defense minister in June 2003; Britain's prime minister, Tony Blair, in July. Meeting U.S. Vice President Dick Cheney in April 2004, Jiang said that China would not allow anyone to separate Taiwan from the motherland in any form. Meeting North Korea's Kim Jong-Il the next week, he called for "in-depth and frank exchanges" to deal with "the complicated and volatile" situation. To the Russian defense minister that same week, he said that their bilateral friendship develops "from generation to generation." To U.S. Assistant to the President for National Security Affairs Condoleezza Rice in July 2004, he reiterated that China "will never tolerate Taiwan independence," a story that was the lead in *People's Daily* (which also noted that Jiang told Rice, with whom he had danced and spoken Russian during President Bush's 2002 visit to Beijing, that she "looks younger than before.")

China's "chief representative" was not reluctant to speak of his own appearance and robustness. "I'm seventy-seven years old," Jiang announced cheerily to some friends. "Many people say that they cannot tell. People even younger than I have more wrinkles." Reportedly, Blair told Jiang that he looked young, to which Jiang replied, "I feel young!" In China, energetic assertions from a supposedly retired senior leader can raise eyebrows.

Jiang dressed smartly in a Western suit and tie. His hair, though thinning, remained black and combed straight back. He appeared vigorous, less heavy, healthier, his voice as strong and vibrant as ever. Perhaps he had more time for swimming and less need to attend formal banquets.

In the early years of Jiang's leadership, foreign critics had derogated him as "uncharismatic." Now he radiated a patriarchal presence and a captivating self-confidence that were both magnetic and charming. In more than metaphor, how Jiang had grown personally epitomized how China had grown nationally.

JIANG KEPT A LOW profile during the second half of 2003, focusing on army issues. As CMC chairman, he sought to accelerate the pace of army modernization to empower the PLA to win the battles of the future, particularly in high-tech and information warfare. He called for further military reform— "fewer but better forces," "winning by quality rather than quantity," "moderate scale, rational structure, expeditious command." He worked on "Party construction" for China's army and a military academies as "major bases" for training military talent, innovating military theories, and developing military technology. "Science and talent are crucial," he said.

In October all China lit with pride as its first astronaut, *taikonaut* Yang Liwei, orbited the Earth fourteen times, making China only the third country in the world, after America and Russia, to launch a manned spacecraft. A beaming Jiang hailed the flight as "one more proof of the will and capability of the Chinese people to surmount the peak of world science and technology."

"I believe," Jiang stated, "that under the leadership of the Communist Party with Hu Jintao as general secretary, we will surely make more brilliant achievements in developing aerospace undertakings and in developing China's scientific and technological undertakings as a whole." As if fulfilling a lifetime dream, Jiang added, "The great rejuvenation of the Chinese nation is definitely come true."

It was a time for giving back, too, for expressing appreciation to some who had helped him over the years. In early January 2004 Jiang invited to Zhongnanhai those television professionals who had long covered his activities, especially his foreign trips—six correspondents one morning, seven producers and editors the next. Reminiscing for two hours, they exchanged stories—like the time when a cameraman, seeking an unusual angle for a shot, jumped over a guardrail on a precipitously steep African dam and began to waver. Jiang by reflex reached out to him, enabling the man to grab his hands and avoid the injurious slide. After the storytelling, Jiang treated everyone to lunch and a tour.

The idea for the television reunion began in a phone conversation between Jiang and CCTV President Zhao Huayong, who attended both days. Zhao's own story was the harrowing one about the mix-up on the *National News*.

In another phone call at this time, Jiang told Zhao that it would be wonderful to help the Chinese people appreciate classical music, noting that many world leaders whom he knew loved such music. While some in China assumed classical music to be elitist, Jiang said that it enriched all people and should be made widely available. Less than three months later, a new national television channel, CCTV's fifteenth, began broadcasting. The mix was 50 percent Chinese classical music and 50 percent Western classical music, much of the latter performed by Chinese orchestras. At the launch, Jiang called Zhao to congratulate him and said that he had been watching and enjoying the programs for several hours.

"The growth of classical music in China is largely due to one man—Jiang Zemin," said Yu Long, the acclaimed young conductor of the China Philharmonic Orchestra and artistic director of the Beijing Music Festival. "The decade between 1992 and 2002 was one of the great revivals in Chinese cultural history. People talk about China's economic resurgence; I believe our cultural resurgence is equally important, and it will enrich multiple generations. No one can doubt how President Jiang's personal passion for the arts, especially classical music, has had national impact."

In late January, Jiang traveled in southern China for three weeks, visiting factories and farms, army bases and theme parks. The Hong Kong press called it "Jiang's Nanxun," after Deng Xiaoping's reinvigorating 1992 Southern Tour, and interpreted it as signifying his continuing power. Front-page photos showed Jiang dancing at the Chinese Folk Culture Village, giving evidence that he was still healthy and still active.

Photos told the story. On various public occasions, Jiang appeared prominently with the nine members of the new Politburo Standing Committee, "nine plus one," as it were. For example, when Beijingers planted three million trees on a day in early April 2004, Jiang and the nine appeared in

Chaoyang Park, Beijing's largest. They all wore similar dark jackets and carried identical green shovels, and they walked in step in a long row, with young boys and girls dressed in red and white between each of them. As always, Jiang Zemin and Hu Jintao were in the center, with four members to each side in precise order of their ranking, inside higher, outside lower. Though protocol dictated that Hu's name come first in the headlines, all, including Hu, respected Jiang as their elder.

Jiang was at peace. At mid-2004, China's economy was sustaining its phenomenal growth, fueling the global economy, and the country's international image was one of stability and strength (if marred briefly by a lockdown of dissidents before the fifteenth anniversary of the crackdown of June 4). The transition to the new generation of collective leaders, with Hu Jintao as general secretary, had progressed smoothly and unremarkably, as would be expected of a normal nation. It now seemed Jiang's responsibility, or prerogative, to complete the transition, to relinquish his final official post as chairman of the Central Military Commission while continuing his overarching role as chief representative.

But Jiang was also on guard. The unrelenting, cleverly couched moves of Chen Shui-bian toward Taiwanese independence (after Taiwan's chaotic and bizarre presidential elections in March) and pressures from various interest groups in Hong Kong, especially prodemocracy parties, seemed to have either encouraged or obliged Jiang to take a larger role in policymaking, strengthening his hold on power. Speaking to local officials in Shenzhen during his visit to southern China in early 2004, Jiang stressed Deng Xiaoping's admonition that "patriots must form the main body" of Hong Kong's leaders, a mandate then publicized in China's national media along with accusations that Hong Kong's prodemocracy personalities were unpatriotic and that foreign forces, particularly the United States and Britain, were interfering in China's internal affairs.

It would be a mistake to assume that in reasserting his influence on policy, Jiang clashed with President Hu Jintao, who was also firm in eschewing independence for Taiwan and in resisting a free, direct election of Hong Kong's chief executive in 2007 and of its entire legislature in 2008. Hu continued to respect Jiang, even on occasion reversing a decision to which Jiang objected, while continuing to appoint colleagues to provincial and municipal posts and to champion the plight of the poor.

Jiang reportedly told Condoleezza Rice in July 2004 that he was "handing over more and more power" to Hu, a statement that was read as confirming that Jiang Zemin, twenty months after turning over Party leadership, still retained ultimate authority and was determining the timing of the yet-incomplete transition. State media highlighted CMC Chairman Jiang's instructions to the army, even ancient ones such as his 1991 exhortation to troops to "master revolutionary theory." It was another signal that Jiang's power was ongoing and that the prerogative to make final decisions on sensitive or contentious issues of foreign affairs and domestic policy remained his.

As for his direction, the former president seemed to be tacking Left, "hard line" as it were, asserting more stringent and uncompromising positions—such as on Taiwan, where he advocated accelerated preparations for potential military action. "We must fight a war with Taiwan" was a quote attributed to Jiang. He also nixed the phrase "peaceful rise," which Hu and his team had developed to define China's emergence as a great power without the use of military force, probably because a "peaceful rise" policy could be interpreted (or misinterpreted) as undermining Jiang's muscular position that China would interdict Taiwan's drive to independence no matter how high the price.

On the home front, Jiang's elevated anxiety about social stability during the multiyear transition moved him to quash activities that he thought politically disruptive. Apparently he was the one who authorized the decision to detain Dr. Jiang Yanyong, the high-profile whistle-blower on SARS who had written a widely circulated letter calling for a revaluation of the 1989 student protests. Since Dr. Jiang was a senior military surgeon and long-standing Party official whose rank was equivalent to a lieutenant general or major general, his case was handled by the Central Military Commission, chaired by Jiang Zemin. (The decision came after a Politburo meeting on the subject—one can assess the importance of subjects by the level and number of meetings dealing with them.) In the light of unpleasant international publicity and conflicting opinions in the Party, Dr. Jiang was released after forty-five days in rather comfortable custody, having acknowledged the threat the Party perceived during the massive demonstrations but without endorsing or condoning the military suppression. In writing his required "thought report," Dr. Jiang used a medical metaphor: the "Communist Party confronted by the student protests was much like a patient with complicated colorectal cancer where, without emergency surgery, death was imminent."

Jiang Zemin considered all his decisions, some of which foreign media swiftly labeled reactionary or repressive, to be necessary to ensure China's political stability and thus not interrupt the country's steadily increasing economic strength and national power. As Jiang saw his motherland (in his paternalistic way), nothing could be allowed to thwart China from growing strong and becoming a leading nation.

How Jiang would adjudicate the competing interests—his need to consummate the leadership transition versus his need to protect China's vital interests—would be a decision, it appeared, that he felt only he should make (and about which he may have been conflicted). Weighing his political sense against the beat of his personal clock, the lifelong patriot sought the patriotic path, perhaps again surprising those who would underestimate Jiang Zemin and his love for his country.

ON SEPTEMBER 19, 2004, Jiang Zemin retired as chairman of the CPC Central Military Commission and Hu Jintao, as expected, was elected by the CPC Central Committee to take his place. The country went about its business as the transition to Hu, now the undisputed leader of China with command of the Party, state, and armed forces, was completed in the first peaceful transition of power since the founding of New China in 1949. Hu's appointment reaffirmed the sacrosanct principle of the absolute leadership of the Party over the military, and it was greeted by virtually unanimous approval. (Since his appointment as CMC vice chairman in 1999 Hu had worked unobtrusively but conscientiously to win the army's respect.)

Jiang's resignation was announced at the Fourth Plenum of the Sixteenth CPC Central Committee, which, led by Hu, focused on bolstering the Party's capacity to rule (and its legitimacy) through increased transparency and accountability. The new reforms stressed checks and balances in the system of governance and advocated open competition in the selection of Party and government officials.

A carefully worded communiqué noted that the Plenum had "highly evaluated Comrade Jiang Zemin's [thirteen-year] outstanding contributions to the Party, the state, and the people," especially "under the extremely complicated international and domestic situation." It credited Jiang for founding the "Important Thought of Three Represents," which, it said, "must be implemented in all areas of China's socialist modernization drive and be reflected in all aspects of Party building."

The communiqué went on to praise Jiang's fifteen years as CMC chairman, stating that he had "grasped the development trends of new military reforms in the world with his great insight" and had enriched the army-building ideas of Mao Zedong and Deng Xiaoping to "found the Jiang Zemin Thought for national defense and army building." (With his name now used as a possessive adjective for his own style of modern military "thought"—likely a negotiated phrase—Jiang's legacy was enhanced.)

Official media had not reported pre-Plenum rumors, exaggerated in the foreign press, of jockeying between Jiang and Hu over positions of protégés and nuances of policy—for example, whether China should maintain high rates of economic growth and emphasize well-developed coastal and urban areas, as Jiang supposedly espoused, or shift to more balanced economic allocations that looked to aid poorer inland and rural areas and those left behind by the rapid reforms, as Hu reportedly supported.

Once the surprising announcement was made, the media spotlighted the two personalities. China Central Television dedicated its prime evening newscast to the transition, showing the seventy-eight-year-old Jiang and the sixty-one-year-old Hu walking together in the Great Hall of the People, shaking hands warmly, and being applauded loudly by all members of the Central Committee who enveloped them.

"Today we are all very happy," said Hu after he and Jiang, who agreed on fundamental policies, posed for pictures. "On the occasion of the successful conclusion of the Fourth Plenum, our respected and beloved Comrade Jiang Zemin has come to join us. Let's welcome him with warm applause to give us an important speech."

"I just want to say three sentences," Jiang said in his short but emotional farewell. "One, I want to offer my sincere thanks to the Central Committee for accepting my resignation letter. Two, I want to extend my heartfelt gratitude to the comrades for your longtime help and support. Three, I hope that everyone will work hard and keep advancing under the leadership of the Party Central Committee with Comrade Hu Jintao as general secretary, and I'm convinced that our Party's cause will witness more and bigger victories!"

According to the official Xinhua account, "Hu paid homage to Jiang for his 'outstanding contribution to the Party, the state, and the people,' and thanked Jiang for his 'support and assistance' to the new central collective leadership of the Party."

Earlier, in a formal letter dated September 1, Jiang had submitted his resignation to the Politburo. With a concise sequence of clear statements Jiang said that he "had always looked forward to complete retirement from leadership positions," and he proposed that Hu Jintao succeed him as CMC chairman, calling Hu "completely qualified for the post." Jiang also praised Hu's leadership of the Party in making "many great achievements in both the Party and China, winning support and trust of the cadres and the people."

Although additional rumors circulated about political pressure and health problems, Jiang regarded his retirement as voluntary, taken to benefit the nation. "After meticulous consideration," he wrote, "I intend to resign from my current post, which is good for the long-term development of the cause of the Party, the state, and the armed forces." Jiang had come to conclude that the Party's success, if not survival, depended on Hu emerging as an unambiguous leader with real power.

At the first meeting of the new Central Military Commission, whose members were expanded from seven to eleven, the new Party military chief praised his predecessor. "He stands high, sees afar, and reckons deep," Hu said of Jiang, who was invited to attend. "Chairman Jiang's noble character, sterling integrity, and broad-mindedness have set a splendid example for us."

Jiang described Hu as a "young and energetic" leader with "rich leading experience" and "excellent qualifications." Remarking that "the top leadership of our Party, state, and military has completely and smoothly realized an old-to-new transfer and transition," Jiang stated: "Now I have accomplished my historical mission and fulfilled my historical duty."

"When Comrade [Deng] Xiaoping handed over the post of CMC chairman to me," Jiang continued, "I really felt that an extremely heavy burden had been put on my shoulders. For fifteen years I tried my best to live up to Comrade Xiaoping's trust. Day and night I was always concerned about our country's sovereignty and security and our army's building and development. Though I'm retired now, my heart will always be linked with the military, with all officers and soldiers of the army, and with the comrades in the CMC."

In his September 1 valedictory letter Jiang wrote that he greatly cherished the Party and the Chinese people, and their well-being has been his life for six decades. "I will be loyal to the undertaking of the Party and the state forever," he said, "and I will always be a loyal member of the Communist Party of China."

IN 1958, WHEN WORKING at the Changchun automotive factory, a young Jiang Zemin had been forced by the Communist Party to purge a man for observing that a Russian lathe "made more noise" than an American lathe. By 2003 that same Jiang Zemin had opened up that same Party to the "new social strata," including private business owners, and had China join the war on terrorism initiated and led by America.

In 1988, when serving as Party secretary of Shanghai, Jiang canceled a beauty contest, because, as he said at the time, "conditions are not yet ripe."

In 2003 the Miss China pageant was a national event, and newspapers delighted in reporting how the winner would compete for the crown of Miss Universe.

In November 2003, at a rally celebrating the country's first man in orbit, Jiang awarded a Space Hero medal to Yang Liwei.

In March 2004 Jiang's Three Represents was written into China's State Constitution, paralleling its earlier inclusion into the Party's Constitution, along with provisions that "the State respects and protects human rights" (marking China's first legal guarantee of human rights) and that "citizens' lawful private property shall not be violated" (establishing personal and public assets on an equal footing).

From beauty pageants and space flights to business owners and private property to the war on terrorism and new laws protecting human rights, China under Jiang Zemin, though still facing endemic and chronic problems, was "advancing with the times."

Conclusion

The Legacy of Jiang Zemin

I
T IS NOT HARD TO MISCONSTRUE China and misunderstand Jiang
Zemin. This includes distorting the meaning of Chinese pride and patriotism, and fearing the country's growing strength. This also extends
personally to Jiang, who many assume to have been a hardline dictator controlling a competitive, totalitarian state. This frustrates the man deeply: it is
surely not the way he sees himself.

Many Chinese complain that Americans do not understand China, yet
many Chinese do not understand Jiang. The new generation in China, educated and increasingly affluent, did not experience the Cultural Revolution,
much less the Great Leap Forward, the Anti-Rightist Campaign, the civil
war, and the Japanese occupation. In Jiang they see a senior elder, now
retired, and they do not appreciate how far China has come under his direction. Yet these young Chinese live where they like, work and dress as they
please, think what they want, and say what they think.

Jiang Zemin came to leadership as neither a founder of the country nor a
military hero. Following the tragedy of 1989, when he became general secretary of the Communist Party, China was politically fractured, socially tense,
economically stagnant, spiritually sullen, and internationally shunned. Jiang
faced intractable problems—widespread unemployment, pervasive corruption, archaic state-owned enterprises, mounting inequalities—and, as he traversed the political corridors of inner-sanctum Beijing, he could at no time
escape ideological assault from both Left and Right.

Yet Jiang persevered and in the end brought stability to society, freed and
accelerated the economy, greatly increased standards of living, and encouraged economic and social freedoms. He also captured the debate on the
major contradictions within Chinese society—rich versus poor, urban versus

rural, coastal versus western, private versus public ownership, management versus labor, spiritual versus material civilization, China's traditional values versus old-line Communism, Western versus Chinese culture, and opening-up versus maintaining China's special characteristics.

The man who once said, "Looking at China's modern history, I see suffering and bullying," restored China's status as a great power for the first time in four hundred years. Jiang visited every important country with which China had diplomatic relations and made China's position on world events matter.

The China that Jiang is leaving as his legacy is a far better place than the one in which he spent his life. Future historians may well conclude that it was during the period of Jiang Zemin's power that the country set into motion fundamental, irreversible transformation, and that it was this habitually underestimated leader who had the consistency of vision and subtlety of action to bring it all about.

ASKED WHAT HER THIRD Brother considered to be his most important accomplishments, Jiang Zehui listed four: revitalizing China through science and education; sustainable development; the Great West; and Three Represents.

Information Minister Zhao Qizheng gave his assessment: "President Jiang modernized the Party and the army, and he fought corruption. He enhanced the rule of law and encouraged the spirit of virtue. He pioneered economic reforms, including state-owned enterprises, finance, rural economy, and foreign investments. Internationally, he brought the Chinese people to the center of the world stage. Only if one is familiar with China's helpless position after World Wars I and II can one understand the deep meaning of my words."

"When Jiang Zemin became general secretary in 1989, China was still largely a planned economy," said Vice Minister Leng Rong. "The transition to the market was all new, and no one knew what to expect. People would ask how to do this or that in a socialist market economy: how to improve the nature of ownership, set macroeconomic controls, reform enterprise management, strengthen the legal system, streamline government, set a value system and moral norms—all consistent with socialism. This was uncharted territory, and as China underwent tremendous changes since 1989, so did Jiang's ideas. According to Deng, the true spirit of Marxism is to 'seek truth from facts.' Jiang added 'advancing with the times.' "

"Economic growth since 1989 has been the fastest in Chinese history," commented Song Ning, a senior adviser on microeconomic policy. "It is all the more remarkable in the face of extraordinary domestic and international challenges, particularly in the early years. If these problems had not occurred, we could have never appreciated President Jiang's wisdom. Because he is so well read, and a natural builder of consensus, he has not made a major mistake. Guiding the transformation of a revolutionary party into a ruling party has taken skill and sensitivity."

As for Jiang himself, he was philosophical about the length and substance of his leadership. "Thirteen or fourteen years [since 1989] are not a very long period in one's life," he mused. "However, they are not a short period either. As for myself, I dare not say how much I have accomplished in these years. I can only say that I have worked in a down-to-earth manner for the Party. I can still recall the days when I first moved to Beijing [in 1989]; I really had a very difficult time. However, after the Fourteenth Party Congress [in 1992], our overall progress sped up quickly."

The big breakthrough, he said, was the validation of the socialist market economy. "When the concept was put on the agenda," Jiang recalled, "some officials said that we should just use the word *market,* and that it was not necessary to include the word *socialist.* I disagreed. Other people said that since Marx never talked about a market economy, and never said that a socialist system could use market mechanisms, we shouldn't either. I disagreed with that too. Look at the past decade: we've done a terrific job! . . .

"When I consider an issue," Jiang continued, "I often try to combine natural sciences with social sciences. I've read many of Marx's papers. In his day, calculus had not yet been applied to economics; therefore the modern concept of marginal utility was not understood. In applying Marx, one must consider the knowledge of the times. . . .

"There are far more variables in the social sciences than there are in engineering," Jiang said, expressing a late-in-life interest. "Therefore social sciences are more complicated. The more I learn, the more I realize how much we have yet to learn. As for political issues, they are more complicated still."

"When President Jiang declared 'revitalizing China through science and education' to be national policy, I was very pleased," recalled Dr. Song Jian, chairman of the new Beijing Institute for Frontier Science. "Chinese scientists had been discussing such a grand vision for years. Now we had a leader who believed that what we were doing was essential for our country's future.

"President Jiang was highly supportive of our scientists," said Song. "He never interfered with our work, and he made sure that other Party or government officials didn't either. Speaking as a politician, Jiang told me that pure scientific research is 'none of our business.' Speaking as an intellectual, Jiang had great interest in our projects."

Jiang not only supported science for what it could do practically, he believed in the scientific method for what it meant intrinsically. A society that appreciates, in Jiang's words, the "unique sensitivities and sensibilities of scientists" and promotes "scientific creativity" is not one that can be, or remain, very much authoritarian.

Jiang took pride in the 200,000 Chinese students who had attended U.S. universities since 1978 (more than 60,000 were studying in the United States in 2002), of whom 50,000 had returned to help build the country. When Jiang met with Chinese young people studying in the United States, he encouraged them to do well, whether they chose to come back to China or remain in America. Either way, an enlightened Jiang would say, they could promote friendship between the two countries.

Although Jiang ruled out political elections for senior leaders, he called for greater social, academic, and personal openness. Westerners may not appreciate how well he succeeded. The electronic messages zipping around China exemplify an increasingly dynamic and unafraid populace. During the two-week Chinese New Year period in 2003, about 5.8 billion text messages were sent on cell phones, five times more than during the same period in 2002. By the time 2003 ended 220 billion cell phone text messages had been sent.

That the Chinese people can poke fun at their leaders with such messaging is a credit to Jiang's legacy. It is light fare compared to the abuse hurled at American presidents, but the jokes epitomize how uninhibited and uncowed the Chinese people have become. They are more personally free today, after Jiang's years of leadership, than at any other time in their five-thousand-year history.

"I've seen President Jiang every year since 1989," said Henry Kissinger, who is often in China. "He has grown in confidence and stature. By the late 1990s it was clear that he was expressing his own views and the government was reflecting those views, whereas in the early 1990s it was just as clear that he was more a spokesman for the consensus. Jiang always stressed that he was not governing by personal rule, but rather by representing China's collective leadership."

JIANG'S PRIMARY ALLEGIANCE WAS to China, the Chinese people, and Chinese civilization, and when he realized that two of nineteenth-century Communism's core tenets were not viable in the twenty-first century, he knew they had to change. The first was the restrictive old-line dictatorship of the proletariat, the theory that workers and peasants alone should rule the state. The second was that the state should own all the means of production. The ideas of class struggle and public ownership were rooted in reaction to abuses of the industrial age and they did not work in the information age. Today intellectual property and commercial enterprises are the wealth of nations, and knowledge workers and business creators are the energizers of economic progress. Jiang had to find a modern philosophy for the Party that would include the new social strata or the Party would lose its relevance, then its legitimacy.

Jiang did not change the people's democratic dictatorship, one of the Four Cardinal Principles of the Party, but he did expand the definition of "people." No longer limited only to workers and peasants, the "people" would now mean, as the third of the Three Represents states, the "overwhelming majority of the Chinese people," a category that would embrace China's elite, those who discover knowledge and those who create wealth.

To most Westerners, Communism is a colossal failure, a despotic, deeply flawed system that consigned one-third of humanity to economic privation and political fear—and it neither can be nor should be modernized. China, however, flouts conventional wisdom. As Nicholas Kristof comments, "We're used to Communist governments that both oppress and impoverish their citizens. But what is challenging about China is that its government is simultaneously brutal to dissidents and is lifting more people out of poverty more quickly than any other country in history."

The West needs to understand why Jiang Zemin, with missionary zeal, set about to transform an outdated revolutionary Party into a contemporary governing Party. His abiding belief in Communism, formed during his late teenage years and reinforced over the ensuing decades, was entwined with his patriotism, but when economic development began to separate what was good for China from what was taught by Communism, Jiang determined to modernize the Party.

To Jiang and his fellow students who were coming of age in the 1940s, Communism was a liberator, the mass movement that defeated the despicable Japanese and then swept out the despised Kuomintang. As young men filled with idealistic fervor, they dedicated themselves to this Communism, first underground in revolution and then openly in victory. Communism was the banner under which the Chinese people marched and fought and ultimately "stood up" before the world. Communism—the idea, the ideal—

became the energizing symbol of China reborn. Those who had worked for its success were imprinted for life with the intoxicating euphoria that often occurs when personal commitment is validated by organizational triumph.

Jiang recalled, "The time I was studying in middle school and in university was precisely the time when the Communist Party was leading the Chinese people toward the climax of the national democratic revolution. I accepted Marxism at that time, joined the Party, and took part in the struggle led by the Party to oppose the aggression of Japanese fascists and the Kuomintang reactionary rule. I take pride in and feel happy about the political faith and the road of life I have chosen."

JIANG ZEMIN'S BELIEF SYSTEM may be described as constructed on four levels. At bedrock, there are twin pillars: Chinese pride and patriotism, and Chinese values and culture. These are Jiang's immutables, the foundation on which all else is built.

The second level is economic development, which, in the modern world, is the only way to strengthen the country and revitalize its culture. Such economic development is impossible to sustain without social stability.

The third level is Party leadership. Jiang believes that only the Party can provide the national stability, unity, and vision needed to develop China's economy, enhance its civilization, and restore its pride.

The fourth level is Jiang's commitment to socialism and Communism, now well modernized with his Three Represents. This means that in Jiang's hierarchy of beliefs, the governance of the Party in leading China (third level) is more fundamental than any specific political precept it espouses (fourth level), not the other way around.

For these core convictions, Jiang has maintained long-term consistency. Observers who think that they see him bob on this policy or weave on that position, then conclude that the man is more political than principled, are not seeing the real man. Sometimes he changes his mind—circumstances change or he may need to bring about compromise or he may come to realize that he had erred—but the underlying reason for his shift is usually the same: to better express his abiding beliefs.

Whenever Jiang experienced a conflict between his Chinese patriotism and his Marxist socialism, patriotism would be the winner. One need only look at Hong Kong. Any who thought that Jiang's promise of not interfering in Hong Kong was a fingers-crossed ruse, and that as soon as the world looked away Beijing would pounce and socialize the territory, did not know

President Jiang at all. His steadfast commitment to support Hong Kong's capitalist system was based not only on his commitment to make good on China's promise of "one country, two systems," it was also based on the simple fact that capitalism worked better there, and if Hong Kong prospered, so would China. Jiang was a Chinese patriot more than a crusading Marxist, and since he wanted Hong Kong's international status enhanced, certainly not diminished, he was deeply serious about keeping the mainland's ministries and mandarins out.

Jiang Zemin was never an ideologue. He was an engineer who spent twenty-five years solving on-the-job industrial problems. When an electrical power plant didn't work, he had to fix it—not with theory but in the cold world of rusted pipes and cracked boilers. So when it became clear that, in a competitive global marketplace, a command economy and a prohibition against private ownership were a recipe for national stagnation, Jiang followed Deng's call to "seek truth from facts."

In his landmark speech on the Party's eightieth anniversary, Jiang put Deng's idea in his own words: "We should take practice as the sole criterion for testing truth."

For Jiang, the challenge was to find a way to maintain the power and relevance of the Party within a rapidly changing society. He believed that the Party was an essential force for unifying and leading the people; without it, he truly believed, the country would disintegrate into chaos. But he also recognized that some of its ideology was no longer applicable. (A sardonic quip gets it half right: "If the Party doesn't reform, it's waiting for death; if it does reform, it's seeking death." The first clause is correct; the second is not—the mistake is conflating the Party as a ruling body with some of its classic but archaic teachings.)

Jiang sought to combine Communist goals, free market methods, and traditional Chinese values in a way that worked in the contemporary world. In focusing on building the Party—"Party construction," as he called it—he used various concepts and campaigns, including "spiritual civilization," "talk more about politics," Three Stresses, and ultimately, Three Represents.

As envisioned by Jiang and his key advisers, Jiang Thought subsumed all of these theories and discourses and expressed the totality of his political philosophy. Central to his legacy, Jiang Thought was promoted as a "further development of Marxism" that built on Mao Zedong Thought and Deng Xiaoping Theory, and he intended that it would become the guiding theory of the Party in the twenty-first century.

Built on a series of maxims and aphorisms, Jiang Thought had three inter-related objectives—material civilization, spiritual civilization, and political civilization—and one unifying mechanism, Three Represents. The three "civilizations" were the intended ends, and "the important thought of Three Represents" was the chosen means. *Material civilization* was economic wealth—products and services of all kinds. *Spiritual civilization* involved culture, morality, ethics, philosophy, literature, art, natural and social sciences, and even (in a way) religion. *Political civilization* represented social and legal systems that would bring about decency, consistency, and ultimately some kind of democratic society.

Jiang believed that in order to develop the three civilizations, he had to strengthen and modernize the Party by aligning its ideology with current realities. The way to do this, he determined, was by giving the Party internal directives for training its members and external goals for leading the country. The internal directives were the Three Stresses. The external goals were the Three Represents. The result, in Jiang's vision, would transform China into a "well-off society in an all-around way."

AT FIRST BLUSH JIANG Zemin's Three Represents, the new governing philosophy of the Party, seems bland and harmless. It is neither, at least not to orthodox Communists. To them, it is disrupting, disorienting, and deeply disturbing.

Often in politics, old ideas are repackaged and dressed up with new names. With Jiang's Three Represents, it is the reverse: The label on the box is the same—Communism—but what's inside is dramatically different.

The First Represent, "advanced productive forces," extends the Marxist phrase "productive forces" in a clever ideological way and works to elevate the status of and bring into the Party the most dynamic strata of society—managers, entrepreneurs, and private business owners. The First Represent, the Party's primary goal in rejuvenating China, promotes the building of "material civilization." For Jiang, it was epitomized by innovation in science and technology. The Party would now be representing intellectuals, and in the process the Party itself would be intellectualized. For this reason China's science and technology communities were early and enthusiastic supporters of Jiang's new theory.

It was a long-deserved turnaround for China's best and brightest. Those who had suffered grievously during Mao's Cultural Revolution had now, three decades later, come to the vanguard of China's new society. Throughout the political campaigns of the 1950s and 1960s, the idealistic young Jiang, a dedicated member of the Party, was deeply troubled by the Party's castigation and dismissal of China's intellectuals, who he believed were China's primary resource for building the country. Now, as leader of that same Party, General Secretary Jiang could praise and empower China's intellectuals, who were the driving talent behind "advanced productive forces."

The Second Represent, "advanced culture," combines morality, civil behavior, high-minded personal traits, progressive social attitudes, shared beliefs, and all the arts. It is the Party's complementary goal for rejuvenating China, and it signifies the building of "spiritual civilization"—in Jiang's words, "lofty ideals, moral integrity, better education, and a good sense of discipline." To Jiang, an appreciation of science is pervasive in this advanced culture.

Advanced culture also signals a pride-filled return to the glories of thousands of years of Chinese civilization—explicitly before the foreigners came, and implicitly before Communism took over. Although the Party is praised for liberating the country, it is criticized for eroding, and at times decimating, traditional Chinese culture. The teachings of Confucius, for example, were for decades derogated as "feudal." With his strong cultural roots, Jiang sought to restore the values and virtues of Chinese civilization, integrating them with Marxism.

The Third Represent, a reaffirmation of the Party's role in serving the masses, reaches out to all Chinese society ("the fundamental interests of the overwhelming majority of the people"). Although it seems to state the obvious, the Third Represent extends the reach of the Party beyond its traditional base of workers and farmers to all society, which includes those who create knowledge (e.g., scientists), and more controversially, those who create wealth (e.g., entrepreneurs). The reason the Third Represent attracted considerable flak from Leftists was that it superseded key elements of the Party's founding theories—class struggle, the vanguard of the working class, and the dictatorship of the proletariat—with a concept of an all-encompassing party that brought in advanced or elite members from all sectors of society.

Jiang was often criticized for making the Party more inclusive and classless, for reaching out to innovators in science and business. To Jiang, only by including within the Party the knowledge and wealth creators could the Party continue to exercise its leadership. To Jiang's Leftist critics, by including "other classes," especially those wealth creators, he polluted the Party's Communist purity.

To Leng Rong, an erudite Party theoretician, Three Represents is a *methodology*. "It doesn't solve specific problems," explained Professor Leng, "but it's a way of categorizing and analyzing problems so that they can be solved. It is consistent with Marxism and extends it by linking traditional theory with current reality." It is the guiding principle for adapting the Party to a high-tech, information-dense world. "Innovation, innovation, and more innovation," said Leng Rong. "Such is how the Party looks to the future under the guidance of Three Represents."

Jiang puts Three Represents at the pinnacle of purpose. To him, it is the reason for establishing the Party, the foundation for governing the country, and the source of national strength. "I put forward the theory," he said, "after thinking about it for a long time."

When asked in late 2001 at the China National Defense University to elaborate on his new political views, Jiang demurred: "People say I've talked too much already; I have to be careful." He then added, defensively at that time, "What I have said is still within Marxism."

How could Jiang defend a "still-within-Marxism" position? Using Communist economics, to be charitable, would be a challenge. However, if the touchstone of Marxism became its methodology or ultimate goal, that could work. To Jiang, the grand vision of Marxism superseded any of its isolated dictates. Thus, Marxism became "a scientific thinking system," a method of political, economic, and social analysis devoid of any archaic baggage that certain things must or must not be done.

As for its ultimate goal, Jiang never wavered: "We firmly believe in the basic Marxist tenet that human society will inevitably move toward Communism. Communism can only be realized on the basis of a fully developed and highly advanced socialist society." Such a society, he said, would have "abundant material wealth, and people would have a very high realm of thought and be able to develop themselves freely and in an all-around way." But he added the caveat that "the realization of Communism will be an extremely protracted historical process."

According to a Party writer, "the three generations of collective leadership" at "the three historical junctures" created "the three exhortations." Mao made "China stand on its own feet" as an independent country; Deng "liberated and unleashed the productivity of Chinese society"; and Jiang "greatly rejuvenated the Chinese nation" and reached "a new milestone in China's development." The relationship between Mao Zedong Thought, Deng Xiaoping Theory, and the "important thought of Three Represents" was said to form "a continuous line of inheritance," even though parts of the latter two negated parts of the first.

Only by securing his theoretical linkage to Mao and Deng could Jiang's practical ideas be protected. Ideological genetics were the Party's political science, and that was why inscribing "the important thought of Three Represents" in the Party Constitution, right after Marxism-Leninism, Mao Zedong Thought, and Deng Xiaoping Theory, was a culminating moment.

"Jiang was very proud of his Three Represents," commented Shen Yongyan. "From our many late-night conversations, it was obvious how passionate he is about its importance."

Asked in early 2004 which were Jiang Zemin's most memorable speeches, Teng Wensheng, his longtime speechwriter, said, "I cannot say; I just take down President Jiang's ideas. They are his achievements, not mine." Minister Teng continued, "There are five speeches," he said, "in which I take special pride. In chronological order: Deng Xiaoping's 'Liberate your thoughts, Seek truth from facts,' given in late 1978 [initiating economic reform]; Deng's 'Reform of the Governing System,' given in August 1980 [initiating political reform]; Jiang Zemin's 'Socialist Market Economy,' given in June 1992 at the Party School [establishing the market]; Jiang's Three Represents, given in February 2000 [modernizing Marxism]; and Jiang's address on the eightieth anniversary of the CPC, given in July 2001 [modernizing the Party]."

ON POLITICAL REFORM, the most sensitive area of China's transformation, Jiang sought a studied and controlled approach to limit the unconstrained exercise of power, such as by institutionalizing regular meetings of Party and government bodies, gradually expanding the scope of reform yet always keeping it within meticulously monitored boundaries. As leader of the nation, Jiang believed that his primary mission was to provide and protect the basic necessities of life for China's vast multitudes, and that assuring such sustenance for all was a far higher good than allowing full political freedoms for a few.

For this reason Jiang unabashedly rejected Western-style democracy, because he was convinced that competitive elections would disrupt society, foment instability, and lead to all manner of trauma for 1.3 billion Chinese. It is a view shared by many of his countrymen. For this same reason—to maintain stability for the good of the masses—Jiang also sought to prevent any dissension, disagreement, personality conflict, or political struggle within the Party or government from being reported, revealed, or leaked, even countenancing cover stories to maintain the semblance of total unity. Then there are the lack of certain freedoms—the absence of free speech, the prosecution of political dissidents, and a notoriously harsh penal code. Yet most Chinese are not troubled by these restrictions and support severe punishment for crime.

To most Westerners, democracy has a simple, one-dimensional test. If a country offers a free and honest one-person/one-vote election for its most senior leader, then it is a democracy. If it doesn't, it isn't. China is either democratic or dictatorial, Westerners believe; the leadership either accepts multiple parties and free elections and the country becomes democratic or maintains its one-party monopoly and the country remains dictatorial. By this test, China is surely not a democracy.

But if one looks at almost every aspect of real life—where to live, where to work, where to travel, how to dress, whom to marry, what to study, what to think, what to say, how to make and spend money, what to write on cell phone messages—Chinese people have more personal freedom today than at virtually any other time in their history. Referring to the period of Jiang Zemin's leadership, Nicholas Kristof states, "China did not achieve political pluralism, but it did move toward economic pluralism, cultural pluralism, social pluralism." Compelling evidence, he says, is that "China now has some seven thousand newspapers, five hundred publishing houses, three thousand TV stations, 250 million mobile phone users, and 70 million regular Internet users." Those who still insist on classifying China as a repressive society must explain why, notwithstanding the strict limitations on political freedoms, it would be the first of its kind to offer such vast arrays of information and expression to all its citizens.

In fact, the personal and social freedoms of most urban Chinese are now just about on a par with those of their counterparts in the West. More important, the entire vast population is finally free from famine, pestilence, homelessness, illiteracy, political mass movements, and many of the social scourges of other eras. This is what Deng Xiaoping formulated and Jiang Zemin implemented. Furthermore, Jiang's government began conducting itself in ways normally associated with democratic systems, such as polling its citizens to assess their attitudes and opinions.

Could Jiang have gone further with political reform? For example, could he have enabled truly free elections in the CPC Central Committee to select the Politburo and its Standing Committee? One would think so, but it is always easy for foreigners to argue for more freedom more quickly in China. As Henry Kissinger remarked, "We are great at telling people how to run their countries, and the older the country is, the freer we seem to tell them."

Jiang's political framework, formed during traumatic times, was founded on the necessity of social stability. If err he must, he would always choose to err on the side of stability. Perhaps this reflected his paternalistic or patriarchal attitude toward the Chinese people. Perhaps he saw deeply into the essence of Chinese society. Certainly he appreciated China's chronicles and had experienced its turbulence. Although Jiang Zemin opposed replicating Western-style democracy in China, the economic, social, cultural, and ethical values he espoused during his time at the helm were arguably more important for the ultimate good of China, Chinese civilization, and the Chinese people.

The question arises: Is being a Western-style democracy the highest good for all countries at all times? If public policy were truly dictated by majority rule, some countries, including a few in the Middle East, would initiate more, not less, aggressive acts against their perceived foes (including the United States) to their own detriment. One Chinese intellectual supports a "one person/one vote" democracy because he believes it is the only way to *oust* his country's pro-American leaders.

In China, a premature democracy would reallocate resources to political debate and thereby sacrifice mid- and long-term economic and social benefits for short-term political freedoms. A premature democracy would also reallocate income among sectors, groups, and classes, which, integrated over time, would likely not build the economy as potently and therefore not bring the greatest good to the greatest number. It is unlikely that if China had instituted a multiparty democracy and freedom of the press in 1989, its people would have the standard of living they do today.

At some point, however, these dynamics invert, so that the absence of a true democracy would thereafter inhibit, not enhance, China's continued development. (For example, corruption is best minimized in a political democracy and by a free press.) China's new leaders will have to figure out when that point of inflection occurs (engineers understand inflection points).

JIANG'S MODEL OF TODAY'S Communist Party is a dynamic, action-oriented vanguard institution, motivated by ideological vision but not bound by ideological dogma. It is the supervisory Party responsible for the well-being, both material and spiritual, of the Chinese people. It is the leadership Party that, in the Chinese system, seeks the "cooperation and political consultation" of eight small non-Communist parties. Jiang's model Party is also the guarantor of the nation's integrity and the holder of the flame of Chinese nationalism, neither of which has any relationship to the political theories of Karl Marx or his Soviet followers. With Three Represents, Jiang kept Communism's unifying name and its ultimate goal but modernized its economic structures and social rules.

As part of his efforts to rejuvenate the Party, Jiang promoted a kind of democracy within the Party, so-called inner-Party democracy. Debate takes place within the one party rather than between separate parties, and because the factions in the one Party can function like multiple parties as they strive to expand influence, affect policy, and promote personnel, a rudimentary, protodemocratic version of checks and balances begins to emerge.

Rather than disparage these factions within the Party—currently, the Shanghai faction associated with Jiang Zemin and the Youth League faction associated with Hu Jintao—foreign analysts would do well to appreciate that these somewhat coherent political groups, as long as they are rational and collegial as well as partisan and competitive, can help strengthen the development of Chinese democracy. For a political system to be *devoid* of competing factions would contradict human nature and group sociology and be decidedly abnormal; such a condition can exist only under the coercive thumb of an absolute dictatorship, which China is not.

"The process of building consensus in the Party," commented Vice Minister Leng Rong, "is not unlike the political process in the American system." Both take diverse, even divergent ideas and drive toward a majority decision that almost everyone more or less accepts. "Jiang Zemin was a master at doing this," adds Leng. The difference in China, of course, is that with only one party, ideas are contested out of public view, but Jiang believed that to be the best way to maintain stability.

Jiang's challenge was to build consensus among his contemporaries, most of whom had more experience working in the central government, without falling back on the intimidating measures of the past to do so. "Jiang Zemin made the Party 'normal,'" commented Leng Rong. During his later years, Mao Zedong's views differed dramatically from those of the majority of the Party's leadership, but he still had the power to enforce his radicalism—that was not "normal." Deng allowed diverse voices to be heard, but he still called the shots—which was probably necessary during his time of transition. During Jiang Zemin's period of leadership, everyone—leaders and masses—became more aware of events and more confident in voicing independent opinions, and only a builder of consensus could be successful in such an increasingly individualistic and cacophonous environment. Part of Jiang's legacy is that China today is a normal country: virtually no one wants to return to the Maoist past; the people would not tolerate it.

"The United States had a history of democracy," explained Zheng Bijian, former executive vice president of the Central Party School under Hu Jintao. "The first American immigrants, remember, came from England, and the United States has had relative peace for over two hundred years to enable its system to develop. China, on the other hand, had a poor, largely uneducated population who had experienced nothing but feudalism, civil strife, and foreign invasion and occupation. . . .

"So as President Jiang has said, give us some time to develop our democracy," Zheng implored. "Please respect our practices, trial-and-error steps, need to go slow. But just like we've done with our economy, we will build our democracy."

Since democracy, such as it is, exists only within the "inner Party," China may be described as a "democracy of the elite," where the elite come from all sectors of society, from peasants and workers to scientists and entrepreneurs. The elite are the Party members, who constitute about five percent of China's population and contend among themselves to determine appointments of leaders and formulation of policy. In this manner, China is run by and large by those who are best educated and most dedicated. It is not a system that can deal well with corruption and it is not a system that can or should last long-term; but it just may be the optimum system for handling the short- and mid-term complexities and contradictions of contemporary China.

In a system where one party maintains a perpetual monopoly, political power is private, personal, and potentially transferable. Those who desire power must curry favor with those who have power. Those who have power seek to protect or increase that power. Each leader has his power base and supporters. Each also has his rivals and antagonists. Jiang Zemin was no exception. Even after he became general secretary, he was not exempt from political struggle. Potential competitors were often probing and testing, seeking occasion to advance at his expense.

As it turned out, Jiang was a fighter. Making a career out of a series of happenstances, and relying on keen political instinct, he emerged as a change-making leader. He surprised pundits who had dismissed him as a transitory lightweight by surviving and then prospering amid more experienced politicians. Notwithstanding his accidental accession and his lack of fierce ambition, Jiang was relentless in consolidating power and methodical in eliminating political opponents.

"It wasn't easy for President Jiang to maintain political stability after Deng Xiaoping died," said Yan Mingfu, a high official under Jiang's deposed predecessor, Zhao Ziyang. "There were many crises, domestic and international, and he provided consistent leadership. My hat is off to him."

Deng had given Jiang four key principles for running the country: Make economic development the primary goal and continue pressing forward with reform; focus on the army and make sure "the Party commands the gun"; watch out for deviations on the Right but mainly guard against attacks from the Left; choose personnel who are both professionally competent and politically reliable.

When Jiang first became CMC chairman, he knew little about the army, and the army cared little about him. Yet he dedicated himself to military matters, winning their loyalty and modernizing their forces. He upgraded the PLA's high-tech capabilities while reducing its size; streamlined its organization to increase efficiency and decrease response time; enhanced the power and pervasiveness of information technology; promoted professional and high-tech-oriented officers; and introduced extensive education and training programs. In one of his most courageous decisions, Jiang separated the army from its vast array of commercial businesses, which were a diversion from national defense and a breeding ground of corruption. He visited hundreds of military facilities, showed concern for ordinary soldiers, spoke at the National Defense University, promoted loyal senior generals, and had the media publicize his activities.

JIANG WAS ALSO A warrior for culture. He often said that the Chinese people would be deprived if they did not know the symphonies of Beethoven and the plays of Shakespeare. Jiang admonished all within earshot that China should absorb the best of foreign ways and things but must not forsake its own traditions, which he called a bulwark against the carnivorous culture of the West. He worried that if Western culture should obliterate Chinese culture, China's integrity as a nation would be threatened. He exhorted Chinese writers and artists to maintain their own vitality, integrity, and autonomy and not allow Western influences to overwhelm them. He encouraged students to be familiar with Chinese literature, art, music, history, and philosophy. As much as he was a proud political patriot, Jiang Zemin was a vigorous cultural patriot.

As China's leader, Jiang promoted a renaissance of science and art. He enjoyed spending time with China's scientists, artists, writers, musicians, actors, and film directors. He considered it a life calling to enrich the Chinese people's mental lives, intellectually and culturally.

Jiang loved the Chinese people and believed he knew best—paternalistically to be sure—how to improve their lives. He had his own image of their ideal, and strove mightily to make it real by combining material prosperity, socialist idealism, traditional morality, and cultural enrichment. When integrated with patriotism, pride, and international respect, it was perhaps the broadest vision ever articulated for the Middle Kingdom.

JIANG ZEMIN NOT ONLY helped shape China, but he was also shaped by China: his patriotism, forged during the Japanese occupation and civil war; his love for Chinese culture and traditions that he learned from his family; his broad education in science and the humanities and the intellectual self-image it engendered; his political training during his days as a student revolutionary; his experience of the chaos and horrors of the Anti-Rightist Campaign, the Great Leap Forward, and the Cultural Revolution; and the problem-solving, team-oriented attitude that he learned as an industrial engineer and manager.

"Like many intellectuals of his generation, Jiang Zemin was driven by his desire to rejuvenate the Chinese nation and revitalize Chinese culture," noted Jin Chongji, the distinguished historian. "Jiang lived through the Japanese occupation and witnessed the deprivations of an oppressed and humiliated China. He was virtually obsessed with two big questions. One, why did China, which for a thousand years had the world's largest economy and leading technology, fall so far behind the West? Two, why did the ruling parties in so many countries ultimately lose power? That's why Jiang set his two personal objectives as rejuvenating China and modernizing the Party. Fulfilling these, he believed, was his noble, sacred mission."

Jiang was painfully aware that China had endured a hundred years of national decrepitude, from the Opium Wars in the mid-nineteenth century to the establishment of New China in the mid-twentieth century. Analytical by nature, he wanted to know why the Chinese nation had become so weak. He came up with three causes: political corruption, economic backwardness, and feeble science and technology. When he became leader, he was determined to change all three. This was the reason why Jiang seemed, at least to the Chinese public, to be overly concerned with American interests: He knew that good relations with America stimulated China's economy and advanced its science and technology.

Jiang's position as a domestic reformer can be viewed through the same prism. He was not an innate, single-minded reformer, as was Deng Xiaoping. Jiang's reformist policies, which he balanced with cultural and moral concerns, were a means to the end of promoting his core beliefs. He was a great advocate of reform because reform was the only way for the people to prosper and for the nation to regain international respect. If Mao's Communism of the 1950s and 1960s had not been modernized, first by Deng and then by Jiang, China today might still look more like North Korea than South Korea.

HAVING BROUGHT CHINA so high up the ladder of international respect, why did President Jiang give such open support to Cuba and North Korea, two of the world's most repressive totalitarian regimes? Jiang publicly praised Fidel Castro, the dictator of Cuba, and Kim Il-Sung and Kim Jong-Il, the sequential father-son dictators of North Korea, stating that the real problem in their countries was American "power politics," which, he said, the people of Cuba and North Korea had to resist by "waged struggles" and "hard work." In effect, Jiang was blaming the United States for their dire conditions.

To Westerners, Jiang's linking China with Cuba and North Korea seemed inexplicable. Why would a worldly-wise, enlightened intellectual do such a thing? Although his reasons were rational, coherent, and internally consistent with Chinese policy, they were largely, as Jiang liked to say about other awkward matters, "left over from history."

Cuba and North Korea wore the same Communist label as did China, and to Jiang Communism was still the ultimate human ideal, even if poor policies had caused recent embarrassments. More germane for the Chinese president's geostrategic realpolitik, supporting these countries asserted China's diplomatic independence, promoted a multipolar world, diverted U.S. focus and resources from China's vital interests, counterbalanced American support of Taiwan, and enabled "strategic trades" (e.g., "we help you with North Korea, you help us with Taiwan"). Furthermore, China should not abandon old friends and, equally important, should not be seen to do so. And finally, after decades of propaganda, China's self-image had in a way become commingled with that of Cuba and North Korea, resulting in a kind of transferred patriotism.

That said, for Jiang and China's new leaders to continue to associate their energized, modernized Communism with the despotic, dreary Stalinist-Maoist model still being enforced in North Korea and Cuba seemed both demeaning to themselves and unhelpful to their old friends. Consistent loyalty is good, but stricter guidance is better—China might encourage its old friends to begin to reform, as China itself did in 1978.

JIANG'S SKIN WAS TOUGHENED by incessant criticism. For example, to get China into the WTO (especially after the embassy bombing), Jiang had to withstand the combined attacks of nationalistic public opinion and anti-West intellectuals while at the same time overcoming the resistance of Leftist officials and political rivals.

Chinese critics lambasted him for acquiescing to American interests. American critics accused him of undermining them. Neither saw the consistency of character of the man who had witnessed the worst of humanity during the ravages of the Japanese occupation and the chaos of the Cultural Revolution, yet remained an optimist about the future. Jiang sought the reemergence of China as a great nation—economically, culturally, internationally—and he did all he could, however imperfectly, to bring this about.

As a leader, the affable would-be professor never succeeded in generating the kind of overwhelming awe that Mao Zedong or Deng Xiaoping had inspired. A street ditty that says, "Mao's word could command thousands; Deng's, dozens; and Jiang's, one," may have been used to denigrate Jiang, but in fact it complimented him. China, under Jiang Zemin, has become an increasingly decentralized society, no longer dependent, thankfully, on the whim and caprice of one man.

Yet it was not simple for Jiang to make his mark; he had no uncomplicated sound bite with which to shape public consciousness. Mao "unified the nation and made China 'stand up' in the world." His grand vision was easy to understand. Deng "ended political strife and freed the economy so that people could prosper." His great deeds were clear and vital. But Jiang had all the hardscrabble details and unintended consequences of implementing Deng's reforms—income disparity, macroeconomic adjustments, controlling inflation, combating corruption, enforcing tax collection, restructuring state-owned enterprises, facing unemployed workers—none of which was either easy to understand or particularly inspiring.

Early in Jiang's career, underground chatter in Shanghai nicknamed him "the flowerpot." "Lots of decoration, no action," explained James Lilley, a former U.S. ambassador to China. Then in his first few years as general secretary, Jiang became known as "the weathervane," because, according to critics, his "ideology and loyalty shifted according to the slightest political breeze." All politicians endure ridicule, but these slings, as it turned out, were superficial. A deeper explanation—that Jiang's actions evidenced his core beliefs and political shrewdness—comes closer to truth. Jiang had a natural talent for "astute shifts in stance that made him acceptable to both sides," for "avoiding ideological battles" and evincing a "malleable practicality." "Well, it turns out," Lilley observed, "he is a good consensus builder, he's a good manipulator."

But what was Jiang called after 1997—succeeding Deng, leading Hong Kong's triumphant return, accelerating reforms, touring America? After 1998—managing the Great Flood, putting the army out of its businesses? After 1999—Falun Gong, embassy bombing, WTO, Taiwan, Three Stresses? After 2000—Great West, Three Represents, international diplomacy? After 2001—spy plane collision, modernizing the Party, winning the Olympics, September 11, and the war on terrorism? And after 2002—close associates on the new Politburo Standing Committee, Three Represents in the Constitution, remaining CMC chairman, and emerging as China's chief representative?

What was Jiang Zemin called after all these momentous events? Critics, scholars, and journalists had many things to say about the man, but two metaphors they did not use were "flowerpot" and "weathervane."

At times Jiang might have cut a comic figure with his humorous remarks and penchant for spontaneous song, but his achievements proved as meaningful as those of Mao and Deng while being less disruptive than Mao's and broader-based than Deng's. According to Professor Frederick Teiwes, Jiang "has had to operate in a much more complex setting than his predecessors [Mao and Deng] without anything like their revolutionary-based authority." Teiwes offers that "the full complexity of Jiang's role" is "captured by the Western business term, 'CEO'—the manager with overall responsibility for a vast enterprise . . . He [Jiang] is perhaps best understood as the 'Chief Executive Officer'—the 'CEO'—of today's China." To judge by results, Jiang's particular brand of leadership, marked by tactful persuasion and careful action, proved to be exactly what a tentative but willing China needed to reemerge as a powerful and prosperous nation.

THOUGH CRITICIZED ON OCCASION for overly accommodating American interests or not sufficiently promoting China's, Jiang directed a measured and consistent foreign policy that provided security and stability through turbulent times and promoted the national interest. He battled American policy and resisted American pressure, yet still set good relations with the United States as a priority so that China could prosper and grow strong.

After Tiananmen this was no easy task, since jingoistic domestic politics in both countries could overwhelm judicious foreign policy. Hardliners in Washington and Beijing restricted the options of both President Jiang and his American counterparts. For example, the more China threatened Taiwan, the more Washington solidified defense commitments to Taipei; and the more American politicians railed about China's human rights abuses, the less China's leaders could accede to specific requests. (These cycles of escalating tensions made Jiang's *60 Minutes* interview all the more daring and helpful.)

While China sought self-reliance, a secure peace, and an independent foreign policy, President Jiang would not compromise its national interests, primarily on Taiwan. Yet he managed to reshape China's Taiwan policy from one of confrontation in the middle 1990s to economic integration by 2004, which, provided Taiwan does not go independent, bodes well for cross-straits relations.

By the end of his term, this unexpected leader had won the confidence of his country, especially the military, for his ability and experience in handling international crises. Many felt secure that Jiang Zemin retained his position as chairman of the Central Military Commission after he stepped down as Party general secretary and State president, even some who objected to his incomplete retirement.

PERHAPS THE NICEST THING about Jiang Zemin is that even though he has been the undisputed leader of 1.3 billion people, he is at heart a simple human being. Jiang loves his family, and he loves his country. He enjoys showing off his physical skills—chin-ups in college, swimming in Hawaii—and he is never shy about trying out his partial knowledge of foreign languages. He can act silly, he can get angry, and he can fuss over his appearance. He has lifelong personal friends in whom he confides, expressing his frustrations and sharing his joys. And when he passes around pictures of his grandchildren, he beams.

Jiang likes food, particularly the simple fare from Yangzhou and Shanghai. He can eat too much and must watch his weight. He drinks in moderation, quite the opposite of Mao, and he detests smoking, much to the contrary of Deng, who was never without a cigarette.

Jiang has been lampooned for his public exhibitions—singing, dancing, playing the piano or *erhu*—and for some of his small talk, which critics deride as unbecoming for a national leader. To some older-generation Chinese, Jiang's extroverted behavior seemed too showy, too individualistic, too apparently self-centered. At a state dinner with Russian President Vladimir Putin, Jiang invited him to sing Russian songs together. "I can do anything in sports," Putin responded, "but I cannot sing." Without missing a beat, Jiang asked Putin's wife to dance, leaving some diplomats with their mouths agape.

He is not at all defensive about his behavior. Jiang loves music and likes to perform; nothing relaxes him more. Yet he also believes that his out-front singing displays the human side of China, showing that its president is a person, not an emperor. A leader a little silly is a lot healthier for his country than one so haughty and unapproachable that he becomes deluded by his own arrogance or self-righteousness. "He certainly isn't one of those dry and rigid Communist leaders that the West has seen in other countries," said Jiang Zehui with a chuckle.

Those who surmised that Jiang's personality puffed when he became China's leader got it wrong. One minister got it right when he commented that Jiang "had been that way his entire life."

Another backroom criticism was that Jiang seemed too desirous of being an expert in everything, from politcal theory and economic analysis to literature and poetry and art and science. Perhaps, some suggested, he was trying to emulate ancient emperors (and Mao) who had to be the leading intellectual thinker while being the leading political ruler. But Jiang was driven more to satisfy an inner need than to crave outer respect. He was always inquisitive and almost obsessed with extending his knowledge.

Always the engineer, Jiang sees problems in light of their potential solutions. He can figure out how to make things work, and he can micromanage and meddle. He can be proud of his achievements, and he can feel hurt if others receive more credit or appreciation than he does. He can change his mind, as he did about private business, and he can stick to old dogmas, as he did about Fidel Castro and Kim Jong-Il. He can overreact, as with Falun Gong, and underreact, as initially with SARS. He makes mistakes, but he tries to learn from them.

On occasion he can put principle over practicality, as when he insisted on a Japanese apology for aggression against China. A fervent student protester himself, he "understood the passion of students who were calling for greater democracy and freedom" in Tiananmen Square, yet he defends the military actions of the Chinese government against them. He yearns for the grand flourishing of Chinese art and literature, yet he restricts the creative freedom of

Chinese artists and writers. It is a conundrum he cannot solve and a theme he cannot avoid. At the same time he is a visionary and a romantic who quotes ancient poetry, enjoys great music, and wonders about the mysteries of existence.

It is hard to name an American president since Woodrow Wilson who had as genuine a love for learning as does Jiang Zemin. Whether it's a fascination with physics or a passion for poetry, Jiang is a true intellectual, the substance without the pretense. He is enamored by culture, Chinese and Western; he is moved by classical literature and marvels at the beauty of mathematics. He entertains philosophical thoughts late at night but will drop everything to help a friend who is ill or infirm. He is zealous about self-improvement and exhorts almost everyone he meets, from senior ministers to common workers, to be likewise.

One secret of Jiang's success was that he was able to integrate different styles of thought. His science-and-math education and two decades of industrial engineering formed his mental mechanisms; during three decades in government, while he learned to maneuver and fight like a politician, he never forgot how to analyze and calculate like an engineer. He was also an intellectual with an inquisitive spirit and a devotee of culture who read and wrote poetry. He enjoyed science and he loved art. Each of these varied strands of knowledge gifted him with its own manner of perceiving the world. Combining them with his Chinese pride and patriotism and his Marxist beliefs, Jiang developed his distinctive way of thinking. Rarely resident in a single individual, even less often in a national leader, it was this combination of interests and experiences that gave Jiang Zemin his special quality.

WHEN JIANG ZEMIN RETIRED an age passed into history. No future generation will have living memories of the brutal Japanese occupation or the debilitating civil war. The post-Jiang leaders will not have experienced the idealistic days of Mao's revolution in the 1950s, and their recollections of the self-destructive Anti-Rightist Campaign and the Great Leap Forward will be weak. Although the new generation did endure the Cultural Revolution, for most it was more a rural delay of their careers than real humiliation, persecution, and suffering.

The new generation of Chinese leaders will be both lesser and greater for this. Not having lived through those decades of true belief and political mania, they will react more analytically and less emotionally to historically encumbered issues, such as Sino-Japanese relations, the changes still needed in China's governance and the Communist Party, and the official judgment of the 1989 demonstrations in Tiananmen Square. Led by Party general secretary and State president Hu Jintao, the new generation will, over time, make its own mark, and in the process, some of Jiang's policies and positions will be altered. Change is inevitable; Jiang said so himself. Just as his generation had exceeded their precursors, Jiang predicted, so too will his successors exceed him.

President Hu has all the markings of the right leader at the right time. He has the perspicacity to guide China as a responsible power in the international community, the dedication to inspire people to work together, the realism to deal with the endemic and chronic problems, the facility to cultivate an enriched development strategy, and the close-to-the-masses feelings to bring all citizens into China's success. To Jiang's credit must be added the first harmonious, nontraumatic transfer of power on the Chinese mainland since the end of feudalism. Though they lamented the secrecy, Nathan and Gilley called the succession from Jiang Zemin to Hu Jintao "a deliberative, meritocratic process."

It may be fashionable to offer various scenarios for China's future, and sensational to warn that China might implode domestically or become an aggressor internationally, but unless there is some kind of disaster, China's road ahead seems reasonably straight. Excluding untoward events, China's economy will grow, standards of living will rise, the middle class will continue its remarkable expansion, and largely due to telecommunications, individual freedoms will increase. China's problems will remain. Income disparity, unemployment, corruption, and the like won't disappear, but they will likely go gradually into long-term amelioration. "Nothing is likely to keep China down for long," writes Ted Fishman ("barring Mao's resurrection or nuclear cataclysm"). "If any country is going to supplant the U.S. in the world marketplace," he concludes, "China is it."

By the middle of the century China will have the world's largest economy in terms of sheer size (though not per capita). As Bruce Gilley forecasts, some form of Chinese democracy is likely to emerge. Nicholas Kristof agrees with Gilley, but thinks "there's a good chance that we'll both turn out to be completely wrong" because, as he says, "China-watchers have a deplorable record, and China's history is one of unpredictable twists and turns." Whatever political form it takes, Kristof concludes, China "will be one of the central stories of this century."

Jiang's way of thinking was often informed by historical perspective. He had long cogitated on the fact that China had been the planet's premier economy throughout much of recorded history. In 1820 China generated about a third of the world's gross national product, about the same proportion as America generates today. If China eventually regains first place, which is its current trajectory, the phenomenon will be of historic proportions. Looking backward, future historians will likely credit the era of Jiang Zemin.

In today's world, differences in social or political systems have become almost meaningless. Economically, the search for efficiency and innovation is creating a vast globalized market in which all countries compete. The real struggle is between the forces of order and modernity on one side, and those of anarchy and sectarianism on the other. In striving for world peace and prosperity, China and the United States are allies not adversaries.

HOW WILL HISTORY JUDGE Jiang Zemin? With his roots in Chinese culture and tradition, a patriotism born of oppression, an idealism colored by youthful socialism, the problem-solving mentality of an engineer, and the interests of an intellectual, Jiang Zemin of Yangzhou, Shanghai, Changchun, Wuhan, and Beijing emerged in the late twentieth century, energized by a grand vision of China's resurgence, to change China forever.

Though he was not an economist, he implemented Deng Xiaoping's vision of reform and opening-up, and (with help) guided macroeconomic and industrial policy safely through chaotic times. Though he had no military experience, he modernized and reformed the army and won its allegiance. Though he was not a politician, he became a master at consensus building, inner-Party maneuvering, rival removal, and power consolidation. Though he was not a lawyer, he worked to standardize laws, rules, and procedures of the Party and government and sought to subject local officials to the supervision of local congresses. Though he was not a judge, he could mete out severe punishment to the few to bring unprecedented prosperity to the many. Though he was not a philosopher, he set forth the contradictions in society and taught appreciation for culture, morality, civility, and virtue.

Jiang Zemin took China through an amazing metamorphosis—from a fretful country traumatized by the turmoil and crackdown in Tiananmen Square into a vibrant and socially open (though politically restrained) nation that became a primary engine of global economic growth and emerged as a center of commerce and culture. In a little over a decade, China went from international pariah to diplomatic power. One measure of Jiang's contribution is that he made governance more normal for all who would follow him. If Jiang Zemin's deepest wish was to revivify his beloved motherland after centuries of shame, the good-natured engineer from Yangzhou had succeeded beyond anyone's wildest expectations—including, no doubt, his own.

How unimaginable all this would have seemed to the twelve-year-old Jiang whose middle school was commandeered by Japanese invaders. Or the seventeen-year-old Jiang marching feverishly in the antidrug demonstration in occupied Nanjing. Or the twenty-three-year-old Jiang distributing ice cream in war-torn Shanghai. Or the thirty-one-year-old Jiang forced to denounce Rightists at the automotive factory in Changchun and then striving mightily to convert its power plant to burn crude oil. Or the forty-one-year-old Jiang deprived of seeing Premier Zhou Enlai by Red Guards during the Cultural Revolution in Wuhan. Or the fifty-four-year-old Jiang working on Special Economic Zones during the first years of Deng's reforms. Or the sixty-two-year-old Shanghai Party secretary Jiang planning his retirement in early 1989. Or even the sixty-six-year-old General Secretary Jiang facing economic challenges and political battles in 1992. Who could have dreamt it all?

China is the most populous country on earth, and it is undergoing one of the most profound transformations in history. As for the life of Jiang Zemin, it is a chronicle of contemporary China. As for the legacy of Jiang Zemin, it is the future of China.

Chronology: Jiang Zemin's Life

1926	Born August 17, in Yangzhou city, Jiangsu province.
1926–43	Raised in an intellectual, traditional family of high Chinese culture; attends primary and middle school during the Japanese occupation; learns and loves literature, music, science; becomes the adopted son of a Communist martyr; Jiang Zehui becomes his sister.
1943–45	Studies engineering at Nanjing Central University; participates in antidrug campaign; meets Tong Zonghai, roommate.
1945–47	Studies electrical and power engineering at Shanghai Jiaotong University; engages in student movements and underground work for Communist Party; joins Communist Party (1946); meets Wang Huijiong, classmate and lifelong friend.
1947–51	First job at Shanghai Yimin Food Factory as apprentice power engineer; works up to general manager; meets Wang Daohan, career-long mentor, adviser, and intimate friend.
1949	Marries Wang Yeping.
1951–53	Deputy director of China (Shanghai) Soap Factory; becomes familiar with Shanghai industry; first son, Jiang Mianheng, is born (1951).
1953–54	Chief of electrical machinery section, Shanghai No. 2 Design Institute, First Ministry of Machine-Building Industry.
1954–55	Helps develop first five-year plan for First Ministry of Machine-Building Industry in Beijing; second son, Jiang Miankang, is born (1954).
1955–56	Apprentices (power engineering) at the Stalin Automotive Works in Moscow; learns Russian language, loves Russian culture.
1956–62	Spends six years in Changchun at First Automotive Works; advances to director of the power plant; converts plant from coal to crude oil in three months; endures Anti-Rightist Campaign and Great Leap Forward; meets Shen Yongyan, longtime close friend.
1962–65	Serves as deputy director, Shanghai Electric Appliances Research Institute.
1965–68	Moves to Wuhan as director of the Wuhan Power Engineering Research Institute; is criticized and "set aside" (but not "pulled down") during the worst years of the Cultural Revolution.
1966–76	Experiences nightmares of the Cultural Revolution.
1968–70	Passes strict personal and political examination and is sent to a May Seventh Cadre School for political reeducation on Bo Ai farm in Henan province.

1970–71   Returns to Beijing; becomes vice director, Bureau of Foreign Affairs, First Ministry of Machine-Building Industry, his first formal government position.

1971–72   Leads Chinese technical team in Romania, conducting feasibility study for construction of fifteen factories.

1972–76   Serves as director, Bureau of Foreign Affairs, First Ministry of Machine-Building Industry; career seemingly slows.

1976   Mao Zedong dies; Gang of Four arrested; the Cultural Revolution, the decade of devastation, comes to an end.

1976–77   Assigned to Shanghai as a member of the fourteen-person "Working Group" sent by the central government to restore order after the Cultural Revolution.

1977–80   Returns to Beijing in his old job as director, Bureau of Foreign Affairs, First Ministry of Machine-Building; passed over twice for vice minister; career seemingly stalls.

1978   Deng Xiaoping assumes power and becomes China's "Paramount Leader" for almost twenty years; China's reform and opening-up policies begin at the Third Plenary Session of the Eleventh Party Congress.

1980–82   Serves as vice chairman (vice minister level) of two new commissions (Import-Export and Foreign Investment), created to implement Deng Xiaoping's new reforms and opening-up policy; helps develop and implement Special Economic Zones (SEZs); heads UN-sponsored, 40-day world tour (including first visit to the United States); member, China's People's Political Consultative Conference (CPPCC); nonvoting member, Standing Committee of the National People's Congress (NPC).

1982–85   Serves as vice minister, minister, and Party secretary, Ministry of Electronics Industry; enters Central Committee of the Communist Party of China (CPC) in 1982; visits the United States, including MIT in Boston and Hewlett-Packard in San Francisco; signs joint venture with Hewlett-Packard, one of China's first.

1985–89   Spends four years in Shanghai as mayor and then Party chief; builds city, promotes growth and investment; greets visitors, such as Queen Elizabeth II and Mikhail Gorbachev; handles student protests in 1986, recites Gettysburg Address; hosts many of China's senior elders (especially Deng Xiaoping), who visit regularly; Zhao Ziyang replaces Hu Yaobang as Party chief (early 1987).

1989   Massive student demonstrations follow the death of Hu Yaobang in April; Jiang fires the editor of and takes over liberal *World Economic Herald;* restores order in Shanghai without bloodshed; is selected by Deng Xiaoping and senior elders to become general secretary of the CPC Central Committee in May; martial law declared, then military action occurs on June 4; Jiang is elected formally as general secretary on June 24 (and announced publicly); brings Zeng Qinghong to Beijing as his first appointment; is elected chairman of the CPC Central Military Commission (CMC) in November.

1990–91   Acclimates to power; traverses country, visiting provinces and inspecting military bases; makes first foreign trips to North Korea and Soviet Union; slows reforms along with dominant group of conservative elders and colleagues (though moderates hardline policies and seeks a more centrist position).

1992   Deng Xiaoping's Southern Tour (Nanxun) reinstitutes and reenergizes reform and opening-up policies; Jiang backs and implements Deng's reforms; presents "socialist market economy" at Party School Speech; economic development formalized as primary goal at Fourteenth Party Congress, where Jiang is reelected CPC general secretary and emerges as the clear leader after political struggles.

1993–94   Elected president of China; economy takes off, but begins to overheat; problems of inflation; "soft landing" of economy is a breakthrough for reform; Jiang makes first trip to the United States as leader of China and has first (less-than-successful) meeting with President Bill Clinton; visits France with his wife, Wang Yeping.

1995   Introduces concept of "spiritual civilization" as a balance to the materialism of reform; offers Eight-Point Proposal for Taiwan, setting policy for years; Chen Xitong, corrupt Party chief of Beijing and Jiang opponent, is removed from office and imprisoned; Jiang establishes initiative to "revitalize China through science and education"; increasing tensions with Taiwan follow Lee Teng-hui's trip to the United States; Jiang visits New York for UN's fiftieth anniversary, meets President Clinton; visits South Korea.

1996   Introduces moral-social message "talk more about politics" as a Party rectification campaign; highest tensions with Taiwan, "military exercises" by both China and the United States; seeks to integrate art and literature with politics.

1997   Deng Xiaoping dies, China mourns, no political struggle; Party, government, and PLA rally around Jiang; triumphant repatriation of Hong Kong; reform breakthrough allowing flexibility in "ownership" at the Fifteenth Party Congress; Qiao Shi, number three in the Party, retires; Jiang is reelected CPC general secretary and emerges as China's undisputed leader; makes high-profile, highly successful state visit to the United States, including press conference with President Clinton and speech at Harvard.

1998   Zhu Rongji is appointed premier; reform accelerates, government is streamlined; Jiang fights the Great Flood; takes the army out of commercial businesses; makes controversial trip to Japan.

1999   Falun Gong surrounds Zhongnanhai in April and is outlawed in July; NATO-U.S. bombing of the Chinese embassy in Yugoslavia triggers heated reaction from Chinese public; Lee Teng-hui's "special state-to-state" theory roils mainland-Taiwan relations; gala parade celebrates fiftieth anniversary of the People's Republic; China and the United States reach agreement on China's entry into the World Trade Organization; Jiang escalates actions against corruption; initiates Three Stresses campaign to rectify Party members; *Shenzhou I* spacecraft is launched.

2000   Develops Great West long-term strategy; formulates and introduces Three Represents to modernize the Party; visits Israel, Palestine, and Turkey; attends UN Millennial Summit in New York; focuses on science and education; has remarkable interview on CBS's *60 Minutes*.

2001   Collision between U.S. Navy spy plane and Chinese jet, stand-off with United States, and strong Chinese public reaction; Jiang visits Latin America; makes controversial speech on eightieth anniversary of the Communist Party (July 1), modernizing the Party by Three Represents and allowing China's "new social strata," including private business owners, to join the Party; wins 2008 Olympics for Beijing; September 11 attacks and war on terrorism; Jiang meets President George W. Bush at APEC forum in Shanghai; new attitude to religion in China.

2002   Prepares for critical Sixteenth Party Congress; meets President Bush in Beijing; encourages heavy promotion of Three Represents; visits President Bush at Texas ranch; at Sixteenth Party Congress (November), sums up condition of China and accomplishments of his leadership, and looks to the future; Three Represents is enshrined into Party Constitution; effects smooth transition of power to new leaders; Jiang is named chief representative of his generation; Hu Jintao succeeds him as CPC general secretary, even as a majority of the new nine-member Politburo Standing Committee are Jiang's close associates; is reelected chairman of the CMC; economy maintains strong growth.

2003   Concludes two terms as president, Hu Jintao succeeds him; maintains CMC chairmanship; is active in military matters and international affairs (while everyone else of his generation has retired); SARS epidemic threatens China but is contained; is involved in diplomacy over Iraq and North Korea; China launches first *taikonaut* into Earth orbit.

1989–2002   Serves over thirteen years in Beijing as general secretary of the Central Committee of the CPC.

1989–2004   Serves almost fifteen years as chairman of the Central Military Commission of the Central Committee of the CPC.

1993–2003   Serves as president of China and head of state (two five-year terms).

2004   As this book goes to press (September 2004), a retired Jiang Zemin continues as chief representative of his generation, giving advice and counsel to China's new leaders.

Names and Abbreviations

ANTI-RIGHTIST CAMPAIGN   A mass movement initiated by Mao Zedong in 1957 to purge and punish intellectuals, some of whom voiced grievances after Mao had called for more open expression ("Let a hundred flowers bloom, let a hundred schools of thought contend").

APEC   Asia-Pacific Economic Conference, a regional forum on cooperation in trade that President Jiang attended regularly along with other state leaders.

ARATS   Association for Relations Across the Taiwan Straits, China's nongovernmental organization for dealing with Taiwan, headed by Wang Daohan.

ASEAN   Association of Southeast Asian Nations, a organization that promotes regional cooperation and economic growth in Southeast Asia.

AUTONOMOUS REGIONS   China has five autonomous regions: Guangxi, Inner Mongolia, Ningxia, Xinjiang, and Tibet. The autonomous regions are similar to provinces, but because much of China's minority populations live in these areas, they are given a special designation that is intended to protect minority culture and tradition.

BEIDAIHE   The seaside resort on the Bohai Sea, about 200 miles east of Beijing, where China's senior leaders gather each summer for political and policy discussions as well as holiday activities, beach sports, and personal comaraderie. Major decisions affecting the Party, the government, national planning, and high-level personnel promotions and retirements are often made at this time.

BOURGEOIS LIBERALIZATION   A vague but disparaging code phrase that seems to represent a tendency to move toward Western-style multiparty democracy (which would abrogate the ruling monopoly of the Communist Party), Western-style economic systems (which would do away with socialism), and Western-style popular culture (which would overwhelm traditional Chinese culture).

BUND   Historic waterfront avenue in Shanghai along the Huangpu River, across from Pudong; features elegant European colonial buildings.

CADRE   Official or functionary of the Communist Party.

CCTV   China Central Television, the state-owned national network; has about fifteen channels, led by CCTV Channel 1, with a daily airtime of more than two hundred hours, attracting more than 1 billion viewers.

CENTRAL ADVISORY COMMISSION   A body of Party elders (with at least forty years of Party service) that provided "political assistance and consultation" to the CPC Central Committee; established in 1982 and abolished in 1992. Deng Xiaoping was its first chairman (1982–92), Chen Yun its second (1987–92).

CENTRAL COMMISSION FOR DISCIPLINE INSPECTION   The highest organ of the CPC responsible for fighting corruption, graft, and all manner of illegal activities of Party members. Its chairman is a member of the Politburo Standing Committee.

CENTRAL COMMITTEE   The leading body of the Communist Party of China; issues all formal policies and Party directives; comprised (in 2002–) of 198 full members and 158 alternate members (356 altogether). It elects the Politburo, Politburo Standing Committee, and general secretary; it convenes Party congresses and meets in plenums between congresses. When the Central Committee is not in session, the Politburo and its Standing Committee exercise its power. Under the Central Committee are the General Office, the Organization Department, the Publicity (Propaganda) Department, the International Liaison Department, the United Front Work Department, the Foreign Communications (Propaganda) Office, and the Policy Research Office.

CENTRAL MILITARY COMMISSION   The supreme decision-making organ for China's armed forces, the People's Liberation Army. The Party and the State each have a parallel CMC, generally composed of the same members (all senior generals except for Jiang Zemin and Hu Jintao). The more powerful Party CMC, which reports to the CPC Central Committee, is responsible for PLA operations, while the State CMC handles interstate military relations. Jiang Zemin was appointed chairman of the CMC in 1989, and he continued in that position after his retirement as Party general secretary and State president.

CENTRAL PARTY SCHOOL   An academy of advanced Party studies, thinking, and training; it schools Party leaders prior to promotions. Hu Jintao was past president (1997–2002); Zeng Qinghong is the current president (2002–).

CHIEF REPRESENTATIVE   The Party's "core" personality, a new term coined and inscribed in the Party Constitution in November 2002. Mao Zedong (retroactively) was "chief representative," 1921–76; Deng Xiaoping (retroactively) 1978–89; and Jiang Zemin since 1989.

CHINA   Consists of twenty-two provinces (or twenty-three with Taiwan in the mainland designation), five autonomous regions, four municipalities directly under the central government, and the two special administrative regions of Hong Kong and Macao.

CMC   Central Military Commission.

COMMUNIST PARTY   The "vanguard" of the Chinese working class, people, and nation; provides leadership to the government; founded on ideology based on theories of Karl Marx as developed by Lenin in the Soviet Union and Mao Zedong in China; modified and modernized by Deng Xiaoping and Jiang Zemin. The Party has some 65 million members in China, about five percent of the population. Its highest body is the Party congress, held once every five years, and the Central Committee elected by it. The Party operates a parallel structure in most organizations, institutions, and agencies, which is responsible for setting policy and providing overall directives.

COMMUNIST YOUTH LEAGUE   Organization of future leaders of the Party, generally associated with General Secretary Hu Jintao, who was a past Youth League president.

CORE   The chief person of each generation: Mao Zedong, Deng Xiaoping, and Jiang Zemin for the First, Second, and Third Generations, respectively; Hu Jintao, though Party chief and state president, has not (as yet) been designated the "core" of the Fourth Generation.

CPC   Communist Party of China.

CPPCC   Chinese People's Political Consultative Conference, a national assembly-like forum designed to unify the country and promote "socialist democracy" through multiparty cooperation and political consultation from diverse sectors of society, all under the leadership of the Communist Party.

CULTURAL REVOLUTION   The decade-long (1966–76) chaotic, self-destructive mass movement, energized by Mao Zedong's obsession to "purify" the Party, rerevolutionize China, eliminate rivals, and purge "capitalist roaders." Institutions, particularly universities, were closed down, and millions, especially intellectuals (i.e., anyone with a college education), were exiled to the countryside to work as peasants and farmers, while fanatical Red Guards terrorized the people and paralyzed the country.

DENG XIAOPING THEORY   The collected teachings of Deng Xiaoping, which take economic development, not class struggle, as the Party's primary mission. They stress reform and opening-up and advocate practical policies over strict ideology. Key sayings: "Seek truth from facts"; "Practice is the only standard to test truth"; "Socialism with Chinese characteristics."

DISCIPLINE COMMISSION   Central Commission for Discipline Inspection.

EIGHT-POINT PROPOSAL   Jiang's specific principles, proffered in early 1995, designed to be the basis for solving the Taiwan issue. Considered moderate, the proposal set policy for years.

ELDER   Retired senior leader or official of the Communist Party of China; it is a term of reverence and is generally applied only to those most senior and respected.

FALUN GONG   A quasi-spiritual, mystical health cult that organized a massive sit-in around Zhongnanhai in central Beijing in April 1999 and was subsequently banned by the government in July. Jiang worried about the dangers of Falun Gong and took particular interest in suppressing it.

FIFTEENTH PARTY CONGRESS   1997 (September).

FIRST AUTOMOTIVE WORKS   The sprawling car and truck factory in Changchun (Jilin province) where Jiang Zemin worked (1956–62) in the power plant. There he met Shen Yongyan, who became his close friend.

FOUR CARDINAL PRINCIPLES   The primary tenets of Chinese Communism, which were articulated by Deng Xiaoping in 1979 and are said to be inviolate: the Socialist road; the people's democratic dictatorship; the leadership of the Communist Party; and ideology based on Marxist-Leninist and Mao Zedong Thought. As China has evolved, the meaning and understanding of each has also evolved.

FOUR MODERNIZATIONS   Agriculture, industry, national defense, science and technology—set by Deng Xiaoping as goals of his reform.

FOURTEENTH PARTY CONGRESS   1992 (October).

FOURTH GENERATION   The generation of Party leaders after Jiang Zemin's time; it was expected to consist of General Secretary Hu Jintao and his contemporaries, but not yet (as of mid-2004) so designated.

GDP   Gross domestic product.

GENERAL SECRETARY   The highest-ranking official of the Communist Party, the most powerful position in China; official title, general secretary of the Central Committee of the Communist Party of China; responsible for calling sessions of both the Politburo and its Standing Committee; in charge of the work of the Secretariat of the Central Committee.

GREAT FLOOD   Massive flooding of 1998.

GREAT LEAP FORWARD   Mao's radical and disastrous campaign in 1958–60 to accelerate the economy by aggregating farmers into massive communes and creating backyard minifurnaces to increase steel production. As a result, widespread famines killed between 20 and 50 million people in 1958–62.

GREAT WEST   China's central and western provinces and autonomous regions (about ten, plus the Chongqing municipality), which lag considerably behind coastal areas in economic development. Jiang initiated a grand multigenerational strategy to build the Great West, which covers more than 50 percent of China's land mass and is home to most of China's minority groups. Accelerated development of the Great West is considered vital for balancing standards of living in China.

GUANGDONG PROVINCE   Located in southern China adjacent to Hong Kong, the pioneer and most aggressive province in economic reform and opening-up policy.

HAN   The majority ethnic group in China, accounting for over 90 percent of the population.

HUNDRED FLOWERS   Phrase symbolizing the open expression of diverse opinions, used by ruling authorities to encourage citizens, primarily intellectuals, to create and criticize. It comes from Mao Zedong's aphoristic use of a line from a poem: "Let a hundred flowers bloom, let a hundred schools of thought contend," which he then turned against those who spoke out (*see* Anti-Rightist Campaign). Jiang's call for a "hundred flowers" policy, such as in the arts, never had Mao's malevolent outcome; nor did it approach the kind of freedom common in the West.

IMMORTALS–EIGHT IMMORTALS   The most powerful elders of the CPC during the 1980s and 1990s, including Deng Xiaoping, Chen Yun, Peng Zhen, Yang Shangkun, Bo Yibo, Li Xiannian, Wang Zhen, and either Song Renqiong, Deng Yingchao (widow of Zhou Enlai), or Wan Li. (The term originally referred to a group of eight Taoist deities in ancient China with powers to give life or destroy evil, but later entered secular Chinese culture.)

IOC   International Olympic Committee.

JIANG THOUGHT   The collective political and social philosophy of Jiang Zemin, epitomized by Three Represents and including "spiritual civilization," "political civilization," "talk more about politics," and Three Stresses. Emphasizing patriotism, socialism, collectivism, and cultural development, it encompasses Jiang's guidelines for building a modern, well-off society.

KMT   Kuomintang (Nationalist) Party, led by Chiang Kai-shek (after 1925). The KMT controlled China (chaotically) in the 1920s to 1940s; fought the Communist Party, led by Mao Zedong, until it was defeated in 1949; then fled to Taiwan, where it controlled Taiwan's government until 2000. The KMT is committed to "one China" and eschews Taiwanese independence.

LEADING GROUP   The policy-setting organ, staffed entirely by members of the Communist Party, that ensures CPC control of organizations and institutions throughout China, particularly government commissions, ministries and agencies, and state-owned enterprises. In general, while Leading Groups formulate overall goals and strategies, they are not involved in implementation or administration. At the highest level of national decision-making, the CPC Central Committee has Leading Groups in key policy areas such as Finance and Economics, Foreign Affairs, Ideology and Propaganda, and Taiwan Affairs.

LONG MARCH   The celebrated, harrowing, year-long (1934–35) journey of about six thousand miles taken by Mao Zedong's Communist Red Army, overcoming natural obstacles and constant attacks, to escape defeat by Chiang Kai-shek's Nationalist Army and reestablish itself around the city of Yan'an in Shaanxi province. Eighty-six thousand soldiers began the Long March, but fewer than 10,000 of them arrived in Yan'an; they included many future leaders of the People's Republic (Zhou Enlai, Deng Xiaoping, Zhu De, Peng Dehuai, Lin Biao, and Li Xiannian). The retreat became a moral victory, inspiring the Communists.

MACHINE-BUILDING MINISTRY   First Ministry of Machine-Building Industry.

MAO ZEDONG THOUGHT   The collected teachings of Mao Zedong, who adapted classic Marxism-Leninism to China (focusing on peasants in the countryside). The ideas included the "people's democratic dictatorship" and strict adherence to Communist principles such as class struggle and collective ownership.

MASS MOVEMENTS   Politically motivated campaigns called by Mao Zedong to instill strict Communist ideology and coerce absolute loyalty to the Party and its leadership. Each mass movement set the country back substantially and visited harm and great grief upon vast numbers of people; mass movements included the Anti-Rightist Campaigns, the Great Leap Forward, and the Cultural Revolution.

MAY FOURTH MOVEMENT   The first patriotic protests and demonstrations in modern China. They were led by students in Tiananmen Square in 1919 to galvanize Chinese nationalism, modernize Chinese society, and inspire the Chinese nation to resist foreign aggression.

MAY SEVENTH CADRE SCHOOL   School named after the day Mao Zedong first issued his call for intellectuals to experience the manual labor of peasants. Used physical hardships (such as pig raising and grain farming) as the refining fire of political purity in the political rehabilitation (indoctrination) process.

MING DYNASTY   Rulers of China from 1368 to 1644.

MINORITIES   China's fifty-five non-Han ethnic groups, which collectively account for just under ten percent of the population. The minorities live largely in China's western and border provinces.

MUNICIPALITIES   China has four municipalities that report directly to the central government: Beijing, Chongqing, Shanghai, and Tianjin.

NANXUN   Deng Xiaoping's Southern Tour, particularly of Guangdong province, taken in early 1992 to reinstitute and reenergize reform: Breaking the conservative hold on the economy, Deng's Nanxun was the key event catalyzing China's accelerated development and economic surge.

NATIONALISTS   Kuomintang Party, led by Chiang Kai-shek (see KMT).

NATO   North Atlantic Treaty Organization, committed to safeguard the freedom and security of its member countries by political and military means.

NPC   National People's Congress, the highest organ of state power. This legislative body enacts and amends the State Constitution, formulates laws, elects government leaders (including the premier and State Council), delegates authority, approves budgets, and supervises other governing bodies.

PAP   People's Armed Police, the internal security force.

PARTY   Communist Party of China.

PARTY CHIEF   Party secretary (the highest Party official).

PARTY CONGRESS   The Communist Party of China's organ of supreme power. Party delegates from the entire country come to Beijing to attend this grand convention (meeting in the Great Hall of the People). It is held every five years (e.g., 1978, 1982, 1987, 1992, 1997, 2002, 2007) and is numbered sequentially. Major policies are presented, and future directions are set. The Party congress elects a new Central Committee and Central Commission for Discipline Inspection.

(The new Politburo, Politburo Standing Committee, and general secretary are elected by the new Central Committee immediately following each Party congress.)

PARTY CONSTRUCTION   The process of strengthening the Party with both theoretical advances and practical programs, fostering rectitude, competence, and dedication in Party members, and vitality, consistency, and legitimacy in Party organizations.

PARTY SECRETARY   In the Communist system of governance, Party secretaries are the most senior official for a geographic area. For a province (or a city), the Party secretary is the number one leader and the governor (or mayor) is the number two leader. In a central ministry or state-owned enterprise, the chief executive officer (minister or chairman/president) is the number one leader (and, not infrequently, the chief executive officer is also the Party secretary).

PEACEFUL EVOLUTION   The (supposed) insidious plan of the West (particularly America) to overthrow the socialist system in China by subtle social transformation (such as "bourgeois liberalization"), not overt military action.

PEOPLE'S REPUBLIC OF CHINA   Official name for the government of China (mainland), founded by Mao Zedong in 1949.

PLA   People's Liberation Army, including all branches of China's armed forces.

PLENUM (PLENARY SESSION)   A meeting of the Party Central Committee in between Party congresses, at which important decisions are presented and enacted. Plenaries are numbered sequentially as a subset of Party congresses. For example, in June 1989 Jiang Zemin was appointed general secretary at the Fourth Plenum of the Thirteenth Party Congress (which was held in 1987).

PNTR   Permanent normal trade relations, a status that the United States awards all but outcast countries. It was a source of contention between China and the United States for years.

POLITBURO   Political Bureau of the Central Committee of the Communist Party of China. The Party's senior leadership comprises twenty-five full members since 2002 (twenty-one members in 1997–2002). Technically, when the Central Committee is not in session, the Politburo and its Standing Committee exercise the power of the Central Committee.

POLITBURO STANDING COMMITTEE   The most powerful ruling body in China, its members are China's highest-ranking and most important leaders. It meets regularly and acts on behalf of the full Politburo. Each member has specific responsibilities, including general secretary of the Party, premier and executive vice premier of the State Council, chairmen of the NPC and the CPPCC, head of ideology and media, head of security, and head of the Disciplinary Commission. It was comprised of seven members when Jiang Zemin was general secretary, and nine when Hu Jintao became general secretary in November 2002.

POLITICAL CIVILIZATION   Social, legal, and political systems that would bring about decency, consistency, and ultimately, a democratic society; guidelines for gradual political reform; a component of Jiang Thought.

PRC   People's Republic of China.

PROVINCES   China has twenty-two provinces, twenty-three counting Taiwan: Anhui, Fujian, Gansu, Guangdong, Guizhou, Hainan, Hebei, Heilongjiang, Henan, Hubei, Hunan, Jiangsu, Jiangxi, Jilin, Liaoning, Qinghai, Shaanxi, Shandong, Shanxi, Sichuan, (Taiwan), Yunnan, and Zhejiang.

QING DYNASTY   Rulers of China from 1644 to 1911.

REPUBLIC OF CHINA   Official name for Taiwan; founded by the Kuomintang, led by Chiang Kai-shek, after its defeat by the Communists in 1949.

SAR   Special Administrative Region (Hong Kong SAR and Macao SAR).

SARS   Severe Acute Respiratory Syndrome; a new highly contagious, often deadly disease that plagued China in early 2003.

SECRETARIAT   The administrative organ of the Central Committee of the Communist Party, responsible for day-to-day operations of the Party; reports to the general secretary.

SETC   State Economic and Trade Commission. The SETC was responsible for facilitating reform of China's industries in adapting to a market economy (especially between 1998 and 2003).

SEZ(S)   Special Economic Zone(s). These areas (Shenzhen, Shantou, and Zhuhai in Guangdong province and Xiamen in Fujian province) were established in the early 1980s to pioneer Deng Xiaoping's reform and opening-up policy; other areas were added later. Jiang was vice chairman of the two commissions responsible for structuring and organizing SEZs (1980–82).

SHENZHEN   The paragon SEZ boomtown. Adjacent to Hong Kong, it epitomized China's reform and opening-up policy.

SHENZHOU   China's spacecraft for manned orbital flights. It was named (Divine Ship) by Jiang Zemin, who approved the program in 1992.

SIXTEENTH PARTY CONGRESS   2002 (November).

SOE(S)   State-owned enterprise(s).

SONG DYNASTY   Rulers of China from 960 to 1279; the Northern Song dynasty ruled from 960 to 1127; the Southern Song dynasty from 1127 to 1279.

SPIRITUAL CIVILIZATION   Moral, social, and cultural development that would parallel and balance economic development (i.e., material civilization). A blending of Marxist philosophy and traditional Chinese culture, it was designed to uplift ethics and reestablish morality. As a key component of Jiang's political philosophy and Jiang Thought, it began to be promoted around 1995 (although initiated earlier).

STANDING COMMITTEE   *See* Politburo Standing Committee.

STATE COUNCIL   The supreme administrative organ of state power, responsible for managing the country, including its economy, society, and international relations; composed of a premier, vice premiers (four), state councilors, ministers in charge of commissions and ministries, the auditor general, and the secretary general. Reporting directly to the State Council (post-2003) are twenty-eight ministries and commissions, seventeen directly affiliated organs, and seven administrative offices, in addition to a number of directly administered institutions and major state-owned enterprises. Ministries and commissions are Foreign Affairs; National Defense; Development and Reform Commission; Education; Science and Technology; Commission of Science, Technology and Industry for National Defense; Ethnic Affairs; Public Security (armed police); State Security (espionage, counter-espionage, and public order); Supervision (law enforcement); Civil Affairs (social care); Justice; Finance; Personnel; Labor and Social Security; Land and Resources; Construction; Railways; Transportation; Information Industry; Water Resources; Agriculture; Commerce; Culture; Health; Population and Family Planning; People's Bank of China; and the National Auditing Office. Directly affiliated organs include state administrations of Customs; Taxation; Environmental Protection; Civil Aviation; Radio, Film and Television; Sports; Intellectual Property; Tourism; Religious Affairs; and Food and Drug Supervision. Administrative offices include Hong Kong and Macao Affairs; Taiwan Affairs; Research Office; and Information Office (international communications). Directly administered institutions include Xinhua News

Agency; Chinese Academy of Sciences; State-owned Assets Supervision; China Security Regulatory Commission; and Development Research Center.

TALK MORE ABOUT POLITICS   Jiang's national campaign to build and strengthen the Party by fighting corruption, disunity, and ideological malaise; a mechanism for creating "spiritual civilization"; initiated around 1996.

TANG DYNASTY   Rulers of China from 618 to 907.

THIRD GENERATION   Jiang Zemin and his contemporary senior leaders. Mao Zedong was First Generation; Deng Xiaoping, Second Generation.

THREE REPRESENTS (SAN GE DAIBIAO)   Jiang's new theory to modernize the Communist Party by changing it from a revolutionary party fomenting class struggle to a ruling party promoting material development, spiritual civilization, and inclusion of all strata of society (thus enabling the "new social strata," such as entrepreneurs and private business owners, to join the Party). It was introduced by Jiang in February 2000, inscribed into the Party constitution in November 2002, and into the State Constitution in March 2004. The Three Represents are: advanced productive forces, advanced culture, and the fundamental interests of the overwhelming majority of the Chinese people.

THREE STRESSES   Partywide reeducation or rectification campaign designed to improve moral quality of Party members and efficacy of Party organizations (promoted in 1999). The Three Stresses are: stress study (ideology), stress politics (loyalty), stress healthy trends (rectitude).

TWO WHATEVERS   Hua Guofeng's policy that slavishly followed Mao Zedong after his death: Whatever Mao decided we uphold; whatever Chairman Mao instructed we do.

WTO   World Trade Organization.

XIAOKANG   Well off, as in a well-off society. This is China's goal for the twenty-first century, as stated at the Sixteenth Party Congress. It is described as equivalent to the condition of a midlevel developed country (like Portugal).

XINHUA   New China News Agency, the official news service of the Chinese government.

YANGZHOU   Jiang Zemin's hometown, located in Jiangsu province, about 150 miles northwest of Shanghai.

YIMIN   Shanghai Yimin Food Company (Factory Number One, specializing in ice cream), where Jiang Zemin found his first job, developed as a manager, and met Wang Doahan, his mentor.

ZHONGGUO   Chinese word for China, meaning "Middle Kingdom" or "Center (Zhong) Country (Guo)."

ZHONGNANHAI   Headquarters of the Communist Party and the State Council (government). In this elegant, walled-off section of central Beijing just northwest of Tiananmen Square, China's senior leaders work (and some live).

Major Figures

BO YIBO   Leading elder, the last surviving "Immortal"; veteran of the anti-Japanese war and the Communist revolution; finance minister under Mao; involved in critical political events during Jiang Zemin's career.

CHEN PIXIAN   Shanghai Party chief before being purged during the Cultural Revolution; after being rehabilitated, he supported Jiang Zemin.

CHEN SHUI-BIAN   First president of Taiwan to openly advocate independence. His election in 2000 ended the Kuomintang's fifty-year control of Taiwan's government.

CHEN XITONG   Ambitious mayor and Party chief of Beijing; instrumental in suppressing student demonstrators in Tiananmen Square in 1989; resisted Jiang Zemin's leadership. He was deposed in 1995 for corruption.

CHEN YUN   Leading elder, "Immortal"; a Politburo member for four decades; vice premier; censured for criticizing Mao's Great Leap Forward. He was removed from office during the Cultural Revolution, then rehabilitated under Deng. He served as chairman of the Central Advisory Commission (elders), 1987–1992. More conservative than Deng Xiaoping, he resisted rapid reform and development during the 1980s and early 1990s.

CHEN ZHILI   As head of the Shanghai Propaganda Department (when Jiang was Shanghai Party secretary), she became state councilor and the first female minister of education; a close associate of Jiang Zemin.

CHI HAOTIAN   Defense minister under Jiang Zemin.

CHIANG KAI-SHEK   The longtime leader of the Kuomintang (Nationalist Party) and mortal enemy of Mao Zedong. A protégé of Dr. Sun Yat-sen, he took over the Kuomintang in 1925–1926. After the Communist victory in 1949, he fled to Taiwan, where he was president from 1950 until his death in 1975.

CONFUCIUS   World-renowned philosopher, sage, and teacher in ancient China (sixth and fifth centuries B.C.). He had enormous influence on Chinese civilization and culture, and he originated many wise sayings and aphorisms, frequently quoted by Jiang. Confucianism, followed by 250 million to 350 million in China and other Asian countries, is more an ethical tradition than a religion.

DENG LIQUN   Propaganda minister under Deng Xiaoping, who openly turned against Deng's reforms. A leading advocate of ultra-Leftist, ultraconservative ideology, he wrote and circulated a number of highly critical public letters ("ten thousand characters") condemning Deng's reforms and Jiang Zemin's modernizations.

DENG XIAOPING   China's Paramount Leader and ardent reformer from 1978 until his death in 1997. Twice purged by Mao Zedong, Deng repudiated the Cultural

Revolution and class struggle and set economic development as the primary mission of the Party. He deposed Mao's successor (Hua Guofeng) and replaced him with Zhao Ziyang as premier (1980) and Hu Yaobang as Party chairman (1981), both of whom Deng later removed. He was chairman of CPC Central Military Commission (1981–1989). Deng set China solidly on the road to reform (Deng Xiaoping Theory), especially with his Southern Tour (Nanxun) in 1992. He chose Jiang Zemin as general secretary in 1989 and confirmed Jiang as his successor in subsequent years.

DING GUANGEN A Politburo member and head of the Publicity (Propaganda) Department of the CPC Central Committee (1992–2002) under Jiang Zemin.

FANG LIZHI A pro-democracy activist. He was the inspiration for and leader of the 1986 student movement and was active in the 1989 demonstrations. A renowned astrophysicist and vice president of the University of Science and Technology in Hefei, Anhui province, he sought asylum in the U.S. embassy in Beijing after June 4, 1989, and was exiled to the United States in 1990.

FU QUANYOU Chief of the PLA General Staff under Jiang Zemin.

GU MU Vice premier and chairman of two commissions established in 1979 to implement Deng Xiaoping's reforms, including the first Special Economic Zones (SEZs). He appointed Jiang Zemin as vice chairman.

GU YUXIU Jiang Zemin's professor at Shanghai Jiaotong University. A distinguished scientist, educator, government official, and master poet, he was a university president and vice minister of education. Respected by both Nationalists and Communists, he emigrated to Philadelphia, where he was known as Yu Hsiu Ku. He remained in touch with Jiang Zemin; he visited Jiang in New York in 1995 and Jiang visited him in Philadelphia in 1997.

HE GUOQIANG Head of the Organization Department of the CPC Central Committee (since 2002).

HU JINTAO General secretary of the Central Committee of the Communist Party of China (since 2002); president of China (since 2003); vice chairman of the Central Military Commission (since 1999); vice president of China (1998–2003); member of the Politburo Standing Committee (since 1992); ranked number seven (1992–1997); ranked number five (1997–2002); ranked number one (since 2002).

HU YAOBANG The Party general secretary (appointed in 1980 by Deng Xiaoping) deposed in early 1987 (also by Deng) for liberal views and supporting student protests. His death in April 1989 triggered the massive student demonstrations that led to the military intervention in Tiananmen Square on June 4. He had been appointed Party chairman in 1981.

HUA GUOFENG Mao Zedong's chosen successor (1976) who advocated the status quo and slavish following of Mao (Two Whatevers). He was replaced by Deng Xiaoping as China's leading personality (1978), by Zhao Ziyang as premier (1980), and by Hu Yaobang as Party chairman (1981).

HUANG JU Executive vice premier of the State Council (since 2003) and member of the Politburo Standing Committee, ranked number six (since 2002); Shanghai vice mayor (1986–1991), mayor (1991–1995), and Party chief (1995–2002); a close associate of Jiang Zemin.

JIA QINGLIN Chairman of the Chinese People's Political Consultative Conference (since 2003) and member of the Politburo Standing Committee, ranked number four (since 2002); governor and Party chief of Fujian province (1991–1996); Beijing vice mayor, mayor, and Party chief (1996–2002); a close associate of Jiang Zemin.

JIA TING'AN   Jiang Zemin's longtime secretary and personal assistant (when Jiang was electronics minister, Shanghai mayor, Party general secretary, CMC chairman, and state president); head of the Jiang Office (minister level); deputy director and director of the CMC General Office (rank of major general); a close adviser to Jiang Zemin.

JIANG MIANHENG   Jiang's older son; Ph.D. from Drexel University (Philadelphia) in electrical and computer engineering; vice president, Chinese Academy of Sciences; information technology expert; state-owned (Shanghai) enterprise investment manager.

JIANG MIANKANG   Jiang's younger son; a software specialist.

JIANG QING   Wife of Mao Zedong and leader of the infamous Gang of Four who helped perpetrate the Cultural Revolution. No relation to Jiang Zemin.

JIANG SHANGQING   A martyred Communist hero (killed in 1939 at age 28) who became, posthumously, Jiang Zemin's adoptive father; he was Jiang's biological uncle and Jiang Zehui's father.

JIANG SHIJUN   Jiang Zemin's biological father.

JIANG SHIXI   Jiang Zemin's grandfather and the family patriarch; doctor of Chinese medicine, scholar, poet, musician, calligrapher, and businessman.

JIANG ZEFEN   Jiang Zemin's older sister, who suffered during the Anti-Rightist Campaign.

JIANG ZEHUI   Jiang Zemin's sister (adoptive) and cousin (biological); internationally known expert on wood science; president of the Chinese Academy of Forestry.

JIANG ZEJUN   Jiang Zemin's older brother; artistic director and writer; died in 1989.

JIANG ZELIN   Jiang Zemin's sister (adoptive) and cousin (biological).

JIANG ZEMIN   General secretary of the Central Committee of the Communist Party of China (1989–2002); member of the Politburo Standing Committee, ranked number one (1989–2002); chairman of the Central Military Commission (since 1989); president of China (1993–2003); Shanghai mayor and Party secretary (1985–1989); vice minister, minister, and Party secretary, Ministry of Electronics Industry (1982–1985); a power engineer by education with more than two decades in industrial management.

JIN CHONGJI   Vice minister, Party Literature Office; distinguished historian; president, China History Society; official biographer of Mao Zedong and Zhou Enlai.

KHRUSHCHEV, NIKITA   Soviet leader who delivered a path-breaking anti-Stalin speech in 1956. He had a falling-out with Mao Zedong and ordered all Soviet advisers to leave China in 1960.

KIM IL-SUNG   President and autocratic "Great Leader" of the Democratic People's Republic of Korea (North Korea).

KIM JONG-IL   Son of Kim Il-Sung; president and autocratic "Dear Leader" of the Democratic People's Republic of Korea (North Korea).

KISSINGER, HENRY   U.S. national security adviser (1969–1975) and secretary of state (1973–1977) under Presidents Nixon and Ford. He was responsible for President Nixon's historic trip to China in 1972. A frequent visitor to China, he has been an informal adviser to U.S. and Chinese leaders.

KOO CHEN-FU   Chairman of the Taiwan-based Straits Exchange Foundation.

KU, YU HSIU   See Gu Yuxiu.

LEE TENG-HUI   President of Taiwan who advocated independence.

LEE, WEN HO   Chinese-American scientist fired from Los Alamos National Laboratory and accused of nuclear espionage for China. The affair caused a media frenzy; the accusation was later retracted. Imprisoned under harsh conditions, he pleaded guilty to one minor infraction and received the court's apology.

LENG RONG   Vice director of the Party Literature Office; Party historian, theoretician, and expert on Deng Xiaoping Theory and Jiang Zemin's Three Represents.

LI CHANGCHUN   Member of the Politburo Standing Committee, ranked number eight (since 2002), responsible for media and ideology; Guangdong Party secretary (1998–2002); close to Jiang Zemin.

LI ENYU   Student leader of the antidrug march in Nanjing in 1943. He was Jiang Zemin's mentor in Communist theory and was protected by Jiang in his aunt's house (1946–1948).

LI LANQING   Member of the Politburo Standing Committee, ranked number seven (1997–2002), and executive vice premier of the State Council (1998–2003); worked in the First Ministry of Machine-Building, including at First Automotive Works in Changchun when Jiang Zemin worked there.

LI PENG   Premier of the State Council (1987–1998); member of the Politburo Standing Committee, ranked number two (1987–2002), just behind Jiang Zemin (1989–2002); conservative on economic and social issues. He ordered martial law in Tiananmen Square in 1989 and was champion of Three Gorges Dam.

LI QIANKUAN   Well-known film director; chairman, China Film Association; chief director, Changchun Film Studio.

LI RUIHUAN   Chairman of the Chinese People's Political Consultative Conference (1993–2003); member of the Politburo Standing Committee, ranked number four (1989–2002); considered more liberal than most colleagues; retired in 2002.

LI XIANNIAN   Leading elder, "Immortal"; president of China (1983–1988) and chairman of the Chinese People's Political Consultative Conference (1988–1992); supported Jiang Zemin's rise, particularly his selection as general secretary in 1989.

LI ZHAOXING   Foreign minister (since 2003); ambassador to the United Nations (1992–1995); ambassador to the United States (1998–2001); deputy foreign minister (1995–1998; 2001–2003).

LIU HUAQING   Member of the Politburo Standing Committee, ranked number six (1992–1997); former commander of the navy and vice chairman of the CMC; a close associate of Deng Xiaoping.

LIU SHAOQI   President of China an.d advocate of moderation (chairman and head of state, 1959–68). He was purged by Mao Zedong, persecuted during the Cultural Revolution, and died in prison.

LIU YUNSHAN   Politburo member and head of the Publicity (Propaganda) Department of the CPC Central Committee (since 2002).

LU BAIFU   Deputy director of the State Council Development Research Center.

LUO GAN   Member of the Politburo Standing Committee, ranked number nine (since 2002), responsible for state security; state councilor (1993–1997); Politburo member (1998–2002); secretary for political and legislative affairs (1998–2003); a close associate of Li Peng.

MA BIN   Former deputy director of the State Council Development Research Center who publicly opposed Jiang Zemin's call to allow private business owners to join the Party.

MAO ZEDONG   Chairman of the Communist Party of China and founder of the People's Republic of China (1949); a Communist ideologue, archetypal revolutionary, and poet. Communist philosophies are described at length in Mao Zedong Thought, focusing on peasants as source of revolution. He was previously adored, even worshiped, as the Four Greats: Great Teacher, Great Leader, Great Supreme Commander, Great Helmsman. He is still respected, and praised for creating an independent New China, making China "stand up" in the world; he is criticized for the extreme excesses and human tragedies of his mass movements (Anti-Rightist Campaign, Great Leap Forward, Cultural Revolution). He died in 1976 after a tumultuous career.

MENG XUENONG Beijing mayor fired for negligence in the SARS epidemic of 2003.

PUTIN, VLADIMIR President of Russia since 1999.

QIAN QICHEN Foreign minister (1988–1998) and vice premier of the State Council (1993–2003) under Jiang Zemin.

QIAN XUESEN Father of China's aerospace industry and space program, China's most revered scientist. He was accused falsely of Communist sympathies by the U.S. government in 1950 and was expelled to China in 1955.

QIAO SHI A member of the Politburo Standing Committee, ranked number three (1987–1997); longtime head of security and intelligence; a contemporary and sometime rival of Jiang Zemin. He retired unexpectedly in 1997.

QIN BENLI Editor of the dynamic *World Economic Herald* who was fired by Shanghai Party secretary Jiang Zemin in 1989 for publishing unauthorized liberal ideas in memoriam to Hu Yaobang.

RUI XINGWEN Shanghai Party secretary when Jiang Zemin was mayor.

SHEN YONGYAN Jiang Zemin's longtime friend from First Automotive Works (Changchun). They met in 1956 and have remained close ever since, often speaking on the phone late at night.

SHENG HUAREN Vice chairman (since 2003) and Standing Committee member (since 2001) of the National People's Congress; chairman of the State Economic and Trade Commission (1998–2001); general manager and chairman of Sinopec (1983–1998).

SHENG ZIJIN Kuomintang (Nationalist) official for whom Jiang Shangqing, Jiang Zemin's martyred adoptive father, worked (secretly) on behalf of the Communists.

SHI KEFA Distinguished, upstanding seventeenth-century general who was martyred defending Yangzhou against foreign invaders; a national hero; role model for Jiang Zemin.

SONG JIAN Chairman of the State Science and Technology Commission (1986–1998) and state councilor (1988–1998). China's top science and technology policymaker, he initiated the Sparks Program (rural enterprises) and the Torch Program (building high-tech industries through science parks and entrepreneurial companies). He served as vice chairman of the CPPCC (1998–2003) and president of the Chinese Academy of Engineering (1998–2003), and serves as chairman of the Beijing Institute for Frontier Science (since 2004). Leading scientist and engineer (cybernetics, aerospace).

SUN, HUN H. Jiang Zemin's former classmate and professor at Drexel University, whose family suffered under Communist rule.

TANG JIAXUAN Foreign minister under Jiang Zemin (1998–2003).

TENG WENSHENG Jiang's chief speechwriter and researcher; vice director (1989–1997) and director (1997–2002) of the Policy Research Office of the CPC Central Committee; director of the Literature Office of the CPC Central Committee (since 2002); member of Jiang Zemin's inner staff (1989–2002).

THIRD BROTHER   Jiang Zemin's name among family members of his generation, particularly used by his sister, Jiang Zehui.

TONG ZONGHAI   Jiang Zemin's college roommate and close friend.

TUNG CHEE-HWA   A shipping magnate who became the Hong Kong SAR's first chief executive officer after its repatriation to China in 1997.

WAN LI   Leading elder; chairman of the National People's Congress in 1989 during the Tiananmen demonstrations. He was considered a relatively liberal Party official.

WANG DAOHAN   Jiang's career-long mentor and intimate friend; vice minister, First Ministry of Machine-Building Industry (1953–1966, 1978–1980); mayor of Shanghai (1980–1985); head of the Association for Relations Across the Taiwan Straits under Jiang Zemin (since 1991).

WANG GUANGYA   Permanent representative of China to the United Nations (since 2003); former vice minister of foreign affairs (1999–2003).

WANG HUIJIONG   Jiang Zemin's college classmate (class leader) and lifelong friend; professor, State Council Development Research Center; expert in applying systems engineering to economic and social problems.

WANG HUNING   Vice director of the Policy Research Office of the CPC Central Committee (director after 2002). A distinguished professor of international politics at Fudan University in Shanghai and a close adviser to Jiang Zemin, he helped develop Jiang's key political philosophies and strategic policies (domestic and international).

WANG, NINA KUNG   Chairlady of Hong Kong–based Chinachem. One of the wealthiest women in the world, she is a supporter of charitable activities in China.

WANG RUILIN   Military leader and closest aide to Deng Xiaoping.

WANG WEI   Pilot of the Chinese fighter jet that collided with a U.S. Navy spy plane and crashed into the ocean in April 2001; lost, presumed dead, declared a martyr.

WANG YEPING   Jiang Zemin's wife, also from Yangzhou.

WANG ZHELAN   Jiang's Zemin's adoptive mother and biological aunt.

WEI JIANXING   A member of the Politburo Standing Committee, ranked number six; chairman of the CPC Central Commission for Discipline Inspection (1997–2002); a close associate of Qiao Shi.

WEI JINGSHENG   Longtime Chinese dissident. He was released from prison and expelled to the United States in 1997 after Jiang Zemin's visit to the United States.

WEN JIABAO   Premier of the State Council (since 2003); member of the Politburo Standing Committee, ranked number three (since 2002); vice premier for agriculture and finance under Jiang Zemin (1998–2003); director of the General Office of the CPC Central Committee (1986–1993); alternate member and member of the Politburo and member of the Secretariat (1993–1998).

WU BANGGUO   Chairman, National People's Congress (since 2003); member of the Politburo Standing Committee, ranked number two (since 2002); Party chief of Shanghai (1991–1994); member of the Secretariat of the CPC Central Committee (1994–1997); vice premier of the State Council (1997–2003); a close associate of Jiang Zemin.

WU GUANGZHENG   Chairman of the CPC Central Commission for Discipline Inspection and member of the Politburo Standing Committee, ranked number seven (since 2002); Party secretary of Shandong province (1997–2002).

WU XIAOLING   Vice governor of the People's Bank of China.

WU YUEQING   Jiang Zemin's biological mother.

XIONG GUANKAI   Deputy chief of the PLA General Staff and chief of military intelligence.

YAN MINGFU   Member of the Secretariat of the CPC Central Committee under Party general secretary Zhao Ziyang; tried to negotiate with students in Tiananmen Square; subsequently vice minister of Civil Affairs and then president of the China Charity Federation.

YANG BAIBING   PLA general in charge of General Political Department; half brother of President Yang Shangkun. He was relieved of office in 1992 for opposing Jiang Zemin.

YANG SHANGKUN   A leading elder, "Immortal," veteran revolutionary, and senior army leader with a strong network in the PLA; president of China (1988–1993); Politburo member (1982–1992). He effectively lost power in 1992.

YAO YILIN   Member of the Politburo Standing Committee (1985–1994) and vice premier of the State Council; conservative leader, close to Li Peng.

YE GONGQI   Vice mayor of Shanghai when Jiang Zemin was mayor and Party secretary.

YELTSIN, BORIS   President of Russia (1991–1999).

YOU XIGUI   Head of Central Guards Bureau (Zhongnanhai security) and Jiang Zemin's personal bodyguard.

ZENG PEIYAN   Vice premier of the State Council (since 2003) and Politburo member; chairman of the State Development Planning Commission (1998–2002); director of the Leading Group for Western China Development (since 2000); key domestic policy adviser and longtime associate of Jiang Zemin.

ZENG QINGHONG   Vice president of China (since 2003); member of the Politburo Standing Committee, ranked number five (since 2002), and member of the Secretariat of the CPC Central Committee; president of the Central Party School (since 2002); deputy secretary of the Shanghai Party (1986–1989); deputy director and director of the General Office of the CPC Central Committee (1989–1999); head of the Party's Organization Department (1999–2002); helped with Jiang's key Party strategies, personnel appointments, and political philosophies; Jiang's longtime chief administrator and confidant in Shanghai and Beijing.

ZHANG AIPING   Division commander of the New Fourth Army during the anti-Japanese war, under whom Jiang Shangqing, Jiang's martyred adoptive father, served in the late 1930s (he was also Jiang Shangqing's friend). He became a general (1955), vice premier, and defense minister (1982) and later supported the rise and leadership of Jiang Zemin.

ZHANG GONGWEI   Jiang's college friend and student leader who worked in the Communist underground and was forced to flee.

ZHANG WANNIAN   A senior PLA general and CMC vice chairman under Jiang Zemin.

ZHANG WENKANG   Former minister of public health, fired for negligence in the SARS epidemic of 2003.

ZHANG ZHEN   Senior PLA general and CMC vice chairman during Jiang's early years.

ZHAO HUAYONG   President, China Central Television (CCTV).

ZHAO QIZHENG   Minister, State Council Information Office (since 1998) and director of the CPC Foreign Communications (Propaganda) Office (since 1998); Shanghai vice mayor (1991–1998) and head of Pudong New Area (1993–1998);

deputy director and director, Shanghai Party Organization Department (1984–1991); a close adviser to Jiang Zemin.

ZHAO ZIYANG   Party general secretary, who was deposed for his liberal views and for supporting student demonstrators in Tiananmen Square in the spring of 1989; reform-minded premier (1980–1987) and general secretary (1987–1989). He was appointed and deposed by Deng Xiaoping, and succeeded by Jiang Zemin.

ZHENG BIJIAN   Executive vice president of the Central Party School (running operations) when the school president was Hu Jintao.

ZHOU ENLAI   Revered premier under Mao Zedong (1949–1976). He tried to limit and then undo the severe damage from Mao's mass movements. He pioneered reestablishing diplomatic relations with the West, especially with the United States. He was a role model for Jiang Zemin.

ZHOU JIANNAN   Former vice minister, First Ministry of Machine-Building Industry, when Jiang Zemin was working in its factories and institutes. He gave Jiang responsibility to convert the power-generating plant at First Automotive Works (Changchun) from coal to crude oil and helped to promote him thereafter.

ZHOU XIAOCHUAN   Governor of People's (Central) Bank of China (since 2002); chairman of China Securities Regulatory Commission (2000–2002); president of China Construction Bank (1998–2000); son of Zhou Jiannan.

ZHU DE   Commander-in-chief of the Communist armed forces under Mao Zedong.

ZHU RONGJI   Premier of the State Council (1998–2003); member of the Politburo Standing Committee, ranked number three (1997–2002), ranked number five (1992–1997); Shanghai mayor (1989–1992); vice premier (1992–1998); aggressive reformer and enemy of government waste.

ZHU ZIQING   Early-twentieth-century writer from Yangzhou; classmate of Jiang Zemin's father; famously refused to eat American-donated grain after World War II.

Notes

ABBREVIATIONS

AFP	Agence France Presse
AP	Associated Press
AWSJ	*Asian Wall Street Journal*
BBC	BBC Worldwide Monitoring Service: Asia Pacific
CNN	CNN (cable) or CNN.com
FEER	*Far Eastern Economic Review*
Gilley, *Tiger*	Bruce Gilley, *Tiger on the Brink: Jiang Zemin and China's New Elite* (Berkeley: University of California Press, 1998)
JEN	Japan Economic Newswire
LAT	*Los Angeles Times*
Lam, *Era*	Willy Wo-Lap Lam, *The Era of Jiang Zemin* (Singapore: Prentice Hall, 1999)
Nathan and Gilley, *Rulers*	Andrew J. Nathan and Bruce Gilley, *China's New Rulers: The Secret Files* (New York: New York Review of Books, 2002)
Nathan and Gilley, *Rulers* (2003)	Andrew J. Nathan and Bruce Gilley, *China's New Rulers: The Secret Files,* Second, Revised Edition (New York: New York Review of Books, 2003)
NYT	*New York Times*
PD	*People's Daily*
SCMP	*South China Morning Post*
ST	*Straits Times* (Singapore)
TKP	*Ta Kung Pao* (Hong Kong)
UPI	United Press International
WP	*Washington Post*
WSJ	*The Wall Street Journal*
Xinhua	Xinhua (New China) News Agency
Yang, *Biography*	Yang Zhongmei, *Jiang Zemin Zhuan (Biography of Jiang Zemin)* (Taipei: China Times Publishing, 1996)
Zong, "Zhu (I)"	Zong Hairen (pseudonym), "Zhu Rongji in 1999 (I)," edited by Andrew Nathan, *Chinese Law and Government* 35, no. 1 (January–February 2002).
Zong, "Zhu (II)"	Zong Hairen (pseudonym), "Zhu Rongji in 1999 (II)," edited by Andrew Nathan, *Chinese Law and Government* 35, no. 2 (March–April 2002).

[following] means that the following section uses or is derived from this source.

INTRODUCTION: THE LIFE OF JIANG ZEMIN

1 *but Jiang did not*   For example, "Jiang, of course, is a figure who cannot remotely compare to Mao or Deng in initiating great historical developments or in political power." Frederick C. Teiwes, "Politics at the 'Core': The Political Circumstances of Mao Zedong, Deng Xiaoping and Jiang Zemin," http://rspas.anu.edu.au/ccc/morrison00.pdf.

1 *"On behalf of"*   Xinhua, September 11, 2001 (BBC).

1 *"the appalling terrorist attacks"*   Xinhua, September 12, 2001 (BBC).

1 *thirty-two counterterrorism specialists* [following]   You Ji, "China's Post 9/11 Terrorism Strategy," *China Brief,* April 15, 2004.

2 *"share common"*   *China Daily,* October 21, 2001.

2 *"absolute gun-boat policy"*   AFP, May 10, 1999.

2 *"bear full responsibility"*   Xinhua, May 11, 1999.

2 *"never be bullied"*   Xinhua, May 12, 1999.

3 *"apologize"*   *Age* (Melbourne), April 5, 2001.

4 *nine thousand bombs*   UPI, May 9, 1999.

4 *"old maps"*   Michael Lans, in *WP,* June 17, 1999.

4 *emergency meeting* [following]   Author's interview with Wang Guangya, Beijing, April 2002.

4 *had been deliberate*   According to Boston University professor Joseph Fewsmith, "The assumption that the bombing was deliberate rested on a perceived pattern of behavior"—that America intended to contain, indeed to humiliate, China—"and the anger flowed from that perception." Joseph Fewsmith, *China Since Tiananmen: The Politics of Transition* (New York: Cambridge University Press, 2001), 1. From selling weapons to Taiwan and supporting Tibetan independence to constant criticism of China's human rights policies and blackballing their bid to host the 2000 Olympics, the Chinese people saw a competitive, superpower America thwarting their national interests and emergence as a great power.

5 *"Tell the U.S."*   Charles Hutzler, for AP, May 10, 1999.

6 *three days . . . sardonic Beijingers . . . three missing persons*   Joseph Fewsmith, "China and the WTO: The Politics Behind the Agreement," The National Bureau of Asian Research, November 1999, http://www.nbr.org/publications/report.html.

6 *1995 poll*   Fewsmith, *China Since Tiananmen,* 155.

7 *"Turtle"*   Zong, "Zhu (I)," 94. In Chinese, "turtle" is a particularly odious epithet due to a nasty double entendre.

7 *"forbids protests"*   Charles Hutzler, for AP, May 10, 1999.

7 *"Mao was great"*   Todd Crowell and David Hsieh, "Growing Backlash in China," *Asia-Week,* June 11, 1999, 24.

7 *"defend state sovereignty"*   Xinhua, May 10, 1999.

7 *"prevent overreaction"*   UPI, May 9, 1999.

8 *Jiang refused   ST,* May 13, 1999.

8 *"I was dumbfounded"*   Bill Clinton, *My Life* (New York: Alfred A. Knopf, 2004), 855.

8 *"I don't blame"*   UPI, May 10, 1999.

8 *"We're inside the embassy"*   Brian Nelson and Chris Black, for CNN, May 9, 1999.

8 *Ding Guangen*   Elizabeth Rosenthal, in *NYT,* May 13, 1999.

9 *public was dictating*   A poll of Chinese youth reported that 90 percent thought that the United States tried to dominate China; the figure was 96 percent for college students. Even more startling, 84 percent of Chinese youth felt that the U.S. censure of China for human rights violations was "based on malice." Although one can question the methodology of the polling process, the fact remained that a large number of China's young people were more suspicious than appreciative of American motives. Author's communication, Beijing.

9 *90 percent*   Jennifer Brooks, for UPI, May 14, 1999.

9 *stupid mistake*   While a few (largely non-U.S.) newspapers hinted that a low-level intelligence officer could have deliberately entered those ill-fated coordinates in Belgrade, the

fact that no credible American news source even wondered whether the bombing of the Chinese embassy might have been intentional was powerful proof, at least to Americans, that it was not. As Henry Kissinger, the former U.S. secretary of state and a longtime friend of China, noted, "Our explanations are so implausible that they have to be true— otherwise we would have certainly invented something better." Author's interview with Henry Kissinger, New York, January 2002.

9 *"strongest condemnation"* Xinhua, May 10, 1999 (BBC).

9 *"seriously infringed"* Xinhua, May 12, 1999.

9–10 *"revolutionary martyr"* . . . *"hegemonist"* Christopher Bodeen, for AP, May 13, 1999; Xinhua, May 13, 1999.

10 *"vigilant"* Xinhua, May 13, 1999.

10 *telephone call from Clinton* Xinhua, May 14, 1999.

10 *"I apologized again"* Bill Clinton, *My Life*, 855.

10 *Clinton's apology* Xinhua, May 14, 1999; *China Daily*, May, 15, 1999.

11 *American side* . . . *"kind of emotion"* Michael Laris, in *WP*, June 18, 1999, A34. A summary of the report, released by Xinhua, cited a variety of failures leading up to the tragedy, primarily outdated maps and databases and no clear markings on the embassy, justifications that most Chinese did not believe. Nonetheless, the detailed presentation of the American position was ameliorating.

11 *GRE* Author's communication, Beijing.

11 *"Since World War II"* The joke was told openly by a Chinese media executive at a private symposium attended by senior representatives of the Chinese and American media industries; the author chaired the symposium, held in Beijing in January 2000.

12 *"I just want to know"* Robert M. Hathaway, "The Lingering Legacy of Tiananmen," in *Foreign Affairs*, September/October 2003.

12 *more outward-looking than* Fewsmith, *China Since Tiananmen*.

12 *Jiang Zemin's life* According to the Communist Party of China (CPC), its history can be divided into seven periods, four before 1949 and three after, each with its own traumas and triumphs: (1) the 1920s, the beginnings of the revolution; (2) the 1930s, the land revolution; (3) the mid-1930s to mid-1940s, the Japanese invasion and occupation; (4) 1945–1949, the culmination of the civil war and the founding of the People's Republic; (5) 1949–1966, the building of New China, with its political mass movements; (6) 1966–1976, the Cultural Revolution, which brought national turmoil (the CPC may not normally count this unpleasant decade among the periods); and (7) 1978 onward, the period of reform, opening up, and great development. Jiang Zemin's life encompassed all seven periods.

Chapter 1. 1926–1943

17 *Year of the Tiger* In the Chinese zodiac, which reflects a cyclical concept of time, a different animal is assigned to represent each year of a twelve-year cycle. As in astrology, certain traits are said to follow from the year of one's birth.

17 *third child* . . . *ze* various sources, including Gilley, *Tiger*, 6.

17–18 *"The making"* Author's interview with Jiang Zehui, Beijing, December 2001. The fact that Jiang Zehui's name is very similar to Jiang Zemin's is no accident. When the grandchildren of a given set of grandparents live in the same household, they may have the same "middle name," or middle character, to show that, even though they are cousins, they are of the same generation in the family tree. For example, although President Jiang Ze Min and his "sister" (biological cousin) Jiang Ze Hui had different parents, they are of the same "Jiang" family and of the same "Ze" generation. From their names alone, one can instantly identify the family name (first character) and the generation (second character) to which they belong.

18 *dueling villages* . . . *"stop guessing"* One claim is made by Jiangwan, located inland in Jiangxi province; another is put forth by Jiangcun, situated in a tea-growing region of

Anhui province, hundreds of miles to the north, where green forests are dotted by charming rural houses of white walls and dark roofs. The competition between the villages is not friendly. The stakes can be high when establishing a claim to China's ruler. It is not only a matter of pride but also tourist dollars. Though Party regulations prevent a cult of personality—such as the one that had deified Mao; for example, it is illegal to sell pendants with Jiang's picture—merchants make a tidy sum in souvenirs. No matter how many tourists these places attract, their link to the president is tenuous. Josephine Ma, in *SCMP*, May 21 and 23, 2002; Ching-Ching Ni, in *LAT*, June 23, 2002, A3.

18 *Yangzhou . . . Marco Polo . . . brides*   Yang, *Biography*, chap. 1; www.magma.ca/ ~mtooker/cities/yangzhou.htm

18 *favorite destination . . . Slim West Lake . . . "ride cranes"*   Yang, *Biography*, chap. 1; www.chinatravel.com.

18 *Eight Eccentrics*   Various sources, including www.bright-spring.com.

19 *Shi Kefa*   Various sources, including *Outlook*, December 1990; Yang, *Biography*, chap. 1; China National Tourism Association, http://cnta.gov.cn; author's communication, Beijing; Gilley, *Tiger*, 14.

19 *"I am a native"*   Yang, *Biography*, chap. 1; Xinhua, July 22, 1995 (BBC); Yang Daojin, *Common Leader* (Hong Kong: World People's Press, July 2001), 686–688. Initially, the author (or someone) sent the manuscript of *Common Leader* (*Pingmin Lingxiu*, literally "Ordinary-Citizen Leader") to the Party Literature Office with the hope that it might be published in China. The manuscript was sent to various leaders for review, but the decision was negative; the book was published in Hong Kong.

19 *"shocked to see" . . . Sundays*   Yang, *Common Leader*, 2001, 686–688; Gilley, *Tiger*, 14 (quoting *Asahi Shimbun*, August 13, 1995).

19 *"eight virtues"*   During the last year of his life, tradition tells that Shi Kefa did eight things, each of which reflected one of his eight virtues: (1) not taking credit for himself after doing worthy deeds; (2) attending to the deteriorating political situation by voluntarily going north to supervise the army; (3) taking risks to mediate among four feudal lords; (4) recruiting talented people to establish a think tank; (5) responding with patriotic defiance to the Qing's demand for surrender; (6) continuing to give loyal advice to the South Ming dynasty; (7) fighting diligently at the battlefront; (8) showing dignity when defending Yangzhou to his death.

19 *"The city lacks"*   Antonia Finnane, "A Place in the Nation: Yangzhou and the *Idle Talk* Controversy of 1934," *Journal of Asian Studies* 53, no. 4 (November 1994), 1150–1174 (quoting Wang Guilin, a Yangzhou native).

19 *Zhu Ziqing*   Yang, *Biography*, chap. 1.

20 *spacious home*   The section on Jiang's home and family background is derived from various sources, including author's interview with Jiang Zehui; Gilley, *Tiger*, 6–19; Yang, *Biography*, chap. 1.

20 *street name*   Yang, *Biography*, chap. 1.

20 *inner courtyard*   Kathy Chen and Joseph Kahn, in *AWSJ*, February 6, 1995, 1. In the mid-1990s ten families were reported to live in the old Jiang family house.

20 *Jiang Zemin's grandfather*   Primarily, author's interview with Jiang Zehui.

21 *"My grandfather"*   Author's communication, Beijing.

21 *artistic and scholarly friends*   For example, a famous calligrapher named Han Guojun, a close friend of Grandfather Jiang's, who would later become a hero in the fight against the Japanese. Yang, *Biography*, chap. 1.

21 *"Mourning Father"*   Yang, *Biography*, chap. 1.

21 *Primary School* [following]   Author's interview with Jiang Zehui; Gilley, *Tiger*, 9–10; Yang, *Biography*, chap. 1.

21 *Jiang walked*   *Nan Feng Chuan*, February 1994.

24 *personal inscriptions*   In China calligraphy makes for powerful symbols. Jiang once re-

marked that in ancient China, poor handwriting was an obstacle to finding a good job (Gilley, *Tiger,* 10). A central technique of the art form is maintaining the brush in an upright position so that the flow of energy from hand to paper can be direct and powerful. To say that someone writes with an "upright brush" carries a connotation of moral strength.

24 *Jiang would sing*   Author's interview with Ye Gongqi, Shanghai, June 2001.

24 *so frustrated*   Author's communication, Beijing.

24 Idle Talk [following]   Finnane, "Place in the Nation." The Chinese title was *Xianhua Yangzhou.*

25 *a critique of the country*   One might surmise that the public humiliation of Yangzhou by the *Idle Talk* book, with its shameful depiction of Yangzhou women and accusations of collaboration, would have stamped onto the impressionable preteen Jiang a distaste for intellectual exposés of social problems and a belief that such contentious issues are best hidden from public examination. After all, the literary controversy must have been discussed in the literate Jiang household. Yet there may be a deeper reading here. The author's question "What's wrong with Yangzhou?" was later metaphorically read as "What's wrong with China?" and by raising the question, as best he could he sought to stir the Chinese people from their long and deepening slumber and reverse their continuing weakness and subservience to foreign powers. Could Jiang Zemin, on later reflection as an adult, have wondered whether the author, who had put himself at personal risk, had the goal of productive self-criticism of the entire land, to push and prod his country, catalyzing national change and revitalizing China?

25 *Communists proposed*   Author's communication with historians, Beijing.

25 *wrote an essay*   Gilley, *Tiger,* 12.

25 *eighteen hundred applicants*   Kathy Chen and Joseph Kahn, in *AWSJ,* February 6, 1995.

25 *refused to eat*   Gilley, *Tiger,* 16. Zhu Ziqing was the founder of a movement known as "new poetry," which selected topics from everyday life.

25 *classical Chinese poems . . . patriotic poems . . . Wen Tianxiang*   Author's interview with Ye Gongqi. Song dynasty poet Wen Tianxiang (1236–1283) wrote these famous lines as the final verses of "The Lonely Ocean," one of the most popular patriotic poems in China. Yang, *Common Leader,* 2001, 686–688.

26 *"You can spend thirty"*   Xinhua, July 22, 1995 (BBC).

26 *many works that had been translated*   Various sources, including Gilley, *Tiger,* 15; Yang, *Common Leader,* 2001, 1078–80.

26 *"three kinds of education"*   Yang, *Biography,* chap. 1.

26 *"Our Jiang family"*   Author's interview with Jiang Zehui. Grandfather Jiang intended for his offspring to become achievers, "dragons"—high officials or well-known people (Yang, *Biography,* chap. 1). The eldest was Jiang Zemin's biological father, Jiang Shijun, who was also named Guanqian (meaning "Champion of a Thousand"), his nickname and pen name (Gilley, *Tiger,* 6, 8, 54). He was born in 1895, considered the beginning of the Japanese Imperial Period, and died in 1973, during the last years of the Cultural Revolution, when Jiang Zemin, his son, was already a government official in Beijing.

Since Jiang Zemin's father was the oldest child, he was required to share the burden of supporting the family. He found his first job at the Tongming Electric Company in Nantong, where, through hard work, he rose to an executive position. Jiang Zemin was three or four years old when the family lived in Nantong, but they returned to Yangzhou before he began school. When Grandfather Jiang retired as first manager of the Grand Canal (*Dada*) Shipping Company—which managed commercial ships that plied the Yangtze River—Jiang Zemin's father became assistant manager of the same company.

Jiang Shijun had married Wu Yueqing, a native of a small village in Jiangdu county, who would become Jiang Zemin's mother. She was born in 1897 and died in 1977, the year that her up-and-coming son, then fifty-one years old, spent in Shanghai as part of the group dispatched, after Mao's death, to reestablish federal control of China's commercial center.

Shijun and Yueqing had three sons and two daughters, among whom Jiang Zemin was the second son; the eldest son, Jiang Zemin's older brother, was Jiang Zejun; the third son, Jiang Zekuan, was the fourth child; the eldest daughter, Jiang Zefen, was born just before Jiang Zemin; and the second female child, Jiang Zelan, was the fifth and final child.

In China children are numbered consecutively, irrespective of whether they are sons or daughters; this is why Jiang Zefen was called Second Daughter—that is, second child—even though she was the first female offspring to be born. Similarly, Jiang Zemin was, to his parents, Third Son, since he was the third child; and he was Third Brother to Jiang Zehui. Cousins of the same generation who live in the same household often call one another brother or sister, and they are numbered chronologically as part of one Big Family. It is as if the biological cousins really are brothers and sisters from the same parents, which is how they actually feel. The Chinese believe that the "cousin" label suggests emotional distance, while the "brother/sister" appellation catalyzes closer attachment. This tradition strengthens the Big Family culture of China.

26 *Big Family* (da jia)   Author's interview with Jiang Zehui. Traditionally in China, even when children married, they did not move away to create their own households but continued living under one roof in one household in a Big Family. The relationship among Big Family members is very close from birth to death, literally from cradle to grave. Any member's success credits all, and all the extended brothers and sisters are expected to help one another. Collective success is stressed; extreme individualism is shunned.

27 *Jiang Shangqing* [following, entire story]   Author's interview with Jiang Zehui; Dong Fanghe, *Zhang Aiping Biography* (People's Press); Yang, *Biography*, chap. 1; Gilley, *Tiger*, 17–19.

28 *under the nose*   At one point Jiang Shangqing even held a part-time job at the private Jiangsu Circulating Library, whose director was also in charge of the investigating department of the Nationalist Party in Jiangsu province.

28 *"My heart is heavy"*   Yang, *Biography*, chap. 1.

29 *horse stable*   Gilley, *Tiger*, 13.

29 *40,000 to 60,000*   Nicholas Kristof, in *NYT*, December 20, 2003. China's official estimate is that 300,000 or more were killed, a claim that Kristof rejects as hyperbole. He relies on contemporary sources, including witnesses and Chinese reports at the time.

29 *Rape of Nanking*   Many sources, notably Iris Chang, *The Rape of Nanking* (New York: Basic Books, 1997).

30 *Zhang Aiping*   One of East China's great military leaders, Zhang became known to Americans after the Doolittle Raiders bombed Tokyo in April 1942. It was the first U.S. attack on the Japanese homeland after Pearl Harbor, and it boosted American morale. Most of Doolittle's B-25 bombers made forced landings in Japanese-controlled areas in China, and Zhang led his Chinese guerrilla force to rescue those American pilots, which he did by securing the cooperation of Chinese farmers and villagers. The Japanese took severe revenge, destroying villages that helped the Americans and killing innumerable Chinese. Zhang Aiping became a general in 1955 and defense minister in 1982, overseeing China's nuclear and atomic programs. General Zhang was an early and consistent supporter of Jiang Zemin.

30 *Sheng could not resist*   Zhang Aiping's primary challenge in creating a joint Communist-Nationalist force to confront the Japanese was a bitter rivalry between Sheng Zijin and another KMT leader, Xu Zhiyuan (Dong, *Zhang Aiping Biography*).

30 *ambushed and captured* [following]   Yang, *Biography*, chap. 1.

31 *solve the problem*   Throughout history in almost every culture, virtually every family has

wanted a son. In China this way of thinking was especially strong. In a line of moral philosophy going back to the Buddha and Confucius, among the traditional unfilial pieties in China—that is, not fulfilling a child's proper obligations to a parent—one of the most serious was to die without a male heir.

32 *became so distraught*   Author's interview with Jiang Zehui.

33 *"a nation ridden"*   Gilley, *Tiger,* 14 (quoting Xinhua, May 12, 1991).

33 *national anthem*   Yang, *Biography,* chap. 1.

33 *"My family"*   Jiang Zejun, Jiang Zemin's older brother, was also a man of high culture—well read in literature and accomplished in classical poetry—and he used his writing skills to promote revolutionary ideas, editing and printing underground Communist Party newspapers. He was also multitalented in music, chess, writing, and painting—just like his grandfather.

34 *Japanese language*   Yang, *Biography,* chap. 2.

34 *"better Japanese"*   Fewsmith, *China Since Tiananmen,* 200. In May 1998 President Jiang went to Beijing University to celebrate its centennial. He spoke to the faculty in English, Russian, and French, and it was when he came to Japanese that he explained why he did not speak it better.

Chapter 2. 1943–1947

35 *Nanjing Central University* [entire chapter]   Primarily author's interview with Tong Zonghai, Changsha, December 2001; see photos of Tong Zonghai, at the interview in 2001 and in the graduating class with Jiang Zemin in 1947. Yang, *Biography,* chap. 2; Gilley, *Tiger,* 19–29.

39 *"Our actions,"* . . . *"shame"*   Author's interview with Tong Zonghai. During the hundred years between the Opium War of 1840 and the end of the anti-Japanese war in 1945, eight developed countries invaded China, which was defeated ignominiously time after time and forced to cede large territories and pay huge indemnities to foreign forces. Beijing, China's capital, was occupied three times. Hong Kong was lost in 1842. In 1860 French and British armies broke into Beijing, killed tens of thousands of citizens, and looted and burned down the Old Summer Palace. In the mid-twentieth century Japan captured half of China; 25 million people perished. The Chinese people are said to cry out over their century-long shame.

40 *Communists . . . provided a means to express*   The antidrug protest march exemplified China's complex political situation. The demonstrators had been followed throughout the night but were never stopped, much less threatened or harmed, even as they protested Japanese policy. The reality was that not even the Japanese army had complete control over the country. Ruling a large hostile people in a large hostile country was tenuous business. A crackdown might trigger social disorder. The Japanese relied on Wang Jingwei and his puppet government to maintain a facade of Chinese autonomy, which was necessary to validate the rationalizing theory that the Japanese had invaded China to protect it from Western powers. Wang, however, was not content merely to be the Japanese government's "Chinese mask" and "running dog." He wanted a piece of the profits from the drug trade. His leverage lay in the fact that the Japanese needed his cooperation. Though neither the Communists nor the Kuomintang ever recognized Wang Jingwei's puppet government, the Japanese feared that he might still have the ability to call the people to revolt. Into this mix stepped the Communists, who were operating underground and seeking opportunities to expand their power base. They swiftly capitalized on the business conflict between Wang and the Japanese by planning the massive antidrug demonstration, an organizing strategy that would have much greater long-term impact than the mere eradication of opium.

43 *Five Items*   Colloquially called the "five zi's," because the five Chinese words for *houses, cars, money, women,* and *golden bars* all end in the character *zi.*

43 *struggle to survive* [following]   He Chongyin, *Shanghai Communist Party History Research,* January 1995 (Digest Weekly, May 4, 1995); Wang Deying, in *Chinese World,* December 2000, 4–5.

43 *Wang Huijiong*   Author's interviews with Wang Huijiong, Beijing, December 2001, April 2002, September 2002, April 2004. (See photos of Wang Huijiong, at the interview in 2001 and in the graduating class with Jiang Zemin in 1947.)

44 *Zhang Xinfu*   Author's interview with Tong Zonghai.

45 *Zhang Gongwei* [following]   Yang, *Common Leader,* 2001, 695–697; Wang, in *Chinese World,* December 2000, 4–5.

46 *senior collective leadership*   Members of the underground Shanghai Communist Party included students who would later become national political leaders, such as Qian Qichen, foreign minister and vice premier under Jiang Zemin, and Qiao Shi, chairman of the National People's Congress, who would become Jiang's colleague and sometime rival.

47 *offered to hide him*   Wang, in *Chinese World,* December 2000, 4–5; Yang, *Common Leader,* 2001, 698–701; He, *Shanghai Communist Party History Research.*

47 *Li Enyu moved in* [following]   Yang, *Common Leader,* 2001, 698–701; Wang, in *Chinese World,* 4–5. Wang Jiaqiu would often join the discussions.

47 *later years*   He, *Shanghai Communist Party History Research.*

47 *twentieth anniversary*   Wang, in *Chinese World,* December 2000, 4–5.

48 *Even the university . . . "Respect Teachers"*   Jasper Becker, *The Chinese* (New York: Oxford University Press, 2002), 207–208.

49 *"Wang Huijiong was the one"*   Author's communication, Beijing.

49 *"I am ashamed"*   Gilley, *Tiger,* 22.

50 *Zhu Wuhua*   Author's interview with Tong Zonghai.

50 *Gu Yuxiu . . . "I come here"*   Yang, *Common Leader,* 2001, 539–541.

51 *"pay my respect"*   Xinhua, July 2, 1993.

52 *called him "Dr. Jiang" . . . words of remembrance* [following]   Yang, *Common Leader,* 2001, 698–701; Wang, in *Chinese World,* December 2000, 4–5.

Chapter 3. 1947–1955

53 *difficulty finding a job*   Author's interview with Tong Zonghai.

53 *Shanghai Haining* [following]   This section is derived from author's interview with Tong Zonghai; Yang, *Biography,* chap. 3; Gilley, *Tiger,* 30–31.

54 *broken motor*   Author's interview with Wang Huijiong.

54 *transaction*   Author's interview with Wang Daohan, Shanghai, June 2001.

55 *Zhang Gongwei* [following]   Yang, *Common Leader,* 2001, 698–701; Wang, in *Chinese World,* December 2000, 4–5.

56 *"northwest wind"*   Gilley, *Tiger,* 33.

56 *"to seek your advice"*   Yang, *Biography,* chap. 3.

56 *remain proud*   *Science,* June 16, 2000, 1950–1953.

56 *he was appointed*   Yang, *Biography,* chap. 3; Gilley, *Tiger,* 33–34.

57 *Factory Number One* [following]   Author's interview with Wang Daohan.

58 *Jiang came to confide*   Author's communication, Beijing.

58 *too bourgeois*   Gilley, *Tiger,* 33.

59 *"training and rectification"*   Ibid., 33. Yang, *Biography,* chap. 3, suggests that Jiang was involved in exposing reactionaries in the factory as well as in increasing production.

59 *Songjiang . . . formal leadership*   Gilley, *Tiger,* 33–34.

59 *"Third Generation" . . . rise to prominence*   Ibid., 34. The First Generation was Mao Zedong and his contemporaries; the Second Generation was Deng Xiaoping and the elders; the Third Generation was Jiang Zemin and his colleagues.

60 *Guangming*   Author's interview with Yimin general manager, Shanghai, June 2001.

60 *"We Workers"*   Gilley, *Tiger,* 34.

60 *marketplace*   Author's interview with Wang Daohan.

60 *food home . . . superiors* Yang, *Biography,* chap. 3.

60 *"an innocent affection"* Gilley, *Tiger,* 36 (quoting *Wen Hui Bao,* July 18, 1989, 3).

61 *Foreign Languages College* Ibid., 36.

61 *Her paternal grandfather* Author's interview with Jiang Zehui.

61 *named Wang* In Chinese the expression *Old Hundred Names*—which is somewhat equivalent to the American term *John Q. Public*—is a humorous reference to the fact that the pool of Chinese surnames is so limited.

61 *a hundred guests* Author's interview with Wang Huijiong.

62 *"For physical education"* [following] Author's interview with Jiang Zehui.

63 *invaded the southern part* Recent access to Russian archives has compelled the Chinese to recognize that North Korea invaded South Korea, not the other way around, as decades of propaganda had claimed.

63 *Soap Factory* Author's interview with Wang Daohan; Gilley, *Tiger,* 35.

63 *Soviet model . . . mass movements* The government also developed its first five-year plan based on the Soviet system. Drafted by the State Council, led by Zhou Enlai and Chen Yun, the goal of the plan was "to build an industrialized, highly modernized, culturally developed country." More specifically, it was to increase the state's share of the national economy between 1953 and 1957. At the time the state sector in China accounted for only 20 percent. In the Soviet Union it was virtually 100 percent.

Between 1952 and 1954 the government established a highly structured planning apparatus that exercised detailed control of the economy, micromanaging industries top down by ministries in Beijing. The Chinese adhered strictly to the Soviet model, investing about 80 percent of resources into the urban economy, even though more than 80 percent of the population lived in rural areas. The vast majority of this investment went into heavy industry, and in pure industrial terms the plan was a success. Agriculture, however, was left in desperate need of resources.

Mao was not happy with China's manufacturing industry, a frustration exemplified by his statement, "We can make tables and chairs, teacups and teapots, grind grain into flour, and make paper, but we cannot make even a single car, plane, tank, or tractor." The fact was that the Party's leadership had little experience in making any kind of economy work, let alone a Marxist-Leninist model, and at almost every decision point they chose ideological purity over economic pragmatism.

By 1952 the Party had initiated three kinds of targeted purges, going after counterrevolutionaries, corrupt cadres, and capitalists. Any Chinese who owned business assets was at risk, and the charges against him—the Five Againsts: bribery, tax evasion, cheating in labor and/or materials, stealing state assets, and theft of state economic intelligence—could be exaggerated or fabricated. Personal friendships and business relationships were shattered as trust broke down and paranoia broke out. It is estimated that as many as 500,000 to 800,000 people were killed during these purges.

64 *promoted to vice minister* Author's interview with Wang Daohan.

64 *transferred to Beijing* Yang, *Biography,* chap. 3. The new job rounded out an already promising résumé.

Chapter 4. 1955–1962

66 *the sprawling Changchun auto plant* [following] Author's interview with Wang Daohan; Gilley, *Tiger,* 37–48; Yang, *Biography,* chap. 3.

66 *"To succeed here"* Guan Yu, "Jiang Zemin at Changchun First Automobile Works," *Children of China* (1994).

66 *Russia's cultural richness . . . khleh* Gilley, *Tiger,* 40; author's communication, Beijing.

67 *his old friend Zhang Gongwei* Yang, *Common Leader,* 2001, 701; Wang, in *Chinese World,* December 2000, 4–5.

68 *When Jiang returned* Author's interview with Jiang Zehui.

69 *a normal promotion* Author's communication with historians, Beijing.

69 *"the Magic Chatterer"* [following]   In the mid-1990s, President Jiang asked Shen Yongyan to supervise research on the First Automotive Works and commission a written history of his times there. Two articles were subsequently published in an in-house publication: Shao Yijie, Li Huile, and Jiang Chengxin, "Jiang Zemin's Time at No. 1 *(Yiqi)* Auto Plant," *Jie Fang,* May 1997 (two parts); and Wang Zhongxue, "Magnificent Younger Years: Jiang Zemin's Time at No. 1 *(Yiqi)* Auto Plant," *Jie Fang,* February 1998.

69 *"was kind to us"*   Jiang remembered Chen Yunheng when, more than forty years later, he visited Changchun. "You're twelve years older than me," Jiang recalled, "but you still look so healthy." Told that Chen often worked out and could run ten thousand meters, Jiang said, "Yes, life depends on exercise." Huang Yi, Li Runmei, and Liu Zhaohui, *FAW Group Economic Research,* nos. 9 and 10, 2000.

69 *"I love talent," . . . "What his father"* [following]   Shao, Li, Jiang, "Jiang Zemin's Time"; Wang, "Magnificent Younger Years."

70 *Shen Yongyan*   Author's interview with Shen Yongyan, Changchun, September 2002.

70 *job in the Party office*   Author's communication with historians, Beijing.

70 *a fourth-floor apartment*   Author's interview with Shen Yongyan; Gilley, *Tiger,* 41.

70 *The plant provided*   Outside this relatively privileged world, however, the situation was very different. The central government had allocated substantial funds to the Changchun enterprise to develop an automotive manufacturing capability but little to the municipality of Changchun itself. The result was a division in the social fabric of the community.

70 *former professors*   Yang, *Common Leader,* 2001, 496.

71 *Hundred Flowers Campaign*   Wikipedia, the Free Encyclopedia (http://en.wikipedia. org). The official Chinese government position, which is always concerned with protecting Mao's image, is ambiguous about his initial motives behind the Anti-Rightist Campaign, although fully admitting that the "extended Campaign," instigated by those who exploited it to accrete unauthorized power, was wrong and injurious. Eventually, every "Rightist" was rehabilitated.

71 *"quota of Rightists"* [following]   Author's interview with Shen Yongyan.

72 *"so many Rightists"*   Ibid.; Guan, "Jiang Zemin at Changchun."

72 *Jiang Zefen*   Gilley, *Tiger,* 42. In the early 1980s, after the death of Mao and the return of Deng, the Communist Party began to rehabilitate the so-called Rightists. But because Jiang Zefen had never been formally charged, she could not be formally rehabilitated— and the county's educational office would not accept her claim for additional support. Later, with the help of friends, her compensation of 70 yuan per month was finally restored, but still there were no benefits. Jiang Zefen's husband was an administrator in the Shanghai Financial Administration Bureau, and they lived together in retirement in a small house.

73 *rehabilitated in 1962*   Huang, Li, and Liu, *FAW Group Economic Research.*

73 *"Comrade Lei Wen"*   Ibid.

74 *forty thousand trucks* [following]   Gilley, *Tiger,* 43.

74 *rolled and cut* [following]   Ibid., 44.

74 *Inferior materials . . . "Ultrasonic Wave"*   Author's interview with Shen Yongyan; Gilley, *Tiger,* 44.

75 *"such braggarts"*   Author's interview with Shen Yongyan.

75 *help the farmers . . . lead workers*   Gilley, *Tiger,* 45.

76 *"the one who inspects for safety"*   Shao, Li, and Jiang, "Jiang Zemin's Time."

76 *young engineer*   Author's interview with Shen Yongyan.

77 *Zhou Jiannan*   Ibid.; Gilley, *Tiger,* 46; Shao, Li and Jiang, "Jiang Zemin's Time." Zhou Jiannan was the father of Zhou Xiaochuan, who served as chairman of the China Securities Regulatory Commission under Jiang and was appointed governor of the People's Bank of China, the top financial job in the country, at the end of 2002 (see Chapter 29).

77 *no margin for error*   Huang, Li, and Liu, *FAW Group Economic Research.*

77 *"too much burden"*   Shao, Li, and Jiang, "Jiang Zemin's Time."

77 *a thousand tons*   Wang, "Magnificent Younger Years."

78 *"not a novelist"*   Ibid.

78 *hosted a reunion*   Author's interview with Shen Yongyan; Guan, "Jiang Zemin at Changchun."

79 *They gave their director* [following]   Shao, Li, and Jiang, "Jiang Zemin's Time."

79 *150 yuan a month*   Ibid.

80 *Jiang began translating* [following]   Author's interview with Shen Yongyan. Shen reported that when Jiang sent him the manuscript in 1965, the entire book had been translated into Chinese. It was handwritten, not typed, mostly in Jiang's own hand—Shen knew Jiang's writing well—except for a small section where the writing wasn't Jiang's. "For that section, whether Jiang had someone who helped with the translation or it was a secretary taking dictation from Jiang, I never asked," said Shen. "Jiang also sent along the original Russian book so that I could check the translation against the original."

80 *"Most books were burned"*   See Chapters 8 and 10 for a continuation of the translation story.

80 *"Lei Wen"*   Shao, Li, and Jiang, "Jiang Zemin's Time."

80 *table tennis . . . not pompous*   Ibid.; Gilley, *Tiger,* 48 (referencing Guan, "Jiang Zemin at Changchun").

81 *inscriptions*   Guan, "Jiang Zemin at Changchun"; author's interview with Shen Yongyan.

Chapter 5. 1962–1976

82 *the catalyst was Wang Daohan*   Author's interview with Wang Daohan.

82 *"more than seven hundred people"*   Author's interview with Zeng Peiyan, Beijing, June 2001.

82 *Wang Yeping*   Li Jiang, ed., *Red Boat Symphony* (CPC Party History Press, February 1998).

82 *bus to work*   Gilley, *Tiger,* 48. The bus ride from their dormlike apartment, located in Caoyang New Village, to the Institute took about an hour.

83 *their own apartment*   Li, *Red Boat Symphony.*

83 *seven thousand Party officials*   Yang, *Biography,* chap. 3.

83 *"main tasks"*   Author's interview with Shen Yongyan.

84 *technical convention*   There was speculation that the Institute was working on military electronics like radar and communications.

84 *in Hong Kong*   Author's communication with historians, Beijing.

84 *Wang Daohan suggested*   Author's interview with Wang Daohan.

84 *The first hint of impending doom*   Various sources, including Gilley, *Tiger,* 49.

85 *purifying its ideology*   Commenting on Roderick MacFarquhar's magisterial *The Origins of the Cultural Revolution,* 3 vols. (New York: Columbia University Press, 1974, 1983, 1999), Jasper Becker wrote that "Mao's ultimate dread" was "the death of the revolution." MacFarquhar, he states, "takes the view that Mao was inspired by a genuine if misbegotten idealism, that he genuinely believed in a spiritual rebirth, and in the search for the revolutionary grail." *London Review of Books,* July 29, 1999.

85 *Liu Shaoqi died*   www.iisg.nl/~landsberger/lsq.html.

85 *"The absurd activities"*   *Time,* October 27, 1997.

86 *by way of Beijing*   Gilley, *Tiger,* 49.

86 *scene in Shanghai*   Yang, *Biography,* chap. 3; Gilley, *Tiger,* 52–53.

86 *"unprecedented destruction"*   Gilley, *Tiger,* 55.

86 *unconfirmed reports*   As Yang Zhongmei tells it (*Biography,* chap. 3), to Jiang's surprise, an old friend from the Communist underground informed him that Chen Pixian, the embattled Shanghai Party chief, wanted to meet him in the early days of the national immolation called the Cultural Revolution. Jiang was supposedly introduced to Chen and gave him a report on the situation in Beijing. United by mutual distress, the pair was said to have formed a fast friendship. On his departure Jiang supposedly said: "My leader is as

calm as ever." According to Jiang biographer Yang, Chen was purged for more than a decade, but years later, after being restored, he would throw his support behind Jiang's candidacy at crucial moments in 1985 and 1989, first for Shanghai mayor and then for Party general secretary (Yang, *Biography*, chaps. 5 and 7). If true, the special relationship between Jiang Zemin and Chen Pixian would be an ironic by-product of the Cultural Revolution.

86 *low profile . . . "expert but not Red"*   Gilley, *Tiger*, 51.

86 *"We must love"*   Yang, *Biography*, chap. 3.

87 *"A small comb"*   Ibid.

87 *"Red" family*   Li, *Red Boat Symphony*.

87 *"unbearable"*   Yang, *Biography*, chap. 3.

87 *Liu Zhenhua* [story]   Yang, *Biography*, chap. 3 (referencing *Southern Daily*, February 2, 1990).

87 *"bourgeois living"* [following]   Gilley, *Tiger*, 53.

88 *bright red graffiti*   Ibid., 52.

88 *"Comrade Yang"*   Yang, *Biography*, chap. 3 (referencing *Southern Daily*, February 2, 1990).

88 *organized lectures and courses* [following]   Wang Xiaopeng, *Chinese Leaders in My Eyes* (Dalian: Liaoning University Press, 1993), 1–18. I learned about Wang's book in Gilley, *Tiger*, 344.

88 *Jiang visited* [following]   Hua Mingchun, "My Days with Comrade Jiang Zemin," *Nanfan Daily*, September 1, 1991.

88 *piled high with books*   Wang, *Chinese Leaders in My Eyes*.

89 *"Personal things"*   Hua, "My Days with Comrade Jiang Zemin."

89 *No matter how noisy*   Wang, *Chinese Leaders in My Eyes*.

89 *roommate's family*   Hua, "My Days with Comrade Jiang Zemin."

90 *Zhou Enlai* [following]   Premier Zhou was accompanying the Albanian prime minister to visit the Wuhan Boiler Factory, which was next to Jiang's institute. Wang, *Chinese Leaders in My Eyes*.

90 *May Seventh Cadre School* [following]   Zhang Jiange, *China Agriculture Reclamation*, October 3, 1996. The Cadre School was located on the Bo Ai farm in Henan province (which Jiang visited during an inspection tour in 1996). During the Cultural Revolution thousands of such schools were established nationwide so that, according to Chairman Mao's worldview, educated people could learn from peasants and workers.

90 *crushed to death*   Author's communication with historians, Beijing.

90 *Jiang Zehui* [following]   Author's interview with Jiang Zehui.

91 *"rustification"*   Gilley, *Tiger*, 55.

91 *Mianheng worked* [following]   Author's interview with Jiang Zehui.

92 *"frontline workplace experiences"*   Yang, *Biography*, chap. 3.

92 *he was the teacher*   Under Jiang's direction, Chinese engineers would later transform the languishing Bucharest Heavy-Duty Machinery Plant into Romania's premier manufacturing plant.

93 *"opened my eyes"*   Gilley, *Tiger*, 62.

93 *Deng resumed his position*   Mao may have also been concerned about Zhou Enlai's growing power and sought Deng Xiaoping as a counterweight.

93 *"standard room"*   Author's interview with Shen Yongyan.

94 *secret negotiations*   The new era in Sino-U.S. relations, after two decades of vitriolic estrangement, had been arranged by Henry Kissinger, who had made a secret visit to China the previous July.

94 *run-down dwellings . . . "Intellectuals cannot"*   Gilley, *Tiger*, 62.

94 *In 1975 . . . Political Research Office . . . article* [following]   Author's interview with Teng Wensheng, Beijing, April 2004.

95 *"major crimes"*   Two other articles were also used against Deng Xiaoping: "20 Plans of Industry" from the State Planning Commission and "Synopsis of Science and Technology Development" prepared by Hu Yaobang, then Party secretary of the Academy of Sciences.

Chapter 6. 1976–1985

96 *1976 was a year*   Yang, *Biography*, chap. 4.

96 *Mao's demise* [following]   Ibid.; Gilley, *Tiger*, 62–64.

97 *caught by surprise*   Author's interview with Wang Huijiong.

97 *the advice of Wang*   Author's interview with Wang Daohan.

97 *Jiang's assignment* [Shanghai story]   Gilley, *Tiger*, 63–64; Yang, *Biography*, chap. 4.

97 *everybody else*   Yang, *Biography*, chap. 4. Yang also tells the unconfirmed story that at this time Jiang, seeking to renew old ties, paid a visit to Chen Pixian, the Shanghai Party chief whom Yang said Jiang had met in the first frenzied days of the Cultural Revolution. Throughout his time in Shanghai, Jiang supposedly kept in contact with Chen, giving him updates and receiving guidance in return. Yang adds that in Jiang's report to Li Xiannian, who would later become president of China, he noted that Chen Pixian had not yet been restored to his prior position of leadership. In 1977 Chen was appointed Party secretary of Yunnan province and then of Hubei province.

98 *the Gang of Four were incarcerated*   The Gang of Four were charged with persecuting and framing more than 700,000 people—some 35,000 of whom had been executed. Jiang Qing was sentenced to death, later commuted to life in prison (where she committed suicide in 1991).

98 *Two Whatevers*   The actual words, published in *People's Daily* on February 7, 1977, were "We will resolutely uphold whatever policy decisions Chairman Mao made, and unswervingly follow whatever instructions Chairman Mao gave."

98 *he was passed over*   Yang, *Biography*, chap. 4. Certain officials who had not yet been reinstated and were jealous of Jiang may have made outlandish accusations to the Party, saying among other things that he had been active in the Anti-Rightist Campaign and, more absurd, that he had been promoted by the Gang of Four. Even though the charges were fabricated, the Party had so many unemployed officials backed up for rehabilitation that they decided to leave Jiang on the side, neither promoting nor demoting him but simply having him remain where he was.

98 *Teng Wensheng* [following]   Author's interview with Teng Wensheng.

98–99 *good timing . . . traumatic period* [following]   Author's interview with Wang Daohan; also Gilley, *Tiger*, 65; Yang, *Biography*, chap. 4. Prior to his reinstatement Wang worked as deputy director of the information and research department in the Machine-Building Ministry, far beneath his previous position as vice minister in the same ministry. Wang returned to power in September 1978 and was appointed mayor of Shanghai in early 1980.

100 *"Marx sits up"*   George Church, in *Time* (1985 Person of the Year), January 6, 1986.

101 *Xiaogang . . . "responsibility system"* [following]   Several sources, including Yang, *Common Leader*, 146–147. The farmers' decision to privatize was extraordinarily risky, because the political atmosphere, so soon after Mao's death, was still unclear. Within a few days, the secret pact was discovered by the county Party secretary, who concluded that these villagers were promoting capitalism, but with starvation imminent, he had no choice but to let them try. With the harvest came the surprise: agricultural production had increased significantly. Soon, the "responsibility system" began spreading to other provinces. While there continued to be ideological debate at the highest level of the Party, Deng Xiaoping used the farmers' success—"Seek truth from facts"—to help shape the nature and mechanisms of early economic reform. The essence of reform in rural areas was giving farmers free access to the market and enabling them to compete in the

market. As a result, China was transformed from a nation always short of agricultural products to a nation abundant with them.

101–102 *SEZs . . . Gu Mu . . . chief task* [following] Yang, *Biography*, chap. 4. The two commissions were the State Administration Commission on Import and Export Affairs, and the State Administration Commission on Foreign Investment.

102 *"Four Transformations"* Nathan and Gilley, *Rulers* (2003), 40. Both editions of this remarkable book are said to be derived from extensive, highly confidential personnel files of the Party's Organizational Department, which is responsible for assignments and promotions of key officials.

102 *general office* Author's communication with historians, Beijing.

102 *"Leading Group"* In China's system of governance, where the Party always plays the "vanguard role," each administrative area has a "Leading Group" of Party members that sets policy and oversees operations.

102 *NPC* The National People's Congress is, according to the Constitution, the highest organ of state power, but in operating reality it has always followed instructions from the Party, the Politburo, and its Standing Committee. It is the legislative body that formulates laws, elects leaders, delegates authority, and supervises other governing bodies. The NPC has the right to enact and amend the State Constitution and to enact and amend basic laws concerning criminal offenses, civil affairs, state organs, and other matters; it examines and approves the state budget and plans for national economic and social development; it elects national leaders, including the state president and vice president, the premier and other members of the State Council, the chairman of the (State) Central Military Commission, the president of the Supreme People's Court, and the procurator-general. Each NPC is elected for a term of five years; it meets during the first quarter of each year; the NPC's permanent and leading body is its Standing Committee. http://english.peopledaily.com.cn/data/organs/npc.shtml.

102 *he gave a briefing* The photograph of Jiang Zemin on the cover of this book comes from this time.

102 *CPPCC* The Chinese People's Political Consultative Conference is the national, assembly-like forum designed to unify the country and promote "socialist democracy" by multiparty cooperation and political consultation; it brings together and enables advisory input from all sectors of society—"democratic parties," ethnic minorities, various organizations, representatives from Hong Kong, Macao, and Taiwan, and public figures from all walks of life—all under the Communist Party, which is the "vanguard" of the people and the nation; the CPPCC meets concurrently with the NPC during the first quarter of each year. www.china.org.cn/english/27750.htm.

102 *"pioneers"* Yang, *Biography*, chap. 4.

102 *balance . . . barbed-wire* Gilley, *Tiger*, 66–68.

102 *UN-sponsored world tour* [following] Private interview of Lu Zifen, delegation member and former Party secretary of Xiamen; the author gained access to notes from the unpublished interview.

103 *The SEZs were controversial* Ibid.

104 *Jiang made his case,* [following] Yang, *Biography*, chap. 4.

104 *Shenzhen* www.nearchina.com/frame/government/cpcjiangzemin.htm.

104 *Zhang Aiping* Dong, *Zhang Aiping Biography*.

105 *Zhao interviewed* According to Gao Xin, Jiang's promotions were supported by a close adviser to Zhao Ziyang, State Councilor Zhang Jinfu, who had been the superior officer of Jiang Shangqing, Jiang Zemin's martyred foster father, during the anti-Japanese war in Anhui province. Gao Xin, *Jiang Zemin's Road to Power* (Hong Kong: Mirror Books, 1997).

105 *major promotion* Jiang's appointment came within two months of his being sidelined at a lesser job. His early career exemplified the Chinese saying, "Wong lost his horse, but he did not know whether it was a blessing or a curse." Yang, *Biography*, chap. 4.

105 *feel at home*   Gilley, *Tiger,* 72. Qiao Shi, who would become a major figure in Jiang's later career, was also elected to the CPC Central Committee in 1982. Qiao's power in the Party would come sooner than Jiang's.

106 *"As an intellectual"*   Yang, *Biography,* chap. 4. The news conference was his first after becoming mayor of Shanghai in 1985.

106 *doctorate at MIT*   Gilley, *Tiger,* 70.

106 *Hewlett-Packard . . . Dr. Liu Chining* [following] . . . *President Ronald Reagan*   Author's communication, Beijing.

107 *"My experience . . . my habit"*   Gilley, *Tiger,* 69.

107 *Jiang was in charge of*   Ibid., 70.

107 *"we are fifteen years behind"*   Dong Huanliang, "Economic and Scientific China," *Weekly Economic Report* (BBC).

107 *"Our level"*   *Jingji Ribao (Economic Daily),* August 1983.

107 *a massive smuggling case*   Yang, *Biography,* chap. 4.

107 *unspoiled by success*   Author's interview with Shen Yongyan.

108 *"Jiang had become more mature"*   Author's interview with Wang Huijiong.

108 *"Most often my brother"*   Gilley, *Tiger,* 71.

108 *appointed associate dean*   Author's interview with Jiang Zehui.

109 *launched . . . congratulated*   Gilley, *Tiger,* 78.

109 *"set goals"*   Author's interview with Zeng Peiyan.

110 *"was not accomplished"*   Gilley, *Tiger,* 71.

110 *Chen Yun*   Ibid., 72–73; Yang, *Biography,* chap. 4. Whereas official reports said that Chen Yun requested the visit, insiders claim that it came at Jiang's initiative after hearing of Chen's interest in electronics. The *People's Daily* article, which Jiang may have had a hand in, was titled "Comrade Chen Yun Noted that We Should Concentrate Our Efforts to Develop Our Electronic Industry and Our Finance and Economic Cadres Should Keep Up with New Knowledge and New Technologies." Nathan and Gilley, *Rulers,* 146.

110 *Jiang wrote an article*   Gilley, *Tiger,* 73. Jiang's mainstream article, entitled "Carry Out Party Rectification in a Thorough Way by Constantly Seeking Unity of Thinking," was published in May 1984.

111 *"I participated"*   Author's interview with Wang Daohan.

111 *delegation to Shanghai . . . Toffler*   Yang, *Biography,* chap. 5.

112 *"chief clerk"*   Gilley, *Tiger,* 75.

112 *maintained his ministerial responsibilities*   Author's communication with historians, Beijing.

112 *as a disguise*   Gilley, *Tiger,* 75–76.

Chapter 7. 1985–1986

113–114 *"heavily loaded cart" . . . "major changes"* [following]   Yang, *Biography,* chap. 5.

114 *minor resistance*   Ibid. One questioner may have been Bo Yibo, who would become one of Jiang's key supporters in later years.

114 *respected elder*   Yang Zhongmei (*Biography,* chap. 5) states that the elder who led Jiang's supporters was none other than Chen Pixian, the former Shanghai Party chief whom Jiang had visited (according to Yang), at great personal risk, during the Cultural Revolution.

114 *visited Yangzhou*   Su Zaiqing, *Guan Jian* ([*Mirror for Officials*] Henan People's Press, 1993).

114 *"few are taking bets"*   David Dodwell, in *Financial Times,* October 29, 1985.

115 *"talk less"*   Gilley, *Tiger,* 75 ("less empty talk and more concrete action").

115 *had to be food* [following]   Author's interview with Ye Gongqi.

115 *"three faces"*   Yang, *Biography,* chap. 5. These included building fifty million square feet of residential areas, passenger bridges at key traffic intersections, and a tunnel under the Huangpu River; adding four hundred international phone lines; improving the water

supply system; erecting hotels, apartment buildings, and office buildings for foreign businessmen; developing a subway and elevated rail system; and connecting Shanghai to its neighbors by freeway.

115–116 *died . . . Qingming . . . General Zhang*   Gilley, *Tiger,* 79–80.

116 *"cold dinner incident"* [following]   Yang, *Biography,* chap. 5.

117 *helped dockworkers*   Ibid.

117 *retail prices shot up*   Gilley, *Tiger,* 81–82.

117 *Tongji University*   Ibid., 82; *LAT,* December 5, 1985.

117 *Comprehensive Plan*   Yang, *Biography,* chap. 5.

118 *$3.2 billion*   www.nearchina.com/frame/government/cpcjiangzemin.htm.

118 *Jiang's management style* [following]   Author's interview with Ye Gongqi.

118 *His office* [following]   Li Jiang, ed., *Red Boat Symphony* (CPC Party History Press, February 1998).

119 *personal life . . . apartment* [following]   Ibid.

120 *piano*   Ibid.

120 *she was stopped*   Ibid.; *SCMP,* October 10, 2002.

120 *health and morale* [following]   Author's interview with Ye Gongqi.

121 *Tong Zonghai*   Author's interview with Tong Zonghai.

121 *Jia Ting'an*   Author's communication, Beijing.

122 *"totally restored"*   Similarly, Jiang also helped one of his former professors, Zhong Zhaolin, chairman of the electrical engineering department at Shanghai Jiaotong University, who had been transferred from Xi'an to Shanghai for medical care. When Jiang learned that his old professor was back in the hospital, he went to visit and discovered that, as an out-of-town patient, Zhong was not getting the treatment he needed. Jiang had him transferred to a better facility and, in spite of his busy schedule, insisted on visiting the elderly academic once a month.

Jiang knew that if it became known that the mayor could carve time out of his hectic schedule to see a patient regularly, this would compel the doctors and nurses to pay special attention and pressure the hospital to give him the best treatment. This personifies the Chinese proverb that "someone has to light up a candle because it cannot automatically give light." It also shows that regarding Jiang's respect for his professors, there was no difference between Jiang the young student and Jiang the powerful mayor. "Every time I saw Professor Zhong, over all the years irrespective of my position," said Jiang, "I was always respectful of him." Author's interview with Tong Zonghai.

122 *seminar*   Yang, *Biography,* chap. 5.

122 *Queen Elizabeth* [following]   Ibid.; Xinhua, October 15, 1986; UPI, October 15, 1986.

123 *Niang, died*   Author's interview with Jiang Zehui.

124 *formal trips . . . hosting*   Yang, *Biography,* chap. 5.

125 *"last cake"*   Kathy Chen and Joseph Kahn, in *AWSJ,* February 6, 1995.

125 *false rumor*   Numerous sources, including Gilley, *Tiger.* 81. China's so-called "princelings" or "red princes"—offspring of elders or high officials who often took advantage of their relationships to advance their government or business careers—were increasingly resented by the masses as reform generated larger income gaps between different sectors of society.

125 *wives*   Nathan and Gilley, *Rulers,* 148.

Chapter 8. 1986–1989

126 *"ultimate leadership" . . . "bourgeois liberalization"* [following]   Yang, *Biography,* chap. 6.

127 *Fang Lizhi . . . Jiaotong University* [following; entire section]   Ibid.; Gilley, *Tiger,* 84–94; author's interview with Ye Gongqi; Ina Chang, for AP, December 21, 22, 1986; Xinhua, December 25, 1986; Daniel Southerland, in *WP,* December 22, 1986; JEN, December 22, 1986; Shanghai City Service, December 22, 1986 (BBC).

128 *more and more posters*   Adding to the tense environment was a rumor that an overzealous guard had pummeled one or more Jiaotong students after they had climbed onstage during a rock concert given by the American singing duo Jan and Dean.

132 *"sympathetic"... "simple-minded"*   Author's interview with Ye Gongqi.

133 *Hu Yaobang* [following]   Yang, *Biography*, chap. 6.

133 *Hu was accused*   Peng Zhen, chairman of the National People's Congress, in a press conference.

133 *Hamlet's soliloquy*   www.nearchina.com/frame/government/cpcjiangzemin.htm

133 *"We should persist"*   Shanghai City Service, January 7, 1987 (BBC).

134 *"If the masses"*   Jim Mann, in *LAT*, June 25, 1989.

134 *regular meetings... look inept*   Gilley, *Tiger*, 95.

134 *broken water pipe* [following]   Author's communication from Xu Jingen, March 2004.

135 *"The Other Side"*   Xu Jingen, *PD*, July 6, 1987.

135 *Xu Jingen*   Xu was a well-known critic who had become popular due to his short, sharp reporting style. His articles were usually published on the front page of major local newspapers.

135 *"Mayor XX"*   In Chinese, *moumou shizhang*.

135 *classic story*   Following is the story told by Xu Jingen in his *People's Daily* article (July 6, 1987) to illustrate the principle *"Shi Bi Gong Qing"* ("the boss must handle every detail himself"), where a leader's concern over apparent trivialities can discern deeper insights. There was once a prime minister named Bing Ji (in the Han Xuan administration of Emperor Liu Xun) who, while riding in a carriage, came across bodies of people who had been killed or injured by mass fighting. Though their bodies were lying by the road, he did not stop. Later on his ride, he noticed a person chasing a cow, which was running and gasping for breath. The prime minister ordered his staff to stop and bring the man over so that he could ask him, "For how many miles have you been chasing the cow?" The prime minister's aides thought that he did not investigate that which he should and he inquired after things that were not worth his attention. Prime Minister Bing Ji answered his aides, "The mass fighting is the responsibility of law enforcement officials; it is not my responsibility to investigate. ['In today's view,' interjects Xu Jingen, 'Prime Minister Bing Ji's statement is not correct. Since it is an issue of life and death that he discovered, he should investigate.'] Now is early Spring; the weather is not supposed to be too hot. If the man had not been chasing the cow for too long and the cow was already gasping for breath, I'm afraid it may be caused by the heat. If it is so hot in early Spring, then this is an obvious abnormality of our climate, which may cause damage to the country's economy. Therefore I could not help worrying and needed to look into it." After hearing this explanation, the prime minister's aides were impressed that he thought so deeply about a matter.

135 *"I was bothered"*   Author's communication from Xu Jingen.

137 *Qiao Shi*   Xinhua, October 28, 1987.

138 *bimonthly seminar*   www.nearchina.com/frame/government/cpcjiangzemin.htm; initiated in early 1987.

139 *126 stamps... "mortified"... "One-Chop Zhu"*   Gilley, *Tiger*, 102; Xinhua, March 14, 1998 (BBC).

139 *ten thousand Shanghai dwellers*   Xinhua, December 5, 1987.

139 *economic reform*   Problems included limited managerial autonomy, chronic imbalances of supply and demand, no national market for price determinations, and capricious regulatory and tax policies.

139 *fact-finding mission to Guangdong... ten thousand officials*   Xinhua, January 24, 1988; Gilley, *Tiger*, 102.

139 *structural changes*   Yang, *Biography*, chap. 6.

140 *"not intelligent"... "shrewd"*   Ibid. In China, the Shanghainese are known for being shrewd (*jing*, meaning astute, sharp, and clever with overtones of canny and cunning).

140 *"one of the most 'Western' "*   Gilley, *Tiger,* 109.
140 *"more like a businessman"*   Author's interview with Maurice Greenberg, New York, January 2002.
140 *his two grandchildren*   Author's interview with Jiang Zehui.
141 *February 1988 . . . 1989*   Yang, *Biography,* chap. 6; author's communication with historians, Beijing.
141 *"no taboo"*   Xinhua, March 12, 1988 (BBC).
142 *a spate of local disasters*   Xinhua, April 13, 1988.
142 *"I should shoulder the responsibility"*   Ibid.
142 *Miss Shanghai*   *Zhongguo Tongxun She* (Hong Kong), May 9, 1988 (BBC); JEN, May 10, 1988. Mayors of other cities used similar reasoning to cancel beauty pageants.
142–143 *inflation . . . "gone whiter" . . . freeze prices*   Colina MacDougall, in *Financial Times,* May 6, 1988; Gilley, *Tiger,* 105–8.
143 *become a professor*   Author's interview with Shen Yongyan.

Chapter 9. JANUARY–MAY 1989

147 *Deng Xiaoping's aggressive reforms*   Fewsmith, *China Since Tiananmen,* 28, 70.
148 *the regular Friday meeting* [following]   Author's interview with a firsthand witness to Hu Yaobang's heart attack.
148 *Tiananmen Square . . .* World Economic Herald [following]   This section is derived from various sources, including Zhang Liang, Andrew J. Nathan, and Perry Link, eds., *The Tiananmen Papers: The Chinese Leadership's Decision to Use Force Against Their Own People—In Their Own Words* (New York: PublicAffairs, 2001), purportedly based on inner-Party documents; Yang, *Biography,* chap. 7; Gilley, *Tiger,* 114–48; *NYT;* AP; Shanghai City Service (BBC); China News Service (Beijing, BBC); Xinhua (English and Chinese [BBC]); UPI; *WP; LAT;* JEN; *Christian Science Monitor; Ming Pao* (Hong Kong, BBC); *TKP* (BBC); *Financial Times; Newsday;* author's interviews with Wang Daohan, Jiang Zehui, and Ye Gongqi; and author's communication, Beijing.
149 *"substantive"* [following]   Yang, *Biography,* chap. 7.
149 *"mourn Hu"*   Nicholas D. Kristof, in *NYT,* April 25, 1989.
150–152 *an advance copy . . . 4:30 . . . 8:30 . . . Comrade Jiang . . . Wang Daohan . . . Foreign newspapers . . . meeting at his home . . . "urgent message"* [following]   Liang, Nathan, and Link, *Tiananmen Papers,* 91–94.
150 *inciting sections . . . Qin cajoled*   Ibid., 92. The offending content, suggesting that Hu Yaobang's record should be reassessed and the condemnation of "bourgeois liberalism" should be reversed, amounted to only a few hundred characters out of about twenty thousand.
150 *Jiang remained in Shanghai*   Author's communication with historians, Beijing.
151 *a nationwide strike*   On the same day in Xi'an, violence broke out between local armed police and people commemorating Hu Yaobang. Vehicles and government buildings were set on fire.
151 *"my help"*   Author's interview with Wang Daohan.
151 *Whether Qin*   Liang, Nathan, and Link, *Tiananmen Papers,* 29, reports that Qin decided to move up publication of the special edition in order to get it to Beijing on April 22, in time for Hu Yaobang's memorial.
152 *"anything wrong . . . self-criticism"*   Liang, Nathan, and Link, *Tiananmen Papers,* 94.
152–154 *"For your information" . . . "intensify" . . . after midnight* [following]   Ibid.
152–153 *Qin was ill . . . "final conclusion"*   Yang, *Biography,* chap. 7; Gilley, *Tiger,* 119.
153 *"I was there!"*   Author's interview with Ye Gongqi.
153 *"He would ask me"*   Author's interview with Jiang Zehui.
153 *"son-in-law"*   *Ming Pao* (Hong Kong), April 28, 1989 (BBC).
154 *"turmoil"*   Gilley, *Tiger,* 119. In Chinese, *dongluan.*

154 *"plot"*   Liang, Nathan, and Link, *Tiananmen Papers,* 73.

155 *"international criticism"*   Ibid., 94.

155 *"moved too hastily"*   Ibid., 105.

156 *"patriotic"*   There is dispute over the impact of Zhao Ziyang's speech. Some say it defused tension and encouraged students to return to their campuses. Other say the opposite, that students were already returning to their campuses until Zhao's speech whipped up their emotions and they returned to the protests.

156–157 *Politburo meeting . . . "fallout" . . . "hasty" . . . "followed Party principles"*   Liang, Nathan, and Link, *Tiananmen Papers,* 135. Government sources claim all this never happened.

157 *"has been provoked"*   *Ming Pao* (Hong Kong), May 14, 1989 (BBC). Government sources claim this never happened.

158 *paper lost its punch*   Gilley, *Tiger,* 124–25. After a difficult year the *Herald* would be shut down, and in contrast to the massive demonstrations in 1989, the move would engender minimal protest. Qin Benli lived under house arrest for that year, then was diagnosed with advanced stomach cancer. The former editor was given a private hospital room and the best medical treatment, a privilege likely approved by Jiang; he was allowed to see Chinese visitors but no foreigners. Qin Benli died on April 15, 1991, two years to the day after Hu Yaobang's death.

158 *high fever . . . "I expected"*   Author's interview with Yan Mingfu.

159 *"We old comrades" . . . "Some people object"*   Liang, Nathan, and Link, *Tiananmen Papers,* 204–5.

160 *"Sino-Soviet weather"*   China News Service, May 18, 1989 (BBC).

160 *"reasonable demands" . . . "extreme shock"*   Shanghai City Service, May 18, 1989 (BBC).

161 *"patriotic feelings" . . . "Such dialogue"*   Shanghai City Service, May 18, 1989 (BBC).

161 *"We have come too late"*   Liang, Nathan, and Link, *Tiananmen Papers,* 217.

161 *martial law*   Ibid., 233–34.

162 *"leading conservatives"*   William Sexton, in *Newsday,* May 18, 1989, 33.

162 *"nominate Jiang Zemin"*   Author's communication with historians, Beijing.

162 *ouster of Zhao*   Liang, Nathan, and Link, *Tiananmen Papers,* 268–72.

162 *four leaders* [following]   Ibid., 278–79. Government sources claim this never happened.

162 *"patriotic enthusiasm"* [following]   Gilley, *Tiger,* 136.

163 *escorted Wan*   Liang, Nathan, and Link, *Tiananmen Papers,* 291. Jiang was accompanied by Zhu Rongji and Ye Gongqi; the party left in two minibuses guarded by the Shanghai garrison. Yang, *Biography,* chap. 7.

163 *"health grounds"*   John Elliot, in *Financial Times,* May 26, 1989.

163 *a formal letter*   Gilley, *Tiger,* 136. Wan Li also postponed the upcoming meeting of the NPC Standing Committee.

163 *historic determination* [following]   Liang, Nathan, and Link, *Tiananmen Papers,* 308–14.

163 *Deng's decision*   Author's communication, Beijing.

Chapter 10. MAY–JUNE 1989

164 *urgent message* [following]   Yang, *Biography,* chap. 7. As for the precise day that Deng offered Jiang the top Party post, opinions differ. *Tiananmen Papers* has Jiang's appointment being voted on during a five-hour meeting of eight elders, led by Deng, on May 27; Jiang is then flown to Beijing on May 30; he meets senior elders Chen Yun and Li Xiannian that night and Deng the next morning, May 31 (323–24). Earlier and without *Tiananmen Papers'* claimed Party documents, Yang said Jiang came to Beijing on May 23; Gilley said May 22 (*Tiger,* 133).

164 *Deng offered* Yang, *Biography*, chap. 7.
164 *"I am afraid"* . . . *"all support you"* Ching Pao (Hong Kong), October 5, 1994, 58–59 (BBC).
164 *"can't bear"* Gilley, *Tiger*, 134.
164 *Jiang wondered* Author's communication, Beijing.
165 *Wang Yeping* Ching Pao (Hong Kong), October 5, 1994 (BBC); author's interview with Shen Yongyan.
165 *"don't survive"* Gilley, *Tiger*, 134.
165 *called upon Wang Daohan* [following] Author's interview with Wang Daohan.
165 *"Lin Zexu"* He was also the one who first introduced America to the Chinese people in a book about world history and geography.
166 *"If the leadership we present"* Gilley, *Tiger*, 131; Robert L. Suettinger, *Beyond Tiananmen: The Politics of U.S.–China Relations 1989–2000* (Washington, D.C.: Brookings Institution Press), 2003, 76.
166 *"factions"* Gilley, *Tiger*, 132.
167 *Li Xiannian* Several sources; *Tiananmen Papers* puts Li with Deng and Chen Yun as the three who supported Jiang prior to discussions with the other elders (309).
167 *Chen Pixian* Yang, *Biography*, chaps. 3, 5, 7.
167 *quashing* Nathan and Gilley, *Rulers*, 147.
167 *"Without electric power"* Gilley, *Tiger*, 137.
167 *emergency call* Liang, Nathan, and Link, *Tiananmen Papers*, 323.
167 *broke the news* . . . *" 'Down with reform!' "* . . . *"former isolation"* . . . *"retire"* Ibid., 324, 325, 327, 328.
167 *"Jiang Zemin as the core"* Senior Party officials state that Deng recommended Jiang be considered as the "core" on June 16. (Author's communication with historians, Beijing.) The various accounts do not yet harmonize.
168 *"On the True Nature"* Liang, Nathan, and Link, *Tiananmen Papers*, 330–338. A similar report by the Ministry of State Security, also prepared on instructions from Li Peng, confirmed "ideological and political infiltration" by clandestine Western sources, including George Soros (338–348).
168 *"clear Tiananmen"* Ibid., 362.
168 *"We must be merciless"* . . . *"No bloodshed"* Ibid., 369–370.
169 *"Infantrymen"* Ibid., 373.
169 *seventeen* . . . *lead tank* James Lilley with Jeffrey Lilley, *China Hands* (New York: Public Affairs, 2004), 371.
169 *Room 202* . . . *Li Peng* [following] Author's interview with Teng Wensheng. The other speechwriter was Lu Zhichao.
169 *"two honorable scholars"* Jiang used the word *xiucai*, which means "scholars" with an honorable connotation.
170 *218 civilians* Liang, Nathan, and Link, *Tiananmen Papers*, 436.
170 *"sizable role"* . . . *"The leadership"* Willy Wo-Lap Lam, in *SCMP*, March 24, 1994.
170 *James Lilley* James Lilley with Jeffrey Lilley, *China Hands*, 297–334 (especially 307).
170 *one-tenth* . . . *"bloody" lessons* Xinhua, September 27, 1989; Gilley, *Tiger*, 141.
171 *reached Shanghai* . . . *forty thousand cadres* . . . *"conceal history"* Gilley, *Tiger*, 143–44; Karl Schoenberger, in *LAT*, June 10, 1989, 1.
171–172 *"core"* . . . *leave politics* [following] Author's communication with historians in Beijing. Attendees at this auspicious meeting were said to be Yang Shangkun, Wan Li, Jiang Zemin, Li Peng, Qiao Shi, Yao Yilin, Song Ping, and Li Ruihuan; Deng Xiaoping, *Selected Works*, vol. 3, 1982–1992, 301; *PD*, "Urgent Tasks of China's Third Generation of Collective Leadership," June 16, 1989, *People's Daily* website: http://english. peopledaily.com.cn/dengxp/vol3/text/d1010.html.
172 *notion of a "core leader"* Frederick C. Teiwes, "Politics at the 'Core': The Political

Circumstances of Mao Zedong, Deng Xiaoping and Jiang Zemin," http://rspas.anu.edu.au/ccc/morrison00.pdf.

172 *characterizes "core"* Fewsmith, *China Since Tiananmen*, 163.

172 *"very serious mistakes"* James Pringle, *Guardian* (London), June 26, 1989.

173 *"accommodated, encouraged"* Fewsmith, *China Since Tiananmen*, 29–30. The public case against Zhao Ziyang, which included the charge of "premeditation," was presented by Beijing Major Chen Xitong to the National People's Congress on June 30.

173 *"I feel the heavy burden"* Xinhua, June 24, 1989.

173 *draft his inauguration speech* Author's interview with Teng Wensheng.

173 *"looked a bit glum"* Richard Bernstein, in *NYT*, June 25, 1989, 12.

173–174 *"his popularity"* Jim Abrams, AP, June 24, 1989.

174 *"succession government"* . . . *"This decision"* Jonathan S. Landry, for UPI, June 24, 1989.

174 *"Beijing protesters"* James Pringle, in *Guardian* (London), June 26, 1989.

174 *"In terms of balance"* William Sexton, in *Newsday*, June 25, 1989 (quoting Stanley Rosen of the University of Southern California).

174 *"very smooth"* Jim Abrams, for AP, June 24, 1989.

174 *"caliber"* Sheryl WuDunn, in *NYT*, June 25, 1989.

174 *"not an iota"* Xinhua, June 28, 1989.

174 *"contribution"* Gilley, *Tiger*, 137.

174 *Jiang's takeover* Lam, *Era*, 51.

174 *For Jiang's family* Author's interview with Jiang Zehui.

175 *Mianheng* [following] Ibid; author's communications, Beijing and Philadelphia.

175–176 *accepted in 1985* . . . *$800* . . . *"dinky"* . . . *Kevin Scoles* . . . *"brilliant researcher"* [following] Matt Forney, *WSJ*, November 1, 1999.

176 *June 4* . . . *June 24* [following] Author's communication, Beijing.

176 *"endeared him"* Ibid; Forney, *WSJ*, November 1, 1999.

176 *"My father"* *Fortune*, July 31, 1989.

177 *"popular in the public"* Ted Duncombe, for AP, June 30, 1989.

177 *doctorate* Jiang Mianheng's thesis was in high-temperature superconductivity (Forney, *WSJ*, November 1, 1999), a "hot" area of research at the time that sought to make practical use of the phenomenon of the disappearance of electrical resistance in certain complex metals, alloys, and ceramics under certain stringent conditions. His adviser, Professor Allen Rothwarf, died in 1998, though a couple of years earlier he was able to visit China as Mianheng's guest. (The Institute [IEEE] Obituaries, September 1, 1998; author's communication in Beijing and Philadelphia.)

177 *"Yuntou"* [following] Author's interview with Shen Yongyan.

178 *book's introduction* Jiang wrote, "The author was my mentor during my internship in the Soviet Union. . . . Before the Cultural Revolution, I completed the translation, but due to the Cultural Revolution and my job changes, I was not able to get it published. . . . Fortunately, through ten years of turmoil, Comrade Shen kept the complete manuscript." The book was published in 1990.

178 *alone in Zhongnanhai* Nathan and Gilley, *Rulers*, 148.

179 *"deep canyon"* . . . *"thin ice"* [paraphrase] Gilley, *Tiger*, 148.

179 *"Li Peng is ruthless"* *FEER*, May 12, 1990.

Chapter 11. JULY–DECEMBER 1989

180 *"bitter fruit* . . . *"We told you so"* Fewsmith, *China Since Tiananmen*, 32–33. The senior leader was Song Ping.

180 *"We practice our socialism"* Xinhua, July 12, 1989.

180 *"boldly learn"* Xinhua, July 15, 1989; *TKP*, August 15, 2001.

181 *"seven things"* Xinhua, July 29, 1989.

181 *regulations would be enacted* Jasper Becker, *The Chinese*, 308.

181 *first trip* Nailene Chou Wiest, in *SCMP*, September 5, 1989.

181 *"The first time"* Author's interview with Jiang Zehui.

181 *grand celebration* [following] Gilley, *Tiger*, 163.

181 *commemoration* Su Zaiqing, in *Guan Jian* [*Mirror for Officials*] (Henan People's Press, 1993).

182 *"Party Center"* Nathan and Gilley, *Rulers* (2003), 7. Zeng's appointment was approved by Li Peng and Yang Shangkun (Ibid., 90).

182 *Zeng Qinghong* [following] Nathan and Gilley, *Rulers*, 84; Gao Xin, *Jiang Zemin's Counselors* (Hong Kong: Mirror Books, 1996); Yang, *Biography*, chap. 8; Gilley, *Tiger*, 135; author's communication, Beijing.

182 *Organization Department* Joseph Fewsmith, "Generational Transition in China," *Washington Quarterly*, Autumn 2002.

182 *"heroes"* Xinhua, August 8, 1989 (BBC).

182 *Party cells* JEN, August 28, 1989: Jasper Becker, *The Chinese*, 308. Strengthening Party cells reinforced the dual system of governance that had been weakened as part of Zhao Ziyang's reforms.

182 Grand Ceremony [following] Author's interview with Li Qiankuan, Beijing, September 2002. The film was produced by the Changchun Film Studio, which is called the "cradle of New China's film industry." Founded in 1946, it created and produced more than six hundred feature and traditional opera films, of which about seventy won awards. Jiang Zemin was quite aware of Changchun's famous film studio, since the city's other major enterprise was First Automotive Works, where Jiang had worked for six years.

"We see in the film the sacrifices and extraordinary efforts of the first generation of leaders represented by Chairman Mao Zedong in bringing a new nation to the people," commented director Li. "Because there are many massive historical scenes, particularly battles, the production was difficult and our team faced substantial challenges. With our limited budget, we couldn't afford multiple takes, so we shot many scenes, including the major battles, under horrible weather conditions."

183 *Censors* "Actually, the film's controversy centered around two factors," noted director Li. "First, I didn't emphasize that the civil war was 'the people's war.' Second, I portrayed Chiang Kai-shek, Mao's sworn enemy, in a reasonably positive light, which represented my personal feelings about the man, even my appreciation of him. When I characterized Chiang, I didn't treat him as a dry, mean militarist, which he was not. In my film he had a fully formed character and expressed diverse emotions. He was a real human being. Traditionally in Chinese films and television programs since 1949, Chiang had been portrayed as an evil, feelingless robot. In my movie Chiang came across as a sophisticated person. To his grandson, he was a kind and loving grandfather; to his son, he was a warm and caring father; to his generals, he was a tough commander-in-chief, the supreme commander of the Nationalist military force. I believe I portrayed him accurately. Yet, some fearful government functionaries felt very uneasy seeing a humanized Chiang Kai-shek on the screen. . . .

"I believe that in artistic creation we have to humanize historical events by emphasizing the key people involved. My film wasn't a history textbook. It used stories of the personalities to touch audiences and stimulate them to think. Human nature doesn't differ among peoples. It doesn't matter whether you're Chinese or American, Communist or Democrat or Republican, human stories reach everyone. I believe that *Kai Guo Da Dian, The Grand Ceremony of the Founding of the Country*, was, for my country, a breakthrough. Yet some government officials and Communist Party historians argued that it wasn't appropriate to portray these historical figures as I did in the film. It's natural to have dissimilar perspectives between Party scholars and independent artists regarding historical events. However, because of a few negative opinions, the decision was that my film was not to be released. That wasn't right." Author's interview with Li Qiankuan.

184 *"another film"*   The earlier film was *The General with a Sword,* which told stories of the civil war. But that film focused only on the prelude to the pivotal Huaihai battle.

185 *Many suggestions followed*   The first to speak was General Hong Xuezhi, who fast-talked in his Anhui accent: "The film is good, accurate; battle scenes are well done, like real battles. It wasn't easy for Chairman Mao to lead us to fight for our new state. Many sacrificed their lives for New China. The film shows this. However, I have a suggestion. The Liberation War [civil war] was a people's war. For example, during the Huaihai battle, there were about six civilians supporting each soldier, including stretcher teams, logistic support teams, ammunition teams, etc. We could have never won the war if our soldiers had fought alone. Without millions of civilians working with us, it would have been impossible. Director Li, I suggest that you add some scenes showing civilians supporting our soldiers on the battlefields."

"I agree, General—I will definitely add such scenes," said director Li, who years later confirmed that he really thought General Hong's advice helpful.

Yao Yilin, executive vice premier, offered his ideas: "Could you possibly add some archival materials of the Chinese People's Political Consultative Conference? On September 21, 1949, the CPPCC convened its first meeting, where the Communist Party discussed with other parties and independent groups how to construct New China."

After everyone had his say, the leaders talked among themselves. Qiao Shi encouraged director Li to incorporate the suggestions in the final cut. Li Ruihuan put his hand on the filmmaker's shoulder and said quietly, "Director Li, take out those two scenes of Jiang Qing. This is an important film for the public to see, and we can't allow those scenes of Jiang Qing to ruin it." Jiang Qing was Mao's wife, one of the infamous, hated Gang of Four who had fomented the Cultural Revolution; she was at the time in prison for life after her death sentence had been commuted.

186 *twice in September*   September 4 and 11; the meetings took place at Deng's residence. Author's communication with historians, Beijing.

186 *"It was a rebellion"* [following]   Xinhua, September 27, 1989; David Holley, *LAT,* September 26, 1989.

186 *"tragedy"*   Xinhua, September 27, 1989.

187 *destroyed army vehicles . . . "sense of irony" . . . "proverb"*   David Holley, *LAT,* September 26, 1989.

188 *"The Yan'an spirit"*   Willy Wo-Lap Lam, in *SCMP,* September 28, 1989.

188 *reaffirm publicly*   Author's interview with Shen Yongyan.

188 *old professors*   Long Qin, in *China Gold Journal,* September 9, 1996. The professors were associated with Jiaotong University's Xi'an branch. The classes Jiang had taken were in electrical machinery design, lighting technology, and radio communications.

188 *"irreversible"*   *SCMP,* September 30, 1989.

188–189 *reform was of two kinds . . . "international reactionary forces"*   Fewsmith, *China Since Tiananmen,* 31, 42.

188 *"Four Cardinal Principles"*   The primary tenets of Chinese Communism, which were articulated by Deng Xiaoping in 1979 and are said to be inviolate: the Socialist road; the people's democratic dictatorship; the leadership of the Communist Party; and ideology based on Marxist-Leninist and Mao Zedong Thought. As China has evolved, the meaning and understanding of each has also evolved.

189 *Wen Jiabao*   Willy Wo-Lap Lam, in *SCMP,* October 4, 1989.

189 *Wen had handled*   Nathan and Gilley, *Rulers* (2003), 97–98.

189 *decision-making*   Author's interview with Dr. Song Jian, Beijing, September 2002.

189 *"Men are not saints"*   Xinhua, October 7, 1989.

190 *Zhu Ziqing . . . "veins"*   Gilley, *Tiger,* 155.

190 *Jiang Zejun*   Ibid. Jiang Zejun was Jiang Zemin's older brother by eight years. After 1949, he moved to Nanjing and eventually became director of the Jiangsu Provincial

Peking Opera troupe, following which he was appointed provost of the Jiangsu Drama and Opera College. He wrote operas and plays based on classical novels and folk stories. *Guangming Daily,* May 14, 1998. He had many children, but because of the Cultural Revolution, several of them did not receive a proper education. The "lost generation" is one of the Cultural Revolution's enduring tragedies.

190 *elegiac poem* [following]   *Guangming Daily,* May 14, 1998.

190 *Ziyege*   The poem is about a girl named Midnight; it can also be read as "Midnight Ode," which gives it the sad feeling.

190 *Dongquanmen is the section*   *Guangming Daily,* May 14, 1998.

191 *"Political power"* [following]   This section is derived from several sources, largely Yang, *Biography,* chap. 8, and Gilley, *Tiger,* 164–67.

191 *not agree*   Willy Wo-Lap Lam, in *SCMP,* November 9, 1989.

192 *"no experience"*   Xinhua, November 22, 1989.

192 *Yang Shangkun as CMC*   Yang, *Biography,* chap. 8; Seth Faison, in *SCMP,* November 22, 1989; Gilley; *Tiger,* 166.

192 *Yang Jia Jiang*   Yang, *Biography,* chap. 8. "Yang Family Army" or "Yang Family Generals" was a play on the title of a classic Chinese novel about a group of legendary female warriors.

192 *Liu Huaqing*   Ibid.; Gilley, *Tiger,* 166.

193 *militarylike gait*   Author's communication in Beijing.

193 *"planned economy" . . . systematic critique . . . "greatest lesson"*   Fewsmith, *China Since Tiananmen,* 35–36.

193 *"the mass media"*   Xinhua, November 30, 1989.

194 *"Private companies . . . "Self-employed traders" . . . military funding . . . reeducation*   Jasper Becker, *The Chinese,* 169, 214.

194 *visited troops* [following]   Willy Wo-Lap Lam, in *SCMP,* December 28, 1989.

194 *"real feelings"*   Ibid.

195 *James Lilley . . . Richard Nixon*   James Lilley with Jeffrey Lilley, *China Hands,* 346–348.

Chapter 12. 1990–1991

196 *"friendly countries"*   JEN, December 22, 1989.

196 *"national flavor"*   Xinhua, January 12, 1990. For guidance, Jiang advised artists to consider Mao Zedong's speech at the Yan'an Forum on Literature and Art, and Deng Xiaoping's speeches on similar subjects. In the Yan'an Forum, Mao mandated the development of "proletarian art and literature," and he admonished artists and writers to integrate themselves with the masses so that their works would serve the workers, peasants, and soldiers.

197 *"flesh-and-blood ties"*   Xinhua, January 26, 1990.

197 *table tennis*   Xinhua, January 29, 1990.

197 *Jiang invited Shen Yongyan*   Author's interview with Shen Yongyan.

197 *"Although I'm the one"*   Ibid.

198 *Pyongyang*   Xinhua, March 15, 1990.

198 *"I was delighted to receive"*   Xinhua, March 24, 1990; Yang, *Common Leader,* 2001, 501–502.

198 *Pudong*   Jim Abrams, for AP, May 4, 1990; Shanghai City Service, September 17, 1990 (BBC). Pudong's strategic location facilitates its commercial success. A 140-square-mile triangular territory between the east bank of the Huangpu River and the point at which the Yangtze River empties into the ocean, Pudong sits at the crossroads of wealthy Jiangsu and Zhejiang provinces and has contiguous access to Shanghai, one of the world's great metropolises, with its strong human resources, science and technology, manufacturing and distribution capabilities, and infrastructure.

198 *urgency*   Author's interview with Wang Daohan.

198 *secondary role*   Gilley, *Tiger,* 173. Deng held several meetings specifically on Pudong, such as one on February 17 with Jiang Zemin, Yang Shangkun, and Li Peng. Author's communication with historians, Beijing.

198 *Zhao Qizheng* [following]   Author's interviews with Zhao Qizheng, June 2001, December 2001. When discussing Pudong, Zhao, who was vice mayor of Shanghai before moving to Beijing in 1998 to become information minister, radiates energy and pride. "In 1918," he noted, "Dr. Sun Yat-sen wrote that since the land price of Pudong was so low, 'shouldn't we develop it ourselves?' " Zhao likened the development of Pudong to "a magnificent symphony." He extended the analogy: "The score was written by Deng Xiaoping; the conductor was Jiang Zemin; and the rest of us were members of the orchestra, each with his own instrument. The orchestra was very large, with millions of people participating." Zhao Qizheng was being overly modest; he, at least, would have been the concertmaster.

199 *international standards*   To become a world-class center of commerce, Pudong would need high-quality infrastructure, a comprehensive free trade zone, attractive tax incentives, and an advanced manufacturing base. Financial expenditures for Pudong's first decade were estimated at $10 billion, a sum to be shared by the central government, the city of Shanghai, and, with luck, foreign investors. Incentives offered to investors included banking privileges, tax breaks, long-term leases of fifty to seventy years, and opportunities to raise capital.

199 *"Economic development"*   Xinhua, June 14, 1991.

199 *"intellectuals"*   In China the term *intellectuals* is sometimes used to describe the educated elite, or, more generally, most college graduates—a broader use than in America.

199 *"We should welcome"*   Xinhua, May 5, 1990.

200 *"bourgeois liberalization"*   In interviews with foreign media, Jiang emphasized that the term *bourgeois liberalization* was not an accurate translation and gave rise to misunderstanding. China, he affirmed, would continue to "learn the fine culture, scientific management, and advanced technologies of capitalist countries. We will not only learn but spend money to purchase these good things" (Xinhua, May 25, 1990).

200 *Barbara Walters*   Xinhua, May 25, 1990.

201 *"hegemonistic" goal*   Seuttinger, *Beyond Tiananmen,* 112.

202 *shocked Chinese military leaders*   Ibid., 116; author's communication, Beijing.

202 *Special Economic Zones* [following]   Liu Hongru, *Transcentury Talents,* February 2000, 16–17.

203 *carefully studied*   Jiang called for further research on the stock market, even asking his old boss, Zhou Jiannan (former minister, First Ministry of Machine-Building Industry), to study the situation.

203 *escort vessel   Jiefangjun Bao* (Liberation Army Daily), August 3, 1993, 1 (BBC).

204 *Asian Games*   Xinhua, July 7, 1990.

204 *flame*   JEN, August 22, 1990.

204 *foreign dignitaries*   The claim is made that when Jiang met with foreigners, Li Peng had to approve each encounter (Nathan and Gilley, *Rulers,* 149). For the Party's general secretary to be subordinate to the State Council's premier would run counter to China's system of governance. Furthermore, the normal practice is for the Foreign Ministry to determine which leader meets which foreigner. More likely, Jiang was simply being cautious and especially respectful after his surprising ascent over leaders who had more experience working in the central government.

204 *circulated to all members*   Author's communication in Beijing.

204 *three patriarchs*   Nathan and Gilley, *Rulers,* 149.

204 *met frequently with Deng*   Other meetings between Jiang and Deng Xiaoping, usually including other leaders (particularly Yang Shangkun and Li Peng), were held on February 17 (on the Basic Law for Hong Kong), March 3 and April 20 (on international and domestic economic matters), June 18 (on U.S.–China relations and Taiwan), and

September 13 (with North Korea's Kim Il-Sung and Song Ping). Author's communication with historians, Beijing.

205 *"savvy man"*   Kathy Chen and Joseph Kahn, in *AWSJ,* February 6, 1995.

205 *"integration of the planned economy"* ... *four articles*   Fewsmith, *China Since Tiananmen* 44–45.

205 *March 1*   Author's communication with historians, Beijing.

205 *Soviet leader*   Reuters, February 28, 1991.

206 *rehabilitated*   Suettinger, *Beyond Tiananmen,* 126. The three officials were brought back in June 1991. Hu Qili became vice minister of Machine-Building and Electronics Industries and then, in 1993, minister of Electronics Industry. Yan Mingfu became vice minister of Civil Affairs, which was responsible for humanitarian activities; later, after he retired, he was appointed president of China Charity Federation, which he developed energetically into a pioneering nongovernment organization for helping China's less fortunate, including the handicapped and victims of natural disasters.

206 *"acquitted himself well"*   Willy Wo-Lap Lam, in *SCMP,* June 19, 1991.

206 *Wang Zhen*   *SCMP,* June 29, 1991. Until this time Wang Zhen had been a proponent of the "twin core" theory that Li Peng and Jiang Zemin together were the center of the new collective leadership, and his praise of Jiang singularly marked a change in attitude.

206 *trip to Moscow*   Xinhua, April 26, 1991.

207 *automotive plant*   Originally named after Stalin, it was now the Lihachov Automobile Works.

207 *reminisced* ... *"very popular"*   Willy Wo-Lap Lam, in *SCMP,* May 18, 1991.

207 *Deng Xiaoping called a meeting*   Author's communication with historians, Beijing.

207 *"good deed"*   Suettinger, *Beyond Tiananmen,* 124.

208 *might be overreacting*   Gilley, *Tiger,* 176–177.

208 *"peaceful evolution"*   Fewsmith, *China Since Tiananmen,* 55.

208 *"We must gradually aim"*   Willy Wo-Lap Lam, in *SCMP,* October 22, 1991.

208 *Kim Il-Sung*   Chris Yeung, in *SCMP,* October 15, 1991.

208 *Beidaihe*   Jasper Becker, *The Chinese,* 349–351.

209 *personal strictures*   Author's interview with Shen Yongyan.

209 *buildings in Zhongnanhai*   These modest-size but breathtaking structures—two dozen or so, each with its own name and history—were located on a small island (Yingtai) in the South Lake (Nanhai), and were connected to the southern end of Zhongnanhai by a stone bridge. Across the water one could almost see the bustle of Chang'an Avenue, which the South Lake abutted. The buildings' intricate, antique patterns of golds, blacks, and reds, restored meticulously by master artisans, suggested the richness and special character of Chinese civilization.

209 *his own style*   The "neoauthoritarian" political philosophy, said to be "Asian" in character, was thought to have fostered the growth spurt in Singapore, Korea, Taiwan, and Malaysia.

210 *"assuage my concerns"*   Author's interview with Wang Daohan.

Chapter 13. 1992

211 *the conservative tide after Tiananmen*   Party hardliners had used the armed suppression of the student movement as a way to promote their own political agenda. Claiming that the dangers of "bourgeois liberalization" were emanating from economic reforms, they urged renewed support for the revolutionary principles of "class struggle" and countering "peaceful evolution."

211 *stumping for reform*   "Deng Xiaoping was fundamentally a reformer," said Henry Kissinger. "I've always believed that the West had a profound misunderstanding of Deng's motivations [in using force in Tiananmen]—he thought he was protecting reform by stopping the chaos, but it blew up around him." Author's interview with Henry Kissinger.

211 *personal journey* Sources for Deng Xiaoping's Southern Tour (Nanxun) are: *SCMP* (many articles); Gilley, *Tiger,* 183–87; Yang, *Biography,* chap. 8; author's communication, Beijing.

211 *Deng boarded* Gilley, *Tiger,* 183. Deng had to rely on his daughter, Deng Rong, who was constantly by her father's side, to help him hear, speak, and on occasion even remember. Observers witnessed her often bending over to whisper to her father and even coach him in what she thought he wanted to say.

212 *"Here's what our problem"* Gilley, *Tiger,* 184; author's communication, Beijing.

212 *"against reform"* Zong, "Zhu (I)," 52.

212 *"liberate their thoughts"* Chris Yeung, in *SCMP,* January 20, 1992.

212 *"nonessential meetings"* Xinhua, January 25, 1992 (cited in Gilley, *Tiger,* 185).

212 *Deng departed* Xinhua, January 19, 1992 (cited in Gilley, *Tiger,* 185).

212 *"working style"* *SCMP,* January 27, 1992.

212 *"no need to worry"* [following] Author's communication, Beijing.

212 *"no common sense"* . . . *"What's wrong"* [following] Gilley, *Tiger,* 184.

213 *"good job"* Ibid., 185.

213 *"escort and protect"* Zong, "Zhu (I)," 52.

213 *absence of press* Official reports would later claim that Deng himself had requested that his trip be kept under wraps, especially during the Chinese New Year period, or that retired leaders are not supposed to get media coverage—but few would believe the ex post facto rationalization. Gilley, *Tiger,* 186; author's communication, Beijing.

213–214 *limited dissemination . . . local papers . . . Qiao himself spoke* Fewsmith, *China Since Tiananmen,* 58, 61.

214 *"bold explorations"* Xinhua, February 4, 1992.

214 *might remove Jiang* [following] Nathan and Gilley, *Rulers,* 150.

214 *agreement with Li Peng* Nathan and Gilley, *Rulers* (2003), 175.

214 *"The Notice About Passing"* [following] Author's communication, Beijing. chap. 16.

215 *Politburo meeting* [following] Author's communication with historians, Beijing. The meeting was held March 9–10.

215 *"sharp differences . . . Yang Shangkun . . . lax in promoting reform* Fewsmith, *China Since Tiananmen,* 59. Wan Li and Qiao Shi supported Jiang Zemin and Yang Shangkun; Yao Yilin, Song Ping, and Li Peng defended the now-superseded conservative position.

215 *"more daring"* Gilley, *Tiger,* 187.

215 *investigative teams* Willy Wo-Lap Lam, in *SCMP,* April 8, 1992.

216 *"could be sacked"* Gilley, *Tiger,* 187.

216 *criticized Leftism* *SCMP,* June 15, 1992.

216 *"conscientious study"* Xinhua, June 15, 1992 (BBC).

216 *change in language* The subtlety of politically tinged descriptions in China is fascinating. For example, private business is called "nonpublic," and the unemployment rate is called the "waiting to be employed rate" (since a core tenet of the Communist system was guaranteed lifetime employment, and Communist propaganda had disparaged capitalism for its unemployed workers and business cycles).

216 *bellwether phrase* Author's interview with Teng Wensheng. Other options, all longer and more awkward, were wisely rejected, including "Planned and Socialist Market Economy," "Market Combined with Planned Economy," "Market Economy with Planning," "Planning Economy with Market Adjustments," "Commodity Economy with Planning," and the ultra-awkward "Planned Economy as the Main and Market Economy as the Minor."

216 *Three days* Author's communication with historians, Beijing. Jiang's speech was on June 9; his talk with Deng was on June 12.

216–217 *capitalist systems . . . Chen Yun . . . Deng then concluded . . . extremely sensitive* Author's interview with Teng Wensheng.

217 *"unprecedented"* *China Daily,* June 16, 1992.

217 *"a warm spring wave"*   Author's communication, Beijing.

217 *"watch out for the Right"*   *AsiaWeek,* http://pathfinder.com/asiaweek/97/0307/cs6.html.

218 *"I can't imagine"*   Author's communication, Beijing.

218 *Emperor Akihito*   JEN, April 6, 1992. Tokyo remained unreceptive, worried that Chinese protests could embarrass the emperor.

218 *Tanaka* [following]   Yang, *Common Leader,* 2001, 1159–1160.

218 *"We have one grandson"*   Xinhua, April 2, 1992.

219 *NHK*   NHK Television, April 9, 1992 (BBC).

219 *camera zoomed*   Even though Japanese and Chinese are totally different languages in terms of the sounds of the words and structure of the grammar, Chinese characters form the core of Japanese characters (kanji), so that a Japanese television viewer could get a good sense of what Jiang Zemin was writing.

219 *"great sufferings"*   Jiji Press English News Service, October 26, 1992.

219 *one hundred new generals . . . machinations and maneuvering . . . old friends*   Nathan and Gilley, *Rulers* (2003), 176–178. Nathan and Gilley refer to the Yangs as cousins, not half-brothers.

220 *all told tales*   For stories about the conflict between the Yang brothers and Jiang Zemin, see Nathan and Gilley, *Rulers;* reports by Willy Wo-Lap Lam in *SCMP;* Gilley, *Tiger,* 193–96; Yang, *Biography,* chap. 8; Laurence Brahm, *Zhongnanhai* (Hong Kong: NAGA, 1998); Zong, "Zhu (I)," 52.

220 *General Zhang Aiping*   According to Gao Xin (*Jiang Zemin's Road to Power*), Jiang's key ally in getting Deng Xiaoping to topple the Yang family was General Zhang Aiping, a former vice premier and minister of defense, who had been the friend and commanding officer of Jiang Shangqing, Jiang Zemin's martyred adoptive father, and one of Jiang Zemin's most steadfast supporters. When Zhang Aiping died at the age of ninety-three in July 2003, both Jiang Zemin and Hu Jintao attended his memorial (*PD,* July 13, 2003).

220 *Deng's son . . . Liu Huaqing*   Nathan and Gilley, *Rulers* (2003), 176–177.

220 *the list*   Yang, *Biography,* chap. 8.

220 *Yang Baibing*   Gilley, *Tiger,* 195.

221 *"clear-cut characteristic" . . . "new revolution"*   Fewsmith, *China Since Tiananmen,* 64.

221 *"We should proceed"*   John Kohut, in *SCMP,* October 12, 1992.

221 *"applaud" . . . "well-organized"*   Author's communication with historians, Beijing. Jiang's political report was given at the opening of the Fourteenth Party Congress on October 10, 1992; Deng appeared with Jiang at the end of the Congress on October 19.

221 *Hu Jintao*   Fewsmith, *China Since Tiananmen,* 66.

221 *Central Advisory Commission*   Deng Xiaoping was its first chairman (1982–1987), Chen Yun its second (1987–1992).

222 *"suggestion" to delegation heads*   The turned-down mayor was Xiao Yang of Changqing, who could only become an alternative member of the Central Committee, thwarting Jiang's plans to promote him to Sichuan Party secretary (he became governor instead). Jiang's two other reelection suggestions—Hua Guofeng (out of respect for Mao Zedong) and two senior generals, Zhang Zhen and Liu Huaqing (as part of Jiang's campaign to free the army of the Yang brothers' control)—were accepted. Nathan and Gilley, *Rulers* (2003), 222.

222 *turning point*   Author's communication, Beijing.

222 *his successor* [following]   Author's communication with historians, Beijing; Gilley, *Tiger,* 197.

223 *refute the common assumption*   Nathan and Gilley, *Rulers* (2003), 43, 90.

223 *remove generals*   On the new Central Military Commission, Zhang Zhen and Liu Huaqing were vice chairmen, and Chi Haotian, Zhang Wannian, Yu Yongbo, and Fu

Quanyou were heads of national defense, army, navy, and air force respectively. General Yu Yongbo replaced Yang Baibing as head of the PLA's pervasive General Political Department.

223 *backing of Generals*   Suettinger, *Beyond Tiananmen*, 223.

223 *CMC . . . "military reshuffle" . . . PLA loyalty*   Gilley, *Tiger*, 196.

223 *Jiang's image*   He was also involved in the appointment of Xu Guangchun, who had been chief of the Shanghai bureau of the Xinhua News Agency, as deputy editor in chief (1991) and then editor in chief (1993) of *Guangming Daily;* deputy director of the CPC Propaganda Department (1995); and minister of the State Administration of Radio, Film and Television (SARFT, 2000).

223–224 *South Korea . . . Kim Il-Sung*   *AWSJ*, November 17, 1992.

224 *"Whenever you have something"*   Author's interview with Dr. Song Jian, Beijing, November 2003.

224 *Lee-Jay Cho*   Dr. Cho was a world-renowned expert in population demographics; Song and Cho had worked together on China's population dynamics in the early 1980s.

224 *reported directly*   "I report my views directly to President Jiang," said Wang in 2001. "If he isn't available, I report to Vice Premier Qian Qichen, who coordinates foreign affairs. The reason I see Jiang every time I go to Beijing is because the Party has a Taiwan Affairs Leading Group, of which I am a member. Jiang is the head of the group, and the deputy head is Qian Qichen. Other members include the Taiwan Affairs Office minister. My organization doesn't have any conflict with this office. I give my opinions to the central government, and the central government makes the decisions." Author's interview with Wang Daohan.

225 *the course of science* [following]   Author's interview with Dr. Song Jian.

225 *Sparks Program*   Approved in late 1985 and begun in 1986 under Song Jian's leadership, the Sparks Program encouraged engineers and technicians to go out to the countryside to help the peasants become more productive. Best practices in agriculture were taught, such as introducing new species from other regions and even other countries. One achievement was aquatic farms, which became a large export industry. "Deng Xiaoping was skeptical at the beginning," recalled Song, "though to his credit he supported us. He was really pleased at our success."

225 *high-tech industrial parks*   A key adviser to Dr. Song Jian was Dr. George Kozmetsky, cofounder of Teledyne, founder of the IC^2 Institute of the University of Texas at Austin, and high-tech-park visionary. Dr. Kozmetsky, who was awarded the National Medal of Technology in 1993, was the person who brought the author to China in early 1989 (for the first time) to advise Dr. Song and the State Science and Technology Commission.

227 *relied on old friends* [following]   Author's interview with Ye Gongqi.

228 *"She manages family business"*   Author's interview with Jiang Zehui.

228 *Hubei*   Gilley, *Tiger*, 201–202; Yang, *Common Leader*, 2001, 112–114.

228 *"It almost doesn't pay"* [following]   Yang, *Common Leader*, 2001, 112–114.

229 *Wuhan . . . Levies*   Gilley, *Tiger*, 202.

229 *"spiritual civilization"*   *SCMP*, November 23, 1992.

230 *sixteen-character slogan*   Suettinger, *Beyond Tiananmen*, 164. In general, two Chinese characters form one English word.

230 *twelve editorials*   Daniel Kwan, in *SCMP*, December 18, 1992.

Chapter 14. 1993

231 *"might not be as dumb"*   Cheng Li, *China's Leaders: The New Generation* (New York: Rowman and Littlefield, 2001), xvii. To Cheng, a young China scholar, Doak's analysis "was the first time that I heard anyone speak positively about Jiang's ability to succeed Deng Xiaoping."

231 *speeches publicized*   Gilley, *Tiger*, 198.

231 *army's loyalty*   Willy Wo-Lap Lam, in *SCMP,* January 27, 1993.

231 *General Ba . . . PAP* [following]   Gilley, *Tiger,* 198–99; Willy Wo-Lap Lam, in *SCMP,* July 26, 1993.

231 *grew the force . . . one million servicemen . . . Ministry of State Security* [following] Jasper Becker, *The Chinese,* 329, 339, 424. Becker references Tai Ming Cheung, *China Quarterly,* No. 146, June 1996, and Yitzhak Shichor, *China Quarterly,* No. 146, June 1996. The claim is made that the Ministry of State Security grew "from a few hundred thousand officials to at least two million."

232 *"Shanghai Faction"   Tokyo Shimbun,* May 17, 1994 (cited in Kyoto News Service, BBC).

232 *"five lakes"*   Willy Wo-Lap Lam, in *SCMP,* July 26, 1994.

232 *"the porcelain teacups rattled"*   Laurence Brahm, *Zhongnanhai* (Hong Kong: NAGA, 1998), 91. Though no one defends Chen Xitong, official sources say this story is fabricated.

232 *marked the end*   Yang, *Biography,* chap. 8.

232 *men promoted*   The promotions included Zhang Wannian, head of the General Staff Department and CMC member; Yu Yongbo, head of the General Political Department and CMC member; Fu Quanyou, head of the General Supply Department and CMC member; and Zhu Dunfa, president of National Defense University.

232 *"Was your position 'arranged' "*   Author's interview with Jiang Zehui.

233 *elders resisted   SCMP,* March 4, 1993 (quoting *Mirror,* a Hong Kong magazine). Official sources call this report fabricated.

233 *out of 2,909 total ballots*   John Kohut, in *SCMP,* March 29, 1993.

233 *"unassuming appearance"* [following]   *Kyodo News International,* March 29, 1993.

233 *Party's Leading Group . . . Zhu Rongji governor*   Suettinger, *Beyond Tiananmen,* 150; author's interview with Wu Xiaoling.

233 *mild heart attack*   Suettinger, *Beyond Tiananmen,* 150; Gilley, *Tiger,* 203–204.

233 *promoted Zeng*   David Shambaugh, "The Dynamics of Elite Politics During the Jiang Era," *China Journal,* no. 45 (January 2001).

234 *Replacing Wen*   Willy Wo-Lap Lam, in *SCMP,* March 26, 1993.

234 *tightening his grip*   Ibid.

234 *"minor reshuffle"*   *Kyodo News International,* March 29, 1993.

234 *island's university* [following]   Yang, *Common Leader,* 2001, 526–528. The visit was on April 14, 1993.

234 *"dazzling"*   *AWSJ,* March 30, 1993.

235 *inflation*   Foo Choy Peng, in *SCMP,* February 1, 1994. Inflation was being fueled by "hot money"—money that was lent short term at very high interest rates—much of it going into real estate, where skyrocketing prices seemed to "guarantee" quick profits.

235 *"from overheating"*   Willy Wo-Lap Lam, in *SCMP,* June 1, 1993.

235 *microeconomic controls*   Author's communication with historians, Beijing.

235 *"frightening specter"*   Author's interview with Wu Xiaoling, Beijing, April 2002.

235 *"crucial year"*   Author's interview with Leng Rong, Beijing, September 2002.

235–236 *"seize the opportunities" . . . "Speeding up"*   Willy Wo-Lap Lam, in *SCMP,* June 1, 1993.

236 *prime interpreter*   Willy Wo-Lap Lam, in *SCMP,* June 4, 1993.

236 *"military thinking"*   Daniel Kwan, in *SCMP,* June 7, 1993.

236 *veneration . . . "neither penetrating"*   Willy Wo-Lap Lam, in *SCMP,* July 3, 1993 (quoting the pro-Beijing journal *Mirror*); *Ching Pao* (Hong Kong), July 5, 1993, 40 (BBC).

236 *ninetieth birthday*   Author's communication with historians, Beijing.

236 *elite group*   Willy Wo-Lap Lam, in *SCMP,* June 28, 1993. The group was coordinated by Zeng Qinghong and Teng Wensheng.

236 *new foundation for reform*   Topics included foreign trade, the socialist market economy, the nature of ownership and the private sector, reforms of the financial and agricul-

tural systems, and the development of a modern management system for state-owned enterprises. "We had to answer three criticisms of our market-centered ideas," recalled economist Li Yining, one of the participants, an expert on ownership and shareholding and dean of the School of Management at Beijing University. "The first was that if we developed a market economy, it would mean that China was going over to the capitalist side. The second criticism was that the Chinese economy needed to be well regulated, and that if we developed a market economy, it would devolve into a mess. The third criticism was that since at that time the prices for various commodities were stable, if we allowed prices to fluctuate according to market conditions, prices would become chaotic. But all three criticisms were proved wrong.

"The market economy could be used in both a capitalist society and a socialist one," Li explained. "If it is helpful for the development of the economy, then it should be used. Why are all those countries that have a planned economy poor? If we had maintained the old system, we would have pushed the Chinese people into a dead end. I turned the second criticism around and argued that if a market economy isn't used and some crisis arises, then society will really be in a mess. To the third criticism I responded that although it appeared that in a planned economy prices are stable, in fact people can't buy the commodities they want, because those commodities aren't available! Furthermore, when the government artificially controls prices, it is actually a kind of inflation." Author's interview with Li Yining, Beijing, September 1999.

But economic reasoning could not placate Party conservatives. A rash of Leftist magazines ran articles exposing negative consequences of reform from "money worshipping" to unscrupulous businessmen and bemoaning the exploitation of workers and consumers. It would take more than one conference to convince some people of the need to reform. Willy Wo-Lap Lam, in *SCMP*, June 30, 1993.

236 *political theoretician*   The underlying reason why China's top political leader should also be its leading political theoretician was, it seems, two parts Communist custom, epitomized by Lenin and Mao, and one part Chinese tradition, personified by literary emperors and generals throughout dynastic history.

236–237 *Ding Guangen . . . Farewell My Concubine*   Willy Wo-Lap Lam, in *SCMP*, June 30, 1993. *Farewell My Concubine* depicts the sweep of twentieth-century Chinese history, from the warlord era through the Cultural Revolution. Upon watching the movie, Ding Guangen allegedly erupted over what he saw as a negative depiction of Communist rule. "Who authorized the script?" Ding supposedly asked. "And who sent the film to international competitions?"

237 *repugnant*   Scarlet Cheng, in *SCMP*, July 25, 1993. There is a report that Jiang Zemin himself ordered the blackout of all publicity for *Farewell My Concubine*, but this is denied by official sources.

237 *Beijing's bid*   Xinhua, June 23, 1993 (BBC).

237 *Buddhism in China*   Xinhua, June 24, 1993. Jiang explained that Buddhism was introduced during the Han dynasty (206 B.C.–220 A.D.) and flourished in the Tang dynasty (A.D. 618–907). Xuanzhuang, China's first Buddhist master, enduring hardships in a pilgrimage to India, brought back the Buddhist scriptures (A.D. 644).

237 *private communication*   James Lilley with Jeffrey Lilley, *China Hands,* 367.

237 *Hong Kong*   SCMP, July 11, 1993.

238 *"trustworthy"*   TKP, August 15, 2001.

238 *beauty pageants*   Cheng Kim Huay, in *ST*, August 31, 1993, 6.

238 *first national pageant*   Tom Hilditch, in *SCMP*, May 9, 1993, 3.

238 *Chinese containership . . . Anthony Lake . . . "tipping the balance"* [following]   Suettinger, *Beyond Tiananmen,* 174–181.

238 *no prohibited chemicals*   Ibid., 176–177. Why the intelligence failure? Did the Chinese dump the contraband at sea? Was it all a ruse to embarrass the U.S. intelligence community? More likely, Suettinger concludes, the original intelligence was good but the

chemicals never made it to the boat; overeager intelligence analysts, he suspects, failed to take into account China's faulty distribution system.

238 *"backlash" states*   Ibid., 179. Anthony Lake later asserted that he never intended to equate China with Iran and Iraq and that China was "opting for liberalization," but the damage had been done.

238 *"weak reaction"*   Ibid., 179–180, quoting *Xin Bao* (Hong Kong), September 17, 1993, 24.

238 *"fully restore"*   Willy Wo-Lap Lam, *SCMP,* July 14, 1993.

238–239 *Jiang's agenda . . . "not to smile"*   Suettinger, *Beyond Tiananmen,* 181–182.

240 *"I am sure"* [following]   *China Daily,* November 19, 1993.

240 *Cary Qualls* [following]   Yang, *Common Leader,* 2001, 834–835.

240 *frosty* [following]   Louise Loca, in *SCMP,* November 21, 1993.

240 *"somber" . . . "nervous"*   Suettinger, *Beyond Tiananmen,* 182.

241 *"came right back"*   *FEER,* December 2, 1993.

241 *constrained*   Nathan and Gilley, *Rulers,* 149.

241 *five areas*   Loca, in *SCMP,* November 21, 1993.

241 *"greater emphasis"*   *FEER,* December 2, 1993.

241 *Shanghai-made saxophone*   Susan V. Lawrence and Emily MacFarquhar, in *U.S. News & World Report,* October 23, 1995.

241 *"I should have brought"*   Gilley, *Tiger,* 212.

241 *"These two countries"*   Louise Loca, in *SCMP,* November 21, 1993.

241 *"attach conditions"*   *Kyodo News International,* November 22, 1993.

242 *"Mr. Clinton said he looked"*   Louise Loca, in *SCMP,* November 21, 1993.

242 *kudos . . . "neither haughty"*   Gilley, *Tiger,* 212.

242 *"backbone"*   Gilley, *Tiger,* 16 ("Louis Cha Meets Jiang Zemin," *Ming Pao Monthly,* June 1, 1993).

242 *Volume III*   Author's communication with historians, Beijing.

242 *hundredth anniversary*   Geoffrey Crothall, in *SCMP,* December 27, 1993.

243 *calligraphy*   Xinhua, August 21, 1993.

243 *"The best way"*   Geoffrey Crothall, in *SCMP,* December 27, 1993.

Chapter 15. 1994

244 *panic buying*   Foo Choy Peng, in *SCMP,* February 1, 1994. This occurred in December 1993.

244 *national inflation*   Lincoln Kaye, in *FEER,* October 27, 1994.

244 *urban inflation . . . Desperate workers . . . "dumplings"*   Julia Leung, in *AWSJ,* April 8, 1994.

244 *"If price controls"*   Author's interview with Li Yining.

244 *"Fuel" . . . "prices lowered"*   Xinhua, January 19, 1994 (BBC).

244 *"To keep prices"*   Xinhua, December 15, 1994.

245 *restrictions*   Liang Kuo-jen, in *Ming Pao* (Hong Kong), November 29, 1994 (BBC).

245 *"overall situation"*   Willy Wo-Lap Lam, in *SCMP,* June 21, 1994.

245 *Yimin Food Factory*   Lam, *Era,* 64.

245 *Liberation Army Daily* [following]   *Jiefangjun Bao,* January 3, 1994 (BBC).

245 *Jiang promoted*   Willy Wo-Lap Lam, in *SCMP,* July 26, 1994.

245 *local army base . . . army salaries* [following]   Laurence Brahm, *Zhongnanhai* (Hong Kong: NAGA, 1998), 26–27.

246 *Mao jacket*   Ibid.

246 *Jiang made it . . . PLA functions* [following]   Ibid. Jiang's attitude toward army events contrasted sharply with that of his predecessor, Zhao Ziyang, who, after arriving late to an officers' graduation ceremony at National Defense University, left so hurriedly that he did not even attend the banquet dinner that had been prepared in his honor.

246 *military documents . . . papers*   Author's communication, Beijing.

246 *army stamp*   Daniel Kwan, in *SCMP,* August 5, 1994.

246 *"Respect professional soldiers"*   Brahm, *Zhongnanhai,* 27.

246 *"a bad thing"*   Xinhua, May 12, 1994 (BBC).

246 *media excoriated*   Chris Yeung, in *SCMP,* May 14, 1994; Gilley, *Tiger,* 224.

247 *"vassal" . . . two dangers*   Chan Wai-Fong, in *SCMP,* June 4, 1994.

247 *"the core"* [following]   Daniel Kwan, in *SCMP,* June 28, 1994.

247 *"threw a fit"*   Danny Gittings, in *SCMP,* January 1, 1995.

247 *"The fat man"*   *FEER,* March 24, 1994.

248 *Jia Ting'an*   David Shambaugh, *Modernizing China's Military: Progress, Problems and Prospects* (Berkeley: University of California Press, 2003), 35, 121; Lam, *Era,* 332. With his rimless glasses, short haircut, pleasant smile, and soft-spoken nature, Jia Ting'an seemed to personify efficient, self-effacing service. With the army rank of major general, he would often represent Jiang at CMC meetings. When complimented on his service to the president, he would say, "It is my job." When praised for helping individuals in need, he would only smile. Author's communication, Beijing.

248 *Zeng Peiyan*   Zeng was born in Shanghai, graduated from prestigious Tsinghua University with a degree in electronics, and joined the Shanghai Electric Equipment Research Institute of the First Ministry of Machine-Building Industry in 1962, which was when the twenty-three-year-old Zeng first met the thirty-six-year-old Jiang Zemin, who was the institute's vice director. In 1966, just as the Cultural Revolution was beginning, Zeng was appointed deputy chief engineer of Xi'an Rectifier Research Institute. He stayed in Xi'an until 1981, when he was appointed secretary of the Commercial Counselor's Office of the Chinese Embassy in Washington. Stationed in the United States from 1982 to 1984, Zeng gained international experience and a command of English. He then joined the Ministry of Electronics Industry as director of its General Office when Jiang Zemin was appointed vice minister, renewing their working relationship (see Chapter 6). When the ministry was reorganized as the Ministry of Machinery and Electronics Industry in 1988, Zeng became its vice minister, a position he held until 1993, when he was appointed vice minister of the State Planning Commission. When the commission's scope was expanded by Premier Zhu Rongji in 1998, Zeng, who was working closely with President Jiang as a lead domestic adviser, became its minister. In 2002 Zeng Peiyan entered the Politburo and in 2003 became vice premier responsible for industry and finance.

248 *presentations*   Author's interview with Zeng Peiyan.

248 *Teng Wensheng . . . Red Flag* [following]   Author's interview with Teng Wensheng. Other leaders at the Academy would have more distinguished careers in the Party Literature Office, Propaganda, and the Chinese Academy of Social Siences.

249 *General Office*   Ibid. With the Gang of Four gone, there was no longer need for competing offices in the State Council and Party. Deng's Politburo speech was titled "Reform of the Governing System of the Party and the Country."

249 *vice minister*   At first, Teng Wensheng was executive vice minister of the Policy Research Office, but he became vice minister when Wang Weicheng, a former vice minister of propaganda, became its minister.

250 *Teng demurred*   Author's communication in Beijing.

250 *"constructive partnership"*   Rajiv Tiwari, for Inter Press Service, September 6, 1994. Still-sensitive subjects remained untouched: dispute over three river islands; illegal Chinese immigrants in eastern Siberia; restricted access to Russian military technology; and allegations of Chinese espionage.

250 *Tolstoy's home . . . MIR*   UPI, September 5, 1994.

250 *literary analysis*   www.nearchina.com/frame/government/cpcjiangzemin.htm.

250 *"terrible misunderstanding"*   Xinhua, September 12, 1994 (BBC).

251 *second time*   The first spouse of a Chinese head of state to travel on an official international trip was Wang Guangmei, the wife of President Liu Shaoqi. Before the Cultural Revolution, the couple had taken a foreign tour together, which contributed to the pair

being condemned and purged. Mao's wife, Jiang Qing, was jealous of Wang and subjected her to public humiliation and torment. *Ching Pao* (Hong Kong), October 1994, 58–59 (BBC). To imply that she was a whore, Wang's captors dressed her in a skirt split up to hip level and displayed her at a mass rally. She was accused of spying and imprisoned in solitary confinement for a decade. See www.sjsu.edu/faculty/watkins/cultrev.htm.

251 *Wang Yeping* [following]   *Ching Pao* (Hong Kong), October 1994, 58–59 (BBC).

251 *charismatic wife*   Gilley, *Tiger,* 219.

251 *"Li Peng has not"*   China Government Guild, http://211.147.20.15/chinagov/main/whois/lipeng.htm.

252 *First Lady . . . constant, excruciating pain*   Author's interview with Shen Yongyan; Gilley, *Tiger,* 220.

252 *"properly report"*   *Ching Pao* (Hong Kong), October 1994, 58–59 (BBC).

252 *a flattering article*   *Lien Ho Pao* (Hong Kong), December 2, 1994 (BBC).

252 *plenum in late September*   The Fourth Plenary of the Fourteenth Party Congress (September 25–28, 1994) is said to mark the end of Deng Xiaoping's active political life. Gao Xin, *Jiang Zemin's Road to Power;* Gilley, *Tiger,* 228; Yang, *Biography,* chap. 8.

252 *decisions on reforming*   Zengke He, "Toward Good Governance: China? Case J," www.11iacc.org/download/add/WS5.3/WS%205.3_P1_He.doc.

252 *no formal document . . . November 11* [following]   Author's communication with historians in Beijing.

252 *final public appearance* [following]   *Cheng Ming* (Hong Kong), November 1994, 6–8 (BBC).

253 *photograph*   Gilley, *Tiger,* 228.

253 *"Here's the problem I'm always"*   Bo Yibo enumerated the five problems about which Deng said he was concerned; most dealt with the country's stability. The first was Deng's own preeminence. "'China should now give less publicity to my opinions and my previous speeches,'" Bo quoted the leader as saying, "'and give more publicity to the central Party with Comrade Jiang Zemin at its core.'" The second issue was the need to improve democratic centralism and guarantee the authority and role of the current leadership. Deng wanted to ensure the support of the whole Party and army for this leadership by opposing any actions that were detrimental to it. He also asked the same of provincial and government officials. He also wanted to make the process of selecting successors quicker, more efficient, and more routine. *Cheng Ming,* November 1994, 6–8 (BBC).

253 *Bo Yibo wrote*   Gilley, *Tiger,* 228–29.

253 *"same ideals"*   *Ching Pao* (Hong Kong), November 5, 1994, 24–27 (BBC).

253 *Huang Ju*   Yang, *Biography,* chap. 8.

254 *APEC summit*   JEN, November 13, 1994.

254 *"further progress"*   Ibid., November 14, 1994.

254 *"without apology"*   Ibid., November 10, 1994.

254 *five principles*   Xinhua, November 14, 1994.

254 *sixteen-character maxim*   Suettinger, *Beyond Tiananmen,* 210.

254 *Nankai University*   Yang, *Common Leader,* 2001, 532.

255 *"Jiang's scientific"*   Author's interview with Zhao Qizheng.

255 *a lecture on law*   Yang, *Common Leader,* 2001, 450–451.

256 *China's national arts*   Xinhua, December 27, 1994.

256 *Peking Opera*   Xinhua, December 20, 1994.

Chapter 16. 1995

257 *"spiritual civilization"*   Xinhua, January 1, 1995.

257 *first put forward by Deng*   Author's communication with historians, Beijing; Stefan Landsberger (http://www.iisg.nl/~landsberger/ssc.html). At the time (1979), Deng Xiaoping had mentioned the idea of a "socialist spiritual civilization" as a way of anchoring the

nascent modernization movement to Communist ideology by strengthening political consciousness and morality based on socialist principles.

258 *provincial leaders* [following]   *Lien Ho Pao* (Hong Kong), January 8, 1995, 7 (BBC).

258 Shanghai Faction   Cheng Li, "The 'Shanghai Gang': Force for Stability or Cause for Conflict?" *China Leadership Monitor*, no. 1, pt. 2, December 2001.

258 *"Some people say we have"*   Tien Li, "Jiang Zemin accelerates pace to secure power in his own hands," *Tangtai* (Hong Kong), January 15, 1995, 8–10 (BBC).

259 *Wu Bangguo*   Willy Wo-Lap Lam, in *SCMP*, January 19, 1995.

259 *"Twelve Rules" . . . "give a hand"*   *Tangtai* (Hong Kong), January 15, 1995 (BBC).

259 *"twenty-point directive"*   Willy Wo-Lap Lam, in *SCMP*, January 20, 1995.

259 *Eight-Point Proposal*   Xinhua, January 31, 1995; *TKP*, August 16, 2001.

260 *Not a single high-level general*   Lam, *Era*, 172.

260 *books exploited*   Gilley, *Tiger*, 249.

260 *"major economic crimes"* [following]   Kathy Chen, in *AWSJ*, February 20, 1995.

260 *Wang Huning*   *Lien Ho Pao* (Hong Kong), March 28, 1995 (BBC).

261 *youngest-ever*   Gilley, *Tiger*, 277.

261 *American films*   Ibid., 278, quoting Wang Huning, *A Political Life* (Shanghai People's Publishing), 1995, 135–144.

261 *"When I'm in Beijing"* [following]   *Wen Wei Po* (Hong Kong), March 9, 1995 (BBC).

261 *Hu Yaobang*   *Chung Kuo Shih Pao* (Taipei), May 3, 1995, 9.

262 *reaching out*   Lam, *Era*, 20; Willy Wo-Lap Lam, in *SCMP*, March 12, 1997. The clever strategy separated Hu's followers from those of deposed Party chief Zhao Ziyang, because even though both groups were on the same liberal wing of the political spectrum, there was residual resentment that Zhao had replaced Hu Yaobang as general secretary after the student protests in late 1986.

262 *shot himself*   *Ming Pao* (Hong Kong), May 9, 1995, A2 (BBC).

262 *Rumors flew*   *SCMP*, April 11, 1995.

262 *"Chen's Money Box"*   Yang, *Biography*, chap. 8. One wild rumor was that Wang's death was really a hit job, ordered by one of Chen Xitong's sons, after other efforts, including blackmail, had failed to coerce Wang to take the fall for the city's corruption. Laurence Brahm, *Zhongnanhai* (Hong Kong: NAGA, 1998), 51–52.

262 *brazenly challenging . . . "The core"*   Gilley, *Tiger*, 243.

262 *"hid his anger"*   Lam, *Era*, 31.

262 *egregiously corrupt*   Yang, *Biography*, chap. 8.

263 *$380 million*   Gilley, *Tiger*, 243.

263 *link to Chen*   Nathan and Gilley, *Rulers*, 155.

263 *"Wang's problem"*   *Ming Pao* (Hong Kong), May 9, 1995, A2 (BBC).

263 *Jiang Zemin's name*   *Hsin Pao* (Hong Kong), April 12, 10 (BBC).

263 *seven Party elders*   *Lien Ho Pao* (Hong Kong), May 5, 1995, 10 (BBC).

263 *Politburo colleagues*   Nathan and Gilley, *China's New Rulers*, 154–57.

263 *Wei Jianxing*   Yang, *Biography*, chap. 8.

264 *"corrupt lives"*   Lam, *Era*, 50.

264 *"took charge"*   Gilley, *Tiger*, 246.

264 *Japanese prime minister*   *Asian Political News*, May 8, 1995.

264 *Zhu Jizhan*   Xinhua, May 5, 1995.

264 *"engineers of the souls"*   Xinhua, May 22, 1995; *PD*, May 23, 1995. The occasion of Jiang's speech was the fifty-third anniversary of the publication of Mao Zedong's *Talks at the Yan'an Forum on Literature and Art*, a classic commentary on the role of the arts in China's Communist society.

264 *annual conference*   Author's interview with Dr. Song Jian.

264–265 *"I sent him a letter"*   Addressed to "Comrade Jiang Zemin," Dr. Song's letter called for a strategic plan to develop China's science and technology over the next ten years, and to mobilize the resources to implement it. Song founded his proposal on two principles: Deng Xiaoping's "Science and technology is the number-one productivity force," and Jiang Zemin's "Science and technology as a productivity force should experience a new revolution and great development." After summarizing how America, Germany, Japan, South Korea, and at times China had used science and technology, Song wrote, "Therefore, we can see that to use science and technology to develop the nation is the common experience of all [developed] countries in the last two hundred years." The letter then noted how most of China's provinces, municipalities, and counties had already begun to "revitalize themselves through science and technology," and how various industries, such as chemical, petroleum, and agriculture, had done likewise. Song concluded, "'To revitalize the nation through science and technology' is a national trend and is becoming a natural strategy for the country," and he suggested that Jiang's speech "should set a high principle and map out a long-term plan" as "a guiding document for the turn of the century." Attaching his latest draft of Jiang's speech, which he had prepared with his team of experts, Song added a note of caution: "We are still not happy with the current version of the speech. We hope the CPC Central Committee Research Office would help improve it."

266 *"quality-oriented education"* Author's interview with Zeng Peiyan.

266 *life at the top* [following] Author's interview with Shen Yongyan.

267 *personally offended . . . "U.S. political figures"* [following] *Ping Kuo Jih Pao* (Hong Kong), July 14, 1995, A10 (BBC). The fiftieth anniversary of VE [Victory in Europe] Day was on May 9, 1995, and many world leaders had gathered in Moscow to celebrate.

268 *"confusing"* Gilley, *Tiger,* 255.

268 *"infringing"* JEN, June 30, 1995.

268 *"out of hand"* Willy Wo-Lap Lam, in *SCMP,* July 7, 1995.

268 *picture of Jiang* Lam, *Era,* 39.

268 *"rebuild Taiwan"* Willy Wo-Lap Lam, in *SCMP,* July 17, 1995.

268 *couldn't sleep* *Lien Ho Pao* (Hong Kong), June 11, 1995, 1 (BBC).

268 *joint venture* China Daily, July 14, 1995.

268 *"an all-around boom"* Xinhua, July 13, 1995.

268 *private letter* Robert S. Greenberger and Eduardo Lachica, in *AWSJ,* July 31, 1995.

268 *uncompromising stand* *Ming Pao* (Hong Kong), August 1, 1995, A2 (BBC).

268 *"relations rationally"* *Lien Ho Pao* (Hong Kong), August 14, 1995, 6 (BBC).

268 *"let Taiwan run away"* *SCMP,* September 10, 1995.

268 *launched six* Katsushi Okazaki, *China's Seaward Adventurism and the Japan-U.S. Alliance,* Japan Ground Self-Defense Force, CSC, 1997.

269 *second missile-launching* *Lien Ho Pao* (Hong Kong), August 14, 1995, 6 (BBC).

269 *"the big winner"* Kathy Chen, in *AWSJ,* September 1, 1995.

269 *"the new situation"* Xinhua, October 18, 1995 (BBC).

269 *Harry Wu* SCMP, August 26, 1995.

269 *Chinese embassy* [following] Xinhua, July 22, 1995 (BBC); Yang, *Common Leader,* 2001, 686–688. The Song dynasty poet's real name was Lu Yu (1125–1210).

269 *Hungary . . . Finland* Ibid.

269 *Twelve Relationships* Willy Wo-Lap Lam, in *SCMP,* October 10, 1995; Xinhua, October 9, 1995. Jiang's speech was given at the Fifth Plenary Session of the Fourteenth Party Congress.

270 *"grasping hold"* Willy Wo-Lap Lam, in *SCMP,* June 12, 1996.

271 *"Certain big powers"* JEN, October 24, 1995.

271 *so positive* *Wen Hui Bao* (Shanghai), October 26, 5 (BBC). U.S. assistant secretary of state Winston Lord described the encounter as the best of the three official meetings between Clinton and Jiang, saying that it laid a good foundation for the future.

271 *joint efforts . . . "Jiang spoke confidently" . . . "it was the first time"* Suettinger, *Beyond Tiananmen,* 241–42.

271 *Clinton reaffirmed*   *Business Times Singapore,* October 26, 1995.

272 *"saxophone playing"*   Inter Press Service, October 25, 1995.

272 *math professor*   Xinhua, October 23, 1995.

272 *historic trip to South Korea*   JEN, November 14, 1995. Trade between the two countries stood at $15 billion and was expanding rapidly; South Korea had invested $5 billion in China to fund about five thousand projects.

272 *"purely defensive"*   KBS Television (Seoul), November, 14, 1995 (BBC).

272 *friendship treaty*   *Korea Economic Weekly,* December 1, 1995.

272 *Japanese militarism*   JEN, November 14, 1995.

272 Opium Wars   Chen Changxi, *Tianjin Seniors Times,* September 13, 1997.

273 *posters*   To see the images, visit Stefan Landsberger's Poster Pages, www.iisg.nl/~landsberger/jzm.html.

273 *"Glad and at Ease"*   Gilley, *Tiger,* 229.

273 *"I shall try to capture"*   Lam, *Era,* 40.

Chapter 17. 1996

274 *"talk more"*   Willy Wo-Lap Lam, in *SCMP,* March 12, 1997; Lam, *Era,* 21. The phrase "talk more about politics" was developed in concert with Jiang's adviser, Wang Huning, who may have coined the phrase. As a political visionary and strategist, Wang was playing an increasingly important role in the plan to modernize the Party. An interesting selling point of the "talk more about politics" campaign was its universality. Different sectors of society could interpret it within the context of their own specific environments. To the army, the phrase meant allocating more of the nation's resources for defense and giving greater respect to soldiers as "the most devoted and trusted offspring of the motherland." But in the Special Economic Zones, "talk more about politics" was transformed "into giving priority to the interests of the people," which was then interpreted to mean accelerating reform. Lam, *Era,* 72.

274 *"By politics"*   Fewsmith, *China Since Tiananmen,* 178–179.

274 *superficially similar*   Gilley, *Tiger,* 267.

275 *"cultural trash"*   *AWSJ,* January 25, 1996.

275 *"We cannot sacrifice"*   Xinhua, January. 26, 1996.

275 *"severe crackdown"*   *ST,* January 26, 1996.

275 *"spiritual civilization"* . . . *"core task"*   Willy Wo-Lap Lam, in *SCMP,* January 26, 1996.

275 *study sessions*   Willy Wo-Lap Lam, in *SCMP,* June 30, 1996.

275 *"a critical moment"*   Author's interview with Leng Rong.

277–278 *"I was worried"* . . . *"unwritten rule"* . . . *"They live with their parents"*   Author's interview with Jiang Zehui.

277 *"I know Jiang Zehui"*   Author's interview with Ye Gongqi.

278 *"My grandchildren"*   *Time,* October 27, 1997.

278 *Spy satellites*   Willy Wo-Lap Lam, in *SCMP,* March 13, 1996.

278 *not in absolute control*   *Ming Pao* (Hong Kong), February, 24, 1996; Willy Wo-Lap Lam, in *SCMP,* March 12, 1996.

278 *General Zhang*   *ST,* March 15, 1996. The PLA Command Center on Taiwan had four functions: monitor Taiwan's military movements, propose strategies on Taiwan, plan military exercises in the Taiwan Straits, and carry out battle commands in a state of emergency.

278 *ground-to-ground missiles*   Katsushi Okazaki, *China's Seaward Adventurism and the Japan-U.S. Alliance,* Japan Ground Self-Defense Force, CSC, 1997; *SCMP,* March 9, 1996.

278 *"peaceful-unification"*   *Asian Political News,* March 11, 1996.

279 *virtual blockade*   Okazaki, *China's Seaward Adventurism and the Japan-U.S. Alliance.*

279 *USS* Independence   Simon Beck, in *SCMP,* March 14, 1996.

279 *"reckless"*   *SCMP,* March 10, 1996.

279 *second carrier*   Avery Goldstein, *China in 1996: Achievement* (A Survey of Asia in 1996, Part I), January 1, 1997.

279 *forty American warships*   Central News Agency (Taipei), August 20, 1996.

279 *"cool tempers"*   *AWSJ*, March 13, 1996.

279 *triggering events*   *Hsin Pao* (Hong Kong), March 22, 1996 (BBC).

279 *Politburo agreed*   Willy Wo-Lap Lam, in *SCMP*, March 26, 1996.

279 *Jiang volunteered . . . "Why were foreign"* [following]   Gilley, *Tiger*, 257–58.

280 *tougher, harder-line*   Suettinger, *Beyond Tiananmen*, 262.

280 *"confrontation behind him"*   Author's interview with Henry Kissinger.

280 *personnel issues*   *SCMP*, March 31, 1996.

280 *third-ranking Qiao*   Willy Wo-Lap Lam, in *SCMP*, April 4, 1996.

281 *"report to the NPC"*   Ibid., April 3, 1996.

281 *Wang Daohan*   Ibid., April 4. Official sources deny the veracity of this description of Jiang's tactics and Wang's advice.

281 *Jiang waited*   Lam, *Era*, 15.

281 *main point . . . "old road"*   Willy Wo-Lap Lam, in *SCMP*, April 4, 1996.

281 *"The direction" . . . anti-Leftist commentary*   *SCMP*, June 23, 1996. The writer accused Leftists of undermining reform by labeling policies like establishing stock ownership companies as "anti-Marxist" or antisocialist, and he asserted that "practice," according to Deng Xiaoping Theory, was "the only yardstick for measuring what was really Marxist."

281 *nationalisic articles . . . "shouldn't give up eating"*   Fewsmith, *China Since Tiananmen*, 173–175. The series of fifteen articles in *Economic Daily* began on June 20; the *People's Daily* rebuttal appeared on July 16.

282 *large network*   Willy Wo-Lap Lam, in *SCMP*, March 12, 1997.

282 *African countries*   Ministry of Foreign Affairs of the People's Republic of China.

282 *route similar*   Willy Wo-Lap Lam, in *SCMP*, June 11, 1995.

282 *sporty, smiling*   Lam, *Era*, 39. In like fashion, a picture of Jiang with PLA units during a 1995 military exercise in the Yellow Sea during the Taiwan crisis evoked a parallel photo of Mao forty years earlier.

282 *Anthony Lake . . . "quirky and strange" . . . "entrusted"*   Suettinger, *Beyond Tiananmen*, 277, 190; see also Jonathan Mirsky, "The Party Isn't Over," *New York Review of Books*, May 13, 2004, 38. Suettinger, a former director of Asian affairs for the National Security Council (1994–97), was present when Lake met Jiang.

283 *target of attacks*   World Tibet Network News, July 13, 1996.

283 *combing his hair*   Lam, *Era*, 13–14; Gilley, *Tiger*, 260–61.

283 *"move" him*   Gilley, *Tiger*, 230 (referencing *Jiushi niandi*, August 1996, 69).

283 *folding stool*   Ibid. (referencing *Jiefangjun bao* [PLA Daily], November 10, 1996).

283 *cult of personality*   Willy Wo-Lap Lam, in *SCMP*, July 1996.

283 *Eight weeks earlier*   The seventy-fifth anniversary of the Party was on July 1; Jiang gave the speech on June 21, since on July 1 he was visiting Romania.

283 *Seven Major Distinctions*   Willy Wo-Lap Lam, in *SCMP*, July 3, 1996.

284 *"distorted the facts"*   Ibid.

284 *consistency with Deng*   Willy Wo-Lap Lam, in *SCMP*, August 24, 1996.

284 *operational role*   Willy Wo-Lap Lam, in *SCMP*, August 21, 1996.

284 *"working committee"*   Gilley, *Tiger*, 231 (referencing *Jing bao*, March 1997, 25).

284 *think tank*   Laurence Brahm, *Zhongnanhai* (Hong Kong: NAGA, 1998), 94.

284 *backlash*   Lam, *Era*, 29

284 *Leading Groups*   Willy Wo-Lap Lam, in *SCMP*, August 21, 1996.

285 *railroad . . . "Solving"*   Daniel Kwan, in *SCMP*, September 23, 1996.

285 *Long March*   Xinhua, October 22, 1996. The harrowing year-long (1934–35) journey of about six thousand miles (other estimates range from under four thousand miles to al-

most eight thousand) taken by Mao Zedong's Communist Red Army overcame enormous natural obstacles and constant attacks to escape defeat by Chiang Kai-shek's Nationalist Army and reestablish itself around the city of Yan'an in Shaanxi province. Eighty-six thousand soldiers began the Long March, including many future leaders of the People's Republic (Zhou Enlai, Deng Xiaoping, Zhu De, Peng Dehuai, Lin Biao, and Li Xiannian); fewer than ten thousand of the original group arrived in Yan'an. But retreat became moral victory, inspiring generations of Communists.

285 *"synthesis"*   Daniel Kwan, in *SCMP*, September 23, 1996.

285 *"spiritual civilization"* [following]   Willy Wo-Lap Lam, in *SCMP*, October 7, 1996.

285 *"sacrifice spiritual"*   Lam, *Era*, 52.

285 *"a positive bid"*   Brahm, *Zhongnanhai*, 72.

286 *"philosopher-king"*   Willy Wo-Lap Lam, in *SCMP*, October 11, 1996.

286 *4,469 people*   CNN.com, April 10, 2002.

286 *new book*   *Time* International, July 22, 1996. The full title is *China Can Say No: Political and Emotional Choices in the Post–Cold War Era.*

287 *"Love Me Tender"*   Anthony Spaeth, in *Time*, October 27, 1997.

287 *stop in India . . . Pakistan* [following]   AsiaWeek.com, www.asiaweek.com/asiaweek/ 96/1213/nat1.html; Xinhua, November 30, 1996.

287 *Tung Chee-hwa*   *TKP*, August 15, 2001.

287 *singled him out*   Some believe that Tung's appointment had been decided even earlier. Jiang had first met Tung in 1989, when he was still the Shanghai Party secretary, and they stayed in touch. When Jiang said that he would send a "Hong Kong patriot" to be the SAR's first chief executive—several years before the handover—he may have been thinking of his old friend. The eldest son of the late shipping tycoon C. Y. Tung, Tung Chee-hwa expressed socially conservative views. "I lived in America during the sixties," he once noted. "I saw what happened with the slow erosion of authority, and the society became less orderly than is desirable. I certainly don't want to see this happen [in Hong Kong]" (BBC, www.bbc.co.uk/politics97/hk/tung.shtml).

287 *allegiance*   CNN.com, http://asia.cnn.com/SPECIALS/1999/china.50/inside.china/profiles/ tung.cheehwa/.

287 *"first Chinese chief executive"*   *TKP*, August 15, 2001.

288 *writers and artists . . . "It is impossible"*   *SCMP*, December 17, 1996.

288 *"literature creation"* [following]   *PD*, May 21, 1997 (BBC).

289 *"ability to create"*   Ibid.

289 *"sounded Western"*   Gilley, *Tiger*, 271

289 *"important chapter"*   Xinhua, December 27, 1996.

Chapter 18. JANUARY–SEPTEMBER 1997

293 *documentary series*   Author's communication, Beijing.

293 *lose consciousness*   *China News Digest*, January 2, 1997; *SCMP*, January 1, 1997.

293 *inflation*   Ibid. In 1996 the GDP growth rate was 9.7 percent, and consumer price inflation, which reached 17.1 percent in 1995, had dropped to a livable 8.3 percent. Nineteen ninety-seven was expected to be another good year.

293 *"We must not"* [following]   Willy Wo-Lap Lam, in *SCMP*, February 12, 1997.

294 Heart-to-Heart   Willy Wo-Lap Lam, in *SCMP*, February 12, 1997. As expected, Leftists criticized the book, which featured a large picture of a laughing Jiang Zemin on its cover. Its primary sins, according to Leftists, were the promulgation of "individualism" at the expense of socialist ideals and the notion that both contemporary Western culture and traditional Chinese culture—twin evils of old-time Communism—could be incorporated into an expanded understanding of socialism. The remnant Maoists were infuriated. They claimed that the book was "an attempt to hoodwink the public" and accused Jiang of ideological inconsistency. Gilley, *Tiger*, 284–85.

294 *"culturally deprived"*   Gilley, *Tiger,* 272.

294 *ideological education*   Lam, *Era,* 81.

294 *lung infection . . . Deng asked* [following]   Author's communication with historians, Beijing.

295 *funeral committee*   *China News Digest,* February 19, 1997.

295 *Qiao Shi*   Willy Wo-Lap Lam, in *SCMP,* February 21, 1997.

295 *"intriguing silence"*   Willy Wo-Lap Lam, in *SCMP,* February, 25, 1997.

295 *declarations of support*   Willy Wo-Lap Lam, in *SCMP,* February 23, 1997. The three senior generals were Chief of the General Staff Fu Quanyou, Chief Political Commissar Yu Yongbo, and Central Military Commission vice chairman Zhang Wannian.

295 *"Out of five working days"*   Willy Wo-Lap Lam, in *SCMP,* January 31, 1997.

295 *Extremes of Right and Left*   Todd Crowell and David Hsieh, "AsiaWeek.com, www.asiaweek.com/asiaweek/97/0314/nat2.html. Reportedly, Jiang refused to allow Zhao Ziyang to attend the funeral, while Deng Xiaoping's family excluded Deng Liqun, who had turned against his former boss—Deng Liqun had been propaganda minister under Deng Xiaoping—and was now openly critical of his 1992 Nanxun (Southern Tour), which reinvigorated reform and jump-started the economy. CNN.com, February, 23, 1997.

295 *February 24*   Author's communication with historians, Beijing.

296 *"The choice of Jiang"* [following]   Gilley, *Tiger,* 293–94.

296 *"deepening of reform"*   Todd Crowell and David Hsieh, AsiaWeek.com, www.asiaweek.com/asiaweek/97/0314/nat2.html.

296 *"multifaceted"* [following]   Willy Wo-Lap Lam, in *SCMP,* February 26, 1997.

297 *"One is to act"*   Joseph Fewsmith, *Elite Politics in Contemporary China* (New York: M. E. Sharpe, Inc., 2001), 137. Deng made the statement when returning to power after one of his purges.

297 *funeral urn*   *SCMP,* December 27, 1997.

297 *General Fu*   Daniel Kwan, in *SCMP,* February, 27, 1997.

297 *nine times*   Suettinger, *Beyond Tiananmen,* 302.

297 *Qiao Shi*   *SCMP,* March 2, 1997.

297 *"system of laws"*   *AWSJ,* March 17, 1997.

297 *"military thoughts"*   *SCMP,* March 3, 1997.

297 *meeting privately*   *SCMP,* February 27, 1997.

298 *the issue of "ownership"*   When an enterprise was "owned" by the state, what did this really mean? Classically, the massive ministries in Beijing were the proprietors of the large national enterprises, while medium-sized and small enterprises were under the administration of provincial or municipal governments. Each administrative agency would determined in advance what each factory was to produce, in accordance with an overall central government plan. What happened when multiple government agencies shared ownership of an enterprise? What about employee collectives, such as rural and township enterprises? Ownership, to put it mildly, was a confused issue.

    Furthermore, managers of state-owned enterprises (SOEs) do not own stock in their businesses. They are prohibited from raising their salaries or obtaining other monetary rewards. Such stringent limitations on executive compensation are designed to prevent corruption. (The actual effect, however, is more often the reverse.) SOEs are not free to run their operations; for example, managers cannot fire employees, because that would exacerbate unemployment.

298 *"capitalist road"*   Willy Wo-Lap Lam, in *SCMP,* April 30, 1997. Leftists ridiculed reform theorists for rationalizing public shareholding as a "form of the social ownership system," the reformist argument being that the shares would be held by many people, not a few "capitalist bosses."

298 *"at least several times"*   Willy Wo-Lap Lam, in *SCMP,* May 21, 1997.

298 *"When I was asked"*   Lam, *Era,* 37.

299 *"Party-and-state power"* Willy Wo-Lap Lam, in *SCMP*, May 21, 1997.

299 *Jiang went public* Ming Pao (Hong Kong), September 19, 1997 (BBC).

299 *losing money* Lam, *Era*, 291. By 1997, 46 percent of the 68,500 SOEs accounted for in the state budget were losing money. Two-thirds of all SOEs were in the red.

299 *bankruptcy* [following] Ian Johnson, in *AWSJ*, May 19, 1997. In 1996 six thousand enterprises had been closed down. In 1997 the bankruptcy program was expanded from 58 to 110 cities.

299 *Zhu Rongji* Lam, *Era*, 62.

299 *"public ownership"* [following] Jasper Becker, in *SCMP*, July 29, 1997.

300 *New and diverse forms* Author's interview with Leng Rong. Though the predominant type of ownership was by the state, the largely rural and difficult-to-classify collectives were becoming an increasingly important sector of the economy. There were also small foreign investments, primarily from Hong Kong and Taiwan. Private business per se was not encouraged in practice and was still condemned in theory.

300 *"I lived the history"* [following] Author's interview with Lu Baifu, Beijing, April 2002.

302 *obvious omission* Asia Times, May 30, 1997.

302 *protocol-appropriate posts* [following] Nathan and Gilley, *China's New Rulers* (2003), 183; Willy Wo-Lap Lam, *SCMP*, July 2 and 9, 1997. Tellingly, Qiao was not in the prestigious VIP delegation at the Hong Kong handover ceremonies.

302 *"reverse the verdict"* Fewsmith, *China Since Tiananmen*, 195.

302 *first leader* TKP, August 15, 2001.

303 *Chris Patten* FEER, September 18, 1997.

303 *handover ceremony* [following] TKP, August 15, 2001.

303 *four thousand guests* [following] SCMP, June 30, 1997.

303 *two flags rose* [following] SCMP, June 23, 1997.

303 *precise time* [following] CNN.com, June 30, 1997.

305 *"Freedom is not"* CNN.com, asia.cnn.com/SPECIALS/1999/china.50/inside.china/ profiles/tung.cheehwa/.

305 *hurried back* Willy Wo-Lap Lam, in *SCMP*, July 9, 1997.

305 *"national disgrace"* [following] Xinhuanet.com, July 1, 1997. The word for "vicissitudes" is *cangsang;* "national disgrace" is *guochi.*

305 *Beidaihe dateline* Ming Pao (Hong Kong), July 25, 1997 (BBC).

306 disunity Fong Tak-Ho and Wu Zhong, *Hong Kong Mail*, July 25, 1997. Jiang was said to be "locked in a battle of wills" with NPC chairman Qiao Shi over Politburo vacancies.

306 *gridlock* Willy Wo-Lap Lam, in *SCMP*, September 3, 1997.

306 *Jia Qinglin* Willy Wo-Lap Lam, in *SCMP*, August 26, 1997.

306 *Machine-Building Industry* Nathan and Gilley, *Rulers* (2003), 122–23. Jia Qinglin and Jiang Zemin overlapped for about three years (1977–1980). Jia was general manager of the China National Machinery and Equipment Import and Export Corporation from 1978 to 1983. Jiang was promoted to director of the Foreign Affairs Bureau in 1976 and resumed this position when he returned from his year in Shanghai in 1977, holding it until he was appointed vice minister of the two new trade-related commissions in 1980.

306 *"the chief architect"* Willy Wo-Lap Lam, in *SCMP*, September 12, 1997.

306 *remain the "core"* Willy Wo-Lap Lam, in *SCMP*, September 10, 1997.

306 *Chen Xitong* China News Digest, September 11, 1997. Chen had been under house arrest since 1995 for embezzling a wildly estimated (and probably exaggerated) $2.2 billion in public funds. Investigators reportedly found that he had amassed almost $300 million in cash along with an assortment of villas, apartments, and jewelry. Chen's fate left people unmoved. He had been the harshest toward student protesters in 1989, the most enthusiastic about the crackdown, and the most vengeful afterward. He was also known to be hypocritical and self-righteous. Meeting with student representatives on April 30, 1989, Chen trumpeted his honesty. "My monthly income is about 300 yuan, a little bit

lower than Party secretary Li Ximing's," he told them, smiling. "This is enough for me." *SCMP*, September 12, 1997.

307 *Zhao Ziyang issued*   *SCMP*, September 11, 1997.

307 *another letter*   *SCMP*, September 16, 1997.

307 *Three Favorables*   *PD*, June 28, 2002.

308 *"historical stage"* [following]   China Central Television, September 12, 1997 (BBC).

308 *370,000*   Kathy Chen, in *AWSJ*, September 19, 1997.

308 *ideological breakthrough*   Mark O'Neill, in *SCMP*, September 13, 1997.

308 *"ideological obstacles"*   Author's interview with Leng Rong.

308 *"emancipating the mind"*   Fewsmith, *China Since Tiananmen*, 193.

308 *too fast with privatization* [following]   Willy Wo-Lap Lam, in *SCMP*, September 12, 1997.

309 *"leap forward" in "inner-Party democracy"*   Willy Wo-Lap Lam, in *SCMP*, September 15, 1997.

310 *military downgrade*   Laurence Brahm, *Zhongnanhai* (Hong Kong: NAGA, 1998), 29.

310 *Now he was history*   Although Qiao Shi had been touted by Western media as a liberal, his taciturn, dour, secretive personality made it difficult for his colleagues to forget that he was China's longtime head of security and spying. Jasper Becker, in *SCMP*, September 19, 1997.

310 *What had happened*   For the web of stories surrounding the retirement of Qiao Shi, see Nathan and Gilley, *Rulers*, 157–161; Willy Wo-Lap Lam's reports in *SCMP;* and Gilley, *Tiger*, 306–307.

310 *technical factor . . . "we set the age"*   Nathan and Gilley, *Rulers* (2003), 184–185; *SCMP*, September 20, 1997.

310 *good relationship with Bo*   Fewsmith, *China Since Tiananmen*, 67.

310 *cutoff date*   Gilley, *Tiger*, 306.

310 *revered Bo Yibo*   Nathan and Gilley, *Rulers* (2003), 185.

311 *cover story*   The official explanation was not only that Qiao Shi's retirement was his own idea but also that his colleagues could not talk him out of it.

311 *"chatting and toasting"*   *Hong Kong iMail*, October 1, 1997.

311 *"Inner-Party democracy"*   Willy Wo-Lap Lam, in *SCMP*, September 24, 1997.

311 *decorum*   In fact, Qiao continued to give speeches at Party meetings, praising Deng Theory and indirectly trying to halt the elevation of Jiang Thought. He sought definitive criteria for the retirement of senior leaders, criticized the granting of multiple titles to individuals, promoted the "rule of law," and tried as always to expand the role of the National People's Congress. Willy Wo-Lap Lam, in *SCMP*, October 9, 1997.

311 *Zeng Qinghong*   Xiao Yu, in *SCMP*, September 24, 1997.

311 *supporting Hu Jintao*   Willy Wo-Lap Lam, in *SCMP*, October 1, 1997.

311 *"When you wake up"*   CNN, May 9, 1997.

313 *"Some nights"*   *Time*, October 27, 1997.

313 *"When Third Brother"*   Author's interview with Jiang Zehui.

313 *iodine-calcium tablets*   Vivien Pik-Kwan Chan, in *SCMP*, April 4, 1998; Yang, *Common Leader*, 2001, 258–259. China has about 40 percent of the world's cases of iodine deficiency, which causes mental illness.

313 *"Jiang usually calls"*   Author's interview with Shen Yongyan.

313 *"My last name"*   Guan Yu, "Jiang Zemin at Changchun First Automobile Works," *Children of China* (1994); author's interview with Shen Yongyan.

313 *"Since our relationship"*   Author's interview with Shen Yongyan.

313 *unusual request*   Author's interview with Dr. Song Jian.

313 *"It will be necessary"*   Bertrand Russell, *The Problem of China* (Nottingham, England: Spokesman Books, 1922), 244.

314 *Song arranged*   Song asked China's ambassador in London to purchase and deliver the case of books to the president's office. Song, who is fluent in English, translated Russell's

last chapter into Chinese and sent it to Jiang. Although Jiang never seems to have quoted from the book, and he had no further discussions with Song about it, much of what Russell recommended seventy-five years earlier seemed remarkably resonant with Jiang's current policies. Russell offered three "chief requisites" for China: (1) the establishment of an orderly government; (2) industrial development under Chinese control; (3) the spread of education. He stressed that a "spirit of patriotism" ("only defensive, not aggressive") would be "absolutely necessary to the regeneration of China." The sequence was not accidental. "Good government," Russell wrote, "is the prerequisite of all other reforms." Russell also encouraged "a new blend of Western skill with the traditional Chinese virtues." One would be forgiven for surmising that Jiang Zemin's philosophy of governance was influenced by Russell. This is not possible, of course, since Jiang did not discover Russell until 1997. Nonetheless, the parallels are striking and Jiang, an intellectual, must have been pleased to find himself corroborated by one of the twentieth century's most profound thinkers.

Chapter 19. OCTOBER–DECEMBER 1997

315 *Human rights activists* CNN.com, October 26, 1997.

315 *briefing books* Lam, *Era,* 3.

315 *researchers were dispatched* David M. Lampton, *Same Bed, Different Dreams: Managing U.S.-China Relations, 1989–2000* (Berkeley: University of California Press, 2001), 326.

315 *the remaking of America* Lam, *Era,* 3, 274.

316 *pre-trip interview* [following] Steven Mufson and Robert G. Kaiser, in *WP,* October 19, 1997, A1, 22 (interview).

317 *private dinner in Zhongnanhai* Ibid. In Washington President Clinton and Vice President Gore returned the gesture by making a special effort to greet Chinese deputy foreign minister Liu Huaqiu, who was meeting National Security Adviser Sandy Berger in preparation for Jiang's trip.

317 *Asian financial crisis* Bad debts of enterprises and governments, volatile currency fluctuations and speculations, slower growth rates, and loss of investor confidence in the "Asian miracle" (which would be blamed on "crony capitalism") conspired to cause a financial meltdown.

317 *"weaker steward"* Lampton, *Same Bed, Different Dreams,* 192.

317 *International Covenant* Office of the High Commissioner for Human Rights, www.unhchr.ch/html/menu3/b/a_cescr.htm.

317 *"There are still violations"* John Pomfret, in *WP,* October 27, 1997, A1.

318 *formal honors* [following] Ibid.

318 *"a shining pearl"* *Strive to Build a Constructive Partnership Between China and the United States—State Visit by President Jiang Zemin of the People's Republic of China to the United States of America* (Beijing: World Knowledge Press, 1997).

318 *"Lessons from that incident"* *WP,* October 19, 1997, A22.

319 *"Dr. Sun Yat-sen"* John Pomfret, in *WP,* October 27, 1997, A1.

319 *"where I acquired"* *Constructive Partnership,* 91.

319 *Jiang ate* Daniel Kwan, in *SCMP,* October 28, 1997.

319 *hula dancing school* John Pomfret, in *WP,* October 28, A9.

319 *"great rhythm"* Daniel Kwan, in *SCMP,* October 28, 1997.

319 *"Aloha, Jiang Zemin"* [following] John Pomfret, in *WP,* October 28, A9.

319 *"I will not surrender"* Gilley, *Tiger,* 337.

319 *"swimming very slowly"* Daniel Kwan, in *SCMP,* October 28, 1997.

319 *outrageous claims* *Time Asia,* September 27, 1999.

320 *"Flopping about"* [following] John Pomfret, in *WP,* October 28, 1997, A9.

320 *played tourist* [following] John Pomfret and John Harris, in *WP,* October 29, 1997, A4.

321 *on to the main event*   Ibid.

321 *"break the ice"* [following]   Ibid.

321 *"the most probing"*   James Bennet, in *NYT,* October 30, 1997.

321–322 *In his autobiography . . . Clinton went to bed . . . "had done well"*   Bill Clinton, *My Life,* 768–792.

322 *high ceremony*   Thomas Lippman, in *WP,* October 30, 1997, A1.

322 *"progress China"* [following]   *Constructive Partnership,* 203.

323 *"a shiny tie"* [following]   James Bennet, in *NYT,* October 30, 1997.

323 *"Yankee Doodle" . . . Hillary Rodham Clinton*   Ibid. Jasper Becker, in *SCMP,* October 30, 1997.

323 *formal part*   James Bennet, in *NYT,* October 30, 1997.

323 *"promote financial stability"*   Author's interview with Robert Rubin, New York, January 2004.

323–324 *"The Treasury Department"*   Lampton, *Same Bed, Different Dreams,* 111.

324 *"one China"*   *Constructive Partnership.*

324 *good rapport*   Other agreements, underreported but significant, were made on legal matters: combating international organized crime, narcotics trafficking, alien smuggling, counterfeiting, and money laundering. The two presidents also agreed that the United States would increase its support for ongoing exchanges of jurists and lawyers. John Broder, in *NYT,* October 30, 1997.

324 *"enormously successful"*   Author's interview with Robert Rubin.

324 *"greater ease"*   Thomas Lippman, in *WP,* October 30, 1997, A1.

324 *"over these five meetings"*   James Bennet, in *NYT,* October 30, 1997.

324 *spirit of candor*   Specific U.S. achievements included China's commitment to purchase fifty aircraft from Boeing valued at $3 billion—50 percent larger than expected. Permission was granted for a U.S. Drug Enforcement Agency office in Beijing. Tariffs were ended on computers and telecommunications equipment. As part of the trade, Clinton agreed to lift a twelve-year ban on the sale of American nuclear technology to China, an action encouraged by American corporations eager to tap into China's $60 billion market for civilian nuclear power plants. In order to secure the deal, China gave written assurances that it would no longer give nuclear support to Iran and that it would terminate two existing contracts. John Broder, in *NYT,* October 30, 1997.

324 *"an evolution"*   John Broder, in *NYT,* October 30, 1997.

324 *smooth process*   Thomas Lippman, in *WP,* October 30, 1997, A1.

324 *protesters* [following]   Simon Beck, in *SCMP,* October 30, 1997.

325 *"I have been immersed"* [following]   Office of the Press Secretary, White House, October 29, 1997.

326 *"Now, questions"*   James Bennet, in *NYT,* October 30, 1997.

326 *Jiang was ready*   Ibid.

326 *"speak a few words"* [following]   Office of the Press Secretary, White House, October 29, 1997.

327 *"I don't suspect"*   John Broder, in *NYT,* October 30, 1997.

327 *dinner guests* [following]   Roxanne Roberts and Tamara Jones, in *WP,* October 30, 1997, C1.

328 *Mao suit*   The tunic was Dr. Sun Yat-sen's innovative sartorial statement that combined China's modernity and independence, more practical and forward-looking than China's traditional dress and sufficiently different from Western business suits to assert China's uniqueness.

328 *"the sweep of a remarkable"*   Office of the Press Secretary, White House, October 29, 1997.

328 *"Asian and American flavors"* [following]   Roxanne Roberts and Tamara Jones, in *WP,* October 30, 1997, C1.

329 *Jiang met privately*   Terence Hunt, in AP, October 31, 1997.

329 *penchant for teaching*   Gingrich showed Jiang the painting of the signing of the Declaration of Independence by the American artist John Trumbull and explained its context. Commissioned in 1817, the twelve-by-eighteen-foot work portrays the committee that drafted the Declaration—John Adams, Robert Sherman, Thomas Jefferson (presenting the document), and Benjamin Franklin—standing before John Hancock, the president of the Continental Congress, in Independence Hall in Philadelphia, which Jiang would be visiting later on that same long day.

329 *"more Congress members"* [following]   *Constructive Partnership*, 109–13.

329 *"You cannot have"*   Helen Dewar and John E. Yang, in *WP*, October 31, 1997, A1.

329 *"almost impossible"* [following]   Simon Beck, in *SCMP*, October 31, 1997.

330 *"Is that how you"* [following]   Online *NewsHour*, October 30, 1997.

330–331 *selective coverage . . . Chinese press*   Kewen Zhang and Guochen Wan in *China Informed*, November 1, 1997.

330 *"This Just In"*   Steven Mufson, in *WP*, October 31, 1997, A20.

331 *"At Home, Rosy News"*   Erik Eckholm, in *NYT*, October 31, 1997.

331 *"ancient Chinese came"* [following]   *Constructive Partnership*, 51–63.

331 *Beijing dinner*   Author's interview with Maurice Greenberg.

332 *"a taste of the unexpected"* [following]   Ron Goldwyn, Myung Oak Kim, and April Adamson, *Daily News* (Philadelphia), October 31, 1997.

332 *"move all the demonstrators"*   Seth Faison, in *NYT*, October 31, 1997.

332–333 *before 5:30 . . . Grinning broadly* [following]   Da-hsuan Feng, in *China Informed*, October 30, 1997, www.chinainformed.com/Archive/x9710/971030.html.

332 *seminar*   Jasper Becker, in *SCMP*, November 1, 1997.

332 *"my heartfelt thanks"*   Ron Goldwyn, Myung Oak Kim, and April Adamson, *Daily News* (Philadelphia), October 31, 1997.

333 *"Ph.D. degree"*   Jasper Becker, in *SCMP*, November 1, 1997.

333 *Flyers jersey*   Seth Faison, in *NYT*, October 31, 1997.

333 *"liked the football"*   Ron Goldwyn, Myung Oak Kim, and April Adamson, *Daily News* (Philadelphia), October 31, 1997.

333 *Hun H. Sun*   Jiang and Sun had been students in a course on Heavyside functions for electrical engineering at Jiaotong University, taught by Gu Yuxiu, the famous professor (see below). (Heavyside was a famous mathematician.) Since Gu was a senior government official during the week, he could teach only a three-hour lecture on Saturday mornings, and he would always arrive with an entourage. Da-hsuan Feng, in *China Informed*, October 29, 1997, www.chinainformed.com/Archive/x9710/971029.html.

333 *Sun, the scion* [following]   John Pomfret, in *WP*, October 31, 1997.

333 *professor apologized*   Da-hsuan Feng, in *China Informed*, October 30, 1997,

333 *Gu Yuxiu*   *SCMP*, September 11, 2002.

334 *Ku's modest apartment* [following]   *Pennsylvania Gazette* (University of Pennsylvania), March 1999; Yang, *Common Leader*, 2001, 539–541.

334 *"It was remarkable"*   Author's interview with Li Zhaoxing.

334 *Jiang gave Ku* [following]   Yang, *Common Leader* 2001, 539–541.

334 *whispery voice*   *Pennsylvania Gazette*, March 1999.

335 *Ku had had the confidence*   Professor Ku had lived an astonishing life. He earned his bachelor's, master's, and doctoral degrees from MIT in four and a half years in the 1920s. In China he had been the dean of engineering departments and the president of two universities before emigrating, in 1950, to America, where he became a celebrated professor at the University of Pennsylvania. Even longtime friends were surprised to learn that the soft-spoken, unassuming Ku was highly regarded, remarkably, by both mainland and Taiwanese leaders. As vice minister of education under former Nationalist leader Chiang Kai-shek during the brief wartime alliance with the Communists, Ku had befriended

Zhou Enlai. Taiwanese president Lee Teng-hui had sent Ku a poem in honor of his ninetieth birthday, which hung on his wall along with that scroll of Jiang Zemin's calligraphy *Pennsylvania Gazette,* March 1999. When Professor Ku had traveled to China in 1986, he was invited by Jiang, then the mayor of Shanghai, for dim sum. "You were my old teacher," Jiang said warmly. Seth Faison, in *NYT,* October 31, 1997.

335 *"I am nonpolitical"*   *Pennsylvania Gazette,* March 1999.

335 *"Watch television"*   Seth Faison, in *NYT,* October 31, 1997.

335 *"When I became ambassador"*   Author's interview with Li Zhaoxing.

335 *Ku died*   Author's interview with Li Zhaoxing; *China Daily,* September 11, 2002.

336 *Museum*   *Pennsylvania Gazette,* March 1999.

336 *Independence Hall*   *Daily News* (Philadelphia), October 31, 1997.

336 *Assembly Room* [following]   Seth Faison, in *NYT,* October 31, 1997.

336 *"To the demonstrators"*   Ibid.

337 *all declined* [following]   Robert McFadden, in *NYT,* October 31, 1997.

337 *"grave concerns"*   *International Herald Tribune,* November 1, 1997.

337 *opening bell* [following]   John Kifner, in *NYT,* November 1, 1997.

337 *seventeen Chinese companies* [following]   John Pomfret, in *WP,* November 1, 1997.

337 *bull-and-bear*   Ibid.

337 *James Sasser*   *WP,* October 27, A18.

338 *IBM headquarters* [following]   John Kifner, in *NYT,* November 1, 1997.

338 *IBM scientist*   John Pomfret, in *WP,* November 1, 1997. The tour-guide scientist was one of the developers of the Deep Blue computer that beat world champion Gary Kasparov at chess. His father had fled to Taiwan when the Communists took over.

338 *visiting technology companies* [following]   John Kifner, in *NYT,* November 1, 1997; Ray Zhang, *China News Digest,* October 31, 1997.

338 *"You can read a hundred"*   John Kifner, in *NYT,* November 1, 1997.

338 *Crossing the Hudson*   Ibid.

338 *"didn't understand"*   Author's interview with Li Zhaoxing,

339 *U.S.–China Chamber* [following]   *Constructive Partnership,* 51–63.

339 *standing ovation*   Jasper Becker, in *SCMP,* November 2, 1997.

339 *hostile public spectacle*   *WP,* October 19, 1997, A1.

339 *American achievement*   Steven Erlanger, in *NYT,* November 2, 1997.

340 *Five thousand* [following]   John Yemma, in *Boston Globe,* November 2, 1997, A30.

340 *twelve hundred . . . fifteen hundred*   John Pomfret and Lena H. Sun, in *WP,* November 2, 1997.

340 *Mini-debates* [following]   John Yemma, in *Boston Globe,* November 2, 1997.

340 *Tibet its independence*   Even the most liberal of China's leaders, Li Ruihuan, asserted that unrest in Tibet was the result of too much freedom, not too little. Nathan and Gilley, *Rulers* (2003), 245–246.

340 *"Free Tibet"* [following]   John Pomfret and Lena H. Sun, *WP,* November 2, 1997.

341 *closed-circuit television*   Steven Erlanger, in *NYT,* November 2, 1997.

341 *"Harvard was among"* [following]   *Constructive Partnership,* 65–83.

343 *"Taiwan is not part"*   David Marcus, in *Boston Globe,* November 2, 1997, A1.

343 *question-and-answer*   Ibid.

343 *fifteen minutes*   Steven Erlanger, in *NYT,* November 2, 1997.

343 *selected questions* [following]   Ibid.; David Marcus, in *Boston Globe,* November 2, 1997; Norman Kempster, in *LAT,* November 2, 1997.

343 *"democracy works"*   David Marcus, in *Boston Globe,* November 2, 1997.

344 *"I did not recognize"*   Norman Kempster, in *LAT,* November 2, 1997.

344 *"Jiang joked"*   John Pomfret and Lena H. Sun, in *WP,* November 2, 1997.

344 *comments about Tiananmen*   David Marcus, in *Boston Globe,* November 2, 1997.

345 *"He was clearly relaxed"* [following] *Boston Globe,* November 2, 1997, A30.

345 *Boston business leaders* [following] David Marcus, in *Boston Globe,* November 2, 1997.

345 *"Jiang asked me"* Author's interview with Shen Yongyan.

345 *Hughes Electronics* In 1972 Hughes engineers set up ground stations to provide satellite television coverage of President Richard Nixon's historic visit to Beijing and his meeting with Mao Zedong. Henry Chu, in *LAT,* November 3, 1997.

345 *GM's cars* *SCMP,* November 4, 1997.

346 *lunch with 750* [following] Henry Chu, in *LAT,* November 3, 1997.

346 *Hollywood Does Protests* [following] Bob Pool, in *LAT,* November 3, 1997.

346 *chatted them* [following] Henry Chu, in *LAT,* November 3, 1997.

346 *Trojan Marching Band* [following] Robert Scheer, in *LAT,* November 4, 1997.

347 *"built with Chinese muscle"* Todd Purdum, in *NYT,* November 3, 1997; Henry Chu, in *LAT,* November 3, 1997.

347 *Republican governor* Attitudes toward China cut across traditional boundaries in American politics, unifying adversaries, separating allies, and defying traditional logic. In the reaction of local politicians to President Jiang's visit, compare New York's odd snub to Boston's proper respect and to Philadelphia's and Los Angeles's warm embrace. Democrats and Republicans were found on all sides. American business leaders, largely Republicans, lauded the Chinese leader and couldn't do enough for him, yet the Republicans in Congress were his most outspoken critics. On the Democratic side, President Clinton maintained a moderate stance compared to the congressional leaders of his own party. To personify the confusion, one need only note the clash between two high-powered liberal Democratic politicians from San Francisco, Representative Nancy Pelosi, a China basher, and Senator Dianne Feinstein, a staunch proponent of closer Sino-American relations. On almost all other issues, their positions were similar. Jasper Becker, in *SCMP,* November 2, 1997.

347 *"nineteen California cities"* Los Angeles and Guangzhou became sister cities in 1981.

347 *"seventeen years"* [following] Henry Chu, in *LAT,* November 3, 1997.

347 *"He's playing to"* Ibid.

347 *"Twenty years ago"* Ibid.

347 *nine hundred leaders* [following] Jim Yu and Guochen Wan, *China News Digest,* November 3, 1997; AP, November 4, 1997.

348 *"'A bright moon'"* *SCMP,* November 4, 1997.

348 *not avoid Taiwan* Henry Chu, in *LAT,* November 2, 1997.

348 *"profound friendship"* *Constructive Partnership,* 145.

348 *Jiang's journey* Seth Faison, in *NYT,* November 3, 1997; John Pomfret, in *WP,* November 3, 1997.

349 *"Jiang's year"* Seth Faison, in *NYT,* November 3, 1997.

349 *Wei Jingsheng* [following] Jasper Becker, in *SCMP,* November 17, 1997. Wei, a former electrician at the Beijing Zoo, was imprisoned in 1979 after writing an essay advocating political reform and posting it on a wall. In 1994 he was released after almost fifteen years, only to be arrested again, this time for fourteen more years. His plight became an international cause célèbre.

349 *"We are very pleased"* Ibid.

349 *APEC conference* *SCMP,* November 27, 1997. The Canadian government recognized the People's Republic two years before the Mao-Nixon summit in 1972, a fact that the Chinese had not forgotten.

349 *"Sporting a leather"* Reuters, November 26, 1997 (quoted in Gilley, *Tiger,* 328).

349 *Stetson hat* Gilley, *Tiger,* 328.

350 *promising not to devalue* *Hong Kong iMail,* December 15, 1997.

350 *"destabilized everything"*   Author's interview with Robert Rubin. Japan's unwillingness to reform was a major part of the problem, making China's decision not to devalue even more crucial.

350 *"never seek hegemony"*   Greg Torode, in *SCMP,* December 17, 1997.

350 *"remarkable"* . . . *"shouldn't be fooled"*   Anthony Spaeth, in *Time,* October 27, 1997.

Chapter 20. JANUARY–JUNE 1998

351 *"On Stressing Decorum"* [following]   *PD,* January 25, 1998 (BBC).

351 *"Our country"* . . . *ultra-Leftists*   Ibid.; Jasper Becker, in *SCMP,* January 26, 1998.

352 *Zhangjiagang country* [following]   Jasper Becker, *The Chinese,* 99–101.

352 *personnel changes* [following]   *Sing Tao Jih Pao* (Hong Kong), February. 28, 1998, 8 (BBC); Willy Wo-Lap Lam, in *SCMP,* March 4, 1998.

352 *"controversial figure"*   Willy Wo-Lap Lam, in *SCMP,* February 28, 1998.

353 *"People overseas"*   *Sing Tao Jih Pao* (Hong Kong), February 28, 1998, 8 (BBC).

353 *Jiang was elected*   Mary Kwang, in *ST,* March 17, 1998.

353 *Zhou Enlai*   *AsiaWeek,* June 19, 1998.

353 *Hu's office*   Willy Wo-Lap Lam, in *SCMP,* March 17, 1998.

353 *a vice chairman* [following]   Willy Wo-Lap Lam, in *SCMP,* March 21, 1998.

353 *"There is no need"* [following]   Willy Wo-Lap Lam, in *SCMP,* October 30, 1998.

354 *restructure*   The state's share of China's industrial output had already fallen markedly—from 80 percent in 1978 to around 35 percent in 1997. Non–state owned enterprises—private businesses, rural township and village enterprises, joint ventures, and foreign-owned companies—had experienced a concomitant rise, accounting for much of China's growth. In 1998, for the first time under China's constitution, private enterprises were officially legalized. Although they had been allowed, indeed encouraged, for years, private businesses were finally made legitimate, thus facilitating their getting bank loans and raising public capital. Yet there were still more than 300,000 state-owned enterprises, employing more than 70 million people, and they still dominated urban labor markets, employing two-thirds of workers in the cities.

354 *major streamlining*   Xinhua, March 2, 1998.

354 *33,000 positions*   Joseph Fewsmith, in *Asian Survey* (China), January 1, 1999.

354 *half a million*   Central News Agency (Taiwan), March 5, 1998.

354 *growth rate target*   Newsmakers, AsiaWeek.com, 1998.

354 *"No matter whether"*   Fewsmith, in *Asian Survey* (China), January 1, 1999.

354 *Zhu's prerogatives*   Willy Wo-Lap Lam, in *SCMP,* March 14, 1998.

354 *Jiang kept*   *SCMP,* February 5, 1998.

354 *international relations*   Willy Wo-Lap Lam, in *SCMP,* March 27, 1998.

355 *"the 'assault' stage"* [following]   *Inside China Mainland,* May 1, 1998.

355 *had their differences*   Central News Agency (Taiwan), March 5, 1998.

355 *"scapegoat"*   *China Focus,* May 1, 1998.

355 *different personalities*   Zong, "Zhu (I)" and "Zhu (II)," an extended essay that claims to have been written by a close associate of Zhu, has a self-proclaimed anti–Jiang Zemin bias, and as such its rich source material must be used with care. Exposing Jiang as a "slippery and devious politician whose priority is holding on to power and whose word cannot be trusted" seems more a purpose than a prejudice in lauding Zhu Rongji's accomplishments. For example, the author traces a ludicrous line of supposed causation from Jiang's "mishandling" of the Falun Gong demonstration to the American attack on the Chinese embassy in Yugoslavia to Lee Teng-hui's move toward Taiwanese independence. This laughably far-fetched theory claims that Jiang's heavy-handed reaction to Falun Gong suggested that China was "ripe for unrest, thus inviting the deliberate bombing," which the essay absurdly alleges was a premeditated plot to probe China's resolve and throw the country into chaos. Then, Jiang's "overly light and casual attitude" toward

the bombing, which was severely criticized in China, "emboldened Taiwan's Lee to declare his two-states policy." Whew!

The material claims to reveal "the increasing distance of the relationship between Zhu Rongji and Jiang Zemin" and seeks to promote Zhu by disparaging Jiang, whom the author characterizes as "jealous." Oddly, the sequence of events and the alleged conversations that the author reports do not seem to support the vigor of his conclusions. One could read the same set of facts and, without excessive twisting, come to an *opposite* cluster of conclusions: Jiang was the one who had always been underestimated in virtually all of his career posts, whereas Zhu always went into his with high expectations; Jiang was the one who supported the advancement of Zhu's career three times (mayor, vice premier, premier—when Zhu was promoted to premier in 1998, Deng Xiaoping was already dead and Jiang was the supreme leader); Jiang was the one criticized by Leftists for the reforms, and he was extending his exposure by backing Zhu; Jiang knew that along with Zhu's brilliance and intensity, he had a mercurial personality that could strike out in unexpected and disconcerting ways, and he sought to protect Zhu, as well as himself, by adding checks and balances. Jiang also knew that conservatives would be out for Zhu's hide, waiting for the time and circumstance to pull him down, since he personified the rapid reforms that they feared; therefore, Zhu would have greater likelihood of survival and success if Jiang would provide political cover for him, and he did so by making sure that he, not Zhu, had ultimate control. All that of course can be spun in the opposite direction, but the fact remains that Jiang Zemin and Zhu Rongji, with their complementary skills and contrasting personalities, with all their imperfections and mutual frustrations, made as good an executive team as could be fielded to deal with China's real-world complexities.

To the author's credit, he lists the areas in which Zhu Rongji worked together with Jiang Zemin: "in surmounting the ravages of the worst floods in a century, in withstanding the enormous pressures of the Asian financial crisis and preventing the devaluation of the renminbi, promptly reforming the management system of the Chinese People's Bank and plugging financial black holes, in vigorously enhancing the intensity of local tax collection and administration, in actively promoting state support for the army and forbidding the army and police to engage in commerce, in forcefully cracking down on smuggling, and in sparing no efforts to advance reforms of the national food grains system. *In all these matters, he [Zhu] received strong support from the general secretary [Jiang]*" (emphasis added).

"On the core issue of Jiang Zemin's character as a leader," Andrew Nathan, the celebrated scholar and editor of this work, concludes, "Western readers may be impressed with his independence from any particular political faction, his knack for straddling all sides of an issue, and his ability to keep rivals and subordinates guessing. If this was what it took to survive in power for ten years in a political system as vulnerable as China's to disabling power struggles, and to steer a middle course that kept the elite together, then perhaps Jiang's political skills deserve to be celebrated rather than deplored."

355 *former subordinates*   These included Zeng Peiyan, a key domestic adviser, to minister of the State Development Planning Commission; Zhao Qizheng, vice mayor of Shanghai and head of Pudong, to minister of the State Council Information Office; Chen Zhili, head of the Shanghai Propaganda Department, to minister of Education; and Zhang Wenkang, Jiang's medical adviser in Shanghai, to minister of health.

355 *"soft landing"*   Leu Siew Ying, in AFP, March 1, 1998.

355 *"pillars of China's economy"* [following]   Author's interview with Sheng Huaren, Beijing, April 2002. There were deep-seated problems, such as a surplus of labor, made worse by life-care obligations to retired as well as current workers for which SOEs were responsible. The rules at the time were that SOEs could hire but never fire, raise salaries but never lower them. All of this was detrimental to building competitive enterprises.

SOEs were saddled with enormous debt, products that no one wanted to buy, and out-dated manufacturing plants that polluted the environment.

"At the same time," said Sheng, "there was tremendous overcapacity since local governments decided to build factories without assessing market needs. In 1996 about half of China's SOEs were running at no better than 60 percent capacity. By early 1997 virtually the entire state sector was losing money. Then, to make matters worse, we were hit by the Asian financial crisis, which slowed exports."

356 *"tell you a secret"*   Author's interview with Li Zhaoxing.

357 Crossed Swords   Fewsmith, *Asian Survey* (China), January 1, 1999, referencing Ma Licheng and Ling Zhijun, *Jiaofeng (Crossed Swords)* (Beijing: Jinri chubanshe, 1998).

357 Titanic [following]   Antoaneta Bezlova, in Inter Press Service, June 2, 1998.

357 *shown to senior officials*   Mark O'Neill, in *SCMP*, April 3, 1998. *Titanic* would become the largest-grossing movie in China's history. Even the steep ticket price of up to 80 yuan—about ten percent of the monthly income of the average Beijing resident—did not dissuade viewers from packing the two hundred cinemas where the film was shown. Xinhua gave a lengthy analysis of the phenomenon, saying that the movie made audiences feel "that they were really in a disastrous situation when they were watching it," adding, "About 80 percent of the films distributed in China are Chinese products . . . and most of them are boring."

358 *surprised American intelligence*   Committee on Disarmament, Peace, and Security, http://disarm.igc.org/.

358 *"In November 1996"*   Sridhar Krishnaswami, in *The Hindu*, June 22, 1998.

358 *Clinton's China trip*   Mary Kwang, in *ST*, June 21, 1998.

358 *go smoothly*   Prior to the visit the Chinese government issued a circular promoting democratic village elections and requiring transparency in the management of village affairs. It also allowed a local venture to operate a website on which orders could be placed for Hollywood movies. For his part, Clinton agreed to have his official state welcome held outside the Great Hall of the People, virtually in Tiananmen Square, a place that had negative connotations for most Americans. The American side also agreed to stay in the elegant but outdated Diaoyutai State Guesthouse rather than in the modern China World Hotel. Mary Kwang, in *ST*, June 21, 1998.

358 *nuclear missiles*   JEN, June 26, 1998.

358 *"we still disagree"*   Jasper Becker, in *SCMP*, June 28, 1998; Mary Kwang, in *ST*, June 28, 1998.

359 *"the main point of the press conference"*   Bill Clinton, *My Life*, 793.

359 *"I specifically spoke"*   Author's interview with Shen Yongyan.

359 *state dinner* [following]   Xinhua, June 27, 1998 (BBC).

360 *Beijing University*   Michael Laris, in *WP*, June 29, 1998.

360 *"The more time I spent with Jiang"*   Bill Clinton, *My Life*, 794.

360 *"I have a very high regard"*   Suettinger, *Beyond Tiananmen*, 349 (referencing *WP*, July 4, 1998, A20).

360 *global leader*   Hsin Pao (Hong Kong), July 8, 1998 (BBC).

360 *"days of Mao"*   Willy Wo-Lap Lam, in *SCMP*, July 16, 1998.

361 *foreign media*   Frank Ching, in *FEER*, July 16, 1998.

Chapter 21. JULY–DECEMBER 1998

362 *"Hong Kong's return"*   TKP, July 1, 1998.

362 *"British officials"*   Benjamin Kang Lim, in Reuters, March 9, 1998.

362 *politician campaigning*   Hong Kong iMail, July 2, 1998.

362–363 *"shake hands"* . . . *"stood up"*   Wang Hui Ling, in *ST*, July 3, 1998.

363 *naval base*   Billy Wong Wai-Yuk, in *SCMP*, July 3, 1998.

363 *Wang Yeping* [following]   Hong Kong iMail, July 1, 1998.

363 *"People believe Mrs. Jiang"*   Alison Smith, in *SCMP,* July 2, 1998.

363 *vast network*   *China Securities Bulletin,* July 23, 1998; *Business Times Singapore,* July 24, 1998. The Rand Corporation, a U.S. think tank, estimated that China's military organs, at national or regional levels, controlled about ten thousand commercial businesses, mostly under the direction of fifty or so umbrella groups. Susan V. Lawrence, in *FEER,* August 6, 1998. Some estimates went as high as 20,000 businesses and 50,000 factories contributing $30 billion, or three percent of China's $1 trillion gross domestic product. *AsiaWeek,* August 7, 1998. Most of the more than $1 billion in earnings was undeclared, and some was sent offshore.

363 *basketball league* [following]   *ST,* September 14, 1998; author's communication in Beijing.

363 *smuggling*   Mary Kwang, in *ST,* July 25, 1998; Susan V. Lawrence, in *FEER,* August 6, 1998.

363 *rogue elements*   *AsiaWeek,* August 7, 1998.

364 *support of the leadership*   *Inside China Mainland,* September 1, 1998.

364 *gave that order*   Suettinger, *Beyond Tiananmen,* 336. The PLA-PAP meeting, which Jiang presided over on July 22, implemented the "Resolution by the Central Committee of the Chinese Communist Party on the Interdiction of Further Commercial Activities by the Military, Armed Police, and Government Agencies."

364 *"without conditions"*   Willy Wo-Lap Lam, in *SCMP,* July 25, 1998.

364 *General Xiong*   Author's interview with Xiong Guankai, Beijing, April 2002.

364 *The decision*   From a purely economic point of view, Jiang's decision also made sense. An example was the Palace Hotel in Beijing, one of the best places to stay in the capital. Almost always fully occupied, it was still losing money. "Why?" asked General Xiong, rhetorically. "Because it was owned by the military—actually the headquarters of the General Staff—the hotel had to accept many guests who did not pay at all! When anyone at high levels in the PLA had guests coming to Beijing, they could be put up at the Palace and treated royally without charge. Dinners and even banquets went for free, even for locals. The large number of 'comped' or nonpaying guests drove what should have been a highly profitable hotel into the loss column. So we had the dual detriment of corruption being nourished and banquets held for free." After Jiang's edict, management of the Palace Hotel was transferred from the PLA to the Everbright Group, then to the Peninsula Hotel Group, which began running the place as a real business.

364 *"anticorruption progress"*   There were complications, primarily replacing army funds that would be lost from shutting down their businesses. Several retired generals facilitated negotiations between political and military leaders over the amount and nature of substitute compensation from the government to the army. They requested the country's leaders show more consideration for the welfare of officers and soldiers who would be laid off as a result of the change in policy. In response, Jiang agreed to have the central government fund the first comprehensive insurance program—covering medical, unemployment, and retirement benefits—for PLA and PAP personnel. *SCMP,* September 10, 1998.

364–365 *harbor doubts . . . tactical retreat*   *Inside Mainland China,* December 1, 1998.

365 *massive flooding* [following]   Various sources, including Yang, *Common Leader,* 2001, 261–276.

365 *"routes flooded"*   Author's interview with Zhao Qizheng.

365 *death toll* [following]   *SCMP,* August 14, 1998.

365 *Epidemics*   More than fifteen hundred cases of cholera and four hundred cases of snail fever were reported, in addition to outbreaks of infectious diseases—typhoid, dysentery, hepatitis, influenza, and epidemic meningitis.

365 *"ensure victims"*   Kai Peter Yu, in *SCMP,* September 5, 1998.

366 *waxed eloquent*   Xinhua, September 4, 1998 (BBC).

366 *Yang Shangkun*   Xinhua, September 14, 1998.

366 *nation's filmmakers* [following]   Author's interview with Li Qiankuan. Also attending were Propaganda Minister Ding Guangen, Politburo member Li Tieying, General Chi Haotian, General Yu Yongbo, Minister Zeng Qinghong, Central Garrison Bureau Chief You Xigui, and senior officials from the Ministry of Culture and the State Administration of Radio, Film, and Television.

366 *"Jiang knew our names"*   Many senior leaders have had a strong interest in China's film industry. Chairman Mao and Premier Zhou Enlai maintained close friendships with artists; Zhou knew the names of most of the leading actors and actresses in his time and in which films they starred. "The same with General Secretary Jiang," said director Li. "He knows us personally; he always supports our work, and respects us deeply."

367 *"admirable character"*   Xinhua, September 22, 2001.

367 *"general public"*   Xu Guangchun, who had become minister of the State Administration of Radio, Film, and Television (SARFT) in 2000, said that Jiang "pays great attention to and has ardent expectations for" China's film industry. Xu hoped that the president's public support would help promote the industry, which had been struggling (Xinhua, September 22, 2001).

367 *controversy* [following]   Author's interview with Li Qiankuan.

369 *Jiang posed*   During the photo session Li Tieying, president of the Chinese Academy of Social Sciences, remarked that he respected Li Qiankuan and Xiao Guiyun as a couple. "They direct together; they're very successful professionally, and in their family and love life as well," he said. "They're not like some in the entertainment industry today who have no respect for Chinese tradition, family values, or even themselves. They divorce again and again; they never take any relationship seriously."

369 *"Jiang calls artists"*   Author's interview with Li Qiankuan.

369 *China Film Museum* [following]   Ibid.

370 *milestone meeting*   *China News,* Chamber WorldNetwork, October 17, 1998.

370 *official contact* [following]   AFP, October 21, 1998.

370 *disagreements* [following]   *ST,* October 19, 1998.

371 *visit to Russia*   JEN, November 23, 1998; Xinhua, November 23, 1998.

371 *"wealth of achievements"*   Xinhua, November 24, 1998.

371 *the idea unwise . . . sweat*   Author's communication, Beijing.

371 *flew to Tokyo*   Xinhua, November 25, 1998.

371 *Japan was now*   *China Securities Bulletin,* November 26, 1998.

372 *issue at hand*   JEN, November 24, 1998.

372 *fundamental difference*   *JEI Report,* December 11, 1998. Some Japanese muttered that if Jiang's state visit had taken place at its originally scheduled time in September (and not postponed because of the floods)—before Japan's apology to Korea had been given during South Korean president Kim Dae Jung's state visit to Japan in October—a similar apology to China would never have been an issue.

372 *On his arrival* [following]   JEN, November 25, 1998.

372 *compromise*   *ST,* November 27, 1998.

373 *embarrassed*   *AWSJ,* November 27, 1998.

373 *ibises*   Xinhua, November 28, 1998 (BBC).

373 *he disagreed*   JEN, November 27, 1998.

373 *"Both sides"*   Kohei Murayama, in Kyodo News Service, November 26, 1998 (BBC).

373 *owabi*   *ST,* November 29, 1998.

374 *doggedness*   Jiang's comments received a positive reception in some venues, noticeably at prestigious Waseda University, where the university president acknowledged his country's difficulty in dealing with its history.

374 *"I, as a witness"*   Xinhua, November 28, 1998.

374 *"visibly paled"* [following]   *Asahi Shimbun Asahi Evening News,* December 16, 1998.

374–375 *sarcastic remarks . . . "two guarantees" . . . diminish* [following]   Zong, "Zhu (I)," 31.

375 *twentieth anniversary*   Xinhua, December 18, 1998.

Chapter 22. 1999

376 *Christopher Cox . . . "sheer fabrication"*   James Kynge, in *Financial Times,* January 2, 1999, 3. The spokesman, Zhu Bangzao, denounced the Cox Report again on January 7: "Obsessed with the Cold War mentality, a few congressmen run counter to the historical trend and fabricate rumors out of thin air in an attempt to obstruct improvement in Sino-US relations." James Kynge, *Financial Times,* January 8, 1999, 5.

377 *visit Switzerland* [following]   Tani Freedman, *AFP,* March 25, 1999.

377 *ten thousand practitioners* [following]   John Pomfret and Michael Lars, in *WP,* April 26, 1999. Some estimates go to 20,000 (Nathan and Gilley, *Rulers,* 169), or 21,000 by afternoon (Zong, "Zhu [I]," 53).

377 *literally means* [following]   Religious Tolerance.org; www.religioustolerance.org/falungong.htm.

378 *"advanced system"*   Numerous Falun Dafa websites.

378 *"largest voluntary organization"*   U.S. News & World Report, February 1999.

378 *never even heard of it*   Although police had been tracking the organization for two years, and Jiang may have seen some of the reports, the sect's sudden appearance on the streets of Beijing baffled and frightened the general secretary. Zong, "Zhu (I)."

378 *"How could it be?"*   Author's interview with Shen Yongyan. The Ministry of Public Security, which has broad police powers, deals with domestic threats; the Ministry of State Security, which conducts espionage and counterespionage, deals with foreign threats.

379 *blamed Luo Gan*   Zong, "Zhu (I)," 60–61.

379 *"The government isn't opposed"*   The claim is made that Zhu Rongji met with Falun Gong representatives on that first day. Zong, "Zhu (I)," 57. The government position is that this story is a fabrication.

379 *Jiang attributed*   Ibid., 61.

380 *Cox Report*   The three volumes were an edited, declassified version of the classified final report that had been delivered to Congress on January 3, 1999.

380 *incendiary charges* [following]   *The United States House of Representatives Select Committee on U.S. National Security and Military/Commercial Concerns with the People's Republic of China.*

381 *another round of thefts*   Jeff Gerth and James Risen, in *NYT,* April 8, 1999.

381 *"I can also state"*   CNN, April 9, 1999.

381 *"great slander"*   PD, June 1, 1999; Reuters, June 1, 1999.

381 *Wen Ho Lee, . . . culprit*   The original *Times* report was James Risen and Jeff Gerth, "China Stole Nuclear Secrets from Los Alamos, U.S. Officials Say," *NYT,* March 6, 1999. Numerous follow-up stories appeared in a publishing frenzy over the next eighteen months, culminating in an unprecedented, self-critical *NYT* "assessment" (in reality a long mea culpa) on September 26, 2000: "From the Editors; The Times and Wen Ho Lee."

381 *presiding judge*   NYT reported that the judge "stunned a suddenly hushed courtroom by implicitly singling out Attorney General Janet Reno, Energy Secretary Bill Richardson and senior officials in the Clinton White House for what he said was a questionable indictment, for misleading him about Dr. Lee's supposedly deceptive behavior and then for ignoring his urgings that the government ease the 'demeaning, unnecessarily punitive conditions' under which Dr. Lee was being held. It was a moment of enormous weight, since it is exceptional for a federal judge to give such an excoriating tongue-lashing to high-level federal officials." James Sterngold, "Nuclear Scientist Set Free After Plea in Secrets Case; Judge Attacks U.S. Conduct," *NYT,* September 14, 2000.

381 *Chinese achievements*   All of the following technologies, Zhao asserted, had been de-

signed independently by Chinese scientists, many of them at a time when the nation had little if any contact with other countries: surface-to-surface missiles, atom bombs, H-bombs, earth satellites, intermediate and short-range missiles, long-range rockets, submarine-launched solid-propellant rockets, recoverable satellites, multiple satellites launched by one rocket, and geostationary communication satellites.

381 *offended*   "The Cox Report is a total lie," said Cui Xinshui, an incensed senior scientist at China Aerospace Corporation. "It completely underestimates the Chinese people's ability to develop our own aerospace industry, which was entirely the result of our own hard work. One must remember that during the times of economic hardship and international isolation—when the Western countries cut us off and when the Soviet Union was isolating us—we depended entirely on ourselves. China had already developed the technology for our missile guidance systems in 1984—work that we had begun in 1965." (Author's interview with Cui Xinshui, Beijing, 1999.)

382 *"archenemy"*   Jiang An, in *ST,* June 12, 1999.

382 *"the atmosphere"*   JEN, June 4, 1999.

382 *"Stick to principles"*   *Ching Pao* (Hong Kong), August 1, 1999, 24–26 (BBC).

383 *"I don't like"* [following]   Author's communication, Beijing. During the 1989–90 period, Jiang, influenced by others in the post-Tiananmen reactionary environment, had sought to limit the growth of private businesses, some of which had bankrolled the student protests. Ching Cheong, in *ST* Asia News Network, *Korea Herald,* March 5, 2003.

383 *"China needs entrepreneurs"*   By early 2002 the private sector accounted for 33 percent of the Chinese economy, up from effectively zero twenty years before and just below the state sector's 37 percent. Nongovernment economists put private output even higher. In Beijing private sector employment overtook public sector employment. All agreed that the private sector was growing much faster than the state-owned sector. In addition, "collective enterprises," which are generally rural and privately run, contributed more to China's GDP than state-owned enterprises.

384 *"state-to-state"*   *China News Digest,* July 13, 1999.

384 *"not a relationship"*   Lee Teng-hui's speech to 3470 Rotary Club, China News Agency, July 20, 1999.

384 *Jasper Becker*   Jasper Becker, *The Chinese,* 347.

384 *"insect"*   PD, July 14, 1999.

385 *"predict the bombing"*   Seth Faison, in *NYT,* July 31, 1999.

385 *"unlawful organization"*   Xinhua, July 22, 1999.

385 unlawful   According to the official decree, newly proscribed Falun Gong activities included displaying or distributing streamers, pictures, insignias, signs, books, magazines, audio and video products, and any other propaganda materials. All gatherings to promote or participate in Falun Gong activities were prohibited, as were assemblies, parades, and demonstrations. To make sure nothing was omitted, a broad miscellaneous category was devised, and the fabrication and distortion of facts and the deliberate spreading of rumors were also outlawed.

385 *"spiritual poisoning"* . . . *Margaret Singer*   Religious Tolerance.org, www.religious tolerance.org/falungong.htm.

386 *"No measures are too"*   Various Falun Gong websites.

386 *new book*   AFP, August 9, 1999.

386 *WTO*   The World Trade Organization is the international body established to promote and protect world trade and includes all provisions for commerce in goods, services, and intellectual property. It is a code of rules and procedures governing the settlement of disputes, a platform for countries to express their concerns regarding the trade policies of their trading partners, and a forum to discuss and resolve trade issues, reduce trade barriers, and expand trade opportunities. China's bid to gain accession to the WTO had indeed been a long march, an arduous fifteen-year process.

386 *"ossified"* Zong, "Zhu (I)," 51.

386 *"Black hair"* Ibid., 38.

386 *"overall situation"* Ibid., 40.

387–388 *"realized his error"* . . . *Joseph Fewsmith* . . . *"posting was widely seen in China"* . . . *"feet to the fire"* . . . *labeled him a "traitor"* . . . *"traitor" was Jiang"* [following] Joseph Fewsmith, "China and the WTO: The Politics Behind the Agreement," The National Bureau of Asian Research, November 1999, http://www.nbr.org/publications/report.html. Referencing "Chinese sources," Fewsmith reports that "President Clinton had written Jiang Zemin a letter on November 6, 1998, expressing hope that the WTO issue could be resolved in the first quarter of 1999. On February 8, 1999, Clinton is said to have written a second letter to Jiang Zemin stating that he hoped that WTO negotiations could be concluded during Premier Zhu Rongji's visit to the United States. A third letter, on February 12, expressed hope that a package deal could be reached." According to Fewsmith, "One version of events argues that before Zhu left for the United States, Jiang Zemin gave a personal authorization to make the concessions necessary to achieve WTO membership. According to this interpretation, the ensuing brouhaha was because the decision was not a collective one. But . . . there was an expanded Politburo meeting in late February. Thus, if there is any truth in this version, it may consist of Jiang's personal encouragement to be as forthcoming as possible. Another version, not necessarily incompatible with the first, suggests that Zhu's 'fault' was in accepting provisions that were at or near China's 'bottom line' across the range of issues rather than, as expected, yielding in some areas while holding fast in others." Fewsmith states that the source of Zhu's problems lay first in the enemies he made among China's bureaucrats as he moved to restructure industry and government; "and second, Zhu became the scapegoat for discontent with Jiang Zemin's policy decisions." The Chinese word for "traitor" is *maiguozei*.

387 *"We had reached"* Author's interview with Robert Rubin.

387 *"The reaction"* Zong, "Zhu (I)," 49.

388 *"look down"* Ibid., 48.

388 *had not wanted to go to the United States . . . redirect blame* Fewsmith, *China Since Tiananmen*, 213.

388 *"harsh rhetoric"* Ibid., 212.

388 *He also modified* Official sources deny any modification to Premier Zhu's responsibilities at this time or for these areas.

389 *begun to differ* [following] Zong, "Zhu (II)," 75–77.

389 *"Wang Yeping* Fewsmith, *China Since Tiananmen*, 223–224.

389 *"very productive"* AFP, September 11, 1999.

389 *Jiang lectured . . . bad taste* Suettinger, *Beyond Tiananmen*, 406.

389 *"The Taiwan problem"* *China Today*, September 12, 1999.

389 *officers were executed . . . freeze pay raises* Jasper Becker, *The Chinese*, 287; AFP, September 14, 1999.

390 *massive parade* [following] PD, October 2, 1999.

390 *public portrait* AP, October 1, 1999.

390 *"calculate political accounts"* Zong, "Zhu (II)," 87.

391 *"Our great motherland"* [following] PD, October 1, 1999.

391 *trip to Britain* CNN, October 19, 1999; PD, October 19, 1999.

391 *Greenwich Observatory* PD, October 21, 1999.

392 *"speed up"* Xinhua, November 15, 1999; JEN, November 15, 1999.

392 *grueling negotiations . . . "Although Premier Zhu"* . . . *"The agreement on China's entry"* Fewsmith, "China and the WTO," The National Bureau of Asian Research, November 1999. On October 16, a month after the meeting between their trade negotiators (Shi Guangsheng and Charlene Barshefsky), President Clinton called Jiang "to urge a resumption of serious WTO negotiations." Clinton again called Jiang on November 6 and

then decided to send Barshefsky and her team to Beijing on November 8 to try to reach agreement.

392 *"driving force"*   Xinhua, November 15, 1999.

393 Shenzhou   Xinhua, November 20, 1999.

393 *Jiang inspected*   Xinhua, November 24, 1999.

393 *corruption*   Wei Jianxing, secretary of the Central Commission for Discipline Inspection, later reported that the Party investigated 130,414 cases and punished 132,447 corrupt officials in 1999. Seventeen were at the ministerial level, and more than 4,400 were heads of bureaus, prefectures, departments, division offices, and counties. In addition, 19,458 companies run by the army, armed police, police, and legal departments were shut down, and 6,494 were transferred to local governments.

393 *tobacco king*   Lynne O'Donnell, in *Australian*, January 11, 1999.

394 *"complicity with smugglers"*   Jonathan Manthorpe, in *Vancouver Sun*, January 22, 2000.

394 *"key role"*   Deutsche Presse-Agentur, August 2, 2000.

394 *"flagrant criminal"*   PD, March 9, 2000.

394 *egregious corruption* [following]   Ching Cheong, in *ST*, January 30, 2000. *People's Daily* (April 29, 2001) stated the smuggled goods were worth 53 billion yuan (about $6.4 billion), with a customs-duty evasion of up to 27 billion yuan ($3.25 billion). Foreign sources put the value at north of $10 billion. Three ministerial officials, twenty-six government department directors, and eighty-six county officials were caught in the scheme. www.China.org.cn.

394 *hou tai*   *Newsweek International*, December 20, 1999.

394 *"grab the big"*   Ibid.

394 *"a hundred coffins"*   *Time Asia*, November 2, 1998; Willy Wo-Lap Lam, in *China Brief*, January 17, 2002. There are several variants of this well-known quote—Lam states it goes back to the middle 1990s—but an original source is not found. Another sardonic statement that Zhu allegedly made was at a convention of entrepreneurs (September 2001), where he supposedly blurted out that his enemies would "get me after my retirement."

394 *"Some comrades' confidence"* [following]   Xinhua, July 1, 1999.

395 *campaign*   The Three Stresses campaign targeted leading officials above the county level and stressed "studying [political] theory, increasing political consciousness, and cultivating healthy trends [conduct]" (Xinhua, December 5, 1998)—in other words, upholding the state ideology of one-party Communist rule ("study"), fostering obedience to the central Party and government ("politics"), and fighting corruption by promoting moral rectitude and decent behavior ("healthy trends"). The program for each participant would last for about two months.

395 *appointed director*   Since Zeng Qinghong's new position put him in charge of all high-level personnel decisions at the ministerial and provincial levels throughout the country, the Three Stresses campaign was a good vehicle for assessing candidates for promotion, particularly with respect to their dedication to Party tenets and loyalty to its leadership.

395 *reached agreement*   The United States agreed to pay $28 million for the destruction of the Chinese embassy in Yugoslavia and $4.5 million to those injured and the families of the three killed. At the same time China agreed to pay $2.87 million in compensation for damages to the U.S. embassy in Beijing sustained in the riots that followed the bombing. AP, January 21, 2000.

395 *patriotic excitement*   According to a government-run survey of 2,500 residents in ten cities, virtually all said they would watch the live broadcast of the return ceremony; 53 percent said that they paid special attention to stories about Macao; and a full 85 percent knew that Ho Hau Wah would be the first chief executive of the Macao Special Administrative Region.

396 *Millennium Monument*   Jasper Becker, *The Chinese,* 341–342.
396 *"The Chinese nation"*   Xinhua, January 1, 2000.
396 *inscription by Jiang*   Ibid.
397 *commemorate* [following]   Author's interview with Jiang Zehui.
397 *his perennial duty*   In Chinese tradition, when the parent's generation passes away, the oldest son and daughter-in-law assume responsibilities for the entire Big Family.

Chapter 23. JANUARY–JUNE 2000
403 *"high-tech wars"* [following]   Xinhua, December 31, 1999.
403 *decree modernizing*   Xinhua, February 23, 2000 (BBC).
403 *"CMC chairman's office"*   Willy Wo-Lap Lam, in *SCMP,* July 27, 2000.
404 *"private enterprises"*   Pakistan Press International, January 5, 2000.
404 *China's stock markets*   In China the use of the terms "public" and "private" in reference to companies differ from their usage in the West. In the United States, a "public" company is one that has issued shares to the general public and is listed on a stock exchange; a "private" company has done neither; and there are virtually no "state-owned" companies. In China, a "public" company is one that is owned or controlled by the state, irrespective of whether it has issued shares to the public and is listed on an exchange; and if a "private" company issues shares to the public and is listed on an exchange, it is still considered a private company because the state has no ownership. Furthermore, Professor Joseph Fewsmith points out that "the notion of 'private' has traditionally been understood quite differently in China than in the West. We have tended to see 'private' as good; the expression of partial interests is central to our notion of pluralism. In traditional China, the term 'private' (*si*) was generally viewed as the antithesis of 'public' (*gong*). The government, specifically the emperor, was supposed to embody notions of 'public' . . . articulating a private, partial interest was taken as by definition in opposition to 'public.'" Statement of Dr. Joseph Fewsmith to the Congressional-Executive Commission on China, July 24, 2003, http://www.cecc.gov/pages/hearings/072403/fewsmith.php.
404 *"The more we do"* [following]   Xinhua, January 14, 2000 (BBC); *ST,* January 15, 2000.
404 *Jia Qinglin* [following]   Ching Cheong, in *ST,* January 30, 2000; *AsiaWeek,* February 3, 2000.
404 *his wife*   Lin Youfang, Jia Qinglin's wife, had been general manager of Fujian province's import-export company (Nathan and Gilley, *Rulers,* 2003, 124), but reports in Hong Kong that she had been arrested, and that this had necessitated a divorce, were denied both by her and a government spokesman. Deutsche Presse-Agentur, January 27, 2000.
404 *promote Jia*   Willy Wo-Lap Lam, in *SCMP,* January 31, 2000.
404 *"Now there is talk"*   *Cheng Ming* (Hong Kong), February 1, 2000 (BBC).
405 *Great West* [following]   Author's interview with Zeng Peiyan.
405 *Economists stated*   Xinhua, February 15, 2000.
405 *"The development of the west"*   Xinhua, February 26, 2000 (BBC).
405 *big brother system*   Willy Wo-Lap Lam, in *SCMP,* September 9, 2000.
405 *"talented people"*   Xinhua, June 21, 2000 (BBC).
405 *retain professionals*   Asia Pulse, June 22, 2000.
406 *Jiang counseled*   Xinhua, June 21, 2000 (BBC).
406 *"from slogans to action"*   Author's interview with Zeng Peiyan.
406 *Qinghai-Tibet*   Perhaps the most challenging railroad construction project ever, the region-transforming Qinghai-Tibet Railroad would be almost 700 miles long, 500 miles of which would be at 13,000 feet above sea level and 300 miles of which would course over frozen ground.
406 *project was military*   William C. Triplett II, "The Dragon in the Indian Ocean," *China Brief,* February 25, 2003. The railroad, critics claimed, would provide a vast new mobile

staging area for rail-based ICBM missiles and effect "the permanent militarization of the entire plateau." Jiang disagreed. "China will never threaten its neighbors," he repeated in several contexts. "No matter how strong China becomes, we have suffered too much to ever become an oppressor."

406 *developing its West*　In March Zeng presented a package of projects for the region, which he said would rebalance inequities and diminish China's dependence on exports to power its economy. The government would transfer low-tech, labor-intensive, and environmentally unfriendly industries to the West as a way of absorbing unemployed workers. Critics, however, saw a dark side, branding it an attempt to suppress independence movements in Tibet and Xinjiang by overwhelming the natives with large numbers of Han Chinese.

406 *speaking in Gaozhou* [following]　Xinhua, February 20, 2000 (BBC).

406 *"Handling China's"*　Xinhua, March 9, 2000 (BBC).

407 *buried the sentence*　Xinhua, February 26, 2000 (BBC).

407 *Three Represents* [following]　Xinhua, March 5, 2000 (BBC).

407 *Li Changchun*　Josephine Ma, in *SCMP,* April 2, 2000.

407 *"Wang Huning and I"*　Author's interview with Teng Wensheng.

408 *"ideological resoluteness"*　Willy Wo-Lap Lam, in *SCMP,* February 28, 2000.

408 *"Success"*　Xinhua, March 5, 2000 (BBC).

408 *school-related cases* [following]　Xinhua, March 1, 2000 (BBC).

408 *"quality education"*　Author's interview with Zeng Peiyan.

409 *"burning beanstalks"* [following]　Xinhua, March 8, 2000 (BBC); JEN, March 8, 2000.

409 *"If Taiwan's voters"*　William J. McMahon, in *China Online,* March 21, 2000.

410 *"never hold"*　Willy Wo-Lap Lam, in *SCMP,* March 22, 2000.

410 *"Anything can"*　William J. McMahon, in *China Online,* March 21, 2000.

410 *"military action"*　Willy Wo-Lap Lam, in *SCMP,* March 28, 2000.

410 *"favoring independence"*　Willy Wo-Lap Lam, in *SCMP,* May 11, 2000.

410 *groundbreaking trip*　Among those along with Jiang were Vice Premier Qian Qichen; State Councilor Wu Yi; Planning Commission minister Zeng Peiyan; Policy Research Office director Teng Wensheng; Central Guards Bureau director You Xigui; special assistant Wang Huning; and Jiang Office director Jia Ting'an. Xinhua, April 12, 2000.

410 *"friendly relations"* [following]　Xinhua, April 13, 2000 (BBC).

411 *Phalcon*　*Jerusalem Post,* April 13, 2000 (BBC).

411 *American law*　Israel Radio, April 13, 2000 (BBC).

411 *"steamroller"*　*Jerusalem Post,* April 13, 2000 (BBC). Implying a double standard, the official, Israeli deputy defense minister Ephraim Sneh, recalled that when the United States sold similar planes to Saudi Arabia in the 1980s, it had assured Israel that they were purely defensive.

412 *deceived, by Barak*　*Times of India,* August 29, 2000.

412 *refuse to meet*　*SCMP,* September 4, 2000 (quoting Israel Radio).

412 *"all civilizations"*　Xinhua, April 13, 2000.

412 *Zohar Agriculture*　Xinhua, April 14, 2000.

412 *ECI Telecom*　ECI Telecom news release, April 18, 2000.

413 *Arafat*　Xinhua, April 15, 2000.

413 *Dead Sea*　*Times of India,* April 16, 2000.

413 *"I visited Israel"*　Author's communication, Beijing, late 2003.

413 *In Turkey*　Anadolu News Agency, April 19, 2000.

413 *major speech*　*Jiang Zemin on the "Three Represents"* (Beijing: Foreign Languages Press, 2001), 14.

414 *"six kinds of errors"*　First, critics said that Three Represents presented neither new thoughts nor new themes in ideological development. Second, since the ideology of Three Represents had been proposed without practice and testing, it might cause ideological confusion. Third, opponents suggested that its ideological and political develop-

ment was weak, making it difficult for people to have a common understanding of it. Fourth, critics doubted whether a new ideological theory was even necessary. Fifth was the charge that Three Represents was aimed at developing a cult of personality around Jiang Zemin. Finally, some wondered whether, if Marxism and Deng Xiaoping Theory were being replaced by the Three Represents, they were still relevant. *Cheng Ming* (Hong Kong), July 1, 2000, 14–16 (BBC).

414 *Hu Jintao defended*   Ibid.

414 *swath of islets*   JEN, May 17, 2000.

414 *"reassured me"*   *BusinessWorld,* May 18, 2000.

414 *"sealed their friendship"* [following]   *Manila Standard,* May 17, 2000.

415 *PNTR*   *Online NewsHour,* www.pbs.org/newshour/bb/asia/china/pntr/house_vote_5-24. html.

415 *legislation then went*   U.S.–China Policy Foundation, www.uscpf.org/news/2000/05/ 052600.html.

415 *"steadily improving"*   Joins.com (Korea), May 29, 2000.

415 *Taiwan issue*   JEN, May 28, 2000.

415 *North Korea*   One report described contingency plans by the Chinese military for a number of huge refugee "reception centers"—each capable of accommodating 100,000 displaced persons—in case desperate North Koreans began streaming across the border. *Newsweek,* June 19, 2000.

416 *inter-Korean summit* [following]   Xinhua, June 16, 2000 (BBC).

416 *"vision and wisdom"*   JEN, June 16, 2000.

416 *weapons technology*   Bill Gertz, in *Washington Times,* June 18, 1997.

416 *curtailed*   *Iranian,* July 3, 2002.

416 *renewed military aid*   American Foreign Policy Council, January 3, 2001.

416 *Zhang Xueliang*   Xinhua, June 2, 2000.

417 *a lifelong passion*   Author's interview with Dr. Song Jian. Song had retired as chairman of the State Science and Technology Commission in 1998 and was vice chairman of the CPPCC when this conversation with President Jiang took place in February 2000. Song divided his paper into two parts: (1) classical physics and electromagnetic discoveries of the seventeenth to mid-nineteenth centuries, and the industrial revolution that accompanied them; and (2) the revolutionary quantum physics of the late nineteenth to mid-twentieth centuries that triggered the technology explosion.

417 *scientific theories*   Xinhua, August 5, 2000 (BBC).

417 *top ten nations*   Research Technology Management, March 2000.

417 *"solid truth"*   Sinofile Information Services, June 13, 2000.

417 *seek innovation*   Xinhua, June 5, 2000 (BBC).

417 *Three Innovations*   David Hsieh, in *ST,* October 30, 2000. For example, at a Party-building conference in Changchun in August, Jiang focused on innovation, especially in economics.

417 *"two core"*   Author's interview with Zeng Peiyan.

417 *"All of society"*   Xinhua, June 4, 2000 (BBC).

417 *long interview*   *Science,* June 16, 2000, 1950–1953; *PD,* May 18, 2000.

417 *"We recognize and respect"*   Jiang Zemin, *Science,* June 30, 2000, 2317.

418 *"My point is that"* [following]   *Science,* June 16, 2000, 1950–1953; Xinhua, June 18, 2000.

418 *world-renowned scientists*   Xinhua, August 5, 2000 (BBC).

418 *"Jiang makes time"*   Author's interview with Zeng Peiyan.

418 *"grandchildren ask . . . younger cadres"*   *Hong Kong iMail,* June 16, 2000 (BBC).

Chapter 24. JULY–DECEMBER 2000

419 *Putin paid*   Xinhua, July 18, 2000 (BBC). One agreement was on energy development; another was on a fast-neutron experimental reactor.

419 *"unilateral superiority"*   Interfax (Russia), July 18, 2000 (BBC).

419 *"I can describe"*   Russian TV, July 18, 2000 (BBC).

419 *"speaks and sings"*   AFP, July 18, 2000.

419 *"multipolar"*   *ST,* July 20, 2000.

420 *Millennium Summit*   China News Service, September 4, 2000 (BBC).

420 *"group photo"* . . . *"the oldest"*   Author's communication, Beijing, late 2003.

420 Zhongguo   The word *China* in Chinese is two characters, *Zhong* and *Guo,* meaning Middle or Center *(Zhong)* Country *(Guo)*—the kingdom, as it were, at the center of the world. China has one of the oldest continuous civilizations in the world, and Chinese science and technology were well ahead of Europe's during the Middle Ages. In addition to gunpowder, the Chinese invented much that underlies modern civilization, such as paper (including paper money), the wheelbarrow, and rockets and multistage missiles. As late as the fifteenth century, China's GDP was the largest in the world. There is also a long history of Chinese literature, music, art, and dance.

420 *cultural extravaganza*   The author, along with colleague Adam Zhu, were advisers to Experience Chinese Culture in the United States, 2000.

420 *exhibition*   *China Daily,* September 7, 2000.

420 *"Through this window"*   *Experience Chinese Culture in the United States, 2000* commemorative book.

421 *"unusually well-planned"*   *AsiaWeek,* September 19, 2000.

421 *As the interview was edited* [following]   *60 Minutes* transcript.

425 Washington Post *called*   "TV Week," *WP,* September 3, 2000, 3. Actually, there were two television specials chosen by the *Post* as "Pick of the Week." The other was *In Search of China,* the PBS documentary of which the author was creator and executive producer (see "Personal Perspective," page 690).

425 *"I see you've taken"*   *China Online,* September 8, 2000.

425 *retrogressed*   *Zhongguo Tongxun She,* September 12, 2000 (BBC).

425 *Christianity*   Greg Torode, in *SCMP,* September 10, 2000.

425 *forty-five-minute speech*   *China Online,* September 8, 2000.

426 *Lincoln Center*   Xinhua, September 9, 2000.

426 *Nina Kung Wang*   Adam Zhu's communication to the author.

426 *"ride on the wind"*   Vivien Pik-Kwan Chan, in *SCMP,* September 8, 2000.

426 *"Quite a few"*   *Wen Jen* (Hong Kong), September 25, 2000 (BBC).

426 *"imperial order"* [following]   Kong Lai-fan and Jimmy Cheung, in *SCMP,* October 28, 2000; Kyodo News International, October 30, 2000; *ST,* October 28 and 31, 2000.

427 *"fought 100 battles"*   Frederick C. Teiwes, "Politics at the 'Core': The Political Circumstances of Mao Zedong, Deng Xiaoping and Jiang Zemin," http://rspas.anu.edu.au/ccc/morrison00.pdf.

427 *Mike Wallace*   Loh Hui Yin, in *ST,* October 28, 2000.

427 *"compliment"*   Susan Shiu and Greg Torode, in *SCMP,* October 29, 2000.

427 *"indignities"*   Author's communication in Beijing.

428 " *'The Party leadership'* "   Willy Wo-Lap Lam, in *SCMP,* September 7, 2000.

428 *videotape*   Author's communication in Beijing; Willy Wo-Lap Lam, *China Brief,* May 23, 2001.

428 *were removed* [following]   China Central Television, September 4, 2000 (BBC).

429 *"Regarding this case"*   *ST,* December 5, 2000.

429 *more grinding*   Author's interview with Shen Yongyan.

429 *right time*   Shen picked this moment to tell Jiang his views on China's problems because he had an emotional story to personify them. It involved Shen's daughter, whom Jiang had known since she was a child. She worked for a local enterprise, where one of her colleagues deceived her and took a cashier's check that her employer had entrusted to her care. His daughter tried to get the check back. When she wasn't successful, she re-

ported the incident to the local public security bureau. The bureau investigated and re-covered the check. But when Shen's daughter went to claim the check, the bureau chief told her that he had "one hundred reasons to return the check" and "one hundred rea-sons *not* to return the check." The chief was hinting, without subtlety, that the only way to get the check would be with a bribe.

"So then I tried to get her check back," Shen told Jiang. "However, I also received the same message. Now I was really upset. Here was our local law enforcement official shamelessly abusing his power." Through Shen's relationships—the Changchun Party secretary used to be a division chief at First Automotive Works, where Shen had been vice president—he eventually retrieved the check. "Without my connections," Shen told Jiang, "I doubt we would have succeeded." Later, when Shen heard that the Party started a national campaign to clean up local law enforcement, he thought that what he had told the president, with its personal example, may have helped.

430 *Olympic Games* Xinhua, October 3, 2000 (BBC).
430 *"support of the Chinese government"* Xinhua, September 9, 2000 (BBC).
430 *ancient China* [following] Erik Eckholm, in *NYT,* November 10, 2000.
430 *2200 B.C.   China Daily,* August 7, 2000.
431 *"an illusion of consensus"* Erik Eckholm, in *NYT,* November 10, 2000.
431 *"vested interests"* Sarah Allan, letter to the editor, *NYT,* November 11, 2000.
431 *"providing fuel"* Bruce Gilley, in *FEER,* July 20, 2000.
431 *Dr. Song Jian . . . Jiang Zemin counseled* [following] Author's interview with Dr. Song Jian. The author is a close friend of Dr. Song; the author's first trip to China, in March 1989, was at the invitation of Dr. Song; and Dr. Song wrote an inscription for the Chinese translation of the author's book on science and meaning derived from his PBS television series, *Closer to Truth (Zoujin Zhenshi,* China Economic Science Press, 2000).
431 *"A history without chronology"* Erik Eckholm, in *NYT,* November 10, 2000.
431 *2,416-seat* Wen Chihua, in *SCMP,* July 31, 2001.
432 *Visitors   PD,* April 18, 2000.
432 *"If this opera house"   Late Line News,* June 30, 2000.
432 *"alien egg"   AsiaWeek,* September 7, 2001.
432 *"nonsense"   Late Line News,* July 15, 2000.
432 *stopped cold* Wen Chihua, in *SCMP,* July 31, 2001.
432 *construction was restarted* The controversy would continue. In May 2004, the fu-turistic Terminal 2E at Paris's Charles de Gaulle airport, also designed by National Theater architect Paul Andreu, collapsed, leaving a 50-by-30-meter hole in the $900 million structure and killing four people, including two Chinese citizens. Critics in China likened the 450-meter-long terminal building, an elliptical tube constructed of concrete and glass rings, to the National Theater in Beijing and demanded, at the very least, a de novo inspection. Responding to the concern, the Theater's safety committee said that it would not be reinspected because it is "safeguarded by a well-rounded qual-ity assurance system . . . constructed through the joint efforts of experts from both home and abroad." *BBC News,* May 24, 2004; *China Economic Net,* May 27, 2004; Xin-hua, June 1, 2004.
433 *longtime confidant* [following] Author's interviews with Wang Huijiong, Beijing, De-cember 2001, April 2002, September 2002.
433 *"I sometimes telephone"* Author's communication, Beijing.
434 *"I enjoy speaking"* Author's interview with Dr. Song Jian.
434 *"divergent physics"* The relationship of quantum mechanics to Einstein's theory of relativity, which seems incompatible, leads to the so-called "theory of everything," for which string theory (in various forms) is a leading candidate.
435 *"When we've met"* Author's interview with Henry Kissinger.
435 *The friendship* [following] Author's interview with Tong Zonghai.

Chapter 25. JANUARY–JULY 2001

437 *rehearsing his lines*   Author's interview with Zhao Huayong, Beijing, April 2002. The taping of Jiang's New Year's greetings was on December 28, 2000.

437 *poems*   PD, March 15, 1999.

437 *metaphor*   Jiang explained the background of his poems: "In January 1991 I revisited Jilin [province] for the third time. I felt particularly close to this place. During my visit the city seemed to be a frosty fog-engulfed wonderland. Icicles were everywhere in the city. I took up a pen to write down these words: 'Snow-clad willows by the ice-covered river; jadelike trees and flowers; no wonder icicles on trees in Jilin are so proverbial.' During the two sessions [of the NPC] in Beijing in March 1998, comrades from Jilin solicited a poem from me. When I recalled the scenes I saw in Jilin during my visit there years ago, I wrote down the following two four-line poems for them" (*PD*, March 15, 1999). The second stanza follows:

> *Spring is here again, among bushes and trees in our divine land,*
> *People have converged into the capital for state affairs discussions.*
> *National revitalization is the common theme,*
> *A child's passion is seen in their words.*

438 The Tiananmen Papers   CNN.com, January 7 and 9, 2001; Andrew J. Nathan, "The Tiananmen Papers," *Foreign Affairs*, January/February 2001; Richard Bernstein, in *NYT*, January 6, 2001; Edward Jay Epstein, in *Nation*, February 5, 2001.

438 *"supreme power"*   The Tiananmen Papers asserts that the appointment of Jiang Zemin as Party general secretary in 1989, approved unanimously by the elders, "violated that Chinese Communist Party Constitution, which stipulates that the Politburo Standing Committee should make such decisions" (314). This view, to be internally consistent, would cede unalterable authority to the Party Constitution, which gives the Party monopolistic and perpetual leadership in China. The elders, especially Deng Xiaoping, saw themselves as among the founding fathers of New China (the so-called "Immortals") and therefore more responsible for safeguarding the nation than for upholding in a technical sense the Constitution (in whose development they had been involved). In addition, a secret 1987 Politburo resolution allowed Deng and two other retired elders the right to insert themselves into Politburo decision-making. Nathan and Gilley, *Rulers* (2003), 75. In the elders' opinion, 1989 was a time of crisis, the existence of the People's Republic was being threatened, and the normal niceties of constitutional procedure had to be suspended. While most Westerners do not buy the argument, one might point to the curtailment of certain freedoms in America following September 11, 2001, in order to ensure national security as a not-too-distant analogue.

438 *resuscitated*   Willy Wo-Lap Lam, in CNN.com, May 23, 2001.

438 *"correct conclusion"*   Xinhua, January 9, 2001.

438 *"reveal his attitude"*   Suettinger, *Beyond Tiananmen*, 412–413.

438 *former student protesters*   One, now a successful businessman, reflected back, "Everyone wanted to see a better China. The differences were how to do it. The government wanted a peaceful solution. The demonstrators knew this and pressed to gain concessions. There was immaturity on both sides. No one had any experience in anything like this.... We have to ask a difficult question: If Tiananmen Square hadn't happened, would economic development in China be where it is today? Probably not. The history of China shows that each time a big event like Tiananmen occurs, everyone must focus on returning things to normal. After Deng Xiaoping's Southern trip in 1992, economic reform accelerated." Author's communication, Beijing.

438 *special reception*   Author's interview with Wang Huijiong.

439 *"ethics and morality"* [following]   Mary Kwang, in *ST*, January 11, 2001.

439 *"rule of virtue"* [following]   Tony Lau, in *SCMP*, February 20, 2001; Xinhua, February 21, 2001.

439 *hybrid system*   Clara Li, in *SCMP*, February 13, 2001.

439 *"This man is no longer"*   Tony Lau, in *SCMP*, February 20, 2001. The researcher was from the National Library in Beijing.

440 *"with virtue"*   Xinhua, February 21, 2001.

440 *"seriously studying"* [following]   Kyodo News Service, January 15, 2001 (BBC).

440 *"greatest building"*   Melinda Lin, in *Newsweek*, July 16, 2001 (quoting a Beijing city press release). If Sydney had gathered 47,000 volunteers to assist in the 2000 Games, Beijing promised to mobilize 600,000. More was required, however, than good public relations. For starters, Beijing's notorious pollution had to be addressed. Emission standards were enforced for the city's vehicles, and the worst polluting factories, including the vast Capital Iron and Steelworks, would be either relocated or shut down. Showers in its Olympic Village would be heated by geothermal energy, and the triathlon course would be laid out to protect the habitat of the rare giant salamander.

440 *IOC* [following]   Xinhua, February 21, 2001 (BBC); *China Daily*, February 22, 2001.

441 *finally relax* [following]   Author's interview with Zhao Huayong.

441 *National News*   More people get their news from CCTV's *National News* than from any other source on Earth. It would be as if the four American evening news shows—hosted by CBS's Dan Rather, NBC's Tom Brokaw, ABC's Peter Jennings, and PBS's Jim Lehrer—were combined.

445 *four editors* [following]   John Pomfret, in *WP*, March 24, 2001, A1.

445 *give-and-take*   Ibid.; Greg Torode, in *SCMP*, March 25, 2001.

445 *"very big question"* [following]   Fred Hiatt, in *WP*, March 25, 2001, B7.

445 *"My life"*   *WP*, March 24, 2001, A18.

445 *"I still trust it"*   Fred Hiatt, in *WP*, March 25, 2001, B7.

445 *"I don't feel"*   John Pomfret, in *WP*, March 24, 2001, A1.

445 *"Years ago"*   Author's communication, Beijing, late 2003.

446 *eavesdropping range* [following]   Federation of American Scientists Intelligence Resource Program, www.fas.org/irp/program/collect/ep-3_aries.htm.

446 *collision* [following]   Various sources, including AP, April 7, 2001; AFP, April 9, 2001.

446 *testimony of the American crew*   Elizabeth Rosenthal, in *NYT*, April 17, 2001, A12. The Pentagon detailed a pattern of increasingly aggressive Chinese intercepts over the previous three months. The American allegation was that Chinese jets would fly directly underneath the EP-3Es and then, without warning, shoot up in front of the slower-moving turboprops in a brazen effort to intimidate the American crews. Experts asserted that the damage to the stricken U.S. plane on Hainan—"a smashed nose cone and shattered left-side propellers"—was "consistent with such a maneuver." AFP, April 9, 2001.

Regarding the missing pilot, U.S. officials claimed that he was a hotshot, who on one occasion had come so close to an American aircraft—within three meters—that the American pilots could take a photo of him holding up his e-mail address. "Obviously he was just being flashy and wanted to show off his stuff," said a Pentagon official. AFP, April 9, 2001, quoting *NYT*.

China responded with its own condemnation of the EP-3E pilots. "In order to shake loose our shadowing, the American planes have created very dangerous circumstances by hiding in clouds, suddenly slowing down or speeding up, suddenly rising or falling in altitude or suddenly veering sharply in different directions," reported Xinhua. Chinese fighter pilots claimed that the EP-3s would often slow to speeds as low as 150 miles per hour in an attempt to force the faster Chinese jets to stall. Neutral experts said that the claims of both the American and the Chinese officials could be true in general and that it would be impossible to determine what had really happened.

Chinese officials also reported that the pilot of the second jet involved in the incident had asked permission to shoot down the American spy plane after the midair collision.

Australian Financial Review, April 10, 2001. His request was denied by Chinese ground control, but it was not revealed from what level the command had come.

447 *contested*   According to U.S. sources, who used a twelve-mile limit for territorial waters, the location was about 60 miles outside of China's sovereignty. According to Chinese sources, the crash occurred 65 miles southeast of South China's Hainan Island, well within China's claimed 200-nautical-mile exclusive economic zone, where air space is "by no means unrestricted." AFP, April 16, 2001.

447 *"without further tampering"* [following]   AFP, April 9, 2001.

447 *fate of the missing pilot*   Author's interview with Li Zhaoxing.

447 *apology* [following]   John Schauble and Gary Alcorn, in *Age* (Melbourne), April 5, 2001.

447 *awkward time*   *Guardian* (London), April 2, 2001. Tensions were already high: America claimed that China was augmenting its missile arsenal targeting Taiwan, and China charged that Washington was planning to sell Taipei advanced antimissile equipment.

447 *first break* [following]   AFP, April 9, 2001.

448 *"Our prayers"*   U.S. State Department transcript, Bush Q&A at American Society of Newspaper Editors Annual Convention, April 5, 2001.

448 *trade and investment*   Channel News Asia, April 1, 2001; Xinhua, April 6–18, 2001.

448 *winemaking . . . Spanish*   Kevin Gray, for AP, April 16, 2001.

448 *learning Spanish*   FEER, April 19, 2001.

448 *"I prepared"*   Author's communication, Beijing, late 2003.

448–449 *Human Rights . . . trade deals* [following]   Betsy Pisik, in *ST,* April 14, 2001.

449 *"the best dish"*   Andres Canizalez, for Inter Press Service, April 17, 2001.

449 *Simón Bolívar*   Xinhua, April 16, 2001 (BBC).

449 *Iglesias*   James Roberts, in *Independent* (London), April 22, 2001.

449 *"excuse me"*   PD, April 6, 2001; Paul Richter and Henry Chu, in *LAT,* April 7, 2001.

449 *Public sentiment*   Calum MacLeod, for UPI, April 12, 2001.

449 *"never gives in"*   Xinhua, April 9, 2001.

450 *"international breakdown"*   Oliver August, in *Times* (London), April 12, 2001.

450 *"adequate solution,"* People's Daily   Calum MacLeod, for UPI, April 12, 2001.

450 *"sincere regret"* [following]   Jasper Becker, Gary Torode, and Tom Mitchell, in *SCMP,* April 12, 2001.

450 *English text*   Henry Chu, in *LAT,* April 14, 2001.

450 *until July 4*   CNN, July 4, 2001.

450 *"If someone peeps"*   Hong Kong *iMail,* April 13, 2001 (BBC).

450 *Another argued*   Lee Seok Hwai, in *ST,* April 12, 2001.

451 *vent their rage*   The softening in Chinese public opinion may have been driven in part by the fact that the American crew's detailed description of the collision had infiltrated the country via the Internet. Elizabeth Rosenthal, in *NYT,* April 17, 2001.

451 *Nicholas Kristof*   Nicholas D. Kristof, "A Little Leap Forward," *New York Review of Books,* June 24, 2004, 59.

451 *Amnesty International . . . 20,000 executions . . . "No government"*   News.com.au, April 25, 2004. This was the third "Strike Hard" campaign; the first two were in 1983 and 1996.

451 *far below the actual number*   Based on purported inner-Party documents, Nathan and Gilley state that for the four-year period between 1998 and 2001, 60,000 people were put to death—averaging 15,000 per year, the highest of the reform period—a figure that includes both those executed and those killed in the act of their crimes or fleeing from authorities. Nathan and Gilley, *Rulers* (2003), 217–218.

451 People's Daily   PD, April 21, 2001.

452 *Internet era*   *China Daily,* July 12, 2001.

452 *his passions*   Xinhua, June 4, 2001 (BBC).

452 *"scientific spirit"* Xinhua, June 22, 2001 (BBC).

452 *nanotechnology* Xinhua, July 3, 2001. Nanotechnology is the science of manipulating materials at the atomic and molecular level in order to build microscopic machines—devices measured in nanometers, billionths of a meter, that are expected to revolutionize twenty-first-century science.

452 *human genome project* Xinhua, August 28, 2001 (BBC).

452 *Three Tenors* [following] *China Daily,* June 25, 2001.

453 *"powerful performance"* Annette Chiu, in *SCMP,* June 26, 2001.

453 *always prepared* [following] Author's communication, Beijing.

454 *Jiang's message* [following] Xinhua, July 1, 2001.

455 *Shen Yongyan* Author's interview with Shen Yongyan.

455 *Leftists erupted* Mark O'Neill, in *SCMP,* August 15, 2001. Objection was also voiced by some old-timers who felt nostalgia for Communism's "golden age" in the early and mid-1950s, when an egalitarian populace had been united by a common vision of a utopian socialist society.

455 *Ma Bin* [following] Letter of Ma Bin, *Monthly Review,* May 2002, www.monthlyreview.org/0502cpc2.htm.

456 *"do not make any sense"* Not satisfied, Ma Bin wrote a second letter, longer and more theoretical. Stating that he had "carefully read" Jiang's speech again, Ma, joined by a former propaganda official, prepared a detailed treatise—more than 8,500 words in English translation—that was circulated on July 15. In this missive Ma invoked the early history of China's Communist Party. If an intellectual or member of "the exploiting class" wanted to join the Party, the letter stated, he "had to rebel against his own class and undergo conscious transformation until he finally came to stand on the side of the working class and was no longer exploiting or enjoying the benefit gained by means of exploitation." To make the argument current, Ma Bin reasoned, "If we consider the exploitation activity of those who painstakingly build up their own business as labor and thus think the exploiters are also workers, we will get into a ridiculous situation." Getting tangled in archaic Marxist theory, Ma Bin, who had also been general manager of the giant Anshan Iron and Steel Company, had to differentiate "chief managers" who are "agents of foreign capitalists" and therefore "belong to a group within the bourgeoisie," from "ordinary managers" who "belong to the working class"—an impossible distinction in a globalized, knowledge-oriented marketplace. He tried to sustain the industrial-age Marxist view that "all laborers and every member of the working class are similarly valuable and equal," another utopian vision broadly at odds with both a competitive economy and basic human nature. Ma Bin concluded by noting, "All the words come to one sentence: we must not admit capitalists into the Party. If so, the nature of the Party will be changed." Letter of Ma Bin and Han Yaxi, *Monthly Review,* May 2002, www.monthlyreview.org/0502cpc3.htm.

456 *Bi Dachuan* Author's interview with Bi Dachuan, Beijing, September 2002. Bi is an old friend and business associate of the author.

457 *"against Ma Bin?"* Author's interview with Wang Huijiong.

457 *Deng Liqun* [following] "The Public Letter to Jiang Zemin from Deng Liqun et al." There had been several earlier "ten-thousand-character" open letters from Leftists that criticized reform policies (the first appeared in 1995).

457 *"political mistake"* [following] Vivien Pik-Kwan Chan, in *SCMP,* August 5, 2001.

458 *"Entrepreneurs"* [following] "The Public Letter to Jiang Zemin from Deng Liqun et al.," referencing *The Important Literature Since the Thirteenth Central Committee,* 584.

458 *Teng Wensheng* Author's interview with Teng Wensheng.

458 *enjoyed support* Jasper Becker, in *SCMP,* August 23, 2001.

458 *"nightmarish"* Chinawn.com, www.websitesaboutchina.com/main/poli/politics_1_1.htm.

458–459 *every member . . . "received strong support" . . . Hu Jintao . . . "historical lessons"* Joseph Fewsmith, "Rethinking the Role of the CCP: Explicating Jiang Zemin's Party Anniversary Speech," *China Leadership Monitor,* No. 1, Part 2, December 2001. The Communique issued at the close of the Party plenum in September voiced "unanimous" approval for Jiang's speech as a "Marxist programmatic document that . . . has great and far-reaching potential."

459 *none too pleased*   Mark O'Neill, in *SCMP,* August 15, 2001.

459 *Ding Guangen*   Vivien Pik-Kwan Chan, in *SCMP,* August 5, 2001.

459 *shut down*   Mark O'Neill, in *SCMP,* August 15, 2001; Jasper Becker, in *SCMP,* August 23, 2001. *Seeking Truth* and *Mainstream* were the magazines closed.

459 *"We should view Marxism"*   Xinhua, August 31, 2001 (BBC).

459 *400,000*   Xinhua, July 14, 2001.

459 *we have won* [following]   AFP, July 14, 2001.

459 *brief speech*   Deutsche Presse-Agentur, July 13, 2001.

460 *balcony of Tiananmen*   AFP, July 15, 2001.

460 *"triple happiness"*   AFP, July 14, 2001.

460 *Technically convicted*   *LAT,* July 15, 2001.

460 *Moscow University*   Mark O'Neill, in *SCMP,* July 18, 2001,

460 *"China-Russian Relations"* [following]   China News Service, July 17, 2001 (BBC).

460 *This time his Russian went well*   Author's communication, Beijing.

461 *Mount Huang*   John Pomfret, in *WP,* July 5, 2001.

461 *In his poem*   *Guardian,* May 30, 2001.

Chapter 26. AUGUST–DECEMBER 2001

462 Times *journalists*   Erik Eckholm, in *NYT,* August 10, 2001, A1, A8.

462 *"our objective"*   Xinhua, August 13, 2001 (BBC).

462 *"thousands of years"*   Communist China divided its approximately five thousand years of civilization into five periods: primitive, slavery, feudalism, capitalism, and socialism. "Capitalism" was said to be the sorry period between the end of the Qing dynasty in 1911 and the founding of New China in 1949. Recent ideological changes are described as the "first stage of socialism"—which will last a "long time"—thus maintaining the five periods.

462 *New China* [following]   Xinhua, August 13, 2001 (BBC).

462 *"I am seventy-five"* [following]   *NYT,* August 10, 2001, A8.

463 *"People think we"* [following]   Erik Eckholm, in *NYT,* August 10, 2001, A1.

463 *"president stresses"*   Author's interview with Zhao Qizheng.

464 *language experts*   Frank Ching, in *SCMP,* January 13, 2002. "Ten language experts" was the report.

464 *"can't communicate"* [following]   Author's communication, Beijing.

464 *Jiang's driver*   Author's interview with Wang Huijiong.

465 *"marvelous English"* . . . *"courageous person"* [following]   Author's communication, Beijing.

465 *"Jiang's facility"*   Author's interview with Zhao Qizheng.

465 *"The knowledge in our world"* [following]   Author's interview with Wang Huijiong. The actual letter is reproduced in the text.

466 *"Palindrome Pythagorean Numbers"* . . . *"Golden Section"*   One article that Wang Huijiong sent to Jiang was on palindromes in Chinese poetry and Palindrome Pythagorean Numbers in pure mathematics. The other was on how the Golden Section in geometry enriches design and enhances human anatomy. Both articles portrayed an intrinsic beauty in the world.

Palindrome Pythagorean Numbers are palindrome numbers—reading the same in either direction—that fit the famous Pythagorean equation of right-angle triangles, $a^2 + b^2 = c^2$. The example used in the article Wang sent was $88,209^2 + 90,288^2 = 126,225^2$, since 88,209 and 90,288 are palindromes, each the reverse of the other. The article then explored issues in number theory, such as how many sets of Palindrome Pythagorean

Numbers exist below a given limit, say, for a triangle whose sides are smaller than ten million. (The answer seems to be forty-two such sets.)

The Golden Section is the division of a line so that the ratio of the larger segment to the whole line is the same as the ratio of the smaller segment to the larger segment. Known to the ancient Egyptians and Greeks, the Golden Section appeared in diverse forms and fields, such as in architectural design and art. The article that Wang sent to Jiang showed how the Golden Section functions in human anatomy, such as in the functioning of joints.

466 *Tian Ran Ju*   A well-known restaurant or café in ancient China.

467 Ke shang   These lines were written by Su Hui, a famous female poet from the fourth century. They were taken from her intricate literary work that presents a riddle both graphically and literally—it has 842 characters, all composing a complex palindrome. People can read the whole poem in different directions and extract many, many different poems and meanings. There is a theory that Su Hui used her poetry as code to communicate with her lover or as lure to regain her wayward husband.

467 *complex example*   The poem is "Late Spring" by Chen Zhaolao. (Jiang seems to have misnamed the poet in his letter.)

> *Xianxian luan cao ping tan,*
> *Ranran yun gui yuan shan.*
> *Lian juan tang kong ri yong,*
> *Niao ti hua luo chun can.*

471 *transfixed*   Jasper Becker, in *SCMP*, October 16, 2001. Jiang was reportedly "shocked" by the images of the hijacked passenger jets crashing into the buildings, and like so many others, he watched pictures of the horrific event multiple times.

471 *reach out to President Bush*   Xinhua, September 12 (midnight September 11), 2001 (BBC).

471 *Bush called to thank*   Xinhua, September 12, 13, 2001 (BBC).

471 *"part of the blame"*   Michael Dwyer, in *Australian Financial Review*, September 13, 2001; Jasper Becker, in *SCMP*, September 14, 2001.

471 *"international cooperation"*   Xinhua, September 19, 2001.

471 *safeguard world*   Xinhua, September 18, 2001 (BBC).

472 *restive Muslim populations*   Jasper Becker, in *SCMP*, October 16, 2001.

472 *a change in the American*   Robert J. Saiget, for AFP, September 17, 2001.

472 *APEC forum*   David E. Sanger, in *NYT*, October 19, 2001.

472 *"I look forward"*   Channel New Asia, October 20, 2001.

472 *" 'one China' policy"*   Kyodo News Service, October 18, 2001.

473 *"no hesitation"* [following]   Kyodo News Service, October 19, 2001,

473 *declared themselves partners* [following]   George Gedda, for AP, October 19, 2001.

473 *Body language* [following]   Jasper Becker, in *SCMP*, October 20, 2001.

473 *enjoying each other's company*   David E. Sanger, in *NYT*, October 19, 2001.

473 *"Public prickliness"*   *WP*, October 18, 2001 (UPI).

473 *"wisest decision"*   Zhang Tianguang, in *SCMP*, October 19, 2001.

473 *gala party*   Xinhua, October 20, 2001.

474 *"your valedictory"* [following]   China Central TV, October 21, 2001 (BBC).

474 *Jiang chaired*   Jason Leow, in *ST*, October 22, 2001.

474 *technology-savvy son . . . "his father's disciple"* [following]   *SCMP*, January 10, 2002.

474–475 *1992 . . . Hewlett-Packard . . . investment company* [following]   Forney, *WSJ*, November 1, 1999.

475 *Chinese Academy . . . deputy commander . . . told friends*   Author's communication, Beijing.

475 *split into two*   *PD*, November 27, 2001,

475 *Miankang*   Author's communication, Beijing.

476 *China's accession*   Xinhua, November 11, 2001.

476 *Religious Affairs* [following]   David Murphy, in *FEER*, December 27, 2001; Xinhua, December 12, 2001; Nailene Chou Wiest, in *SCMP*, December 17, 2002; Dian Tai, in *China Daily*, December 13, 2001.

476 *"socialism and religion adapt"*   Nailene Chou Wiest, in *SCMP*, December 17, 2002.

476 *"Asking religions"*   Daniel Kwan, in *SCMP*, December 13, 2001.

476 *"infiltration"*   Ibid.; Channel New Asia, December 13, 2001

476 *more constraints*   The Party stepped up its training courses for Muslims in Xinjiang province, which had been initiated earlier in the year with the education of eight thousand imams. The classes focused on the struggle "against the ethnic separatist, religious extremist and violent terrorist forces" in Xinjiang, and the curriculum centered on the study of Jiang's speeches on religious issues and the Party's ethnic and religious policies. China Central Television, January 11, 2002 (BBC).

477 *"social phenomenon"*   Ye Xioawen, in *Foreign Affairs Journal*, June 2002, 10.

477 *religious adherents*   The 100 million were mostly Buddhists and Taoists and included 18 million Muslims, 10 million Protestants (up from only 700,000 before 1949), and 4 million Catholics. www.index-china.com/index-english/people-religions-f.html. A 2002 U.S. government report estimated that China had more than 200 million believers, including 100 million Buddhists; 20 million Muslims; 5 million belonging to the official Catholic Church; another 5 to 10 million belonging to unofficial Catholic-related churches; 10 to 15 million registered Protestants; and anywhere between 30 and 80 million who worshiped in Protestant "house churches" that were independent of government control. The number of Taoists was difficult to assess, though there were more than ten thousand Taoist monks and nuns and more than a thousand Taoist temples. www.state.gov/g/drl/rls/irf/2002/13870.htm.

477 *new view* [following]   Ching Cheong, in *ST*, January 10, 2002.

477 *"rule the country by virtue"* . . . *Buddhist temple*   Vivien Pik-Kwan Chan, in *SCMP*, June 21, 2002.

478 *"Meditation can lead"*   Ibid. According to medical research, meditation and other stress-reduction techniques can help ameliorate some kinds of gastric illness. In no way does this justify any of the irrational and dangerous healing claims of cults like Falun Gong.

478 *Dr. Qian Xuesen*   Xinhua, December 11, 2001.

478 *"equipped with modern scientific"* [following]   Tu Yuanji, *PD*, June 24, 2002.

478 *superstring theory* [*Chao Xian*]   The so-called "Theory of Everything" that seeks to explain the structure and behavior of elementary particles and the fundamental forces of nature, particularly gravity, postulates minute, vibrating "strings," which are about 10^{-33} centimeters in length (or about a millionth of a billionth of a billionth of a billionth of a centimeter) and exist in ten dimensions. String theory seeks to unify the conflicting claims of quantum mechanics, which explains elementary particles, and Einstein's Theory of General Relativity, which describes gravity over astronomical distances.

479 *"a great renaissance"* [following]   Xinhua, December 18, 2001 (BBC).

479 *"It is impossible"* [following]   Vivien Pik-Kwan Chan, in *SCMP*, December 19, 2001.

479 *"The West has"*   Maggie Farley, in *LAT*, May 7, 1999, F1.

480 *In a side story* [following]   Author's interview with Li Qiankuan.

480 *three objectives* [following]   Willy Wo-Lap Lam, on CNN.com, November 28, 2001. These moves would echo Deng Xiaoping's. After he retired Deng kept his post as chairman of the Central Military Commission, and in 1987 the Party Central Committee, led by General Secretary Zhao Ziyang, agreed to defer to the retired leader on issues of vital significance.

481 *The assumption was* [following]   AFP, December 13, 2001.

481 *"sue for compromise"*   Willy Wo-Lap Lam, on CNN.com, November 28, 2001.

481 *"negotiation, consensus"*   AFP, December 13, 2001.

Chapter 27. JANUARY–JUNE 2002

482 *rumors*　For the most insightful, see the pieces by Willy Wo-Lap Lam at www.cnn.com and in *China Brief* (Jamestown Foundation, www.jamestown.org); and Nathan and Gilley, *Rulers* (particularly the second, revised edition, published in 2003). More fanciful tales were told by Hong Kong tabloids and posted in Internet chatrooms.

482 *"lack of power struggles"*　Frederick C. Teiwes, "Politics at the 'Core': The Political Circumstances of Mao Zedong, Deng Xiaoping and Jiang Zemin," http://rspas.anu.edu.au/ccc/morrison00.pdf. Teiwes notes that "the aversion to the elite strife of the Cultural Revolution and the divisions surrounding the Tiananmen crisis has been crucial in the absence of 'power struggles' . . . Jiang Zemin's ability to sustain his pre-eminence can perhaps be summarized in a simple formula—the powers of office *plus* fear of disunity *plus* tolerable results." Even the removal of Chen Xitong (1995) and the involuntary retirement of Qiao Shi (1997) "were handled well within existing procedures and without major drama."

483 *"no matter when"*　Ching Cheong, in *ST,* February 14, 2002.

483 *sought symmetry*　Jasper Becker, in *SCMP,* January 10, 2002.

483 *"Zeng mostly"*　Ching Cheong, in *ST,* February 16, 2002.

484 *Middle Eastern* [following]　Xinhua, January 17, 2002 (BBC); *China Daily,* January 18, 2002.

484 *"your costume"*　Xinhua, January 24, 2002 (BBC).

484 *bugging devices*　The spying electronics, most of which were buried in the upholstery, were detected after a "static whine" was heard during test flights in China in September, shortly after the twin-engine long-range jet had been delivered in August. Intelligence experts in China said that the tiny bugs, which were operated by satellite, were more technically advanced than those available on commercial markets. James Kyrne, in *Financial Times,* January 18, 2002.

After the discovery the plane, which was supposed to have made its maiden flight taking President Jiang to the APEC forum in October 2001, was parked on the runway of a military airfield north of Beijing with much of its interior gutted. Chinese security forces launched a large-scale investigation, fearing negligence or worse from the state-owned enterprises responsible. More than twenty air force officers were being questioned, and two executives were said to be in custody. *AWSJ,* January 21, 2002.

The long-range aircraft had been originally built by Boeing for Delta Airlines. It was then purchased, at Boeing's suggestion, by a Chinese air force company in June 2000 and flown to San Antonio for an electronics upgrade and interior remodeling. The commercial passenger seats were removed and replaced by luxurious accommodations with plush upholstery. Sophisticated satellite communications and other special equipment were added. (Ibid.) The aircraft was completed in August 2001 and, after refueling in Hawaii, had flown directly to China.

Three U.S. companies and one Singaporean firm were involved in the remodeling— all of which denied knowledge of the more than two dozen bugs. Boeing also forswore any responsibility. "We're not in the business of bugging airplanes," said a company spokesman. Greg Torode, in *SCMP,* January 20, 2002. Boeing's chief of commercial aircraft said that he "panicked" after learning the news of the bugging, telling a Seattle newspaper, "I about died when I saw this." *SCMP,* February 3, 2002.

484 *officials braced*　Torode, in *SCMP,* January 20, 2002.

484 *"subdued reaction"*　Willy Wo-Lap Lam, on CNN.com, January 21, 2002.

484 *American diplomats*　Elizabeth Rosenthal, in *NYT,* January 27, 2002.

485 *millions of dollars*　Harvey Stockwin, in *Times of India,* January 28, 2002.

485 *Li Peng*　Bill Gertz, in *Washington Times,* February 15, 2002.

485 *"preposterous"*　David Hsieh, in *ST,* February 18, 2002.

485 *Bush might feel*　Harvey Stockwin, in *Times of India,* January 28, 2002.

485 *weaken Jiang*　Ching Cheong, in *ST,* February 14, 2002.

485 *mystery*　About a year later, in April 2003, another bizarre story, this one out of Los Angeles, may have shed some light on the bugs. A prominent Chinese-American woman, Katrina Leung, was arrested as a double agent. According to the charges, the forty-nine-year-old social lubricant with large stylish glasses and a radiant confident smile had been paid $1.7 million over a twenty-year period to spy on China for the FBI, and for virtually the entire time she had carried on a sexual affair with her high-level handler—who was the FBI's top expert on Chinese counterintelligence in Los Angeles. Allegedly, the fetching Leung had used their intimate encounters to copy untold secret documents, which she then sold to Chinese intelligence. Eric Lichtblau and Barbara Whitaker, in *NYT*, April 10, 2003.

The FBI feared that Leung may have tipped off the Chinese that their president's plane had been bugged. In the disclosure, it was noted that the National Security Agency, the United States' supersecret electronic spying agency, had conspired with the FBI and other intelligence agencies to install the bugs. Red-faced officials surmised that macho "pillow talk" with Leung might have included hints about the intelligence community's plot to bug the plane. James Risen and Eric Lichtblau, in *NYT*, April 15, 2003.

485 *"thirty hours" . . . local women*　SCMP, February 16, 2002.

485 *shared intelligence* [following]　Michael Sheridan, in *Sunday Times* (London), February 17, 2002.

486 *treasure trove*　Ibid.; John Pomfret, in *WP*, February 2, 2002.

486 *listening stations*　Michael Sheridan, in *Sunday Times* (London), February 17, 2002.

486 *"not China's enemy,"* [following]　John Pomfret, in *WP*, February 2, 2002.

486 *press conference*　Xinhua, February 21, 2002 (BBC).

486 *"strategic dialogues"* [following]　*China Online*, February 21, 2002.

486 *pointed question* [following]　Jason Leow, in *ST*, February 22, 2002.

487 *"With respect"* [following]　China Central Television, February 21, 2000 (BBC).

488 *American officials*　"China is going to be told that any future dealings between Beijing and Iraq's military establishment will be viewed in the most serious light," said a senior Pentagon source. Gary Torode, in *SCMP*, February 25, 2002. The United States wanted China to enforce more stringent licensing requirements. In exchange, China expected the United States to restart approvals of export licenses for U.S.-made satellites to be launched on Chinese rockets. Jim VandeHei and Charles Hutzler, in *AWSJ*, February 22, 2002.

488 *"treasure peace"*　China Central Television, February 21, 2000 (BBC).

488 *banquet* [following]　Daniel Kwan and news agencies, in *SCMP*, February 22, 2002.

488–489 *he called . . . allies*　Xinhua, February 23, 2002 (BBC).

489 *Financial Work Conference*　Xinhua, February 7, 2002 (BBC). Problems presented and labeled urgent included weak financial regulation, unsound operating mechanisms of financial institutions, slack management, shortage of financial professionals, low standards of financial services and innovation, and disorder in the financial markets. Recommendations included intensifying financial reform, guarding against financial risks, strengthening supervision, advancing reform of state-owned banks, and giving full play to the role of monetary policy in economic regulation.

489 *Attending the conference* [following]　Author's interview with Wu Xiaoling, Beijing, September 2002.

489 *Bubbles Act*　This act was an early corporate reform that followed from the spectacular collapse of the South Sea Company—a story featured in Adam's Smith's eighteenth-century classic *Inquiry into the Nature and Causes of the Wealth of Nations*.

489 *China's banks*　In this policy-setting speech, Jiang focused on China's four major state banks—Bank of China, Industrial and Commercial, Construction, and Agriculture. The problem was self-evident: China's banks were not, in fact, banks. Prior to 1993 they were vehicles for "adjustments"—that is, mechanisms for the state to funnel money to cash-

draining state-owned enterprises, which were saddled with unnecessary workers and costly social services. They were not commercial banks in any meaningful sense, and all had heavy loads of nonperforming loans on their books. For years three of the four had been technically insolvent: the size of their bad loans was greater than the value of their net assets. Worse, many SOEs saw no need to pay the banks back (since everything was owned by the state anyway); sometimes SOEs and local government conspired not to repay their debts, since it seemed only a transfer of resources to the central government.

489 *"a real test"* . . . *"go swimming"* Xinhua, February 25, 2002 (BBC).

489–490 *"truth clarification video"* [following] Falun Dafa Clearwisdom. Net; Falun Dafa Information Center, http://faluninfo.net/DisplayAnArticle.asp?ID=5474.

490 *"Jiang called me"* Author's interview with Shen Yongyan.

490 *Libya and Iran* Ray Cheung, in *SCMP*, April 16, 2002.

490 *oil companies* [following] Antoaneta Bezlova, for Inter Press Service, April 18, 2002.

491 *"Beijing's policy"* *Hindustani Times* (AFP), April 23, 2002.

491 *poet Hafez* . . . *Persepolis* Xinhua, April 19, 2002 (BBC).

491 Shenzhou III Xinhua, March 25, 2002 (BBC).

491 *"philosophy and social sciences"* Xinhua, May 7, 2002 (BBC).

491 *forum with experts* Xinhua, July 16, 2002 (BBC).

492 Guide for Implementing China Central Television, April 14–30, 2002 (BBC).

492 *graduation speech* Xinhua, May 31, 2002 (BBC).

492 *mainland scholar* *TKP*, July 18, 2002 (BBC), quoting Wang Tianyi, professor at Yantai University and vice mayor of Jinan municipal government.

493 *"new dynamics"* Workers and managers would have parallel functions: workers would be "basic laborers" *(jichu laodong)*, and business owners would be "management laborers" *(guanli laodong)*. But both groups would be "career laborers" *(zhiye dong)* or, in other words, members of the same group or class. Vivien Pik-Kwan Chan, in *SCMP*, July 30, 2002.

493 *left out* Ibid.

493 *peacemaker* . . . *missiles* [following] Charles Hutzler, in *AWSJ*, June 7, 2002.

493 *mediator* [following] *Kyodo News International*, June 3, 2002.

493 *public call* [following] Xinhua, June 4, 2002 (BBC).

494 *Latvia, Estonia, Lithuania, and Iceland* Xinhua, June 10, 12, 13, 16, 2002 (BBC).

494 *Jiang Zehui* Fong Tak-ho, in *SCMP*, June 9, 2002.

494 *When she told* . . . *"Wow, Zehui"* Author's interview with Jiang Zehui.

Chapter 28. JULY–OCTOBER 2002

495 *petitions* Charles Hutzler, in *AWSJ*, July 2, 2002.

495 *Jiang's wisdom* [following] Lung Hua, in *Hsin Pao* (Hong Kong), August 16, 2002.

496 *treasure* Vivien Pik-Kwan Chan, in *SCMP*, July 24, 2002.

496 *seventy-fifth anniversary* [following] Cary Huang, in *Standard* (Hong Kong), August 2, 2002.

496 *"a grand journey"* Entitled "Xinhua Hails Jiang's Contribution to National Defense," the article commended Jiang for "bringing the PLA into line with international developments, while keeping its nature as a people's army under the absolute leadership of the Party." Highlights of Jiang's leadership, according to Xinhua, included an increase in modern quality (emphasizing science and high technology) accompanied by a decrease in inefficient quantity (a reduction of half a million personnel); reforms in recruitment, housing, insurance, military academies, and the command system; using the army to fight natural disasters (such as the 1998 Great Flood) and poverty; proscribing the army from engaging in commercial activities; enhancing information technology and innovation; and developing a robust space program in commercial satellites and manned space flight. Xinhua, July 30, 2002 (BBC).

497 *provocative theory*   *Cheng Ming* (Hong Kong), September 1, 2002 (BBC).

497 *"push at Beidaihe"*   Ching Cheong and Goh Sui Noi, in *ST,* September 8, 2002.

497 *later than usual*   Nathan and Gilley report that Hu Jintao, deferring to Jiang, was the one who proposed the November date for the Party Congress. *Rulers* (2003), 58. The primary reason for the delay, they state, was the still-unresolved position of Li Ruihuan.

497 *Jiang would be retiring*   Since the Fifteenth Party Congress in 1997, when at the time of Qiao Shi's surprise retirement Jiang had said he would step down from his Party and state positions at the Sixteenth Party Congress in 2002, he repeated his pledge several times. According to sources quoted by Nathan and Gilley (*Rulers,* 2003, 66), these reconfirmations were given at a Party plenum in 1998, at Beidaihe in 2001, and "at least five times in documents circulated by the Central Committee."

497 *reports out of Beidaihe* [following]   Ching Cheong, in *ST,* August 22, 2002.

497 *bid to remain*   John Pomfret, in *WP,* October 21, 2002.

497 *"He staked out"*   Ibid.

498 *prostate cancer*   Author's interview with Wang Huijiong, Beijing, September 2002.

498 *Stephen Hawking*   Xinhua, August 19, 2002.

498 *Fields Medal*   *China Daily,* August 21, 2002.

499 *wanted to head off*   Vivien Pik-Kwan Chan, in *SCMP,* August 30, 2002.

499 *Google*   *SCMP,* September 3, 2002.

499 *Internet cafés*   Dali L. Yang, "China in 2002," *Asia Survey,* January/February 2003.

499 *Jiang's name*   John Pomfret, in *WP,* October 21, 2002.

499 *"the important thinking"*   There are numerous official articles where Jiang Zemin's name was used as a possessive adjective describing Three Represents. References for the quotes in the text are from the Xinhua news agency: July 30, 2000; February 15, 2001; May 12, 2002; May 20, 2002; and June 24, 2002 (quoting a *People's Daily* editorial).

499 *name no longer attached*   According to Nathan and Gilley, Li Peng was the one to suggest that Jiang's name be taken off Three Represents. *Rulers* (2003), 157.

499 *Hu Jintao evinced strong*   *PD,* September 3, 2002.

499 *blockbuster story* [following]   Erik Eckholm, in *NYT,* September 5, 2002, referencing Zong Hairen (pseudonym), *Disidai* (Fourth Generation) and the shorter English translation, Nathan and Gilley, *Rulers.*

500 *"resounding send-off"* [following]   Andrew J. Nathan and Bruce Gilley, "China's New Rulers I. The Path to Power," *New York Review of Books,* September 26, 2002, 12–16.

500 *"the era following"*   Author's communication, Beijing, September 2002.

501 *"outdated information"*   Ching Cheong, in *ST,* September 6, 2002,

501 *prospects of Li Ruihuan*   Nathan and Gilley, *Rulers.* The book also seemed to commend Zeng Qinghong and Wu Bangguo for their independent thinking. Was this a subtle effort to undermine Jiang? The appeal to Zeng and Wu assumed that both men held a private belief in the desirability of faster political reform, and that personal expediency would compel them, in effect, to desert their mentor and join the winning camp of Li Ruihuan. (This analysis may overstate the degree to which considerations of political reform among China's senior leaders dominate all other issues.) The two senior leaders who were considered the more robotic supporters of Jiang, Beijing Party chief Jia Qinglin and Shanghai Party chief Huang Ju, were largely ignored. Neither was expected to make the Politburo Standing Committee.

501 *inscription*   Author's communication, Beijing.

501 *five agreements*   These included a major petrochemical project for Exxon-Mobil, telecommunications contracts for Motorola and Lucent, and an increase in Anheuser-Busch's investment in China's Tsingtao Brewery. Charles Hutzler, in *AWSJ,* October 17, 2002. To facilitate trade, temporary regulations allowed the continued import of genetically modified U.S. soybeans. *SCMP,* October 27, 2002.

501 *export control*   The new regulations affected dual-use biological and chemical agents—materials that could be used to produce weapons of mass destruction. Beijing

said that the new procedures would have "a significant bearing on fulfilling China's international nonproliferation obligations." Antoaneta Bezlova, for Inter Press Service, October 20, 2002.

501 *Tibetan nun* Louisa Yan, in *SCMP*, October 19, 2002. Incarcerated for ten years, she was the longest-serving female political prisoner in China; she was also the fifth prominent political prisoner to be freed in 2002.

501 *North Korea* Jason Leow, in *ST*, October 19, 2002.

502 *"prestigious event"* Kenneth Lieberthal, in *SCMP*, October 14, 2002.

502 *Landing in Chicago* Channel News Asia, October 23, 2002.

502 *runways* Vivien Pik-Kwan Chan, in *SCMP*, October 24, 2002.

502 *Ritz-Carlton* *Chicago Tribune*, October 23, 2002.

502 *"closing performance"* *Chicago Tribune*, October 24, 2002.

502 *Jiang greeted staff* Xinhua, October 22, 2002 (BBC).

502 *felt dizzy* Vivien Pik-Kwan Chan, in *SCMP*, October 24, 2002.

502 *Houston* Gao Anming, in *China Daily,* October 25, 2002.

502 *"China is the largest"* [following] Xinhua, October 24, 2002 (BBC).

503 *informal summit* Vivien Pik-Kwan Chan, in *SCMP*, October 28, 2002.

503 *"Welcome to the ranch"* [following] Xinhua, October 25, 2002 (BBC).

504 *"in the dark"* Ron Hutcheson, in *Philadelphia Inquirer*, October 26, 2002.

504 *"nuclear-free"* Xinhua, October 26, 2002.

504 *After the talks* Ron Hutcheson, in *Philadelphia Inquirer,* October 26, 2002.

504 *perfunctory notice* *SCMP*, October 30, 2002.

504 *APEC forum* Xinhua, October 25, 2002.

504 *Yasukuni Shrine* [following] *Asahi Shimbun,* October 28, 2002. The shrine, which claims to enshrine the "deities" of all Japan's war dead (in the form of mortuary tablets with inscribed names), honors Japan's fourteen convicted Class A war criminals along with the nation's 2.47 million war dead. Kyodo News Service, September 25, 2001.

505 *San Francisco* AFP and Reuters, October 30, 2002.

505 *Party announced* Wang Xiangwei, in *SCMP*, October 25, 2002.

505 *thwarted from bringing Huang Ju* Nathan and Gilley, *Rulers* (2003), 187; *Ming Pao* (Hong Kong), May 9, 1995, A2 (BBC); Willy Wo-Lap Lam, *SCMP*, October 31, 1996.

505 *Zeng Qinghong* Xinhua, October 24, 2002.

506 *Liu Yunshan* Mark O'Neill, in *SCMP*, October 25, 2002.

507 *retirement home* Vivien Pik-Kwan Chan, in *SCMP*, November 7, 2002.

507 *Li Ruihuan . . . leaving* Ching Cheong, in *ST*, October 25, 2002.

Chapter 29. NOVEMBER–DECEMBER 2002

508 *The construction of the political report* [following] Author's interview with Jin Chongji, Beijing, September, 2002.

510 *H. Lyman Miller* H. Lyman Miller, *The Road to the Sixteenth Party Congress.* www. gbcc.org.uk/iss22analysis.htm.

512 *record-breaking* Itar-Tass, November 9, 2002.

512 *achievements* [following] Xinhua, November 8, 2002.

514 *China's prosperity* Channel News Asia, November 10, 2002.

514 *"necessary to implement"* Xinhua, November 8, 2002.

514 xiaokang Xinhua ("All About Xiaokang"), November 10, 2002.

514 *"midlevel developed nation"* A per capita annual GDP of more than $3,000 would put China well along toward becoming a *"xiaokang"* society. Xinhua, November 10, 2002, quoting Zeng Peiyan. The ambitious agenda would require China to almost quadruple its 2000 GDP figure by 2020, meaning that the country's GDP would top $4.2 trillion, or 35 trillion yuan, in less than two decades. By comparison, in 2002 the U.S. GDP was about $10 trillion and China's GDP was about 10 trillion yuan, or around $1.2 billion. In order to reach Jiang's goal, the Chinese economy would have to sustain an average annual

growth rate of just over 7 percent for the next twenty years, a task that gets progressively more difficult as the economy gets larger. *China Daily,* December 16, 2002.

514 *"nonpublic sector"*   Xinhua, November 8, 2002.

514 *privately owned firms*   Susan V. Lawrence, in *AWSJ,* November 21, 2002. Supporting private businesses made sense. Their numbers had skyrocketed from ninety thousand in 1998 to more than two million at the end of 2001 while at the same time China's state-owned enterprises (SOEs) had shrunk from 102,300 in 1989 to 42,900 by mid-2002. "One thing is quite certain," Planning Minister Zeng Peiyan observed two days after Jiang's report, "the number of SOEs will drop even further." Charles Hutzler and Peter Wonacott, in *AWSJ,* November 11, 2002. Zeng noted that while 24 million to 25 million people had been laid off from SOEs, a high number of them, about 17 million, had found new jobs, largely in small and midsize private firms, or had begun working for themselves. Mark O'Neill and Wang Xiangwei, in *SCMP,* November 11, 2002.

515 *loose definitions*   Since "public ownership" (i.e., state ownership) was a core value of a socialist system, some economists were offering the idea that shareholding companies that were listed on the stock market could be considered "public" because many citizens owned shares and the state, in most cases, still owned a large part. Jiang seemed to be advocating this interpretation when he declared, "We should deepen the reform of state-owned enterprises and further explore diversified forms for effectively realizing public ownership, especially state ownership." Xinhua, November 8, 2002.

515 *"never copy"*   Channel News Asia, November 8, 2002.

515 *Political reform*   Wang Xiangwei, *SCMP,* November 9, 2002.

515 *regular annual conferences*   *China Business Weekly,* July 5–11, 2004, 18. Following the Sixteenth Party Congress, experiments on standing Party congresses began in Guangdong, Hubei, Sichuan, and Zhejiang provinces.

516 *"our culture"*   Xinhua, November 8, 2002.

516 *research on how such military takeovers*   Nicholas D. Kristof, "A Little Leap Forward," *New York Review of Books,* June 24, 2004, 59.

516 *"Jiang's victory"*   John Pomfret and Phillip P. Pan, in *WP,* November 14, 2002.

516 *elect Central Committee*   Earlier in the congress, delegates had voted in a primary election in which the number of names on the ballot had slightly exceeded the number of places available, giving the voters the chance to eliminate a few of the candidates. Susan V. Lawrence, in *AWSJ,* November 7, 2002. At this point there were only as many candidates as there were seats—Party politics and horse trading had determined which names would appear. Voting options were "approved," "opposed," or "abstain," but the results mattered—both as a matter of pride to full members, and because alternate members were ranked according to the number of "approved" votes they collected.

516 *first time*   One trendsetting new face was that of Zhang Ruimin, the millionaire founder and CEO of Haier Group, a multibillion-dollar collectively owned corporation, who was elected as an alternate member. The subject of the documentary film *CEO,* Zhang was the first head of a non–state-owned company ever elected to the CPC Central Committee. Haier was China's largest appliance manufacturer and on its way to becoming an international brand with numerous foreign operations, including a $30 million plant in South Carolina.

516 *average age*   Xinhua, November 14, 2002.

516 *ethnic minorities*   The thirty-five members of ethnic minorities constituted ten percent of the CPC Central Committee, reflecting their percentage of the total population. Willy Wo-Lap Lam, on CNN.com, November 14, 2002.

517 *applause . . . peaceful transition*   Xinhua, November 14, 2002; Josephine Ma and Wang Xiangwei, in *SCMP,* November 15, 2002.

517 *Three Represents*   Xinhua, November 15, 2002.

517 *"paramount authority"*   Eric Eckholm, in *NYT,* November 12, 2002.

517 *vote was called* [following]   Josephine Ma, in *SCMP*, November 15, 2002.
518 *"waved his hand"*   Ibid.
518 *walked off the stage*   Xinhua, November 14, 2002.
518 *new members*   Xinhua, November 15, 2002.
519 *a confident Hu*   Erik Eckholm, in *NYT*, November 15, 2002.
519 *Every leader . . . was an engineer*   General Secretary Hu Jintao was a water conservation engineer; Wu Bangguo, an electronics communications engineer; Wen Jiabao, a ge-
ological structure engineer; Jia Qinglin, an electrical power engineer; Zeng Qinghong, an
automation control engineer; Huang Ju, an electrical machinery engineer; Wu
Guanzheng, a thermal measurement and automation engineer; Li Changchun, an industrial automation engineer; and Luo Gan, a mining and metallurgical engineer.
519 *Nicholas Kristof noted*   Nicholas D. Kristof, "A Little Leap Forward," *New York Review of Books*, June 24, 2004, 56.
520 *"In our times"*   Author's communication, Beijing, late 2003.
520 *daringly*   Jonathan Mirsky, in *Times Literary Supplement*, January 24, 2003.
521 *dramatically revised edition* [following]   Nathan and Gilley, *Rulers* (2003), 55, 59–61.
At the same October 17 meeting, Jiang Zemin is reported to have recommended that the
next Politburo Standing Committee be expanded to nine members to accommodate Jia
Qinglin and Huang Ju after Li Ruihuan proposed Wu Guanzheng as the seventh member. Li Peng and Hu Jintao supported Jiang's proposal.
521 *"A new era"*   Wang Xiangwei, in *SCMP*, November 16, 2002.
521 *"seek instruction"*   Erik Eckholm, in *NYT*, November 21, 2002.
522 *formal arrangement*   Willy Wo-Lap Lam, in *China Brief*, March 11, 2003.
522 *"close to awe"* [following]   Susan V. Lawrence, in *FEER*, November 28, 2002,
522 *"At the strong request"*   Shin Pao (Hong Kong), March 23, 2003.
522 *"at least three years"*   Susan V. Lawrence, in *AWSJ*, November 28, 2002.
523 *"I always value"*   Xinhua, December 12, 2002.
523 *clear signal* [following]   Shin Pao (Hong Kong), March 23, 2003.
523 *senior generals*   Zhang Liang, in *Hsin Pao* (Hong Kong), March 18, 2003 (BBC).
523 *it was Hu*   Shin Pao (Hong Kong), March 23, 2003; Nathan and Gilley, *Rulers* (2003),
73.
523 *"Seeking instruction isn't"* [following]   Erik Eckholm, in *NYT*, November 21, 2002.
524 *That afternoon*   Xinhua, November 15, 2002 (BBC).
524 *"I hope"*   Susan V. Lawrence, in *FEER*, December 26, 2002.
524 *"with Jiang Zemin"* [following]   Xinhua, November 15, 2002 (BBC).
525 *"shelving the idea"*   Willy Wo-Lap Lam, on CNN.com, August 30, 2002.
525 *"chief representative"*   Frank Ching, in *SCMP*, December 8, 2002; Frank Ching, in
Business Times Singapore, November 27 and December 11, 2002; Xinhua, November
15, 2002.
525 *Mao had remained, . . . "come and go"*   Frank Ching, in *SCMP*, December 8, 2002.
526 *"underestimating him"*   ABC News, http://abcnews.go.com/reference/bios/zemin.html.
526 *Sino-Russian partnership*   Xinhua, December 2, 2002.
526 *military hardware*   Russian media reported that China and Russia had decided to
maintain secrecy on all arms deals, citing public relations as well as national security reasons. Although officials on both sides declined comment, speculation was rife that China
was seeking nuclear submarines, high-tech surface ships, and advanced fighter aircraft.
China needed the weapons to speed the high-tech transformation of the People's Liberation Army, one of Jiang's primary objectives. Indeed, by 2000 China had become the
world's biggest arms importer. As for Russia, whose domestic demand for its military
technology was greatly reduced, it desperately needed the business to keep its defense
industry solvent and its R&D capabilities current. Russia's defense minister put it bluntly:
"Russia's defense industry complex can be preserved only by supplying military equip-

ment and arms to China." David Lague and Susan V. Lawrence, in *FEER*, December 12, 2002.

526 *Kazakhstan president* *China Daily*, December 24, 2002.

527 *trusted advisers . . . "big power diplomacy" . . . "Fifth Generation"* [following] Vivien Pik-Kwan Chan, in *SCMP*, November 20, 2002.

527 *"I was with President Jiang"* Author's interview with Teng Wensheng.

527 *"self-perfection"* Dong Yuyu and Shih Binghai, *Political China: Facing a New Era of Selection of New System* (China Today Publishing).

527 *attended meetings . . . "charge you"* Author's communication, Beijing.

527 *the gift* For example, a magnificent two-volume set *Paintings of Zhongnanhai* that exemplifies the richness of Chinese culture.

527 *Foreign media speculated* The speculation was that in the "Fifth Generation" Wang Huning could become responsible for ideology. Vivien Pik-Kwan Chan, *SCMP*, November 20, 2002.

528 *public pilgrimage* [following] Susan V. Lawrence, in *FEER*, December 26, 2002; Vivien Pik-Kwan Chan, in *SCMP*, December 9, 2002; *PD*, December 8, 2002.

528 *photograph* *PD*, December 8, 2002.

528 *"white smoke"* Andrew J. Nathan and Bruce Gilley, "China's New Rulers 1. The Path to Power," *New York Review of Books*, September 26, 2002, 12–16.

528 *similar outlooks* Susan V. Lawrence, in *FEER*, December 26, 2002,

528 *to the poor* Willy Wo-Lap Lam, in *China Brief*, December 20, 2002.

528 *Wen Jiabao* Willy Wo-Lap Lam, on CNN.com, November 25, 2002.

529 *petroleum industry* Nathan and Gilley, *Rulers* (2003), 136.

529 *Social discipline* Willy Wo-Lap Lam, in *China Brief*, December 20, 2002.

529 *Zhou Jiannan* Lam, *Era*, 17.

529 *chief representative* Xinhua, November 15, 2002; *Business Times Singapore*, November 27, 2002; *SCMP*, December 8, 2003.

529 *"contrary to rumor"* Susan V. Lawrence, in *FEER*, December 26, 2002.

529 *a year later* Author's communication, Beijing, late 2003.

529 *Peking Opera* Xinhua, December 31, 2002.

530 Shenzhou IV Xinhua, December 30, 2002.

Chapter 30. 2003–September 2004

531 *arms inspections* *PD*, February 8, 2003.

532 *Colin Powell* AFP, February 25, 2003; Xinhua, February 25, 2003.

532 *Taiwan* Xinhua, February 24, 2003.

532 *expected something* John Pomfret, in *WP*, February 24, 2003.

532 *four hundred short-range missiles* *AWSJ*, February 24, 2003, A9.

532 *Fidel Castro* Xinhua, February 26, 2003; *China Daily*, February 27, 2003.

533 *Bill Gates* Xinhua, February 28, 2003.

533 *North Korea* Xinhua, January 10, 2003; *PD*, February 8, 2003.

533 *While some Chinese* Ching Cheong, in *ST*, January 16, 2003.

533 *For decades* North Korea also downplayed China's huge sacrifice in the Korean War.

533 *"If Kim tells"* Gordon G. Chang, in *China Brief*, February 25, 2003.

533 *8 percent . . . 9.1 percent* *PD*, December 30, 2002; *China Daily*, January 20, 2004. The torrid economic growth in gross domestic product (GDP) in 2003 was all the more impressive considering the SARS slowdown, said to have cut 0.8 percent (*PD*, October 18, 2003).

534 *only Jiang* Xinhua, February 28, 2003 (BBC).

534 *Zhu Rongji* Xinhua, March 5, 2003 (BBC).

534 *"darker complexion"* China News Service, March 6, 2003 (BBC).

534–535 *"form of dialogue" . . . "Iraq must"* Xinhua, March 10, 2003.

535 *main elections*   The first election, on March 13, was of Jia Qinglin as CPPCC chairman. Had Jia, who was close to Jiang, been tainted by the huge corruption scandal in Xiamen? He received 92.8 percent of the 2,151 votes cast, higher than some observers had been expecting though lower than Li Ruihuan's results for the same position five years before. Kyodo News, March 13, 2003. Sounding a progressive theme in his closing speech, Jia said that the CPPCC had to adapt to the changing face of society, noting that "new interest groups and social organizations have emerged." *SCMP*, March 15, 2003.

535 *folk music*   *China Daily*, March 16, 2003.

535 *shake Hu's hand*   Xinhua, March 15, 2003.

535 *"top vote-getter"* [following]   Kyodo News, March 15, 2003.

535 *cyclical fashion*   For all of his heroism and popularity during World War II, Winston Churchill lost the general election in 1945, just months after the great victory. (When his wife told him that it might be a "blessing in disguise," Churchill famously replied that it was "very well disguised.")

535 *Wen Jiabao*   Willy Wo-Lap Lam, in *China Brief*, March 25, 2003.

536 *"never let down"* [following]   Xinhua, March 18, 2003.

536 *"created by Jiang"*   Chinese News Service, March 18, 2003 (BBC).

536 *parallel CMC*   The Party CMC commands the People's Liberation Army while the State CMC conducts state-to-state military relations.

536 *full five-year terms . . . "help Hu Jintao"*   Ching Cheong, in *ST*, March 15, 2003.

536 *"relationship between"*   Elizabeth Rosenthal, in *NYT*, March 4, 2003.

536 *"Historically"*   Author's communication, Beijing, late 2003.

537 *fresh, controversial ideas* [following]   Ray Cheung, in *SCMP*, April 8, 2003; Elizabeth Rosenthal, in *NYT*, March 4, 2003.

537 *press should report*   Nathan and Gilley, *Rulers* (2003), 61.

537 *rank order correct*   Author's communication, Beijing.

537 *not to "misunderstand"*   Elizabeth Rosenthal, in *NYT*, March 4, 2003.

537 *"transparency"*   *PD*, March 4, 2003.

538 *News of the contagion*   Gordon G. Chang, in *China Brief*, April 22, 2003.

538 *China's newspapers*   For example, see *China Daily* during late March and early April 2003.

538 *"effectively controlled"*   John Pomfret, in *WP*, April 21, 2003,

538 *twelve cases . . . went public* [following]   John Pomfret, in *WP*, May 13, 2003, A1; Matt Pottinger, in *WSJ*, April 22, 2003.

538 *"never cover up"*   *Apple Daily News* (Hong Kong) and *Chinese Net News*, April 28, 2003.

538 *news conference . . . fired* [following]   *PD*, April 30, 2003; John Pomfret, in *WP*, May 2 and 13, 2003; A1; Erik Eckholm, in *NYT*, April 20 and May 1, 2003; Arnold Zeitlin, in *China Brief*, July 1, 2003.

538 *mayor of Beijing*   In October 2003, former Beijing mayor Meng Xuenong was quietly rehabilitated (partially) with his appointment as vice director of the cabinet-level office of South-North Water Diversion. Willy Wo-Lap Lam, *China Brief*, March 3, 2004.

539 *If SARS had not spread*   In 1989, when China had little to lose, the government had stubbornly maintained its position in the face of the world's disapproval. In 2003, though it took its time, the government owned up to its wrongdoing. It had no choice: If the world didn't believe China about SARS, it would express its distrust by not visiting and not investing.

539 *By not warning*   Ching Cheong, in *ST*, April 22, 2003.

539 *Literally overnight*   Erik Eckholm, in *NYT*, April 23, 2003. On April 21 the top six articles on the *People's Daily* website were related to SARS.

539 *"Sacked" . . . "To strengthen"*   Josephine Ma, in *SCMP*, April 22, 2003.

539 *"rare, blunt"*   Erik Eckholm, in *NYT*, April 20, 2003.

539 *"rise to the challenge"* PD, April 30, 2003.

540 *Critics worked* Apple Daily News (Hong Kong) and *Chinese Net News*, April 28, 2003.

540 *first public statement* PD, April 27, 2003.

540 *twelve hundred medical* Apple Daily News (Hong Kong) and *Chinese Net News*, April 28, 2003.

540 *Navy submarine* PD, May 3, 2003.

540 *military disasters . . . condolences* CNN.com, May 2, 2003.

540 *Jiang and Hu* Fong Tak-Ho, in *SCMP*, May 6, 2003.

540 *CMC meetings* For example, when *People's Daily* reported on CMC leaders visiting an exhibition on military logistics and transport equipment, Jiang was listed first and Hu second; everyone else, all the senior generals, came afterward in a separate paragraph. PD, April 29, 2004.

541 *unprecedented coverage* Stratford's Global Intelligence Report, March 26, 2003.

541 *Miss China* Xinhua, April 20, 2003.

541 *"not important"* Xinhua, April 15, 2003

541 *"major role"* Karen DeYoung and Doug Struck, in *WP*, April 17, 2003.

541 *first meetings* PD, April 30, 2003

541 *"We've got nukes" . . . "in disbelief"* [following] Glenn Kessler, in *WP*, April 24, 2003.

541 *"major slap"* Joseph Kahn, in *NYT*, April 25, 2003. The Chinese authority was Shi Yin-hong, a foreign policy expert, whose commentary in *Ta Kung Pao*, the pro-Beijing Hong Kong newspaper, stated that "China's first objective is to firmly cause North Korea to get rid of its nuclear weapons." Gordon G. Chang, *China Brief*, February 25, 2003.

542 *blamed China* [following] Author's communication, Beijing, late 2003.

542 *"does not obey China"* Reportedly, Kim Jong-Il had for several years been "weeding out" many "pro-Chinese" advisers and officials in North Korea's senior echelons. Willy Wo-Lap Lam, *China Brief*, April 29, 2004.

542 *"new round of study"* [following] PD, April 28, 2003.

543 *Hu Jintao surprised* Xinhua picked President Hu's July 1, 2003, speech, which called on Party members to study the "important ideology of the Three Represents," as its third most important news story of 2003, right after the election of China's new leaders and the battle against SARS. Xinhua, December 28, 2003.

543 *"three close to's"* Willy Lam, *China Brief*, July 1, 2003.

544 *"scientific development concept"* Joseph Fewsmith, "Promoting the Scientific Development Concept," *China Leadership Monitor*, No. 11, Summer 2004, http://www.chinaleadershipmonitor.org/20043/jf.html. He references Xinhua, September 2, 2003.

544 *senior retirees . . . Brahm* [following] Allen T. Cheng, in *SCMP*, January 13, 2003.

544 *"lead quiet lives"* According to state media, the former numbers two, three, and four in the Party, Li Peng, Zhu Rongji, and Li Ruihuan, were enjoying their retirement. Li Peng was writing his memoirs. (His first volume, *Three Gorges Journal*, was published in 2003.) Zhu Rongji was reading Tang dynasty poems and avoiding publicity. Li Ruihuan was playing tennis and attending Peking Opera. AFP, January 3, 2004.

544 *rumors* John Pomfret, in *WP*, August 27, 2003.

544 *"considerable influence"* Wang Xiangwei, in *SCMP*, July 17, 2003.

545 *"no pressure"* Author's communication, Beijing, late 2003.

545 *inner staff* In addition to Jia Ting'an (promoted in January 2004), this included Wang Huning, director of the Party's Policy Research Office; Zhao Qizheng, minister of the State Council Information Office; Teng Wensheng, director of the Party's Literature Office; and You Xigui, head of the Central Guard Bureau.

545 *When he asked . . . "Big Brother" . . . "I'm seventy-seven"* Author's communication, Beijing, late 2003.

545 *Dick Cheney* PD, April 15, 2004.

545 *Kim Jong-Il . . . To the Russian China Daily,* April 22, 2004, 1.

545 *Condoleezza Rice PD Online,* July 8, 2004.

546 *army issues* In early January 2004 Jiang met Richard Myers, chairman of the U.S. Joint Chiefs of Staff, and stressed a familiar theme: Taiwan, he said, is the "most important and sensitive issue in Sino-U.S. relations." *PD,* January 15, 2004.

546 *army modernization . . . information warfare* [following] *PD,* November 5, 2003.

546 *"Party construction" PD,* December 12, 2003.

546 *A beaming Jiang PD,* October 16, 2003. China's manned space program had been initiated by Jiang to promote national pride, stimulate national technology, and support national defense.

546 *television professionals* Author's interview with Zhao Huayong, March 2004.

547 *Zhao's own story* See Chapter 25

547 *In another phone call* Author's interview with Zhao Huayong, March 2004. CCTV's culture and classic arts station began broadcasting eighteen hours a day on March 28, 2004.

547 *"growth of classical music"* Author's interview with Yu Long, Beijing, April 2004.

547 *"Jiang's Nanxun" Ming Pao* (Hong Kong), February 11, 2004. It was the Chinese New Year period; Jiang stayed a week in Guangzhou after twelve days in Shenzhen. Traveling with him were Politburo Standing Committee member Li Changchun, Vice Premier Zeng Peiyan, and Guangdong's Party chief and governor. The mainland media did not cover Jiang's journey.

547 *three million trees Beijing Morning Post,* April 4, 2004, 1.

548 *strengthening his hold on power . . . "patriots must form" . . . reversing a decision* Philip P. Pan, *WP,* May 31, 2004, A1.

548–549 *"handing over more" . . . ultimate authority . . . "master revolutionary" . . . "fight a war" . . . "peaceful rise" . . . detain Dr. Jiang Yanyong . . . Politburo meeting* Joseph Kahn, "Former Leader May Still Hold Sway in China, *NYT,* July 16, 2004, 1. Jiang's alleged comment to Rice (said to be volunteered) about "handing over more and more power" to Hu Jintao was reported by an American official who attended the Zhongnanhai meeting. Jiang's alleged comment—"We must fight a war with Taiwan"—was quoted in an essay by Liu Yazhou, the deputy political commissar of the Chinese Air Force, which dealt with preparations for conflict with Taiwan and was circulated on Chinese websites in May 2004.

549 *senior military surgeon . . . Dr. Jiang was released . . . Party perceived . . . "colorectal cancer"* Joseph Kahn, *NYT,* July 20, 2004; Philip P. Pan, *WP,* July 20, 2004.

550 *Jiang Zemin retired* [following] Xinhua (several reports), September 19 and 20, 2004; Joseph Kahn, *NYT,* September 19 and 20, 2004; Wang Xiangwei, *SCMP,* September 19, 2004; Edward Cody, *WP,* September 20, 2004; Ray Cheung, *SCMP,* September 20, 2004; and *PD,* September 10, 19, 20, and 21, 2004.

551 *"I just want to say"* Edward Cody, *WP,* September 20, 2004.

553 *Miss China* Moreover, *People's Daily,* the Party mouthpiece, highlighted "China's Top 10 Sex-Related News Stories," www.peopledaily.com, November 13, 2003.

553 *State Constitution . . . "private property" PD,* December 22, 2003; *PD,* March 8, 2004. The Three Represents was written into the Party's Constitution at the Sixteenth Party Congress in November 2002 and into the State Constitution at the Second Plenum of the Tenth National People's Congress in March 2004. By formally asserting that "the State respects and protects human rights," China was providing, for the first time, the legal basis for the implementation of human rights processes, though no one expected this to be easily interpreted or rapidly enforced. The State also committed itself to protect citizens' rights to private property, including its inheritance, and "shall make compensation" whenever such property is expropriated or requisitioned. *PD,* March 8, 2004; *PD,* March 15, 2004; Chris Buckley, *NYT,* March 15, 2004.

CONCLUSION: THE LEGACY OF JIANG ZEMIN

555 *"I see suffering"* David M. Lampton, *Same Bed, Different Dreams: Managing U.S.–China Relations, 1989–2000* (Berkeley: University of California Press, 2001), 256.

555 *Third Brother considered* Author's interview with Jiang Zehui.

555 *Zhao Qizheng gave* Author's interview with Zhao Qizheng.

555 *"When Jiang Zemin"* Author's interview with Leng Rong.

555 *Song Ning* Author's interview with Dr. Song Ning, Beijing, April 2004.

556 *"Thirteen or fourteen years"* [following] Author's communication, Beijing.

556 *" 'revitalizing China' "* Author's interview with Dr. Song Jian.

556 *Beijing Institute* Founded by Dr. Song Jian in April 2004, the Beijing Institute for Frontier Science brings together leading Chinese and foreign scientists—physicists, mathematicians, biologists, space scientists—to explore novel theoretical ideas, catalyze new ways of interdisciplinary thinking, and facilitate fresh expressions of scientific freedom. The author is vice chairman of the Beijing Institute.

557 *"unique sensitivities"* Jiang Zemin, *Science* (editorial), June 30, 2000, 2317. See Robert Lawrence Kuhn, "Science as Democratizer," *American Scientist*, September–October 2003, 388–90.

557 *took pride in the 200,000* Author's interview with Zheng Bijian, Beijing, January 2003.

557 *220 billion cell phone text messages* There are more text messages being sent in China than in all the rest of the world put together. In July 2004, the Chinese government began "filtering" these text messages to eliminate pornography, false or deceptive advertising, and information or news deemed inappropriate for maintaining social order or the authority of the Communist Party. The creative contest between senders and filterers would have no end. Joseph Kahn, in *NYT*, July 2, 2004.

557 *"I've seen President Jiang"* Author's interview with Henry Kissinger. Jiang met repeatedly with Kissinger not only because the Chinese president was interested in the views of the erudite former U.S. secretary of state, but also because Jiang has extraordinary respect for Kissinger's historic role in opening relations between China and the United States. "The Chinese in general and President Jiang in particular believe that for cultural and moral reasons, as well as for practical ones, friends should be valued and old friends should be valued greatly," commented Dr. Kissinger. "Chinese always greet their old friends; they do not treat people as dispensable even if they're long out of active life."

558 *Nicholas Kristof comments* Nicholas D. Kristof, "A Little Leap Forward," *New York Review of Books*, June 24, 2004, 56.

559 *"The time I was studying"* Xinhua, October 25, 1999 (quoting Jiang's interview with *Le Figaro*).

562 *combines morality* Under Jiang, the Party's concept of morality changed. The old, coercive idea that equated ethical behavior with political obedience was quietly abandoned, and a new, more humanistic form of morality was encouraged, one that also lauded the modern carriers of the social order, such as science and education.

562 *high-minded personal traits . . . "lofty ideals"* [following] Xinhua, July 1, 2001 (Jiang's speech on the eightieth anniversary of the Communist Party). In addition to morality and civil behavior, the Second Represent encompasses four categories: (1) high-minded personal traits, such as decency, honesty, courtesy, graciousness, commitment to education, hard work at one's job, and dedication to one's family; (2) progressive social attitudes, such as self-reliance, competition[!], efficiency, democracy, a [well-functioning] legal system, and a pioneering and innovative spirit; (3) shared beliefs, customs, and traditions; and (4) all the arts collectively, Chinese and Western.

563 *methodology* Author's interview with Leng Rong.

563 *reason for establishing* Xinhua, July 15, 2000 (BBC).

563 *"I put forward"* Xinhua, July 15, 2000 (quoting from a speech published in *Seeking Truth* magazine).

563 *"People say"* Author's communication, Beijing. Two hundred officials attended this closed session.

563 *"a scientific thinking system"* Jasper Becker, in *SCMP,* September 23, 2001.

563 *"We firmly believe"* Xinhua, July 1, 2001.

563 *"three generations"* China News Service, November 15, 2002 (BBC).

563–564 *"a continuous line"* *PD,* December 26, 2003, quoting Li Changchun at a symposium in honor of Mao Zedong's 110th birthday.

564 *"very proud"* Author's interview with Shen Yongyan.

564 *Teng Wensheng* Author's interview with Teng Wensheng.

564 *prevent any dissension* The use of cover stories to conceal high-level disputes—for example, that Qiao Shi's retirement in 1997 was Qiao's own idea (see Chapter 18)—elicits the question of how Jiang Zemin, who always respected intellectual honesty, could allow (or encourage) such inaccurate (or incomplete) accounts to be propagated. The answer, such as it is, lay in his hierarchy of values, the pinnacle of which was preserving stability, because at the current stage of China's development, Jiang fervently believed that only by maintaining stability could the government ensure that its 1.3 billion citizens would continue to have the necessities of life. He also believed that to the extent that dissensions, disagreements, personality conflicts, and political struggles in the Party became known, the people's confidence in the Party would become eroded, thereby weakening the Party's capacity to maintain stability and provide the necessities of life. Keeping a pretense of total unity in government is not limited to China. The administrations of American presidents also try, with varying degrees of success, to present a unified image. Secretary of State Colin Powell and Secretary of Defense Donald Rumsfeld were not always successful in keeping their disagreements out of the press.

565 *"China did not achieve"* . . . *"seven thousand"* Nicholas D. Kristof, "A Little Leap Forward," *New York Review of Books,* June 24, 2004, 57.

565 *polling its citizens* Even though China is not a democracy, Joseph Fewsmith and Stanley Rosen argue that government polling indicates some recognition of the legitimacy of popular opinion ("mass legitimacy"), even if it views popular opinion only in negative terms (i.e., sets boundaries on what policies would be unacceptable). Joseph Fewsmith and Stanley Rosen, "The Domestic Context of Chinese Foreign Policy: Does 'Public Opinion' Matter?" in David M. Lampton, ed., *The Making of Chinese Foreign and Security Policy in the Era of Reform* (Stanford, Stanford University Press, 2001), 155.

565 *"We are great"* Author's interview with Henry Kissinger.

566 *One Chinese intellectual* Fewsmith, *China Since Tiananmen,* 219. Wang Xiaodong states that without individual (democratic) rights, the people "will have no way to stop [China's] ruling clique from selling out the country for its own self-interest."

566 *non-Communist parties* China's political systems is said to be founded on "multiparty cooperation and political consultation under the leadership of the Communist Party." It differs from the multiparty or two-party systems of Western countries in that all the non-Communist parties are "friendly parties" rather than opposition or out-of-office parties. They are said to "participate in the discussion and management of state affairs in cooperation with the Communist Party" (*China Daily,* December 5, 2003). There are about 600,000 members in the eight non-Communist parties, less than one percent of those in the Communist Party.

567 *ultimate goal* A common fallacy in understanding China's Communism is confusing its continuing ultimate goal (the social ideal of total equality in a prosperous society) with its archaic, no-longer-applicable economic ideology (full state ownership and total central planning) and its traditional method of control (authoritarianism, if no longer the totalitarian "dictatorship of the proletariat"). By modifying its economic ideology (reducing state ownership and encouraging private business; developing a market economy and minimizing central planning), and by changing its method of control (gradually loosening

the authoritarianism in all walks of life), Jiang Zemin modernized Communism, thus preserving its idealized vision of society as the ultimate goal of China.

567 *inner-Party democracy*   Most foreigners are surprised to learn how the Party and the government select and promote personnel, and refine and establish laws. There were many modest examples of political reform during Jiang's term. About ten thousand central and local laws were enacted, two-thirds of them economic. Delegates to the annual national assemblies (NPC and CPPCC) began expressing independent views, even if still casting their ballots largely in unison. Real voting is increasingly common at lower levels of government, and surveys are extensive, even within central ministries, where employees comment (often electronically) and vote (nonbinding) on the potential appointment of superiors up to the vice minister level, thus bringing the rudiments of public exposure and competition into civil service. In many rural areas, residents choose their village committees through direct, secret ballot elections.

In the Politburo Standing Committee, where ultimate decisions are made, the number of members is always odd. (Under Jiang there were seven; after the Sixteenth Party Congress, under Hu, nine.) A strict majority always carries the vote. In one sense, this is purer "democracy" than exists within the administration of the American president, who has a cabinet and many advisers but is not required to heed their advice and certainly does not take their vote. In the American system, the final decision is made solely by the president; "The Buck Stops Here," said the famous sign on the White House desk of President Harry Truman. Not so in China, where all major decisions are made by a noncircumventable majority vote of the Politburo Standing Committee.

Of course, the U.S. president is elected by a direct vote of the American people, whereas the members of the Politburo Standing Committee are elected by a very small circle of high-level Party leaders. In addition, the American system is based on strong checks and balances among the executive, legislative, and judicial branches of government. Although in China there are no such independent controls on power, inner-Party political maneuvers mix shared interests, group alliances, personal friendships, and good old arm twisting, the totality of which gives rise to a rudimentary form of balance of power among the factions and sectors that begins to function as a protodemocratic system of checks and balances.

568 *Maoist past*   Many Chinese have mixed feelings about Mao Zedong. Though he perpetrated or enabled incalculable harm for almost two decades from the Anti-Rightist Campaign and the Great Leap Forward in the late 1950s through the end of the Cultural Revolution at his death in 1976, he also brought independence and international respect to China and many of his thoughts conveyed timeless wisdom and great artistry. "I don't like him," said one patriotic Chinese official of Mao, "but I can't hate him."

568 *"history of democracy"*   Author's interview with Zheng Bijian.

569 *"It wasn't easy"*   Author's interview with Yan Mingfu.

570 *"Like many intellectuals"*   Author's interview with Jin Chongji.

571 *"power politics"*   Xinhua, September 5, 2000.

572 *encourage its old friends*   Was Jiang Zemin really trying to convince world opinion that the reason why the Cuban and North Korean people were suffering was not because they were dominated by dictators, not because their freedoms were repressed, not because their economic system did not work, but because the United States was somehow oppressing them? Such arguments would resonate only with those given to reflex anti-Americanism or remnant bands of ultra-Leftists. In fact, Jiang's underlying rationale was historic, strategic, psychological, and, in parts, even subtle.

For decades, China (like the Soviet Union and the United States) saw a bipolar world—socialist versus capitalist—and had the simple notion that a Communist state, ipso facto, was a "fraternal state." (There was also the "enemy of my enemy must be my friend" mentality.) In addition, since there were so few countries left in the world that continued to call themselves Communist or socialist, perhaps Jiang felt a paternal need to protect this endangered political species.

Supporting the anti-American regimes of Castro and Kim certainly declared China's foreign policy to be independent of America's. But if relieving U.S. pressure on Taiwan was an objective, the more China set itself as America's adversary, the more the U.S. Congress would wax emotional in its support of Taiwan. If loyalty to old friends was an issue—discarding them could seem uncivil and even humiliating to China—the "tough love" of helping change self-inflicted, debilitating behaviors would be, just like with drug addiction, the actions of a true friend. (Jiang did discuss, but did not demand, economic reform in his private talks with Castro and the father-and-son Kims.) Building a multipolar world is a laudatory goal supported by many Westerners, but Cuba and North Korea are hardly exemplars of the "spiritual civilization" that Jiang described as his ideal.

Castro and the Kims personified the worst qualities of ultra-Leftists against whom Jiang had waged protracted battle, and their cults of personality and stringent social controls matched all the excesses of pre–Deng Xiaoping China that Jiang and his generation had forsworn. Just because Castro or Kim claimed his country to be socialist did not mean that either was anything like China. Cuba and North Korea were totalitarian; China was not. Cuba and North Korea had lifelong dictators; China did not. Yet by appearing with Castro and Kim, Jiang inadvertently blurred the vision of the unsophisticated in distinguishing China.

Just as Stalin's Communist Soviet Union had far more in common with Hitler's fascist Germany than with the socialist-like countries of Scandinavia, Castro's Cuba and the Kims' Korea were more political soul mates of, say, Allende's fascist Chile than of Jiang's socialist China. It's not the name on the door, the sign on the system, that determines true commonality. What counts are the degrees of freedom in citizens' lives, the energetic growth of an innovative economy, the improvement in standards of living, and the progressive developments in society and governance—these are what determine similarities among systems. Simply put, today's North Korea and Cuba are more akin to the China of the Cultural Revolution—destitute and deteriorating, with a personality-cult leader and a coerced and subjugated citizenry. Jiang Zemin's China is nothing like that.

In April 2004, President Hu Jintao, CMC Chairman Jiang Zemin, and every member of the Politburo Standing Committee welcomed North Korea's Kim Jong-Il on a state visit to Beijing in a remarkable show of high-level protocol not often afforded to other state leaders. A large picture of Kim and Hu dominated the newspapers, though there may have been frustration beneath the surface after Kim reportedly refused to consider free-market reforms suggested by the Chinese leadership. It seems that while Kim expressed willingness to make concessions on nuclear weapons, he worried, with good reason, that "economic liberalization would lead to the unraveling of his orthodox socialist society." Willy Wo-Lap Lam, *China Brief,* April 29, 2004.

572 *"Mao's word"* Gilley, *Tiger,* 231.

572–573 *"Lots of decoration"* . . . *"consensus builder"* BBC News Online, October 21, 2002, www.news.bbc.co.uk.

572 *"political breeze"* AsiaWeek, December 26, 1997.

573 *"astute shifts"* Time, October 27, 1997.

573 *"avoiding ideological battles"* ABC News, http://abcnews.go.com/reference/bios/zemin.html.

573 *Frederick Teiwes* Frederick C. Teiwes, "Politics at the 'Core': The Political Circumstances of Mao Zedong, Deng Xiaoping and Jiang Zemin," http://rspas.anu.edu.au/ccc/morrison00.pdf.

574 *domestic politics* Robert M. Hathaway, "The Lingering Legacy of Tiananmen," in

Foreign Affairs, September/October 2003, quoting Robert Suettinger, *Beyond Tiananmen,* who argued that after Tiananmen "the bilateral relationship lost its insulation from domestic politics" and was susceptible to wild swings of emotion. Fewsmith and Rosen state, "As compared to Chinese foreign policy in the Maoist era, the domestic context of Chinese foreign policy today has become both more important and more complex." Fewsmith and Rosen, in David M. Lampton, ed., *The Making of Chinese Foreign and Security Policy in the Era of Reform.*

574 *drinks in moderation*   Gilley, *Tiger,* 229–30.

575 *"anything in sports"... One minister*   Author's communication, Beijing. The minister was Fang Yi and he made his comment in the mid-1980s when Jiang was major of Shanghai (and acting the same).

575 *"dry and rigid Communist leaders"*   Author's interview with Jiang Zehui.

575 *more credit*   Reportedly, Jiang wore an involuntarily long face when, on occasion, Zhu Rongji received louder applause than he did.

577 *"deliberative, meritocratic"*   Nathan and Gilley, *Rulers* (2003), 260.

577 *middle class*   Forecasts estimate that the percentage of middle-class people in China (defined as those with family assets of 150,000 to 300,000 yuan, about $18,000 to $36,000) will reach 40 percent in 2020, up from 19 percent in 2004. In 2004, 49 percent of urban households met this middle-class standard, a remarkable testament to China's reform policies. *PD,* March 10, 2004.

577 *"Nothing is likely"*   Ted C. Fishman, "The Chinese Century," *NYT Magazine,* July 4, 2004, 27.

577 *Chinese democracy*   Bruce Gilley, *China's Democratic Future: How It Will Happen and Where It Will Lead* (New York: Columbia University Press), 2004.

577 *Nicholas Kristof agrees*   Nicholas D. Kristof, "A Little Leap Forward," *New York Review of Books,* June 24, 2004, 56, 59.

578 *In 1820*   At that time America accounted for about two percent of world output, ranking ninth.

578 *historic proportions*   Dmitry Kosyrev, for Russian Information Agency Novosti, November 5, 2002.

579 *most profound transformations*   Economist Jeffrey Sachs, who has advised dozens of developing countries and originated "shock therapy," said that "China is the most successful development story in world history." Fareed Zakaria, in *Newsweek,* January 6, 2003.

Acknowledgments

PREPARING THE BIOGRAPHY of Jiang Zemin has been an exhilarating, consuming experience, and only now, when both the euphoria and the anxiety are almost over, can I reflect on the process. My first feeling is angst: There is so much more to know; what have I left out? My second is gratitude: I am honored by those people I interviewed in China (some of whom I do not name); they gave of their memories and emotions and put their words into my trust. These interviews, conducted between June 2001 and April 2004, form the backbone of the biography.

I offer my deep appreciation to former Shanghai mayor Wang Daohan, Jiang's mentor and friend, whose candor, clarity, depth of understanding, and firsthand presence elucidates Jiang's early and middle career; Jiang Zehui, Jiang's sister and family historian, for her family experiences, intimate reflections, and personal warmth; Wang Huijiong, Jiang's university classmate and lifelong friend, for his remembrances, insights, private encouragement, and special support; Shen Yongyan, Jiang's former colleague and close friend from Changchun, for his keen-eyed observations and openness in relating personal conversations; and Tong Zonghai, Jiang's college roommate, for animating and enriching the university years.

I am honored to thank those whom I interviewed: Zeng Peiyan, vice premier and former chairman, State Development Planning Commission; Dr. Song Jian, former state councilor and chairman, State Science and Technology Commission; Zhao Qizheng, minister, State Council Information Office; Sheng Huaren, vice chairman, National People's Congress, and former chairman, State Economic and Trade Commission; Li Zhaoxing, foreign minister; Teng Wensheng, minister, CPC Literature Office; General Xiong Guangkai, deputy chief, General Staff, People's Liberation Army; Wang Guangya, permanent representative of China to the United Nations; Zhao Huayong, president, China Central Television; Leng Rong, vice minister, CPC Literature Office; Ye Gongqi, former vice mayor, Shanghai; Zheng Bijian, former executive vice president, Central Party School; Jin Chongji, biographer and president, Chinese History Society; Lu Baifu, vice minister, State Council Development Research Center; Wu Xiaoling, vice governor, People's Bank of China; Yan Mingfu, former member, Secretariat, CPC Central Committee, and former president, China Charity Federation; Song Ning, senior economic policy adviser and longtime friend; and Li Qiankuan, film director and chairman, China Film Foundation.

I am much appreciative of the observations and insights of former U.S. secretary of state Dr. Henry Kissinger, former U.S. secretary of the treasury Robert E. Rubin, and AIG chairman Maurice Greenberg.

ALTHOUGH I HAVE SPENT a good deal of time in China, I am neither a China scholar by training nor a China hand by profession. I do not speak serious Chinese and cannot read it at all. I conducted interviews and read sources in English or in English translation. My doctorate was in science (anatomy / brain research), and while I have written and edited a number of books, my career has been in finance (mergers and acquisitions) and television, not China studies, journalism, or biography.

In addition to my interviewees, I am indebted to the China scholars, analysts, commentators, and writers on whose books, articles, essays, and reporting I have relied. Though my interpretations may, at times, differ from their own, I admire their works, have drawn upon them extensively, and recognize their contributions to China's emergence and development.

Bruce Gilley's pioneering, well-researched biography, *Tiger on the Brink: Jiang Zemin and the New Elite* (Berkeley: University of California Press, 1999), is an important source from which I have drawn and to which future biographers will certainly refer. A former journalist for the *Far Eastern Economic Review* and more recently a graduate student at Princeton University, Gilley has made available, in English, a host of heretofore inaccessible information. In general, I do not give Gilley's Chinese-language sources; readers can check his book for references and find there further information, ideas, and stories.

The articles and essays of Willy Wo-Lap Lam, a preeminent "China watcher" and author of *The Era of Jiang Zemin* (Singapore: Prentice Hall, 1999), offers snapshots of the inner workings of Chinese policies and politics.

For many years with the *South China Morning Post,* he has more recently reported for CNN and written for the Jamestown Foundation's *China Brief.*

Yang Zhongmei's biography, *Jiang Zemin Zhuan (Biography of Jiang Zemin)* (Taipei: China Times Publishing Co., 1996) is a rich source of material, primarily for historical contexts and political events.

Andrew J. Nathan has written or edited several important works on contemporary China from which I have drawn, especially *China's New Rulers: The Secret Files,* coauthored with Bruce Gilley (New York: New York Review of Books, 2002; and Second, Revised Edition, 2003).

I have been informed by the works of Joseph Fewsmith, James Lilley, Robert L. Suettinger, Donald M. Lampton, Kenneth Lieberthal, David Shambaugh, and Cheng Li. I note in particular Joseph Fewsmith's *China Since Tiananmen: The Politics of Transition* (New York: Cambridge University Press, 2001). Political economist Laurence Brahm, based in Beijing and the author of *Zhongnanhai* (Hong Kong: Naga, 1998), provided special insights.

In constructing the sequence of events of Jiang's later career, I have integrated reports from many newspapers and news services, including the *South China Morning Post* (with acknowledgment, after Willy Wo-Lap Lam, to Simon Beck, Jasper Becker, Vivien Pik-Kwan Chan, Allen Cheng, Daniel Kwan, Josephine Ma, and others), Xinhua News Agency, *People's Daily,* the *Washington Post* (especially John Pomfret), *The New York Times* (especially Erik Eckholm, Seth Faison, and Elizabeth Rosenthal), the *Straits Times* (Singapore, especially Ching Cheong), *Far Eastern Economic Review,* the *Los Angeles Times,* Associated Press, Agence France Presse, China News Service, United Press International, and various Chinese publications in Hong Kong and the mainland, through the superb translations provided by the BBC Monitoring Service (Asia Pacific).

IT IS A PLEASURE to recognize several extraordinary publishing professionals whose contributions have been invaluable: Youngsuk Chi, chairman of Random House Asia, whose vision and commitment have been essential to this project; Annik La Farge, my editor at Crown Publishing, for her sense and sensitivities; Ann La Farge, whose elegant edits and editorial advice have been invaluable; and Leslie Chang, who helped transform a long manuscript into a manageable one. My appreciation goes to Yee-Wah Chow for her thorough, persistent, and creative research; to Adam Zhu, Daniella Kuhn, Brian Knowles, and Jacki Slater for editorial advice; to Xu Yongjun for fact checking; to Mario Rojas for logistics; to Camille Smith for production editing; and to Yang Yang, director general, State Council Information Office, a personal friend, who facilitated the process and was a source of insight and encouragement throughout this not-always-easy expedition.

I thank my wife, Dora, my mother, Lee, and my children, Aaron, Adam, and Daniella, for their understanding during the years of work; Pamela McFadden, my assistant, for her tireless support; and my friend and partner, Adam Zhu, without whose energy, ideas, creativity, sensitivity, perseverance, dedication, and all manner of help this book would not have been possible. To describe the challenges Adam and I faced, and the adventures we had, would require, it seems, another book. And to all those who put up with my obsessive-compulsive behavior, I offer my gratitude but no regrets.

Personal Perspective

THREE TIMES I HAVE SEEN Jiang Zemin in person, two of which related to music. The first was in November 1993, when I was startled to walk past him on an upper floor of the Hotel Nacional in Havana, Cuba, where he was on a state visit and I was accompanying my wife, Dora Serviarian-Kuhn, who was appearing as piano soloist with the Cuba National Symphony Orchestra. The second time was at a reception in New York in September 2000, when President Jiang attended a concert in Lincoln Center as part of Experience Chinese Culture in the United States, 2000, an exhibition of art and fashion that my partner, Adam Zhu, and I helped organize.* The third time was in Beijing in November 2003, where I heard him speak informally on a number of subjects.

I FIRST WENT TO CHINA in March 1989, one month before students began gathering in Tiananmen Square, but it would be years before I would begin to understand what was really going on there. I had been invited by the State Science and Technology Commission to advise Chinese research institutes in their fledgling efforts to adapt to the incipient market economy. As an investment banker trained as a scientist, not as a lawyer, I've joked that perhaps I seemed less threatening.

I was hooked from the moment I arrived, drawn by the country's remarkable transformation and the energy and optimism of its people. The Chinese had a fresh, if naïve, enthusiasm; they were eager to learn and determined to

---

*It so happened that I appeared with President Jiang in the official photo of the event taken by the Xinhua News Agency. It was published on the front page of major newspapers in China, including *People's Daily*, on September 10, 2000.

improve their material and civic lives. I knew then that the culture, history, economics, and politics of the world's most populous country would matter a great deal to America. What I didn't know then was how much China would matter to me.*

Since that initial visit, I have been much occupied in China.† I've worked with enterprises and agencies, particularly in science, finance, and media. In the early and mid-1990s I lectured and conducted seminars on mergers and acquisitions (M&A), arguing that an open and free M&A market would not only help develop well-managed companies and eliminate poorly managed ones but would also protect the value of state-owned assets (the reverse of prevailing opinion) by inhibiting well-connected people from taking advantage of special relationships.

In 1996 a translation of my book *Investment Banking* (*Touzi Yinhang Xue;* Beijing Normal University Press) was the first of its kind published in China. In 1999 my book on dealmaking (*Jiaoyi Ren*—literally, *Transaction People*—China Economic Science Press) targeted a broader audience. In 2000 *Closer to Truth* (*Zoujin Zhenshi;* China Economic Science Press), the companion book to my U.S. public television (PBS) series on science, meaning, and the future (www.pbs.org/closertotruth), was published simultaneously in the United States and China.

In 1999 I created and coproduced with China Central Television an eight-part documentary entitled *Capital Wave*—the first series on mergers and acquisitions that was broadcast on China's national network. I also created and coproduced with CCTV a vérité documentary exploring China's transformation, *In Search of China*, which was broadcast on PBS in the United States on September 8, 2000—the same night that President Jiang attended the concert at Lincoln Center in New York.

Since CCTV insisted on veto power over the final cut of *In Search of*

---

*What I also didn't know then was that I was meeting my future partner, Adam Zhu—at the time an energetic, resourceful, twenty-two-year-old cadre (with degrees in literature and linguistics), who was assigned to be my translator and, as I would later learn, my chaperon. Adam earned his MBA in finance at Temple University in Philadelphia; we began working together in 1994.

†Two members of my family have also been involved in China. My wife, Dora Serviarian-Kuhn, a concert pianist known for her performances of the Khachaturian Piano Concerto, has appeared as a soloist with three orchestras in Beijing. My daughter, Daniella Kuhn, an actress, has played leading roles in two dramatic series on China Central Television, including a yet-to-be-released multiepisode epic on the Korean War directed by Li Qiankuan.

China for American audiences, I insisted on parallel veto power over the final cut of CCTV's *Capital Wave* series for Chinese audiences—a contractual right that, surprisingly, I was granted. (For the record, CCTV never exercised its veto power; after brief internal discussions, CCTV executives decided not even to screen *In Search of China* prior to its premiere broadcast on PBS.)

The issue of editorial control was sacrosanct. In an early meeting with a high-level media official, I stated that if our documentary appeared 100 percent positive about China, Western audiences would believe none of it. I said our team would have little concern about the ratio of "positive" to "negative"; rather we would strive to tell the truth, as best we could, using a diversity of real-life stories that personified contemporary China. In the end, we were pleased that Chinese officials appreciated our PBS documentary, even the "negative" piece about the Acheng Sugar Factory (Harbin, Heilongjiang province), China's first major bankruptcy, and the human tragedies of its incredulous, laid-off workers (with whom our CCTV crews lived through the fierce Manchurian winter). Chinese professors of communications and journalism said that they would use our documentary as a teaching aid in their courses.*

TWO MISCONCEPTIONS FORM A grand rationale for writing this book: the assumption that China is inherently hostile to America, and the perception that the Chinese leader, Jiang Zemin, was a "dictator." If peace and prosperity in the twenty-first century depend to no small degree on bilateral relations between America and China, such misconceptions are a detriment and perhaps dangerous.

I like China, the culture of the country and the character of the people, and I admire Jiang Zemin, an underestimated intellectual who defied disdain, criticism from all directions, controversies of all kinds, and even apathy to change forever the largest population on earth. I also relish a little psychohistory—trying to discern the conceptual and emotional antecedents of Jiang's political philosophy and leadership strategy.

The book is anchored by exclusive interviews and special (though limited) access, for which I have made no concessions. I received many suggestions and much advice—some helpful, some contradictory—but always with agreement that all editorial decisions would be mine and mine alone.

This book is more a personal biography of Jiang Zemin as told by his friends and colleagues than a political one as told by his critics and opponents. I try to

---

*The PBS video *In Search of China* is available at www.shoppbs.org.

concentrate on what I believe to be true and minimize that which I cannot confirm. A comprehensive, dispassionate biography must wait until the primary material—original documents and widespread interviews—is openly accessible. That time will come. What I tell here is surely not Jiang Zemin's whole story, but it is, I submit, a good part of it.

ONE CANNOT UNDERSTAND Jiang's actions and beliefs without understanding the texture of his times. My previous book, *Made in China: Voices from the New Revolution,*° focused on two overarching themes needed to comprehend China—the intense *pride* of the Chinese for all things Chinese, and their monomaniacal concern (particularly of their leaders) for social *stability*. When one can recognize the twin themes of pride and stability in their countless themes and variations, one knows a good deal about this country and its leadership.

In September 2000 I watched President Jiang being interviewed by Mike Wallace on *60 Minutes.* Although I thought I knew China well, I had not appreciated his significance until that moment. With a new sense of China's transformation, I first thought to learn and write about Jiang Zemin. My interviews explored how he modernized the Communist Party and reformed the country—subjects about which most people in the West remain oblivious (or harbor distortions). I found myself drawn to Jiang's personal story, and what I found was more than I had expected. What began as a book on his role in reform became an exploration of his life and legacy, how he thinks and what he feels—a biography of Jiang Zemin.

It is considered improper for Chinese leaders to encourage self-promotion, and although there are never shortages of their quotations and pictures in the official media, biographies seem singled out for special proscription. If one considers China's chronicles, there are good reasons for concern. Personality cults, from the ancient emperors to Mao Zedong, have repeatedly plunged the country into chaos. Of all the reforms initiated by Deng Xiaoping, none was more important than his rejection of personal veneration. But China has matured, and as the country reaches out and becomes a leading nation of the world, honest biographies of its leaders cannot fail to promote international goodwill. In a media-intense, personality-driven world, biographies can help China "advance with the times."

°*Made in China: Voices from the New Revolution* (New York: TV Books, 2000) was the companion to my PBS documentary *In Search of China.*

I AM PROUD TO BE considered an "old friend" (*lao pengyou*) of China, a high compliment indeed, earned by fifteen years of learning and teaching, working and joking, eating and exploring, giving and receiving. I dedicate this book to those good people, particularly my friends and colleagues in China, whose commitment, foresight, persistence, and courage are strengthening economic, social, and political reform, and helping China to understand the world and the world to understand China.

In the spirit of full disclosure, I have business interests in China. To the perfectly natural question of whether financial participation in the country alters or affects my views of its leader, I can only say I hope not. This is not a complete answer but my ego, odd as it is, seems a good deal more involved with my intellectual reputation than with the size of my bank account. Everyone has predilections and biases; mine are exposed on these pages.

I do not claim to be a dispassionate observer of China. I root for China, like a loyal fan of a local sports team; I cheer when the actions of its government show China in a favorable light, and I lament when I must admit the reverse. I try to distinguish fact from opinion, what is from what could or should be. Akin to the ethos of science, I respect truth insofar as I can currently determine it. This book is what I can currently determine to be truth about Jiang Zemin.*

Robert Lawrence Kuhn
Pasadena, California
New York, New York
Beijing, People's Republic of China
July 2004

---

*A word about the title. While this book was in production, it came to my attention that there had been a children's book with the same title, Pearl Buck's *The Man Who Changed China: The Story of Sun Yat-sen* (New York: Random House, 1953). I was concerned, but my editor (and others) at Random House noted that the other book was a half-century old, and that it was not uncommon for new books to come out with titles that have been used before. More important, she said, we had a strong, provocative title that took a clear if controversial point of view about our subject. I thought about how Sun and Jiang each "changed China," how their changes differed so markedly yet were each essential for making China what is today. This same-but-different title, though inadvertent and rationalized a posteriori, I came to like. If the similarity of titles highlights the importance and diversity of change that enabled China to reemerge in the twentieth century as one of the world's great nations, that, I thought, is not a bad thing.

Index

About the Author

Robert Lawrence Kuhn is creator and executive producer of the PBS television documentary *In Search of China;* creator and host of the PBS series *Closer to Truth: Science, Meaning and the Future* (www.pbs.org/closertotruth); and producer of the China Central Television (CCTV) series *Capital Wave* (on mergers and acquisitions). He is the author or editor of numerous books, including *The Library of Investment Banking, Handbook for Creative and Innovative Managers, Dealmaker, Closer to Truth: Challenging Current Belief,* and *Made in China: Voices from the New Revolution;* three of his books have been translated into Chinese, including the first investment banking book of its kind published in China *(Touzi Yinhang Xue).* He was president and co-owner of The Geneva Companies, a leading mergers and acquisitions firm, prior to its sale to Smith Barney/Citigroup, where he is a managing director. He is a trustee of Claremont Graduate University and serves on the Committee on Scientific Freedom and Responsibility of the American Association for the Advancement of Science (AAAS). He holds a Ph.D. in anatomy/brain research from UCLA and an M.S. in management from MIT. Since 1989 he has been an adviser to the Chinese government on economic policy, mergers and acquisitions, science and technology, and media and television. He is vice chairman of the Beijing Institute for Frontier Science.